VICTORIAN OXFORD

I have made another discovery in my travels which you will not consider as a perfectly new one, and that is no less than that Oxford is a very curious place.

Anthony Storer to Lord Auckland, Sept. 28, 1790.
Auckland Corr. ii.371.

One may fancy Cambridge a very excellent and useful big place of education, but Oxford is the place for the education of statesmen and great political men, and the influence of Oxford and its place in relation to the Commonwealth is far higher for good or evil.

Correspondence of Arthur Hugh Clough, July 18, 1836,
ed. F. L. Mulhauser (Oxford, 1957), i.49.

In a European state like England, where Church and State have been so inextricably intertwined, where political life has been bound up so intimately with every subordinate form of association, a national academical organisation was certain to reflect, as in a mirror, all the political or semi-political, movements of the contemporary age.

W. Ince, *The internal duties of the University in prospect
of external changes* (Oxford, 1878).

VICTORIAN OXFORD

W. R. WARD

FRANK CASS & CO. LTD.
1965

First published in 1965 by
Frank Cass & Co. Ltd.
10 Woburn Walk, London, W.C.1

Printed in Great Britain by
Thomas Nelson (Printers) Ltd, London and Edinburgh

CONTENTS

Chief MS. Collections and Abbreviations   vii

Chief Newspapers and Journals   x

Preface   xi

Introduction   xiii

Chapter I   Oxford and the Court   1

        II   Oxford and the Church   21

        III.   Oxford in the Post-War Era   40

        IV.   Oxford and the Constitution   61

        V.   Oxford in the Age of Reform   80

        VI.   The Constitutional Crisis in the University   104

        VII.   The Liberal Revival   128

        VIII. The Great Blue Book   156

        IX.   The Triumph of Reform and the Executive
               Commissioners   180

        X.   Oxford Reformed   210

        XI.   The Liberals and the Tests   235

        XII.   Oxford and National Education   263

        XIII. The State and the Settlement   291

Index   417

CHIEF MS. COLLECTIONS
AND ABBREVIATIONS

Acland MSS. in the Bodl[eian Library, Oxford].

Add[itional] MSS. in the B[ritish] M[useum].

especially	31229 — 31232	Bexley Papers
	34455 — 34458	Auckland Papers
	34569 — 34582	Bliss Papers
	37845 — 37913	Windham Papers
	38195 — 38580	Liverpool Papers
	40182 — 40880	Peel Papers
	44091 — 44755	Gladstone Papers

Apsley Ho[use] MSS. being the correspondence of the 1st duke of Wellington at Apsley House, London, W.1.

Bryce MSS. in the Bodleian Library, Oxford.

Burgon MSS. in the Bodleian Library, Oxford.

Chatham MSS. in the P[ublic] R[ecord] O[ffice] especially P.R.O. 30/8/176.

Colchester MSS. in the P[ublic] R[ecord] O[ffice] especially P.R.O. 39/9/15–16, 33–4.

Exeter College MSS. in the archives of Exeter College, Oxford, including the College Register, 1826–82, the Order Book, corr. of the Rector with the University Commissioners, 1854, and the minute book of the committee for drawing up the statutes of 1854.

MS. Diary of John Hill in the library of St. Edmund Hall, Oxford.

Jenkyns MSS. in the library of Balliol College, Oxford.

Jowett MSS. in the library of Balliol College, Oxford.

Keble College MSS. in the library of Keble College, Oxford, including
Corr. of E. B. Pusey and J. Keble, 1837–66, in two bound volumes.
Corr. of J. Keble with Elizabeth Keble and Charlotte M. Cornish.
Corr. of J. D. Dalgairns presented by Dr. Hermitage Day.
Corr. of J. Keble with J. Davison, 1814–37.
Corr. of J. Keble with his sisters.
Corr. of E. B. Pusey with J. Keble (further series).
Corr. of Archdeacon Froude with J. Keble.
Corr. of Sir J. T. Coleridge with J. Keble.
Corr. of W. E. Gladstone with J. Keble.
Corr. of H. J. Rose with J. Keble.
Corr. of Bp. Philpotts with J. Keble.

MS. Knowsley Papers being the correspondence of the 14th earl of Derby at Knowsley Hall.

MS. Diary of H. P. Liddon in the library of Liddon Ho[use], 24 South Audley Street, London, W.1.

Magdalen College MSS. in the library of Magdalen College Oxford, including B II.2.2, C I.2.13, C II.3.9, D 4.1, D 4.3, D 7.4 and MS. Bloxam Diary.

Monk Bretton MSS. in the Bodleian Library, Oxford.

MS. Oriel College Letters in the library of Oriel College, Oxford, also MS. Gladstone-Hawkins Letters (series MS. Oriel College Letters G1.).
Also papers on college and university affairs in a large iron trunk in the Treasurer's Muniments.

Oxford topographical MSS. in the Bodleian Library, Oxford, especially
    MS. Top. Oxon, a 6.
    MSS. Top. Oxon. b 23, 66, 252.
    MSS. Top. Oxon. c 31, 101, 236, 286, 296, 309.
    MSS. Top. Oxon. d 15, 16, 35, 353–6.
    MSS. Top. Oxon. e 80, 165.

Pattison MSS. in the Bodleian Library, Oxford.

Pusey Ho[use] MSS. in the archives of Pusey House, Oxford, including
    Ollard Papers.
    Corr. of Charles Marriott with E. B. Pusey.
    Corr. of E. B. Pusey with Dr. Bull.
    Corr. of R. W. Church.
    Corr. of E. B. Pusey with Sir William Heathcote.
    Papers relating to Pusey's campaign against the removal of the tests, 1835.
        Chest B, drawer 4.
    Corr. of G. Rolleston with E. B. Pusey.
    Corr. of Isaac Williams with Thomas Keble.
    Pusey's monograph on the Middle Class Examinations.
    Letters to Dr. Robert Scott, Master of Balliol.
    Corr. of C. P. Golightly with W. S. Bricknell, 1842–5.
    W. Tuckwell's reminiscences of E. B. Pusey.
    Corr. of the earl of Radnor, 1834–5.
    Liddon's transcripts of Pusey's corr. with J. Keble.
    Corr. of Sir J. T. Coleridge with E. B. Pusey.
    Liddon's transcripts of corr. of E. B. with Philip Pusey.

Routh MSS. in the library of Magdalen College, Oxford, especially D 5.8–22, D 6.2–20.

Salisbury MSS. temporarily deposited in the library of Ch[rist] Ch[urch], Oxford.

MS. Sidmouth Papers in the Devon C[ounty] R[ecord] O[ffice].

MS. University Papers in the keeping of the Custos Archivorum at Oxford, including

Minutes of the Hebdomadal Board 1788–1803, 1803–23, 1823–33, 1833–41, 1841–54.

Minutes of Hebdomadal Council 1854–66, 1866–79.

Reports to Hebdomadal Council 1855–64, 1865–9.

Reports and papers on university requirements and reform, 1874–8.

Parliamentary papers on university affairs, 1833–95.

Memoranda respecting the Professorships of Pastoral Theology and Ecclesiastical History.

Minutes of the committee appointed by the Hebdomadal Board to consider the Commissioners' recommendations, 1852–3.

University Commission letters.

Convocation Register, 1776–93, 1793–1802.

Also many other miscellaneous papers in the following series:

W.P. 3. (7), (9).

N.W. 4.1, 2.

8.6, 8.

21.1, 4, 7, 8, 10.

MS. University Commission papers in the P.R.O. H.O. 73/37–40.

MS. Letter-book of John Wills, Warden of Wadham, 1792–6 in Balliol Coll. MS. Jenkyns VI.

MS. Wynter Papers in the Bodleian Library, Oxford.

CHIEF NEWSPAPERS AND JOURNALS

British Critic	(Tractarian)
British Quarterly Review	(Congregational)
Christian Observer	(Evangelical)
Christian Reformer	(Unitarian)
Christian Remembrancer	(High-Church)
Christian Witness	(Congregational)
Contemporary Review	(Liberal)
Edinburgh Review	(Whig)
Fraser's Magazine	(Liberal)
Guardian	(High-Church)
Inquirer	(Unitarian)
Jackson's Oxford Journal	(Tory)
Macmillan's Magazine	(Liberal)
Nonconformist	(Congregational)
North British Review	(Liberal)
Oxford Magazine 1847	(Anti-tractarian)
Oxford Protestant Magazine 1847–8	(Liberal)
Oxford University Magazine 1834	(Conservative)
Quarterly Review	(Tory)
Saturday Review	(Conservative)
Times	(Liberal)
Wesleyan Methodist Magazine	(Methodist)
Westminster Review	(Benthamite)

PREFACE

OF the making of books about Oxford there is (quite rightly) no end, and it will not escape any reader that nineteenth-century Oxford is a subject so rich in interest and material that this book, despite its concessions to terseness, could easily have exceeded its already substantial limits. The main object has been to give an account of the development in the constitutional organisation, the political standing and the studies of the university; to keep the scale of treatment within bounds and to permit a reasonable amount of quotation from the piquant original material (a luxury which gives the leisurely Victorian biographies an enduring value), this object has had to dictate the handling of incidental matters. The Oxford Movement which appears here for example is not that which (for better or worse) changed so much of the church, and in Newman gave rise to important discussions of the relations of faith and reason; it is the (equally real) movement which was vexed by the tactics of agitation, and, until driven to reappraisal by defeat, was almost wholly destructive in the university world. There are many portraits; but the Jowett, for example, of this book is not so much the tutor who did well by his pupils, as the politician with an infinite capacity for making enemies. Politics and preferment are pursuits which bring the worst out of dons (as out of parsons), and they are the staple topics of this study. It is the same with the treatment of ideas. The development of the professorial and tutorial ideals described here gave rise to sharply differing notions of the organisation, instruction and social function of a university, but so complex was the university constitution, and so complicated was English parliamentary life for much of the period, that a head-long clash of ideals could hardly ever take place. If the reader is asked to bear with an often intricate narrative, the fact is that confusion was generally the order of the day, and could hardly be worse confounded than in 1854, for example, when the admission of dissenters was carried against the government by surprise with the aid of conservative votes. In the realm of theology the conflict of ideas can only be described from a personal standpoint; while not attempting to disguise this, I hope I have given a fair account of the parties in the field. Finally, it should be said that the writing of this book was completed in 1962, and that it has not been possible to take account of archive material which has been catalogued or finished work which has been published since that date.

xi

Many obligations are incurred in a work of this kind. I am very grateful to the Duke of Wellington and the Earl of Derby for hospitality and permission to examine their private papers; and to the Marquess of Salisbury and Lord Monk Bretton for permission to examine and quote from their family papers. The Warden of Liddon House granted me access to Liddon's MS. Diary, and the Principal of Pusey House to the rich collections in his charge. The Custos Archivorum and his deputy opened the university archives to me; and the Keeper of Western MSS. granted access to the Acland and Pattison papers. No one can work on a subject of this kind without becoming enormously indebted to members of his staff. One of Oxford's unsung assets is the large number of college librarians and archivists to whom no trouble is too much when visiting students intrude upon their vacations; I am particularly grateful to those of Balliol, Exeter, Keble, Magdalen and Oriel Colleges, and to the Principal of St. Edmund Hall, for permission and facilities to use their archives. The footnotes will show how heavily I have trespassed upon the patience of the staff of the MSS. Room in the British Museum. The Rev. Roger Thomas as on earlier occasions has assisted me with the resources of Dr. Williams's library. To Messrs. Cordeaux and Merry of the Bodleian Library I am again grateful for access to their great bibliography of university history while it was in progress; and to the latter for many other favours beside. Dr. J. F. A. Mason of Christ Church eased my passage through the Salisbury papers and lent me a transcript from the Ottley and Pitchford Hall MSS. Dr. J. R. Western and Mr. J. P. R. Roach kindly read my typescript at different stages and made helpful suggestions. Miss R. Bridgman nobly typed the final draft. The Leverhulme Trustees generously forwarded the work by a grant, while the University of Manchester and my colleagues in the history department made possible a term's sabbatical leave. To them all I owe much, and much also to my wife who (as is the way with students' wives) put up with the whole enterprise.

Department of History,   W.R.W.
University of Manchester.   1965.

INTRODUCTION

There has, indeed, been a good deal of port and prejudice at Oxford, and in the common rooms and cloisters vestiges of both may still occasionally be traced; though no-one is any longer forced to imbibe either the one or the other.

H. H. DRUMMOND, *Observations suggested by the strictures of the Edinburgh Review upon Oxford* (Edinburgh, 1810)

IN the last years of the eighteenth century the University of Oxford which for two generations had dabbled in opposition or even treason, came to regard itself as a bastion of the protestant order in church and state, a pillar of the establishment in the broadest sense. How this far-reaching transformation was brought about has been discussed in an earlier volume;[1] by 1800 the university was avowedly a privileged oracle of the *ancien régime* looking to the state for the maintenance of its exclusive rights, and requiting its obligations by its public pronouncements, its influence upon the clergy, and the election of members of parliament similar in social character to those of the early Hanoverian period, but wholly different in their disposition towards the political order. Formerly the colleges had stressed their legal status as lay corporations; now Oxford appeared again as the defender and faithful son of the church. Until the state enforced university reform in the 'fifties, Oxford history mirrored that of the church. But a generation later a second reforming commission had left the university, according to the wilder sort of conservatives, 'de-christianised', and no longer in any official sense an ecclesiastical institution. The old universities, and especially Oxford, afforded almost the sole triumphs of the bitter campaign for disestablishment and disendowment in England; dissent and scepticism which had first gained academic toleration with the establishment of the University of London, not only entered the old strongholds of the church, but profited by the transfer of endowments from purposes ecclesiastical and clerical to purposes secular and lay.

If Oxford had ceased to be an arm of the church, she had also ceased to be an arm of the state, 'an integral part of our constitution.'[2] The university still elected her burgesses to parliament, and still chose a political magnate as her Chancellor, but these functions retained only the vestigial remnant of their former importance. For

[1] W. R. Ward, *Georgian Oxford* (Oxford, 1958).
[2] T. Hodgskin, *Travels in North Germany* (Edinburgh, 1820) ii. 265.

xiii

the seat which Peel regarded as 'the paramount object of my ambition, and one to which I should have looked forward as the ample reward of a long political life,'[1] and for which Canning schemed to the end of his days, no statesman of the first rank was returned after the defeat of Gladstone, and the ultimate abolition of university representation made no perceptible difference to the political system. Similarly the election of a Chancellor which had been a political event of note in 1715 or 1772, and in 1809 had occasioned a savage conflict between the Lord Chancellor and an aspiring Prime Minister, carried no consequences for the outside world and few for the university itself.

This sorry decline was, nevertheless, regarded by many, especially of liberal inclinations, with great satisfaction, for it enabled the university to concentrate upon what they regarded as its true functions, teaching and research. Teaching had hardly figured at all in the public image which the apologists of the university sought to create in the eighteenth century, and consumed a very small proportion of the endowments, while after the middle of the nineteenth century there were still conservatives like Newman who could argue that research had no proper place within a university, and was best sponsored by private learned societies. By this time, however, both teaching and research had taken institutional shape; many fellowships had been converted into scholarships, many more devoted to the support of tutors, and others to the sustenance of professors who were expected to set new standards of scholarly investigation. The active controversies now related not to the prospects of ministers, nor to the nature of the church, but to the number of schools which the university should compass, how it could extend the usefulness of its education, and whether its fundamental business was not research rather than teaching. The framework of the discussion had also changed, and the controversies of the 'thirties whether professorial teaching was not a subversive, and tutorial teaching a conservative, form of education, were now extinct.

In many ways the purview of the university had diminished. It no longer manned the political and ecclesiastical ramparts of society, nor cast its weight into the struggles of church and party. Like the East India Company, the Civil Service, and the church, it had been reformed by being taken out of the field of strife. 'Oxford has pronounced her judgement', declared Vaughan Thomas, with infinite unction, when Convocation opposed the abolition of tests in 1834;[2]

---

[1] C. S. Parker, *Sir Robert Peel* (London, 1891–9) i. 252.
[2] Apsley Ho. MSS. Vaughan Thomas to duke of Wellington, April 26, 1834. Cf. F. D. Maurice's view of the universities as 'the true National Church Councils in educational matters.' F. Maurice, *Life of F. D. Maurice* (London, 1884) i. 286.

but by the 'eighties Oxford was an oracle no more. On the other hand in important respects the context of university life and thought had broadened immensely in the course of the century. Having set itself to be useful, the university found its usefulness compared with that of universities in Scotland, France, and especially Germany. Oxford tutors were soon teaching from classical texts edited in German universities, and Oxford theologians were championing or assailing novelties conceived in German universities. Oxford dons found themselves inescapably members of an international fraternity engaged in study and criticism, and the animosities which had formerly been absorbed by party battles and college feuds, now went into contests between tutors and professors, or advocates of three, four or five schools.

This great transformation arose from developments both inside and outside the university. Oxford's political importance was bound to decline as the vested interests for which she stood diminished in importance. As the produce of industry rivalled that of the land, as dissent and popery challenged the church, the political significance of a university supported by agricultural rents and pledged to the Anglican cause shrank inexorably. But the whole process was aggravated by animosities within the university, and obsolete forms of political etiquette which made the seat impossible for front-bench politicians. A university which preferred Inglis to Peel, and Gathorne Hardy to Gladstone, courted political insignificance. Similarly, the teaching and curriculum of the university was overhauled partly in response to outside criticism, and its constitution was reformed by the state, but the spirit of improvement which flowed through myriad channels in the nineteenth century flowed through Oxford too, breathing new life into the dry bones.

The shape of Oxford in the 'eighties with her exaggerated emphasis upon the ancient classics, but her recognition of other studies, her tutorial system and incongruous professoriate, her crowd of parsons and her infidelity, her members of parliament and her political unimportance, sprang from the interaction of forces within and without, and bore the marks of Manchester as well as Westminster, of Berlin as well as Christ Church, and of religious zeal of every shade from unitarian to anglo-catholic.

CHAPTER I

OXFORD AND THE COURT

It may be thought that [Samuel Parr] entertained an unfavourable
opinion of the Oxford men, since he used to say, 'they are very good
men; but too orthodox in religion, too rampant in loyalty, and too
furious in politics.'

W. FIELD, *Memoirs of the life, writings and opinions of
Rev. Samuel Parr* (London, 1828) ii.186.

THROUGHOUT the reign of George III powerful forces were drawing
the University of Oxford away from its old opposition shibboleths
into the orbit of the Court. The loaves and fishes of clerical preferment in the government gift, always a tempting bait, increased
steadily in quantity even as the lay system of influence waned. Still
more important, the protecting hand of government seemed increasingly attractive as issues of substance came back into politics.
Wilkes's attacks, the far-reaching implications of the agitation by
the religious liberals, the threat to parliamentary sovereignty created
by American resistance, all imbued the university with ministerial
politics. Royal visits to Oxford were resumed in the 'eighties for the
first time since the reign of Queen Anne. The most famous, in August
1786, was immortalised by Fanny Burney's account of the uncourtly
enthusiasm of the dons. William Crowe, the Public Orator,
heralded the visit in a great paean upon the king from the pulpit
of St. Mary's,[1] and the royal family and whole assembly were
touched by references in the university address to the king's escape
from assassination. The king pledged himself to uphold the university
in its dual role,

> to encourage every branch of science, as the more my subjects
> are enlightened, the more they must be attached to the excellent
> constitution established in this realm.

The king and university impressed each other;[2] there was another
visit in 1788,[3] and when in 1789 the king was restored from insanity,
there were great rejoicings.[4] Henceforward loyalty was the order of
the day in Oxford; visits from royal personages were frequent, and
in 1801 the past could be so far forgotten that Tom Grenville could
speak of 'the tendency which Oxford always professes to government.'[5]

When the dissenters moved against the Test and Corporation Acts

2

the majority in the university would give no ground. In 1787[6] and again in 1789[7] when Beaufoy's motion for repeal came before the Commons, Lord North, the university Chancellor, and Sir William Dolben, her burgess, stoutly defended the present liberal constitution. The university was not yet, however, a committed defender of the church, and was careful to make no public appearance in her cause. According to George Horne, President of Magdalen,

> it was thought more liberal, as the sentiments of our Chancellor and members were well known, to leave them to themselves, than to importune them with fresh solicitations . . . since it is more honourable to the cause that it should be so carried, than by the interest and effort of bodies corporate.[8]

The motion of 1789, however, was defeated by only 20 votes, and the Hebdomadal Board laid plans against the next campaign with the Chancellor and the Primate. The Clarendon Press reprinted a pamphlet for distribution to members of both houses, and a petition against repeal was prepared, though it was held back at the instance of the Primate and the political advisers of the university.[9] This time the feud amongst the whigs and fears of the revolution in France swelled the majority against the motion to 189,[10] and John Randolph, regius professor of divinity, and a bitter opponent of dissenters, foresaw that this defeat would settle the question for another generation.[11]

Oxford high-churchmanship displayed a new vehemence. In 1791 Edward Tatham, Rector of Lincoln, made a characteristic onslaught upon that 'phalanx of political literati . . . the dissenters,' upon their 'specious, but flimsy productions,' and their 'Sunday Schools, those pious but ill-judged institutions;' 'they dissent from the church and constitution of England, and are united to each other only by that dissent.'[12] The minister of the New Road Baptist Chapel replied with a spirited vindication of the constitutional loyalty of dissenters, but he could hardly stem the tide.[13] In 1799, John Randolph was talking in almost the Tractarian manner of

> an *increasing danger* of which people are scarcely aware, which is the adopting and forwarding religious projects without the authority and assistance of the church and its rulers. The end is ostensibly good, and the intention perhaps is such, but inasmuch as it tends to dissolve or weaken the tie by which the established church is held together, it becomes a cooperation with levellers and reformers (falsely so-called) and is a parallel case with the present attempts to dissolve the tie of civil government. [14]

And even the Bible Society was not yet born.

The changed political circumstances of the university stood out boldly when a new Chancellor was elected in 1792. The whigs were divided in their attitude towards the French Revolution, and in the summer Pitt sought reinforcement for his government from Portland and their conservative section. These negotiations had a crucial influence upon the Oxford election. Within the university the new feature was the predominance of Christ Church, the most ministerial of houses in an age when Court influence was no longer abhorrent to the majority. Christ Church already claimed a proprietary interest in one of the university seats in parliament. In the university's opposition days, the Deans had not been invited to serve as Vice-Chancellor, and now made a virtue of declining; Cyril Jackson, however, was plotting for the House to capture the Chancellorship.

The great object was to secure 'a minister of state with great patronage,'[15] but Prime Minister Pitt was doubly disqualified as a commoner and a Cantab. Next to him in influence was Lord Grenville, his kinsman, foreign secretary, and a scholar worthy of Christ Church. He was put forward by a group of self-styled 'independent colleges.' The duke of Beaufort, like his Jacobite fathers, was also canvassed as an independent candidate.[16] Long before North's death, however, Jackson had 'it in agitation to strike a bold stroke'[17] in the interests of the man who had appointed him Dean, the duke of Portland. Portland's conservatism was no longer in question; he might regain ministerial patronage at any time; if he could be adopted as a ministerial candidate he could unite the Oxford friends of both parties, and supported by the well-drilled host of Christ Church, must win. The House then could claim special access to his patronage.

The plan worked to perfection. Portland's nomination was still a secret from Pitt on August 9,[18] by which time Grenville had withdrawn in favour of the official candidate of the House.[19] The Dean was already canvassing furiously and unashamedly declaring

> that we have the most thorough approbation of government itself—and that we are even assur'd that it would be consider'd as a fortunate circumstance for the great and constitutional interests of the country if the D. of P. should be elected by the university.[20]

Only Beaufort was now in the field, supported by Routh of Magdalen in the name of independence from Court and Christ Church,[21] but by the middle of August the fight was over,[22] and Portland duly acknowledged 'the harmony and union of sentiment which . . . so happily distinguished' his uncontested return.[23]

When, however, Portland was installed in July 1793, Fox was still staving off the junction with Pitt, and the tension was felt in the celebrations. The eccentric whig Samuel Parr who emulated his father's devotion to Jacobitism by dabbling in opposition causes of all sorts, even unitarianism, described the Encaenia as

> tumultuous and shewy, and full of novelties. Posterity will find the Chancellor of a Tory university, accompanied only by Whiggish aristocrats . . . not a single English Bishop, glutted with preferment, or panting for it, appeared at this ceremony, excepting the two who were officially present . . . your sermon will be preached by an alien academic, and an alien Prelate . . . after a Christ Church triumph, and at the enthronement of a Christ Church Chancellor, two Christ Church Archbishops, and three Christ Church Bishops, in a most unexampled manner absented themselves. . . . Who could have expected the splendour of the houses of Bentinck, Cavendish and Russell, to cast its meridian beams upon the Tory land of Oxford?[24]

A list of honorary doctors including the duke of Bedford and William Windham, and panegyrics upon whig leaders, made undeniably odd reading.[25]

Even stranger was the presence of Edmund Burke.[26] In 1790, 49 resident masters had petitioned the heads to recognise the *Reflections on the Revolution in France* by conferring the degree of D.C.L. by diploma. This request the heads refused, and Burke received the lesser honour of a laudatory pamphlet from Edward Tatham.[27] In 1793, however, as Tatham later related, it was a different story.

> His friend was now the Chancellor. To cover the disgrace of their opposition to his degree by diploma, and, at the same time, to sleeve-creep the new Chancellor, they [the ruling party of heads] had recourse to the finesse of proposing his name at the Hebdomadal Board, among the many other names who were to be complimented with Honorary Degrees at the time of the Public Installation . . . [Tatham vainly opposed this as no real honour] But . . . in consequence of a short note which, though totally unacquainted with his person, I wrote to him that very day, the Right Honourable Gentleman saw clearly through the finesse, and magnanimously rejected the proferred degree so dexterously prepared for his acceptance; notwithstanding the earnest entreaties of the Chancellor himself, and of the highest nobility, male and female, in the nation; holding as he did the Vice-Chancellor and his fawning crew in that sovreign contempt they so sovreignly deserved.[28]

While garbled versions of what had actually happened went round, Burke appeared in the train of the party magnates.

Though the Encaenia of 1793 was disappointing, and Jackson's

feud with Tatham was to echo down the years, the Dean had calculated well. Portland became Home Secretary in 1794, to the delight
of a Vice-Chancellor who put the maintenance of order as the first
function of the university.[29] The spirits of the dons varied with the
tide of war.[30] Great subscriptions were raised for the war effort.[31]
In 1797 the Vice-Chancellor and Proctors enrolled an enthusiastic
body of 500 volunteers for the defence of the place, who ordered
uniforms, drilled zealously under regular sergeants, and were commanded by senior dons.[32] Portland presented them with colours; the
duke of York reviewed them in Port Meadow, and by the time of
the peace £1900 had been spent upon a loyal hobby which for a time
diverted Oxford men from their country walks.[33] Such chauvinism
mortified Foxite whigs like Samuel Parr,[34] and by 1797 Fox himself
had almost given up hope of keeping whiggism alive in Oxford.[35]
John Randolph spoke for many when he declared that the ministers
'have done so much for us lately that . . . they have a right to all
the assistance we can give them.'[36]

Such political criticism as the university received came therefore
from political outsiders. As late as 1781 the Commons had been
treated to the ancient legend that Oxford still inculcated principles
of tyranny,[37] and in 1796 the *Monthly Review*, denouncing the celibacy
of fellows as an 'absurd relic of popery,' revived the fiction of the
enlightenment that the universities were the haunts of thinly disguised
papists.[38] Another old but sounder cry was revived by Samuel Parr
in his blast against

> the strange, absurd, nugatory, and immoral practice . . . of
> requiring oaths to be taken for the observance of statutes which
> it is impossible to enforce.[39]

Vicesimus Knox, headmaster of Tunbridge School and former
fellow of St. John's, pressed a plan of reform on Lord North in 1789
and urged that

> all useless and antiquated forms whatever, which savour of
> monkery, popery, slavery and Gothicism should be utterly
> abolished,[40]

but oaths of immense complexity, and others by nature absurd, went
on unchallenged. Much later in December 1826 the Vice-Chancellor,
Richard Jenkyns, the shrewd Master of Balliol, urged the Hebdomadal
Board to dispense with the more eccentric requirements; in 1827 the
oaths 'never to consent to a reconciliation with Henry Simeon' and
'not to give or attend lectures at Stamford' and some others were
repealed.[41] But when the storm broke in the 'thirties the university
had done little, and the colleges nothing, to avoid public reproach.

In other directions Oxford men had an eye to improvement. John

Napleton, fellow of Brasenose, for example, who had attacked the matriculation test[42] during the fracas of 1772,[43] now questioned the requirements for residence and the examinations for degrees. He claimed that by liberal construction of the statutes, and by dispensations habitually granted, the seven years' residence nominally required for the M.A. degree had been reduced to eleven months, and that further concessions were always being sought.[44] Chancellors' letters of dispensation continued to fill the Convocation register, but the university became steadily more scrupulous in granting exemptions, and the grant of a term's grace in celebration of the coronation in 1820 was widely felt to be an abuse.[45] Napleton also called for examination changes upon the rumour that the Vice-Chancellor had raised the matter in the Hebdomadal Board.[46] The present examinations were notoriously an empty form, and Napleton advocated serious public examinations in classical, mathematical and religious knowledge.

The absurdities of the examinations were also attacked by Vicesimus Knox, and were held responsible for the dissipation of the junior and the idleness of the senior members of the university. Knox made a hodge-podge of the journalistic common-places of the day. Classical learning must be the staple of a liberal education, but it ought to be united with science. 'Attainments merely ornamental, and those of a mere modern linguist' had no educational worth; nevertheless the university should open a fully staffed department of modern languages.[47] The university should offer a liberal education; but it should also provide professional training in medicine, law and divinity.[48] The office of tutor was 'chiefly active in saving appearances'; nevertheless the number of tutors should be increased, and the professors required to lecture.[49] There should be examinations in every college, 'but . . . they should be conducted with such delicacy as not to hurt the feelings of the diffident and modest;' university examinations should be reformed.[50] There should be strict enforcement of sumptuary and disciplinary regulations.[51]

Knox's lack of intellectual coherence suggests that he was a reporter of current gossip rather than an educational pioneer, but some of his criticisms were reinforced by a genius. Gibbon's comments on Oxford in his autobiography,[52] his sneer against 'idle monks,' attracted much attention from the time when they were first published with his *Miscellaneous Works* in 1796. Yet there were always those who recognised that his criticisms related to a past generation, and were those of a most unbalanced youth. Sir James Mackintosh roundly rebuffed his call for state intervention.

Ought a philosopher really to lament that the rights and privileges of great societies are not, even for the special object of reformation subjected to the discretion of the legislature? If, even for the most apparently salutary objects, these rights and privileges could be trampled underfoot, there could no longer be either fixed law or secure liberty in a nation.[53]

Throughout the eighteenth and nineteenth centuries the whigs sought to compensate for their weakness in the university by calling in the state; the tories protected their supremacy by pleading chartered liberties. Mackintosh's argument showed that his feud with Burke was almost over, and that he was turning to the side of counter-revolution.

Other friends of Oxford also made their replies. James Hurdis, poetry professor, claimed that undergraduates at Magdalen had to work, and that the professors were active.[54] Even the Foxite Samuel Parr sang the praises of the English universities in his most turgid prose, rehearsing in two quarto pages of tiny print the roll of distinguished alumni (not including Gibbon), a cloud of witnesses for 'the excellency of our strength, and the joy of our glory;' the universities were the saviours of society, the 'pillars, not only of the learning, but of the virtue and piety *whether seen or unseen*, which yet remain among us.'[55]

The most interesting of Oxford's defenders was also one of her sharpest critics, the eccentric Dr. Tatham, Rector of Lincoln.[56] A man given to strong aversions,[57] Tatham made a violent assault in his Bampton Lectures of 1789 upon the prejudice and bigotry which still sustained the Aristotelian logic in the Oxford schools. Yet Tatham thought that Knox's criticisms overlooked altogether the chief effect of the obsolescence of the public exercises for degrees.

> The consequence is, that the university discipline, in every branch of learning, out of the *public* is forced into more *private* channels; in which every part of a learned and liberal education is cultivated with advantage, and inculcated with success. Since the schools were neglected, the colleges have improved ; and, however the mainspring of the great literary machine may be worn out by time, and never yet replaced, there are other wheels in action of better mechanism, improving and to be improved: which move to the honour and emolument of general learning.

The colleges would move faster if university requirements were overhauled, but were already providing an efficient and up-to-date education.[58]

Among Tatham's 'private channels' were the lectures of professors. The public lectures prescribed by the Laudian code had ceased, but private courses were being delivered and attended with enthusiasm towards the end of the century. Among the most popular were those in scientific subjects not much taught in colleges.[59] For years, though subject to epilepsy, Thomas Hornsby, professor of experimental philosophy, and an astronomer of note, had delivered a perspicuous course each term to classes which generally numbered over fifty.[60] Even larger were John Williams's botany classes,[61] supported by the splendid benefactions of his predecessor, John Sibthorp, and others. Sibthorp, who occupied the Sherardian chair from 1784 to 1796, spent much time abroad collecting materials for the Greek Flora which was published after his death. One of Lord North's last acts as Chancellor was to secure a substantial endowment from the king for both his chair and the botanical garden.[62] Thomas Beddoes, who was attracting large classes as reader in chemistry, also hoped for an endowment, and foresaw a great future for scientific studies in Oxford; but he was a stormy petrel. In 1787, he violently attacked the Bodleian Library as quite the worst organised in Europe, and in 1792 when negotiations were in train for a royal benefaction he imprudently glorified the French Revolution, and denigrated the English Church. A great clamour followed. He lost his endowment and resigned his place. Deterred from going to France by the September Massacres, he established a 'Pneumatic Institute' at Clifton for the treatment of disease by inhalation.[63]

Some chairs which had formerly been sinecures were now laborious offices. Thomas Nowell, regius professor of modern history, was old and ill, but gave his courses.[64] The divinity professors had long slumbered, and even in the 'nineties the Margaret Professor lectured only once a term; John Randolph, the regius professor, however, regularly put classes to sleep with courses drearily delivered by candle-light.[65] Thomas Wenman, regius professor of civil law, never gave his statutory lectures, but delivered an annual course adapted to modern needs until in April 1796 he was drowned in the Cherwell upon a botanical expedition.[66] Dr. Smith, Savilian professor of geometry, was non-resident, but lectures of great repute were given by his deputy Abraham Robertson, who succeeded to the chair in 1797, and was soon employed upon budgetary calculations for the ministers.[67]

The medical staff were of varied reputation. In 1790 Convocation degraded William Thomson, the former anatomy reader and a man of 'ready eloquence and extraordinary perspicuity,' for 'some unnatural & detestable practices' with a servant boy. Thomson is credited with having thereupon become physician to the Pope.[68] Martin Wall who secured the clinical chair by 196 votes to 194 in 1785 was an unorthodox practitioner, for 'his exhilarating conversation, his lively anecdotes, his urbanity, contributed more to the relief of his patients than could be effected by medicine alone.'[69] George III commended Addington for appointing the anatomy teacher Sir Christopher Pegge to the regius chair of medicine in 1801 for 'merit not solicitation,'[70] but Pegge had solicited his knighthood, both for equal status with his opposite number at Cambridge and for his services as 'the real father of all the Oxford armed associations.'[71] Even those who doubted Pegge's scientific soundness allowed him ability as a lecturer.[72]

In Oxford in the 'nineties, as Tatham insisted, there were obvious absurdities, but education of a reasonable standard and of a varied and modern character was to be had in at least some of the colleges and from the courses regularly delivered by most of the professors.[73] Tatham argued that the university needed the double stimulus of a really high standard in some colleges together with public exercises for degrees which would raise the general level. There was no reason why, under such reforms, the teaching and examining should be a college monopoly, or why the value of the teaching in scientific, legal and humane subjects given in the 'nineties by professors should not be recognised. The last years of Tatham's life were embittered by the fact that the man who achieved both the college triumph and the establishment of new examinations was the head whom he detested beyond all others, Cyril Jackson, Dean of Christ Church.

By any standards a remarkable man, Jackson's force of character won him submissive obedience or outright hostility in the university, and few dons have ever been so cordially loathed and respected by politicians. As Oxford returned to Court, college animosity towards the House decayed, and the way was open for Christ Church to establish her supremacy by exploiting her assets of size, wealth, and Court connexions. These assets Jackson turned first to his personal profit, then to that of his society. A favourite pupil of William Markham at Westminster, he was elected head to Trinity College Cambridge in 1764, but was diverted to Christ Church by the prospect of a studentship. In 1767 Markham himself returned to Christ Church as Dean, and becoming preceptor to the Prince of Wales and Prince Frederick in 1771, got Jackson appointed sub-preceptor. Such appointments never lasted long, but when Jackson was turned out in 1776 he had established a claim upon the reversionary interest of the Prince and his parliamentary allies. Jackson's turn came in 1783, in the Indian summer of the whigs, when Portland secured him the deanery of Christ Church.[74]

The cancellarial election of 1792 gave Jackson the opportunity to oblige Portland and Pitt as well, and as Christ Church contemporaries of his own generation (such as Auckland and Abbott) and men he had launched into the world as Dean (such as Canning and Peel) came to the fore, Jackson developed an astonishing facility for listening at statesmen's keyholes.[75] Private information of the downfall of

Pitt's ministry in 1801 filled him with gloom. 'Nothing,' he declared, 'yet presents to me any idea of an efficient administration to be formed from the remaining materials of the old one, & the friends of the old one;' the obligation to form a ministry might almost have been his. 'My general idea in all such cases is, that the university shd. make itself felt before it makes itself heard,' a doctrine which he shortly expounded at Addington's expense.[76] In 1802 and 1803 there were perpetual rumours that Pitt would return to office, and when war broke out it became more than ever desirable to strengthen the ministry. For Jackson the issue was crucial, for if Pitt stormed his way to power at the head of the Grenvilles, Canning and the whigs, there would be a fresh attempt to emancipate the Catholics, a proposal he abominated. In May 1803, therefore, he brought the two sides, in the dukes of York and Portland, into a negotiation with the object of bringing in Pitt at the head of a new ministry, and 'placing Mr. Addington upon a bed of roses, in a dignified and official station.'[77] The outbreak of war, however, strengthened Addington's parliamentary position; he refused to budge, and held on till over-come by Pitt's onslaught in April 1804. Having failed in the attempt to settle the destinies of state on the basis of Christ Church free-masonry among Addington, Abbot, Portland and himself, Jackson confined himself to collecting gossip about Pitt's efforts to fill offices in 1804,[78] and to stiffening the king's protestant resolution through the duke of York.[79] At Christmas 1808 Jackson pulled the political wires for the last time, attempting to persuade Portland, a sick man at the head of a sick ministry, 'to resign, that he might even then render the King the service of superintending the formation of a new government.' Thomas Grenville believed that it was the Dean who finally persuaded Portland to resign in September 1809, but Jackson insisted that Portland refused to discuss the matter again as he was under the king's command to hold on.[80] At the same point the Dean also resigned, and although in 1812 he was still advising his old pupil, the Prince Regent,[81] he assumed the character of one withdrawn, the hermit and philosopher of Felpham[82] dispensing moral advice to politicians,[83] and blessings to the Regent.[84]

Jackson hardly possessed the 'mighty power with the clergy' with which he has been credited;[85] he owed his influence to the extra-ordinary ascendancy which he established over his royal pupils and over loyal sons of the House who entered politics. Even in retirement he received lengthy confessions from the hard-boiled Canning (who in his youth had elaborately concealed from the Dean his intention to enter politics);[86] Peel was not put off by a lecture that the way to political success was to read through Homer four or five times a year;[87] and the political memoirs of the period abound in the con-fidences Jackson received. Clearly he was no ordinary Dean.

On the other hand the shafts of those who would not bow to him often found their mark *regnante Cyrillo*. Holland described him as 'a worshipper of rank'—and he encouraged absurd exclusiveness in the House.[88] J. W. Ward, later earl of Dudley, found him 'something of a mountebank,' a character not unjustified by the literary opinions which he enforced after dinner.[89] The cruellest cut came from Samuel Parr who

> said, 'Stung and tortured as he is with literary vanity, he shrinks with timidity from the eye of criticism' &c. meaning that Jackson had never presented himself to the public through the medium of the press.[90]

Parr saw in Jackson's literary silence the tactics the Dean affirmed in politics, that it was better to be felt before being heard. To a man with Jackson's connexions no church preferment was closed, and he is said to have refused various bishoprics and the primacy of Ireland.[91] His preference for his deanery, and what so charitable a man as Reginald Heber described as 'an absolute monarchy of the most ultra-oriental character,'[92] to a fully public station, owed as much to weakness as to affection for the House. Indeed he resigned when it was clear that the imminent death of Portland was going to be acutely embarrassing. Tatham, Rector of Lincoln, uncouth as he was, took the measure of his man when he accused him of trying to save a new Examination Statute in Convocation not by open debate but by '*beckonings*! and *crossings*! and *whisperings*! and *consultations*!' and 'the tricks of a common borough.'[93]

Jackson's politics bore directly upon his government of the House. He told Liverpool in 1809, not simply with the mock modesty of a successful man about to retire, that his achievements were

> principally owing to the gracious mention wch His Majesty was so often pleased to make of my conduct, by the favourable terms in wch he always condescended to speak of Christ Church. That was in fact the protection & support wch enabled me to overcome opposition, & even to set it at nought.[94]

Favour at Court, and the access to patronage conferred by his influence with the powers of the day, were the great inducements by which Jackson attracted the political nation to Christ Church, and secured obedience to his sway.[95] His connexion with the duke of Portland he turned to the profit of innumerable Christ Church men,[96] and by persuading the duke to appoint Lord Chancellor Eldon as High Steward of the university in 1801, he furnished 'to the blackcoats a fair access to the ecclesiastical patronage of the Chancellor and a more ample fund of solicitation than he will well know how to satisfy.'[97] Charles Abbot's influence was put to Christ

Church use,[98] and even Edward Copleston, later Provost of Oriel, who admired and in some ways resembled Jackson, admitted that 'he carried too far his attachment to the "little platoon he belonged to in society."'[99]

One patronage scheme intimately connected with the discipline of the House, the Dean failed to carry through.

> There was a system of espionage transmitted in various ways, originating with the Dean—then to his favourite, a young man, then only a bachelor, called *Carissime Carey* to distinguish him from another *Carey*, a translator of Italian. Well, *Carissime Carey* had his spies, graduating down to the lowest servants.

No wonder the Dean 'well knew the character of all the members.'[100] Carey was destined for Westminster School on the way to higher things, and Jackson got Addington to remove Dr. Wingfield, the headmaster of Westminster, to a stall at Worcester.[101] Jackson next planned to bring Carey and his espionage back to the House by carefully timing his own resignation. By October 1809, however, Liverpool had secured the reversion of the deanery for his handsome but incapable tutor, Charles Henry Hall.[102]

Jackson was nevertheless far removed from the college heads of the early eighteenth century who governed their houses by a private system of influence. He inculcated a gospel of unremitting work, and strove to restrain the riotous propensities of the Westminster students.[103] In 1792 it was a not implausible joke 'that all undergraduates at Christ Church read the *Principia*,'[104] and he kept up a supply of able tutors. This supply was sustained by the students, 101 in number, who apart from the two or three annually elected from Westminster, were nominated in turn by the Dean and Canons. Jackson bequeathed to the House the tradition that he nominated students for merit rather than interest, and when Samuel Smith began to pull the society together again in the 'twenties, it was to Jackson's example that he appealed.[105] It was a testimony to Jackson that his impulse outlived even the rule of his successor, C. H. Hall, who was probably the worst Dean Christ Church has ever endured.

Jackson was not, however, entirely absorbed in his college; as Copleston later pointed out, 'by the disinterested part he took in establishing the system of examination for degrees . . . the *comparative* importance of his own college was proportionally reduced.'[106] The origins of the momentous examination statute of 1800 are almost wholly obscure. A large gap in the minute book of the Hebdomadal Board lends some colour to the charges of improper conduct of business later made by Dr. Tatham.[107] Press reports that action was contemplated appeared in April,[108] and there is no reason to doubt the tradition which ascribed the statute to the combined labours of Cyril Jackson, John Eveleigh, Provost of Oriel, who is said to have secured action by offering a large endowment for the best candidates under a reformed examination,[109] and John Parsons, Master of Balliol, whose college derived the greatest ultimate benefit from the new system. A number of tutors led by Copleston of Oriel and 'Horse' Kett of Trinity opposed two sections of the statute as not going far enough, but 15 of the 18 sections were accepted by Convocation unanimously.[110]

The new examinations were to be fully public examinations, the statute declaring that 'it is a most desirable and momentous object, that as many members of the university as possible . . . should be present.' There should be six examiners, three to be a quorum, who should examine six candidates *viva voce* each day. The scope of the examination barely exceeded Oxford's ancient repertoire,

> that is to say for the degree of A.B., Grammar, Rhetoric, Logic, Moral Philosophy, and the Elements of Mathematics and Physics . . . For the degree of A.M. Mathematics, Physics, Metaphysics and History. And to these there is to be added, for the last degree, the Hebrew tongue. . . . Again at every examination, on every occasion, the Elements of Religion, and the Doctrinal Articles . . . must form a part.

The chief novelty lay in the last point. It had long been orthodox doctrine in Oxford that the first signs of the revolutionary upheaval abroad had been 'the want of subordination, the impatience of discipline in the seminaries of learning,' which itself had been due to the decay of religion.[111] In the autumn of 1792 French priests took refuge in England and appeared in Oxford to embody the principle of health and order on which the French had turned their back. The Hebdomadal Board launched an appeal for financial help for them with a gift from the university chest,[112] and the colleges astonished the Vice-Chancellor with their subscriptions.[113] Three of the refugees settled in Oxford, and in 1795 Convocation voted that 2000 copies of the New Testament in Latin should be produced at the press for the French priests in England.[114] As the persecuted apostles of a conservative order, a glamour surrounded the émigré priests which survived even the bitter controversy with the Irish Catholics after the Union, and channels were then opened through which new currents of catholic sentiment flowed into the church. Compulsory examination in religious knowledge which, so far as anyone knew, Oxford was the only university in the world to require for the first degree, was her defence against the fate which had overtaken the émigré priests. The high-church press acclaimed it as a means of ending profligacy, and checking the plague which had issued from the seminaries abroad to overthrow the dearest interests of the human race, 'the sophisms of that reptile philosophy which would materialise and brutify the whole intellectual system.'[115] Oxford was pledged against revolution.

The other compulsory test was the 'grammar,' 'an examination in humane literature . . . especially in the Greek and Roman writers, three of whom at the fewest, of the best age and stamp are to be used.' There was to be a further competition for honours, candidates for which were to be examined by the whole board upon a larger range of books, and the best twelve were to be listed in order of merit. As it was several years before twelve candidates presented themselves, this provision amounted to very little.[116]

Once the Hebdomadal Board began to remodel the examination system, they did not find it easy to stop. The scope of the examination was defined more clearly in a statute of 1803 which explained that Aristotle was 'the master of logic,' that logic must have its due importance, and that 'nothing severe or harsh' was intended.[117] In 1807 decisive changes were introduced. A school of mathematics and physics was created for candidates who had already taken the Greats school, and the Cambridge system of awarding honours in order of merit was abandoned in both schools in favour of classification in two classes.[118] At the same time the examination for the Master's degree was abandoned; few candidates were under any professional obligation to take the degree, and rather than face another examination, dispensed with it or took it at Cambridge.[119] In 1808 a new examination for responsions was introduced, in which two Greek and Roman authors were required, together with the rudiments of logic and the elements of mathematics.[120] In 1809 the second class of the honours schools was divided into two parts,[121] and for more than a decade the Oxford tutors were left to make the best of a settled system.

Already the constitution of the university was proving better adapted to preserve a system like the Laudian code, than for passing radical legislation. The competition for honours was much criticised. The invitation to a public challenge to the examiners, with the prospect of a public disgrace in case of failure, daunted all but the boldest, and created a rapid demand for a non-competitive system of classification. Since Convocation could not amend a statute, it behoved the heads to produce an acceptable draft. No formal machinery existed for consultation between the masters and heads, who were naturally chary of risking defeat. Inevitably the deliberations of the heads were protracted, and great frustration was engendered among the M.A.s. The Proctors pressed changes upon the Board in June 1804, a committee appointed did not report till June 1806, and it was December before a draft statute was circulated.[122] During the next six months the draft was twice brought into Convocation, twice rejected and amended by its framers, and finally put through in what Tatham insisted was an 'artful,' 'smuggling' way after Commemoration, when all academic business was at an end, and most of the residents had gone down.[123] Even then fresh botching had to be done in 1809.

Tatham declared that the whole process reflected badly upon the framers of the original statute; he viewed it as part of a process (exemplified in the much disputed statute of 1804 establishing the select preachers) by which the rights of M.A.s were being whittled away,[124] and accounted for it by a variation of the theory by which his hero Burke had accounted for the ills of state forty years before: a cabal of heads, of whom Cyril Jackson was the chief, had usurped the legitimate power of the Vice-Chancellor and Hebdomadal Board as a whole, and were exerting undue influence upon the independent members of Convocation. The basic trouble with the university was this usurped influence.[125] This theory owed too much to Burke to carry conviction, but it was already clear that the total separation between government and teaching in the university would make the reform of the educational statutes very difficult. When, in the next generation, these difficulties were aggravated by bitter religious divisions, progress became impossible.

Tatham's main complaint, however, was that the requirements of the new examination statutes were narrow and obsolete. 'A violent affectation of Peripatetic learning has seized of late the fashionable college' (Christ Church) and all must follow suit.[126] Tatham had for years raved against the reign of Aristotle in Oxford, and had rejoiced that under the unreformed system progressive colleges had been in no way inhibited by the official forms. Now, 'that obsolete and exploded discipline [was] . . . revived and restored to practice to the total exclusion or marked neglect of more modern and useful learning.' Likewise with moral philosophy.

> The old moral philosophy of Aristotle, Cicero, or Epictetus, however admirable in their days, is today not worth a louse . . . how much worse than absurd is it to send the youth of a Christian university in the nineteenth century, to learn their moral philosophy from Aristotle, that uncircumcized and unbaptized Philistine of the Schools?[127]

Nor was Tatham alone in asserting that the statute did not compel candidates to master their Greek grammar.[128] Still worse was the treatment of science which had formerly been a useful ingredient of Oxford education. The statute of 1800 had provided for 'the elements of mathematics and physics'; when they attained the dignity of a separate school in 1807 they ceased to be obligatory subjects, and there was still no provision for the other sciences.

This omission immediately affected the teaching system. Tatham bemoaned the decline in the professorial classes in science after the new statute. Chemistry classes fell to a quarter of their old numbers, and often could not be held for lack of support. Botany classes fell away. Respectable classes in anatomy and medicine dwindled to nothing.[129] The Rector's account is confirmed by the other sources.[130] Mathematics, segregated to a second school, languished as honours candidates of moderate standard found that an aquaintance with the elements contributed nothing to the one thing needful, their inescapable obligation to satisfy the examiners *in literis humanioribus*.[131] Shelley found the lectures on mineralogy languid and ill-attended,[132] and the *Edinburgh Annual Register* reckoned that in 1809 only 9 of the 23 professors offered courses, and not all of them could raise a class.[133] In a dozen years there had been a woeful change. Tatham, never reluctant to wound, regarded the new monopoly of classical learning as a compliment to the regius professor of Greek 'because he has been completely dormant for more than twenty years;'[134] this was William Jackson, brother of the Dean of Christ Church.[135]

If examinations narrowed undergraduate reading, they nevertheless made it more intensive. Observer after observer noted the new spirit of diligence,[136] and not observers only. Reginald Heber, a year after the examination statute was passed, declared 'we are . . . in the economy of time, perfect Cartesians; we admit of no vacuum,'[137] while Keble, though three years from his examinations, was induced by the statute of 1807 to give up his French exercises and 'to read for [his] degree immediately.'[138] In character and talent Heber and Keble were quite unlike the average passman who still had too little to occupy his time; but success in the schools soon became a matter of prestige, and bred a race of tutors who took pride in the successes of their pupils.

There were, moreover, powerful minds in Oxford which were well content with the quality and range of the current studies, and none more so than the redoubtable Edward Copleston, fellow of Oriel. The key to Copleston's character was unwittingly revealed by his pupil, friend, admirer and editor, Richard Whately.

> All the most remarkable steps of his elevation in life took place *without any application whatever* on his part. He was elected fellow of Oriel College, Provost of the same, Doctor of Divinity by Diploma, Dean of Chester and Bishop of Llandaff (and at the same time Dean of St. Paul's), *all* without his having *offered himself* for any one of these appointments.[139]

Copleston, in short, was a man whose intellectual superiority immediately impressed his contemporaries (and ultimately himself); a

man of undoubted talent who never fulfilled his potentialities because
success came too easily; a man whose natural tendency to arrogance
was ultimately aggravated by the knowledge that he would leave no
literary memorial;[140] a man who had the misfortune to attain high
office in the church at the very moment when his own religious ideal
was to be shouted down by those whom he regarded as the twin
prophets of irrationalism, the evangelicals (who were nowhere
stronger than in his diocese) and the apostolicals (who dominated
the lower ranks of his college). For to Copleston and his school
Anglicanism represented rational Christianity. With his liberal
toryism Copleston combined something of the temper, though not
the doctrinal conclusions, of the liberal rationalists of the previous
century; he abhorred the enthusiasm of the Welsh Methodists,[141]
found Bulteel, the evangelical fellow of Exeter, 'incurably enthusiastic,'[142] and condemned Tractarianism as 'folly,' 'mystical divinity,'
and the substitution of pious opinion for evidence.[143]

Copleston and his pupil Whately survived into the middle of the
nineteenth century, extinct volcanoes in their championship of logic
in religion. Copleston had only taken up logic when required to
expound it as tutor at Oriel in 1797, but he quickly became the
foremost advocate of logic in the schools, ferociously demolishing a
text-book written by 'Horse' Kett, one of his fellow examiners on
the first board appointed under the statute of 1800.[144] In these
halcyon days Copleston had the makings of a literary terror. In
1807 he wrote a scathing attack upon the reviewing methods of the
high-church *British Critic*;[145] by 1809 he had come to despise the
Quarterly,[146] and was working himself up to 'declare open war
against' the *Edinburgh*.

From its foundation the *Edinburgh Review* had regarded the
English universities with supercilious superiority, but had spared
Oxford any direct onslaught such as that which it delivered against
the appropriation of university chairs by the clergy of the Scottish
capital.[147] Jobbery was no longer the whig charge against Oxford,
and although broad hints that the universities contributed little to
the formative intellectual movements of the day could hardly be
rebutted, they infuriated Copleston. Three successive attacks in 1808
and 1809 brought him into the field. A learned review of La Place's
Traité de mécanique céleste concluded gloomily that although the
foundations of modern astronomy had been laid in England, although
interest in the subject remained widespread and its importance for
navigation grew no less, English scholars no longer advanced the
subject. The universities had failed.

In one of these, where the dictates of Aristotle are still listened
to as infallible decrees, and where the infancy of science is

3

mistaken for its maturity, the mathematical sciences have never flourished; and the scholar has no means of advancing beyond the mere elements of geometry.

In the other, mathematical studies had got into a rut.[148] The rhetoric of all this was offensive, but it could not be denied that Oxford contributed little to mathematics. Another review argued that the unchallenged predominance of the classics at Oxford and the English public schools was unhealthy, and that the instruction was of a limited and mistaken kind.[149] Finally, Oxford classical scholarship was impugned in an attack upon the Oxford Strabo of 1807, and the Grenville Homer published by the university under the Chancellor's patronage. 'For,' declared the *Edinburgh*,

> though this learned body have occasionally availed themselves of the sagacity and erudition of Rhunken, Wyttenbach, Heyne, and other *foreign* professors, they have of late added nothing of their own, except what they derived from the superior skill of British manufacturers, and the superior wealth of their establishment, namely, whiter paper, blacker ink, and neater types.[150]

It was hard when the aesthetic standards of the press were made a reproach, but the dependence of Oxford classical teaching upon texts edited in Germany became steadily more obvious, and even that Oxford glory Thomas Gaisford, who became regius professor of Greek in 1811, 'was content to collate manuscripts and assemble the best work of other scholars.'[151]

In rebutting this formidable indictment,[152] Copleston sought to show that the criticisms of the *Edinburgh* were either misconceived or out of date, and that Oxford education, crowned by the new examination system, constituted a liberal training. The reviewer's sneer about 'the elements of geometry' derived some substance from the wording of the examination statute of 1800, but Copleston pointed to the establishment of the school *in disciplinis mathematicis et physicis* in 1807; nevertheless his list of its mathematical requirements, apart from 'fluxions,' was entirely classical in scope, and could not meet the charge that the university was not advancing the study.[153] Copleston gave no ground in defence of Aristotle, and his curious argument that the Organon was improved for undergraduate consumption by being taught in Aldrich's abridgement, enabled him to claim that Oxford logic was not as out-moded as it looked, for

> the method of induction is there accurately explained; and . . . the vulgar error . . . by which people are led *to oppose* the Organon of Bacon to the Organon of Aristotle is directly pointed out and refuted.[154]

He also undertook a vigorous defence of the Grenville Homer which now has little interest.

Copleston's main aim was to establish that Oxford education was liberal education. The cultivation of literature raised men above an illiberal absorption in their specialised pursuits, and strengthened the basic qualities of the mind. Educated men were agreed that no literature fulfilled this high office better than 'the choicest fruits of human genius' embodied in the classical authors.[155] College teaching enabled ordinary men to get the best results from their reading. Copleston painted a rosier picture of the way in which college teaching in the classics was supplemented by professorial teaching in science than the circumstances of 1810 justified, but he was insistent that no ancillary teaching could rival the liberal discipline of the classics, and the examination system ought not to pretend that it could.

> 'Never let us believe,' he wrote, 'that the improvement of chemical arts, however much it may tend to the augmentation of the national riches, can supersede the use of that intellectual laboratory, where the sages of Greece explored the hidden elements of which man consists and faithfully recorded all their discoveries.'[156]

Liberal studies at Oxford comprised, in the highest sense, a useful education.

To this assertion the *Edinburgh*, like Tatham before, returned an absolute denial.

> Our objection is not that classical knowledge is not a good, but that it is not the only good . . . that we are making only one article, when we ought to be making many.[157]

In the end the university came to the same conclusion, but for the moment Copleston remained in the field, fortified by two anonymous puffs in the *Quarterly* written by his brother fellow, John Davison.[158] The later stages of the controversy are of no great interest,[159] and Copleston had already made his mark. He had defended the new examination system from first principles, as its supporters had failed to do against Tatham,[160] and had caught out the *Edinburgh* on some matters of fact. His prestige secured him the offer of the headship of Magdalen Hall, the unchallenged succession as Provost of Oriel in 1814,[161] and the unusual distinction of a doctorate of divinity by diploma.[162] The modern reader may sympathise with the standpoint if not the manners of the *Edinburgh*, but so unquestioned in Oriel was the tradition that Copleston had won an outright victory, that forty years later Newman was deploying all his eloquence to persuade an Irish Catholic audience that in this protestant source was the true doctrine of the nature of a university.[163] Certainly Oxford studies continued to be dominated by the examination system, the results of which inspired much less deference in Copleston than he had inculcated in the reviewers. To the end of his days he denounced

> the quackery of the schools. Every election to a fellowship which tends to discourage the narrow and almost technical *routine* of public examinations I consider an important triumph.[164]

Oriel, nevertheless, became one of the successful colleges in the schools, though with its smaller numbers it could never challenge Christ Church.[165] Encouraged by his pupil John William Ward, Copleston sought to rival his neighbour's repute as a place of fashion and education,[166] and in so doing laid up some ugly problems for his successor. At the same time Copleston isolated himself in the university on the other great controversy of the day, that of Catholic emancipation.

CHAPTER II

OXFORD AND THE CHURCH

The university of Oxford has long since ceased to exist except for the purpose of electioneering.

Westminster Review, 1831.

At Gloucester they think County Halls, & at Oxford they think Court addresses, more clerical and important objects than the making boys & girls Christians & Churchmen.

J. KEBLE to J. E. TYLER, Sept. 4, 1816.
MS. Oriel College Letters no. 992.

Why should there be more caprice, and more jealousy in universities and colleges, than in other collections of men? I know not but so it is.

C. H. HALL to LORD HAWKESBURY, June 12, 1805.
B.M. Add. MSS. 38473 fo. 220.

MATTERS in Oxford stood favourably towards Court and church when in 1801 Francis Page, who for a generation had occupied one of the university's two seats in parliament with complete lack of distinction, resigned from age and infirmity.[1] In the course of the university's struggle with the Court early in the eighteenth century, the convention had been established that no sitting member should be opposed, and Page, who had slipped in during a confused contest in 1768, had enjoyed complete tranquillity. With the same view of countering outside influence, canvassing by outside parties was frowned upon, and of course, any canvassing against a sitting member. Candidates themselves were excluded from the constituency during the election, and only afterwards were the burgesses permitted to return for ceremonial visits to the heads. Election itself was gratis, and combined with the long record of the members in opposition to justify the university's boast of independence. That Oxford elections and Oxford members should be free and independent was the tradition evolved in and for opposition. Now that Oxford had made its peace with government and the whole political order was changing, the tradition was thoroughly inconvenient; its *raison d'être* was already forgotten, but it encumbered the constituency throughout the new century.[2] Sir William Dolben, the university burgess, spoke of the

free & unsolicited choice of Convocation which stands paramount over all other places in purity of principle, & has

ever so eminently decided the election of the representatives of
the University of Oxford.[3]

Election could hardly be 'free & unsolicited' in this sense once the
electorate was divided by fundamental political issues, nor could the
member be free if the voters insisted in knowing on which side of the
crux he stood. Similarly the squires who had for so long been Oxford's
independent representatives, became incongruous when the university
wanted ministerial protection, yet the tradition persisted that

> the first requisite is a gentleman of good family and independent
> fortune who will give an unbiased constitutional vote, not a
> professional man, who will barter the honour and interests of
> his seat for promotion in his profession.[4]

A professional man, however, was precisely the burgess the university
now obtained.

Since Christ Church spoke 'pretty peremptorily of *dictating*' a
successor to Sir William Dolben,[5] they left the other seat to the
university. New College which had carried Page, talked of putting
forward John Coker, an irascible barrister with a thirst for controversy, but never formally proposed him.[6] A more distinguished man
who dearly coveted the seat was William Windham, the disciple of
Burke, who had been turned by events in France into a strong
conservative and unyielding advocate of war against the revolutionary
government. He had resigned with Pitt, giving up the secretaryship
of war and a seat in the cabinet, and was about to be rejected by his
constituents at Norwich for opposing the peace. Security as well as
honour were at stake. Windham fulfilled the canons as a model
country gentleman, a keen scholar and a polished linguist. Important
issues of policy divided him from the majority in the university,
but he was regarded as a serious candidate for both seats. For the
moment his hopes were deferred because his society, University
College, had already sponsored another candidate,[7] Sir William Scott.

Twenty years before Scott had contested the university seat with
Dolben as an independent,[8] and the passage of years had turned him
into a strong conservative. In his youth he had been reputed 'the
most enlightened tutor' of his day,[9] and had been a creditable Camden
professor. A man of surpassing classical acquirements and taste,[10] a
luminary in the world of letters, an intimate and executor of Johnson,
he attained a peculiar eminence in the legal profession in the ecclesiastical and admiralty courts. In these quiet channels Scott developed
a unique power and refinement of reasoning. From the great range
of cases which came before him during the Napoleonic War, Scott
created a system of prize law embodying definite principles and
rules.[11] At the same time his eminence in ecclesiastical law gave him

special authority as parliament began to overhaul the machinery of the church.

Scott had often been in difficulties about a seat, and in 1793 when Page had been expected to retire, he and Henry Addington had been favourite candidates for the succession.[12] Addington had recently given up his claim;[13] Christ Church, while perfecting tactics against a resignation by the aged Dolben,[14] supported Scott; and on March 23 he was elected unopposed.[15] In one respect at least Scott remained a true independent. Elections at Oxford had long been free to the members, except for small fees and gratuities to the bedells who brought tidings of the result, and other officials. Scott now 'put an end to all fees whatever, except some shillings to bell-ringers.'[16] Purity could hardly go further.

Scarcely had Scott been returned as virtual member for the church than he encountered the embarrassments which were to be the common lot of Oxford burgesses when the age of ecclesiastical reform began. In 1800 a small group of lawyers began to claim the rewards due under the acts of Henry VIII to common informers against non-resident clergy. Gross injustice was done to clergy who were techni-cally non-resident, though performing their spiritual duties, and chaos was threatened in a church whose parish life was dominated by clerical poverty and lack of parsonage houses. Scott was clear that an equalisation of clerical stipends would be useless and would be subversive of a hierarchical English society,[17] nor would he have sympathised with later doctrines of a separated ministry. He strongly advocated that the clergy should be freed from the restrictions imposed by Reformation statutes upon their participation in the gentlemanly profession of agriculture. In 1803 at the third attempt, and solely by means of government support,[18] he carried an act enlarging the grounds of clerical non-residence, broadening the clergy's scope for earning a living, and strengthening the authority of the bishops. This last point was unpopular,[19] but even worse was his bill to assist stipendiary curates, attention to whose interests had been promised in order to get the Clergy Non-Residence Bill through.

The Hebdomadal Board were particularly angry at the authority to be given to bishops to compel non-resident incumbents to employ curates, a provision which might prove costly to heads and professors to whose offices were annexed benefices with cure of souls. Nor did they relish the financial arrangements. The arguments of the Board convinced neither Scott nor the laity in parliament; but after two attempts, Scott thought better of the campaign, and every time the bill came forward he and the university Chancellor received instruc-tions to take the sting out of it.[20] Scott was threatened with the opposition at elections of which Oxford's later reforming burgesses were to have bitter experience; and already the alienation of the university from lay opinion which characterised the age of reform was foreshadowed.

No-one in Oxford yet rose up to denounce national apostasy, for, unlike the leading politicians, the majority in parliament was still sound on the crucial question of Catholic emancipation. Oxford was nevertheless very sensitive to the constitutional issues raised by the emancipation question and to the way those issues were confused by the demands of war. Conservatives who saw the fundamental menace in the revolutionary spirit in France favoured concessions to Irish Catholics in order to save English protestantism by winning the war. On grounds of this sort a minority of 110 in Convocation opposed a petition against the Catholic claims in 1805,[21] and Windham still nursed hopes of winning the university seat.

Sir William Scott sat for Oxford for twenty years, but from the beginning there were rumours that he was about to follow his brother Lord Eldon, to the House of Lords.[22] By June 1805, when these rumours reached their first climax, cynics already regarded them as 'the old story repeated . . . to feel the pulse of the university.'[23] The pulse now showed a strong protestant beat, but Windham had friends even among protestants.

Foremost was Martin Routh, President of Magdalen, now only fifty, but a victim to the 'almost morbid inactivity of [his] disposi- tion,'[24] and settling down into an eternity of venerable seclusion, largely cut off from the university.[25] Routh was an old-fashioned radical tory whose survival into an alien age is of singular interest. While most Oxford politicians were becoming ardent church-and- state men, Routh embodied the traditions of the old high-church opposition. His life's work was an edition of patristic writings,[26] and, deeply interested in the Stuart period, he also edited Burnet's *History of his own time*.[27] In his youth, a devoted admirer of Johnson,[28] Routh was later intimate with those stormy petrels of opposition, the whig Samuel Parr,[29] and the radical Sir Francis Burdett, whom he always defended, and who delivered a warm panegyric upon him in the Commons. In 1789 he favoured Fox's plan of a regency during the king's insanity rather than Pitt's;[30] he thought it unconstitutional to describe the united parliament created upon the Act of Union with Ireland as an 'imperial parliament;'[31] and even after the publication of Tract XC could still find sympathy for the angry young rebels of the Oxford movement[32] who reproduced so much of what Routh described as 'my general dislike of the superiors of my own order.'[33]

He represented himself as 'one of those persons who by their small, or rather no, number, now become useless, who follow principles more than connections,' and his general principle in matters of church and state was that 'this church I am bound in conscience never in the smallest degree or remotest bearing to act against, not because it is established, or because I enjoy emoluments in it . . . but because I believe it to be really Catholic.'[34] He had no love for dissenters,[35] and thought that papists excluded themselves from the catholic church by using the name catholic as a denominational distinction.[36] Nevertheless, though aware of Windham's advocacy of emancipation,[37] he consistently supported him in Oxford, and probably still considered that Catholic relief could be combined with adequate securities for the church. He admired Windham as 'a man of probity' and 'a most elegant scholar'; the two had been brought together in 1792 by Samuel Parr, who exerted all his influence to secure the election of Robert Lukin, Windham's nephew, as a demy.[38]

Though a scholar, Routh was no politician, and the heads to whom Windham poured out his philosophy of emancipation were John Cooke, President of Corpus, and David Hughes, Principal of Jesus, a rough Welshman who had been a repository of his Oxford hopes for five years. To Cooke, whose college rule, like that of Routh, was 'mild and inert,'[39] Windham wrote at length explaining that if Ireland were lost to a French invasion neither church nor state would survive.[40] Among Windham's other friends, neither Septimus Collinson, Provost of Queen's, nor William Cleaver, Bishop of Bangor and Principal of Brasenose, was free to assist. Cleaver had been tutor to the marquis of Buckingham, under his aegis had enjoyed rapid preferment in the church,[41] and had been intimately concerned with the notorious Grenville Homer.[42] As the leader of the Grenville party in the Commons, Windham must have expected strong support from B.N.C. Cleaver, however, reckoned the Oxford seat 'quite hopeless for any who have given a decided vote for the Catholic question,'[43] and, moreover, had a candidate from his own college.

This candidate, Richard Heber, had many of the same assets and liabilities as Windham. Even at college Heber had acquired a scholarly reputation and laid the foundations of the famous book collections which led him into the society of the leading men of English letters, and eventually exceeded in size anything hitherto known. In 1804 he succeeded to his father's estates in Yorkshire and Shropshire which he augmented by purchase and considerably improved.[44] Rich and popular, Heber rivalled Windham as a cultivated gentleman; through his half-brother Reginald,[45] than whom no evangelical was more respected outside the party, he had access to clerical support. On emancipation Heber was equivocal; he had always associated with the catholic Grenvilles, but he was able to satisfy rabid protestants.[46] The truth was that he was not a serious politician, and had no experience of affairs; he was further reproached

with being too young and having come into his estate too recently
to qualify for the Oxford seat. Even his friends at B.N.C. scolded
him for canvassing in Oxford after the Commemoration in 1805.[47]
Like Windham, Heber found some doors closed; his second cousin,[48]
Dr. Routh, was firmly pledged to his opponent, while Pitt whom he
approached through Lady Hester Stanhope, 'gave his usual answer
to such applications that he made it a rule never to interfere in any
election whatever.'[49]

Dr. Collinson, Provost of Queen's, was more cordial but equally
embarrassed. A party in Queen's wished to propose Richard
Richards,[50] a Chancery lawyer who had matriculated at Jesus, and
subsequently migrated to Wadham and Queen's. He might expect
votes from all three societies. As Richards was a man of no reputation,
Samuel Parr could only account for his appearance by the 'dirty and
dark machinations' of Scott and Eldon to safeguard the protestant
interest by dividing Windham's following.[51] It was certainly serious
for Windham that David Hughes could not guarantee half the Jesus
votes against the attraction of a Welsh lawyer.[52] Another barrister
was also being started from All Souls, William Dickinson, one of
Pitt's junior lords of the Admiralty; he had matriculated at Christ
Church and so had a personal following in two colleges.[53]

Windham needed every vote, and now felt the full force of the
protestant interest. Nathan Wetherell, Master of University College,
deprived Windham of the unanimous backing of his own society.[54]
Michael Marlow, President of St. John's, a devoted disciple of
Burke and Portland, promised his personal assistance, but despaired
of success.[55] Whittington Landon, Provost of Worcester, who had
been appointed by Portland, had a prior engagement,[56] and Portland
himself discovered a scruple against interfering.[57] David Hughes of
Jesus elaborately double-crossed Windham, 'conceiving the Catholic
question to have altered the situation.'[58] Berdmore, Warden of
Merton, Parsons, Master of Balliol, and the Dean of Christ Church
were implacably protestant,[59] and even Dr. Routh was asking for
assurances that Windham would maintain the Test and Corporation
Acts.[60] Even worse, that ferocious abettor of lost causes, Dr. Tatham,
'declared himself loudly against all professional men,'[61] which left
him a millstone round the neck of either Heber or Windham.

As the Long Vacation dragged on, the truth gradually dawned
that Scott was not going to the House of Lords after all, and in
September Pitt 'expressed his astonishment that such an idea should
ever have existed.'[62] The futile conspiracies of the summer were not,
however, without effect. The strength of protestant feeling in Oxford
was unmistakable, and Windham abandoned his claim to the representation until Oxford should see eye to eye with him on emancipation,[63] a day he never lived to see. And when in the following year a

vacancy arose by the retirement of Dolben, several candidates were well prepared and in the field.

During the winter the protestant pot was kept well boiling by the preachers at St. Mary's[64] and Christ Church prepared to reassert her property in one of the university seats.[65] The system was that the Chapter determined the college candidate by a majority decision; any Canon in the minority might vote for his friend, but might not canvass the college for him.[66] In Jackson's day, the decision as to the suffrage of the House was largely his, and he had kept out of other contests to ensure the succession to Dolben.[67] Since 1801 the candidate of his choice had been Charles Abbot.[68] Abbot had come up from Westminster to Christ Church in 1776 and became eminent among the Old Westminsters at the House at a time when they were taking many of the classical prizes in the university. Abbot became Vinerian fellow, and in 1792 began legal practice in London. Finding this life too strenuous, he had accepted a lucrative office in the King's Bench, and began a notable career as an administrative reformer. He served with distinction as chairman of the select committee on finance of 1797, introduced the first Census Act of 1800 and in 1801 went over to Ireland for a year as Chief Secretary. This appointment Abbot owed to his intimate friend Addington; in 1802 Addington supported him for the Speakership, and he assumed Addington's mantle as prospective Christ Church candidate for the next Oxford vacancy. Abbot, a fervent admirer of the Dean, had two great political recommendations. Jackson believed in playing safe, and of the leading political figures, none was less of a party man than Abbot; on the other hand, on the inescapable emancipation issue, he was an immovable protestant. Abbot, however, became intensely attached to the Speaker's office,[69] and would not embarrass the conduct of parliamentary business by resigning his seat to fight a by-election; still less did he wish to risk a defeat, for the duke of Marlborough could no longer promise to return him again for Woodstock if he were defeated in the university. It was plain that Abbot could only stand at a general election.[70] In the summer of 1806, therefore, Jackson secured a letter of resignation from Dolben to produce at whatever moment he judged most favourable for Abbot's return.[71]

One more obstacle lay between the free suffrages of the university and the result so carefully contrived by the Dean. Under the charter, burgesses must be members of the university, and it had often been held that the statute *de semel non fruendis* debarred office-holders in the town from membership of the university; Abbot, who was the Oxford Recorder, found the cry revived against him. There were enough precedents to the contrary to convince Jackson that Abbot was qualified,[72] but when polling began Cholmondely, the Dean of

Chester, a relative of Richard Heber, and Frodsham Hodson, a respected tutor of B.N.C., made an immediate attempt to disqualify him. Jackson, whose best friends admitted that 'he cannot utter three sentences in publick', made an indifferent reply, and the Vice-Chancellor permitted a disorderly debate in English to drag on for a couple of hours before admitting an utterly unorganised flood of voters.[73]

Only now was it clear whom Abbot would have to oppose. Richard Heber had been canvassing and would certainly stand. He was strong in B.N.C. and Oriel and in Magdalen, the society of his cousin Routh, and Jackson's elaborate electioneering only lent point to Heber's cry of independence. The Speaker's chief worry, however, was caused by the persistent candidacy of Richards. When Richards came forward as a successor to Scott in July 1805 Abbot derived the apparently unwarranted impression that he would not oppose his plans to succeed Dolben. When Richards announced his intention of standing, Abbot was terrified that he had lost the support of Grenville's government, and submitted the issue between them to the adjudication of Spencer Perceval.[74] In the nick of time Richards withdrew, and once polling began, though the Dean was on tenterhooks, the result was never in doubt. A record number of voters came to the poll which read:

Heber 275:   Abbot 404:   Scott 651.

Both Abbot and Heber professed satisfaction, each claiming that the other had done all the canvassing. Abbot's majority was less than the Christ Church poll;[75] Heber claimed an equality of resident votes, and a total which would normally have secured election, even though 'Royal Dukes and Dukes not Royal, Committees of the Treasury, E. India Company and that great body of Ch. Ch. overpowered us.'[76] To Abbot the seat meant independence but his opponents claimed that the independence of the university was forfeit—'the Univ. is turned into a dirty rotten minister's borough.'[77] The next election showed vividly how far Court politics might jeopardise Oxford's most treasured doctrines.

Where the Court interest lay was itself obscure in the next few years. After Pitt's death, that Oxford luminary, Grenville presided over an alliance of Grenvillites, Foxites, and friends of Addington, and in Oxford gave government support to Abbot, to whose views on the Catholic question he was totally opposed. In 1807 the Ministry of All the Talents fell owing to a misunderstanding with the king over a measure of relief for Catholic officers in the Irish army, the king's suspicions being aroused by that staunch friend of Oxford, Lord Sidmouth. The new ministry, which from the outset was a weak one, was headed by the Oxford Chancellor, Portland, and among its

leading members were the High Steward of the university, Lord
Eldon, and the most influential of the younger generation of Christ
Church politicians, Lord Hawkesbury, later 2nd earl of Liverpool.
Portland was an inefficient premier, and the ministry was soon
wrecked by the famous quarrel between Canning, another son of the
House, and Castlereagh. George III set his conscience between the
politicians and Catholic relief, but his days appeared numbered, and
no one could foresee that in office the conscience of the Prince of
Wales would turn stoutly protestant. Thus the fall of the Talents in
March 1807, in no way precluded the early return of a ministry
pledged to emancipation and able to carry it through. The politicians
of Oxford might have to decide whether, in fundamentals, they
were Court politicians or apostles of the protestant constitution.

The issue for the Talents came to a head early in March 1807 over
a bill to repeal the military test, and on the 11th, Sidmouth and
friends attempted to resign. On the eve of this crisis, Portland and
Eldon (both of whom had resigned office on the death of Pitt in 1806)
and the two university burgesses got the Hebdomadal Board to put
an immediate petition against the bill through Convocation.[78] With
this encouragement the king stood firm, and in a few days the
ministers were out of office. Should the university now go further
and put on a demonstration of gratitude to the king for his defence
of the establishment? To many Oxford men the question was simply

> whether we should adhere to the wholesome institutions which
> our ancestors had purchased at the price of much blood and
> bitter persecution, or whether we should agree to give the
> ascendance again to that pernicious sect from which they had
> endured all this, and which was harmless now only because it
> had no power.[79]

Some protestants, however, thought that the university would be ill-
advised to take up a position permitting of no compromise with a
future catholic ministry, and in the middle of April 1807 several
heads thought that the university had done enough by its petition
of March 16.[80] The avowed Grenvillites, the chief of whom, William
Cleaver, Principal of Brasenose, had lately been raised to the see of
St. Asaph by Grenville, had fought the petition,[81] and would bitterly
resist anything further.

The majority of the Board, however, were willing to answer
Hawkesbury's call for a public demonstration of support for the new
ministry, despite the threat of a procuratorial veto.

> Many persons here have a hankering after the Grenvilles, from
> whom they expected promotion. The whole B. Nose College for
> instance certainly expected that Ld. Temple wd. make them

Deans at least. Now of the Proctors who enter'd office the first
day of the present term, the senior (Deane of B.N.) is a decided
Grenvillite, or at least decidedly under the influence of those
that are, & the junior (Copplestone of Oriel) is not much
better. Both voted against the addressing, but professing to vote
as individuals, & not as uniting in the procuratorial veto.
Nevertheless I am not clear that they might not be persuaded,
and if they shd. be exasperated I am very clear that they wd.
work themselves up to go even that length. So that you will see
some management is necessary.[82]

The management, however, was provided; an address congratulating
the king upon 'his firm support of our happy Establishment' put
through,[83] and the Proctors were left to justify their conduct on
another day.

When in September 1809, Portland resigned, a dying man, the
ministry was reconstructed under Perceval, and in the following
month, upon the golden jubilee of his accession, Convocation voted
the king a fulsome address, rejoicing that amid the perils of the
reign, 'our public seminaries of education have not been disturbed
. . . the foundations of our civil and religious establishments have
remained unshaken.'[84] At any time, however, those establishments
might be threatened by Lord Grenville's return to power, while the
peace of Oxford was shattered as Portland's life ebbed away, and
Grenville prepared to succeed him as Chancellor.

One of the humours of the violent contest for the Chancellorship
was the indignation with which each candidate denounced the others
for canvassing before there was a vacancy, and for bringing undue
pressure to bear. Since 1805 Portland had more than once seemed
likely to die, and Grenville had marred his hitherto irresistible claims
by taking up emancipation again. In June 1805, upon a rumour that
Portland was already dead, a party in New College put forward
Lord Sidmouth,[85] and in 1809 he received a fresh invitation to stand.
This he declined partly because the Chancellorship was no honour
unless unanimously conferred, and partly because he had no taste
for 'distinction unconnected with real usefulness.' In truth Sidmouth
was among the members of the Perceval ministry who hoped to
recruit the support of Grenville and Grey,[86] and in the great Oxford
contest, Sidmouth, a pillar of the protestant interest, remained
officially neutral, and rendered Grenville some private assistance.[87]

Liverpool who had risen rapidly to high office, and who in
September 1809 secured the Deanery of Christ Church for his old
tutor Charles Henry Hall, was more anxious for the Chancellorship.
Hall had long claimed to be canvassing for him against the opposition
of Dean Jackson,[88] and now bore the full brunt of Liverpool's

insistence that Grenville must be defeated or 'the severest mortification' would be inflicted upon the king. Hall was in no position to support his pupil, for Grenville had not only given him the regius chair of divinity in 1807, but as the outstanding Christ Church statesman of the older generation, and a polished scholar, had a considerable following in the House. Hall claimed that his common room had begged him to take no part, that Grenville's party in the House could not be broken, that Liverpool would be beaten if he stood. Liverpool therefore withdrew,[89] and must have reflected how skilfully Cyril Jackson had timed his retirement.

The other protestant candidates, the duke of Beaufort and Lord Eldon, clashed acrimoniously for reasons which are still not altogether clear. A distinguished former fellow, as Lord Chancellor the head of his profession and patron of hundreds of livings in the church, High Steward, a consistent protestant,[90] Eldon had every conceivable claim to the Chancellorship, and when University College put him forward in 1805,[91] Eldon seems to have intended to stand.[92] Certainly Portland was no sooner dead than Eldon was pressed by the Vice-Chancellor, Dr. Parsons, Master of Balliol, Dr. Eveleigh, Provost of Oriel, and Dr. Marlow, President of St. John's, to stand upon the protestant constitution and the consistency of the university.[93] Eldon, however, did not want to risk defeat, and created an impression in some quarters that he would not stand.[94] Moreover, he was the quintessential court candidate, and it still behoved Oxford candidates to defer to the shibboleths of independence.

The duke of Beaufort, a local magnate whose family had long aspired to the Chancellorship, and was 'still considered as a sort of hereditary chief of the friends of Ch. & Kg.', was launched by protestants of independent sympathies of whom Dr. Routh, President of Magdalen, was the most distinguished.[95] Even Canning favoured Beaufort,[96] and he would perhaps have been the strongest candidate had he begun his canvass before the first week in November.[97] During this week certain ministers concluded that Beaufort would not stand, and even after nomination continued to expect that he would transfer his interest to Eldon, should the latter take the lead.[98] Much later to assuage his pride Eldon said that he only stood upon the assurance that Beaufort would not be candidate, and at the king's command, a command from which the king refused to release him when Beaufort refused to withdraw.[99] This division in the protestant interest became deeper as the contest proceeded.

Meanwhile Grenville, who before 1805 would probably not have been opposed, had been canvassing bishops and burgesses, catholic and protestant alike.[100] By the autumn of 1809 his prospects were obscure, and he himself reckoned his success merely as 'not out of the question.'[101] A few days before Portland's death the situation changed dramatically. 'The Dean of Christ Church removed, and a tottering ministry,' rejoiced Cleaver, had altered the whole situation.[102] Cyril Jackson had always refused to credit Catholic disavowals of the doctrine of papal infallibility, and while he was Dean, Christ Church as a body would never take Grenville up. But Dr. Hall ought enormously to reinforce Grenville's chief agents in Brasenose. As for the 'tottering ministry', Tom Grenville perceived that

> one of the great features of your strength in Oxford is in their expectation of a change of government; everybody sees and knows that this speculation sustains you against the overbearing influence at Oxford which any fixed government would have.[103]

Grenville's unabashed touting among the bishops now met with astonishing success,[104] and if Eldon enjoyed the support of the king, Grenville was favoured by the rebellious royal dukes; the Prince and Princess of Wales canvassed for him, and the duke of Clarence procured for him the support of Dr. Cole, Rector of Exeter, who became Grenville's first choice as Vice-Chancellor.[105] By the middle of November Grenville's friends had collected 350 promises, and were full of confidence, though on the 17th Henry Beeke, regius professor of modern history, computed that it was a very close call, and that Eldon's strength in London put him slightly ahead.[106]

Eldon was exploiting his patronage, and was said purposely to have kept livings vacant till the election.[107] He wrote desperately to the king for fresh assurances of support, and circulated the quip (attributed to others also)[108] that 'the King today said it would be hard if Cambridge had a unitarian Chancellor,[109] and Oxford a popish one.'[110] Eldon was most wounded by the treachery of the Princess of Wales,[111] his ally Liverpool by the inactivity of the Dean of Christ Church. The Censors circulated letters declaring that the House was officially neutral, but were said to be canvassing for Grenville as individuals. Liverpool threatened the utmost displeasure of the Lord Chancellor, the government and the king,[112] and had he seen the Dean's fulsome letter of congratulation to Grenville at the end of the election, his suspicions of duplicity would have been confirmed.[113]

Meanwhile Grenville's Brasenose friends were working like beavers, Principal Hodson being for weeks inseparable from his canvassing lists. Copleston and the rising generation at Oriel served devotedly.[114] Outside Oxford, Lord Auckland and the duke of Marlborough, the marquis of Buckingham and Tom Grenville, the Foxite peers[115] and William Wickham,[116] all toiled for new promises. In this election for the first time the candidates set up committes in Oxford and London. The secretary of Beaufort's Oxford committee was James Ingram, the future President of Trinity;[117] University College and Brasenose

were bases for Eldon and Grenville, an active member of whose
London committee was Richard Heber, the equivocal protestant of
1806.[118] For the first time also committees undertook to get voters
to the poll. Grenville's committee urged personal attendance,[119] and
warned his friends not to be deceived by specious proposals for
pairing.[120] His London committee promised to reimburse travelling
expenses or provide transport for friendly voters, and the Principal
of Brasenose, a month before the poll began to urge that the Oxford
coaches from London and Birmingham be engaged.[121] The Oxford
committee deplored this step; it put an end to the tradition of election
without expense, and immediately provoked Lord Eldon's side to
allegations of immorality,[122] and to designs upon the post-horses.[123]
But the promises having been made had to be redeemed.

To these preparations Dr. Parsons, the protestant Master of
Balliol, who as Vice-Chancellor was returning officer, made a curious
riposte. He determined to adjourn Convocation during the polling
so that voters delayed by Grenville's inroads upon the public
transport could vote at an adjourned session. Grenville immediately
secured a legal opinion that a Convocation held for the purpose of
electing a Chancellor could not be adjourned. Dr. Hodson, who
feared the consequences of appearing to coerce the Vice-Chancellor,
doubted the prudence of publishing the opinion, but Parsons himself
sought to obtain an opinion that he might adjourn the poll and
failed to get it. Nevertheless, though 'suffering exceedingly from a
very painful attack of the gout,' the Vice-Chancellor secured two
days of voting by keeping the poll open all night.[124]

The election arguments about emancipation were bitter and did
not attain the later refinement of the age of Peel. Eldon's friends
urged that the university must act with consistency if it wished to
preserve any political reputation. In almost Tractarian terms a
pamphlet urged:

> If this nation has hitherto escaped the almost general ruin, it
> must be attributed to the influence of its moral and religious
> principles . . . And shall this university be the place that shall
> set the pernicious example of the dereliction of all principle?[125]

Grenville's arguments were often unimpressive. His friends hoped
'the university would for once sacrifice party and even high-church
feeling to the interests and credit of learning,'[126] but the election
could hardly be unpolitical if Grenville was to enjoy a political
triumph. As Auckland put it,

> the object there is, at best, rather honorary than important;
> but it happens to be intermixed with a consideration which alone
> impedes the prompt establishment of such a government as
> might save the empire.[127]

4

Grenville had not fought so hard for an object 'rather honorary than important.' His propagandists yielded to none in abuse, claiming that the protestant cause was fundamentally illiberal The university should

> use milder and more Christian language—language which breathes more of the tolerant religion she professes, than she did in 1805 and 1807.[128]

Or without pretence of reason:

> A poor gentleman of good parts, and liberal education, has of late become disordered in his mind, and wanders about making a great outcry about Catholics, monks, mass-books and James the Second . . . It is useless to reason with him.[129]

Again the Grenvillites claimed that past university petitions were not genuine corporate acts like the present election, but the work of a minority,[130] which, as Churton said, was 'a republican or worse than republican argument.'[131] And Grenville's committee published reports that Eldon was about to withdraw alternately with claims that a junction of the protestant forces could only be conceived by personal malice.[132]

Grenville's complaints that he was unfortunate with the press need some discounting. Dr. Hodson sent paragraphs to the *Morning Chronicle*,[133] and had to make a public apology to Dr. Routh for a letter that journal published from another ally.[134] Copleston wrote effectively for Grenville,[135] but few in Oxford read the *Chronicle*,

> whereas the *Courier*, in which the answers are inserted is read probably by nine-tenths of our outlying voters and by every resident member of the university.[136]

Walter of the *Times* was specially sympathetic with Grenville, but by paying for material as advertisements and by exerting general pressure, Eldon's committee got him to accept their paragraphs.[137]

On one matter press comment became especially vehement. Grenville always claimed to be a friend of the church,[138] and in response to queries from President Routh, he wrote an open letter to Dr. Hodson, explaining that he had never brought forward the question of emancipation on his own initiative, that his refusal to promise the king never to bring the question forward did not imply his 'having determined to act upon it rashly, and at all hazards,' and that there must be securities (unspecified) for the establishment.[139] This letter Hodson kept private for about a month, giving out that Grenville promised adequate securities for the church, and creating an impression that he had undertaken to support a royal veto on appointments to the Catholic hierarchy, or even to renounce his support of the Catholic petitions.[140] Protestants soon began to clamour for a sight of this remarkable document,[141] and a week before the poll put up a tremendous howl when they discovered that it contained no specific promises at all. The *Courier* pointed out that the oath of abjuration and the subscriptions would not survive in the university if abolished in the state.[142] The protestants posed as the victims of a great deception.

At this stage the Grenvillites were very confident, even though their promises had barely increased in the last two or three weeks, and when on December 10 they cast up their books for the last time they divided the vote thus:

Grenville 456: Eldon 351: Beaufort 216.[143]

Almost every voter in the constituency was accounted for, and Grenville should win provided that voting reached the astonishingly high figure expected,[144] and provided there was no protestant coalition. This was now Grenville's chief fear, and he even offered to bring up Beaufort's voters with his own.[145] Nevertheless the Eldonites were reported to have printed letters announcing their victory, and to have offered the High Stewardship to Lord Radnor.[146] After two days and a night of polling, with the nerves of all parties at breaking point, the Convocation House 'filled with suffocating smoke' from burning voting papers,[147] 'a King's messenger . . . waiting to carry the happy news to Windsor and Sir William Scott standing at the door,' the result was announced to 'an hysterical scream of joy and sorrow from the different parties'[148]—'the tumult and uproar . . . was very considerable.'[149] By virtue of rank Eldon's name was announced first: 393 votes; then came Grenville with 406 and Beaufort with 238. Grenville's friends were so delighted with even their diminished poll that they received with charity the studied rudeness with which the Vice-Chancellor reported the result.[150] Eldon's party was furious. John Coker of New College 'stood forth in the Convocation House and declared the university to be ruined,'[151] and prolonged the controversy in a series of pamphlets, reserving his worst blasts for the Brasenose contingent and for the Proctors of 1807, who, if emancipation was their politics, ought to have vetoed the petition of that year.[152]

Copleston elaborately defended his conduct as Proctor, and put the ablest case for emancipation to arise from this conflict.

> The argument of abstract right and justice, 'he declared,' has always appeared to me untenable, and inconsistent with the principle that the Church establishment is part of the Constitution. That principle I maintain in its fullest extent . . . Still it is an undisputed maxim of English government that an equal

> participation of civil rights shall be enjoyed by all ranks and persuasions, as far as is consistent with the public good. The imposition, therefore, or the relaxation of these disabilities will ever be a varying and not a fundamental rule of policy . . . Unless this position were admitted, with what conscience could one carry up an address to the throne, talking of the *wisdom of our fore-fathers* who imposed restraints on Catholics, yet expressing satisfaction at the repeal of the greater part of them within the present reign.[153]

But Coker was not to be put down and the dispute dragged on into the next year.[154]

Eldon's mortification[155] and recriminations occasioned various comic stories after the poll,[156] and he finally ascribed his defeat to defections of Beaufort's voters to Grenville.[157] Grenville's observers, however, claimed that Eldon had run him close because Beaufort's voters had turned to him.[158] Yet Grenville's final canvass suggested that the ultimate transfer of votes must have been from Grenv le to Eldon. Bitter recriminations went on for years,[159] and the voting record of 1809 influenced the disposal of patronage long afterwards.[160]

The venom of the campaign bore no relation to its final consequence. Grenville failed to return to office, and became more of a spent force with every year that passed; his whig allies deplored the way in which his Oxford connexion hardened his conservatism in church matters.[161] Nor did his triumph dispose the clergy towards emancipation.[162] As early as the following May a numerous and unanimous Convocation instructed the university burgesses to resist fresh Catholic petitions.[163]

Grenville's friends did not desert him at the installation, well knowing (in the inflated language of the *Times*) that

> it is here that a great and free people, through many a revolving century, from the earliest dawn and infancy of their science up to the brightest blaze of their illumined maturity, have told learning herself to place herself in a state of moral and political exaltation.[164]

In March 1810, Grenville's abettor the Prince of Wales made a bequest of papyri and other MSS. to the Bodleian,[165] and was awarded the degree of D.C.L. by diploma.[166] He was expected to appear at the Encaenia,[167] and although he finally stayed away, Oxford was packed. Grenville was welcomed by an ode written by Copleston, and some rather uncomplimentary verses.[168] Partisans of Grenville received academical honours, though Sheridan's name had to be withdrawn for fear of opposition,[169] and a balloon was put up in Merton Field which eventually came down at Newport

Pagnell.[170] But splendid though it was, the celebration accomplished nothing for the university or the parliamentary opposition.

In February and again in June 1812, Grenville's last hopes of a return to power with the whigs were disappointed, and the gulf between him and the university on the Catholic question was re-emphasised. Early in 1812, Grenville resolved to move for a committee upon the Catholic disabilities,[171] and the wheels in Oxford began to turn against him. On April 17, in what Dr. Parsons described as the fullest Convocation he had ever seen 'except in cases of election,'[172] petitions against the Catholic claims were moved.

> Upon the question being proposed several non-placets were given loudly. Then arose Mr. Copleston of Oriel & having previously translated a quantity of commonplace arguments against the question into reasonably good Latin, he pronounced a short oration to which nobody gave any answer.[173]

The majority in favour of the petitions was about eight to one, but the *Times*, still sympathetic to Grenville, reported that the petitions were carried 'after much opposition'[174] and unpleasant comments in the Commons followed.

Sir John Coxe Hippesley attacked a column in the *Morning Post* slandering the Chancellors of the two universities for sacrificing their office to their party views,[175] and claimed that Convocation had been rushed into voting. Another speaker, echoing Grenville's speech in presenting the petition,[176] claimed that

> a very respectable portion of the resident members, including the Vice-Chancellor, the two Proctors, and several heads of houses and others of the most learned and estimable men in the university decidedly opposed it.[177]

This group consisted of Dr. Cole, Rector of Exeter, Grenville's ally, Dr. Hodson, the Grenvillite pillar of B.N.C., and the heads of Jesus and Pembroke, from which colleges the Proctors of the year also came. How isolated Brasenose and Exeter had become was shown in the following year. After the great victory of Leipzig, the Hebdomadal Board sanctioned a general illumination;[178] the heads of Exeter and Brasenose refused to comply and had the windows of their lodgings 'completely demolished.'[179] It was true that in both universities some of the leading scholars were sympathetic with the Catholics. As the whig[180] Peter Elmsley, a great Greek scholar remarked,

> there certainly must be some connexion between Greek and Popery. Besides Messieurs Blomfield and Elmsley, there are Doctors Parr, Butler and Raine—all men conversant with the subjunctive mood, and all supporters of the Catholic claims.[181]

But Elmsley obtained no preferment in the university until Grenville appointed him Principal of St. Alban Hall in 1823, and the progressive intellectuals of Oriel helped to give themselves a bad name by their attachment to the liberal side.

In November 1812, the university again prepared to petition against the Catholic cause. Grenville warned the Hebdomadal Board that he would present the petition, but would state his total dissent from its policy,[182] and his friends agitated the university with broadsheets attacking the petition and printing letters written by Windham in 1805 urging that the danger to church and state came not from the Roman Catholics but from the military power of France.[183] But again, in a crowded Convocation, despite speeches from Copleston and Davison, the majority against any concession was so large that no scrutiny was needed.[184] The *Times's* gloss upon this was that 'the minority was larger than ever was known on a similar occasion.'[185] Sympathy for Grenville among the 'time-serving gowns and cassocks and mitres of Oxford' was diminishing, and when in January 1814 an address of congratulation to the Regent was drawn up, 'in the worst manner of the worst paragraphs of the *Courier*,' confusing in Grenville's view 'the goodness of the Creator and the merits of the Prince of Wales,' the Chancellor's willingness to sink his personality in his office was exhausted. He insisted on numerous changes in the draft (which was ascribed to Dr. Parsons, Master of Balliol, the newly created Bishop of Peterborough, as 'the first-fruits of his acknowledgements to Carlton House') and finally refused to present it.[186]

If there was one man more disappointed by the cancellarial election than Grenville, it was the Dean of Christ Church, Charles Henry Hall. Jackson resigned rather than battle with the division opened in the House by Grenville's candidature, and Hall's abstention from the contest began a lifetime of misery. Liverpool was furious and rebuffed all attempts at reconciliation; Cecil Jenkinson took his name off the books.[187] Still worse the tribes of Christ Church, no longer marshalled by an overbearing Dean, threw off obedience altogether, and Hall was soon 'as little attended to . . . as the peishwar of the Mahrattas; the whole government resting on an oligarchy of tutors.'[188] 'Nothing wd. save Ch. Ch. but the excellence of the tutors,' concluded a former tutor in 1817.[189]

The wretched Dean then became financially embarrassed, and made humiliating attempts to touch Abbot and Peel for loans; his appeals varied, but he always claimed to be the victim of financial guarantees he had given for others.[190] His son became disastrously involved with 'a vile connexion' at the House, and had to be sent abroad for two years to reform. Returning 'a totally altered creature,' he went up to Cambridge to prepare for ordination, for which, however, he soon declared himself unfit. Hall now touted among his former political friends for some civil preferment.[191] By this time Liverpool had concluded that it was 'a great publick object to place some other person in the station which he holds in Oxford.'[192] The Regent would have made Hall a bishop during the royal visit to Oxford in 1814, but Liverpool would not countenance a bishop in embarrassed circumstances.[193] Only one resort remained, the fat Deanery of Durham; thither Hall was translated on the next vacancy in 1824, and having given a promise to reside, immediately made the condition of the Deanery an excuse for going abroad.[194]

Throughout this period of feeble government a succession of able tutors was fortunately maintained; students appointed in Jackson's time continued to set a valuable tone; Liverpool took care in his appointment of Canons;[195] and in 1818 the House was said to flourish 'at least as much as under the cloud-compelling wig of the venerable Cyril.'[196] The number of first classes in the schools declined but little, and it was not until Hall's last year that the gradual relaxation of discipline resulted in a protracted bout of rioting in the House, in the course of which Lord Castlereagh was expelled.[197]

CHAPTER III

OXFORD IN THE POST-WAR ERA

It is necessary to ascertain forthwith . . . the one vital and decisive question, which will be evaded as long as possible: How is the enormous mass of patronage bestowed? Have they ever given anything to the right person? If they have, what, and to whom?

T. J. HOGG, *Life of Shelley*.

THE intimate association of Oxford with the establishment in church and state was never more vividly illustrated than in 1814. As part of the peace celebrations (from which the Hebdomadal Board prudently excluded illuminations)[1] the Regent brought over the allied sovereigns on a state visit, and 'every heart fluttered with expectation and delight; . . . in the sacred swell of enthusiasm . . . every bosom heaved.'[2] The visit followed the pattern of Oxford's great celebrations of the previous century; the dense crowds and exorbitant price of lodgings; the ludicrous mistakes—Lord Yarmouth and Lord Cathcart, arriving in a post-chaise were hailed as the Emperor of Russia;[3] the disorder, with Blucher fighting his way out of the Theatre, declaring that 'it was the hottest struggle he had ever been in';[4] an enormous banquet costing £2135.[5] Both guests and hosts, however, were immensely satisfied with the mêlée. The Regent asked for an extension of the Long Vacation and the grant of a term towards the degrees of all members of the university at the time of the visit,[6] and arranged with Lawrence to gratify the university's request for his portrait.[7] Royal benefactions multiplied,[8] and Oxford became a regular resort of visiting royalty. The duke of Clarence in 1816, the Grand Duke Nicholas of Russia in 1817,[9] the Grand Duke Michael of Russia and Archduke Maximilian of Austria in 1818 were all received with special attention.[10] The university appeared as the cynosure not merely of triumphant toryism at home, but of the pillars of conservatism on the continent.

The succeeding years brought home the perils as well as the advantages of adherence to the establishment, and exposed Oxford to the dangers which threatened all privileged corporations in an age of criticism and reform. And by none were the tensions between consistency and political necessity, between conservative instincts and the need for reform, felt more acutely than by Peel, who became the university's representative in 1817.[11]

For some years there had been rumours of an impending vacancy, and Scott had been confidently tipped for the peerage in 1811,[12] 1812,[13] and 1814.[14] When finally the vacancy was created in May 1817, it was brought about by Abbot's retirement from the Speakership owing to ill health, and his elevation to the upper house as Lord Colchester. For the Christ Church seat which thus came open, two distinguished sons of the House had been prospecting with differing degrees of urgency for some years. From at least 1811 Canning, who badly needed the seat, had been hoping for it, supported by the duke of Beaufort,[15] the protestant candidate for whom he voted in 1809 despite his own notorious support for Catholic emancipation.[16] In 1812 he negotiated with Abbot about a vacancy and the Dean of Christ Church began to canvass for him.[17] In 1814 Canning again tackled Abott, who promised to give him the first information should he ever receive a peerage.[18] This promise Abbot redeemed on May 29, 1817, when on the same day he wrote to the Vice-Chancellor, to Christ Church and to Canning, giving the latter one post or twelve hours more notice than the others of his resignation.[19]

Since 1813 Peel also had been coveting the seat;[20] as the rising hope of the protestant interest and the pride of Christ Church in the schools, he had the blessing of the tutors who now ruled the House, and especially of his own tutor, Charles Lloyd. He was a favourite with the aged Cyril Jackson,[21] and received a tremendous reception in 1815 when invited to receive an honorary degree.[22] In 1816 and again in May 1817 he strengthened his claim upon the ordinary members of Convocation by taking the lead on the catholic question from the nerveless hands of Sir William Scott, and securing unexpected majorities.[23]

Abbot thus resigned with Peel's protestant reputation at its peak. Immediately the Dean summoned a depleted chapter and proposed that they should support Canning. He was supported by the Sub-Dean, Barnes, and Goodenough, one of the Censors, and vigorously opposed by the other Censor, Corne, and by Peel's old tutor Charles Lloyd. The two last declared that Canning could not carry the college, and by threats of resignation drove the Dean to give him up. The Sub-Dean then made an attempt to carry Vansittart, the Chancellor of the Exchequer, which foundered on Van's connexion with the Bible Society,[24] and Corne and Lloyd, supported now by Van Mildert and Laurence, two famous canons, won the day for Peel.[25] On May 30, the Dean wrote to Peel informing him of the College's support,[26] sent Charles Lloyd up by night with the letter, and obtained an immediate acceptance. On June 1 an extremely successful canvass by the Dean and Corne showed that Peel must win.[27]

After seeing Lloyd, Peel announced his good fortune to Canning, and found him surprised.[28] Canning, indeed, had half thought that Abbot's letter implied his resignation at the end of the session,[29] but the chapter proceedings at Christ Church show that he was wrecked by his political reputation rather than by lack of speed off the mark. His friends, however, complained bitterly that Abbot had defrauded him of the seat.[30] Abbot's defence was that the timing of his resignation, so peculiarly favourable to Peel, had been dictated by his doctors,[31] but the Canningites[32] put some unpleasant paragraphs in the *Morning Chronicle*. These frightened Charles Lloyd whose nerves were never strong, because he was convinced that Copleston and Davison of Oriel, in disgust at Canning's failure, were plotting to promote J. W. Ward on the interest which had carried Grenville at the last election.[33] Ward was never heard of as a candidate; an attempt to propose Joseph Phillimore, regius professor of civil law, as a Christ Church Grenvillite came to nothing;[34] the Warden of New College gave up his hopes of Bragge Bathurst, and Brasenose resolved to keep Heber in reserve for the next vacancy.[35] Thus Peel received the coveted prize[36] unopposed, though Lloyd prophetically warned him not to tamper with what he quaintly termed the university's increasing attachment to the principles of Mr. Pitt.[37]

During the next difficult years Oxford stood aloof from the problems of economic distress and political radicalism. Her college revenues sheltered by the Corn Laws, her glories admired by kings, the university became a quiet prop of royalty,[38] and left the economic situation to the judgment of the few individuals such as Tatham[39] and Copleston[40] who felt equipped by an Oxford education to pronounce upon it.[41] After the Peterloo Massacre in 1819, Lord Grenville called on the university to declare its attachment to king and constitution, and an address was at once sent up promising to instil respect for religion and the Regent, and lamenting the 'rapid and connected progress of blasphemy and sedition.'[42] In the following autumn, however, the causes of public order and monarchy became harder to reconcile. On January 29, 1820, the Regent assumed full majesty as George IV, and when in June, his queen, much sinned against and much sinning, returned to claim her rights, she was soon the heroine of a popular agitation of almost revolutionary proportions. As the crisis reached its peak in the middle of November 1820 riots broke out repeatedly in Oxford, with a town mob demanding illuminations, a gown mob replying, the Vice-Chancellor reading the Riot Act, and Oxfordshire Yeomanry called in.[43]

The Hebdomadal Board appointed a committee to investigate its police resources, recruited two servants from each college to be sworn in as special constables and occasional Proctors' men, and arranged successful and peaceable illuminations to celebrate the coronation the following July.[44] Of more immediate advantage, in December 1820, a university deputation headed by Lord Grenville took up an address in favour of law and order which won the heart of the king.

> 'It is impossible to describe,' wrote W. H. Fremantle, 'how full the king was of the Oxford address . . . He described over and over again all the enthusiasm of loyalty betrayed in the forget-fulness of all decorum after he had left the throne. He spoke of their clapping him on the back; of their numbers; but above all, of the dignified and proper manner in which the Chancellor read the address.[45]

The king's warmth towards Grenville was significant. The Grenvillites were now courted by both ministry and opposition,[46] and already the wheels were in motion which led at the end of 1821 to their joining the ministry, and in 1822 to the elevation of the marquis of Buckingham to a coveted dukedom. In July 1820 Grenville was flattered by the disposal of the regius chair of divinity to his election manager, Dr. Hodson of B.N.C.[47] And the new favour of government towards the Grenvillites assisted also in the election of the Brasenose candidate for the parliamentary seat, Richard Heber.

In July 1821, after a year of the usual tantalising rumours,[48] Sir William Scott received his long-awaited peerage. Heber's friends were immediately ready; at Brasenose a committee was set up under the declining Dr. Hodson, Dr. Routh, President of Magdalen, canvassed with unexampled energy,[49] and there was loyal backing from the old friends of Grenville and Canning at Oriel.[50] St. John's was nevertheless ready with another candidate, Sir John Nicholl, Dean of Arches, judge of the prerogative court of Canterbury, and at present M.P. for Great Bedwin.[51] Nicholl was a former fellow of St. John's, and had advised the college during a curious transaction in 1814, when Lord Liverpool had pressed them to sell their property in Bagley Wood to the duke of Wellington, and so plant a duke on each side of the university.[52]

The issue between Nicholl and Heber was much the same as that between Abbot and Heber in 1806, or between Eldon and Grenville in 1809, complicated by the fact that Catholic emancipation was no longer a cabinet matter, and by the rapprochement between the court and the Grenvilles. Nicholl was a reactionary protestant[53] of a kind common at St. John's in the nineteenth century; and Heber's canvassing gave him an additional cry.[54] Heber was now generally recognised to have prevaricated on the matter of emancipation;[55] consistent protestants drew the worst conclusion from the facts that he had helped Grenville in 1809, and was now championed by

Grenville's caucus in Brasenose and Oriel.[56] Repeated attempts were made to compel him to declare his position.[57] On the second day of polling Vaughan Thomas distributed free copies of his sermon on *The impropriety of conceding the name catholic to the Church of Rome*, a personal altercation with Archdeacon Churton followed, and finally Heber's evangelical half-brother, Reginald, assured the university of Richard's 'determined hostility to the enlargement of the power possessed by the Roman Catholics;' though Reginald sympathised with emancipation, he had never been able to convince his brother.[58]

Even when refurbished as a protestant, Heber was still no politician. Moreover, since Dr. Hodson, by virtue of the canonry annexed to the divinity chair, was now a member of the Christ Church chapter, it was alleged that through him Christ Church would capture the second parliamentary seat.[59] In fact Christ Church remained neutral and ultimately voted in the proportion of 3 to 2 for Sir John Nicholl.[60] But Heber's campaign was equivocal enough: his friends gave it out that he had the full backing of the ministry,[61] which Nicholl's party strenuously denied.[62] A correspondent to the *Courier* also accused Brasenose of deliberately manufacturing votes by pressing gentlemen to take the M.A. degree who would not otherwise have done so. This charge was piquantly illuminated by the poll, for after allowing the Johnians to take the lead on the first day, and hold 'a sort of Belshazzar's feast,' Hodson sent down a written order, '"Let forty B.N.C. men go up and vote," which was obeyed with military precision.'[63] In 1806 this effort would have exhausted the Brasenose vote, but now Hodson polled 161, only one less than Christ Church, and more than twice as many as any other society. Finally Heber triumphed by 612 votes to 519, the majority being considerably smaller than the margin by which the Brasenose vote of 1821 exceeded that of 1806.

As a member Heber did not justify the trouble which had been taken to elect him; he never spoke, and when in 1822 he was thought likely to speak, it was in favour of Canning's motion to permit Roman Catholic peers to sit.[64] He was handicapped by poor eyesight, and admitted his impatience with the way attendance at the house interfered with his book-collecting tours abroad;[65] consumed with bibliomania, confronted with murmurings in Oxford,[66] attacked in *John Bull*, he resigned his seat in 1826,[67] and spent most of his remaining years abroad.

With the return of the Grenvilles to court, Oxford seemed more closely knit with government than ever, but she was not immune from the tide of legal and administrative reform, and her defence of her privileges created an image of the university in the radical mind as a corporation of the narrowest and most self-centred sort.

Characteristic of the new issues were the agitations on the subject of copyright. By 1802 the number of copyright libraries had grown to eleven, but publishers intending to claim no copyright need not register a book at Stationers' Hall, nor supply the eleven free copies. In 1812, however, in the case of the University of Cambridge v. Bryer, the King's Bench decided that the libraries could claim the eleven free copies whether or not the book had been entered at Stationers' Hall. As a result in the next four years more books were registered than in the first seventy years of the Copyright Act of 8 Anne c.19,[68] the publishers began a great agitation for the redress of a grievance, and their petitions were referred to a committee of the Commons. Sir William Scott reported to the Vice-Chancellor that the committee was bent on reducing the number of privileged libraries, and denying the privilege where books were not registered under the act; some members of the committee were opposed altogether to the delivery of free copies.[69]

In the end the university escaped lightly. Under a new act[70] only the British Museum was entitled to delivery of a free copy of every new book registered at Stationers' Hall, but the other ten libraries might obtain a copy of any book by applying to the publisher in writing within twelve months of publication. The Hebdomadal Board nevertheless insisted that the cost of supplying eleven free copies was no burden to the publishers, and petitioned against the bill.[71]

The new act annoyed both sides. By 1817 the publishers were agitating again, while Bulkeley Bandinel, Bodley's Librarian, complained to the Vice-Chancellor of the irregular delivery and poor condition of the books.[72] When the issue came to a head early in 1818 Sir William Scott feared that the privilege of the Bodleian was shared with an indefensibly large number of other libraries; probably all except the British Museum would lose their rights.[73] Lord Grenville also despaired of maintaining the Bodleian privilege, but thought that Lord Liverpool might compound it for a grant of £500 p.a., subject to periodical revision according to the value of money.[74] It was believed in Oxford that the difficulty had been created by Cambridge efforts to extend their rights,[75] and that the Cambridge librarians abused their privilege by selling or throwing away privilege copies.[76] The commons then required a return of books received since 1814 which had not been placed in the library. Macray recounted that the Oxford list was 'but a trifling one,' though it contained some works of merit; the Cambridge list, however, showed a culpable 'recklessness of rejection.'[77] The Hebdomadal Board nevertheless would give no ground, and instructed Peel and Scott to join with the Cambridge burgesses in a last ditch fight for the rights of the university.[78] If all else were lost they might accept a compromise like that advocated by Grenville.[79]

The Commons committee was plied with favourable witnesses,[80] but it reported that the British Museum should henceforth be the only copyright library, that the other libraries should be granted a fixed allowance in lieu of their privilege, and that books surrendering all claim to copyright be exempt.[81] These resolutions were carried in the committee by a majority of only six to five, but four of the minority were university burgesses.[82] It was abundantly evident why Lord Grenville and his allies at Oriel recommended the surrender of the privilege.[83] The copyright report appeared too late in the session for any fresh legislation, but in 1819 the agitation was renewed and the *Quarterly* prompted the universities to give way. This the Board would not countenance, and in the end, overshadowed by the greater political crises of 1819 and 1820, the copyright question died away, leaving the privileges of the university publicly impugned, but unimpaired.

While the rights of the Bodleian were under fire, college endowments were coming under the scrutiny of that most ferocious of critics, Henry Brougham. In 1816 Brougham had obtained the appointment of a committee upon the education of the lower classes in London. This committee reported that there were enormous abuses in the administration of educational charities, and urged that the enquiry be extended throughout the country. The committee obtained this power in 1818 and thus the educational charities in college hands were opened to them. Brougham's draft bill exempted the universities, but he sarcastically called upon them to vindicate their reputation by inviting inquiry.[84] The Hebdomadal Board, however, instructed Peel to widen the university's exemptions as far as possible,[85] and Charles Lloyd urged him to get Brougham's bill thrown out in the Lords, for 'everybody is frightened of these predatory commissioners.'[86] Brougham later produced evidence of mismanaged college charities at Cambridge, but though he obtained his committee, he could not get the universities included.[87] The Hebdomadal Board nevertheless took fright at 'the dangerous tendency of the power indiscriminately exercised' by the committee in the last session, and the Vice-Chancellor was despatched to London to take counsel from the university representatives and Chancellor.[88] Grenville was by now thoroughly alarmed at Brougham's national education proposals and wanted to free the university from the 'threatened inquisition of a parliamentary visitation to be kept hanging over them at the pleasure of any chairman of any committee of the House of Commons.'[89]

The result of all these alarms was an astonishing outburst by Peel in the debate on the third reading of the Charitable Foundations Bill on June 23, 1819, attacking the committees of 1816 and 1818 for grossly exceeding their powers, and interfering with the universities.

Had parliament intended an inquiry into foundations controlled by colleges, he declared, they would have selected commissioners associated with the universities;[90] as it was the commission was packed with Brougham's friends, and their behaviour especially towards the Master of St. John's College, Cambridge, had been atrocious. Brougham tore Peel's evidence to shreds and accused him of framing the whole allegation to catch the committee unprepared. Why had he kept silent during the public sittings of the committee?

> Then was the time for him to come down, protesting and declaiming, and imploring—but no—he saw Oxford menaced, Cambridge invaded, Eton insulted, Winchester sacked, and still he made no sign. The imminent danger even of his own *alma mater* could not draw a word from him; he left her to be defended from the outrages of a revolutionary committee by the prowess of the worthy and Horatian members for the city.

Peel's humiliation was completed by J. H. Smyth, member for Cambridge University, and Wilberforce declared succinctly that

> if it had been any other person who had shewn such fatuity of intellect, he should have said that the man was totally insensible to the admirable administration of justice in this country.[91]

Once again the privileges of the university escaped unimpaired, but its reputation was impugned. To avoid public inquiry by the methods of Peel invited the liberal public to draw the worst conclusions.

In a further matter, the treatment of prostitutes, the university authorities were liable to the reproach of tyranny if they exercised their special powers, or of conniving at indiscipline if they did not. In 1814 Cobbett's *Political Register* ran a campaign against the Proctors' powers over non-matriculated persons in the town, and the procedure of the Vice-Chancellor's court. Cases of abuse were reported such as an occasion when the Proctors took up some girls of ill repute in a cottage two miles out of Oxford, though they were not associating with gownsmen, and the Vice-Chancellor committed them to the county gaol. An active correspondence in the *Times*, *Oxford Herald* and *Morning Chronicle* showed that the Proctors were trying to clear the streets of undesirable women, and their tyrannies were remembered against them. But the problem was intractable. The same women were

> constantly brought up every quarter for having returned to Oxford after having been passed to their parishes. Being unable to obtain employment . . . they are compelled to return to

Oxford by extreme distress, and are again committed to prison where they live the greater part of the year.

If the Proctors hounded one set of prostitutes from the town, and got the Mayor of Abingdon and other officers to imprison those who took refuge locally, London harlots came to fill the gap, and the last state was worse than the first.[92]

While the university was being impugned as a chartered tyranny and folly, her own more thoughtful members recognised that an overhaul of the local police arrangements, and with it, the relations of city and university, was overdue. The position was that

> after 9 o'clock no officer of any sort or kind [has] power in the streets of Oxford to quell disturbances, take up rioters &c. except the V.C. the Proctors & their officers under them. The City Constables are not allowed in any way to interfere—and the university is excessively jealous on this point; which the City have on some occasions much reason to complain. In the long vacations, for instance, when the Univ. is now quite empty, the V.C. & Proctors & everybody in connection with the discipline & police of the place is absent . . . The harlots & scoundrels unchecked by any magistracy, turn out in numbers & the High Street resembles Fleet St. & Drury Lane.

Furthermore Oxford was expanding rapidly especially towards Headington and along the Woodstock road, and the new industrial populations had scant respect for academic authority.[93] Thus even before Peel's Vagrant Act brought the matter to a head, the special jurisdictions of the university were known to be not merely anomalous, but inefficient and in need of reform.

On February 26, 1825 the Vice-Chancellor himself put all this before Peel as a matter of urgency. The sole police officers at the university's disposal were the two Proctors and their four deputies, and counsel's opinion was that they could not be reinforced by effective constables. More immediately the university's power by charter to banish prostitutes was of little use, but under the Act 17 Geo. II c.5, the Proctors apprehended, and the Vice-Chancellor committed, prostitutes as *lewd idle & disorderly persons* and sent home those without a settlement in Oxford.

> But the new Vagrant Act, 5 Geo. IV c.88, authorizes no commitment of a prostitute who is not proved to have behaved *in a riotous & indecent manner* & gives no power of sending such women to their parishes. Hence our discipline has most grievously suffered . . . [alterations in the law] have alarmingly increased the number of prostitutes in this place & emboldened them in a contempt & defiance of the Procuratorial authority.

In short this state of things threatens to involve our youth in shameless & habitual vice, and already draws down on the University the reproaches of friends as well as enemies. The Proctors it is apprehended will ere long be completely disheartened in the execution of their office.

Even more alarming was the isolation of the university.

Any local or particular enactment of the legislature might be open to many serious objections, & even the application to Parliament for obtaining any such enactment, might, in the present state of public feeling expose our institutions to rude attack, & perhaps endanger many privileges which we now enjoy.[94]

Endless embarrassments threatened. The Speaker insisted that any bill relating to Oxford police was a private bill, must be preceded by petition, and, therefore, must arouse the very publicity which the Vice-Chancellor wanted to avoid.[95] The only way to turn the bill into a public bill was to include Cambridge in it, but the Cambridge authorities, having adequate powers by charter, had no desire to be included.[96] In the end a short public act was put through empowering the Vice-Chancellor of each university to appoint constables to exercise normal constabulary powers within four miles of the university, and to take up prostitutes as idle and disorderly persons within the meaning of the Vagrant Act.[97] In order to get this act through, Peel had to make the constables subject to actions in the common law (not the university) courts and to silence the objections of the City of Oxford by a mixture of browbeating and half-promises of financial assistance.[98]

Although the university appointed no constables, a more effective bridle was now placed upon the Oxford prostitutes,[99] with the result that in November 1826 the Town Clerk applied to the Hebdomadal Board for a contribution towards the cost of supporting them in the city gaol. Under the Vagrant Act the average daily number of prostitutes in gaol from university commitments had declined from nine to less than one, and the City held that if the university wished to act with a rigour now unknown to the general law, they should bear the cost. This amounted to $7\frac{1}{2}$d. per day for women in health, but one third needed medical attention,[100] at a cost of a further 7d. a day. Peel denied absolutely having made a promise of financial assistance, though the tenor of his remarks may be gauged from his admission that he 'certainly felt that the city had had the power without the least difficulty of defeating the measure.'

The Hebdomadal Board was profoundly relieved to have turned an awkward corner, and offered the City 10d. per day towards the cost of maintaining each prostitute committed by the university authorities.[101] This whole episode was an unsavoury prelude to Oxford's vapourings against the university in London, and illuminated significantly the extreme weakness felt by Peel and the university authorities in reclaiming an old privilege for the university against the recent trend of the law. The unreformed constitution of which the university was a part was still intact, but the university like the church was in an exposed position.

While the tempest was gathering outside the university, the bent within was all towards improvement. The improvement of the professoriate became a concern even of the government. Henry Beeke who had accompanied Addington on his mission to Denmark in 1801, and advised him on foreign affairs, was appointed regius professor of modern history in the same year.[102] For many years Beeke was a financial adviser to Nicholas Vansittart,[103] and his official duties took him away from Oxford a good deal.[104] Beeke, however, had been appointed on condition that he lectured not only in history, but in political economy, and satisfied the requirements of that improving diehard, Addington, by whom he was appointed.[105] When Beeke resigned his chair in 1814, Sidmouth again settled the terms of appointment of the new professor,[106] Edward Nares, and bound him to reside 90 days, to pay two modern language teachers, and give courses of a very modern flavour upon historiography, political economy, the art of political biography and international affairs.[107] For good measure Liverpool added advice on the sources for his lectures.[108] Before his marriage with Lady Charlotte Spencer in 1797, Nares had been an intimate at Blenheim and took a prominent part in the high-church review, the *British Critic*, founded by his cousin Robert. In subsequent years as Bampton lecturer, select preacher, reviewer, and pamphleteer, he built up a considerable reputation in religious controversy.[109] He now turned his attention to history, and in 1816 began his first course before a huge class of dons and undergraduates. Unfortunately Nares exhausted his market and in the next year the numbers fell to seven. However, he began a course on political economy, a 'curious science,' his ignorance of which had shamed him at the time of his appointment; he now raised a class of 37, consisting, ominously for the future, of noblemen and tutors, the undergraduates being much too preoccupied by work for the schools to attend professorial lectures. In subsequent years classes were hard to come by, and so were lecture-rooms, so ill-provided was the university with basic necessities.[110] The expense and trouble of coming up from his living in Kent to reside and lecture made the office unprofitable. He applied for the regius chair of divinity in 1820,[111] was defeated in a contest for the Margaret chair in 1827,[112] and became altogether embittered.[113] The good intentions of the Liverpool ministry had been frustrated by the reformed Oxford system.

Liverpool was 'bitten with the mania for modern sciences in preference to the ancient studies of the university, and [thought] very lightly of Greek and Latin;'[114] certainly his ministry nobly supported the new studies. In 1812, John Kidd, the chemistry professor, began to agitate for an increment to his small salary from the Exchequer, like that which had long been enjoyed by the botany professor, had been granted to the chemistry professor at Cambridge, and had been intended for his own place before the indiscretions of Thomas Beddoes.[115] Pressed by the Chancellor and Hebdomadal Board, the Regent graciously complied with this request early in 1813.[116] Immediately S. P. Rigaud, professor of experimental philosophy, applied and obtained equal recognition.[117]

The government also recognised the lectures in mineralogy given by the famous William Buckland, fellow of Corpus, by a grant of £100 p.a.. Buckland attained great celebrity not only as an eccentric, but as a geologist, and his work was supported by a further grant in 1818.[118] Buckland, however, could neither meet the expenses of his geological expeditions[119] from the £200 p.a. he received from the government, nor find time to increase his earnings by tutoring, and convinced Lord Grenville that but for the researches by which he justified the Mosaic account of the flood, geology would have become the tool of atheism. Without substantial preferment in Oxford he would have to leave the university. Grenville had no difficulty in persuading Liverpool to find him a canonry at Christ Church in 1825, to the intense annoyance of Charles Lloyd who wanted the place for Gaisford, and deplored Buckland's 'loose and desultory habits.'[120] Until Buckland became Dean of Westminster in 1845, Christ Church had to bear with them, and with his son and his collection of wild animals.[121]

Equally with Edward Nares, the science professors found themselves short of room for even their diminished classes, and for their growing amount of apparatus. In 1806 the Hebdomadal Board hoped that Sir Roger Newdigate's proposal to pay for the rehousing of the Pomfret Marbles would release more room for the natural philosophy lectures and experiments.[122] In 1811 they found it 'expedient for the advancement of chemical science that the reader in chemistry should be provided with a permanent habitation adjoining to the laboratory,'[123] and rooms were set up for Dr. Kidd in the basement of the Ashmolean. Subsequently Charles Daubeny went to great expense in fitting up the laboratories, which the Hebdomadal Board refused in 1826 to reimburse, on the ground that the whole work had been unauthorised; and they gave notice that no unauthorised work would be paid for in the future. In 1828

Daubeny was given permission to improve his living quarters and the entrance to the lecture rooms at his own expense, though he received a small grant in aid in the following year.[124] Meanwhile in 1819, the Anatomical Theatre had received a present from Florence of 'some beautiful models in wax, formed with so much accuracy as to supersede the necessity of having recourse to the human body for anatomical instruction and experiment.'[125] Limited as the facilities for university teaching were, they were slowly being improved, and if by 1830 the *Quarterly* could join hands with the *Edinburgh* in bemoaning the decay of science, the fault lay more in the organisation of university studies,[126] than in any neglect of science in the Hebdomadal Board.

It was the same story with that lavishly endowed pariah of Oxford studies, theology. After Charles Henry Hall, the university had enjoyed two distinguished regius professors, William Howley who became Primate, and Van Mildert, who became bishop of Durham; both lectured, the latter with distinction.[127] In 1820 Frodsham Hodson, Principal of Brasenose, was put into the chair by Grenville,[128] but died in 1822 before leaving any mark. Hodson's appointment was a cruel blow to the House, for through the canonry annexed to the chair it introduced into their sadly disorganised governing body a man who was already the head of another society. There was an eighteenth-century precedent for this anomaly,[129] but the appointment was carried over the furious protests of the whole Christ Church body.[130] This episode had some influence upon the next appointment, for the issue lay between Davison of Oriel and Charles Lloyd, student and tutor of the House, and Lloyd was carried home not simply by the efforts of his pupil, Peel, but by Liverpool's desire to assuage the ruffled feelings of the college.[131]

Lloyd was a fat, ambitious and unpleasant man, determined to extract the last ounce of advantage from his connexion with Peel, but he had energy and talent and knew that some evidence of merit was now necessary for higher preferment in the church. He claimed that only his labours as a tutor at Christ Church and as Preacher of Lincoln's Inn (a place he obtained with Peel's assistance in 1819 after some anxious electioneering) had kept him from publication.[132] Having obtained his chair he set out to make himself 'a great divine & to be accounted the best in England . . . and to become the founder of a school of theology in Oxford,'[133] a wish which Lloyd urged as a special qualification for the see of Oxford, which Peel obtained for him in 1827.[134] Neither of Lloyd's hopes was fulfilled, but he was the most influential Oxford professor of his day.

Since Potter had ended the theological disputations in Queen Anne's day, successive regius professors had given little beyond the short statutory course of lectures, attendance at which was the church's sole meagre requirement of ordinands beyond the arts degree. Lloyd successfully introduced post-graduate courses which attracted a loyal following, including some of the later Tractarian leaders. Lloyd's instruction was of the old high-church kind, and introduced his classes to a wider range of theological reading than had been offered in the church for many years.[135] It was Lloyd rather than Martin Routh, the venerable recluse of Magdalen, who (in Newman's phrase) was 'reserved to report to a degenerate age the theology of our fathers.'[136] He trained up his chaplain and learned successor, Edward Burton, and together they met the two-fold challenge to the church, Lloyd attacking Roman Catholicism in the *British Critic*, Burton assailing unitarianism in his *Testimonies of the ante-Nicene fathers to the divinity of Christ*.[137] Lloyd also sought to end the farce by which the candidate for the B.D. degree obtained the requisite answers to the standard questions for a payment of five shillings; instead he was to present a latin thesis upon a subject approved by the professor. Unfortunately latin theses were to be bought as readily as the old standard forms, and the regulation merely increased the incidental expenses of a divinity degree from five shillings to eight guineas.[138] No exercises whatever were required for the D.D. degree. Divinity, like science, could find little place in the general education of the university and no place at all as a superior faculty.

Other improving influences were brought to bear by the Chancellor, Lord Grenville. He helped to persuade the ministry to augment the endowments of the science lecturers in 1813, secured a generous grant from the Regent in 1814 for that perennial desideratum, a new catalogue for the Bodleian,[139] supported measures of improved discipline in Christ Church in 1825,[140] and insisted that the new Drummond professor of political economy be required 'not to read only, but to *publish*.'[141] At the same time he took up a new cause, that of university extension. There seems little doubt that the numbers in Oxford ebbed steadily in the middle of the eighteenth century and again during the long wars at the end; at a census taken in May 1811 the small number of 1015 residents was counted.[142] After the war numbers increased again. Cyril Jackson had helped to revive the fashion of university education among the aristocracy and those who followed their cue and there were fewer alternatives to university qualifications. The number of commissions to be purchased in the armed services was drastically reduced, and easy openings in the civil service were constantly falling victim to the administrative reformers.[143] The result of increased pressure was that many who were by no means sympathetic to the projected London University, came to think that the universities could only justify their monopoly by admitting all who wished to come; even if the legendary throngs

of medieval Oxford were discounted, it could not be denied that the
university was educating fewer now than in the tiny England of the
seventeenth century. To utilitarians and critics of 'Church of
Englandism' this was an abuse, but the first man to take up university
extension was within the fold, Oxford's burgess and public defender,
Robert Peel.

In 1824 colleges were empowered to borrow from the Public Works
Loan Commissioners to finance the building of extra accommodation
for students, the loans to be repaid within twenty years at 4 per cent
interest.[144] These terms were not generous and in the next year
Palmerston launched a bill to enable the universities and colleges to
borrow for new building by mortgaging their revenues.[145] Peel
pressed this bill upon his constituents, warning them not to be left
behind by Cambridge,[146] but met with a mixed reception. The heads
considered the bill dilatorily; the Vice-Chancellor wanted facilities
for the university to borrow on behalf of halls;[147] Lord Grenville
was whole-heartedly in favour;[148] Charles Lloyd attempted to
discourage it altogether.

Paradoxically, although undergraduate accommodation in Oxford
was less than it had been a generation earlier,[149] it was in some
respects too lavish. The great pressure for admission was felt in
colleges such as Christ Church, Oriel and Brasenose, which had
established a reputation for sound education and fashionable society,
and then by others such as Wadham and Balliol which offered
merely sound education. For a generation these societies had had
waiting lists for entrance of two or three years. Oriel had recently
built and filled its site; Balliol had suppressed a fellowship to start a
building fund; Brasenose was accumulating money for building.
Christ Church, as in every generation, claimed to have no money,
and the Dean's view that they had already admitted more undergraduates than they could manage was borne out by a succession
of serious riots. In any case the popular colleges could never meet
the demand on their own, and their waiting lists created the illusion
that Oxford was over-crowded. But there was always plenty of
unoccupied accommodation. Christ Church, Oriel and Brasenose
apart, the enthusiasm of colleges for education varied inversely with
their endowments. All Souls had never admitted undergraduates,
and angered the radicals by sitting loose to its statutes.[150] The
Warden of Merton was said to preserve the college amenities by
rejecting two applications out of every three; Lloyd believed that
Magdalen and Corpus would do the same did their statutes not
prohibit the one from admitting more than 20, the other from
admitting more than 6, independent members. New College similarly
vegetated in tranquillity,[151] and there were small colleges and halls
which were never likely to be full. While the papers talked of founding

a university at York, and of turning the lodgings of the canons of Christ Church into undergraduate sets, there were always rooms in Oxford unlet.[152] Even the stronger societies might be emptied by a war or other adverse circumstances. Lloyd's belief that colleges ought not to borrow for new building on anything resembling commercial terms was justified by the fact that the number of matriculations remained stationary for a generation, and declined for a time thereafter. In any case the bill of 1825 failed to pass before the end of the session, and so the advocates of university extension had to turn to existing resources.

Lord Grenville's eye was drawn to the halls, the principals of which (other than St. Edmund Hall) he appointed. The property of the halls was held in trust for them by the university; there were usually no endowments other than the buildings, and the principal benefited simply from the rents of rooms. Members of the halls with no social standards to keep up lived cheaply, but were commonly recruited from men who had parted company with their colleges through delinquency or marriage or failure in examinations.[153] Macbride made a success of Magdalen Hall during his long headship (1813–68); while John Hill was Vice-Principal of St. Edmund Hall (1812–51) evangelical parents were glad to put their sons in his charge; Whately gave a great impulse to St. Alban Hall (1825–31) and built and filled extra rooms;[154] but the halls usually attained a very low standard indeed, and were not often full.

While trying to persuade the university to build a new hall, Grenville discovered that at New Inn Hall not only was the Principal non-resident, but there had been no students for probably a hundred years. New Inn Hall had long been a retreat for celebrated lawyers; William Blackstone had been Principal (1761–1766), then Robert Chambers (1766-1803), one of whose absences abroad had enabled John Scott, the future earl of Eldon, who had lately eloped with Bessie Surtees, to set up house in the principal's lodgings.[155] In 1803 Cyril Jackson got the duke of Portland to appoint James Blackstone, son of the famous Vinerian professor and a successor in the chair, legal adviser and political manager to the duke of Marlborough,[156] fellow of All Souls, deputy High Steward of the university,[157] and Lieutenant-Colonel of the Oxford Volunteers.[158] Grenville, unimpressed by this record, insisted that he must either reside and make the hall available for education, or resign.

To this invitation Blackstone made the remarkable reply that he had been admitted by Portland upon the

> strict engagement ... that I should upon no pretence admit any undergraduate whatever upon my books ... Subject to this provision I was totally absolved by his Grace from the necessity

of residing . . . and beyond this I had the peculiar privilege conceded me of retaining & residing upon my fellowship at All Souls College.

No one could remember the existence of any undergraduate accommodation at New Inn Hall; the Principal's lodgings consisted only of 'two sitting rooms on the ground floor & a few bedchambers & garrets,' and to prevent his misusing these the university had forbidden his admitting undergraduates. The lodgings he had restored and occasionally occupied. This reply convinced Grenville that New Inn Hall could not be restored to educational service without new building. The Vice-Chancellor was unwilling to squander the profits of the press upon a dubious project, and the affair dragged on for years.[159] In 1831, however, Blackstone was induced to resign, and was succeeded by J. A. Cramer of Christ Church, the Public Orator. He entirely rebuilt the hall at his own expense, and added a large room to serve as a chapel, hall and lecture room, but never made the place thrive.[160] The story of New Inn Hall formed a melancholy preface to the various schemes of university extension by hall building or reform in the middle of the century.

The burning domestic topic in Oxford in the 'twenties, however, was that of examinations. The new system as modified between 1807 and 1809 had given rise to considerable dissatisfaction in three related respects, the burden upon examiners, and the importance attached to logic and denied to mathematics and other scientific subjects. Examiners became hard to find, ostensibly because of the labour of examining all the candidates orally at six per day, and the serious interruption to college work twice a year.[161] However, although mathematicians were scarce in Oxford, there was no shortage of mathematical examiners after the boards were separated, and the truth seemed to be that in Greats the burden was not so much the volume as the range of the work.[162] The mechanics of examining therefore began to provide arguments for the advocates of more numerous and more specialised schools.[163] It was admitted that if Hebrew or Anglo-Saxon were introduced into the Greats school, the supply of examiners would dry up altogether.

This argument might have served the scientific professors who for years had been complaining that their labours were nullified by a narrow examination syllabus,[164] had not they sought their advantage within the present system. S. P. Rigaud claimed that Dr. Parsons, Master of Balliol, one of the authors of the original examination statute, intended to comprise chemistry in Disciplinae Physicae, and urged that it should now form part of the second school.[165] The mathematicians, however, whose recognition in the second school had formed one of Copleston's chief shots against the *Edinburgh*

Review, were equally dissatisfied. Mathematical examiners kept reporting that the study was declining in Oxford,[166] and even Charles Lloyd who had no sympathy for science complained.

> That the mathematical sciences are in the lowest possible state in Oxford may be assumed as an indisputable fact. They have rather gone backwards than forwards for the last 20 years.[167]

Some of the mathematicians, especially Baden Powell, wished to increase the prestige of their study by separating it more completely from the Greats examination, and by increasing the competitive element by creating a prize, or by adopting the Cambridge system of an order of merit.[168] Robert Walker, fellow of Wadham, (and Powell too with one side of his mind) hankered after the notion of science as an indispensable ingredient of a liberal education and after the old days of crowded lecture classes in mathematics and physics.[169]

The only hope of strengthening the mathematical content of the basic school was to permit candidates to offer an alternative to the most unpopular compulsory subject, logic. Oxford's attachment to Aristotelian logic had always been attacked in some quarters as out of date,[170] and was felt by many undergraduates and some tutors as a useless burden. This feeling was powerfully reinforced in 1826 and again in 1829 by the publication of Whately's textbook on logic; in the preface he asserted that the universal requirement of logic at Oxford demeaned the subject, and that logic should be compulsory only for classmen.[171] In 1829 these sore feelings were exacerbated by attacks in the London and Oxford press on H. A. Woodgate, fellow and tutor of St. John's, who ploughed an unprecedented number of candidates, including five of the six he examined in one day, by introducing questions on logic in every part of the examination.[172]

With this discussion in progress the heads resumed the work of reform and once again aroused intense suspicion. In 1826 they appointed a committee which included all the heads who had ever served as examiners, and by March 1829 their draft was ready for Convocation. It proposed to ease the examiners by increasing their numbers from 4 to 10, to grade the candidates in three classes, with a fourth class of those who satisfied the examiners. Mathematics might be offered instead of logic.[173] When Convocation met, Tyler of Oriel pleaded for English to be permitted; the Vice-Chancellor refused, and had the mortification to see the first and crucial clause of the statute defeated by 13 votes.[174] This defeat was effected by diehards and progressives jointly. The former held that the original statute had been framed by men far superior to the present governors of the university, that the burden on examiners could easily be lessened, and that the present mediocre heads would be much better employed in shutting up shops on Sundays and clearing the streets of prostitutes.[175] The liberal Thomas Arnold resented the slight put upon his beloved Aristotle, and urged, with some reason, that if the studies of the place were to be altered something more radical was needed.[176] The heads then botched their draft to meet what they thought were the views of the M.A.s, but in June suffered the loss of two further clauses by small majorities, after the Proctors had been urged to veto an act of tyranny.[177] Further botching took place in 1825, and the heads secured their main points. The mathematical examiners were separated from the classical, the divided second class disappeared for good, in favour of a third class, and a fourth class of men who satisfied the examiners; logic remained undisturbed.[178] Even now there was fresh tinkering, and in 1826 another statute was passed, permitting the candidates for honours in mathematics to take the examinations in Greats and have a three-week rest before their next ordeal.[179]

None of these changes satisfied those who felt that the examination system was cramping the development of the university, and on March 23, 1829, the Hebdomadal Board appointed a committee which included those old progressive allies Richard Whately, Principal of St. Alban Hall, and Edward Hawkins, Provost of Oriel, 'to discuss the construction of a new examination statute, with a discretionary power to consult with, and to receive communications from, other members of Convocation.'[180] These communications now form a small volume,[181] and shew how change was delayed by the large variety of schemes canvassed.[182] Arnold looked for a radical reconstruction of the Greats school, and the introduction of civil law,[183] others for mechanical changes for examination convenience. After months of consultation the committee produced a report which bore the mark of the powerful mind of Richard Whately, and of his old Oriel friends such as R. D. Hampden.[184]

The report strongly condemned the burden which the present system imposed upon examiners, and the unequal treatment of the candidates to which it led. The recent policy of appointing more examiners gave immediate relief at the cost of expending the available supply more rapidly. The examination permitted inferior candidates to pass far too easily by the mere exercise of memory, while honours candidates were not sufficiently warned of the recent policy of extending the range of literature to be examined. Above all logic suffered by being a compulsory requirement; mathematics, deficiency in which was a reproach to the Greats school, should be offered as an alternative.[185] The committee's other recommendations clung to familiar ground, merely making explicit recent tendencies to broaden the examination. The statute should recognise the current practice in divinity of questioning the candidates in biblical history. In Lit.

Hum. candidates should be able to illustrate their author by 'reference to modern writers, but strictly retaining the treatises of the ancients as the basis of the examination.' Through this narrow crack was squeezed the later philosophical development of the Greats school. Mathematics should be encouraged by allowing attainments insufficient for a mathematical class to count towards a class in Greats. The committee divided on the question whether an ambiguous clause should be repealed which had been interpreted to mean that examiners should take into account 'the supposed moral character of each candidate, particularly his diligence or idleness;' Whately, of course, was quite sure that they should not. An appendix recommended Whately's evergreen of a matriculation examination to raise the standard of university entrance.[186]

By this time disaster had befallen the constitution to which Oxford had pledged herself, and for the next quarter of a century she was to be drawn into the political maelstrom. Already proposals for examination reform suffered the impact of Peel's by-election struggle in 1829, and the passions aroused by the reform crisis. The mild proposals of the Hebdomadal Board were assailed in one inflammatory flysheet in the clap-trap dear to the Tractarians:

> they pride themselves in marching with the march of mind and Spirit of the Age; and they think with the great agitator [O'Connell] that importunity must at last prevail, and extort from our weariness what our judgement would refuse.[187]

Nor would others now countenance the old Oriel heresy that the schools were a test of intellectual achievement. The object of the university, declared a pamphlet with delicate satire, was not to produce statesmen guided by theories or 'churchmen of mis-called liberal views and habits of studious trifling' (like Whately) but

> to keep up a succession of sound orthodox Protestants in Church and State; men of true English growth, who are convinced that sterling honesty is not only the best policy, but that it will suffice to teach true policy in all departments; men who despise the frivolous refinements of the age, and are determined to put a stop to all the dangerous innovations of the boasted march of intellect, as destructive of the stout-hearted complacency of the true British character, and utterly useless to the man whose mind has been cast in the mould of our ancient institutions.[188]

The all-pervading spirit of liberalism which was already bemusing future Tractarians was seen as animating Peel and the emancipators, compassing the overthrow of the Anglican ascendancy, and even permitting candidates to illustrate ancient with modern authors.[189] As usual the heads' proposal was defeated in Convocation,[190] and it is wonderful that the main proposals of the committee went through in November 1830.[191]

The opportunity lost in 1830 was not to recur for twenty years. Copleston bewailed the lack of progress, and foretold the early supremacy of Cambridge.[192] The examiners in mathematics protested against the heads' refusal to recommend the listing of candidates in order of merit[193] (a proposal which could certainly not have been carried), Baden Powell resigned from the board of examiners in disgust in 1832,[194] and the struggle to establish 'physical and mathematical studies *as an essential branch of a liberal education*' was still proceeding eighteen months later.[195] At the end of 1832 the classical examiners reported to the Vice-Chancellor

> an almost universal inattention to Latin composition, to critical scholarship, to the proprieties of idiom, translation, and to the practical application of logic; but above all they must note a general tendency to inaccurate and superficial habits of reading and thinking. They attribute these evils, in a great measure, to the distraction of the student's mind among a variety of subjects at the same time.[196]

At this stage, however, the university was in such dire political trouble that the Hebdomadal Board would not reopen the issue. In 1833 changes were made in the requirements for degrees in medicine and divinity, but in one sense the age of reform was over. What was in question now was not the efficiency of the university but its ecclesiastical status.

CHAPTER IV

OXFORD AND THE CONSTITUTION

We ... regard our ancient universities as an integral part of constitution, which it would be almost sacrilege to amend or destroy.

T. HODGSKIN, *Travels in the North of Germany*
(Edinburgh, 1820)

It is my fervent and anxious wish that, while we clear away gradually the rubbish of some of our old prejudices, the *essence of the old Oxford principles* should still remain inviolate—that no shuffling or trickery shd. be introduced among us—no condescendence to new opinions for the sake of popularity, no change of our ancient sentiments, or anct. institutions.

Professor CHARLES LLOYD to ROBERT PEEL, March 23, 1825.
B.M. Add. MSS. 40342 fo. 229.

IN the 1820's public criticism fastened not merely on the discipline and privileges of the universities, but on their constitution and political role. The liberalism of the students and professors of the German universities was well known, and was publicly demonstrated in the burning of Kotzebue's *German History* and other symbols of absolutism at Wartburg in October 1817. On March 23, 1819, Charles Louis Sand, a student of Jena, assassinated Kotzebue. The German princes under Metternich's influence adopted the Carlsbad decrees and resolved to keep a close watch on the universities and press. Among the butchers of academic liberties were the very princes whom Oxford delighted to honour. The public, liberal and conservative, had forgotten that not long ago Oxford had been suspected of treason, and thought that differences in constitution explained the contrast between Oxford's present conservatism and the subversiveness of academies abroad.

Not long after the murder of Kotzebue a pamphlet was published[1] justifying the German and reflecting obliquely upon the English universities. The German students had

> adopted the universal wish of the nation, and the professors so unlike the generality of their brethren in other places, [were], almost without a single exception, the strenuous supporters of national liberty and unalienable rights of mankind.[2]

No disciplinary regulations could check their 'irresistible spirit of freedom,' or their desire for a parliamentary system of the

English style.[3] The achievements of the German universities, impoverished as they were, contrasted brilliantly with those of the 'opulently endowed establishments of England in which a desire for patronage and place must influence so many.'

In the following year Thomas Hodgskin gave a much more circumstantial account of the German system. He held that much of what was taught there was trivial, and that the student politicians were an unpractical lot, but he questioned the faith of English tories in the superiority of academic self-government guaranteed by chartered privileges and endowments.

> Accustomed as we are to regard our ancient universities as an integral part of our constitution, which it would be almost sacrilege to amend or destroy, this rising and sinking of universities so that they scarcely last longer than the life of their founder, appears very strange. The facility to change is derived from the institutions being the mere bubbles of the monarch's will . . . German universities are, therefore, essentially different from the universities of England, which are corporate bodies, regulated by laws of their own, possessing large revenues, and independent of everything but the laws of the land . . . That philosophy which considers the control of sovereigns over the education of society as an evil regards this state of the German universities as a matter of deep regret. But . . . universities which living men can alter are better than those which slumber on, century after century, and take no note of all the improvements that rise on every side . . . Without placing much confidence in sovereigns, it may at least be supposed that, checked and informed as they now are by public opinion, they are as capable of organising a university as the same class of men were three or four centuries ago . . . There is probably no country of Europe in which larger funds are appropriated to this purpose than in England, and, owing to our rigid adherence to Gothic regulations, there is no one in which so little is effected by them.

The revenues of Göttingen, the most lavishly endowed of all the German universities, amounted to little more than £11,000 p.a., or the income of four heads of houses in England. Of course,

> Göttingen has no good things to bribe its younger members to a continued adherence to taught opinions. There is no warm and well-lined stall of orthodoxy, and no means are taken to influence the students' conscience through their stomachs.

There being no collegiate system or corporate discipline, there was no need for those unpopular English survivals, the university courts.[4]

Hodgskin revealed the full paradox of liberal hostility to chartered liberties and preference for state control rather than 'influence.' Even more sharply, Brougham in 1822 sought to demonstrate that the influence of the Crown was increasing by pointing out the uncanny alacrity with which the University of Oxford scented a shift of power.[5] Here was a case to be answered, and some of the main lines of later controversy were laid down in a discussion in the *Quarterly* in 1820.

According to the *Quarterly* the German university system failed at precisely those points where it differed from the English system, its lack of college organisation, the poverty of its endowments, and its reliance upon professorial instruction.[6] Students with the liberty to migrate enjoyed in Germany could never be kept in order. English university education was based on the study of well established texts—'the safer round of wholesome learning'—but German lectures upon the latest scholarship produced students who

> are all speculative to a degree surpassing even the highest flights of those in our northern capital; and are all puffed up . . . with their perfect fitness to introduce a new order of things and to become the regenerators of Europe.

The professors, instead of restraining the follies of youth, led their agitations; but what could be expected of men who gained their livelihood by dispensing novelties for fees? The 'superabundance of professorial knowledge with which Germany is deluged,' the overgrown intellectual proletariat, only spurred them on. To this statement of the intellectual and disciplinary superiority of tutorial instruction by books over professorial instruction by lectures, Pusey, Newman, H. L. Mansel and other conservative writers of the middle of the century had little to add.

The reviewer, however, said nothing of the religious anxieties already created by the German intellectual upheaval. In 1801 even Samuel Parr rejoiced that Oxford men escaped

> the contamination of these metaphysical novelties which are said to have gained a wide and dangerous ascendancy in some places of education upon the Continent,

though not the University of Göttingen 'which deservedly flourished under the auspices of Mr. Heyne.'[7] In 1818 Wilberforce learned that even here 'a system of unqualified scepticism was maintained and diffused', and appealed to the duke of Cambridge to use his influence in Hanover to stop the rot.[8] Small wonder that, as an undergraduate, another evangelical, Reginald Heber, defended the 'Gothic regulations' which Hodgskin despised, because

> these remnants of Gothicism tend very much to keep us in a

sound consistent track; and that one cause of the declension of the foreign universities was their compliance, in such points as these, with the variation of manners.[9]

Meanwhile a series of theologians, Conybeare, Bishop Jebb, and the celebrated dissenter, Pye Smith, were sounding alarms at the progress of rationalism in Germany, which were taken up comprehensively by Hugh James Rose in 1825 in his famous course of Cambridge sermons on *The state of protestantism in Germany*. According to Rose the rationalist party in Germany had 'used their utmost efforts to convince the world that Christianity is a human invention,' and now monopolised the divinity chairs in the universities.[10] Rose was careful to argue that in their effort to get rid of the historical element in Christianity the rationalists were false to reason itself, but among the Oxford liberals, Thomas Arnold rightly feared that Rose's sermons would raise a hue and cry against all 'impartial investigation and independent thought,'[11] and the young E. B. Pusey first came before the public in 1828 with a defence of the German protestants.[12] But even Pusey and Arnold found much to lament in Germany, and despite Liddon's assertion to the contrary,[13] there was real anxiety about the negative tendencies of German theology.[14] No-one doubted that these arose from the prestige and peculiarities of the German professorial system. Liberals might harp on the superiority of German ways, but conservatives replied that they were fatal to order in the state, and, much more important, that they drained all truth and fervour from religion.

This issue came home with the launching of a German university in London. The idea of a London University was conceived by Thomas Campbell in 1820 in the course of discussions with professors at Bonn, and was supported by Benthamites, whigs and dissenters who wanted a place of higher education for the middle class, free from religious tests, cheaper and better disposed to modern studies than the existing universities. In 1825 the plan was put forward of a university organised on the professorial principle, established by means of a joint-stock company, and evading insuperable religious disagreements by omitting all instruction in religion and all common worship.

The promoters of the university from the first desired incorporation though not a power to grant degrees. The government refused to grant a royal charter, so in May 1825 Brougham moved in the Commons for an incorporation bill. Peel assumed at once that the bill must be defeated, and wrote to Charles Lloyd for arguments against it.[15] Lloyd thought that Brougham envisaged an institution purveying cheap education of no very advanced kind and was little concerned.[16] The bill was finally ruled out of order, and knowing the opposition, Brougham went no further.[17] It was Peel, rather than Lloyd, however, who had gauged the temper of his constituents and conservative opinion in general.

The *Quarterly* made its familiar attacks against German universities, and deplored the absence of religious teaching from the London scheme, for religion was intimately associated 'with the progress of the human mind in every liberal pursuit.' Nevertheless extensive changes were needed before the old universities could meet the needs of the day.[18] In 1827, following Peel's commission of inquiry into the Scottish universities,[19] the *Quarterly* began to complain that the syllabus at Oxford was narrower than anywhere else, and narrower than it used to be even there; that the total exclusion of professional education in the superior faculties of divinity, law and medicine was a mistake; that it was disgraceful that the English universities should produce fewer graduates than the Scottish; that Oxford tutorial teaching was far too unspecialised, and that in Scotland at least, the professorial system had not produced a deluge of German novelties.[20] By 1829, with the protestant constitution in a parlous state, the *Quarterly*'s regret at the exclusion of religion from the London system had turned to a rabid championship of a coarse popular clamour, and the assertion that the Gower-street college could be no university at all.

> There was . . . a curious and three-fold impropriety in assuming the title of University for a *single* college, which the *crown* has not created, and from which the science of *divinity* was specially to be excluded.[21]

This crude abuse and fallacious etymology could hardly conceal the concessions which the defenders of the old academic monopoly had had to make. The defects of Oxford which the *Quarterly* admitted with regret, the *Edinburgh* denounced with enthusiasm, and especially ridiculed the idea that there was any substance in Oxford religious instruction. But the basic weakness in the English universities

> might be summed up in two words, their wealth and their privileges. Their prosperity does not depend upon the public approbation. It would therefore be strange if they deserved the public approbation . . . Like manufacturers who enjoy a monopoly, they work at such an advantage that they can venture to work ill.[22]

Even the Wesleyans, who in this generation generally followed the Anglican line in education, were dissatisfied, and ascribed the foundation of a godless university to the supine neglect of government and church to extend the facilities of Oxford and Cambridge. The Wesleyan desideratum was a university, or colleges in the old universities, free of tests to students, and guaranteeing orthodox teaching by binding the dons to the articles.[23] This object was ultimately achieved in the Oxford University Act of 1854 to the applause of whiggish churchmen like Dr. Hawkins, but meanwhile the Wesleyans thought the ancient universities inadequate, and 'the religion taught . . . too partial, too sectarian, and too little Christian.' The *Edinburgh Review* could say no more.

The church now made a great effort to retain its hold upon higher education, which took a characteristically two-fold form. On the one hand King's College, London,[24] St. David's College, Lampeter and the University of Durham were established to increase the supply. On the other hand Oxford used all her political influence to block the incorporation of the Gower-Street body. The advent of the whig government in November 1830 encouraged the latter to apply for a charter and the power to grant degrees. On January 21, 1831, Sir Robert Inglis reported to the Vice-Chancellor that

> one of the members of the Council of the King's College, London, happening yesterday on other affairs to wait on the Lord Chancellor, his lordship mentioned that the London University had applied for a clause enabling them to grant degrees & that he had struck it out.[25]

Already, however, the Hebdomadal Board had scented danger and had requested the Chancellor to obtain 'full and precise information on a point so deeply concerning the established Church of England as well as its ancient universities.'[26]

On January 31, they obtained an opinion from Sir Charles Wetherell, the university counsel, that a power to grant degrees might be claimed under the proposed charter, and recommending that a precluding clause be inserted.[27] For this clause the university immediately pressed. Inglis's story may indicate that the Hebdomadal Board had an unexpected sympathy in a government they abhorred; at any rate they resolutely rebuffed a private negotiation opened between Leonard Horner, the Warden of London University, and Shuttleworth, the whig Warden of New College,[28] and rejected the London offer to surrender divinity degrees only, on the grounds that it did not cover cases where ecclesiastical privileges were annexed to arts degrees.[29]

Thus the London proposal to grant degrees in arts both threatened the grip of the old universities upon entrance to the professions, and, as theoretically-minded Tractarians were to argue, bore an ulterior menace to the relations of church and state. William Tooke, one of the council of the London University, admitted that it was the representations of Oxford that had held up their charter in the Home Office at the last minute, and in vain begged the Hebdomadal Board to negotiate with him direct.[30] Oxford had won the first round in the battle, but had the prospect, after the Reform Bill, of fighting the next under much less favourable circumstances. Nor had the university any counter to the 'march of mind' in the name of which liberal and dissenting groups in the provinces were planning the creation of new German universities.[31]

The collapse of the old tory party, the great displacement in the relations of church and state which took place in 1828 and 1829, and the upheavals which led up to the Reform Act of 1832 were powerfully felt in Oxford. The liberal toryism of Liverpool's last years was not unpopular and it provided a meeting ground for old friends of Grenville and Canning with the court politicians of the university. In 1823, when Grenville's health was thought to be failing, C. H. Hall tried unsuccessfully to make his peace with Liverpool by inviting him to stand as Chancellor.[32] Canning, the great luminary of the ministry, remained the object of much distrust, but his claims to the university seat were renewed upon the resignation of Richard Heber in 1826.

The first candidate to appear was the Solicitor-General, Sir Charles Wetherell, with strong support in Magdalen, University College, Jesus and Queen's. Wetherell's father had been Master of University College, an odious courtier and pluralist who was reputed in Oxford to have left £150,000;[33] he himself inherited much of the Master's personal unpopularity, and confronted by a strong canvass from Henley Eden, was about 'to be turned out of the City [of Oxford] for parsimony.'[34] Peel detested him,[35] and he was cordially hated in most colleges. Nevertheless, Wetherell had all his life been involved in university affairs,[36] and at first seemed likely to meet no opposition.

The obvious opponent was Sir John Nicholl who had run Heber hard in 1821, but his patron at Bodmin, Lord Aylesbury, was unwilling to have the seat vacated except at a general election.[37] In his absence Copleston and the progressive party at Oriel began to stir for Canning in the belief that he might be returned by 'the friends of the catholic claims, the moderate party' and those who favoured the most distinguished candidate.[38] Reactions to this proposal varied widely. Some Grenvillites like Joseph Phillimore, regius professor of civil law, thought Canning almost assured of success;[39] others, such as C. W. Wynn, had long taken the view that Canning's unsavoury reputation made him an impossible candidate.[40] In the chapter at Christ Church, Canning was detested,[41] and the House had a ready excuse for abstention in the fact that it was not their seat which was vacant. Canning himself seems to have waited for some college to take up his cause as a body,[42] but within a week of the poll a laudatory paragraph in the *Times* assured his friends, 'the friends of light and learning in this celebrated seat of his early distinction,' that he would stand, and that the odds accepted in London were two to one that he would go to the poll, and evens that he would be successful if he did.[43]

The Oriel faction, nevertheless, had to hedge against the possibility of his refusal. The position was that

> a respectable country gentleman of known attachment to things as they are, and one who would upon proper occasions say a few words . . . would certainly be chosen,[44]

but the gentry were as unwilling as Canning to draw a bow at a venture. Ashurst, one of the members for the county, was invited but declined,[45] and then the President of Corpus produced the name of Thomas Grimston Bucknall-Estcourt. Estcourt who had a country seat in Gloucestershire, belonged to a well-known Wiltshire family, and had long represented the family borough of Devizes. He was a man well calculated to heal the breaches in the tory ranks in Oxford. On friendly, though not familiar terms with Canning,[46] in no sense a rabid church-and-state man like Wetherell,[47] he nevertheless implored the advice of Sidmouth at the outset of Wellington's government in January 1828 in the most antiquated terms:

> I cannot help feeling strongly disposed against a government in which nought but the signs of weakness, discontence [sic] innovation and hostility to Church & King are found to console us in our embarrassments. I hate faction as much as I do Whiggery, and am therefore anxious to ascertain when & where I am to find the real friends of the Sovereign, and the supporters of the constitution, that I may take care not to be found wanting in support of their principles, and to be at my Post.[48]

Always independent in outlook, Thomas Arnold inquired as to Estcourt's sentiments on the Corn Laws and Game laws.[49] Oddly enough, Estcourt opposed the Game Laws,[50] and proved ultimately a more advanced free-trader than Peel.[51] He spoke regularly on questions relating to rural poverty.[52] Estcourt in short, though a protestant, was a candidate whom the progressives of Oriel could whole-heartedly support if Canning did not stand. Copleston, therefore, making the curious proviso that if Canning came into the field he should be free to join him, became Estcourt's most strenuous canvasser, and an old member of the college became chairman of his London committee.[53] The success of their canvass speedily made it impossible not only for Canning, but also for Wetherell, to go to the poll. By the middle of February, Estcourt had more than twice as many promises as Wetherell, who accordingly withdrew.[54]

After this events proceeded steadily towards the disruption of the old constitution. A year later Canning was Prime Minister, Copleston was raised to the bench, and Charles Lloyd, his inveterate rival, was growling that 'the Church of England has seldom been subject to such a terrific invasion of undue influence.'[55] By September 1827 Canning was dead, and Goderich was making ineffective efforts to hold his followers together. In January 1828, Peel returned to office under the duke of Wellington, and the church was truly in danger. The new cabinet with its group of Canningites contained eight catholics to six protestants, and invited challenge upon the issues which had so often divided Canning from the other tories; and the first challenge had been prepared during Canning's ministry. On several occasions since 1820, the nonconformist pressure groups had agitated for the repeal of the Test and Corporation Acts, and in May 1827 they established a united committee of dissenting bodies, and gave notice that a motion for repeal would be put on May 31. A vigorous campaign was put on, and although Canning's government was given respite by the postponement of the motion till the next session, petitions were presented, and William Smith, the unitarian chairman of the Protestant Dissenting Deputies, insisted in the House that exclusion from Oxford was among their practical grievances.[56]

When after a brisk autumn campaign, the dissenters confronted Wellington's new government with their motion in February 1828, it appeared that Oxford might not after all be a guardian of the ascendancy. Peel applied to Charles Lloyd for 'arguments for people who know very little of the matter—care not much about it—half of whom have dined or are going to dine.'[57] In Lloyd's view

> the sentiments of the university in regard the C. & T. Acts may be considered as none at all. The Vice-Chancellor without consulting me, proposed a petition to the heads of houses; but he had several voices against him, and said no more about it. He then came to me and I advised him to let the matter drop. I did this, partly from my opinion of the inexpediency of petitioning, wch. wd. only have fettered you, and made it more difficult to concede—& partly because I have great doubts whether the Masters of Arts wd. not have the petition thrown out if brought before Convocation.[58]

Oxford clearly was forewarned when Peel made the motion a government matter and was beaten by 237 to 193. This defeat settled the fate of the tests. The only hope of separating those who voted in the majority because they considered that the sacramental test was a profanation of the rite from those who objected to all religious discrimination, was to propose a declaration in place of a test. Dr.

Tournay, the evangelical Warden of Wadham, pressed hard for a declaration to be imposed upon all office-holders binding them not to act in opposition to the church, but Peel insisted that to impose this upon all office-holders was absurd, while to draw up a list of specified officers would be to invite ridicule.[59] Much bargaining ensued; Russell insisted that the dissenters must accept a declaration if they wanted their act, and the dissenters bargained shrewdly for acceptable terms. The bill passed quietly and even the Warden of Wadham was satisfied.[60]

Throughout the campaign the dissenters had been in touch with the Catholics, and the extreme protestant press accused them of 'union';[61] before the Test Acts were repealed the Catholics were moving their own claims, and subjecting both Peel and the university to a further test of consistency. Russell had challenged the university in the Commons to defend the Test Acts;[62] their refusal to accept the challenge had been used by the Lord Chancellor as an argument in the Lords to beat down Eldon's opposition to repeal.[63] The Catholics might well hope to succeed by the same tactics, and there was some evidence for their optimism.

It was true that the university petitioned against every concession to Catholics with monotonous regularity,[64] that in 1825 only three members of New College opposed the petition,[65] and that, with the avowed object of stemming the tide of popery, a proposal for a Martyrs' Memorial (in the shape of a special print) was put before the university in 1826.[66] At the same time Blanco White, now midway in his evolution from popery to unitarianism was created M.A. by diploma on account of his anti-Roman writings.[67] But since then the promotion of the Canningites had had its effect, and the political situation had deteriorated both at home and in Ireland. There had been considerable nervousness in Oxford in 1825 at the effect on the young men of rumours that Liverpool had changed his mind on the Catholic question,[68] and to discourage wavering Lloyd had always insisted that Peel should give no countenance to Canning.[69] When in March 1828, as the Test Acts were going by the board, the annual petition against the Catholics was brought on there was new opposition. A flysheet urged that instead of reproducing old petitions the university should show that some of its gloomy prophecies had come to pass.[70] When the petition came before Convocation, J. D. Macbride, the evangelical Principal of Magdalen Hall, demanded a scrutiny; the petition was carried by 60 votes to 32, but the striking feature of the division was not merely the size of the minority but the fact that it was now led by four heads,[71] Macbride, Shuttleworth, the whig Warden of New College,[72] and the two Oriel progressives who after 1830 became the hopes of the whigs, Edward Hawkins and Richard Whately. Edward Hawkins had won golden opinions as

Dean of Oriel,[73] and only a month previously had been elected Provost in succession to Copleston; assured of a majority from the first, he was enabled by Keble's refusal to stand to be elected with a cordial unanimity which gave no hint of the squabbles which were soon the ruination of the college.[74] Whately had been appointed Principal of St. Alban Hall by Grenville in 1825, and had begun to argue that 'consequences subversive of Christ's spiritual kingdom must follow from the alliance' with the state.[75] So different a man as Keble also confessed that in the present times 'the chief comfort is in persuading myself that an establishment is not on the whole so great a benefit to men's spiritual interests as most of us have been taught to think.'[76] If this was the temper of both the rationalist and high-church strains which had mingled in a cocksure Oriel common room in the time of Copleston, and if they were now allied with whigs and the senior Oxford evangelicals, there was ground for Eldon's gloomy conclusion that the university would not struggle against the great interests in church and state which were taking up the Catholic cause.[77]

The very formation of the Wellington government brought on the final emancipation crisis, for one result of the ministerial changes was the by-election in County Clare which was triumphantly carried by O'Connell. By the end of 1828, Peel and Wellington had decided that they must carry emancipation, and on January 31, 1829, before any public announcement had been made, Peel intimated his intentions privately to the Dean of Christ Church and offered to resign his seat.[78] The Dean immediately consulted Gaisford and Lloyd who were not agreed as to the best course, and were in any case put in an impossible position by the fact that Peel had not announced his policy. Peel finally sent an unconditional resignation to the Vice-Chancellor to arrive on February 5, the day of the opening of parliament, but also, unfortunately, the day on which Convocation met to vote an anti-Catholic petition; after the petition had been despatched Peel's letter of resignation was read, and an election campaign began which exceeded in acrimony even the cancellarial campaign of 1809.

The Dean was generally expected to propose Peel again; Thomas Vowler Short, Censor of Christ Church, who was a fervent Peelite, pressed hard for Peel to state clearly that he would stand. Robert Bullock-Marsham, Warden of Merton, also helped to beat down Charles Lloyd's remaining scruples about putting Peel forward, and on February 9 the Christ Church common room agreed unanimously to support him. On the 10th, however, Lloyd, whose inflated ego had been punctured by this crisis, took fright at the news that other colleges were meeting in order to oppose Peel with a candidate yet unchosen, and so on the following day, receiving a letter in which Peel put himself in his hands, he put a stop to his candidature.

No opposition had yet been organised against Peel, but his cause seemed lost, 'all the heads of houses favourably disposed . . . were sunk in hopeless apathy.' Many, however, were attached to Peel, and many did not want to let in Sir Charles Wetherell by default. Finally Whately was galvanised into action by Hinds, his Vice-Principal, and a meeting at Merton set up a committee for Peel under the chairmanship of the Warden, with the support of seven heads.[79] Two days later a London committee was set up under Granville Somerset, one of the tory managers,[80] and Peel's campaign was in full swing. Lloyd's initial indecision, nevertheless, cost Peel the corporate support of the House.

Meanwhile tempers were rising on the other side. A friend of Philip Bliss, Keeper of the Archives, pressed him to turn Peel out

> not because I am *clear* that I am not a friend to the Duke's measure, but because I detest a fellow who would bait George Canning into his coffin & then go smack round like the Duke's flugelman to keep his Grace's foot out of his breech—hang him, this shows the baseness of the cotton-spinner's breed.[81]

Three candidates were considered by the protestant party. Lord Encombe, son and heir to Lord Eldon, had both principles and unpopularity guaranteed by his father. S. L. Gifford, the editor of the protestant *Standard*, was despatched to consult both the marquis of Chandos, the rising hope of the Grenville family, and Sir Robert Harry Inglis. He reported that he had seen them both, that Chandos would not stir from Buckinghamshire, but that Inglis would stand. Chandos later denied having been approached, but by then Inglis had taken the field.[82]

Inglis was the thirteenth and youngest child of Sir Hugh Inglis, a director of the East India Company, and in 1820 succeeded to the baronetcy. At Eton he became a friend of Henry Addington, the son of Lord Sidmouth, and eventually became private secretary to Lord Sidmouth himself.[83] Inglis thus grew up in the straitest school of protestant constitutionalism. With this, he was accepted in the inmost circles of the evangelical elect. He was a friend of Reginald Heber, corresponded with him on theological matters, helped in the publication of his works, and, after his death, edited his sermons.[84] He was intimate with another evangelical East Indiaman, Charles Grant, and in 1815 became joint guardian with his wife of Marianne Thornton. The Grants and the Thorntons were chief pillars of the Clapham Sect, and Inglis's connexion with them made public his own evangelical faith. It immediately occurred to Philip Bliss that this 'would not "go down" with a large majority of . . . members of Convocation,'[85] but this Oxford prejudice was confused by two others. Among evangelical churchmen there had always been a 'high' and a 'low' party, and Inglis was as high and exclusive as any Oxford churchmen could desire, being 'more high-church than most of the bishops . . . in the matter of the Test and Corporation Acts.'[86] Again, Oxford high-churchmen of all schools cherished the prejudice that evangelicalism was built not merely upon an incomplete theology, but also upon enthusiasm and the neglect of reason. To this pattern Inglis refused to conform.

> Sir Robert adored travel—he was the typical tireless tourist—
> . . . There was something of the courteous dilettante about him; he was interested in Public Records, he founded a literary club, he was Antiquary to the Royal Academy, he encouraged young artists. One of these, George Richmond, requires particular notice . . . Sir Robert detected him when he was very young, encouraged his early marriage, and provided him with a sitter in William Wilberforce. The portrait brought him fame instantly.[87]

An amateur of science, he had been pressed in 1827 to become chairman of the Royal Society.[88] As a man of culture, not to mention as a lay theologian,[89] Inglis was in every way Peel's superior, and had the university fulfilled Newman's outrageous description of 'a religious, straightforward, unpolitical body,'[90] it could not easily have found a better representative. No election on the issue of emancipation, however, could be unpolitical, and as a politician Inglis could offer two merits only, those of assiduous effort and consistency. Bred of the East India Company, Inglis regarded the church and university as beleaguered monopolies like the Company, capable of surviving only by standing on every tittle of their chartered rights. Inglis was the last man to reconcile the university with her enemies in state and society,[91] but he was absolutely dependable (which could not be said of Heber and Peel), a worthy and lovable person, one who bore so little the conventional Oxford image of an evangelical that S. L. Gifford could deny that he was an evangelical at all, and to boot, a Christ Church man who could counter Peel's influence in the chapter.

The election was fought throughout with great bitterness.[92] Lloyd's first reaction to Inglis's committee list was that 'there is not a name except Dr. Routh's known out of the precincts of the university,'[93] and Peel's friends 'everywhere styled themselves the "talent" of the university.'[94] Even after the election, the *Times* went on analysing the voting on the same principle: 101 first-class men had voted for Peel, 51 for Inglis; 23 prize-men for Peel, 4 for Inglis; 12 professors for Peel, 6 for Inglis. Peel's six strongest colleges included the most distinguished in the university, whereas those of Inglis were

> six of the very lowest order of colleges, the members of which are generally remarkable for nothing more than the obscurity

of their station, the mediocrity of their talents, and the insignificance of their character.[95]

Newman's retort to this was that Peel's strength consisted of the London lawyers, tied to the interest of the ministry, and (with all the arrogance of the Oriel set) that the only men of talent on the other side were Whately and Hawkins.[96] The general reply was in terms which the Tractarians were to make their own, that 'the advocates of emancipation and the patrons of the march of mind are one and the same,'[97] that

> the point now is, not whether we humbler residents in this place should be hewers of wood and drawers of water for these philistines of literature, but whether our absent members also must submit to a yet more galling subjection to these *Men of mind*.[98]

If the university changed front on this occasion, it would for ever stand condemned for 'an interested and pliable judgment.'[99] Peel's friends yielded nothing in abuse, and represented Inglis's party as a coalition united only by hatred of Catholics, as 'crazy and prophetical.'[100] Convocation had neither the information nor the judgment to challenge the advisers of the Crown.[101] Letters supporting Peel were published from two such prominent anti-Catholics as Henry Philpotts and Blanco White, who were thereupon overwhelmed with vituperation as rats.[102]

Argument continued to the very commencement of the poll. Marsham made a long and boring speech proposing Peel; there were speeches urging on the one side that emancipation was no cure for the economic ills of Ireland, and on the other that the penal laws embodied no Reformation principles, and that the age of intolerance was past;[103] the Vice-Chancellor finally interrupted one speaker in full flow by taking the votes.[104] Once the polling began, the issue soon became clear; to the dismay of Peel's confident committee, Inglis led the whole way and ultimately triumphed by 755 votes to 609. In countless rectories there were scenes of joy as delighted protestants rode home, answering inquiries all the way, declaring 'a majority of 146 against the united exertions of the government, the whigs & radicals. Oxford never yet stood on so high a pinnacle of renown.'[105]

The election left an unpleasant backwash. The affray in Oxford could only sharpen the differences in the tory ranks, and there were recriminations among Peel's friends themselves. Whately offered comfortable words,[106] but Grenville epitomised much disillusionment in the comment that 'there never was anything so mismanaged.'[107] Nor would the majority in Oxford forgive the superior tone adopted by their opponents.

In no college was the division keener than in Oriel. The senior fellows who had built up the society supported Peel and pressed Blanco White to write in his favour; Keble, pleading that 'we are lowering the standard of political integrity to suit the times, instead of trying to raise the times to our standard'[108] had taken most of the young men with him and had written in favour of Inglis. In February 1828, Newman had warmly approved Hawkins's election as Provost; in February 1829 he abused him as a meddler, though Hawkins had not swerved an inch from the college line over many years. Within a year this bad blood disrupted the college tutorial arrangements. Newman and his friends claimed that the college had begun to go downhill in 1823 with the admission of an idle set of men. They wished to end the Gentlemen Commoners' privilege of dining with the fellows and to strengthen the grip of individual tutors over their pupils by limiting the men's opportunities to attend the lectures of other tutors. They hoped also to invest the Dean with the Provost's authority to exclude men from the sacrament. Hawkins felt entitled to resist changes which by tightening discipline and restricting specialised teaching must ruin the college reputation built up by Eveleigh and Copleston for liberal[109] and fashionable education.[110] But the younger set now affected to despise 'the philistines of literature,' the tutors resigned and Hawkins secured the fateful services of a distinguished former fellow, R. D. Hampden. Samuel Wilberforce took Peel for 'either a rogue or a poltroon,'[111] and evolved from a radical into a 'very high tory.'[112] Already this high toryism was out of date as protestant politicians began to turn against the unreformed constitution, and it was to be transformed, as soon as a whig government was in office, into a high and unyielding doctrine of the church. This whole development was foreseen and deplored by another former Oriel fellow of the older generation, Thomas Arnold.[113]

Inglis's election, moreover, began a period not of triumph but of demoralisation for the Oxford evangelicals. During the 'twenties they had been growing in influence, and moderate in their politics; Heber rather than Nicholl, and Estcourt rather than Wetherell had been their choice. In 1829 they were divided. J. D. Macbride had come out in favour of repeal, supported by James Garbett (who succeeded Keble in the poetry chair in 1842) and Daniel Wilson: but H. B. Bulteel of Exeter, B. P. Symons of Wadham, R. L. Cotton of Worcester, the erratic R. W. Sibthorp of Magdalen, and John Hill with the tribes of St. Edmund Hall, were all on the other side. The evangelicals were as perplexed as to the church's future as those who became Tractarians, and in 1830 and 1831 they began to fraternise with the Plymouth Brethren and Irvingites.

Most notorious among the waverers was H. B. Bulteel, who in

November 1826 had become curate of St. Ebbe's. Bulteel's ministry among undergraduates there proved so fruitful that in May 1828, his churchwardens tried to get the Hebdomadal Board to exclude them 'on the plea that they prevent the parishioners from coming.' On May 11, they tried on the Vice-Chancellor's authority to keep out members of the university and take their names. The Vice-Chancellor soon found that he could not sustain this attempt to forbid gownsmen to attend a parish church against the attacks of Whately and Shuttleworth on the Hebdomadal Board,[114] but once the establishment had been called in question in 1829, Bulteel got into deep waters. On February 6, 1831, he concluded a forcible exposition of the doctrine of free grace at St. Mary's with the nagging question, 'are we collectively, as a Church, led by the Spirit of God?' Bulteel began to think that the church was subject less to the spirit of God than to the spirit of the world, abetted by the Oxford college authorities who granted testimonials for ordination to improper persons.[115] To this charge Edward Burton, regius professor of divinity replied,[116] not to the satisfaction of others[117] besides Bulteel,[118] and a regular pamphlet war developed, in which Bulteel was censured by that stout evangelical, Daniel Wilson. Bulteel proceeded to preach in the open air and in dissenting chapels, and his licence was withdrawn by the bishop. He therefore abjured the church as anti-Christian before a congregation of a thousand assembled in his garden. 'Thus Oxford is left,' bewailed John Hill the Vice-Principal of St. Edmund Hall, 'destitute of a single faithful pastor in any church among a population of 20,000.'[119] But worse was to come.

A few weeks later Hill noted that

> Bulteel has been spending a week with some of Mr. Irving's friends & is come back satisfied of the genuineness of the miracle of healing & tongues: and convinced moreover of their doctrine of general redemption. For myself this does not appear the testimony of scripture.[120]

Six months later Hill went reluctantly to see a girl possessed of devils at Bulteel's house,[121] doubtless one of those he claimed to cure by prayer and intercession.[122] In May 1833, however, the hard rock of Calvinism triumphed in Bulteel and he confessed to John Hill

> his gracious deliverance from the awful delusions concerning supernatural gifts (of miracles, tongues, prophesyings and visions) which he had so long been carried into . . . He spoke with horror of two of Irving's errors concerning the human nature of Christ, & perfectibility on earth.[123]

Thus partially restored, Bulteel conducted the chapel built for him by his friends in St. Ebbe's on ordinary Strict Baptist lines.[124]

The New Year of 1832, however, found John Hill in unparalleled gloom conducting a spiritual inquest not only into the state of his heart, but also into the state of the nation and church. Finally he concluded:

The state of this place and neighbourhood is humbling. In the university, little, very little, goes on which betokens an outpouring of the Spirit of God. Not one minister fully preaching & living the Gospel in charge of any one of the parishes in Oxford. Bulteel, Tiptaft, Brenton, have deserted the English church. Lambert my co-Secretary in the Church Missionary Society, has left it & the Church of England—Newton, my co-Secretary in the Jews Society is on the verge of doing the same. I have scarcely a friend left in Oxford who is not altogether like-minded.[125]

The evangelicals in Oxford as elsewhere were to prove loyal defenders of the church as the church revival gathered way, but the shattering blow of emancipation demoralised them for the time, and made them incapable of giving a lead.

The university's relations with the new court of William IV began as auspiciously as possible. The university sent up a deputation with an address.[126]

The delegates were most graciously received—& after allowing them all to kiss hands according to rule, [the King] followed it up by shaking hands with them—saying something to each: 'Rigaud[127]—I have known you all my life, there is not a more honest man in England.' 'Mr. Proctor, take care you keep up discipline'—to Dornford.[128] 'Dr. Macbride,[129] I knew your father the admiral very well.' After this reception Oxford is sure to be as loyal as ever.[130]

In the university the election occasioned by the late king's demise passed off with complete tranquillity,[131] but in the country as a whole it led to the overthrow of the tory government, and with public opinion inflamed by economic distress and tidings of revolution in France, a revolutionary situation developed. To the demand for a reformed parliament was added a violent clamour against the privileges of the church. As the establishment in church and state tottered, Oxford trembled too.[132]

The university had its share of the general disorder. In November 1830, when Wellington's government collapsed and Grey came into office, the town called upon the university to take special measures. The Vice-Chancellor called upon the heads to keep the undergraduates in order by closing the gates early, and enrolled M.A.s from each college to patrol the streets after dark. After one 'decided

attempt to riot,' peace was preserved.[133] Again in May 1831 during
the county election similar measures were taken, and George
Anthony Denison, fellow of Oriel, a storm-centre in later years, was
thrown to the ground by a mob in front of Balliol in the course of
his duties as a special constable.[134] The university election went
uncontested in spite of newspaper talk about a whig opposition to
the sitting members for opposing the Reform Bill.[135]

The first reform bill reached its crisis at the end of March 1831
when it received its second reading by one vote. Already the differences in attitude towards the government between the heads of
houses and the rank and file which were a regular feature of the
next decade were visible. Edward Hawkins, Provost of Oriel,
conscious that reform would come and that the university had better
come to terms with it, proposed to the Hebdomadal Board that they
should try simply to moderate the bill.[136] Pusey and Copleston from
different points of view had urged the Provost that it would be
disgraceful for the university to do nothing at all,[137] but the Provost's
draft petition against the bill actually asked for

> such modifications in the representative system, as without
> endangering the stability of our best institutions, and the balance
> of the constitution itself, may check corruption among the
> electors, and render the representation better adapted to the
> circumstances of the country.[138]

To the wilder spirits who saw an opportunity to put an end to the
whole bill this was dreadful; Keble described it as 'a plentiful flow
of water-gruel . . . being handed round to the old ladies' on the
Hebdomadal Board, and made a vehement speech in Convocation
to get it withdrawn in favour of something stiffer.[139] In the event
Estcourt was unable to get the petition presented before the king
dissolved the House.[140]

Before the next bill was brought in, in the summer of 1831, Keble
was urging Hawkins to petition the king against it both as a matter
of duty and as a means of strengthening the resolution of the House
of Lords.[141] The Hebdomadal Board, however, was more taken up
with technicalities in the new bill,[142] which were eventually circumvented by a simple clause exempting the universities from its
operation, a clause that was to prove an unexpected embarrassment
to Gladstone a generation later. But the university was growing more
hostile to reform, and at the end petitioned against it as hazardous
and 'at variance with the acknowledged practice of the constitution.'[143]

The statesmanship of the Hebdomadal Board was now to be very
seriously tested. They had fought half-heartedly against the bill and
lost. The enemies of the university made capital out of their tactics.

The *Times* attacked the university for wanting to go back on the revolution of 1688, and for 'inferiority to the bulk of their country-men in the most important branches of general knowledge.'[144] The reforms of the last generation availed the university nothing, and even their older tradition of returning sitting members unopposed was made a reproach by the radical press. In 1831

> the opulent, the costly, the cherished universities alone dared to betray the people, by whose toil and illrequited bounty they are fed. Not a breath moved the stagnant waters of that dark and sullen pool . . . They chose as heretofore, such members as would have come from Madrid if a writ had been sent to the Holy Inquisition, and that venerable and execrable corporation had obeyed the command.[145]

When the Reform Bill passed, power might be in the hands of propagandists of this kind, certainly reverence would pass out of politics;[146] since it seemed impossible for Oxford to please, perhaps the best tactics would be to oppose the heads' efforts to do so.

CHAPTER V

OXFORD IN THE AGE OF REFORM

Never has learned institution been more directly political and national than the University of Oxford. Some of its colleges represent the talent of the nation, others its rank and fashion, others its wealth; others have been the organs of the government of the day; while others, and the majority, represent one or other division, chiefly local, of the country party.

J. H. NEWMAN, *Rise and progress of the universities* (1854).

IN the first age of reform the university recapitulated the stormy history of the early days of the Hanoverian era. Now as then, Oxford was confronted with a sudden whig triumph, and now the whigs were the abettors and not the enemies of a popish threat to the church. Now as then, a whig triumph let loose a torrent of rationalist and nonconformist abuse against the university and its privileges, a scurrilous vein in which convinced many Oxford men that whiggism and liberalism threatened all things sacred. Now as then, a whig government considered legislation against the university, and it behoved the heads to keep their peace with the ministers as best they could. Now as then, the juniors abused them as Laodicean and stupid, and urged intransigeant high-church resistance. The Hebdomadal Board had never been more solidly high-church than in 1830, and in seeking to go beyond them the livelier juniors went behind protestant high-churchmanship into catholic antiquity. A churchmanship which should be catholic against both dissenters and Romanists was likely to be abstract in character, but at first this was no disadvantage;[1] abstract considerations were all that could be opposed to the whig ministry's utilitarian designs upon the Irish bishoprics. As long as there was pressure upon the university from without, the juniors were sure of support, and set the heads, as in the early Hanoverian years, an almost insoluble problem of government.

From 1830 the pressure upon Oxford was intensified by the common cause made by critics of the most varied hues. Oaths and subscriptions in particular were abhorrent to three great groups, the dissenters, the radicals and the evangelicals. The power of the dissenters and of radical 'march of mind' men was enormously increased by the reform agitation and the new electoral arrangements, and it was a serious matter for the university (and for men like

Newman personally) that evangelicals often took the liberal side. The *Christian Observer* persistently campaigned against university and college oaths at Oxford as profaning sacred things,[2] and deplored the university subscriptions, though with no intention of breaching the church monopoly. It was wrong to exact subscription from untaught youths, and it encouraged the 'bigotry, Popery and intolerance' which the *Christian Observer* detected in the early stirrings of the Oxford Movement, and the 'very excellent Loyolan Popery' of Philpotts's 'extraordinary declaration . . . that the youth subscribes first, and learns to understand what he has subscribed afterwards.'[3] Nevertheless, in July 1834, the *Observer* could still find 'the whole aspect of our universities, moral, religious, and literary . . . highly cheering.'[4]

Dissenters, especially the unitarians and congregationalists who led the attack on the establishment, were commonly less genial. A stiff-necked determination to claim their right of entry into what they described as 'national universities'[5] had triumphed over their suspicion that they were better off without it.[6] The abolition of the university test had been canvassed occasionally among them for a century past,[7] and was now in the forefront of their demands. Unitarians who would probably profit most from repeal, campaigned vigorously against the tests as an insular abuse.[8] Yet few dissenters had any real knowledge of the universities, and their claims were mostly those of the have-nots upon the haves. Indeed their great savant, Pye Smith, who had a unique acquaintance with the university theologians, was converted to the view that since the colleges had swallowed up the university, and were by nature private foundations, the dissenters could not justly force their way in.[9]

While dissenters attacked the university system only by the side door of the tests, radical writers assailed it at all points and on all levels from philosophy to superstition. Oaths and subscriptions,[10] fees[11] and tithe,[12] preferments[13] and morals,[14] all stood in the way of the neat and inexpensive utopia which the radicals saw within their grasp. In July 1831, the *Westminster Review* published a scurrilous assault upon the whole system,[15] which derived both in matter and in style from the liberal rationalist pamphlets of the early Hanoverian years. The petulant demand 'that the chairs of theology [be] filled, not by drones and sluggards, but by professors whose talents and learning would adorn the science they taught,' had no bearing on the age of Lloyd and Burton. In the old manner the reviewer threatened that the bells of St. Mary's would soon ring for the reforming commissioners of the king who would 'transfer the entire sovreignty over the realms of learning to the hands of laymen' and revive 'the drooping spirits of the scholar.'

7

The wealth of the universities was immense yet 'not a shilling of their enormous income is truly applied to the purposes for which it is designed.'

> Each college . . . is a clerical tontine; an abominable institution alike hostile to learning and subversive of piety . . . The instant a young man is elected fellow, he has but one object, to outlive his brethren, and thus to receive in succession the valuable benefices attached to his college, which were designed to reward the most learned, but which are blindly and dishonestly handed over to the longest liver.

If this was liberalism and the spirit of the age, it was small wonder that Oxford men began to worship the spirit of ages remote.

With narrow pertinacity the radicals also attempted a novel manoeuvre in parliament. The grants in aid of professorial salaries formerly made from the civil list were now dependent upon a parliamentary vote, and in 1831 Hume challenged them in the interests of economy, while Orator Hunt declaimed that the poor should never be taxed for such a purpose.[16] In the following year, Hume objected again, and the motion proved a convenient peg on which to hang the grievances of the dissenters and the University of London.[17] The Oxford reply, apparently invented by Charles Daubeny, professor of chemistry, and urged incessantly by Inglis, was that the university received in professorial salaries only £1000 p.a. while it paid out in stamp duty upon matriculations and degrees £2500 p.a.[18] Hume's tactics never won more than a handful of votes, and contrasted pitifully with a philosophical analysis which raised the whole university question to a new plane.

In the *Edinburgh Review* in 1831, Sir William Hamilton began a series of articles upon Oxford, 'of all academical institutions at once the most imperfect and the most perfectible,' which in breadth of view excelled all previous contributions to the debate, and focused the whole academic history of Europe upon the immediate problem.[19] Hamilton outflanked the tory doctrine that the defence of Oxford's chartered privileges was the defence of liberty, by claiming that the whole present system was illegal, 'a flagrant usurpation, obtained through perjury and only tolerated from neglect.' As a brilliant Snell foundationer at Balliol twenty years before, Hamilton had thought very little of his college tuition,[20] and the colleges now bore the brunt of his attack. Hamilton impressed indelibly on the public[21] the distinction between

> the *university proper* and . . . the *colleges*. The former original and essential, is founded controlled and privileged by public authority, for the advantage of the state. The latter, accessory

and contingent, are created regulated and endowed by private munificence, for the interest of certain favoured individuals . . . The university as a national establishment is necessarily open to lieges in general: the colleges as private institutions, might universally do as some have actually done—close their gates upon all except their foundation members . . . If the university ceases to perform its functions, it ceases to exist; and the privileges accorded by the nation to the system of public education legally organised in the university, cannot—without the consent of the nation—far less without the consent of the academical legislature—be lawfully transferred to the system of private education precariously organised in colleges, and over which neither the State nor the University have any control. They have, however, been unlawfully usurped.[22]

At one stroke he required the present system to prove its innocence, established the right of the state to intervene, and disposed of the university test. The university as a teaching body had been displaced by the colleges, and in Hamilton's view the substitute was contemptible.

On the average there is to be found among those to whom Oxford confides the business of education, an infinitely smaller proportion of men of literary reputation than among the actual instructors of any other university in the world . . . *As at present organized*, it is a doubtful problem whether the tutorial system ought not to be abated as a nuisance.[23]

On the other hand 'a tutorial system in subordination to a professorial (which Oxford formerly enjoyed) we regard as affording the condition of an absolutely perfect university.'[24] The whole usurpation had been brought about 'furtively' as 'a private job' by the colleges through their heads. Hamilton knew how in Scotland it was the colleges that had withered away, and he called for a royal or parliamentary visitation to restore the English universities to their rights.

Conservative writers eventually attempted serious answers to most of Hamilton's points, but for the moment the defence was left to the protestant propagandist, Vaughan Thomas of Corpus, whose eleven proofs of the legality of the Oxford system were no match for the breadth and simplicity of his opponent's conception.[25] Tempers rose as reply and counter-reply came out, and Hamilton directed his missiles against the three superior faculties of medicine, law and divinity, and against the oaths at Oxford.[26]

His attacks on the colleges were reinforced by John Stuart Mill. Hamilton had urged that as the colleges were private foundations, the state should merely end their usurpations in the university. Mill claimed that as endowed bodies colleges were peculiarly subject to state oversight. The common law abhorred perpetuities, and for centuries entails had steadily been narrowed. The governments of France and Germany ensured that their endowed universities were places of vigour and learning, and the British government should do likewise.[27] The state had interfered with founders' wills on a huge scale at the Reformation,[28] and when taunted with this in the house by Macaulay, Inglis could only reply that if the Catholic founders 'had lived to the age of the Reformation . . . they might . . . have seen the error of their former doctrines,' and that if Christ Church were reckoned a protestant foundation, more fellowships had been established since the Reformation than before.[29]

By the end of 1833 the university had produced no convincing defence, had scant encouragement in parliament, and was the victim of scurrilous libels widely diffused. Lord Grenville, however, was in decline, and his death on January 12, 1834 enabled the university to seek a fresh champion as Chancellor. The Oxford Movement was already in being, but Newman and his friends had not yet mobilised the power to overawe the heads, and their romantic suggestion that the university should elect the Archbishop of Canterbury, powerless as it was to increase the political resources of the university, fell on deaf ears. They nevertheless put on a demonstration of anti-erastianism by refusing to give public support to any other candidate.[30]

Meanwhile various parties of heads were sounding the ground. F. R. Bonham, the conservative party agent,[31] distinguished

> four parties, the whigs very inconsiderable in themselves but not so in govt. patronage; that headed by Macbride & I presume the Oriel Common Room,[32] calling themselves liberal tories, which was our party of 1829[33] *shorn of the influence of Govt.*; the tory party headed by Wintle [Vice-President of St. John's] . . . ; and quoad this election the Ch. Ch. common room.[34]

The whig candidate was Lord Carlisle, who had sat in Canning's cabinet, and was now a cabinet minister without portfolio under Grey; his prospects, however, depended upon a deadlock among the other parties which never materialised, and he was never nominated.[35] The other three parties moved simultaneously and were soon accusing each other of bad faith.

The first committee was constituted at St. John's, a college which under the presidency of Dr. Wynter was a hot-bed of reaction. They represented the party which had carried the election of Inglis, and they sent a deputation to the Dean of Christ Church affirming their wish for the best possible conservative candidate, irrespective of college, and promising to support any respectable Christ Church nominee. This offer testified to the bitter division in the tory ranks, for an alliance with Christ Church offered the only sure hope of defeating a liberal tory candidate. The Dean, however, failed to persuade either Lord Talbot or Lord Mansfield to stand, the St. John's committee refused to parley further, and opened negotiations with their own candidate, the duke of Wellington.[36]

The choice of the duke was in every way ironical. The engineer of emancipation, he was now endeared to the ultra-protestant party because he had differed from Peel and attempted to form a reform government in 1832. The duke confessed that he 'had not received a university education . . . knew no more of Greek or Latin than an Eton boy in the remove,' and was a model of the non-academic made good; moreover he was on the worst of terms with Christ Church. In 1825 undergraduate discipline in the House deteriorated to the point where 'a positive rebellion' was expected.[37] A series of outrages were perpetrated without the culprits being detected, and the chapter resolved to let matters proceed until they could '*pounce* upon somebody.' Dr. Bull sat up till 2 a.m. one night and then caught three members of the college, including the duke's second son, Lord Charles Wellesley, forcing open a college gate with tools. They had no ulterior intention, but were all rusticated for a year. The duke who thought Bull was at fault in not acting much sooner, sent the Dean some home truths on the state of discipline in the House, and removed both his sons to Cambridge.[38] He was not therefore the Dean's favourite for the Chancellorship.

Nor did he wish to stand. Wellington's popularity in Oxford had nevertheless revived towards the end of the struggle against the Reform Bill, and Keble had raised a testimonial fund to procure his bust.[39] The St. John's committee impressed on him that it was his duty to answer the call of the university.[40] Still he would consent only on condition that Talbot would not stand,[41] and the latter's friends accused the St. John's men of concealing from the duke that Talbot's son had induced him to retract his refusal. Neither party was willing to give up its candidate.[42]

The possibility that tory feuds might let in a whig was increased by the conspiracy of the fourth party, the liberal tories, to bring in Peel. In 1827 when Grenville, had seemed to be failing, Peel had been talked of as Chancellor,[43] and now men like J. D. Macbride, Principal of Magdalen Hall, and Robert Marsham, Warden of Merton, who had proposed him in 1829, saw an opportunity to reverse the verdict of that year. Peel was naturally cautious about an Oxford contest without government support, and could not win unless Christ Church and the St. John's committee were friendly or neutral.[44] Nevertheless while the prospect of deadlock among the grandees 'led other persons to look out for a tertium quem,'[45] he had a hope, and two days after Grenville's death, a meeting in Marsham's lodgings addressed him a requisition to stand. This was signed by liberal tories like the Warden and Macbride, by a liberal evangelical in Francis Jeune of Pembroke, by J. C. Jones, Rector of Exeter, who was to befriend the Tractarians, by J. A. Cramer, Principal of New Inn Hall whom Peel pressed for preferment,[46] but most prominently by the old Oriel Noetics and their friends—Provost Hawkins, Bishop Copleston, R. D. Hampden, Principal of St. Mary Hall, Baden Powell, Savilian professor of geometry, and Samuel Hinds who had been Vice-Principal to Whately at St. Alban Hall.[47]

The day before, however, the St. John's Committee got a requisition to the duke signed by both the evangelical and high-church pillars of the old protestant interest,[48] overcame his final demurrers, and dictated to him a strong letter to Peel's supporters. Christ Church withdrew with patent reluctance,[49] but Talbot would not stand against Wellington, and the Dean had to admit defeat.[50] An appeal from Haywood Cox of Peel's committee was quite unavailing,[51] and Peel had no alternative but to withdraw.[52] A committee under Sir Charles Wetherell established itself in London to provide against surprise among the outvoters, and the battle was over.[53]

Wellington's triumph had been brought about with the characteristic unscrupulousness of the politicians of St. John's, and feelings were sore. Talbot felt slighted; Peel sulked because Wellington had not communicated with him;[54] Eldon deplored the apparent volteface of the protestant heads.[55] Yet the duke's election helped to reunite the party and revive its morale. Eldon, for example, reluctantly attended Wellington's first official dinner, but was conciliated by his speech;[56] he made a penance of attending the installation in June, but found the enthusiasm 'affecting beyond anything I ever met.'[57] The duke also circumvented the embarrassments which threatened when Talleyrand, the renegade bishop, and that wayward defender of the protestant constitution, the duke of Cumberland, intimated their intention of attending the celebration.[58] He struggled manfully with his Latin speeches[59] (said to have been written by Philip Bliss, the Registrar),[60] and at the Encaenia the tory nobility deserted Ascot[61] and poured into Oxford to witness a tremendous triumph. For once even the undergraduate turbulence contributed immensely to the occasion; the ministers were hysterically hissed, tory leaders of all sections prodigiously cheered, and the spirits of the party rose[62] under this powerful suggestion that there was still life in their cause. The two chief figures, the new Chancellor and Eldon, the High Steward, were deeply and visibly moved by the warmth of their welcome.[63]

From this time forwards the duke became noticeably more zealous

in defence of the church,[64] and the fillip given to the party may be
gauged by the torrents of abuse directed against the celebrations by
the whig and radical press.[65]

This revived tory enthusiasm[66] for church defence came none too
soon for the university, for a great attack by the dissenters was
gathering force. They had been disappointed by the first session of
the reformed parliament. Their campaign for disestablishment had
fallen flat, and, with Ireland in a state of insurrection, their grievances
had gone unredressed. Ministers assured them that their case would
be heard in the next session, and during the winter of 1833-4 the
dissenters were exercised by what became their familiar dilemma,
whether it was more profitable to trust the whigs or to harry them.
The influential unitarians were for trusting whig generosity and
dropping far-reaching demands such as disestablishment.[67] The
Protestant Dissenting Deputies whose object was to protect the
civil rights of nonconformists, also favoured a limited programme.
But apocalyptic fire was still burning bright in the baptists and
congregationalists of the north, and they pressed strongly for
disestablishment. The United Committee formed of the various dissenting pressure groups drew up a minimum programme. The
opening of the ancient universities figured largely in it,[68] and when
on March 21, 1834, the dissenters of Birmingham presented a petition
to Lord Grey, they strongly opposed the university tests, and in an
interview urged the separation of church and state.[69] At once the
tactics of government became plain. On disestablishment Grey

> explicitly but candidly signified his entire disagreement with
> them; yet was happy that no such topic had found its way into
> the memorial . . . But on no point did his Lordship declare so
> cordial a concurrence with the views of the memorialists as
> on that of opening *the universities* to our youth for degrees,
> independently of religious tests . . . At the same time he acknow-
> ledged that he was not a little desirous of the relief being
> granted by the universities, rather than by the legislature.

For some weeks the Commons had been bombarded with nonconformist petitions demanding, *inter alia*, the opening of the
universities,[70] and Grey himself warmly introduced a petition to the
Lords signed, he claimed, by almost half the resident members of
the Cambridge senate, for the free admission of dissenters.[71] Liberal
rationalist whigs disliked the tests and it was good policy to head
the dissenters off serious topics by attacking them. And the danger
to the tests was multiplied by the conservative tactics of seeking to
save the ministers from the radicals; to conservatives as well as
whigs, repeal might seem cheaper than disestablishment.[72]

Nonconformist animus was aggravated by the continued misfortunes of the University of London. An attempt to secure the power to grant London degrees had been defeated, largely by Oxford opposition in 1831;[73] in 1833, William Tooke sought the support of the Commons for the grant of a royal charter.[74] Inglis opposed the motion as an interference with royal prerogative, and it was finally withdrawn upon Lord Althorpe's assurance that the matter was under government consideration. The Hebdomadal Board, however, refused absolutely to make concessions,[75] and the whole issue was deferred again. In February 1834, the Council of the London University announced that they had brought the objections of the ancient universities before the Privy Council for settlement.[76] At once Wellington urged the Hebdomadal Board to fight to the last ditch and arranged for a petition (which was approved in a crowded Convocation with only one dissentient vote) to go up to the Privy Council; the University's case was to be put by Sir Charles Wetherell.[77] The university objected to the grant of degrees in arts in London because immense endowments were annexed to arts degrees on the assumption that graduation implied conformity with the church;[78] in characteristic fashion William Sewell, fellow of Exeter, a unique mixture of talent, woolly idealism and coarse prejudice, saw in the proposal a threat to the connexion of church and state.[79] The result of the opposition of the universities and the medical profession before the Privy Council in May was that no further action was taken. The following winter Melbourne fell from office, and on his return was as dilatory as ever; not till 1837 did the proprietors of what became University College, London, receive a charter. It was significant that on April 4, 1835, the Hebdomadal Board deferred action upon the Vice-Chancellor's proposal to petition against the London charter;[80] the defence of the Oxford test was now a matter of acute anxiety, and prudence counselled a concession to Socinianism and the march of mind in London.

The debate on the Cambridge petition presented by Grey on March 21, 1834, began a passionate controversy on the university tests both in parliament and in the country. On April 17, George Wood obtained leave by 188 votes to 44 to bring in a bill for the abolition,[81] and the battle was openly joined. The Cambridge liberal cause was supported by a pamphlet from Connop Thirlwall in which he denied that the colleges were in any sense theological seminaries, and generally depreciated the worth of their religious instruction and observances. He also quoted a damaging passage from Pusey's *Remarks on the prospective and past benefits of cathedral institutions* which came close to admitting that under the present university regime the Church of England obtained the worst trained clergy in Europe.[82] Christopher Wordsworth, Master of Trinity, thereupon dismissed Thirlwall from his tutorship and wrote sternly upon the dissenting menace.[83] The Oxford liberals were inspired, now and for many years to come, by Thomas Arnold, whose broad and sanguine views were expounded to Gladstone by Bonamy Price:[84]

> The improvement of the dissenters, both moral and intellectual, appears to me one of the most important objects which good men can labour to promote: and no method seems more promising than to give them access to the moral culture, sound scholarship and learning, and gentlemanly feeling to be found at our universities. The dissenters form a large mass of our population: they are our legislators: and it is of the utmost consequence to rescue them from the low-mindedness and illiberality to which their social position condemns them. We conscientiously believe that not one essential part of Xtianity need be compromised.[85]

In 1833 the Rugby plan had been to comprehend the dissenters in the church;[86] in 1834 it was to comprehend them in the universities.

The Oxford high-church writers set themselves to destroy the two latest liberal arguments, that the religious content of university education was insignificant,[87] and that no harm could come from the admission of dissenters. William Sewell made a virtue of the changes with which Hamilton reproached the Oxford system and dropped altogether its recent claim to purvey universal knowledge. The university was

> no more a mere collection of learned men explaining the metaphysics of antiquity to crowds of undisciplined boys; nor the scene of that ardour and zeal which once used to animate its followers, and not rarely terminated in bloodshed. It has become a society for education . . . Students . . . are brought here to be governed and formed, and instructed in those rules of thought, and courses of study which in its public and corporate capacity, the university has thought proper to encourage.

Among these religion formed an essential part, and nearly a third of the regular lectures at Exeter were devoted to religious studies. Religion must be dogmatic, and there could be no question of accommodating the dissenters.[88] On this score Sewell became increasingly hysterical; the admission of dissenters would inflict on the university

> the most deadly blow at its religion, next to the starvation of its ministry, which in all strictness of logical conclusion must very soon follow, that man ever dared to attempt who believed in a God and his Bible.[89]

George Moberly, fellow of Balliol, claimed that theological teaching of a catechetical kind took up two full days in the week at Balliol and concluded with a great hostage to fortune: 'how fearful a prospect of religious animosity is opened to us! Controversy is now unknown to us.'[90]

The high-church writers related the principle of authority to the tests very variously. Vaughan Thomas attempted to have the argument both ways. Against liberals and evangelicals he affirmed that men now coming up were of sufficient age and education to subscribe at matriculation from rational assent, but if they were not, it was still a good argument that they signed from faith in church authority.[91] This turn of mind increasingly fascinated the younger men— Newman, for example, was shortly yoking both dogmatic and experimental religion with subscription, and with a characteristic scepticism about the articles themselves:

> The advantage of subscription (to my mind) is its witnessing to the principle that religion is to be approached with a submission of the understanding . . . the great lesson of the gospel is faith, an obeying prior to reason, and *proving* its reasonableness by making experiment of it . . . I should say the same of a person in a Mahometan country or under any system which was not plainly and purely diabolical . . . Subscription . . . actually does I believe impress upon the minds of young men the teachable and subdued temper expected of them. They are not to reason, but to obey; and this quite independently of the degree of accuracy, the wisdom &c. of the articles themselves. I am no great friend of them—and should rejoice to be able to substitute the creeds for them, were it not for the Romanists.[92]

It casts much light on Newman's deep-rooted sense of persecution that when in later years simple men accused him of lack of candour, he could be surprised and hurt. In any case, as Radnor pointed out in the Lords, the Oxford matriculation test could hardly be supported by the appeal to authority because it exempted boys below the age of twelve over whom authority might most reasonably have been exercised.[93]

The election of the duke and the flood of propaganda were insufficient of themselves to rally the conservatives to the tests. The dissenters were making their pressure felt to the tune of 1003 petitions to parliament, containing 344,000 signatures,[94] and a similar show of strength must be put on in Oxford. None of the juniors knew that in November 1833, Shuttleworth, the whig Warden of New College, had proposed to the Hebdomadal Board to substitute some less objectionable matriculation test for subscription to the articles, and had raised 7 votes against 14.[95] Though the board was unanimous against the admission of dissenters, there was a party disinclined to defend the present subscription which the wilder young men were representing as fundamental to religion and all things sacred. Though this temporising was unsuspected, the heads were clearly loath to lead a contest with the government on such an issue. Agitation, as in the early days of George I, must be led by the juniors, whose appetite for action had been already whetted by the cause of church defence.

On April 21, 1834, a meeting of tutors and others engaged in religious education was held in the rooms of Dr. Burton, regius professor of divinity, to frame a declaration against the admission of dissenters. At further meetings on the next two days the declaration was drafted,[96] and it was immediately signed by almost all the Oxford tutors. Burton could 'never remember any occasion on which so strong or unanimous a feeling [had] been shewn in Oxford.'[97] Vaughan Thomas now took charge of a committee which whipped in immense numbers of M.A.s to support the tutors' declaration, and hoped to win 'the parentage of the country' by 'the fact that Oxford has pronounced her judgment and insists upon standing upon the fundamentals of religion.'[98] Gladstone was enlisted to rally the Christ Church M.P.s,[99] and even Pusey, only yesterday a liberal, insisted upon the

> interference with the education of our own members in conse-
> quence of the proposed admission of dissenters; we are to have
> no tests for the faith of those who professedly belong to our
> church in order that others may be admitted among us.

Cambridge required no doctrinal subscription at matriculation and collected all the sceptics who could not get in at Oxford.[100]

Unknown to Pusey the duke of Wellington was much embarrassed by the difference in the matriculation requirements of the two universities, and could not answer the charge that since dissenters had long been admitted at Cambridge without ill effects, there could be no justification for the matriculation test at Oxford.[101] The Hebdomadal Board were also embarrassed by the extraordinary success of the juniors in raising a clamour for the defence of church and university. As long as it appeared that the church was being persecuted by a coalition of liberals, dissenters and papists, the Oxford agitators were on the crest of a wave, and the Board lagged lamely behind. The Vice-Chancellor, George Rowley, Master of University College, confessed to the Chancellor that Burton had acted

> without any communication with the weekly Board—the more
> influential members of which, as well as myself, had we been

consulted, would probably have disapproved. It was not, however, judged expedient to express dissent under circumstances which could not be controlled, and we were therefore compelled to proceed with as great an appearance of unanimity as possible.[102]

With these sentiments unconfessed,[103] the Hebdomadal Board adhered to the tutors' declaration on May 2.

By this time the government was in confusion over the disposal of Irish church revenues, and conservative opposition to concessions in the universities was hardened not merely by the sight of ministerial weakness, but by the assurances of dissenters, like Edward Baines, that nothing short of disestablishment would suffice.[104] The conservatives could not defeat the bill in the Commons, but they had now no compunction in throwing it out of the Lords on August 1, 1834.[105] This triumph put the tory peers in fine fettle and on the following day the duke assembled an enthusiastic 'omnium gatherum of all the party,' exhorting them to stick together for the rest of the session.[106] The battle of the university tests would soon have to be fought again.

During the summer Richard Whately had been in touch with Lord Grey urging him to restore the rights of independent M.A.s to teach and open halls, so that when tests were abolished dissenters might not be excluded by a college embargo against them.[107] Before the next session began, Lord Holland was negotiating with Joseph Fletcher, the celebrated independent minister of Stepney, the terms of a bill which might satisfy the dissenters, and was preparing to press it upon the government.[108] Moreover, Lord Radnor was studying Sir William Hamilton's articles in the *Edinburgh Review*,[109] and Hamilton delivered another onslaught upon the tests. The argument was as before. The present state of education in the universities was 'contrary at once to law and reason;' the rulers of the university had violated a public trust and subverted a national establishment for the benefit of private foundations. Dissenters and other citizens were entitled to demand that the universities (as distinct from the colleges) be restored to an efficient and legal state. Hamilton recounted how the halls had out-weighed the colleges in importance before the Reformation, and how simple it had been to establish them. Were they revived, dissenters could be received without intruding upon Anglican foundations. As for the religious basis of Oxford education, religion had nowhere been essential to instruction in arts, until the Oxford examination system was introduced thirty years before. The scepticism of German universities could not be attributed to the absence of tests, for in no universities outside England were there tests except in the theological faculty.[110]

An unexpected broadside came from an admirer of Hamilton,[111] Renn Dickson Hampden. Twenty years earlier Hampden had accomplished the remarkable feat of obtaining a double first without a private coach.[112] His subsequent career among the Oriel Noetics was cut short by early marriage, and he served as a pillar of orthodoxy in church journalism, and, among the straitest of high-churchmen, as curate in South Hackney to H. H. Norris, brother-in-law of Joshua Watson. In 1832 he delivered the Bampton lectures on *The scholastic philosophy considered in its relation to Christian theology*; Provost Hawkins found the early lectures 'most masterly' and 'admirable,' and concluded that 'Hampden will be abused: but if the work proceeds as it has begun, I should expect it to form quite an aera in theology.'[113] Hampden attempted to investigate the influence of philosophy upon theological language, and to distinguish between revelation and the theological systems by which it was expounded. In 1833 Lord Grenville acknowledged the reputation he had won in Oxford[114] by appointing him Principal of St. Mary Hall. When early in 1834 Hampden adhered to the tutors' declaration against the admission of dissenters, he was still in favour, and in March was elected White's professor of moral philosophy.

Hampden, however, like many of the old Oriel school, now leant towards the whigs, and in the autumn of 1834 unexpectedly turned the argument of his Bampton lectures against the matriculation test. In Hampden's view contention among the sects arose less from religious difference than from formularies, 'matter of human opinion and speculation.' The church ought not to require all who entered the university to adopt her particular formularies. Moreover, the practical benefit of the present system was grossly overrated. As an examiner Hampden found many graduands 'very imperfectly acquainted with the doctrines of the church. How much more must this be the case at matriculation!'[115] The test had been imposed from motives of politics not piety, and

> the present religious character of the university is not owing to subscription at Matriculation, but to the awakened spirit of religion generally throughout the country. The secondary and more immediate cause of the improvement is the examination in divinity for the first degree.

Undergraduate subscription was not required in the new church colleges in London, Calcutta or New Brunswick, nor in the old foundation at Dublin.[116] Hampden's one reservation was that the tests should be abolished by the university, and not by the legislature; and it was for this reason that he had concurred in the tutors' declaration against Wood's bill.[117]

While the storm heralded by the press campaigns was gathering, the Hebdomadal Board was being urged to reform by none other than the Chancellor, whose election had seemed so sure a guarantee of the *status quo*. For a century past cancellarial activity in Oxford had been only sporadic, and now even the Chancellor's annual choice of the Vice-Chancellor was formalised; the appointment went always to the senior member of the Hebdomadal Board who had not served before and was willing to accept appointment, and it was renewed annually for four years. Lord Grenville had been a friend to improvement, but on the most controversial matters his opinions had been so alien from those of the majority in Oxford that his hands were tied. Wellington, however, regarded himself as commander-in-chief of a new army, and marshalled the campaign against the London University and the admission of dissenters with pristine vigour. As a plain man the duke made no claim to understand the details of academic organisation, but he assumed authority to interpret to dons the sentiments of the world outside.

In a long letter to the Vice-Chancellor on August 27, 1834, the duke pointed out that every aspect of university life would be made a matter of parliamentary inquiry in the next session. The present House of Commons had no respect for established institutions, and the university should take care not to defend the indefensible. It was widely said that many statutes were obsolete, and others were contravened by custom; the objects of some foundations were said to have been subverted for private benefit. Without passing judgment on the charges, the duke urged the heads to overhaul every university and college statute, to abolish what was obsolete, and bring regulation and practice into harmony. A further embarrassment was the matriculation test, for here the universities stood on a different footing; many conscientious men, even bishops, felt it wrong that young men should have to subscribe articles far beyond their understanding. Would not a declaration of church membership suffice? Finally it was far too easy for undergraduates to get into debt in Oxford, and the wrath of parents was constantly on his head.[118] This comprehensive indictment kept the Board occupied for the 18 years of the duke's reign. The hazards of overhauling the statutes provoked a severe constitutional crisis, and finally helped to discredit the constitution of the university altogether; disputes over the meaning of the university subscriptions aggravated the constitutional crisis, and helped to discredit the ecclesiastical character of the university; scandals of undergraduate indebtedness drew attention to the high cost of Oxford education generally as the chief obstacle to university extension. On the other chief subject of the next twenty years, that of university studies, the duke as a plain man forbore to comment.

The duke's letter made a strong impression on the Board, and after further pressure they agreed in November (by 11 votes to 10 with 5 members absent) to propose the substitution of a declaration for subscription at matriculation.[119] This decision was rapidly followed by the fall of Melbourne's government, and Wellington's assumption of all the chief offices of state; immediately the heads reversed their vote, the Vice-Chancellor declaring that in any case no change could be put through Convocation.[120] News of the duke's pressure had leaked out and began to create an ugly mood among the juniors.[121] With the advent of a conservative government the subscription issue was temporarily shelved, but Wellington was insistent

> that no change can render unnecessary an investigation by the authorities of the university into the state of their affairs, and the application of such temperate remedies . . . as may be found necessary; because no changes can effect the existing constitution of parliament and allay its inquisitatorial jealousy of the institutions of the country.[122]

This was a prudent comment on the eve of the ecclesiastical commission and the Municipal Reform Act; it doubtless encouraged New College to surrender the right of its members to obtain degrees without examinations, and it helped to produce new Aularian Statutes in 1835, which contained no new principles but repealed obsolete provisions.[123]

On March 6, before Peel's hundred days had expired, Lord Radnor moved for a return of the oaths taken at the universities, with some tart remarks on the way academical authorities encouraged perjury by lightly administering oaths which no-one intended to keep.[124] Edward Cardwell, Principal of St. Alban Hall and Chancellor's private secretary in Oxford, warned the duke that he would 'be surprised at the number of them,'[125] and the Chancellor recurred to his old theme; all inessentials must be conceded,[126] and amongst them was the matriculation test.

During the winter the majority of the heads remained averse to any change,[127] but the prospect of Melbourne's return to power worked an immediate transformation, and on March 23, by a majority of one, a board of 23 resolved to substitute a declaration for the matriculation subscription, and committed the drafting to Provost Hawkins.[128] As soon as the proposal was published pandemonium began, and Oxford rang with hostile pamphlets. Protestant high-churchmen like Godfrey Faussett, Margaret professor,[129] William Sewell,[130] or Vaughan Thomas,[131] were aghast and denounced

> the proposed change [as] . . . a modified indication of that restless

spirit of innovation and spurious liberality, which would abandon every *test*, reject all *authority*, [and] resolve faith into individual knowledge.

F. D. Maurice brought out a tract arguing that

the subscription to articles on entering Oxford was not intended as a test, but as a declaration of the terms on which the university proposed to teach its pupils, upon which terms they must agree to learn; that it is fairer to express those terms than to conceal them,

while Hawkins's declaration was a test embodying a principle of exclusion and nothing else.[132]

John Hill was mobilising the evangelical posse of St. Edmund Hall to vote against the measure,[133] while the Tractarians who had been on the boil all winter, convinced that the university had been abandoned by Peel, Wellington, the heads and the bishops, and committed to their defence alone,[134] burst forth in full extravagance. In Hawkins's declaration (which Maurice rightly regarded as in principle more exclusive than subscription) Henry Wilberforce saw the foundations of the faith assailed; for him it was proof enough that Hampden supported the change upon theological grounds.[135] Pusey inevitably descried the threat of German scepticism. The candidate was required to declare his assent to the doctrines of the church so far as his knowledge extended: was not this analagous with the German system of subscribing articles 'as far as (quatenus) they are agreeable with Holy Scripture,' a system which permitted intolerable laxity?[136] This parallel Edward Hawkins vigorously denied; it was not promoting scepticism for the university to recognise in matriculants a defect of knowledge which it would labour to remove.[137] In view of the later development of the Tractarian party, perhaps the most curious comment was that of C. P. Eden of Oriel, who succeeded Newman at St. Mary's. The great benefit of subscription was

SELF-PROTECTION; protection of self against self; protection for your proper self against the thousand extravagant fancies which will run away with you if they can.[138]

Not content with flooding the university with propaganda,[139] the politicians among the juniors had long been preparing to bring up non-residents.[140] Out-voters were told that a scheme designed by the heads to keep dissenters out on respectable grounds was a plan to let them in, and on May 20 there were chaotic scenes as the throng, too large for the Convocation House, poured into the Theatre, and threw out the declaration by 459 votes to 57. The mood was captured in a lampoon:

> This vile declaration, we'll never embrace it,
> We'll die ere we yield—die shouting '*Non placet*.'[141]

The blow which the juniors aimed at the enemies of the church had the chief effect of producing a constitutional crisis in the university. For among the defeated seniors were represented the same parties as among the juniors.[142] Besides Hawkins and Hampden who were regarded as liberal rationalists, there were sound high-churchmen in Dr. Routh, President of Magdalen, and Professor Burton, who had launched the declaration against the admission of dissenters a year before;[143] and the most vigorous defender of the Board was the evangelical apostle, B. P. Symons, Warden of Wadham.[144] The enemies of the church were of the same hues as her defenders but of superior status. Moreover, the rejection of the declaration brought the university immediately under the hammer of Lord Radnor.

In March, Lord Radnor who had been all his life a champion of liberal causes, had been disposed to drop his campaign against oaths and tests in the belief that there was 'a more liberal spirit growing up in Oxford.'[145] This was now clearly a delusion, and even R. D. Hampden who had at first opposed state intervention urged him to resume the struggle.[146] Radnor now consulted with Lord Holland who advised on parliamentary tactics, with Sir William Hamilton to whose coaching he owed the immensely broadened perspective of his next opening speech, and with R. D. Hampden who contributed more than anyone to the final shape of the bill.[147] Hampden, be it noted, favoured legislative action only as a last resort, and was throughout intent upon maintaining worship, government and teaching in the hands of the Church of England. The main object was to put Oxford on the same footing as Cambridge as to matriculation, and at most to admit dissenters to degrees but not to the governing body.[148] There was prudence as well as principle in this course, for many of the Oxford opponents of Wood's bill in 1834 did not object to the admission of dissenters on the basis of a temporary conformity, but expected that if they were admitted as dissenters, Oxford would find, as London had already found, that no religious education would suit all parties, and that she would be reduced to a completely secular system.[149]

When the bill was published in June 1835, there was the expected reaction from the juniors,[150] but the duke was totally unsympathetic. He told the Vice-Chancellor that the subscription requirements must be harmonised with the sentiments of the day, and that boys of 16 or 18 could not possibly understand what they were subscribing.[151]

Caught between the Chancellor and Convocation the Hebdomadal
Board wavered. By 10 votes to 8 a committee was appointed to draw
up a petition objecting to the bill altogether. But when the draft was
presented, the Board resolved by 12 votes to 10

> that it was desirable to abandon subscription to the 39 Articles
> at the time of matriculation, & that no petition should be
> presented in justification of that practice. But considering the
> division which has recently taken place in Convocation . . . it
> is thought better to bring no notice at all before them rather
> than one which would surrender the practice so recently & so
> strongly approved by them . . . There was a general & anxious
> wish to retain subscription on taking degrees.[152]

This decision was reached after a discussion of four hours and a
half,[153] but was immediately nullified by a requisition from the juniors
to the Vice-Chancellor to petition against the bill. The only point
on which the Hebdomadal Board were agreed, was in deploring the
interference of the legislature with the internal arrangements of the
university, and on this general ground the petition went forth.[154]

On July 14, 1835, Radnor moved the second reading of his bill in
a speech which bore the impressive hall-mark of Sir William
Hamilton. To attribute the scepticism of German theologians to the
absence of university tests was absurd, because the divines alone
were subject to a test. Over the whole of Europe, protestant and
catholic, there were no tests for laymen. Nor was the alliance of
church and state involved in the university test, for neither church
nor state normally required lay subscription. The bill proposed no
interference with private foundations, for the universities and colleges
were totally distinct bodies.[155] The Archbishop of Canterbury urged
that in Catholic countries the church needed no test, because it
could invoke general laws against heretics, and that in England the
tests had proved themselves beneficial. But the weight of the
opposition was in votes rather than argument, and the bill was
rejected by 163 to 57, with three bishops in the minority and 18 on
the other side.[156] Oxford had escaped again.

As long as the whigs retained even their reduced majority of 1835,
danger must be expected and Wellington pressed the Board to
appease the critics of the university in the only remaining way, by
passing an explanatory statute defining the meaning of the matriculation subscription. After its recent experiences the Board refused,[157]
but applied itself instead to reducing the number of oaths required
by the statutes.[158] This work involved such a considerable revision
of the statutes, that Edward Cardwell was in hopes that a complete
overhaul might follow.[159] In the present temper of Convocation there
were those who would argue for every ancient oath,[160] but a number

of superfluous oaths was abolished. Further revision was checked not by conservatism, but by a renewed outburst of religious spleen.

Circumstances had made R. D. Hampden a peculiar target for the juniors. The Hebdomadal Board was divided very evenly on the question of the test, but Hampden alone had spoken out openly in favour of a change, and Hampden alone had cooperated with the liberal Radnor and sceptical Holland to enforce change by act of parliament. If Hampden could be discredited a majority for the tests might be preserved in the Hebdomadal Board; furthermore, Hampden's services marked him out for promotion by the ministers,[161] and to destroy his character might reduce the usual power of ministerial influence to form a party. This last point impressed itself especially upon Hugh James Rose who on January 1, 1836, urged Newman to declare war against the Principal of St. Mary Hall.[162] On this advice Newman acted with alacrity.

Hampden seemed predestined to thwart the crusades of Newman and his friends. He had helped Provost Hawkins to break the tutors' strike at Oriel. He had defeated Newman in the contest for the moral philosophy chair. He was being pushed in ministerial favour by those pillars of the old Oriel school, Whately and Copleston,[163] to whose advice Provost Hawkins still turned in every crisis, and whose influence must have seemed to the younger set a dead hand upon the college.[164] Immediately upon the death of Dr. Burton, the widely respected regius professor of divinity,[165] Newman foresaw that Hampden would obtain the chair in preference to Keble and himself.[166] The stage was therefore set when on February 8, 1836

> someone saw at the Post Office . . . a letter addressed to Dr. H. by Lord Melbourne, which was forthwith concluded to be an offer of the Professorship, and Dr. H. not denying it tho' he wd. not otherwise have thought himself at liberty to speak on the subject, the report spread quickly thro' the place.[167]
>
> That very day Pusey[168] gave a dinner to the leaders of orthodoxy in the university at which Newman and Hook of Coventry . . . and others were present. A petition was agreed to, to be signed by the resident Masters, expressive of their condemnation of Hampden's tenets.[169]

A public meeting at Corpus was prepared, and Newman sat up all night dashing off his *Elucidations of Dr. Hampden's theological statements*. The Principal seemed delivered over to him as a faction leader.

> Were H. or other such appointed, numbers would approximate to us and open themselves to our views, from fear of him, who at present are suspicious of us. Really, thank God, it would seem as if for our comfort, it were graciously explained to us

by sight, what we know by faith, that all things must work for us.[170]

When in a buoyant mood, Newman's judgment did not often desert him. Hampden's politics had offended many; and his treatment of theological language distressed those to whom the *sacrum depositum* was constituted by a set of familiar credal propositions. He was the perfect Aunt Sally for the coalition of juniors and country parsons which had defeated the declaration the previous spring.

On February 20, a meeting of M.A.s at Corpus voted an address to the king[171] against the appointment, and rapidly obtained the signatures of half the residents. Melbourne absolutely refused to give way,[172] and so Newman sought a censure from the university. On February 24, another meeting was held at Corpus to vote a requisition to the Vice-Chancellor. Three forms of requisition were discussed. The first, the standard form in heresy cases, recommended that the Bampton lectures be submitted to the Vice-Chancellor and six D.D.s with a view to excluding Hampden from the university pulpit (the procedure later applied to Pusey's sermon on the Eucharist); the second recommended that the Hebdomadal Board extract erroneous theses from Hampden's works and submit them to condemnation by Convocation (the procedure later applied to W. G. Ward); the third requested the Board to submit an address to the hierarchy asking them to accept attendance at the lectures of the Margaret professor rather than the regius professor as a qualification for ordination. A series of meetings followed at which the second and third requisitions, involving no judicial process,[173] were adopted.[174]

This democratic pressure offered the conservative party among the heads an opportunity to regain a majority on the Board; Edward Cardwell, for example, who had loyally supported the Chancellor's efforts to get rid of the matriculation test 'was going about . . . quite furiously, with a passage from Hampden's moral philosophy lectures in his pocket, and declaring that he ought to be turned out of his professorship and hall, and house and home and everything.'[175] A party of heads now anticipated the Corpus committee in bringing the case before the Board. Hampden had been universally expected (notwithstanding a recent precedent) to resign his headship on appointment to the chair,[176] but knowing that he would need every weapon of defence, he clung to it and his place on the Hebdomadal Board. Despite broad hints from Edward Hawkins and the Vice-Chancellor to stay away, Hampden appeared at his own trial, and after three hours' stormy discussion secured his acquittal by his own casting vote.[177]

The two requisitions of the Corpus committee came before the

Board on February 29. The proposal to condemn Hampden's propositions in Convocation was defeated by 21 votes to 4, and that for
accepting ordinands' certificates from the Margaret professor went
down by 14 votes to 10, Hampden voting for himself in each case.[178]
The heads would not condemn one of their own number. When
this decision was announced to the juniors they set up a formal
organisation with Vaughan Thomas, Pusey, Sewell, Newman and
John Hill on the committee.[179] This committee representing all shades
of conservative opinion was an ideal camouflage for the Tractarians,
and the next day they adopted Sewell's draft petition with modifi-
cations.[180] The petition again raised the question of taking certificates
from the Margaret professor, but when the Warden of Merton
moved at the Hebdomadal Board that no action be taken till
Hampden had given his explanations in his inaugural lecture, the
regius professor again survived by 13 votes to 12, his own vote
and those of the Proctors being in the majority.[181]

Desperate activity on the part of the Corpus committee followed
(John Hill gave up teaching altogether)[182] but in fact only delayed
the bringing of the measure before Convocation, for the single defection necessary to put Hampden in a minority on the Board had taken
place, and the heads were already preparing a statute suspending
him from part of his functions.[183] Events moved rapidly before this
statute came before Convocation on March 22. Pusey pressed the
attack with *Dr. Hampden's theological statements and the Thirty-
Nine Articles compared*, and there was a flurry of replies saying that
the extracts were garbled,[184] and that the Corpus committee were
anything but sound themselves.[185] A. P. Stanley found Hampden's
inaugural

> one of the most pathetic and impressive sights I ever saw—the
> regius professor defending himself before the whole university
> against the charge of heresy in the old magnificent school of
> divinity.[186]

But all the time the Corpus committee were whipping in the votes.[187]
Hampden's defence was now the proctorial veto, and a week before
the Convocation the Proctors announced that they would exercise it
in his favour. The Corpus committee nevertheless brought up over
400 non-residents, and Vaughan Thomas began to argue that the
Proctors could only pronounce their veto after the votes had been
taken, not before.[188] Frustrated by the veto, the non-residents held a
meeting at Brasenose, their rancour against Hampden fanned as they
perused Arnold's slashing attack on the 'Oxford Malignants' which
was timed to the day.[189]

Hampden gained little respite as the Proctors were about to retire
from office. The Corpus committee immediately sent up a fresh

requisition to the Vice-Chancellor with 389 signatures.[190] As in the previous May the Board felt powerless to resist the tide, and enormous pressure from country clergy who knew little about scholastic philosophy, but saw an opportunity to strike a blow against whiggism, latitudinarianism and the chastening power of dissent, left no doubt as to the verdict of Convocation on May 5.[191] Hampden had already appealed in vain to the Chancellor. His last recourse was to the law. He obtained from the Attorney-General and Dr. Lushington the opinion that the university had no authority to abridge his statutory powers since it was *ultra vires* to alter the Laudian Code.[192] The Vice-Chancellor was naturally reluctant to put this opinion before the Board (for it threatened the legality of much university legislation since powers to change the code were assumed in 1759); Philip Bliss, the Registrar, disputed its validity at length; and on May 5, when Hampden was deprived of his unimportant powers in the appointment of select preachers by 474 votes to 94, it was disregarded altogether.[193]

The Tractarian agitation in Oxford had reached its apogee. In important matters the government of the university had been taken out of the hands of the heads, the ministers had been defied, and the clergy had been brought into a political manoeuvre with unwonted precision. On the other hand Wellington's counsel that the university should agree with her adversary while he was in the way, had gone unheeded, and the new powers of the juniors combined ominously with their intention to stand on old ways. Moreover, it was now generally appreciated that there was something new on foot in Oxford, and that the discontents in the church had been manoeuvred to the advantage of a party. The whig *Globe* carried a long series of articles in Hampden's favour by Nassau Senior,[194] and the *Times*, though losing no love for Hampden, was more hostile to Oxford than ever.[195] It was difficult to rebut Whately's comparison of the Tractarians with Addison's 'Tory-Freeholder' who declared, 'I am for passive obedience and non-resistance; and I will oppose to the utmost any ministry and any king that will not maintain that doctrine.'[196] Some old friends were uneasy; the *Wesleyan Methodist Magazine* thought that Hampden's orthodoxy was sufficiently guaranteed by his inaugural lecture and that the fuss was due to the inadequate study of theology in Oxford.[197] The evangelical *Christian Observer* was much less complacent towards Hampden,[198] but had reached the limit of its limited patience with Tractarians. There were two especially threatening signs. The *Globe* reported that in the new *Dublin Review*, Dr. Wiseman 'identifies the pretensions which are now put forth by the Oxford high-fliers with those of the Roman Catholic Church, and having identified, most justly reclaims the *stolen property*.'[199] And the counsel's opinion obtained by Hampden not only gave unexpected support to Hamilton's allegations that the present organisation of the university was illegal, but if taken seriously put an end to all hopes of reform from within. Certainly doubts continued to be felt inside the university, and Provost Hawkins, hitherto a reformer, is said to have declined the Vice-Chancellorship from the feeling that it would be his duty to impose a veto on any statute which altered the provisions of the Laudian code.[200]

CHAPTER VI

THE CONSTITUTIONAL CRISIS IN THE UNIVERSITY

Universities never reformed themselves; everyone knew that there was too much competition and jealousy, too many and varied motives constantly in play, to prevent the desired effect.

LORD MELBOURNE in the House of Lords, April 11, 1837.

The Oxford parties . . . consist of Hampden and the Arians, Newman and the Tractarians, Palmer and the Retractarians, and Golightly and the Detractarians.

Diary, reminiscences and correspondence of Henry Crabb Robinson iii.260. Oxford, the *Salamanca* of England. *Christian Reformer* 1839 p. 81.

THE events of 1836 suggested strongly that without outside pressure little formal change would take place in Oxford. This pressure was renewed in February 1837 when George Pryme, the Cambridge whig economist, proposed to move for a university commission. The burgesses for the universities interviewed Lord John Russell and gathered that

> the government not only do not object to such a commission, but that they will be glad to promote it; only they do not like to have it taken out of their own hands, or rather forced into their hands by another.[1]

Lord John Russell in his already familiar role of champion of the royal prerogative was a more formidable proposition than Lord Radnor, who, Copleston reckoned, had 'no weight in the House.'[2] Nevertheless Radnor, early in March, gave notice of a bill for a university commission; there were hurried consultations among the Hebdomadal Board, the Chancellor and the Cambridge authorities, and a flurry of petitions went up from the university and colleges.[3] On April 11, 1837, Radnor concentrated his attack on the colleges arguing that they should be released from their ancient statutes, and accusing them of misapplying endowments intended for poor men. Copleston replied that colleges only departed from their statutes with a view to fulfilling founders' intentions, and the Archbishop of Canterbury claimed that 'poor scholars' were simply those whose parents could not afford to maintain them at the university. Wellington abused the bill as a bill of pains and penalties.[4] Radnor

had chosen weak ground in seeking to disturb private corporations
which were already subject to visitatorial jurisdiction, and failed to
get a second reading;[5] but the defenders of the university had earned
no laurels, and there was prudence in Wellington's renewed counsel
to the Vice-Chancellor that the colleges must purge their statutes of
abuses and anomalies.[6] A week later the duke learned that Russell
intended to issue a royal commission for inquiry into the
universities.[7]

The Hebdomadal Board at once responded by advising the colleges
to go through their statutes, and appointing a committee for the
systematic revision of the statutes of the university. Edward Cardwell,
the duke's private secretary, was much less optimistic as to the outcome than the Vice-Chancellor, A. T. Gilbert, Principal of B.N.C.[8]
Some colleges, however, began to stir,[9] and discover the vested
interests which blocked their way.[10] The visitors themselves were
sometimes averse from reasonable change.[11] Nevertheless, when on
May 4 Pryme moved for a royal commission, and on May 8 Radnor
moved for a committee on the college statutes, the defenders of the
university had a cause to plead, and Radnor withdrew his motion
upon Wellington's assurance that reform was in hand.[12] The duke
was jubilant.

> No consummation of this affair could be more satisfactory . . .
> neither the govt. nor the H. of C. will interfere till the local
> bodies have had ample time to consider what they will do.[13]

For this ample respite the whig losses at the general election soon
afterwards were sufficient guarantee.

The juniors who regarded the present organisation almost as a
principle of faith, were only encouraged by this reprieve to refuse any
further parley with the spirit of the age. The *British Critic*, already
under Newman's influence,[14] insisted that the Oxford system could
not be illegal because it attained the legal end of maintaining literature and the virtuous education of youth by legal means of internal
legislation.[15] The *Quarterly* whose sympathies Newman had also
engaged, published a blimpish effusion after the cloudy manner of
William Sewell. According to the reviewer the basic struggle was not
of parties, but of the only

> two generic forms of society . . . one growing naturally and
> unconsciously out of the instinct of faith, or if faith is a term too
> theologically restricted, out of natural reverence, attachment
> and submission to a moral power above us—the other, artifi-
> cially built up and cramped together, for the purpose of holding
> in some sort of association individuals each claiming and
> exercising a selfish, capricious, independence.

The universities were of course of the former kind, kept steady in their course by their ancient statutes and their religious sense. The state could not get men to perform the chores of education except through the church and its mysteries. 'Darkness . . . and infinitude, and invisibility, and all other elements of mystery are not mere invention of priestcraft . . . They are in some shape or another necessary conditions of education.' Moreover, the universities remained public oracles. They were not bound to comply with a church lapsed into error, but at the present time they were the voice of the church, and they needed all their power and privileges to make their voice heard.[16] By such devices the Tractarians blinded their followers to simple questions about the fulfilment of statutes. They twisted the screw of faith too hard, and in a surprisingly short time were to rue their rashness, and bitterly denounce their own assertions that the university system was legal and formed the conscience of the church. But the tide as yet flowed with them.

Throughout the summer the statute committee of the Hebdomadal Board[17] had been working steadily, and by the end of October 1837 had produced drafts of the first three titles.[18] An attempt by one head to defer the question until they were assured that Convocation had the power to alter the Laudian statutes won no sympathy,[19] though a proposal to abrogate the matriculation subscription was defeated by 16 votes to 4, many of its old supporters not wishing to inflame the suspicions of Convocation against the revision as a whole.[20] By this time the juniors were in a furor and Oxford was flooded with broadsheets. The heads were said to be usurping the rights of Convocation. The initiative in proposing a new statute was undoubtedly the Board's, but a general revision was another matter. Convocation had never agreed that a general revision should be undertaken, and would in any case, it was said, have committed the task to a delegacy of its own. The difficulty (as Newman privately admitted)[21] was that since the Hebdomadal Board had been created under Charles I there had been no general revision, but arguments must be found to justify the present university system against the Chancellor, Hebdomadal Board and parliamentary critics, as the offspring of catholic truth. William Sewell insisted that the

> remodelling of a large body of statutes is a very difficult and complicated work, tending to unsettle the minds of those who live under them, to disturb principles, and to introduce a spirit of change particularly inexpedient in the present day.[22]

The Tractarians ought to have argued that Convocation had no independent power to abrogate the Laudian code, but they had jettisoned that argument to compass the ruin of Hampden, and now had to define the powers of Convocation by reference to the pre-

Laudian constitution. On behalf of the Board, B. P. Symons, Warden of Wadham, and Edward Cardwell, Principal of St. Alban Hall, argued that reform was absolutely necessary, and that the Hebdomadal Board had been originally created to end the squabbles of Convocation delegacies.[23]

On the eve of the Convocation, Sewell was deputed by the juniors to warn the Board that its proposals would be resisted as unconstitutional, but the heads, still under the lash of the Chancellor,[24] 'unanimously dissented from the proposition.'[25] Events in Convocation took a better turn for the heads than for some time past. Vaughan Thomas, Sewell, Pusey and their friends pertinaciously divided upon all 16 propositions, but were heavily defeated,[26] and the heads established their right to initiate a general revision. On December 21 Radnor returned to the Lords with accusations that despite the legislative activity in Oxford no material changes were being made, but Wellington now replied with great cheerfulness.[27] Six months later Radnor again demanded a report upon progress. The *Oxford Herald*, now under the management of that arch-tory, Philip Bliss, the Registrar,[28] exultingly reported that 'the house listened with impatience, and the subject dropped amid loud cries of "order of the day" '.[29] At any rate the whig ministry was too weak to be dangerous.

Meanwhile the revision had reached points of serious controversy. Wellington's early complaints about student debt had been brushed aside by the Vice-Chancellor,[30] but in November 1837 the statute committee presented the Board with a scheme for restricting undergraduate credit to one term, and compelling tradesmen to deliver copies of unpaid bills to the debtor's tutor.[31] The difficulty was that while the university had some authority over tradesmen in Oxford, it had none in London, and no good would be accomplished by restrictions which simply drove spendthrifts from one place to the other. The Board therefore resorted to the lame substitute of a solemn exhortation to the college authorities to be vigilant.[32] This pleased neither the Chancellor nor the tutors,[33] and on March 24, 1838, it went down in Convocation by 71 votes to 20.[34]

The Board now returned to its consecutive revision of the statutes, and found itself in even deeper waters, for Title IV concerned the duties of public lecturers. The day was long past when sinecure chairs might pass without question,[35] but professors, especially in subjects which could not be offered in the schools, found it more difficult to raise a class with every year that passed.[36] In order to find work for them the Board resolved that graduands should be required to attend two courses of public lectures before the B.A. degree, and a further course before the M.A. Only one of the six members of the statute committee could stand this invasion of the college teaching monopoly, and a special committee had to prepare the draft.[37] The next nine months were spent by the heads protecting the college system,[38] and the plan did not come before Convocation till March 14, 1839.

By this time a lively interest had been created among the residents. It was generally agreed that the university could not continue with statutes prescribing the appointment of praelectors in grammar, rhetoric and logic, who were not appointed, and enjoining attendance at lectures which were not given. Professors in scientific subjects published melancholy figures of the steady decline in their classes; numbers had generally dropped by half over the last decade, and but for the college requirements at Christ Church and Balliol, some classes would already have closed.[39] Again, although the tutorial system was the sacred cow of Oxford conservatives, it was widely held that the tutors were overburdened, that some of what was now left to private tutors ought to be done by the public professors, and that the university as a whole suffered from the lack of the oracular authority of profound scholars. If professorial teaching was to be revived, many salaries ought somehow to be augmented; for the miserable endowment of many chairs made a full-time devotion to scholarship impossible. The universities ought to move quickly, for the Ecclesiastical Commissioners were steadily diminishing the support which the church could give to learning through cathedral benefices.[40] The range of support for a revived professoriate was very striking; liberals like A. C. Tait and A. P. Stanley,[41] protestant high-churchmen such as Hussey,[40] evangelicals like Robert Walker,[42] Tractarian fellow-travellers like William Sewell,[43] were all unwilling to regard the professorial system as 'a beautiful excrescence on the university and nothing more.'[44]

The Vice-Chancellor subsequently admitted having under-estimated the strength of this feeling which the draft statute did not go nearly far enough to meet. The courses which undergraduates were to attend were defined as consisting of eight lectures; profound scholarship could not be encouraged by forcing professorial instruction into this procrustean bed, nor by the proposal to limit the tenure of chairs to five years. To compel undergraduates to attend merely two courses of eight lectures might even reduce the attendance at professorial classes. Moreover, since the professors suffered from their isolation from the main stream of university work, it was arguable that they could only be helped by basic changes in the examinations. In short, the revival of the professoriate required altogether broader treatment, and the material parts of the draft were thrown out by a margin of 2 to 1.[45]

On April 25, 1839, therefore, the Board appointed a committee to consider examination requirements in relation to professors' duties.[46] By mid-summer the committee proposed that the mathematical school should be postponed for a year after Greats, and that two new schools of Natural Sciences (experimental philosophy, anatomy, chemistry, botany, mineralogy and geology) and Political Sciences (modern history, civil law, common law, antiquities and political economy) should be created as options for men who had taken the Greats school. By making the examinations voluntary the committee hoped to evade the charge of increasing the expense of university education; by keeping Greats as an indispensable qualification, they hoped 'to disarm the hostility of another body' (the university of Cambridge).[47] This bold plan failed to get through the Hebdomadal Board.[48] Discussions dragged on into 1840, and in May the scientific professors complained of their embarrassment in being required to lecture to diminishing classes.[49]

By June 1840 the Board had agreed on another plan under which all graduates must display competence in arithmetic, mathematics and experimental philosophy, but Convocation was full of men with panaceas and men who felt it a duty to defeat the heads, and the material portions of the statute were all lost.[50] Cardwell despaired of progress. Towards the end of Michaelmas Term 1840, the proposal of March 1839 was revived and again defeated at the Board,[51] there was another memorial from the professors on February 1, 1841,[52] and a third in May 1842,[53] but the heads could see no way through all the difficulties. For forty years every alteration of the examination system had produced long drawn-out battles; in times of religious animosity when a man like Newman did not scruple to accuse the heads of revolutionising the university by introducing a professorial system,[54] the cause was hopeless.

While the university was thus groping for employment for her professors she was embarrassed by the endowment of two more. The Ecclesiastical Commissioners had been willing to relax their strict regimen of a dean and four canons per cathedral in favour of Christ Church, and had recommended that a canonry be annexed to the Margaret chair in place of a stall at Worcester.[55] In 1837 with a view to improving the vocational training of the clergy, a private individual offered to found a liturgical chair, the first holder to be the Rev. William Palmer of Worcester. The Hebdomadal Board would not have the divinity faculty invaded by another Tractarian, and rejected the offer.[56] In June 1840, however, Russell raised the matter again in connexion with the reorganisation of the Christ Church chapter, renewing the offer of a canonry for the Margaret professor, and offering two more to be annexed to new chairs of ecclesiastical history and biblical criticism.[57] The following August a circular went round the university urging that better practical training for the clergy be provided, and Thomas Gaisford

Dean of Christ Church, took up with Archbishop Howley the possibility of doing this through the new endowment. Two years later these negotiations ended in the foundation of the regius chairs of ecclesiastical history and pastoral theology[58] (part of whose duties were in the field of the liturgical chair proposed in 1837), and in the passing of a new statute on theological instruction.

Gaisford's idea was that instruction upon a voluntary basis should be undertaken by the whole board of professors, leading to the 'quasi-degree' of candidate in theology. The Archbishop who was anxious to resume schemes for practical training in the universities which he had dropped on the appointment of Hampden, and to check the growth of 'private schools of theology' in the country, was willing to commend any reasonable scheme to the government.[59] These efforts were reinforced early in 1841 by the impression created in Oxford by Charles Perry's plea for professional training for the clergy.[60] Unless the professors had work to do the proposed benefaction might be withdrawn, and the Archbishop's chief fear was that the three present professors, Hampden, Pusey and Faussett, whose mutual hatred was now of grandiose proportions, might not be sufficiently on speaking terms to reach agreement. The scheme for the voluntary theological examination was therefore finally concerted between the Hebdomadal Board and the Primate early in 1841, and the first professors took office in the following year.[61]

This scheme never fulfilled the high hopes of the Primate, and vividly illuminated the cognate difficulties of revising the statutes. After its failure to improve Title IV the university could not receive (and would not get from the government) any further chairs without preparing a working scheme for the faculty. The plan was contrived for church benefit by Hampden's bitterest enemies, who not only baulked his efforts to exclude Pusey from the board,[62] but changed the scope of the second new chair from biblical criticism to pastoral theology partly because Pusey himself covered Old Testament exegesis. Pusey, however, took umbrage because his only specific assignment in the new statute was instruction in Hebrew grammar.[63] With consummate egotism Newman put the whole scheme down to the heads' jealousy of Durham and the theological colleges, and their determination to curb Tractarian influence.[64] The *British Critic* abused the plan,[65] the calumny was put about that the new examination would add a year's residence to the cost of a B.D.,[66] and, most astonishing of all, it was condemned after the event as a means of undoing the censure upon Hampden by trickery.[67]

This preposterous inference was made from an ill-considered manoeuvre by the heads immediately after the new statutes were passed. The papers reported that Hampden's duties as teacher and examiner under the new statute virtually rescinded the censure of

1836, and a few days later the heads promulgated a draft statute proposing formally to repeal the censure.[68] This proposal had been occasionally canvassed before, and was now moved by J. A. Cramer, Principal of New Inn Hall, and Dr. Marsham, Warden of Merton. Cramer insisted that the censure upon Hampden had been accepted only as a temporary measure, to be repealed if his conduct was satisfactory.[69] In December 1839, in Hampden's absence, the Board had admitted that he had worked his theological passage, but they did not like his continued tenure of his headship and did not propose repeal.[70]

Hampden's orthodoxy was now accepted by some high-churchmen and by both the evangelical schools represented by the *Christian Observer* and the *Record*.[71] These testimonies and the sense that they must now 'contend with opinions in the opposite extreme'[72] led the heads to support Cramer's motion. Golightly dreaded

> a union of evangelicals and latitudinarians in Dr. H's favour under the idea that in so doing they would strike a blow at Tractarianism.[73]

But too many attitudes had been struck for Hampden to escape. The statute was supported by evangelicals, and by some liberals such as A. P. Stanley,[74] but a coalition sprang up against it led by protestant high-churchmen like Vaughan Thomas, Sewell, the Greswell brothers (of Corpus and Worcester), E. C. Woollcombe of Balliol, lesser lights among the Tractarians such as Isaac Williams and F. W. Faber,[75] and influential liberals such as A. C. Tait.[76] There was the same excitement,[77] the same heavy poll, the majority against Hampden still vast, though reduced from 380 to 115. The heads gave up Hampden's cause,[78] but they were to be humiliated by the juniors only once more on an issue which the Tractarians made their own.

The Tractarian leaders never recaptured the glamour of 1836. Their power had been based on the sense that they were the dedicated defenders of a persecuted church.[79] The Melbourne government which forced Hampden upon conservative churchmen in 1836 was too feeble to do more, and had only a precarious majority after the election of 1837. Its measures of church reform now were mostly those initiated by the tories during Peel's hundred days. Church and dissent alike were now threatened not by the liberalism which obsessed the Tractarians, but by Chartism and social revolt. In so far as Tractarianism was the assertion of churchmanship against dissent it became equally irrelevant, for in politics militant dissent fell upon hard times. The dissenting politicians knew that if they held their peace they would be neglected by the whigs; but if they exerted pressure on a weak government or put up candidates of their own at elections, they might let in the tories. Nothing would help the tories more than an agitation for disestablishment, and influential congregationalists began to follow the wealthier unitarians in playing it down. Moreover no sooner had the dissenters' attacks upon the establishment begun to flag, than they came to blows in furious attempts to disendow each other, and the litigation arising from Lady Hewley's case reached an acrimonious crescendo. And when in 1839 it seemed likely that the dissenters might derive some support from Wesleyan hostility to the Tractarians, the Methodists were driven back to the tory fold by Russell's education proposals.

As the external threat to the church relaxed, so the clerical coalition headed by the Tractarians began to fall apart, its dissolution hastened by the reaction of other church parties to the logic of Tractarian development. Tractarians had from the beginning assailed liberalism as the spirit of the carnal world, and liberals replied in kind. Peter Maurice of New College enforced the parallel with the early Hanoverian period by reprinting in his *Popery of Oxford confronted, disavowed and repudiated* the latitudinarian sermon preached by his namesake in 1718 on *The true causes of the contempt of Christian ministers*.[80] Charles Dickinson, one of Whately's Irish protégés, produced a *Pastoral epistle from his Holiness the Pope to some members of the university of Oxford* in 1836, while the *Edinburgh Review*[81] scoffed at Pusey's fondness for the age of Charles II and non-resistance, and advised Tractarians to emulate the non-jurors 'not in their visionary notions about hereditary right, but in that strong principle which regarded the letter of an oath as binding, and scorned to interpret it away.'

Evangelicals fell away rapidly after 1836. The *Christian Observer* began a controversy on the doctrine of baptism as taught by Pusey which was not wound up till after the Gorham judgment. Evangelical innuendoes resembled those of the liberals; it was well that the Martyrs' Memorial should not be a church 'because there is no adequate security that the pulpit may not be made to defame the doctrines for which those martyrs sacrificed their lives.'[82] The establishment of the Martyrs' Memorial committee in November 1838 showed how isolated the Tractarians might become; there were three heads and three juniors, two of them evangelicals (Macbride, Principal of Magdalen Hall, and John Hill), the whig Shuttleworth, Warden of New College and the tory Cramer (both of whom had befriended Hampden in different ways) and two high-churchmen, Golightly, the inveterate enemy of Tractarians,[83] and their wayward friend William Sewell who separated from them on the publication of Tract XC.[84]

The question of the meaning of subscription came inexorably to the fore, embittered by Tractarian extravagance on other matters.[85]

Only yesterday the Tractarians had been the stoutest defenders of the university test, but even in 1838 some were poised on a knife edge between a catholicism that to plain men looked Roman, and scepticism. In July 1838 W. G. Ward reported a conversation with H. H. Vaughan;

> He says he is perfectly certain of this, that there is no mean between Newmanism on the one side and extremes *far* beyond anything of Arnold's on the other; . . . for his own part he trusts himself to the progress not knowing whither it will carry him, but not feeling confident that any part of Xtianity will remain, except the truth of the main facts (miracles and Resurrection of our Lord) and those virtues (humility, forgiveness etc.) which though first brought to light by Xtianity, carried their own evidence with them. Neither the canonicity nor authority of Scripture he thinks will remain; further he thinks Newman sees to the real bottom of the question.[86]

'Newmanism' proved to be no permanent ground for Newman or Vaughan. A year later

> poor Vaughan was avowedly standing on this principle; that a professor of logic or any other -ic or -ology besides theology need not be called to account for his religious opinions,

and Keble was shocked.[87] It was not a Tractarian but the White's professor, William Sewell, 'morality's bright gem,'[88] who undertook to stay the faithful by demonstrating the logical basis of the moral and natural sciences in catholic theology. Sewell's inaugural had been a 'contemptible farrago of unconnected scraps of nonsense,'[89] and the *Edinburgh Review* was not too hard in regarding his *Christian Morals* (1840) (in which the demonstration was offered) as 'a strange instance of the lengths to which the ravings and hallucinations of an individual may go.'[90] It was hardly open to the Tractarians to seek a change of subscription as Whately and Arnold were now doing,[91] and so in Tract XC Newman undertook to show that if read literally the XXXIX Articles were not inconsistent with authoritative as distinct from popular Romanism.

As in the palmy days of the Tractarian movement, the heads were more responsive to outside opinion than the juniors liked or expected. In parliament Lord Morpeth made an odious comparison between the ethics of subscription at Maynooth and at Oxford, and Wellington hoped to defeat Tractarianism by a combination of heads and bishops.[92] Whately counselled succinctly that 'just at this crisis a good hard thrust might thoroughly overthrow the party.'[93] The heads had heard the fruits of Newman's teaching in November 1839, when J. B. Morris

9

preached *totidem verbis* the Roman doctrine of the Mass, and, not content with that, added in energetic terms that everyone was an unbeliever, carnal and so forth, who did not hold it.[94]

They now solemnly warned the university against the evasive modes of interpretation contained in Tract XC and declared them contrary to the statutes. Here the heads moved astutely for their word of counsel did not need to be submitted to Convocation, and it took the ground most likely to appeal to plain men. So warm a friend as Sir John Taylor Coleridge told Keble that

> No. 90 was a great mistake—the strain of reasoning is of a kind which, even if it were conceded to be perfectly logical, is so subtle & distinguishing, so much *like* quibbling, that plain, honest, it may be blunter, minds rebel against it.[95]

Moreover, as Keble knew, the Tractarian position must deteriorate with the revival of the tory party.[96] Newman expected that as soon as the tories were in office the whigs would move for a university commission, and the tories would not resist it.[97] The Tractarians had begun their rake's progress with the defeat of Peel, they had sulked at the election of Wellington, and appeared to the heads of the new ministry as men bent on overthrowing settled academic government, and on obstructing that prudent reform which the university owed to public opinion. In church preferment the whigs had neglected Oxford men;[98] now Peel proposed to put this right[99] and to do all that preferment could to stem the tide. Dr. Gilbert, Principal of Brasenose, had begun as a violent enemy of Hampden,[100] had turned against the Tractarians,[101] and was rewarded by the see of Chichester for taking the lead against Isaac Williams in the contest for the poetry chair.[102] Dr. Cramer, Principal of New Inn Hall, had no sooner moved the repeal of the censure upon Hampden than he became regius professor of modern history, though pleading his lack of qualifications.[103] Peel's chief embarrassment was that an injudicious promotion might not only weaken the general staff in Oxford, but even let in a Tractarian head. When the deanery of Carlisle came vacant in 1844, Peel offered it to Edward Cardwell, the Chancellor's secretary, who found Tract XC 'jesuitical and mischievous.'[104] He, however, was a man of means, and refused to leave the scene of battle;[105] Cramer was persuaded to add the deanery to his Oxford preferments.[106] Of the old Oriel school, Hawkins was too well endowed to be tempted by a move, and might make way for Newman as Provost,[107] but Copleston secured a canonry for J. E. Tyler.[108] Finally in 1845 the deanery of Wells went to Richard Jenkyns, Master of Balliol, who could be comic in his protestantism;[109] but Peel first made sure that if the Mastership came vacant it would go to Robert Scott, not W. G. Ward,[110] and finally arranged for the deanery to be held with it. While Newman's spirit sagged under the weight of attacks from the bench, horror at the Jerusalem bishopric, and the notion that the security of the Church of England was somehow involved in the theological contests of the fourth century, lesser men who regarded the conservatives as friends of the church could not but be influenced by the unequivocal testimony which those friends gave.

Tractarian fierceness in elections also began to lose them friends. In 1837 they had pushed F. D. Maurice for the political economy chair on the strength of *Subscription no bondage*, but dropped him again when his letters to Quaker[111] revealed a view of the church which was broad rather than high.[112] At the end of 1841 the election of a successor to Keble in the chair of poetry clearly showed the turn of the tide. The Tractarians put up Isaac Williams, A. T. Gilbert put up James Garbett, a non-resident evangelical. Pusey, innocent of all worldly wisdom, published a foolish letter alleging that Garbett was put forward only to prevent the election of Williams, and that the professor should be resident.[113] (Keble had not resided.) This letter though censored by Newman before publication, was bitterly regretted by the Tractarians,[114] and loaded the scales against Gladstone's attempt to get both candidates withdrawn. To ask Garbett to withdraw when he not only appeared the injured party, but was in the lead, merited the worst possible construction of catholic principles of compromise.[115] Neither Newman nor Pusey wanted to withdraw,[116] but on a comparison of votes they proved to be in arrear by 921 promises to 623, and the contest was given up.[117] The violence of this contest exposed the university to the coarsest of radical abuse,[118] and it did not end with the polling. In a university sermon of 1844 Garbett sharply condemned the exclusive episcopalianism of the Tractarians, and described their 'gigantic sacramental system' as a 'sacerdotal usurpation.'[119] This sermon was denounced as heretical by Charles Marriott, but Dr. Wynter, the Vice-Chancellor, refused to take action.[120]

In 1843 the decisive crisis approached. On May 14 Pusey preached a sermon on the eucharist, and was accused by Dr. Faussett, Margaret professor, who had inherited Hampden's functions as a judge of orthodoxy. The rest of the story was long ago told by Liddon.[121] The Vice-Chancellor, Dr. Wynter, appointed five other D.D.s to judge the case with himself. The sermon was condemned in Pusey's absence, Wynter considering that the sermon itself was all the evidence necessary.[122] Five of the six judges condemned the sermon, and the sixth Dr. Jelf, was deputed to inveigle Pusey into a confidential negotiation with a view to securing a recantation; this failed and Pusey was suspended from preaching. At last the university had publicly pledged its opposition to dangerous teaching; the duke of Wellington commended the Vice-Chancellor on the performance of his duty, and forbade him to publish any of the judges' reports,[123] so that the grounds of Pusey's offence were never divulged.

The heads had won a Pyrrhic victory, for the university tests were altogether discredited. It had long been urged that the subscription was beyond the understanding of boys at matriculation; but now Pusey and Hampden, the professors of the Old Testament and the New, were each under suspension for breach of their undertakings. The tests must be incomprehensible or useless.[124] At the moment when the Anglican monopoly in Oxford appeared in this odious light, there was public alarm at efforts elsewhere to reassert a clerical hold upon university education. In France the ultramontane party was reviving its claims to authority in education and the lectures of Michelet and Quinet at the Collège de France were being broken up by demonstrations in favour of the Jesuits.[125] It was complained that at King's College, Toronto, endowments intended for the general benefit of the colony were being usurped by the Anglican Church.[126] Nearer home, and most bitterly contested, were the Scottish subscriptions which, after lying fallow for a century, were being revived by the church to dispossess the academic heads of the Disruption.[127]

The Oxford tests would certainly survive until there was a change of ministry, but the wrath of the Tractarians began to threaten the collapse of the university constitution. There had always been a gap between the Tractarians' public professions of respect for the heads, and their private contempt which now boiled over.

> If ever there was a despicable oligarchy it is the heads of houses. The whole world has been in progress about them and not one jot have they advanced: all Oxford is shrieking about them 'What shall I do to be saved?' and yet not one iota of feeling have they shewn, not one symptom that they had a heart among them all. There they remain impenetrable in their leather arm-chairs, ensconced in cod-fish and oyster-sauce, without caring or seeing that hearts are bleeding and breaking about them. But when they have turned out all the learning and earnestness that there is in the English Church, they expect to go back in their arm-chairs and go to sleep . . . Alas for Oxford! Rome, Rome, Rome will be the only shelter for weary feet.[128]

The heads' real offence was that they were too closely in touch with outside opinion, but Dr. Wynter invited criticism when he pompously admonished an effort by Gladstone to mediate as 'an unbecoming and unstatutable attempt to overawe the Resident Governor of the university.'[129] And the Board seemed to be running into trouble from both sides when on the occasion of the honorary degree given to Edward Everett, the American ambassador, a former unitarian minister, Wynter ignored or failed to hear non-placets of which notice had been given.[130] Numerous masters unsympathetic to the Tractarians felt their rights had been infringed,[131] while Wellington was furious about the undergraduate pandemonium behind which Wynter had sheltered, and demanded that on the next occasion the galleries be cleared by the civil power.[132]

The following session saw the climax of the Macmullen case, which in tortuousness and obscurity exceeded all others. R. G. Macmullen, a young fellow of Corpus, was required to proceed B.D. in order to retain his fellowship. For some years the old divinity disputations had been suspended, and Dr. Burton, while regius professor, had accepted English theses on subjects of the candidates' choice, or had offered titles to candidates not otherwise provided. But the whole system was informal. In the summer of 1842, Macmullen, a Tractarian whose impetuosity was later demonstrated at St. Saviour's, Leeds,[133] applied to Hampden for a subject and was given two theses to defend on the Eucharist and the authority of scripture. This task Macmullen professed himself unable conscientiously to perform, and Hampden refused to offer an alternative. Macmullen, thereupon, sought to perform a disputation under the ancient statutes, but Hampden refused to preside, and could claim that the rejection of the theses he offered created a presumption that Macmullen was unsound and unqualified for a degree. Macmullen talked of storming the schools and disputing in the professor's absence, and finally began a chequered progress through the university courts.

Edward Cardwell confessed to the Chancellor that the two were 'very intractable persons,'[134] and that the statutes were intolerably vague, but the Tractarians regarded the whole proceeding as an attempt to turn the opinions of the regius professor into a new test. This view was strengthened when in February 1844 the Board proposed to end the abuse of Oxford divinity degrees by making the voluntary examination of 1842 compulsory upon all candidates, thus putting them into the hands of the divinity faculty. As there was deep-rooted prejudice among the juniors against examinations of any kind for divinity degrees, there was a storm against this proposal, and the statute was withdrawn. Macmullen now, under protest, took up the theses which he had so long refused, and in April 1844, after the reading of the first thesis, Hampden made the unprecedented ruling that the exercise was insufficient. A modified version of the February statute came before Convocation in May, and was rejected by 341 votes to 21. The heads now instructed the regius professor 'to recur to the legitimate statutable exercises of the B.D. degree.' Finally after Dr. Wynter had vetoed his grace four times, Macmullen obtained his degree, and the college found a device by which he could retain his fellowship.[135] But the Tractarians now not only regarded the Hebdomadal Board as a usurped power, but the office of Vice-Chancellor as an inveterate menace.

When Dr. Wynter had been nominated for his last year of office in October 1843, the Tractarians had talked of opposing him. But time for conspiracy was short and nothing was done.[136] In October 1844 he was due to retire and the next senior head willing to serve was B. P. Symons, Warden of Wadham, the leading evangelical in the university. From midsummer onwards some of the Tractarians plotted to oppose him.[137] On the appointment of the Vice-Chancellor, as on so many other matters, the statutes were not unequivocal. The Chancellor had an unconditional right to nominate his deputy annually, but it was not absolutely certain that the consent of Convocation to his choice was a pure formality. Moreover, when Gilbert's nomination had been challenged in 1839 he had conceded a scrutiny in which two votes were cast against him. The lead was taken with a pseudonymous letter in the *English Churchman* by J. B. Morris, efforts were made to beat up votes, and by the end of September the national newspapers were joining in the fray.

Newman and the Littlemore group were content to follow the agitators with little expectation of success,[138] but Keble and Pusey plunged warmly into the battle. Pusey looked upon it as a theological question; the heads had attacked sound doctrine, therefore the university must dissociate itself from them. In the Macmullen case the Vice-Chancellor had usurped a power to veto divinity degrees, so Convocation must break through all precedent and assert a power over the Vice-Chancellor.[139] When in this mood (which he later regretted)[140] Pusey was impervious to all persuasion, but the lay friends of the party leaders did their best to teach them the elements of political ethics. Sir John Taylor Coleridge shook Keble's confidence in the cause.[141] Sir John Awdry held that 'men who will insist on making such a post a matter of party, do all they can to justify . . . attempts to proscribe them,' and Heathcote tackled both Pusey and Keble.[142] Gladstone was even more brusque. The scheme was 'a *mad* one,' and for all the Tractarians' allegations about Symons's conduct in the trial of Pusey, they had no firm evidence of how he voted.[143] And Symons explicitly denied Pusey's allegations that he wished to drive the Tractarians out of the church.[144]

When in September it became certain that he would be opposed, the Warden of Wadham was in Boulogne, and his college was empty, but C. P. Golightly was mobilising the heads, and Provost Hawkins assured the Vice-Chancellor that since his refusal to serve was exposing Symons to trouble, he would step into the breach if necessary.[145] The immediate worry of the Vice-Chancellor, however, was to tranquillise the duke of Wellington. The Chancellor first learned of the approaching contest through the newspapers, and wrote passionately to Dr. Wynter recalling his unwillingness ever to serve the university, declaring that he would not be disgraced by Convocation, and announcing that he would resign by return of post were Symons's nomination not accepted.[146] The Vice-Chancellor obtained a legal opinion from Sir Charles Wetherell that Convocation had no power to refuse the nomination, but if, as in the case of Everett's degree, he disregarded the *non-placets*, and installed Symons in office, the two Proctors, the Tractarians Guillemard and Church, would probably refuse to tender the oaths.[147] Wynter would be deemed to have resigned already, Symons would not be appointed, and if Wellington resigned as he threatened, the university would be without its two chief officers. Had this happened, Peel's government would have had to perform another *volte-face* and state intervention in Oxford would have been advanced by ten years. That such a pass could have been seriously contemplated is a measure of how nearly the university constitution had collapsed under the animosities engendered by religion and reform.

The Tractarians had, nevertheless, grievously miscalculated, and their enemies plotted to destroy them.[148] John Griffiths, Sub-Warden of Wadham, formed a committee and began to whip in the voters. With the encouragement of new catholic recruits such as Dr. Hook and Sir William Heathcote, and new Tractarian extravagances on the right of bishops to excommunicate the queen and on the prospect of replacing Wellington by Bishop Philpotts, their propaganda breathed a new confidence.[149] On October 8 over a thousand graduates crowded into Oxford for the Convocation. Proceedings were delayed for over an hour by the admission of 150 masters to their Regency, but Symons's nomination was then approved by 882 votes to 183.[150] Newman read the writing on the wall.

> The country parsons are of unfathomable strength: they and the conservative feeling which moved with them turned out Sir Robert Peel in 1829, brought in the duke of Wellington in 1834; censured Hampden; and made Symons Vice-Chancellor in 1844.[151]

The Tractarians could run the rapids no longer.

The heads put the constitutional question before a committee which after many months of consideration could only resolve by a majority to ask the Chancellor to solicit counsel's opinion.[152] This opinion strongly supported the Chancellor's absolute right of nomination, and the duke concluded that Dr. Wynter had been wrong even to allow a scrutiny. Assuring himself of the Vice-

Chancellor's ready compliance with his directions, the duke subscribed himself the Board's most obedient humble servant.[153] In
October 1845 C. P. Eden pursued Symons again, but won no
response.

During the furor Provost Hawkins inquired from the Vice-
Chancellor whether there was any way of ridding the university of
W. G. Ward; Dr. Wynter replied that his power extended only to
making him subscribe 'which he would not hesitate to do.'[154] On
October 26 Archbishop Whately gave a decisive push to the Hebdomadal Board in a long and fierce letter pointing out that the university
could not afford to forfeit the confidence of the bishops, and the
bishops in turn were entitled to call on the university to remove their
'well-founded alarm.'[155] He put pressure on Copleston and Hawkins,
and at the latter's suggestion the Vice-Chancellor required Ward to
subscribe again, while Copleston cheered on the heads to take penal
measures against him (though not to run the risks of litigation).[156]
The game was thus begun by the older generation of liberals.

W. G. Ward had become fellow of Balliol in 1834 and had subsequently shared in the tuition as mathematical lecturer. There was no
middle way in Ward's mind between outright scepticism and sub-
mission to church authority; deeply religious in nature he fell under
Newman's influence. Ward was nevertheless the most uncomfortable
of disciples, and in 1841, in defending Tract XC, he went further in
accepting Roman teaching than Newman had done. There was at
once a division in the college. A. C. Tait, who had urged the heads
to censure Tract XC, and who claimed merely to have been 'a passive
instrument' in the hands of the Balliol high-churchmen, began an
agitation which led to Ward's dismissal from his lectureship.[157]
Ward had also caused offence among those champions of the church
revival who were hurt by his persistent denigration of the English
church. In this character William Palmer, the 'retractarian,' replied
to him, and received a great counter-blast in July 1844 in Ward's
Ideal of a Christian Church. In this book the ideal seemed always
to be realised in Rome and never in England, the fruits of subscribing
to the English formularies in a 'non-natural' sense were reaped to
the full, and the Tractarians knew that firm measures must follow.
Pusey found the book 'very strong;'[158] Dalgairns confessed that
'Ward is a most aggravating fellow (in Pickwickian phrase),'[159] and
Charles Marriott admitted that if he had been a protestant he
would not have been as forbearing with Ward as Symons now
was.[160]

On November 30 Ward was summoned by the Vice-Chancellor to
disavow certain portions of the book, and on his refusal was censured.
The heads then prepared three statutes; the first condemned passages
from the *Ideal* as inconsistent with the XXXIX Articles and Ward's

good faith in subscribing them; the second annulled his degrees, and the third required graduates to subscribe the articles in the sense in which they were first published, and now imposed by the university. To each of these motions there were substantial objections, but against the last, which constituted a new test, there was a violent storm from all sides. Whately was furious: 'Ward had given them a great advantage which they were throwing away.'[161] Tait and the younger liberals such as A. P. Stanley began to write against the folly of new tests.[162] Gladstone wondered 'what spirit of dementation possesses these our guides and governors in the university.'[163] Dr. Hampden still held that

> It is no question whether Mr. Ward is Arian, Sabellian, Athanasian, Transubstantiationist, Calvinist, Arminian or what not; but whether he should be allowed to trample on the articles.[164]

But it was clear that the new test could never be carried, and on January 13, the Board withdrew it.

For the moment attention was concentrated upon Ward. His friends procured counsel's opinion that the measures against him were not legal, and the Board replied with the opinion of other counsel that they were.[165] Rapidly the Board was outpaced by the juniors. Golightly, Dr. Ellerton of Magdalen and Dr. Faussett, Margaret professor, got up a requisition to the Vice-Chancellor to submit to Convocation the censure on Tract XC which it had issued in 1841.[166] Nearly 500 signatures were rapidly obtained and on February 3, the Board, deeming it impossible to bring up non-residents twice, agreed to comply with this proposal on February 13 after the condemnation of Ward.

The storm which had threatened over the proposed new test now burst in full fury. The Tractarians believed that the power against them on the Board was Provost Hawkins,[167] whom Gladstone took severely to task; Hawkins admitted to being in a cleft stick, and merely claimed that the Board could not refuse to comply with the requisition.[168] Some insisted that the time allowed was too short, others that the condemnation was in terms altogether too vague.[169] Robert Hussey, professor of ecclesiastical history, urged that no-one should be tried twice for the same offence, and that the new censure was in effect a second trial of Tract XC. Moreover, at the end of 1843, an address to the present purpose numerously signed by laymen had been presented to the Board, who refused to take action on the grounds that the university was sufficiently protected by its subscriptions.[170] A. P. Stanley drew elaborate parallels between the condemnations of 1836 and 1845; he claimed that in each case the liberals had been against persecution, and pressed the voters to stop the practice before it was too late.[171] Others complained that Convocation was not a fit court for a case of this kind.

The scene of February 13, when '1300 wild country parsons' crammed the theatre, was unsurpassed in the dramatic annals of nineteenth-century Oxford, and formed a set piece in many a letter and memoir.[172] Ward was given leave to defend himself in English, and pressed the view that all parties subscribed in a non-natural sense. The plain sense of the articles was abhorrent to the high-churchmen, that of the prayer book to the evangelical; they should all be honest together. But the passages from the *Ideal* were condemned by 777 to 386, and the degradation voted by 569 to 511. The Tractarian Proctors, Church and Guillemard, who had held their hand on the nomination of Symons, now vetoed the censure of Tract XC, and 400 M.A.s subscribed a vote of thanks for their services.[173]

This was the end of the story. 180 M.A.s signed a requisition to bring up the motion again after the Proctors had retired from office, but the Board would have none of it.[174] Frederick Oakeley whose Romanism was as advanced if not as pawky as Ward's, explained casuistically to the Vice-Chancellor how he stood his ground in the English church,[175] and Pusey breathed again. 'My whole self is concentrated about N[ewman]: he is God's special instrument towards us & upon him seems to hang most of ye future fortunes of our church.'[176] Yet before long, though Convocation had not censured Tract XC, Ward,[177] Oakeley, Newman and a multitude with them had entered the Roman Church. The self-appointed defenders of the Anglican cause capitulated to the enemy, and the efforts of the remnant to obstruct university business were ludicrously ineffective.[178] Benjamin Symons reported contentedly that

> the seceders have for the most part been young, inexperienced & uninformed. It is observable that no undergraduate has been influenced by the example of Mr. Newman, nor has anyone holding a university or college office.[179]

Weakened now by secession, attenuated still further by the losses which followed the Gorham judgment, its hold over the parish clergy broken for the time being, the Tractarian party never again functioned in the old way, and in the next decade influence in the university passed to its rivals, the evangelicals (from whom came Vice-Chancellors Symons (1844–8) and Cotton (1852–6) and a succession of Bampton lecturers)[180] and the liberals (who had the ear of Russell's government). Moreover, the old landmarks were disappearing. Bitter experience of opposition had drawn the Tractarians and Gladstone together,[181] and, young reactionaries as they had begun, was leading them both into strange liberal paths. The illegality of the university constitution they now denounced with the vehemence of the *Edinburgh Review*. They still abhorred the notion of dissenters in Oxford,[182] but they were now the chastened victims of the tests and were ready to seek liberal support against new tests. Gladstone had been soured with both the constitution and the behaviour of the university. On June 21, 1845 he wrote a long letter to Peel, bitterly denouncing his old chief's support of the *status quo* in Oxford, accusing the heads of driving men to Rome and doing nothing to meet the needs of the day. He referred

> to the almost entire absence of any efforts to raise the religious tone of the university, to remove its scandals, to enlarge (in particular) its theological studies, to increase its means of meeting the wants of the country, to resist by works of solid learning the renewed and (in our present ill-trained state) really formidable controversial attacks of the Church of Rome. Here are five heads of positive duty.[183]

The thin end of the reforming wedge had been driven into the mind of Gladstone and his Oxford friends, the stout opponents of reform in the 'thirties.

On one matter they were especially sensitive. Ten years before William Sewell had defined universities as incorporations for the education of 'Englishmen who, from their wealth and connexion, form the highest ruling ranks in society,'[184] but now the whole catholic party wanted to enlarge the flow of ordinands for the new parishes by providing cheap education for the sons of poor clergy. Unfortunately the generally high cost of Oxford education was advertised by occasional cases of gross indebtedness among undergraduates. These were Gladstone's 'scandals.' For many months in 1843 a committee of the Board wrestled with the problem of debt on which proposals had been defeated in Convocation in 1838,[185] but finally to the disgust of the duke, and of important sections of the press, they gave it up as hopeless.[186] The one positive proposal for cheaper education came from R. L. Cotton, the evangelical Provost of Worcester, himself a church-builder.[187] He pressed his college to erect what later became known as an affiliated hall, in which more frugal board should be provided than in the college itself. The fellows, however, feared that 'their college would lose caste in the university' if it acted alone, and referred the Provost to the Hebdomadal Board for the backing of other societies.[188] This was not forthcoming and the Board got no further than a discussion upon licensed lodgings.[189] On questions of debt and university extension the Board, after one defeat, failed to produce fresh proposals, and incurred the united hostility not only of evangelicals and Tractarians who wished to cater for the poor clergy, but of liberals who were alarmed at the rapidly shrinking proportion of the population served by the university.[190] This issue like that of the university constitution was to be a leading theme for the next decade.

Another great question, that of Oxford studies, could hardly be postponed much longer. In 1833 the university had responded to public changes in the medical profession by a new statute on medical examinations which recognised modern as well as classical medicine.[191] But only three medical graduates were produced per year, and when in 1837 the College of Physicians deprived the graduates of Oxford and Cambridge of the privileges it had hitherto offered, the supply seemed likely to dry up altogether. The regius professor of medicine and the other Oxford physicians petitioned the Board to keep some connexion with the profession by regularly conferring the degree of D.M. by diploma.[192] In the early 'forties the odious comparison between the hundred doctors annually produced at Edinburgh and Oxford's exiguous handful was very damaging,[193] especially when Sir James Graham and others were trying to reform the profession by act of parliament. These proposals were carefully watched by the Board, but their resistance to medical examination by a central board of health on the grounds that the university had an efficient system of its own had a hollow ring.[194]

The other sciences flourished no more vigorously. Efforts to find useful work for the scientific professors had foundered on party animosities, even at a time when there were Members of Parliament to urge that the social importance of their work justified greater public subsidies.[195] Worst of all, the efforts of so many tutors of the generation of Newman and Sewell to counter the pride of intellect which they regarded as the essence of liberalism by instilling right principles and tastes, seeking to form the character rather than the mind, had ended disastrously.[196] J. D. Dalgairns had pictured young Oxford crying 'What shall I do to be saved?' while the heads looked on unmoved; but the tutors who encouraged the question now fought acrimoniously over the answer. The *Edinburgh Review* was not too severe when it wrote that

> the fruits of the recent fashion of decrying mere scientific pursuits or mere literary studies, as unworthy, frivolous or dangerous are terribly apparent in the present condition of Oxford . . . The utter absence of all spirit for investigation of every sort, except in polemic theology and one or two inferior pursuits of taste, is the subject, even there, of general lamentation.[197]

As soon as the smoke of battle cleared the question of studies would certainly be reopened.

Finally, though overshadowed by the Tractarian crisis, the pattern of external pressure upon the university had also established itself. The stir created by the Chancellor's demand for the revision of the statutes led to the publication of several colleges' statutes in English translation. These were the work of G. R. M. Ward, a contemporary of Newman at Trinity,[198] and a most difficult character. He began by waging 'a vindictive war' against the Hebdomadal Board for resisting his efforts to obtain emolument from his honorary office of Deputy High Steward,[199] then fell foul of his college and was removed from his fellowship for failing to enter holy orders at the proper time. Obtaining no satisfaction from the visitor, the bishop of Winchester, Ward wrote a violent pamphlet against him and the university authorities, and threatened ulterior measures.[200] First with T. W. Lancaster of Queen's (who had crossed Dr. Hampden) he opposed the nomination of Dr. Gilbert as Vice-Chancellor in 1839. He then published English translations of the statutes of the colleges of which the bishop of Winchester was visitor 'for the purpose of showing that they have been neglected & violated without any interference on the part of the visitor,' and in particular that endowments for the poor had been misapplied.[201]

His edition of the Magdalen statutes created a sensation. A number of the fellows obtained an injunction to prevent the publication, but were finally glad to withdraw it and pay costs.[202] The fellows of Magdalen were known to have sinned against the statutes in not paying the demies at half the rate of the fellows, and in compensating them unstatutably by allowing them to retain their demyships until they succeeded in turn to fellowships.[203] The Vice-Chancellor conveyed the wrath of the duke of Wellington to Dr. Ellerton, the head of the conservative party among the fellows, only to be assured that any change would be too much for their aged President, Dr. Routh.[204] Nor was the reputation of the college enhanced when one of the fellows provoked Ward to a duel.[205]

Ward's translation was reviewed in the Tractarian *British Critic* by J. R. Hope-Scott, who savagely denounced the appeal to 'the triple-crowned popedom of self-will, hastiness and party spirit which rules amidst the popular assemblies,' while at the same time getting grist for his own mill of restoring colleges on monastic lines.[206] Ward's appeal to liberal opinion in the country showed the direction which agitation would take, for his translation of the Corpus statutes was published at the expense of James Heywood of Manchester,[207] who also completed and published the translation of the university statutes upon which Ward was engaged when he died in 1846.[208] James Heywood who was to play a crucial part in the history of university reform, was at once an embodiment of the culture of that other England which lay beyond the purview of academic apologists like Newman and Copleston, and a link between it and the university liberals.

The Heywood family who were prominent in the public life of

South Lancashire throughout the nineteenth century, were descended from Nathaniel Heywood, a Lancashire presbyterian minister ejected in 1662. By the end of the eighteenth century they were distinguished unitarians and bankers both in Manchester and Liverpool. James was the youngest son of Nathaniel, a partner in the Manchester bank of Benjamin Heywood, Sons and Co., and a Liverpool Russia merchant as well. His mother, Ann Percival was the daughter of a fellow of the Royal Society. As a boy James was one of the many eminent pupils of the famous Bristol unitarian, Dr. Lant Carpenter. In dissenting fashion he then went to Edinburgh and studied natural history and geology. A year at Geneva followed, then a spell in the bank, and in 1831 he entered Trinity College, Cambridge, under Whewell. In 1833 he obtained the place of Senior Optime in the honours list, but could not graduate because of the subscription. Subsequently he was called to the bar as a member of the Inner Temple, and he devoted the rest of his life to science and to radical causes of all kinds. A keen geologist, he read a paper on the Lancashire coalfield before the British Association at Liverpool in 1838, and was elected Fellow of the Royal Society on the nomination of Sedgwick two years later. He was among the founders of the Manchester Geological Society in 1838, and his liberal gifts to the society eventually passed into the collections of the university. He was one of the chief founders of the Manchester Athenaeum, a trustee of Owens College, and in later life built a free library at Notting Hill at his own expense. He contributed to many causes of a scholarly kind, helping, for example, to launch the revision of the English version of scriptures.

In the 'forties two enthusiasms consumed his time and energy, the Anti-Corn Law League, and university reform.[209] Heywood had a stout unitarian faith that if the true facts were known about universities at home and abroad, reform would follow. He not only supported Ward's translations, but promoted a translation of the Merton statutes.[210] He got Walter C. Perry of the university of Göttingen to write a temperate account of *German university educa-tion*[211] which stressed the role of the state in university reform, and persuaded Frank Newman, the brother of John Henry, who at this stage in his career was a unitarian and a professor at Manchester New College, to abridge and edit an English translation of Huber's *English Universities*.[212] This massive work by the professor of Western literature at Marburg is the only study of the English universities which attempts to set their whole development against the political and social development of the country, and though Huber's zeal far outran his knowledge, it is still worth reading. At the time it was unrivalled, and Newman's edition gained in piquancy from the radical notes which ruffled the pietistic and conservative author.

Even Huber, however, was ready 'to excuse or pity the academicians, who, from fear or disapproval of parliamentary interference have attempted to raise objections to its *legality*,' and had no doubt that state action would soon come.[213]

This barrage of propaganda was designed to support parliamentary action. On May 25, 1843, W. D. Christie, M.P. for Weymouth, a young Cambridge liberal, moved for leave to bring in a bill to abolish the university test. There was not much hope of carrying such a motion against the government,[214] and Christie arranged to bring the Protestant Dissenting Deputies into the campaign in the following year,[215] but the ball had been set rolling and Inglis had to answer questions about the university's progress in revising their statutes. In the following year Christie asked for an address to the Crown to issue a general commission of inquiry into the universities and colleges. The Oxford burgesses arranged for Philip Bliss, the Registrar, to sit in the body of the House to prompt them, but the precaution was superfluous. The debate came on on the eve of Whitsuntide during Epsom week, and the House was counted out before Christie could begin his speech.[216] On April 10, 1845, Christie finally put his motion, and made a long attack on the state of religion and learning in Oxford. In reply Inglis denied the faults complained of, and insisted that in any case a royal commission could work no improvement. The motion was duly defeated by 61 votes,[217] but Christie had now made it a hardy annual; he had established links between the academic liberals and dissenters, and when the tories had fallen from office, he might well succeed.

CHAPTER VII

THE LIBERAL REVIVAL

A Whig Commission! The very sound is enough to make us lock our drawers and see that the plate is safe.

Guardian May 31, 1848, p. 345.

Whether it be from that 'alloy of dulness' which Fuller tells us 'sorteth well with the Headship of a College,' or that fatality which sometimes waits on usurped authority, so it is that the heads seldom call Convocation together without being plainly informed by its vote how utterly they have failed to understand the wants of the university, and how entirely indisposed their subjects are to yield to their authority and respect their wisdom.

Guardian June 25, 1851, p. 453.

ALL the commentators noted the radical change in the Oxford atmosphere after the secessions to Rome. Many of the old controversies seemed played out,[1] Cox in a famous passage described how dons turned from speculation in theology to speculation in railway shares,[2] and for a time the Tractarians lost their spirit. Pusey talked of an alliance with the 'religious evangelicals'[3]—always a sign of desperation with him. The *Times* campaigned for the extirpation of secret jesuitism in Oxford, and the Oxford Architectural Society, with its gothic propensities, was said to be instrument of popery.[4] When the *Times* fell silent the Tractarian remnant were pestered by the brethren who had gone over to Rome.[5] Their fellow-traveller, William Sewell, described them from the university pulpit as

> lying, even in this place . . . under a proscription and a ban Kept apart from each other by that terrible suspicion which hands over all alike, paralysed in their efforts to do good, excluded . . . from offices of responsibility, scarcely daring to look for support even to their bishops, distrusted by those whom they have to rule, branded with names of opprobrium . . . wearied out and exhausted by a lengthened conflict . . . and only craving for solitude and silence as a refuge for a wounded spirit.[6]

According to William Sewell the young saw in the 'suspension of conflict . . . a suspension of life.'[7] At the opposite theological pole the young liberal Goldwin Smith reported that

torpor and apathy prevail. . . . The better sort of men are turning
to practical matters, new Examination Statutes, and university
reform. The worse sort are becoming more careless and more
sensual. There are great fears and rumours of infidelity, which
from what I can learn, seem to me to be so far well founded,
that a certain number of men may be growing up, not exactly in
infidelity, but in the belief that Christianity is an open question.[8]

In almost identical terms the evangelical *Christian Observer* reported
that former Tractarians were now saying that 'the historic truth of
Christianity was . . . an open question,'[9] and Archbishop Whately
repeated the charge.[10] Pusey maintained that the only scepticism in
Oxford had been imported by Germanising liberals.[11] But although
he tried to close his mind to Mark Pattison's plain assurances that
his 'faith and perception of Divine things . . . was withdrawn,'[12]
there was no contesting the evidence of *The Nemesis of Faith*, a
novel published in 1849 by that favoured pupil of Newman, James
Anthony Froude,[13] and publicly burnt by William Sewell, the sub-
rector of his college; with the Rector of Exeter moving the college
meeting, and Bishop Philpotts calling for his degradation, Froude
checked proceedings by a timely resignation of his fellowship.[14]

His Oriel friend, Arthur Hugh Clough, explained their difficulties
to Provost Hawkins.

> There is a general feeling that miracles are poor proofs. . . .
> Can we be sure that anything is really a miracle? . . . Again,
> books like Strauss's *Life of Jesus* have disturbed the historical
> foundations of Christianity. And people ask further what has
> History to do with Religion? The worth of such a doctrine as
> that of the Holy Ghost as the Lord and Giver of Spiritual life
> is intelligible, but what is the value of biographical facts?
> External evidence is slighted: but I think the great query is
> rather as to the *internal* evidence. Is Xtianity really so much
> better than Mahometism, Buddhism or the old heathen philo-
> sophy? Are those virtues and graces which are our religious
> and moral tradition, really altogether Christian?[15]

Gone was the comfortable assurance of Oxford tutors of only
yesterday that 'it is not more the characteristic *excellence* of Revelation in the comparison with heathen ethics, than its own coincidence
with them in certain remarkable instances, which speaks of its
Divine origin.'[16] Gone was the Tractarian conviction of the moral
significance of every Christian dogma. And H. H. Vaughan, who
had earlier slipped through the Tractarian net, was engaged in a
great study of the origin of moral ideas, which, true to form, he
never completed.[17] The battle over the articles had made it impossible
to take any doctrine on trust, and the *Edinburgh Review* preened

itself on having foreseen that 'the desperate assertion that 'the
evidence for Christianity' was no stronger than that for 'church
principles' must by reaction lead to an outbreak of infidelity.'[18]

The Tractarian collapse gave new prominence to the Oxford
liberals who were reinforced by former high-churchmen like Vaughan
and Mark Pattison, and who still had a vigorous gospel to preach.
Stubbs later classified the reading men as '(a) religious men, (β) the
classical school and (γ) infidels,' a class which he subdivided into
'Rugby' and 'Wadham.'[19] Rugby and Wadham were two important
elements in Oxford liberalism and were already under suspicion of
infidelity.

Arnold was a father figure to a large group of Oxford liberals.
Foremost among these was his favourite pupil, A. P. Stanley who
matriculated from Balliol in 1833; W. C. Lake came up to Balliol in
1834; Arthur Hugh Clough who even at school had been full of the
mission of the Rugby set to 'leaven the whole lump' at Oxford,
followed in 1836.[20] Ten years later all were men of influence. Stanley
was fellow and tutor of University College, and had struck a
powerful blow in the liberal cause in his tremendously successful
Life of Arnold (1844), which portrayed its hero as a prophet who
though dead still spoke powerfully. W. C. Lake, as a tutor at Balliol,
held a position in educational strategy rivalling Rugby itself. Arthur
Hugh Clough, a more delicate plant than even Stanley, and much
bruised by contact with W. G. Ward,[21] was tutor at Oriel. His faith
was fading fast and he was anxious for relief from the agonies of
subscription. Another old Rugbeian who came up to Wadham in
1837 was Richard Congreve; he too was now a fellow and tutor,
and a 'great Arnoldite' in his religious principles.[22] J. A. Froude
later claimed that his faith had been temporarily shattered by the
revolutionary events of 1848; Congreve went to Paris and came back
a positivist. Frederic Harrison, later the best known of the English
positivists, was his pupil.

Rugby was the shrine as well as the breeding ground of liberals.
A. C. Tait, the Balliol tutor who had led the attack on Tract XC
succeeded Arnold as headmaster; Frederick Temple,[23] another
Balliol liberal, was offered the succession to Tait in 1849, and
actually became headmaster in 1857. A Blundell's scholar from
Tiverton, Temple could not have been more alien in origin, yet 'from
that day there was only one school for a Temple,'[24] and there was
still much of Arnold's churchmanship in Temple's son William.
Lake also toyed with the idea of a return to Rugby in 1849,[25] and
one of the assistant masters was Bonamy Price, always good for a
pamphlet on Oxford issues, and flowing 'with a continuous stream
of German Divinity and Bible-Philology.'[26]

It was the pride of the Rugby connexion that 'at Oxford we only form part of a large set,'[27] and their influence was multiplied by that of their friends. By virtue of his intimacy with A. P. Stanley, the closest and most important of these was another fellow of Balliol, Benjamin Jowett. As an undergraduate Jowett had lost sympathy with his evangelical background, and began to develop a resistance to the fashionable catholicism of the day which was barely weakened by personal affection for W. G. Ward. Jowett found comfort in the text that 'they that do the works shall know of the doctrine',[28] and on this ground entered holy orders, though Goldwin Smith reckoned that his first impulse was always to deny whatever doctrine was advanced.[29] At the time of Tract XC Jowett was hoping for a simplified version of the articles; despairing of this, he became an implacable foe of subscription,[30] even while advising young men that they should subscribe if they were in general sympathy with the existence of the Church of England. In early life Jowett's liberalism set him against dissenters, partly from the belief that 'the gentlemanly virtues . . . exist tenfold among the aristocracy for one 'gentleman by nature' you find among the middling classes,'[31] partly because dissenters constantly degenerated 'into unitarianism, and never into latitudinarianism.'[32]

At the time of Tract XC Jowett was compiling a paper 'On Strauss's Theory of Christianity,' and he was deeply influenced by visits to Germany with Stanley in 1844 and 1845. Jowett returned an ardent Hegelian,[33] began to lecture on the history of philosophy, and by 1848 had been captivated by Baur and the negative theologians of Tubingen.[34] The dogmatic content of Jowett's faith diminished so steadily with the years that he could not carry through the theological reconstruction which he began with Stanley in his youth. His ultimate residuum of 'belief in the existence of God and in the Christ ideal' justified the conviction shared by Pusey with so thorough-going a liberal as Goldwin Smith, that Jowett was not a Christian in any more than intention. For religious and philosophical reasons Jowett was also a liberal educationalist. Impressed with the power of education to change the world, he looked to the new studies, and to the reign of Bacon, Locke, Mill, and the history of philosophy in the Greats school, to overthrow the old doctrines of authority.[35] A liberal in theology and education, Jowett was also a strong liberal in politics. With none of Stanley's hereditary whiggism, Jowett became one of the rationalistic liberals who were always impatient with Gladstone. He was the nearest thing Oxford ever produced to the German liberal professors who took the stage in the revolution of 1848, and it was hardly surprising if conservatives of the middle of the century, such as H. L. Mansel, thought that if this was what Hegel led to, it was time to reach again for Bishop Butler.

Jowett, like Newman, believed that the world was unjust to him, and harboured a grudge against another Oxford liberal, whom he thought even less orthodox than himself, yet who flourished as the green bay tree, H. G. Liddell of Christ Church.[36] A favourite of Dean Gaisford, Liddell became a tutor at the House in 1836, and from 1843 when he and Scott published their celebrated *Lexicon* he enjoyed increasing favour. In 1844 he preached a university sermon on '*unity*, not *uniformity*; an attempt to persuade people to *agree to differ*' which was praised by both Gaisford and Hampden.[37] In 1845 he became Censor and White's professor of moral philosophy, attracting large classes. In 1846 he was made domestic chaplain to the Prince Consort, and left Oxford to become headmaster of Westminster. But from time to time he reappeared in the university pulpit, declaring 'that he desired to get rid of the definitions of the Trinity, sacraments &c.'[38] and creating the impression inside the university and out that he was the rising leader of liberal Oxford.[39] From a theological viewpoint Liddell proved an even damper squib than Jowett, and in his later days rarely even preached, but in university affairs he was in some respects more useful. A man of grace, whose varied accomplishments reminded Goldwin Smith of Leonardo da Vinci,[40] Liddell never had Jowett's struggles, nor his facility for making enemies; on his return to Oxford in 1855 he was at once elected to the Hebdomadal Council, and, except for one short break, sat continuously till 1891.

Another liberal from a central Anglican tradition was Goldwin Smith. The son of a Reading physician and railway company director, Goldwin Smith longed to escape from the compulsory Anglican conventions of his youth, and though many of his pronouncements now bear the marks of hasty dogmatism, he rapidly established a great reputation in Oxford as a prophet[41] and a devotee of progress. His disappointments after a brilliant classical career guaranteed that he would be a university reformer. Oriel made a poor bargain by disqualifying him on grounds of his private means and electing J. W. Burgon into a fellowship; at Queen's he was defeated by a coalition of non-residents and reactionaries.[42] Finally he was elected Stowell civil law fellow at University College, and his repute as tutor, journalist and thinker grew steadily. His refusal to take orders foreshadowed his later loss of faith, and as an old man he was severe upon former allies like Jowett, Liddell or Bishop Thirlwall, who had, he believed, succumbed to 'the pressure of the white tie.'

With these younger liberals worked a number of older men and especially Baden Powell, Savilian professor of geometry. Baden Powell was interested in reform as a professor, as a scientist and as the author of a long series of works of liberal theology. Jowett vented his spleen on him,[43] but was ultimately glad of his support in the *Essays and Reviews*. H. B. Wilson was a senior man of evangelical origin and advanced liberal views. A fellow and former tutor of St. John's, he had joined Tait in the protest of the four tutors in 1841. From 1849 he was Rawlinsonian professor of Anglo-Saxon, and though he took a college living in 1850, he created a sensation in 1851 with his Bampton Lectures on *The communion of saints*, and suffered perhaps worst of all the contributors to the *Essays and Reviews*.

With these liberals, all convinced that there was virtue in the times, and especially in the scholarship of the times, all believing in progress, there acted as on earlier occasions others moved by evangelical scruples. Eminent among them was Francis Jeune, who became Master of Pembroke in 1843. A dozen years before Keble had remarked that

> as light dawneth in a cellar from a decayed mackerel, even so it is bruited that in Pembroke, the cellar and dusthole of the university, there are those who send forth sparks of reform,

and had described Jeune as 'the most radical of all the tutors.'[44] After serving as examiner in 1834, however, Jeune departed to the headship of King Edward's school in Birmingham, which he reformed on modern lines, introducing English and scientific studies. Here he obtained the notice of Lord John Russell, who in 1838 made Jeune dean of his native Jersey. Again Jeune laboured for the improvement of the local clergy, and the establishment of Victoria College, St. Helier. Meanwhile a handful of liberal fellows had done what they could to rescue Pembroke from the evils of its congeries of close foundations by rejecting fellows and scholars who were not *sufficientes doctrina*,[45] and on the death of the Master, Dr. Hall, they brought back the scholarship and business acumen of Jeune.

Jeune who was connected through his wife, the niece of Dr. Symons, Warden of Wadham, with the Vice-Chancellor-to-be, had already given offence with his liberal politics and evangelical theology. The election to the headship ended in a tie, 4 votes to Jeune, and 4 to C. F. Parker,[46] who had gone off to a country living a quarter of a century before, and Jeune was carried home by the casting vote of the Vice-gerent T. F. Henney, one of the youngest fellows, and a strong liberal. Pembroke still retained traces of its former status as Broadgates Hall, however, for the Chancellor was Visitor, and the Vice-Chancellor admitted the Master. The defeated party claimed that Jeune was not validly elected, Dr. Wynter was not loath to refuse him admission,[47] and Parker's supporters secured a summary decision from the duke of Wellington that the election was void. Jeune's party now began a long struggle to gain a hearing, and, finally, after taking legal advice, the duke came down on Jeune's side 'in the handsomest and most flattering manner' and resolved never again to decide a case upon the statements of one party 'even though such party should consist of men deserving implicit confidence in their character of clergymen of Church of England.'[48]

A new era of progress for Pembroke now began. In 1843 there had been only two matriculations; by 1848 the intake was the third largest in the university. Extensive new building was begun, and Jeune excelled in keeping down the battells.[49] Dr. Hall had attempted to revise the statutes, but had yielded before the opposition of the conservative fellows;[50] Jeune spared the feelings of none and kept the pot continuously on the boil.[51] In the university Jeune pleaded for better training for the clergy, and though he began by arguing that an education based upon the Bible must be broad enough, since the whole of knowledge was required for its exegesis,[52] he favoured the foundation of new schools. He held a low view of German criticism and continued to assail the Tractarians from an evangelical standpoint;[53] and though he did not, as expected, obtain the regius chair of divinity in 1847,[54] great things were in store. His character, after long service to his college and university, was acutely assessed by Dr. Cardwell:

> A thorough reformer, with great talent and all sorts of information: energetic and impetuous, but clear-headed and good-tempered: low-church politically rather than doctrinally: vehement as a preacher, but not impressive: his pervading faults are ambition and restlessness.[55]

A link between the liberal evangelicals and the Rugby men was provided by John Conington. He came up from Rugby in 1843, and in the following term carried off both the Hertford and the Ireland. Other brilliant successes followed, and he was confirmed in a fellowship at University College after a rival had appealed against him to the courts; nevertheless his hopes of an academic career seemed blighted by his refusal to take orders and his distaste for law. In 1854, however, an ideal opening was provided by his appointment to the new chair of latin. Conington was early regarded as a dangerous radical,[56] and he wrote on university reform in the *Morning Chronicle* in 1849 and 1850. Always deeply interested in religious and moral questions, he underwent, at the turning-point of his career in 1854, a profound spiritual crisis.[57] This upheaval confirmed him in the evangelicalism in which he had been brought up, and made him something of a saint. This lapse from progressive doctrine some liberals found hard to forgive.[58]

Thus while the Tractarian remnant were grouping themselves round the *Christian Remembrancer* and the *Guardian* and salvaging what they could from the wreckage of the party, the liberals and liberal evangelicals were recruiting much of the most formidable talent in the university. Suspicion of each side towards the other was embittered by the fact that neither side could foresee the movement of theological opinion away from both entrenched positions. To Stanley and his friends the loss of faith of men like Vaughan, Froude and Pattison was evidence that without the liberal insights the church would fail the age altogether; to Pusey the loss of faith of Clough and Goldwin Smith, and the increasingly impoverished religion of Jowett, showed that liberal reconstruction was a device of the devil for the destruction of faith, and that hope lay solely in the full catholic programme. Moreover, in Convocation numbers counted as much as talent, and the liberal group was still a small minority. Its real strength, talent apart, consisted in the fact that after 1846 it had the ear of Russell's government, and was in touch with the reviving pressure groups of dissenters. These were the threats against which the original Tractarian protest had been raised, and which had aided Newman to form a party. After 1846 his ancient enemy regrouped his forces.

The *Prospective Review* declared that the dissenters had 'effectually stopped their mouths against demanding' the repeal of the university tests by steadily founding colleges with tests of their own,[59] but they were soon caught up in Christie's continued campaign. Stanley and Jowett also linked up with him, submitting a memorandum and a draft of questions which might be asked by a parliamentary committee of inquiry.[60] In return Christie fired a shot for them by moving for a return of the professors in Oxford and Cambridge, the number of their lectures and pupils and their stipends;[61] this return, declared the *Times*, showed the extraordinary inefficiency to which the Oxford system had reduced the professors, and the independent *British Quarterly* also pleaded for them.[62] The parliamentary advocates of national education also joined in; Thomas Wyse, chairman of the Commons committee on legal education, called witnesses upon the facilities for legal education at Oxford,[63] and James Kay-Shuttleworth came down to Oxford in 1847 to collect information with a view to state action.[64] In September 1846 James Heywood delivered a smart attack on the university in a paper read to the British Association on 'Oxford University statistics.' Jowett and his friend R. R. W. Lingen who succeeded Kay-Shuttleworth as secretary to the education office, were conspiring with Edward Horsman, the whig member for Cockermouth, whose life was largely devoted to harrying bishops and exposing ecclesiastical jobs. The forces were now in line, though Jowett still had little precise idea of the object of the campaign. The opening of the fellowships, the admission of dissenters to the university but not the colleges, something for professors, legislation against 'the double corruption upstairs in elections, downstairs in the scoutocracy'—these were the ends vaguely in view.[65]

The tory press and the high-church *Guardian* began to suspect that the government had a royal commission on the universities up its sleeve.[66] Rightly assuming that a revived professoriate was part of every liberal scheme, the *Guardian* formulated a conservative reply to the arguments which derived from Sir William Hamilton. It claimed that the counterparts of the ancient university teachers were not the professors but the private tutors who taught simply by virtue of their degree;[67] the modern professors had never educated the bulk of the undergraduates and never would. As Christie gave notice of his intention to move for a commission the temperature of the press rose. The *Guardian* claimed that the universities received no privileges from the state which were not received by dissenting academies, and Christie's object could only be to create a precedent for the subversion of church property. The liberal daily press regurgitated the usual arguments,[68] and in March 1847 the Oxford liberals launched the heavily-loaded *Oxford Protestant Magazine*[69] to the enthusiastic applause of unitarian and congregationalist journals.[70] Yet it is clear that there was as little enthusiasm among dissenters for sending their sons to universities as there was in Jowett for receiving them, and the *Times* pointed out that their uneasy alliance had led Christie's arguments astray.

> To prove that Baptists should be admitted to fellowships, he has endeavoured to show that Churchmen have misused them. To obtain an infusion of new blood, he has represented the academical constitutions as wholly effete, decrepit and corrupt. . . . Whatever reform may be expedient it is utterly impossible to prove that Churchmen have so egregiously failed in managing the universities that they ought to be replaced by Independents.[71]

Ultimately the cause of university reform had to be separated from that of the tests, and for the present Christie made no progress.

By the following winter the whigs had made some gains in the elections and were 'shewing their teeth' in a manner which alarmed the leaderless tories.[72] Jowett still had hopes of Horsman, but cast his net wider with an elaborate appeal to Roundell Palmer 'under the idea that [he was] half an M.P. for the University of Oxford.'[73] After many Oxford successes Palmer was now on the threshold of his parliamentary career, and was a lay sympathiser of the Tractarian remnant second in importance only to Gladstone. If Palmer took up the cause, he might unite Oxford opinion and answer in advance charges that reform was the work of enemies of the church. Jowett pleaded that the experience of the last decade showed that the colleges and university could not reform themselves, and that he had no desire 'to see Oxford turned into a German or a London University.' His programme was still rudimentary; parliament should open the fellowships, establish adequately paid professorships from the proceeds of suppressed fellowships, and, from the same source, raise scholarships into demyships 'to provide means for many more persons of the middling class.' This invitation Palmer declined, feeling bound by the oath not to change the statutes which he had taken as a fellow of Magdalen.

For lack of a parliamentary champion the agitation perforce proceeded on an extra-parliamentary basis. Unitarian propagandists, notably Francis Newman, continued to plead for the abolition of tests, and for a reconstruction of university studies,[74] and James Heywood, who was now M.P. for North Lancashire, resolved upon a direct approach to the Premier. From Russell there was real hope; in November he proposed a commission to inquire into schools and colleges of royal foundation, but was dissuaded by the Prince Consort.[75] During the winter of 1847–8 a petition for a university commission was circulated for signature;[76] 138 signatures were obtained, only 39 of them from Oxford men, and few of these were of any note apart from a liberal group including Baden Powell, A. H. Clough, Matthew Arnold, Richard Congreve, H. Wrightson, fellow of Queen's, and Granville Bradley, fellow of University College. In July a deputation presented this petition to Russell with complaints of the backwardness of the universities in the field of modern studies, the inconveniences of the college system and the hold of the clergy upon tuition. Lord John promised to give the matter his serious consideration,[77] but the unitarian initiative had obviously made a fiasco of the petition in Oxford.[78] There were, however, two significant straws in the wind. In August there were the usual radical parliamentary challenges to the Treasury grants for professorial stipends, to which Inglis made the usual replies. But in a quite new way Russell recommended changes in the professorial system and concessions for dissenters, while Gladstone almost promised that something would be done about university extension.[79] Perhaps the former was considering reform in earnest; the latter certainly voiced very important changes of opinion in the university, and not least in the high-church party, which became public in the summer of 1848.

Ever since teaching and examining had revived in the university, the opinions of the tutors had been of consequence, and in the later 'forties their relations with the party men, whether liberal or Tractarian, were of far-reaching importance. The Tractarians had once been able to speak for them and on one issue in particular they still took the lead, intensified the unpopularity of the heads, and swelled the growing demand for reform. This was the question of the poor men's college.

The first efforts to provide cheaper accommodation in Oxford promoted by the evangelical Provost of Worcester had been frustrated, but the evangelicals had sought support from the other parties, and in 1845 a memorial urging what was called university extension, and bearing the signatures of laymen as various as Lord Sandon, Lord Ashley and Gladstone was presented to the Hebdomadal Board.[80] The opportunity seemed ripe to Charles Marriott, fellow of Oriel and former principal of Chichester Theological College, to found a new cause for the Tractarian remnant, preserved altogether from evangelical contamination.[81] The Tractarians had developed a mystique both of colleges and of the poor scholars whom they claimed the ancient colleges had been intended to benefit.[82] Sewell maintained that

> monasteries were the temptation and the curse of the Church of Rome, colleges have been the pride and the strength of the Church of England. And unless now in our hour of trial, we can multiply and expand them, how are we to retain our hold of the millions of the populace, how spread the Gospel among the heathen?[83]

Colleges were anti-professorial and enabled the tutor to exercise a pastoral vocation.[84] In Marriott's scheme a new college should inculcate the catholic virtues of poverty and obedience.[85] To the Tractarians the poor scholars were more than a means of staffing the new parishes and colonial sees, more than an argument from the statutes to oppose to the liberal virtues of intellectual competition; they embodied a religious principle. Originally distinct,[86] the poor scholars and the *pauperes Christi* became merged in the glow of Pusey's imagination, till in 1851 he was assuring Convocation that 'poor scholars, rich in faith and sterling character, are the very wealth of the university, of the state and of the church.'[87] On this plan Gladstone, Coleridge and others were interested in the scheme in the summer of 1845.[88]

It was a question where the new institution was to be and whether it was to be a hall or a college. Keble thought it would be better out of Oxford for the hostility of the heads and the prevailing social tone would undermine the spiritual ends of the foundation—it would be better to unite it with St. Augustine's missionary college recently founded at Canterbury by A. J. Hope.[89] Pusey and Marriott, however, had an eye to the reform of Oxford as well as the church, and their enthusiasm, together with the advantages of Oxford as a place of study, carried the day by the early summer of 1846.[90] On the other issue, a hall needed no endowments beyond the buildings, but Marriott saw no chance of the Chancellor's agreeing to make him head; there was a possibility that Peel's interest might be aroused, and that he would secure a charter for a college. Marriott regarded

Peel as a charlatan, and knew that to found an endowed college would require much more money, but felt no alternative but to make the attempt.[91]

Meanwhile on March 16, 1846, the Hebdomadal Board replied to Sandon's memorial with a dose of official realism. They declared that it was idle to establish new foundations while there were still unfilled places in the old. Poorly endowed new foundations were not likely to be cheaper than the old, and it was undesirable to create a new class of servitors in affiliated halls.[92] At no stage did the heads show any enthusiasm,[93] and on financial grounds they were justified. Matriculations had not increased for twenty years,[94] but during the 'forties some 200 sets of rooms were built,[95] and Exeter burst its bounds by providing freshmen with sitting rooms in lodgings and sleeping them in college in the third room of sets belonging to seniors.[96] There was wisdom in the heads' view that money would most profitably be devoted to founding bursaries for poor men. Finally they regarded unrestricted credit as the most urgent abuse.

This opinion was borne out by spectacular cases in the courts. Late in 1847, Edward Napleton Jennings, commoner of Worcester, appeared in the insolvent debtors' court, having in two sessions run up debts in Oxford to the tune of £1697 and in London of £600; his sole asset was a silver cigarette case worth three shillings. Two bad features of the case were that he was the son of a Yorkshire clergyman with eight children, and that a money-lender had granted him £55 for two £100 bills. Mr. Commissioner Phillips made some severe reflections on the tradesmen and the system, and the *Times* was overwhelmed with letters from anxious parents insisting that something be done. On the other side the Oxford tradesmen had no use for the misplaced sympathy which enabled Jennings to get off lightly, for he was a practised swindler who had dealt with 76 different tradesmen to avoid suspicion and postpone the day when he could be arrested for a debt exceeding £20. The Oxford Trades-men's Association made resolutions of better conduct, but they were soon complaining that the university authorities obstructed their efforts, especially by refusing to say when young debtors were about to graduate. Despite solemn warnings from the Hebdomadal Board, other serious cases followed.[97] The most highly coloured occurred in 1851 at a very serious time for the university. A number of under-graduates made a midnight attack upon the house of a notorious money-lender, one Caudwell. He replied to their stones with a gun-shot which wounded one of the attackers. They then retired to prosecute their enemy at the assizes. The undergraduates behaved so badly that the jury, in the teeth of the judge's direction, returned a verdict of not guilty, which was received with protracted cheering by the mob outside the court. But at the same assizes Caudwell was convicted of aggravated perjury.[98] A solution to the problem of gross indebtedness would not reduce the general cost of Oxford education, but it would remove the most lurid blot upon the reputation of the university.

Not only the Board but experienced tutors like Osborne Gordon of Christ Church and E. C. Woollcombe of Balliol,[99] objected to Marriott's plan, and advocated halls affiliated to present colleges. There were the risks that such a connexion would raise the level of extravagance or create a new depressed class,[100] but they were risks worth taking. This was the strength also of Marriott's case against the Board. Oxford could hardly defend its privileges when it received only half the number of undergraduates for whom it had found room in 1612.[101] And his persistence in the cause won the grudging admiration even of Jowett, who wanted a Balliol Hall to save the clergy from Marriott's clutches and found none of his friends, not even Stanley, willing to take charge of it.[102]

During 1846 Marriott collected a number of interested friends, including Manning, Gladstone and Sir John Taylor Coleridge who, it was hoped, would divert a sum of £14,000 for which he was trustee, to the new project.[103] Marriott himself gave a site near Joe Pullen's Tree on Headington Hill,[104] and great efforts were made to raise money. Marriott's estimate for building and endowment was £20,000 in 1846, £35,000 in 1848, and £40,000 by the time public advertisement was made in 1849. Despite support from the high-church press,[105] only a small proportion of the money was raised. By 1851 the proposal had been reduced to a hall,[106] Sewell had despaired of getting anything done,[107] and Provost Hawkins began to tell Marriott that his health would be unequal to the management of a hall if he ever obtained one.[108] By 1856 Marriott's ill-health had finally killed the scheme,[109] and when his party opened Keble College in 1870, it was not a foundation separated from the rest of the university by strict discipline or dedication to the training of poor ordinands. In at least the later stages there were hopes of some support from the Hebdomadal Board, but despite the efforts of R. L. Cotton, Edward Hawkins and Richard Harington, Principal of Brasenose, nothing was obtained. In 1851 high-churchmen and low campaigned furiously to divert the funds proposed for building the museum to providing accommodation for poor students. But after 1853 they could not carry Convocation, and Dr. Jeune defeated their friends at the Board.[110]

Jeune opposed the plan on business grounds. Marriott hoped to emulate Bishop Hatfield's Hall at Durham, and to keep a man for a session for between £65 and £80.[111] Jeune perceived, what subsequent experience has confirmed, that an unendowed hall was not likely to be cheaper than a well-organised college.

'My arrangements', he related, 'consist in turning the kitchen into a cook's shop—fixing a price on every article supplied—allowing all that a young man may be fairly expected to give to his friends, so as to exclude pastry-cooks—and keeping a careful watch over the weekly expenditure . . . the men are satisfied, and I believe no smuggling goes on . . . I believe the men are as comfortably kept in this college (Pembroke) as in any in Oxford. But I should be sorry if the highest account in the college for rent, tuition, servants, college and university dues, coal, washing, glazier and food, including breakfast parties, exceeded £85 or £90 per annum.[112]

Without glorifying poverty the average man lived as cheaply as the most optimistic had hoped from the poor men's hall. Here was the way to fill the redundant sets in Oxford's less fashionable colleges.[113]

However reasonable, the obstructiveness of the Board aggravated the mood of dissatisfaction among the juniors, and the risk that they might again, as in the 'thirties, seize the initiative was exemplified in a spectacular way in 1847. Estcourt was known to be unwilling to serve the university in another parliament, and when he declared his intentions early in May the first steps to settle the succession had already been taken. The first candidate to take the field, with the blessing of the Hebdomadal Board, was Edward Cardwell,[114] a former scholar and fellow of Balliol and a double first. An intimate of Peel, his former secretary of the Treasury, and already highly regarded as a public servant,[115] Cardwell was nephew to his namesake, Principal Cardwell of St. Alban Hall, the Chancellor's private secretary. Cardwell was formally proposed by Warden Williams of New College and supported by 11 other heads;[116] his following showed again that the politics of the Board was less the bigoted toryism of which they have often been accused than the ministerial conservatism which had infuriated the Tractarians. Nor was Dr. Jeune the only liberal who thought a Peelite the best hope for the Oxford seat: Cardwell's committee also included G. H. S. Johnson of Queen's and Hayward Cox, the liberal protestant mouthpiece of Professor Hampden.[117] High-church and low, tory and liberal, thus put forward Cardwell as a man of business in politics who yet fulfilled the ancient canons of being 'independent in circumstances and in mind, and dutifully attached to our institutions in church and state.'

Meanwhile Gladstone's cause had been advanced by an alliance of

London Puseyites, who atone for their religion by their rank, mixing with Tyler, Hume Spry, Saunders of the Charterhouse, Hallam (the whig historian) etc. and . . . an Oxford committee of barefaced Puseyites whom nobody in Oxford but themselves will join.[118]

The *Guardian* ground its usual axe against the Hebdomadal Board alleging that they had surprised the university with Cardwell, and were usurping power,[119] but the first moves on behalf of Gladstone had been made the previous February by R. J. Phillimore, a rising London barrister, and one of his contemporaries at Christ Church.[120] At the last, confusion between the Oxford and London committees almost led to the nomination of Sir William Heathcote in his place, but Gladstone came forward with alacrity, for at the moment he was out of parliament,[121] and there was no other seat from which he could so readily do his life's work for the church.[122]

Not a single head appeared on his committee. His chairman was Richard Greswell, tutor of Worcester, who enjoyed a remarkable influence in this decade.[123] Greswell was one of the five sons of the perpetual curate of Denton in the parish of Manchester, all of whom won Oxford fellowships, and one of whom, Edward, became a theological scholar of some note.[124] Richard became involved in the Tractarian upheaval, and when he vacated his fellowship upon marrying a fortune in 1836, he set up house in Beaumont Street and retained his tutorship. The rest of his life was devoted to good works on behalf of Oxford and the church. He created the gardens at Worcester, and improved the amenities of Port Meadow.[125] After the failure of Graham's Factory Education Bill in 1843 he secured the patronage of Peel and the Primate for one of the most successful of all efforts to raise money for church schools. In 1844 he fought off the compromises proposed by the Warden of Merton, Provost Hawkins and Dr. Cardwell in an agitation for an exclusively church cemetery in Oxford.[126] In 1839 the Vice-Chancellor, Dr. Gilbert, had recommended him very strongly to the duke for appointment as Provost of Worcester; he had reformed the financial and electoral systems of the college, he had provided money for the retirement of aged and inefficient masters from Bromsgrove School (from which Worcester received scholars on Sir Thomas Cooke's foundation), and his scholarship had been acknowledged by a fellowship of the Royal Society.[127] Greswell never attained the dignity of a headship,[128] but remained full of schemes for an institute for the study of art,[129] a museum for the study of science, 'a Tabularium, or Public Registry, for the Diocese of Oxford,'[130] and for raising £50,000 for church building at Denton. As a B.D. he was the senior resident on Gladstone's committee, and acted as chairman until in the 'sixties Gladstone's liberalism proved too much.

Gladstone's committee was composed mainly of resident fellows and tutors of whom only Frederick Temple had liberal inclinations at this time. Gladstone always irked the Oxford liberals and was now bitterly attacked as a Tractarian by the *Oxford Protestant Magazine*.[131] He claimed never to have read the tracts, and to be libelled on account of his votes for Ward in 1845,[132] but even before the election his churchmanship caused concern to friend and foe alike. Gladstone was moving towards the ideal of a free church in a free state, and was already convinced that the Anglican ascendancy could hardly be defended in its present shape. As a matter of religion the friends of the church should be prepared to revise it according to circumstances. The immediate question was whether he would support the endowment of the Irish Catholic priesthood from the funds of the Irish Church. Gladstone refused absolutely to give a pledge, and admitted privately that although he could not see his way to such a scheme, he doubted whether it was just or prudent for the Irish Church to retain the whole of its revenues.[133]

The ancient Oxford orthodoxies were affronted by both Cardwell and Gladstone. Each advocated free trade which was expected to reduce tithes by a quarter; each had favoured the Maynooth grant, and in the famous phrase of the *Times*, the anti-popery fire-engine played on both candidates with absolute impartiality.[134] It was clear that the orthodoxies were now less dear to residents either senior or junior, than to the clerical mob in Convocation, but candidates pressed forward to stand on the double platform of protestantism and protection.[135] An attempt to launch Dr. Marsham, Warden of Merton, whose protectionism had long made him the butt of the *Times*,[136] failed, and finally a meeting at the house of Dr. Ogilvie, professor of pastoral theology, adopted the member for North Essex, Charles Gray Round. Round had been a first-class man at Balliol thirty years before, and had consistently voted in the interest of church and protection. Behind him were protestant high-church men like Faussett, Ogilvie, Vaughan Thomas, and Golightly, evangelicals such as John Hill[137] (and the more rabid evangelical journals), and also the Tractarian fellow-traveller Sewell, who had protested and walked out of Gladstone's adoption meeting, because Gladstone had supported a ministry which encouraged heresy and schism.[138] Six heads also supported his cause.[139] In Oxford as elsewhere party was falling into confusion. The favour of tories and protestant high-churchmen was divided among the three candidates, and liberal support between Cardwell and Gladstone with a preponderance to the former. Most of the evangelicals supported Round, but the more intelligent favoured Cardwell or Gladstone.[140] The Tractarians mostly backed Gladstone, but Sewell came out for Round. Even the college was no longer an electioneering unit. Old Dr. Routh could not vote for Gladstone because his election would give both seats to Christ Church;[141] on the other hand, both Cardwell and Round were Balliol men.

The election was fought with great acrimony. The friends of Round and Gladstone represented them as friends of the church. But Round was shown to have supported Peel against Inglis in 1829, and to have attended a dissenting chapel on a few occasions in recent years. The other side alleged that Gladstone's sister, under his influence, had gone over to Rome; they magnified his votes for Ward into sinister horrors, and pointed out that to return Gladstone and Inglis would nullify the voting power of the university in the house.[142] In this affray there was very little room for Cardwell, who appeared like Gladstone but on every count inferior, and a creature of the Hebdomadal Board to boot. His London committee was Peelite in the narrowest sense,[143] and on June 21 Cardwell's friends acknowledged defeat and withdrew him.

The issue was now much simpler. Most of the liberals now came over to Gladstone,[144] and F. D. Maurice pleaded powerfully for protestant voters to support him rather than Round.[145] The *Times* summed up the contest in his favour.[146] Preparations were made for a record poll, and Arthur Haddan of Trinity, one of Gladstone's Oxford secretaries, who had learned his canvassing in the contest for the poetry chair in 1842, tracked down all but 600 of the names in the university calendar.[147] Only the heads, their candidate gone, were outside the mêlée (five ultimately abstained). On the day the horde of electors, who had been brought up in fleets of special coaches, stampeded in to vote. When voters began to faint under the pressure the Vice-Chancellor ordered the windows of the Convocation House to be broken to admit the air; but he could not cope with the press and 240 voters were paired off by the rival committees.[148] Both parties agreed to support Inglis, but Gladstone held the second place all the way and defeated Round by 997 votes to 824.

At once the analysts got to work. Sixteen heads had voted on the losing side, only four with the majority. J. B. Mozley was jubilant:

> First we have bowled out eleven heads of houses and Cardwell. Secondly we have bowled them all out again, and Round. And thirdly—which is a spice for the simply malignant to relish— Round himself has lost his seat in Essex in consequence.[149]

The Hebdomadal Board had not been so badly outmanoeuvred by the juniors since the Hampden affair of 1836. Equally striking was the distribution of talent. Gladstone polled 157 firsts against Round's 46, 45 Chancellor's prizemen against Round's 12, 218 foundationers against Round's 128. These statistics vividly illuminated the changes in the university since the great election of 1829. Then Peel had been defeated, but he had polled almost half the heads, and the great preponderance of talent; Newman had reviled his party as intellectual philistines. The Peelite candidate still attracted the talent among the voters, but he was now the choice not only of the majority, but also of the Tractarians. The men who had denounced the 'march of mind' in 1829 were now by force of circumstances allied with it, and the political evolution of Gladstone was to have a profound influence on their development as a party. In 1829 Keble had insisted that the university should not swerve by a hair's breadth from its old constitutional doctrine. In 1847 he declared that Gladstone (who avowedly expected revision of the ascendancy) was 'Pusey in a blue coat: & what can be said more for any layman? . . . I am so sure of him that I dont at all mind here and there a speech or a vote wch. I cant explain.'[150] The older leaders' personal trust in Gladstone was often tried, but Keble's loyalty was lifelong,[151] and the enthusiasm of the younger men, nourished weekly by the *Guardian*, took them with him gradually into liberalism, and enabled them to transform the rigid orthodoxy and high tory politics of the early apostolicals into the liberal catholicism of Gore and the *Lux Mundi* group.

Before the year was out there were new demonstrations of hostility by the juniors towards the heads, and of the trials to which Gladstone was to expose his friends; the reforming progress of the Tractarians was also interrupted. In November Lord John Russell announced the appointment of Dr. Hampden to the see of Hereford, and at once a great storm broke. Jowett who despised Hampden, was nevertheless willing to write on his behalf,[152] but Charles Marriott prepared charges of heresy,[153] and the Tractarians found themselves again a ginger group in a wildly indignant body of juniors.[154] At this inauspicious moment the majority of the heads, ignoring the warning of Edward Cardwell and Richard Jenkyns, chose to publish an address of confidence in Hampden's character and orthodoxy,[155] and obstructed the efforts of his opponents to obtain extracts from the university registers to use against him.[156] Fourteen of the fifteen heads who signed the address had been supporters of Round at the last election, and generous as their act was, they could hardly have emphasised more imprudently their isolation from university opinion.[157] The episode was also calculated to imbue the whole university with the high-church party's suspicion of Lord John. For as Whately came out with an angular defence of Hampden,[158] it was confidently reported that his old vice-principal at St. Alban Hall, Samuel Hinds, who had followed him to Ireland, was to be preferred to the regius chair of divinity.[159] This provocative appointment never came to pass,[160] and the chair went to William Jacobson, vice-principal of Magdalen Hall, whose opinions were 'moderately liberal, and not tory.'[161] Nevertheless the appointment of Prince Lee,

11

a former assistant master at Rugby, to the new see of Manchester, suggested that the hour had struck for the connexion of Whately and Arnold, [162] and within a few weeks John Graham, who had advocated the admission of dissenters at Cambridge, was made bishop of Chester. In the eyes of all except the small liberal group at Oxford, Russell was now damned, and any suggestion of university reform promoted by his ministry was rejected out of hand. If there was anyone against whom university independence must be maintained, it was Lord John Russell.

In December 1847, while this controversy was at its height, Gladstone created a rival sensation by voting with the government for the removal of Jewish disabilities. The previous September he had admitted privately that if the admission of Jews to parliament could be made to enlarge liberties for the church he would support it,[163] but his constituents and even his father were taken by surprise. The Hebdomadal Board, against the advice of Dr. Jeune,[164] had prepared a petition against the Jews which had passed Convocation by 52 votes to 10.[165] Pusey told Gladstone he would never have voted for him could he have foreseen this issue; for his soul's sake he should be out of parliament.[166] Haddan reported that he would have no hope of re-election should he have to face his constituents for some time to come.[167] Even Provost Hawkins who as a young man had advocated the admission of Jews, now turned against them,[168] and the Rector of Exeter thought that the Hebdomadal Board would not recommend the new burgess's usual honour of a D.C.L. degree.[169] This indignity Gladstone was spared, and he regained some ground among his constituents by publishing his speech with an explanatory introduction;[170] but already he experienced two great inconveniences in his coveted seat. Every readjustment of the relations of church and state must grieve some of his clerical constituents, and because of the outmoded convention that no politician might canvass in the constituency, he could not come down to explain his votes. Gladstone was muzzled, and muzzled he remained till he went off to South Lancashire in 1865.

The opposition between the heads and the talent in the university revealed in Gladstone's election, was revealed again as the tutors began to take up the cause of university reform. The most obviously vulnerable point in the university system was the useless professoriate, and in the spring of 1846 the professors submitted a memorandum to the Board, urging that the examination system be modified to include the modern sciences and literature upon which they lectured, or, at the very least, that they be provided with classes by requiring undergraduates to attend their courses as they had recommended in 1839. Proposals for changes in the examination system opened the door to panaceas of all kinds. Whately revived his old plan of a matriculation examination to raise the level at entrance to the present pass degree standard, and recommended the award of superior degrees upon a competitive basis.[171] On June 13, a leader in the *Oxford Herald* urged that residence for the B.A. degree be reduced, and natural science be incorporated in the examination.[172] More important the Hebdomadal Board appointed a committee to consider the whole matter,[173] and Dr. Jeune began to press upon the board a plan which underlay the whole later discussion. More work should be exacted from undergraduates by increasing the number of their examinations from two to three, and making responsions early enough to fulfil some of the functions of a matriculation examination.

The year 1847 with its mounting threat of state intervention increased the urgency of the whole matter.[174] Osborne Gordon, tutor of Christ Church, produced an elaborate development of Jeune's plan, which considerably increased the burden upon passmen and proposed to require two honours schools from the classmen, Greats and one of three new options: history and philosophy, disciplinae mathematicae, disciplinae physicae.[175] High-churchmen no longer believed that Oxford studies as they stood were superior to all others; the *Guardian* urged the tutors to take the matter into their own hands, and, emboldened by their success in carrying Gladstone's election, they did so.

Early in March 1848 a memorial based on Jeune's scheme[176] was presented to the Hebdomadal Board with the support of 59 of the 63 college tutors. The request was for three examinations, the last of which should 'comprise theology, moral philosophy, history (ancient or modern) or mathematical and physical science.'[177] This memorial arose from deliberations among the tutors during the winter which revealed an unexpected degree of agreement,[178] and which foreshadowed the more formal organisation of the Tutors' Association five years later. In this revolutionary year even the Hebdomadal Board responded to the winds of change; a committee was appointed and the principle of the three examinations accepted at once.[179] The heads almost agreed to create a joint delegacy of heads and masters to draft a statute. Their committee was accessible, and they circulated their report privately among the tutors, and willingly received a deluge of suggestions.

The earliest and most celebrated of these was an anonymous tract put out by Jowett and Stanley.[180] They urged the general view that the passmen had not enough to do, and while disclaiming any intention of transforming Oxford into a Scottish or a German university, they wished in the new final schools to find something for the professors. One of the peculiarities of Jowett's plan was that there should be a final school of theology; immediately the objection came from Robert Hussey, professor of ecclesiastical history, which was constantly to be heard in the next twenty years, that sacred studies would be demeaned by being made 'the vehicle of academical honours.'[181] Moreover, high-church critics swiftly perceived that the theology recommended was like Hamlet without the Prince of Denmark, for it consisted solely of biblical criticism, and ommitted dogmatic works such as Pearson on the Creed. Even Butler gave place to Adam Smith and Ricardo.[182]

The evangelical Robert Walker thought that theology was better retained as a post-graduate study, and that Jowett had not classified the physical sciences properly. But with the general scheme he was in sympathy.[183] Charles Daubeny also thought little of Jowett's classification of the sciences, and pointed out that the effect of the present examination system was not merely to displace professors by college tutors, but to displace college tutors by private tutors. There should be a natural sciences school as well as a mathematics and physics school.[184] Henry Acland pleaded for the inclusion of some elementary science in the basic arts course, and although he was not yet ready for the formation of a medical school, thought that the university ought to catch the tide of medical reform by founding 'a school for the branches of knowledge introductory to the study of practical medicine.'[185] And the friends of the other defunct superior faculty, that of civil law, pleaded for new life to be breathed into the dead bones.[186]

During the Trinity Term 1848 the heads did their best to digest this barrage of comment, and after fresh rumours of state intervention in the Long Vacation, a majority was found for a draft statute during the Michaelmas term. Early in 1849 the crisis of actual legislation was reached, to the accompaniment of high-church growls that the tutors had not been taken into partnership, and the examiners not consulted at all. Discussions began towards the formation of a 'Tutorial Society' to keep a continuous pressure on the Board.[187] The main principles of the heads' plan had underlain the discussion from the beginning; there were to be three examinations and all candidates were to graduate in Greats and one of three other schools, mathematics, natural sciences or history. Attendance at two professorial courses was to be required. Points of detail apart, criticism of the draft fastened on two chief issues, the fourth school and the appointment of examiners. To high-churchmen the proposed history school was at best a soft option to be prepared for by 'historical novels or novel-like histories, as Macaulay's,' and at worst a liberal conspiracy.[188] Provost Hawkins feared that it would allow some of the best men to leak away without a proper mental discipline,[189] while even the liberal Clough thought that the school needed the 'stronger aliment of political economy.'[190] To the Oxford devotees of standard texts the project looked impossible.

Where is the *standard-author,* like Thucydides, Xenophon, Herodotus or Livy? And if there be none, and the examiner and candidate have studied *different* historians, as they well may, the acquirements of the candidate may be most praiseworthy, and yet be wholly inappreciable by the examiner.[191]

The appointment of examiners proved a controversial question for a generation. The draft proposed to transfer the nomination of examiners from the Vice-Chancellor and Proctors to professorial boards. Since the examiners called the tune to which the whole university danced, this provision was potentially very important, and was debated with more than the normal abuse and confusion. The defenders of the colleges talked about 'the jobbery of boards' and regarded 'the patronage of the Proctors . . . [as] patronage in the hands of the resident body of Masters.' On the other hand it was pointed out that the Proctors

> are . . . appointed according to an unequal cycle, which as a general rule gives the greater number of turns to the colleges least interested in the promotion of education; who are commonly elected by seniority by their own colleges and are under strong temptation to elect others according to the same rule from their own colleges; who, further, being often non-residents before and after their year of office, have neither the knowledge nor responsibility which residence would involve.

To which it was replied that the calendars showed very little correspondence between the colleges from which the examiners and the Proctors came.[192] Bedevilling the question was the ancient rivalry between the colleges and the university.

Convocation assembled to pass judgment on March 20, Jowett trembling for the statute after the *Guardian* had declared against it.[193] The interesting feature of the Convocation was that the colleges dissuaded non-residents from coming up to disturb the patient labours of the residents, and few appeared apart from the headmasters of the great public schools. Here was plainly foreshadowed the Congregation of the reformed university, and an acknowledged initiative in the hands of the residents. The Hebdomadal Board divided the statute into 28 parts, and in the course of a five-hour session divisions were taken on each, so that the loss of some parts did not involve the loss of the whole.[194] The effect of the voting was to preserve the main lines of the statute, but to reject most of the details, including those most dear to the liberals. The principle of three examinations was carried by 197 votes to 23, the establishment of a natural sciences school unanimously, and compulsory attendance at professorial lectures by a huge majority. On the other hand the appointment of examiners by boards was decisively defeated, and the modern history school went down by six votes. The significance of the voting was two-fold. Important changes of principle had been adopted, and the statute as it now stood embodied the professors' ancient nostrum that a liberal education should include compulsory science; but many details remained to be filled in. The only changes which the Hebdomadal Board had been able to carry were those which the general body of tutors and professors approved. The case for making the body initiating legislation more representative of the opinion of the residents had been underlined.[195]

The revised statute was not ready for Convocation till the following December, and with the political sky darkening the heads showed a surprising penchant for liberal lost causes. The fourth school re-appeared as a school of history and jurisprudence, and so did the appointment of examiners by boards. As passions rose it proved impossible to confine the issue to the residents; the liberal *Globe* appealed to sympathetic out-voters, and the *Guardian* replied on the other side. Again slow progress was made. The principle of a modern history school was accepted by 14 votes, but on the plea of the new regius professor, H. H. Vaughan,[196] all the details were lost; George Anthony Denison made his famous 'nolumus Germanizari' speech, and J. W. Burgon groaned that the university had yielded to the spirit of the times.[197] Convocation would not have the boards, nor the principle that a candidate might have the highest honours by allowing great strength in one subject to compensate for mere laudable proficiency in another.[198] In March 1850 the deferred portions of the statute were promulgated again. The history syllabus bore a closer correspondence with the schemes of H. H. Vaughan,[199] and the introduction of Adam Smith testified to 'the stronger aliment of political economy.' But the appointment of examiners was to be in the hands of boards at least for the final schools in the new subjects.[200] There was clearly a case for having boards where a new system had to be established, but the opposition had taken root,[201] and when Convocation met on April 23 the boards were again thrown out by 163 votes to 90.[202] The syllabus of the modern history school was strongly criticised by E. A. Freeman, for whom the initial date of 1066 was not nearly early enough, and attacked root and branch by G. A. Denison, but it was accepted by 127 votes to 74.[203] Dean Gaisford made a last despairing attempt to save something for professors,[204] but the Board decided to give way on the appointment of examiners, and in May the powers of the Vice-Chancellor and Proctors were extended to the new schools.[205]

It had thus taken four years to secure a new examination statute which was in principle similar to that proposed by Jeune in 1846, and even then the college interest had carried the day in the appointment of examiners. The Oxford liberals were dissatisfied with this progress, and were not reassured by the chequered history of two other schemes for the diversification of Oxford studies, the Taylorian Institute and the new museum. In 1848, after long delays, the Taylorian, a foundation for the teaching of modern languages created under the will of an eighteenth-century architect, was at last ready, and the curators were expected to elect to a new chair in the field. The chair had been advertised in 1847, and an election had been expected in the Michaelmas term; no election was made, and early in 1848 rumours circulated that the curators were trying to secure the services of Guizot.[206] There was at once a public outcry. The *Times* denounced the idea as 'nothing less than a gross *job*,' partly because of the affront given to English philology, partly because Guizot was not a philologist at all.[207] The *Guardian* urged Convocation to reject a man who was not an Anglican and had behaved disgracefully over the Spanish Marriages.[208] Jowett conceived that the evangelicals were trying to sacrifice modern literature to science.[209] Guizot declined the offer,[210] but it was not till 1850 that another non-Anglican and liberal, Max Müller, was appointed deputy professor.[211]

If the university got into a scrape in the inauguration of a lavish endowment, the prospects were dim for the creation of a new scientific museum for which the funds had to be raised. Kidd, Richard Greswell and others had long made use of the Ashmolean Society for extending scientific studies in Oxford. As soon as the natural sciences school was created a meeting was held in New College to raise funds for the creation of a new museum which should house the existing scientific collections, Hope's new entomological bequest, the laboratories and lecture-rooms which would be needed for the new teaching, and the scientific library which Greswell had been building up. Greswell undertook to raise funds, but he was now too well known as a sturdy beggar. His appeals to the five wealthiest men in the university (Gaisford, Jenkyns, Cardwell, Ogilvie and Canon Bull) were fruitless, and the subscription was a total failure.[212] The Vice-Chancellor, however, considered it 'very important at this crisis that the university should appear to the world to be doing something,' and accordingly persuaded the Board to propose to Convocation that a large part of the sum of £60,000 which had just accrued from the profits of the press should be devoted to the museum. The fate of the proposal might have been foreseen. Although Pusey and Marriott were on the Museum Committee the Tractarians could not allow that the profits from prayer books should be expended upon sciences which attracted no students, rather than upon the sons of poor clergy and university extension. The *Guardian* ridiculed such extravagance 'in building a receptacle

for dried insects,' and the scheme was rejected by 88 votes to 47.[213]
University reform was needed before the museum could be
established.

Almost everything that had happened since 1848 confirmed the
high-churchmen in the belief that the heads had lost their senses,
and convinced the liberals that Oxford would not be saved without
outside intervention. Their nonconformist allies now renewed their
pressure. Neither the *Edinburgh* nor the *Prospective Review* was
satisfied with the reforms of 1849, and the *Inquirer* called for the
abrogation of University oaths and tests. In the summer James
Heywood gave notice of a motion for a commission of inquiry into
the ancient universities with a view to the improvement of national
education, but made no progress.[214] In Oxford, Stanley and Jowett
were at work on the history of the university and a plan for its
reform, and were not only laying the foundations of the blue book
of 1852, but were recruiting help from men like Goldwin Smith,
Temple and Johnson, who were to take a leading part in the enforcement of reform from the outside.[215] Before this work could be finished
it was suspended, because the longed-for commission was appointed,
and Stanley was its secretary.

On April 23, 1850, James Heywood again introduced his motion
for a royal commission on the universities. His speech, like some of
his books, was a farrago of all the charges which the radicals had
levelled at the universities in the last generation.[216] Few expected
anything to arise from this hardy annual,[217] and even the unitarians
were disillusioned and confused. They had just obtained their ideal
of an undenominational, professorial and German university at
Owens College, Manchester, only to find that the Trustees were
trying to promote religious education by the Principal, and the
Inquirer made an astonishingly blimpish attack upon Heywood (one
of the trustees) which wound up by pleading for the admission of
the dissenters into the ancient universities and against all other
innovations.[218] The Oxford liberals, however, were not only dissatisfied at the rate of progress in Oxford, but suspected from Russell's
reception of the deputation in 1848 that he might yield to pressure.
Stanley who had influence in whig circles, pressed him privately to
take up their cause now,[219] and Jeune stated a case for a commission
which Russell made the basis of his speech.[220] Just before the
adjournment of the debate Russell announced that he could not agree
to Heywood's motion which amounted to an indictment of the
universities, but that he would advise the Crown to issue a royal
commission of inquiry.[221]

In the following week Prince Albert begged him to leave the
inquiry to the universities,[222] the resumption of the debate was twice
postponed, and each side exerted pressure on Lord John.[223] Jowett,

Stanley, Lake and Goldwin Smith wrote privately to the Premier urging him to live up to his resolution,[224] William Thomson of Queen's obtained an interview,[225] and Goldwin Smith reinforced their pleas by a series of letters in the Times over the signature 'Oxoniensis', setting forth a scheme for a reformed professoriate and fellowship system.[226] Lake made a desperate appeal to Gladstone, urging that the university was crippled for lack of the profound learning which a professoriate might supply.[227] The Hebdomadal Board, on the other hand, in the absence of Dr. Jeune, published a manifesto asserting that all was well with university,[228] but Wellington recommended them to hold their peace,[229] and although a group of tutors was formed at Exeter to watch events with a view to agitation,[230] the main effort went into briefing the university members.[231] When the debate came on on July 18, Roundell Palmer challenged the legality of a royal commission, and argued that a commission was in any case irrelevant to the real tasks of university reform which depended on the education of public opinion. Gladstone strongly opposed the commission, while not doubting that its inquiries must redound to Oxford's credit. The commission would be contrary to 'the principle of local freedom of independence in local institutions' which was basic to our way of life, and no convincing case had been made out for an inquiry. The government, however, would not yield, and they obtained a majority of 22.[232]

During the Long Vacation Russell attempted without success to obtain the cooperation of the Hebdomadal Board in the nomination of the commissioners,[233] and after casting aside Professor Daubeny and H. H. Vaughan,[234] he produced a distinguished liberal team. At the head was the Bishop of Norwich, none other than Samuel Hinds, Whately's old henchman. A. C. Tait had led the liberal assault upon Tractarianism, and Dr. Jeune after pushing the Hebdomadal Board into reform, had propelled Lord John Russell towards appointing the commission.[235] J. L. Dampier was appointed 'to keep the commission right in its law,' and Baden Powell to uphold the interests of science. Of equal distinction were H. G. Liddell, headmaster of Westminster, and G. H. S. Johnson, fellow of Queen's, who had had an outstanding career in both the classical and mathematical lines, and had held the chairs of both astronomy and moral philosophy.[236] The secretary to the commission was A. P. Stanley, whose recent studies of university history were reinforced by Goldwin Smith's appointment as assistant secretary; for his contribution to the work projected by Jowett and Stanley, Goldwin Smith had had the access to college muniments which was to be denied to the commission.[237]

This eminent body was coldly received. Jowett regarded Baden Powell as 'odious,'[238] while old Dr. Jenkyns, Master of Balliol, exploded with 'indignation and resentment.'[239] The appointment of Dr. Jeune posed an acute problem for the heads. On October 21 the Principal of Brasenose carried a motion at the Board that 'all matters relative to the commission of enquiry should be referred to a committee to consist of all members of the Board with the exception of the Master of Pembroke.' The conscience of the majority was not easy at this device, and a week later after Jeune had given assurances that he would not attend when the commission was under discussion, the motion was rescinded.[240] The commission had no powers to compel witnesses to give evidence, and Brougham argued from the beginning that this would mean that evidence would be offered only by its friends;[241] the *Guardian* continued to insist that the report must inevitably be partisan.

Many doubted whether the commission was legal. In 1839 a Cambridge don had argued that

> one of the objects of the Ecclesiastical Commissions issued by James II was to visit 'the universities;' yet as that, and 'all other commissions of a like nature,' were then declared to be 'illegal and pernicious,' our institutions may be regarded as secure from the invasion of Royal Commissioners, so long as the Bill of Rights is suffered to remain unmutilated.[242]

J. W. Pycroft, a tory barrister, argued that the rights of the Crown were excluded by the act of 13 Eliz. c.29 which declared that 'all letters patent of the Queen and her predecessors should be as good and effectual as though the said matters were recited in that Act of Parliament.'[243] Nothing short of another act could destroy 'the protection of legislative incorporation'. Early in 1851 the Hebdomadal Board obtained counsel's opinion that the commission was illegal, and that most of the 57 others which had preceded it since 1815 had probably been illegal too.[244] Brasenose College which had never intended to cooperate,[245] obtained a similar opinion, and gave a general lead to the colleges in refusing to give information.[246]

In May the Hebdomadal Board resolved to petition the queen to withdraw the commission (whose legality was affirmed by the Crown lawyers),[247] and in Convocation could command the support both of those opposed to outside intervention in general, and of the large body who distrusted Lord John Russell. Charles Neate of Oriel pressed that it was much too late to begin resistance, and that a request for voluntary information could not possibly be unlawful;[248] the commissioners whipped in their non-resident liberal friends, but the most strenuous exertions could only raise them 105 votes against 249.[249] Russell of course did not yield, but there were expectations that his government was breaking up, and would be replaced by the Peelites.[250] In this case Gladstone would put a stop to the commission. In the event Russell survived another year, and Derby who succeeded him was surprised by the Bishop of Norwich into allowing the commission to continue work in Downing Street as before.[251] Much now depended upon the report.

CHAPTER VIII

THE GREAT BLUE BOOK

There is no political power in England like a College in the Universities;
. . . it has allies in every part of the country . . . wherever you look, to
the North or South of England, to the East or West, you find the
interest of Colleges dominant; they extend their roots all over the
country, and can scarcely be overturned, certainly not suddenly overturned, without a revolution.

J. H. NEWMAN, *Rise and progress of the universities* (1854).

CONSERVATIVE opponents of the royal commission spared no pains
to discredit the report in advance. The commission, it was urged, had
been packed with liberals; its conclusions must therefore be a fore-
gone conclusion,[1] and the only witnesses who would appear before
it would be liberals equally dyed-in-the-wool. Neither of these prog-
nostications was fulfilled in the event. The commissioners each took
special responsibility for a portion of the inquiry—Tait for oaths
and university extension, Liddell for the university constitution,
Jeune for the colleges, and so forth. But there were many differences
of opinion,[2] and all Tait and Stanley's soothing syrup was needed
before an agreed report could be presented.[3] Nor was the evidence
all of one kind. H. L. Mansel, fellow and tutor of St. John's, who
rapidly became the philosophical apologist of the Oxford tories,
gave a spirited testimony that undergraduate expenses could not be
reduced by any measure within the grasp of the university, and that
university extension was a delusion in an age of great commercial
and professional competition, for a general education could never
supply the means of making money. Moreover, each intellectual
specialism tended to develop its own habitat, and it was hopeless to
try to centralise all learning within the universities. Mansel yielded
an inch to the liberals on the professorial system. He did not 'believe
that a tyro is likely to be well *grounded* in any branch of study by
being *talked at in large classes*,' but he thought that almost the only
hope in this country for the growth of 'speculation . . . not directly
applied to the invention or improvement of material comforts' lay
in the provision of university endowments.[4] Another good conservative, Robert Scott, who in 1854 succeeded to the headship of
Balliol also testified in favour of the professors,[5] and among the
liberals who gave evidence was that most eccentric of them all,
E. A. Freeman, who had fought tooth and nail against the new

examination statute, and especially against the establishment of a
school of modern history.[6]

Nevertheless, the evidence was of a predominantly liberal cast,
and most of the leading liberals of the past and present generation
submitted memoranda, H. H. Wilson, Robert Walker, Richard
Whately, Hayward Cox, John Conington, Frederick Temple,
Richard Congreve, W. C. Lake, Bonamy Price, Mark Pattison,
Jowett and H. H. Vaughan among others. The evidence of the last
three was of special importance. Vaughan was the object of 'idolatry'
on the part of Liddell,[7] who made the regius professor's proposals
the basis for the commission's discussions on the reorganisation of
the university constitution.[8] Vaughan pleaded the orthodox liberal
case that what Oxford needed was more, more prosperous, more
learned and more influential professors.

> That a university in the higher sense of the term should exist
> without such a class seems almost impossible; and it would be
> wasteful to possess it, or call it into existence, without assigning
> to it an important place in legislation and management.

Vaughan proposed to create a new administrative and legislative body
out of the present Hebdomadal Board reinforced by the Professors
and a small number of M.A.s elected by Convocation. The tutorial
system should be adjusted so as to permit compulsory attendance
upon professors' lectures, and professors should also control the
examination system.[9] Jowett had not the immediate access to the
ear of the commission enjoyed by Vaughan, but his intimate
association with the two secretaries was bound to give weight to his
views. Jowett averred that

> the unsettled state of opinion in Oxford during the last 15 years
> is in a great measure attributable to the want of a Professorial
> System. There have been 'no oracles at which to go and inquire.'

The loss of Thomas Arnold, the one prophet of Stanley's generation
of Oxford liberals, proved indeed irreparable, but Jowett set out to
fortify the remnant, whose strength might be expected to lie among
the professors, so many of whom were appointed by the Crown.
Jowett would have no truck with any system of representation, which
he thought likely to put down the 'minority . . . possessed of the
greater share of intelligence and talent,' and recommended that the
government of the university be entrusted to the Hebdomadal Board
together with a revived professoriate. The tutors must be content
with appointment by grace on special delegacies.[10] So much for
Sewell's conservative doctrine of 14 years before that

> a tutorial system of education has always been connected with

monarchical principles and institutions—a professorial almost always with a democracy.[11]

Mark Pattison later admitted that his 'evidence acquired a peculiar importance and notoriety as being the solitary defence of the *status quo* coming from the Liberal side.'[12] He contributed a characteristic defence of the tutorial system from the standpoint of a successful tutor, and damned the professorial system as producing an 'inferior stamp of mental cultivation.'[13]

On many important points there was widespread agreement among the witnesses. No-one now regarded the Hebdomadal Board as an adequate governing body, and some thought that Congregation might be revived to give the working residents a lead in the government of the university. There was also almost universal agreement on the need to strengthen and develop the professoriate; most witnesses believed that professorial teaching could be fitted in with the tutorial system,[14] though on the one side A. H. Clough doubted the use of high-grade lectures for low-grade passmen, and on the other John Wilkinson, Rector of Broughton Gifford and sometime postmaster of Merton, thought there was very little at all to be said for college tuition. There was strong support for the opening of all foundations, and a great deal of favour for the idea that the university could attract larger numbers by permitting halls of various kinds to be opened. Jowett, it is true, thought it unlikely that unendowed halls would be cheaper than colleges, and both Hayward Cox and Henry Wall thought that new halls would, like the old, become asylums for students ejected from the colleges. The belief that independent halls offered a practical means of opening the university to new classes consorted oddly with the universal pessimism at the possibility of reducing the cost of the ordinary college education. Almost all the witnesses thought that fees and battells admitted of little reduction, and that in an imperfect world the extravagance of young men was only to be expected. Even Henry Wall, fellow of Balliol and Vice-Principal of St. Alban Hall, who thought that sharp reductions in college charges were possible, despaired of putting down private extravagance, and could only hope that financial prudence would be encouraged if much more work were demanded.

The commissioners met assiduously to digest the mass of information put before them and in eighteen months produced a report of the first importance. They began by insisting that the university must have undisputed power to alter the Laudian Code.[15] Then after stressing the weight of dissatisfaction with the Hebdomadal Board, they proceeded to constitutional reforms which they claimed would secure the advantages of the various schemes which had been pressed upon them. Their object was to give the working members of the

university some share in the initiative at present monopolised by the
Board, and to give the residents more effective opportunities to
discuss legislative proposals than were provided by Latin speeches in
Convocation. Their proposal (much influenced by Vaughan) was to
revive Congregation, the ancient house of the teachers of the university. It should be composed of the Hebdomadal Board together with
the professors and public lecturers, and as a sop to the rank and file,
with the senior tutor of each college as well. They should deliberate
in English upon measures proposed by themselves or by the Hebdomadal Board, meeting whenever the Vice-Chancellor received a
requisition from a given number of the members. The inconveniences
of preparing measures in an assembly of over a hundred could be
overcome by appointing delegacies. The Hebdomadal Board would
retain its administrative functions, and Convocation its veto. The
other chief constitutional change proposed was a variation upon the
standard liberal doctrine; the professors should enjoy improved
status and be formed into a standing delegacy for the supervision of
studies, examinations and libraries. This implied the establishment in
Oxford of a body very like the Senate recently created in Owens
College, Manchester, which was the prototype of a series of new
university constitutions.[16]

The commissioners did not believe that Oxford's educational
achievement was commensurate with the endowments. They could
see no satisfactory solution to the problem of student extravagance,
but they devoted much thought to enabling frugal students to withdraw from expensive society. Halls affiliated to colleges and independent halls both received their blessing though they admitted that
they did not know how the capital cost was to be met. The only way
in which cheap accommodation could be provided quickly was by
permitting the use of lodgings both to members of colleges and to a
new race of non-collegiate students who should receive their instruction from the officers of the university.[17] Vaughan's arguments
in favour of lodgings told with the commissioners, with Tait
especially,[18] and their recommendations opened a curious chapter
of Oxford history. The university test was excluded from the terms of
the commission, but they criticised it as a barrier to university
extension, and pointed out that in practice it neither excluded all who
were not members of the Church nor included all who were—a
matter which shortly proved embarrassing.[19]

More than half the report on the university was devoted to examinations. The commissioners thought that the principles of the new
statute of 1850 ought to be taken further. A matriculation examination ought to be introduced even at the risk of diminishing the entry
for a time. The new studies promoted in the statute of 1850 should
be encouraged further by ending the privilege of Greats as the

compulsory school. Classical studies (and the rudiments of religion) should be wound up at an intermediate examination, and for the final school there should be four options, Theology, Mental Philosophy and Philology, Jurisprudence and History (including political economy), Mathematical and Physical Science. By this means the increasing narrowness of Oxford studies even within the Greats school would be checked, and some concession made to the need for professional training.[20] For the second time the Oxford liberals affirmed their faith in theology as a discipline for the schools.

A dramatic broadening of the examination system such as the commissioners envisaged would certainly break the back of the tutorial system. Mark Pattison admitted that the college tutors often worked to an indifferent standard, because even within the Greats school, their energies were spread over too broad a field. Private tutors flourished upon their failings and were indispensable for distinction in the schools. A revived system of university teaching would not only raise Oxford's literary repute, it would make possible instruction in new schools with which the colleges could not cope, and might even raise the level of college teaching by opening a career to tutors beyond the college living. Even theological controversy might be stilled in the presence of professorial authority. There was no incompatibility between professorial and tutorial teaching, and, provided the tutors regarded certain hours in the day as sacred to professorial oracles, the two could be harmonised. The professors should be organised in boards corresponding to the four final schools.[21]

The professors and their assistants ought to be chosen as freely as possible and improvements were needed in the patronage of chairs. Of the four chief modes of appointment at present, the commissioners followed the witnesses in condemning elections by Convocation and by small university committees, and approved of appointments by the Crown and by boards of eminent persons outside the university. They were not prepared, however, to recommend that Oxford men should be deprived of all choice; appointment to new chairs should be in the Crown, but elections by Convocation could be transferred to the new Congregation.[22]

To complete a system of four faculty boards new chairs would have to be founded, and since tutors received about £500 per annum, the chairs would have to be endowed with a least £800 if they were to attract men of real eminence.[23] Outside the divinity faculty no Oxford chairs carried anything like this stipend, and in order to find it the commissioners had to deal in detail with the organisation of the colleges.

If the commissioners' recommendations for the university bore the marks of Sir William Hamilton,[24] their discussion of the colleges

sprang from the researches of Jowett, Stanley and Goldwin Smith.
The colleges were shown to have been founded for a variety of
purposes, few of which they now fulfilled.

> They may be defined as charitable foundations for the support
> of poor scholars, with perpetual succession, devoting themselves
> to study and prayer, administering their own affairs, under the
> presidency of a Head within, and the control of a Visitor without,
> according to Statutes which were to be neither altered nor
> modified, and which were sanctioned by solemn oaths.[25]

The colleges were no longer eleemosynary; the children of the poor
were not received at All Souls; and the only wealth against which
colleges discriminated was landed property. Even in the seventeenth
century there had been between 400 and 500 poor students, many of
them at Magdalen, All Souls and New College which now received
small numbers and men of a very different kind. Nowhere did the
fellows observe the rule of common life to which they were bound,
and for 300 years masses and prayers for the dead had been illegal.
Few fellows resided for purposes of study in the sense intended by
the founders, and the bulk of those who were educated in the colleges
studied at their own expense and not that of the foundation. The
Visitors had long since ceased any regular inquiry into the observance
of the statutes.[26] Founders' wills had little relevance to contemporary
practice, and there was no impropriety in replacing college statutes
by others more in harmony with the times. Oaths to retain statutes
unchanged should in future be prohibited.

Foremost among the changes demanded by the commission was
the opening of the fellowships. Free trade in talent was as much a
liberal dogma as free trade in goods; only 22 of the 542 fellowships
in the university were reckoned to be really open, but the repute
they had won seemed to settle the issue. The commission did not
acknowledge the fact that closeness unaccompanied by other vices
did not destroy a college reputation; the Christ Church record for
example had once been unrivalled in the schools, and Brasenose, a
very close college, had provided itself with first-class men as tutors
almost without a break since classes had been introduced.[27] Moreover,
so many fellowships came open every year that practically all first-
class men who wished were elected somewhere, and a good proportion of the seconds too. The common rooms of Balliol and Oriel
might be less dazzling once they lost the monopoly of creaming off
the talent. Nevertheless, a general opening of foundations would
simplify the whole system and offer the means of cleansing such
Augean stables as the Blundell's foundation at Balliol and the
Abingdon scholarships at Pembroke.[28]

The commissioners did not recommend that the obligation upon fellows to reside should be enforced; fellowships should continue to give men the means of beginning a professional career away from the university. On the other hand fellows should not be required to take orders, an obligation which the commissioners regarded as an invincible temptation to hypocrisy. Conington argued strongly against the obligation of fellows to remain celibate, and instances (such as Hampden at Oriel and Greswell at Worcester) were not rare of colleges employing married men as tutors who were no longer fellows. The commissioners, however, thought it impossible to provide married quarters in college for any but the heads, and thought that if fellows were allowed to marry they would almost all do so and move into the town, leaving the undergraduates without super-vision within the walls. Subsequent experience bore out this expecta-tion, if not the hope of the commission that an enlarged professoriate would enable the university to retain the services of able teachers who wished to marry. The other major question was whether the succession to fellowships maintained at present by marriage and ecclesiastical preferment should be accelerated by direct enactment. All the Pembroke witnesses and Dr. Jeune were in favour of limiting the tenure of fellowships to a certain number of years in order not only to increase the turnover, but to compel fellows to qualify themselves for a profession within a limited time. The majority on the board however, were unwilling to impose any new restrictions upon fellow-ships until it was absolutely necessary.[29]

The most revolutionary proposals sprang from the conviction that there were too many fellowships. An average of 35 fellowships fell vacant each year, and there was an average of 13 first-class men. At present one in every eight graduates could be provided for, and the appropriation of such an enormous capital to sinecures could not be justified. Some fellowships ought plainly to be devoted to the new studies, but the dismal history of Oxford mathematics suggested that the colleges would give little voluntary encouragement to any-thing other than Greats. Some fellowships should therefore be compulsorily appropriated to other studies. Other fellowships should be suppressed in order to increase the number and value of open scholarships, and to endow university teachers. The tutorial system was not only intrinsically faulty; it was likely to get worse as places worth much more than £500 per annum multiplied in the church, the professions and the public schools. Some at least of the college founders (as at Magdalen and Corpus) had appropriated college funds to the support of university lecturers, and colleges should now support the professors and their deputies by suppressing fellowships or uniting them with chairs like the canonries at Christ Church.[30] Here was the tangible evidence that the university was to be built up at the expense of the colleges, and the commissioners wound up their report by applying their recommendations to each society in detail.

The reception of the report in the press and influential society marked its publication as a point of no return. Few blue books had ever sold as well, and as the subject was one on which members of the educated classes all reckoned to have opinions, there was protracted discussion in the press. From the moment of publication in May 1852 the tone of the comment was set in journals as politically various as the *Times* and the high-church *Guardian*; each agreed that the report was a notable achievement and must be taken seriously.[31] The

> attack on the independence and self-action of the universities and the Church at large, which it essentially belongs both to the traditional policy and the substantial interest of the Russell clique to organize and prosecute by every means in their power

and which the *Guardian* had confidently prophesied,[32] had not come to pass, and the *Times* thought the colleges had been fortunate to escape the recommendation that their property should be handed over to centralised management as capitular property had been taken over by the Ecclesiastical Commission.[33] In the autumn the liberal press prepared for the next session of parliament by using the report to support a crusade against chartered privilege.[34] The *Edinburgh Review* acknowledged the report as its offspring, but felt that the commission should have claimed more for professors, and taken more seriously the fact that college tuition, having supplanted that of the university, was now largely supplanted by that of the private tutors.[35] The nonconformists also hailed the report, but in a variety of tones which exposed their deep divisions on all the educational issues of these years. The unitarian *Prospective Review* saw no alternative to outside interference with the university, but was deeply impressed with the affection which Oxford had inspired even in those of her sons who called most loudly for change, and with the philosophical temper inculcated by the Greats school.[36] The *British Quarterly* revealed the bitterness of the congregationalists towards the educational policies of the establishment, and while paying a tribute to the commissioners' 'entire absence of clap-trap' insisted that their proposals did not go nearly far enough. Their concessions to the Hebdomadal Board were ludicrous, and their distrust of public opinion in the university, which underlay their hostility to Convocation and the over-weighting of the official element in their Congregation, would not do. The apple of the congregational 'voluntaryist's' eye was the private tutor; private tutors should be encouraged to take pupils into their homes and they should have sectional representation in Congregation. Undergraduates should not only be free to seek tuition from whom they liked, but they should come and go at will; the recommendation of a matriculation examination, tying the schools to Latin and Greek, was a retrograde step, and students should be allowed to take advantage of the educational facilities of the place for whatever period they found convenient.[37] The dissenters might press Russell to attack the universities, but they would probably fall out over the spoils.

Russell in opposition was almost certain to take up university reform, and the most significant feature of the press comment came from the church and conservative side. The manoeuvres of the *Guardian*, which was soon defending the report against the calumnies of the radicals, showed that if the tutorial system and college independence could be maintained, an alliance between anglo-catholics and liberals to which, against their dearest theological prejudices, both sides were being driven by university politics, was a genuine possibility. The *Guardian* sympathised with the schemes for university extension, and if it could not swallow 'unattached' students, this was because it thought the proposal sprang from scorn of the tutorial system.[38] It heartily cheered the demand for a constitutional revolution in the university, while deprecating an extension of Crown patronage.[39] Finally it produced a plan of reform of its own. Collegiate reform without the iniquities of state intervention could be promoted by an enabling act which would empower colleges to open or suppress their fellowships, and which by force of competition would soon lead to a change throughout the university. The university must keep its church connexion and do something about the level of expenses and the licence it allowed to the rich.[40] By the beginning of the next session the *Guardian* was looking for a parliamentary combination of liberal-conservatives and liberals 'to free the universities from their shackles, increase their usefulness, but not destroy their principles.'[41] How far the shibboleths had been eroded was borne out by that other Tractarian organ, the *Christian Remembrancer*, which also called for state intervention and the conversion of redundant fellowships to better uses, especially to scholarships and exhibitions.[42]

The one really spirited reply from the conservative side was produced by the *Quarterly Review* early in 1853.[43] The reviewer poured scorn on the idea of reviving Congregation and entrusting the initiative in legislation to a body of over 100 members. The truth was that the commissioners had no real constitutional plan apart from 'a general wish to stuff in professors.' It was hopeless to try to recapture professional and scientific education for the universities, and in any case the universities served modern society valuably by giving a good general education, which the universities of Germany, France or Scotland did not. The affection of the commissioners for professors had led them astray in the proposals about teaching. The real counterpart of the university teaching of the middle ages was provided by the private tutors who taught simply by virtue of their degree. The university would be in a sad state if it was handed over to the professors and the professorial system failed to revive. Let the professors work their passage. College property moreover was church property, and the commissioners' proposal to divert it to the support of professors who need not be members of the church was a mistake. Not only did the nation prefer clerical instructors, but peculiar dangers beset the lay teacher 'thrown on the world of pure intellect as his home . . . for human nature requires . . . the balance of a moral or religious tie.' The commission was quite wrong in its interpretation of what was meant by poor scholars, who were simply men of insufficient means—though it was true that at present 'neither the claims of middle-class poverty nor those of lower-class intellect [were] sufficiently attended to.' The commissioners, however, would make this much worse, for by giving away all the prizes to merit as revealed by examination, they were putting the endowments in the lap of the affluent classes which could afford a first-class education. Instead of insisting with the founders that poverty had some claim to endowments, the commission proposed to import unattached students under the romantic delusion that they would regenerate the university.

> You are bringing them, as country squires import foxes into their estates, and German barons wolves; as fine specimens of the intellectual *ferae naturae*; a rough unshorn collection, which ornate academics may point out to polished savants and delicate ladies at commemorations, with the finger of a showman, and the remark, 'That is an unattached student; isnt he a fine animal in his way?' . . . The moral sense is bewildered as we contemplate the labyrinthal involutions of this self-disciplining process.

Nor could the commissioners really distinguish what was meant by 'close' foundations. Only about a third of the fellowships were subject to restrictions by the place of birth, and these did little harm; the real trouble was with the school restrictions on which the commissioners were unhelpful. Their basic flaw was enthusiasm.

> From such a temper has proceeded a scheme of university reform, of which the university constitution is a blunder, the university instruction a theory, and the university education a joke.

All this was good polemic, but it was a sign of the times that it produced protests from the conservative side. The *Guardian* cheered, but differed fundamentally on the question of close foundations, claiming that both the figures and conclusions of the reviewer were in error. Again while it was true that three-quarters of the classical firsts got fellowships, it was also true that only one third of the mathematical firsts succeeded in doing so.[44] Charles Daubeny also vigorously denied that science could play no part in general education, or that scientific studies could not be revived in the university. In Germany it was the small universities which advanced science and the large towns which did not.[45]

The upshot of the press comment was that things could not be allowed to go on as they were, and there was a similar sense in the university. If action were not taken soon the university would have very little defence against state intervention. Within a few days of the publication of the report 56 resident M.A.s including 3 professors and 25 past or present tutors had signed a memorial to the Hebdom-adal Board asking that a delegacy of Convocation should be appointed at once to report on university extension, the best mode of improving the professorial system, and other questions. As in 1837 the heads refused to concur in this derogation from their authority, claiming that they had already taken up the matter themselves, and they received another protest from the juniors. These manoeuvres were designed

> as an evidence that a considerable part of the residents are most anxious for *well considered* reforms carried in a constitutional way, after *mature deliberation* by the university itself—and at the same [time] as a protest on their part, against such an abdication of our corporate *deliberative functions* as would be involved in the passive acceptance of the Report of a commission . . . [46]

Gladstone too reflected a considerable body of university opinion. In June 1852 A. P. Stanley pumped him to state whether he felt committed by his original opposition to the commission to oppose reform, or whether he would use his unique influence to induce the legislature and the university to co-operate harmoniously in bringing about the necessary changes. Gladstone in a characteristically involved reply confessed that he was now in favour of reform and that he had no doubts about the competence of parliament to bring it about; he was in the last degree reluctant to ask for more than an enabling act to untie the hands of the Oxford authorities; nevertheless parliament must see that sinecures were abolished, and 'if need be . . . require that the whole powers, influence & services of the university should be applied in the most effective manner to the promotion of its proper work.'[47]

In various colleges reformers began to stir while there was yet time. New College called upon its Visitor to carry out 'a thorough investigation of all points within his province' with a view to making whatever improvements were statutably possible.[48] Magdalen, a society which rendered little educational service for vast revenues, was in an exposed position, and from 1850 a party there had sought to improve the election of the demies and to discipline the class of gentlemen commoners. Even now it was asked only that the latter should not be admitted unless 'able to construe and parse some portion of the works of at least one Greek and one Latin Standard Classic Author,'[49] but the difficulty was to get round the wooden obstinacy of President Routh. In February 1851 a college committee was appointed which recommended that the admission of gentlemen commoners be tightened up, that ordinary commoners be admitted and that an affiliated hall be built to accommodate 60 poor scholars. Demies should be examined more strictly. Nothing was said about the succession of demies to fellowships, but, nevertheless, Routh refused to allow the scheme to come forward at all.[50] Few improvements had been made when an account of progress was demanded by the government at the end of 1853, and in January 1854 a college meeting decided by a considerable majority that it would be contrary to their oath to ask for enabling powers to alter the statutes. The Magdalen oath was a celebrity, Roundell Palmer holding to the view that it bound the fellows not to seek for change, J. B. Mozley that it should be interpreted as liberally as the oath to obey the statutes.[51] At the same time the fellows put the question of the succession rights of the demies before the Visitor, who ruled that demies should in future retire at the age of 25 according to the statutes, and have no right of succession to the fellowships.[52] The committee also resolved to open the fellowships and to assist the university by reviving the three praelectorships established by the founder as new chairs.[53] But it was already too late for the college to take independent action, President Routh was still unmoved, declaring himself

> ready to concur in the execution of such measures of improvement as . . . have been mutually agreed on by the President and Fellows,[54]

and when he died in December 1854, the choice of his successor, Frederic Bulley, was 'determined . . . by dislike of reform.'[55]

There was a similar situation at Corpus. In June 1853 the Latin lectureship of the college was reestablished as a university chair, but there was distrust between the President (who wanted an enabling act permitting changes to be made under the sanction of the Visitor) and the liberal party among the fellows led by J. M. Wilson, professor of moral philosophy, who wanted a parliamentary commission and great extension of the lay element in the governing body of the college.[56] At Queen's the rival factions began to wash their dirty linen in public. For some years the college had been in ill odour, and sharp remarks in the press occasioned by the rejection of Goldwin Smith had been underlined by the report of the commissioners.[57] The situation was that

> a minority small in number are strongly of opinion that the foundation which had been practically confined to Cumberland and Westmorland is by statute open with certain preferences *caeteris paribus*, the majority on the other hand maintain that the words of the statute amount really to an exclusive preference.[85]

and John Barrow attempted to defend the majority from public criticism and to show that the college was improving.[59] On their view what was at fault was not the close system, but the practice grafted on to it of electing taberdars into fellowships by seniority. This system had diverted able men to Cambridge, but it had been inoperative since 1825. Now the difficulty was that the examination system worked against boys from the north whose proficiency in logic and philosophy did not compensate for their backwardness in classics. In 1837, nevertheless, it had been resolved to open the scholarships completely if there was not a larger supply of well qualified northerners. The schools had petitioned them not to do this if they would send up better candidates, and in fact since 1846 the scholars of the college had been exclusively from Cumberland and Westmorland but had acquitted themselves well. William Thomson replied on behalf of the liberals that Barrow had suppressed the fact that the preference given the northern counties was not statutably a monopoly, and that Provost Collinson had drawn up a paper proving the point.[60] From 1825 to 1837 fellowship candidates had been required to obtain a third class; from 1837 to 1847, a second class had been required and obtained. But it was bad for the college that a man's prospects should depend not upon his own merits but upon the shifting balance of college factions.[61] This difficulty was urged upon Gladstone by another fellow, H. B. Barry, as a reason for having a settlement imposed quickly by outside authority. At present progress depended on converting a minority into a majority, and valuable energy was wasted in college intrigue.[62]

In Pembroke there was disillusionment of a different kind. The masterful Jeune was in no way satisfied with the progress that had been made, and was encountering strenuous opposition from the schools which would suffer by the opening of the college scholarships.[63] Jeune complained to Lord Derby, the college Visitor:

> We have done all we can . . . and the Duke of Wellington nobly supported us; but the result is abuse from parents (I have been insulted on the railway platform at Swindon before a train disgorging its contents for not electing a youth whose father,

uncle and cousins had been plucked, and who has himself been
plucked since, as a thief robbing a family of their birthright.) All
that the College gets at the best is a class of men not bad enough
to keep from a fellowship, not good enough to become teachers.[64]

On June 3, 1853 the college resolved that its only hope was to apply
for an enabling act, and communicated its resolutions to Lord John
Russell and Lord Derby. The latter professed himself willing to help
the college as far as he could without over-turning founders' wills,
but this was the question in point. Russell referred the matter to
Gladstone and an interesting correspondence between them and
Jeune followed. The upshot of this was that the ministry felt that it
was too late in the session to promote a special bill and that Gladstone
felt that even in a special act the general implications of the proper
tenure of fellowships could not be avoided.[65]

Jeune had nevertheless set the ball rolling, and early in the next
session, on December 12, 1853, Palmerston as Home Secretary
applied to Lord Derby to know what progress the colleges had made
'and what they may desire from Parliament in the form either of
prohibitions, of enabling powers, or of new enactments.'[66] The
replies of the heads to the inquiry made by the Vice-Chancellor on
behalf of Lord Derby form a fascinating conspectus of the state of
college affairs under the shadow of state intervention.[67] Old Gaisford
of Christ Church was truculent:

> As this college has no statutes it has no need of prohibitions,
> of enabling powers or new enactments.

Jenkyns of Balliol was obstinate. His fellows were full of reforming
schemes with which he would have no truck; *they* would certainly
need an act of parliament. Dr. Wynter of St. John's, who proved
the most stubborn opponent of reform, was evasive; a college
committee had been through the statutes and would shortly recommend changes which would require an enabling act.[68] University
College, Oriel and Worcester put a good face upon the changes which
had been made in the past generation, and suggested that all was well.
All Souls might not even propose changes without an act, but prayed
they would be spared the wholesale butchery of the fellowships to
found chairs which the commissioners had proposed. New College
and Trinity were in the hands of their visitors, and President Wilson
feared that though the legislature might annul the legal force of the
college oath, it could not annul the moral force. The liberal heads
Jeune and Cradock of Brasenose[69] and Dr. Richards of Exeter, a
high churchman whose society had drawn up elaborate plans for
opening and reforming their foundations, were all in favour of
legislation. By the end of 1853, therefore, the threat of outside inter-

vention had driven the Oxford colleges to examine their statutes, and a good many wanted changes which would require legislation. It was also clear that the forces of conservatism were not dead and that in many colleges influential heads and diehard fellows would obstruct any progress under an enabling act.

The power of the reactionary element in Oxford was revealed three times within a few months of the commissioners' report. The extreme protestant and protectionist leaven which had promoted Round in 1847 was still active, and if protectionism was now sick, there had been a great protestant ferment in 1851, and the Ecclesiastical Titles Bill had been rushed through by great majorities. Gladstone, while claiming that he had for years advocated measures which might have prevented the 'papal aggression,' had opposed the bill;[70] at the same time his intimate friend Manning had seceded to Rome, and inevitably weakened Gladstone's standing in protestant eyes. Moreover, in 1852 the mid-Victorian equipoise could not be foreseen, and a radical revision of the relations of church and state appeared imminent. So far as Gladstone's standpoint could be divined, it was satisfactory to no party. With Archdeacon Denison he was at loggerheads over the rights of the state in the management of National Schools.[71] There had been widespread protests against his support for Jewish emancipation. Gladstone was convinced that if the church was to obtain the free synodical action which it needed, it could not resist the claims of others to liberties for themselves. This plea for 'plenary religious freedom,' underlined in Gladstone's mind by his distaste for the Gorham Judgement, he had recently expounded in an open letter to the bishop of Aberdeen.[72] To the protestant constitutionist Gladstone's refusal to stand by what was left of the ark of the covenant could only mean that he was out for the separation of church and state.[73] Among Gladstone's friends, J. B. Mozley could not understand

> how so large a sacrifice of the privileges of an establishment as you seem to contemplate can be necessary for securing a limited synodical action, wh[ich] is all the present move for Convocation contemplates,[74]

and Sir William Heathcote, sympathetic as he was, told him that while Inglis seemed content to make a protest on behalf of the church,

> you . . . are so full of a statesman's appreciation of practical difficulties & advantages, and of the best modes of dealing with the actual temper of the House of Commons, as to seem sometimes as if *you had lost faith* in your principles.[75]

Among the politicians, the liberals believed that in asking for university reform to be left to the university, Gladstone was preparing to thwart any effective measure, while conservatives were angry that Gladstone and the Peelites were not coming to the rescue of Lord Derby's ministry.

To protestants who could desire no better theatre for a demonstration than Oxford, the prospects seemed auspicious,[76] but there were two difficulties. The eighteenth-century tradition that sitting members should never be opposed, still flourished among the residents; and there was no candidate. Nevertheless, early in May 1852 Gladstone's Oxford friends discovered that an opposition was being got up in London by Sir Brook Bridges, a tory baronet from Kent, who had been chairman of Round's London Committee in 1847, and his ultra-protestant friends in the National Club.[77] The National Club was notorious among high churchmen for having exhorted all churchwardens at the peak of the No-popery furor in December 1850 to check Romanising practices in the church by agitating against suspect parish priests.[78] Bridges began to canvass voters on a purely anti-Gladstone platform, assembled the organisers of Round's campaign and cast about for a candidate. The marquis of Blandford was turned down, perhaps as being too much a church reformer himself, and J. C. Colquhoun adopted. Now forgotten, Colquhoun was then prominent in the bitter Scots element in English evangelicalism, chairman of the general committee of the National Club, of the Irish Church Mission to Roman Catholics and other enterprises.[79] At once the spirits of Gladstone's friends rose, and those of his opponents fell, for it was perfectly certain that not even the anti-Popery mania would carry a candidate of Colquhoun's stamp in Oxford. At this moment the Oxford contacts of the London conspirators did not extend beyond the evangelical Dr. Macbride, Principal of Magdalen Hall (who in earlier days had been a steady friend of liberal causes) and Edward Rowden of New College, formerly secretary to Round's London committee; but it was soon clear that Colquhoun would not do. The reluctance of the resident members to break with their own conventions was now a serious drawback to the Bridges party; many prominent residents (William Sewell of Exeter, for example),[80] who had opposed Gladstone strenuously in 1847, could see no case for plunging the university into turmoil again. By the middle of May Greswell, Woollcombe, Haddan and Gladstone's Oxford organisers had published a numerously signed address in the press deploring the conspiracy by which a contest was being forced on Oxford from the outside, and were hoping that their show of strength would carry the day.[81] The immediate effect, however, was to produce a counter-declaration from the other side signed by comparatively few residents but by a conspicuous number of heads. The fact that a group of the heads were prepared to carry on the fight against Gladstone and the juniors where they had left off in 1847 not only gave some local sanction to the schemes of the National Club, but provided a candidate, Robert Bullock-Marsham, Warden of Merton, a protectionist, a man of moderate talents and small influence, but almost alone among the heads in not being disqualified from a parliamentary career by holy orders.[82]

The contest was now fairly joined, and when early in July the Provost of Oriel and Sir William Heathcote, armed with promises of over 1300 votes for Gladstone, approached Marsham's organisers, Dr. Wynter, President of St. John's, and Dr. Ogilvie, regius professor of pastoral theology, to try to persuade them to withdraw, they were rebuffed.[83] The press went into action. H. A. Woodgate of St. John's defended Gladstone's consistency, and Keble his protestantism;[84] the *Guardian* never failed him. On the other hand Christopher Wordsworth, Warden of Glenalmond, reinforced his reply to the *Letter to Skinner* by denouncing Gladstone in the *English Churchman* for advocating the 'political equality of all religions,' and the *Catholic Vindicator* did him no good by calling upon some Irish borough to return him when the evangelicals hounded him from Oxford.[85]

Once the polling began the issue was never in doubt. Wynter's last throw was to seek the open backing of Lord Derby, but the prime minister still had hopes of Gladstone, and would make no move.[86] The final result read

Sir R. H. Inglis	1369
W. E. Gladstone	1108
R. B. Marsham	758

Not only did Gladstone decisively defeat Marsham, but if his committee had not asked his voters to support Inglis also, he would have headed the poll. Even in Merton only 21 of the 55 voters polled for the Warden. Furthermore the church-and-state shibboleths of Marsham appeared to be weakening in their appeal; the heads still voted 12 to 5 against Gladstone (5 abstaining), but Haddan computed that of the voters who had proceeded M.A. since 1847, Gladstone had a majority of 5 to 1. His analysis showed that the voting had followed expected form. Of Gladstone's opponents

> of the pro-Commission party, the largest number held aloof altogether. A certain portion, perhaps two score voted for you.[87] Consequently those who did elect you, although undoubtedly as a body anxious for reform from *within*, are none the less, speaking generally, of the party opposed to compulsory Government or parliament interference as utterly ruinous.

Of the parties who did take a part in the contest your opponents consisted of 1. the low Church to a man

2. the old protestant tories &

3. a few of your former supporters (perhaps 30 or 40), good Churchmen (ecclesiastically speaking) but shocked by the Jew Bill & a few of them, but not many, by Wordsworth's pamphlet. The Ecclesiastical Titles Bill, I believe, did not [lose] you *one vote* . . .

The bulk of Gladstone's supporters were

Churchmen of all sorts of mere politics, most of them clinging to Ld Derby as (not good indeed but) the only resource to keep out Ld. J. Russell & Cobden &c., most of them disliking & very many *excessively* disliking the Jew Bill, but all uniting in this that they wished for a Church representative.

There was no question but that the election had a bearing upon the issue of reform. No sooner had the heads been the subject of strong criticism in the blue book, than a party of them had broken through a strong political convention in the effort to get rid of the burgess favoured by the great majority of the juniors. According to Haddan

of your supporters i.e. of nine-tenths of the *residents, all* wish reform. A large number, but not so large as they would fain appear wish it from *any quarter.* A still larger [number] dread the *Ho. of Commons* more than *existing* evil, and wish reform only from within—not to say that they think *statutes binding.* Of non-residents, fewer still . . . than among residents can endure the bare idea of Government interference, but *almost all* among your own friends would gladly hail effective reform from within.

The question of state intervention, in short, still separated Gladstone's juniors from the liberals, but if the Hebdomadal Board (which could not be reformed from within) continued to behave as at present, the gap would certainly narrow.[88] This was the significance of an acrimonious interchange between Gladstone and Dr. Wynter which took up the Long Vacation.

After the election Marsham's Oxford committee published a statement signed by Wynter, saying that they rejoiced that they had enabled more than 750 electors to protest against all further attempts to sever the union of church and state. At this Gladstone boiled over. Earlier in the campaign he had publicly denied a very much milder assertion that he was out for disestablishment, and he protested that in twenty years of political life it was the first time that his 'deliberate assertion [had] been met, by a responsible person, with contemptuous disbelief.' To this Wynter returned the remarkable reply that he conceived it no part of his duty to read election documents and that

> in every official position which I have occupied, I have uniformly made it a point to avoid as much as possible reading any documents which have appeared in newspapers or other periodical publications.

Gladstone then insisted that their correspondence should be published, but finally after Wynter had repeatedly sheltered behind his election committee which he said could not be assembled in the long vacation, Gladstone withdrew.[89] When one of the most influential heads could only defend himself by insisting that he took no account of the organs of outside opinion, more of the juniors could only conclude that it was time outside opinion made itself forcibly felt. And almost at once the heads showed how far they could still commit the university.

On September 14, 1852, the report of the royal commission claimed its most illustrious victim. The duke of Wellington retired to bed with

> the Oxford Blue Book, with a pencil in it; and he said to Lord Charles Wellesley, who was with him, 'I shall never get through it, Charles, but I must work on.'[90]

His death during the night removed an obstinate university reformer, and exposed the university to a most embarrassing election. It was believed that for a year past a committee had been sitting in London ready to launch a candidate at a vacancy,[91] and this could only mean that some body like the National Club was preparing to promote Lord Shaftesbury. The high-church factions in the university were therefore under the strongest pressure to act quickly, and above all to avoid a division of their forces which would enable Worcester, Wadham and St. Edmund Hall to carry an evangelical. With such cancellarial patronage, groaned Pusey, they would soon have five St. Edmund Halls.[92] Immediately the news reached Oxford a group of Tractarians met in Oriel common room with Robert Hussey, regius professor of ecclesiastical history, in the chair, and resolved not only that the duke of Newcastle, Gladstone's friend, was the best candidate, but that he was the best man to keep out Lord Shaftesbury even if Lord Derby should be nominated. Sewell, who promoted Newcastle, Charles Marriott, Hussey and Canon Marshall were deputed to sound opinion in the university, and Sewell went down to Clumber to see the duke.[93] Gladstone's friends, however, were handicapped not only by their terror of Shaftesbury, but by an ambiguous attitude towards their own candidate. Some were for Newcastle because they thought Derby (whose youthful onslaughts

on the Irish Church and the university test had not been forgotten)
as bad as Shaftesbury; others thought that if there were any doubt
about Newcastle's success they ought to support Derby, while a
party in Christ Church including Professor Hussey looked with
favour upon Lord Harrowby, who was anathema to Tractarians as
'Shaftesbury-and-water'.[94]

The ruling knot of heads also moved quickly and were all out for
Lord Derby. The head of the old protectionist tories, prime minister
with church preferment in his gift, a man who 'declared himself as
decidedly hostile to the Puseyite tendency, and ready to watch over
the Protestant character of the Church,'[95] and not least an accomplished classical scholar, Derby was an ideal candidate; moreover if
anyone could stave off unpleasant legislation it was he. On the
afternoon of September 16, 16 heads gathered in the Delegates'
Room (where the Hebdomadal Board usually met), and under the
leadership of President Wynter resolved to invite Derby to stand.[96]
Derby agreed to do so provided he could succeed without a contest,[97]
and Wynter's agents set about whipping up signatures in his favour.[98]

The support which Derby received immediately ruled out the outsiders who had been fancied, Lord Redesdale, Lord Ellesmere, Lord
Carlisle and Lord Harrowby, and forced a decision upon the friends
of Newcastle. A meeting was arranged at Oriel on September 17 at
which a decisive and characteristically slippery part was played by
Samuel Wilberforce, Bishop of Oxford. Voted into the chair, the
Bishop

> after a long speech setting forth, . . . the *superior merits* of the
> Duke of N. finished with recommending, on the ground of
> *expediency* that Lord Derby should not, under the *present
> circumstances of the case*, be opposed . . . Lord Derby was sure
> to be carried in, & . . . the High Church Party (so-called) had
> better not oppose him at a disadvantage, or it would be con-
> strued as a triumph by the Low Church!!

Richard Michell, Public Orator, could hardly credit this report,[99]
but it was true and not as odd as Wilberforce's letters after the
meeting. To Newcastle he explained that the sense of the meeting
was that 'it would be wrong under present circumstances to the
Church, the University and yourself, to ask you to come forward,'
and that in a contest 'the whole effect of Gladstone's contest and
success would be lost.'[100] To Lord Derby he explained that he had
written the previous day 'to put the question . . . whether if properly
requested you would allow us to nominate you as our future
Chancellor,' but had thought it better to wait till he had had the
opportunity to attend the meeting of Derby's opponents at Oriel;
this meeting he had persuaded to take no action.[101] Wilberforce had

thus made his peace with both sides, and contributed powerfully to the rout of Newcastle's forces. Newcastle's only hope now was that Derby might be insufficiently impressed with the requisition to him to stand. William Sewell wrote a passionate sheet in his favour attacking Derby's record, and pleading the disasters which fell upon Oxford when she put her trust in politicians; her one hope of salvation now lay in self-reform under an independent Chancellor such as the duke of Newcastle.[102] His plea was reinforced by letters in the *Times* and by the *Guardian*, but already he was too late.[103] High-Church and low were scrambling on to the bandwaggon to avoid appearing isolated, and Derby was carried home unanimously. W. C. Lake made a public protest at the formal election that the whole affair had been rushed, but the true criticism was that the university had made a dangerous intrusion into party politics, and the strongest political group among the residents had reason to feel that they had been outmanoeuvred by the heads. Before the year was out the contest had been renewed.

On December 17, just before 4 a.m., the government of Lord Derby was beaten on its budget proposals after a great speech by Disraeli had been powerfully answered by Gladstone. The outlook for government was grim. Within a year a tory and a whig government had foundered; on the one side Palmerston and Russell were at loggerheads, and on the other the relations between the Peelites and Derby's tories were worse than ever. Gladstone was in especial ill odour, and a few nights later a group of drunken tories who had been entertaining Major Beresford at the Carlton—he having been acquitted upon a charge of bribery at Derby—came across Gladstone reading the papers, insulted him, and threatened to throw him out of the window into the Reform.[104] Instead they shortly made a desperate effort to throw him out of Oxford.

Both parties having failed to maintain a majority, the queen commissioned Lord Aberdeen to construct a coalition ministry. The cabinet consisted finally of six Peelites, including Gladstone as Chancellor of the Exchequer, six whigs including Russell and Palmerston as Foreign and Home Secretary respectively, and the radical Molesworth, who was anathema to the orthodox as the editor of Hobbes. Immediately a howl of anguish went up from tory quarters, intensified by Lord Derby's allegation that his defeat had been brought about by a deliberate combination. Archdeacon Denison denounced the coalition as latitudinarianism in politics which must lead infallibly to latitudinarianism in the church; Russell would undoubtedly seek to extend state influence over the schools.[105] Gladstone could not have taxed his high church friends worse than by letting Russell into office, and then accepting him as a colleague,[106] though Pusey converted a few by insisting that Russell had joined the Peelites, not they him.[107] From the other wing, Hugh Stowell, the evangelical firebrand of Salford, declaimed that the university could not endorse 'a cabinet more deeply tainted with the leprosy of Tractarianism than any which has yet existed;' and 'which owes its elevation to the alien brigade of the Pope, and whose tenure of office must depend on the adhesion of that traitorous band.'[108] Nowhere was the shock greater than in Oxford, where Gladstone had now to face a by-election. The university burgess had given the *coup de grâce* to the Chancellor, and 'loaves and fishes, deaneries and bishoprics were all knocked over.'[109] Letters poured in to the pillars of the old church interest in Oxford, Dr. Wynter of St. John's and Dr. Bliss, Principal of St. Mary Hall, demanding that Gladstone be opposed.[110] The problem, as usual, was to find a candidate. The first breath of conspiracy reached Gladstone from Greswell, who related how the two Misses Plumptre on a social call had been shown by error of a servant into the drawing room of Dr. Faussett, Margaret professor, and found it full of strange men, who could be there for only one purpose.[111] But as in July 1852 it was not from Oxford that the decisive moves were made.[112]

Dr. Lempriere, fellow of St. John's College, conservative agent, London secretary and promoter of Colquhoun and Marsham at the last election, and one of the revellers who had annoyed Gladstone at the Carlton, had been seeking furiously for a candidate.[113] J. W. Henley, member for Oxfordshire, Lord Blandford, Travers Twiss, a former Drummond professor, Sir J. D. Harding, the Queen's Advocate, were talked of but declined, and Lord Chandos also refused. On Saturday, January 1, the Derbyite *Morning Herald* announced that Gladstone's return would not be opposed, and receiving private assurances to the same effect, Gladstone dispersed his committee and left town. On the same evening, however, the *Standard* announced that there would be a contest and that either Chandos or Harding would stand, and on the following day Lempriere passed through St. John's, bearing a mysterious message for Lord Chandos. On that day and the following Monday Chandos again refused to stand, but the Monday post brought Oxford electors a circular signed by Lempriere announcing that Chandos would be a candidate, and in the evening the *Standard* related that he had 'consented' to come forward. Only on nomination day two days later, January 5, did it come out that the candidate was in fact to be Dudley Perceval, the son of Spencer Perceval, a man who had not even kept his name on the books of the university. But Lempriere had had time to complete his coalition, for Perceval, another member of the Committee of the National Club and supported by the venerable evangelical Macbride, was actually proposed by the high-church extremist Archdeacon Denison.[114]

13

Gladstone's friends were consumed with indignation at what they considered the shabbiest of all election tricks, and his position was serious. Even his best friends were baffled at the latest turn in his career, and Sir William Heathcote was only induced to remain chairman of his London committee by anger at the Carlton conspiracy.[115] Gladstone's defence was that he had opposed Disraeli's budget as dishonest, and not as a means of overthrowing the government, that the coalition had been formed only to meet a great national emergency which the major parties had been unable to overcome singlehanded, and that he would never have entered it had not he been certain that ecclesiastical patronage would be as safe in the hands of the presbyterian Aberdeen, as in those of Derby. This defence was finally circulated as a leaflet, and together with passionate denunciations of Lempriere's intrigues, did some thing to revive the flagging spirits of Gladstone's voters.[116] For at an early stage, to the intense grief of Hawkins and Greswell, his senior friends,[117] Gladstone fell behind in the polling, and a frantic appeal went out from his committee.[118] By the eighth day of the poll Gladstone was over a hundred ahead but his rivals were determined to keep the poll open till the last possible moment, and it transpired that, as the university was excluded from the Reform Act, the poll could be kept open for fifteen days.

> A portentous whisper . . . spread through the metropolis that the university statutes interposed no obstacle to a perpetual poll, and that instead of members sitting for life, we were now to have candidates standing for life.[119]

The extension of the poll proved only a vexation to all concerned, and a proof to Gladstone's party of the utter unscrupulousness of the other side. At the end he still had a lead of more than a hundred.

The pamphlet warfare which followed was even more protracted than the poll, and the result had none of the appearance of permanence of the victories of 1847 and 1852. Even in the last contest Gladstone had been much grieved by the bitter conflict which had raged around him, and had wondered whether for the sake of the university he ought not to move elsewhere;[120] now his doubts were renewed,[121] and although he resolved to hold the fort for the time out of loyalty to his allies, his hesitations could only encourage his opponents to try to frighten him off in future. It was certain that he would be opposed as long as candidates could be found to stand. Gladstone's opponents, however, had done themselves no good by the unseemly protraction of the polling. The *Times* declared that voting ought to be by proxy,[122] and even the Hebdomadal Board began to discuss improvements.[123] In August 1853 an act was passed limiting the polling in the universities to five days.[124]

The iniquities of the polling lent point to the usual distribution of the heads; 7 voted or paired for Gladstone, 13 against. For the third time the influential party on the Hebdomadal Board had tried to defeat Gladstone, and they had been worsted in peculiarly discreditable circumstances. There can be no doubt that this last experience helped to move Gladstone quite sharply towards the view that the university needed overhauling by outside authority. By the same token it brought him nearer to the liberals. In 1852 most of the liberals under the leadership of Goldwin Smith held aloof in distrust,[125] and even now Jowett was hostile.[126] But about fifty liberals now came to his side, there was support from the liberal press, and it was widely noted that he was liberalising his Tractarian friends.[127] The decisive liberal-catholic coalition was getting nearer, and the future allies on both sides were no doubt delighted by the spectacle of the National Club becoming an embarrassment to the Derbyites.[128] Even Perceval began to claim that he had bent every effort towards keeping it in check.[129]

CHAPTER IX

THE TRIUMPH OF REFORM AND THE
EXECUTIVE COMMISSIONERS

If my college cannot be opened, I for one would decidedly prefer to
see the property revert to the heirs-at-law. Close foundations are not
only useless, they are injurious. Magdalen Hall which has not a penny,
is infinitely more beneficial than the noblest foundation in Oxford,
Magdalen College.

F. JEUNE to LORD DERBY, June 15, 1853.
MS. Knowsley Papers Box 8.

WHILE parties in the university were clashing in these elections, they
were also making the first responses to the great blue book of May
1852. As we have seen the Hebdomadal Board rebuffed the suggestion
of appointing a delegacy of heads and masters, but they appointed a
committee of their own,[1] and early in the following session invited
members of Convocation to submit written evidence upon matters
arising from the royal commission report. The retiring Vice-Chancellor declared that the university and colleges must undertake
essential reforms, and the queen's speech announced that the report
had been sent to the governing bodies of the universities, and that
parliament should be prepared to remove any legal impediments to
reform.[2] With Derby prepared to go so far, and the heads who
secured his election as Chancellor also moving, it behoved the juniors
to make their views known. At first it was proposed to ask the
Chancellor to press the Hebdomadal Board to appoint a delegacy,
but after a pamphlet had recommended the M.As. to exert their
potential power, the committee of the Tutors' Association which had
met during the long gestation of the new examination statute, revived
the body, and a large meeting in the Oriel Common Room on
November 8 resolved that the association should meet formally
twice a week.[3]

The revival of the association very greatly furthered the crystalli-
sation of Oxford opinion; the outright conservatives were strongly
represented on the Hebdomadal Board and had the machinery for
publishing their opinions; the outright liberals already had their
programme in the blue book and gathered round Dr. Jeune at
Pembroke; now the great bulk of the working residents who liked
neither the authoritarianism of the one nor the fondness for professors
and state compulsion of the other, were formally organised. The

association drew together men of disparate views. Among the influential were the conservative H. L. Mansel, and the liberal Lake; there were Tractarians like J. B. Mozley, George Rawlinson, late fellow of Exeter, and Mountague Bernard, one of the founders of the *Guardian*; Gladstone's organisers Woollcombe and Haddan reflected his influence among the working residents.[4] Before their first report was published he was in office, and the association then possessed the advantage of access to the man in power which, during Russell's ministry, had been enjoyed by the liberals.

The first report on university extension was hastily compiled by a committee by the second week in December and accepted by the association in the last week of January 1853. The tutors would not countenance the commissioners' suggestion of lodgings, but were clear that the college monopoly must be broken. They recommended that a cheap education, the cost of which could be known in advance, should be provided in affiliated, independent and private halls, and existing college buildings should be extended.[5] The real bone of contention was the private halls which many tutors expected to give rise to theological strife, but when the committee had finished its work the draft was submitted to Gladstone, and his approval helped to save the halls when the association met to accept the report.[6]

Later in the term another committee which had been appointed to discuss the university constitution produced its draft, which was accepted at the end of April.[7] The tutors had no sympathy for either the Hebdomadal Board (which they characterised as isolated, irresponsible and in some ways unqualified) or the plan of the royal commission. The proposed new Congregation was grossly overweighted with professors, was much too large for an initiative body and would hardly help to harmonise draft legislation with the opinion of residents. The harmonising principle in the constitution should be that of representation; there should be a new Hebdomadal Board in which nine members should be chosen by the heads, nine by the professors, public examiners and moderators, nine by the tutors and other resident M.A.s, together with the Vice-Chancellor and Proctors sitting *ex officio*. The tutors as a body were pledged to the cause of representation, and the great battle came over the concessions to be made to the professors. A good proportion of the association including Gladstone's allies Woollcombe and Haddan wanted no concession at all, and advocated a two-section board, twelve members to be elected by the heads and twelve by the M.A.s The committee finally carried a professorial section only by diluting it with public examiners who were about equal in number to the resident professors. Again their hand was strengthened by the knowledge that Gladstone had seen their draft and much preferred their proposals to those of the blue book.[8] The *Guardian* had praise for both the tutors' schemes of representation, and somewhat prematurely concluded that they had given the *coup de grâce* to the idea of a remodelled Congregation.[9]

While these discussions were proceeding J. B. Mozley persuaded the association to seek out the evidence of expert opinion, instead of merely waiting upon the testimony of witnesses as both the commissioners and the Hebdomadal Board had done.[10] In May 1853, therefore, questionnaires on university and college organisation went out, partly with a view to sounding the opinion of non-residents, and partly to collect solid information from professional men on the still obscure possibility of reviving professional education in Oxford.[11] The answers to these questions eventually formed an interesting series of appendices to the associations' reports. The other great work of the Trinity term was to make a start upon the third report on the vexed question of the relations of the professorial and tutorial systems. This was a very contentious matter which the tutors rightly asserted had been left unclarified by the commissioners. George Rawlinson made their attitude quite clear to Gladstone, declaring that while they wanted professors more learned, better paid and more often resident, they wanted professorial teaching to remain subordinate to the tutorial system.[12] The report was not accepted until November.[13] The tutors admitted Oxford's lack of the professional scholarship which was the glory of Germany, but could see no case for putting the teaching and studies of the university in the hands of a completely new and untried body of men, and depressing the status of tutors who had hitherto been the principal teachers and examiners of the university. They supported Mark Pattison's criticisms of professorial teaching, found the blue book hopelessly vague on the subject of assistant professors and thought professorial control of examinations dangerous. The patronage of new chairs certainly ought not to be in the Crown, nor ought professors to be exempt from the tests. Professorial influence should be moral and indirect, and the reader is left with the feeling that they hoped it would be negligible. Nevertheless, undergraduates should be required to attend professorial courses. Gladstone perceived at once that the prejudices of the tutors led them to skate over the question of the endowment of the new chairs for which they called, and he was privately informed that the tutors having reluctantly accepted a much reduced professoriate wanted the maximum freedom for colleges to decide how to finance it; there was bitter opposition to the compulsory suppression of fellowships.[14]

The final report on the college system was begun at the same time as that on the professorial and tutorial system and it was not finally accepted till the university crisis was at its peak in March 1854.[15] In this respect the fourth report was less important than the others, for decisions had already been taken elsewhere which would settle the future of the colleges in advance of the tutors' final views. Inevitably the college system brought out all the tutors' conservatism. Colleges should remain the centre of the university and nothing should be done to destroy their moral and religious influence. The statutes of each college were a separate problem and no uniform system could be applied to them. Local restrictions on fellowships should be relaxed, but only a proportion of fellowships should be completely open. It was most important to maintain the obligation to take holy orders; few able laymen, it was alleged, had been driven from the university by it. Some colleges nevertheless might benefit from a larger proportion of lay fellowships. It was important to find work for fellows to do—and there would be openings in the new halls—but the great object of fellowships was to promote study. Some machinery for overhauling college statutes from time to time was needed, and parliament must act now. In the first instance parliament should provide enabling powers (though a compulsory power to break college oaths was required) with compulsory inter-ference later. If parliament were to try to lay down detailed regula-tions for colleges, a parliamentary committee would be needed to discuss them with the colleges. This last point revealed how far the tutors had been driven against their instinctive inclinations, and it was a point with which Gladstone had to reckon in his act.[16]

While the tutors—or those of them who managed the Association[17] —were preparing their scheme in consultation with Gladstone, the heads also were at work, and were gradually undermining the reluc-tance of Gladstone in the ministry and his supporters in the university to face coercive action by the state. By the beginning of November 1852 the committee of the Hebdomadal Board had completed its report, and the Vice-Chancellor wrote to Lord Derby requesting royal licence to repeal three statutes of the Caroline code, the first prescribing the nomination of collectors in Lent, which was now a meaningless form, the second establishing the proctorial cycle which was now out of date and the third constituting the Hebdomadal Board. This was all the assistance which the university needed on the side of legislation, but they would also like a licence to increase their holding of lands in mortmain. To neither of these requests was Derby sympathetic. He could not ask the Crown to abandon its controlling power without being informed of the intended changes; it was clear that the committee had no programme and that the colleges were not ready to be included in a comprehensive enabling measure. He was also extremely reluctant to grant a request so completely contrary to general public policy as a fresh licence to hold lands in mortmain. The Board readily agreed to defer its petition for enabling powers, but pleaded that the gold strikes in various parts of the world made it absolutely necessary that new academic

departures should be financed by landed investments; one of Lord
Derby's last ministerial acts was to direct their attention to 'other
securities with at least equal profit and safety.'[18]

The heads had now to find an explicit answer to the blue book, and
on February 10, 1853, Gladstone assured the ruling spirit, Provost
Hawkins, that they had better move quickly as Lord John Russell
must shortly state the intentions of the government in reply to
parliamentary questions.[19] Russell was briefed by Gladstone with
correspondence from Hawkins and the Tutors' Association, and with
Gladstone's own conclusion that the crux of the whole university
problem was the constitutional question.[20] Russell's parliamentary
statement indicated that already he was content to follow Gladstone's
lead. The government, he announced, would allow the university the
grace of the present session to settle its affairs, but they would be
satisfied with no plan of reform which did not meet five requirements:
the opening of fellowships so that they became real rewards of merit
and of work; constitutional reform so as to secure the representation
of the main elements of the university in the governing body;
measures to increase the number of students and to limit the dis-
advantages of poor students; and the application of some part of
the college endowments towards the support of a revived professoriate. He also suggested that it might be prudent to limit the tenure
of fellowships.[21] The statement convinced the delighted Jeunes that
the government had accepted the programme of the blue book,[22]
and led Derby to insist that the heads must have a well-considered
programme ready by the beginning of the next session. They must
find some means of ending the college monopoly without going to
the heresy of unattached students, and they must also relax the
stranglehold of classics in favour of newer subjects.[23] At his installation in June 1853 he renewed his counsel publicly with greater
urgency.[24]

During the summer the Board proceeded with their work and
Pusey not only submitted a substantial treatise as evidence, but
canvassed his friends to do the same to give the heads' report when
it appeared a respectable appearance.[25] It soon became known that
unlike the general body of high-church juniors Pusey and his *alter ego*,
Charles Marriott, had veered towards the defence of the *status quo*.
Marriott was now the complete prisoner of an organic theory. The
founder's will, he declared

> is *everything* as a *typical germ*, giving the principles and organi-
> sation of the Foundation. And I look upon a diminution of a
> Founder's numbers as almost sure, in one way or another, to
> truncate the living body which he intended to exist.

The university like the colleges was an organism of miraculous harmony. Unwittingly Henry VIII had created in Christ Church the perfect instrument for aristocratic education, while Oriel and Balliol were 'the best for a brisk training of clever men as undergraduates,' and other colleges, if their peculiarities were untouched, would 'ere long excel in history, or law, or physical science, others in divinity, etc.'[26] If Pusey and Marriott were encouraging their old enemies with this kind of doctrine, the report of the Hebdomadal Board would be a thing of little account, and when, with infinite labour, Hawkins finally produced it in December 1853, so it proved.[27]

With some reason the heads' committee felt that the new examination system ought to be allowed to prove itself before further changes were made, but they could not conceive a matriculation examination of a standard low enough not to exclude some candidates who were now properly admitted. They expressed prudent doubt about the demand for university extension, and were resolutely opposed to unattached students and private halls. They favoured affiliated and independent halls, and were prepared to grant £10,000 to the latter under stringent regulations for diminishing the expenses of students. Marriott's experience showed, however, that this offer was little more than a token of goodwill. The professorial question was burked almost altogether; the Board supported that combination of professorial and tutorial teaching which had been envisaged in the new examination statute, looked for the endowment of new chairs to the resources of the university as distinct from the colleges, and to concessions in taxation from the government. Assistants to professors should be appointed only in cases where the burden of teaching justified them. The Board was not unnaturally well satisfied with the university constitution, and pointed to the great amount of legislation which had been passed during the present century. However, as a gesture, they were prepared to appoint non-members of the Board to their delegacies more often, and to enlarge the Board by the addition of eight elected members of Convocation. They were against the wholesale opening of fellowships, and would only recommend marginal relaxations of the obligation to enter holy orders. In general they relished the enthusiasm with which their witnesses attacked the commissioners' desire to overturn the present system in the interests of uniformity and merit.[28]

There was not the least prospect that these recommendations would satisfy either Lord John Russell or the tutors, and the *Guardian* did not err in prizing chiefly the massive evidence of Dr. Pusey.[29]

Dr. Pusey has been the first to show clearly what the real question is between those who support the Commission and those who oppose it—that it is, indeed, a question between religion and irreligion—between moral restraint and licence—

between belief and unbelief—between discipline and dissolute-
ness.

Certainly Pusey's evidence, unlike that of the Board, was governed
by a master idea, and worked out ingeniously with his personal blend
of percipience and prejudice. The issue between the professorial and
the collegiate system in his view was virtually between the idolatrous
authority conferred on a person and the sound authority of a literary
tradition. Pusey believed that scientific education (which he admitted
could be well provided by professorial lectures) consisted of 'the
reception of *information* as to matters of fact,' and that for this
reason it had nowhere been a vehicle of liberal studies.[30] On this
premise it was not unreasonable to claim that professorial lectures
could not replace the study of standard texts. At the bottom of his
heart Pusey felt that the literary heritage of the Catholic past was
the sole defence of faith and morals against the destructive
modernisms of the day, and for this reason also he insisted on
keeping teaching in clerical hands. On the constitutional question,
Pusey insisted that weight must be given to the heads, but that some
means must be found to end their isolation and put them in touch
with the views of the residents. Pusey suggested that Convocation
should elect a second board of residents equal in numbers to the
Hebdomadal Board; each should have the power of recommending
measures to the other, and measures accepted by both should be
put to Convocation. This cumbrous system which did nothing to
weaken the grip of the heads upon legislation, would afford a
guarantee against revolutionary change.[31]

The publication of the report and of Pusey's evidence with its
imaginative power came at a crucial moment, for on December 12,
1853 Palmerston wrote to Lord Derby asking for a report on the
progress made by the university and colleges towards fulfilling the
aims outlined by Russell in April.[32] Through the Vice-Chancellor,
Derby set on foot an inquiry into the achievements of each college
with the results that we have seen, and it behoved the Hebdomadal
Board to turn their report into legislation at the earliest possible
moment. The senior Proctor, D. P. Chase, moved that a delegacy
be appointed to prepare constitutional changes, and was defeated,[33]
and when the heads' proposals were published they revealed themselves to be hiding behind their old enemy Dr. Pusey; Convocation
was to be asked to petition the Crown for a licence to repeal the
Caroline Code in favour of precisely his system of two boards.[34]

The constitutional issue now dwarfed every other, and there were
three schemes before the government and university, that of Pusey
(now sponsored by the heads), that of the tutors and that of the
royal commission which had all along been championed by the

'Pembroke' party which now included Jeune, Johnson, Cradock, Goldwin Smith, Conington, H. B. Barry and others. A final counter-blast against the other schemes was now delivered from this quarter by H. H. Vaughan, regius professor of modern history.[35] Vaughan had no difficulty in exposing the animus of the Oxford tutors; the moral influence which they wished professors to wield amounted to no authority at all, and they wished to end even the traditional authority in examinations exercised by the professors in divinity, medicine and law. In the scheme of the Hebdomadal Board, pro-fessors were among the victims of the heads' determination to mono-polise power. Pusey also was ridiculed for ascribing all the troubles of the church since the Reformation to German professors, and taking a very ideal view of the Oxford system as it stood. The controversy between Vaughan and the conservatives went on at length,[36] but it is not worth following, because even Vaughan's first pamphlet had now been left behind by the tide of events. The great demand of the Pembroke party had been for substantial power for professors sealed by their standing in a delegacy of studies, examinations and libraries, and in Congregation. Now 41 of the liberals led by J. M. Wilson, professor of moral philosophy, signed a petition and sent it up to Lord John Russell by deputation, urging a tripartite Hebdomadal Council (after the manner of the Tutors' Association) elected by a Congregation which should consist of all university and college officers, the powers of Convocation remaining unchanged.[37]

There were three reasons for this major concession to the position of the tutors. In the first place the liberals saw that tutors were now willing to accept a broadly based Congregation, and in this respect the latest Pembroke proposals marked a further stage in the reconci-liation of liberals and high-church men which had been going on for some time.[38] The second was a lively fear, that without an approach of this kind, nothing whatever would be obtained for professors. The liberals had concluded that the government had given up the idea of a full professorial and university system, and on the strength of Gladstone's unofficial warnings that the government would not be satisfied with the plans of the Hebdomadal Board, W. C. Lake and the junior Proctor, J. W. Knott, had gone about boasting that 'the Tutors' Association would have it all their own way with Mr. Gladstone;' as a *pis aller* therefore the liberal party gave reluctant consent to measures which must entrench the college interest.[39] And, thirdly, the power of Gladstone's connexion was displayed once again in January 1854 in the election of Sir William Heathcote as a university burgess.

In the middle of January Sir Robert Inglis resigned his seat on grounds of ill health, and at once the factions which had divided the university so frequently in recent years took the field. A high-church meeting at Oriel with Hussey in the chair decided by 13 votes to 9 to invite Roundell Palmer, in preference to Sir William Heathcote, to stand.[40] Heathcote, however, had been chairman of Gladstone's London committee from the beginning, and was at present out of the house, so Gladstone's London connexion absolutely declined to surrender his claims, and Palmer, who moved in the same political and church circles, withdrew. There were Tractarians who thought the party should put the claims of talent first and prefer Palmer, but as the pupil and patron of Keble, a lay sympathiser of the party, and a cultivated gentleman of the old school who was on easier terms with the Derbyites, Heathcote was a strong candidate.[41] Gladstone's committees immediately reformed for Heathcote, but there was no contest. Lord Robert Cecil was talked of by the heads, but at 24 was thought too young. Dudley Perceval's Oxford committee tried to entice Sir John Pakington from Droitwich but without success. There was talk of running Travers Twiss, Vicar General of the Province of Canterbury, on liberal protestant principles, but in the present state of Oxford politics there was no room for such a candidate, and, with evangelicals and protestant constitutionists making pretence that Heathcote was not as high-church as he looked, opposition faded away. Thus declared the *Times*:

> the representation of the University, which might fairly claim that both of its great phases of opinion should be heard in Parliament, has passed entirely into the hands of one, and that one directed by a committee acting on the university from without. This is what comes of fighting a battle with impossible candidates, with incurables averse to all reform either in Church or State, and with men who were simply set up to be knocked down, and of whom noone has ever heard after they were beaten.[42]

Heathcote represented himself as an independent conservative, and in due course a great political gulf opened between him and Gladstone. But all that was apparent in January 1854 was that through being unwilling to share the spoils, the evangelical and protestant constitution party had lost all to the Gladstonians, with whom accordingly the liberal rank and file sought to make their peace.

The government was now known to have legislation of its own ready to introduce, but the heads determined to put their trust in the magic of Pusey's name and proceed with their plan. Pusey negotiated privately with Gladstone to postpone the government's announcement until Convocation had passed verdict on the scheme of the Board. Like most of Pusey's private negotiations this ended in ll-feeling and misunderstanding, for although the government allowed the heads another week they had no intention of agreeing to their constitutional proposals, and informed Lord Derby accordingly. Derby on his side concluded that the government intended to introduce a complete professorial system (as the liberals knew was not the case) and encouraged the heads to do everything in their power to resist.[43] Convocation was a curiously confused occasion. The juniors assumed until too late that this technical discussion would be left to residents, and, in any case, since it was generally known that the government would recommend the queen not to grant a licence to alter the constitutional arrangements of the Caroline Code as the heads (with Pusey and Marriott)[44] wished, there was no point in beating up the outvoters. The heads, however, did so, and brought up some of the diehards who had fought for Perceval and Marsham. When Convocation met on February 24, Thorold Rogers on the liberal side attacked the heads for producing a hastily botched scheme parts of which were only twenty-four hours old, and George Butler, another liberal, attacked them for serving the ends of party. But the outvoters defeated the residents and carried the motion by 212 votes to 161, the minority being almost entirely composed of resident fellows. The heads' vote of confidence could carry no conviction, and the general body of residents were looking to the bill being drawn for the government by Gladstone.[45]

On this as on later occasions Gladstone's personal evolution was to have an important influence on the development of English institutions, and the blow to his natural conservatism given by the heads' opposition to the Tractarians, had been followed by a series of others. In January 1852 before the publication of the blue book, he had still insisted that

> no course of events . . . can be really safe and satisfactory, but one which shall *avert* Parliamentary interposition altogether.[46]

Gladstone was impressed by the blue book, but in June 1852 he still thought

> legislative interference of a compulsory character so great an evil in itself, that until I shall have abandoned all hope of seeing just expectations satisfied by improvements adopted spontaneously or under enabling powers, I shall never allow myself to conclude in favour of the necessity of such interference.[47]

By the end of September after the animosity of the Hebdomadal Board had been manifested in the parliamentary and cancellarial elections, his doctrine was that 'unless a tolerable bill of fare' could be exhibited by the university authorities, parliament would intervene, and it would then become a duty to prefer positive enactments, because in this way the danger of repeated interference would be more effectually obviated.[48]

Nor was there any real hope that the heads would meet the need.

Their position is too much a false one with regard to university reform to allow of such results from their labours as would be adequate to the emergency.[49]

After the bitter experiences of the by-election of January 1853, at a public luncheon in Oxford, he made it as clear as his public circumlocutions ever made anything clear, that there would be parliamentary intervention with his support.[50] When, about the same time, the cabinet discussed the matter Russell found him 'very radical,' and was content to leave the management of the question to him.[51] All this was before Hawkins had laboriously produced the report of the committee of the Board; when in December 1853 the report was published, Gladstone gave him the cold comfort that it was now impossible to preserve the independence of the university, and only substantial changes could safeguard it for the future.

As there must be intervention of some kind, I hope it may be an intervention strictly limited indeed by the real necessity of the case, but measuring that necessity with especial reference to the advantage of placing the whole matter as it were out of arm's length; and providing at once, whether directly or indirectly, for all the main and leading objects which the reasonable demands of the country may embrace, and the fundamental principles of the university allow. By her fundamental principles I mean for the present purpose this: that nothing shall be done to endanger 1—the essential connection between the university and the church of England; 2—the predominance of the higher studies; 3—the religious and domestic spirit of the discipline of the place.[52]

On these principles, and to the accompaniment of an astonishing barrage of advice from interested parties, Gladstone began to construct the government's bill.

The first move was made by Jowett who, after taking little recent part in the reform agitation, wrote to Gladstone on December 14, 1853, urging that a general measure of university reform be introduced before the colleges began to apply for individual enabling acts. Such a measure could be based on a single intelligible principle and would ease consciences which shrank from proposing interference with founders' wills. Moreover, in a general measure those with vested interests in close foundations could be compensated by the general opening in a way which was impossible in individual settlements.[53]

Jowett outlined the plan he had in mind and was invited by Gladstone to call on him.[54] Within a few days Jowett had cast his ideas in the form of a draft bill, and anticipated the resolutions of the Pembroke party as a whole by adopting the Tutors' Association principle of a Hebdomadal Council elected in three sections, restricting the election simply to the tutors. Foundations were to be opened as far as possible; schools with special privileges were a great problem, but no school should keep close scholarships unless it was giving a classical education to more than 100 scholars. There were to be no undergraduate fellowships, and the fellowships at St. John's and New College and the Christ Church studentships were to be divided into senior and junior classes to correspond with the distinction between fellows and scholars elsewhere. Colleges were also to be given extensive powers to redeploy their wealth; they might suppress a sixth of their fellowships to provide open scholarships, and appropriate a similar proportion to new studies. Jowett dared not plunder any further proportion for the endowment of chairs, but looked to the state and other traditional benefactors. Two other noteworthy features of this plan were that the details were to be settled in the bill without any subsequent negotiations by an executive commission, and the qualification of 'indigence' was to be abolished.[55] In January 1854 Gladstone circulated this draft among the ministers and the members of the Committee of the Council on Education together with another of his own which incorporated a commission,[56] and, in the middle of the following month, the two drafts were given an extensive private circulation in Oxford in order to give Gladstone a guide to the views of the working residents.

One of the great issues between Gladstone and Jowett was the question of a commission. Gladstone thought

> that by means of a Commission Parliamentary reluctance may be softened—more careful adjustment of details . . . secured—a more complete and yet a somewhat milder measure accomplished—and the question thus rescued from the risk of the serious evils attending repeated parliamentary interpositions.
>
> I am, however, convinced that the question is one of necessity rather than of policy. Every Oxford man whom I have yet been able to consult except Mr. Jowett agrees with me in thinking that in the Colleges characterised by the oath against change in Statutes—and they are by far the most glaring cases—the *enabling* powers would never be exercised during the present generation.[57]

To which Jowett replied that

> a Commission would be unpopular and that it would be difficult

to find persons fit to be Commissioners. . . . The great objection to a Commission is that it will work unjustly or not work at all. It will have to treat in detail and in a semi-legal manner matters which can only be treated by laying down a new general principle.[58]

Again Gladstone felt that it was justifiable to retain some college oaths, and as Russell had said nothing on the subject in 1853 it was

open to serious doubt whether the absolute proscription of oaths of obedience or observance would be consistent on our part with good faith.[59]

Jowett on the other hand had a violent animus against college oaths of every kind.[60] Gladstone had the high-church faith in private halls; Jowett had none, and thought the best hope of expansion lay in multiplying scholarships.[61]

An immense and confused correspondence followed the circulation of the drafts, to which Gladstone replied with infinite patience. Every don had his own nostrums, but the two chief topics of comment were the election of the proposed Hebdomadal Council and the tenure of fellowships. A. W. Haddan, his conservative election secretary, favoured dividing the electorate into the same sections as the Council, and Gladstone suggested this to Liddell as a means of securing more power for professors.[62] His other secretary Woollcombe was against sectional election, and like Lake wanted Congregation to be extended to include all residents.[63] To him Gladstone admitted that the government were moving in the same direction, influenced partly by the evils inherent in very small electorates, and partly by the initiative of the Pembroke party (the main advocates of professors) in agreeing to congregational election.[64]

Fellowships presented innumerable difficulties, not the least of which arose from Gladstone's conviction that endowments would never be safe as long as fellowships were formally sinecures. He himself was thinking of requiring fellows who were not office-holders to produce certificates that they were engaged in study, a plan which teemed with difficulties.[65] There was general opposition to the idea of compelling fellows to fit themselves for the world by limiting their tenure,[66] for the small financial return of fellowships (and still more of studentships) was little inducement in itself; but permanency enabled a man to wait until professional security was assured.[67] A good many of Gladstone's friends such as Lake, Haddan and Woollcombe were very strongly opposed to any reduction in the number of fellowships, or to any attempt to suppress fellowships as canonries had already been suppressed.[68] He carried them with him in his desire to increase the number of lay fellows to a quarter of the whole, if only for the sake of assisting the new studies,[69] but there were vigorous protests from liberals that the scheme was far too favourable to the clergy.[70]

The bill which was finally introduced by Russell on March 17, 1853 was in the main a compromise between the schemes of Gladstone and Jowett (who both warmly supported it),[71] and it bore the marks of the strenuous discussion in Oxford. Gladstone secured his commissioners, and Jowett his tripartite Hebdomadal Council elected by Congregation (though the Chancellor was to nominate one head and one professor). Congregation was to be composed of university officers, the senior tutor of each college and such other residents as could produce a certificate that they were habitually engaged in study. This last provision brought a howl from Rawlinson that the Pembroke scheme had been swallowed entire.[72] Congregation was to discuss proposals of the Hebdomadal Council in English, and its members might submit amendments to the Council in writing, but Congregation itself had no power of amendment. Gladstone obtained his point about oaths which were to be restricted but not prohibited, and also the opening of private halls under licence from the Vice-Chancellor. Half the fellowships were to be opened, certain preferences to schools on lines suggested by Jowett were to be retained. Colleges were to allot up to a quarter of their fellowships to laymen, and restrictions were placed upon non-residence. Fellows must not only reside, but must be tutors, office holders, incumbents of parishes within three miles of Carfax, or hold a certificate of study. Colleges might produce ordinances for the approval of the commissioners overhauling their statutes, and redeploying their revenues. A maximum of one fifth of their income might be devoted to the support of chairs, and they might suppress fellowships to raise the income of fellows to a sum not exceeding £250 p.a., to erect new buildings or to establish affiliated halls. Here Jowett's suggestions had been developed in the direction of the blue book. The principles set forth in the bill respecting oaths, private halls, special preferences and examinations of candidates for university and collegiate emoluments, and the tenure of fellowships were to be embodied in statutes to be approved by the commissioners before the beginning of the Michaelmas Term 1855; failing this the commissioners were to make the statutes themselves. These, subject to the approval of the Queen in Council, and to lying on the table of both houses of parliament for forty days without an address being carried against them in either house, should become binding. For the purposes of the act Christ Church was to be regarded as a college, and, as Jowett had urged, its studentships, like the fellowships of St. John's and New College, were to be divided into fellowships proper and scholarships; nothing, however, was said about his further proposal to quarter more professors upon the canonries of Christ Church.[73] Finally the

14

colleges were to present a statement of their affairs to the Visitor once at least in every seven years.[74]

Once published the bill went down to Oxford again for comment. Dean Gaisford truculently declared that he could not

> agree either with the principle or details of the measure, I must add that I think it not merely inexpedient but unjust and tyrannical.[75]

Other conservatives like Vice-Chancellor Cotton, Provost of Worcester, and Dr. Pusey were querulous,[76] but Gladstone could fairly reply that

> we have not sought in one single point to attract influence to the Crown. We have not strengthened the Professoriate by securing to it a factitious majority. We have left the restraints of celibacy and Holy Orders applicable, the first wholly, the second generally to fellowships. We have not founded elections upon the naked test of intellectual proficiency, but we propose to base preference upon fitness, of which the actual electors, such as the actual Oxford has produced, are to be the exclusive judges. We have repudiated the proposal to let young men be their own masters: and we declare that domestic discipline should be the rule and condition of admission into the university . . . [The bill] emancipates the emoluments of the university from restraints which have made . . . three fourths of them ineffective: and it emancipates the depressed classes of the university from a state of artificial and unnatural subordination which . . . had at length brought about it's certain but most unhappy consummation in a thorough divorce of *power* from influence.[77]

Nevertheless, the admittedly complex subjects of the tenure of fellowships and the special connexions of colleges with schools occasioned a good deal of disagreement and enabled the heads to fight their last action against the bill. Convocation was moved to petition against it lock stock and barrel. Sir William Heathcote urged the board to negotiate with the government on the question of the university constitution, but confident that Lord Derby would throw the bill out of the Lords if they made a demonstration, the ruling party on the board were adamant, and they could rely on all the threatened interests in the schools supporting them in Convocation.[78] The Tutors' Association immediately got out a statement against the Board, and the *Guardian* faithfully supported them, declaring that the petition was a folly which could be accepted neither by this government nor by any other.[79] On March 31 a vacation meeting of Convocation approved the petition by only 193 votes to 191, a result which meant virtual defeat for the Board, and guaranteed a second reading for the bill in the Commons.[80] Once again the residents acted generally against the heads, except in the case of colleges with strong close foundations such as New College, St. John's and Brasenose.[81]

The really serious feature of the voting was the abstention of a party of extreme liberals whose connexions in the House of Commons might render them acutely embarrassing to the government. Bonamy Price and Liddell (who had expected strong action from the government and who was reputed to be personally piqued at not being appointed to the executive commission)[82] together with J. B. Blackett, James Heywood and other radical M.P.s began to lobby support for the view that the bill was worse than no reform at all, and got up a petition to Russell attacking the provision for professors, and declaring that the bill aggravated the clerical character of the university. This was signed by A. P. Stanley, B. C. Brodie, H. H. Vaughan, Baden Powell, J. M. Wilson, A. H. Clough, Richard Congreve and others. Gladstone's reply was simply that there was no hope that a clause abrogating the obligation of fellows to enter holy orders could be passed through the Commons let alone the Lords, and

> as to the election of professors by themselves . . . this was our plan, and . . . we gave it up in deference to a strong representation from decided reformers at Oxford, and adopted in the main their proposal.

Jeune indeed was satisfied with the 'Pembroke compromise,' tried to restrain the extreme liberals, and deplored undue deference to the details of the blue book.[83] Nevertheless, the parliamentary prospects of the bill were not improved now that the alliance of liberals and catholics in Oxford in support of the bill had been weakened on the one flank by the secession of Pusey and Marriott, and on the other by a clique of high-powered reformers. The bill could no longer be represented as a measure agreed by everyone in the university but the heads, and Gladstone began to despond. He reckoned later that he had never had so rough a time with a bill as he was now given by Dean Liddell's conspiracies, and the wound was slow to heal.[84]

It was his misfortune to introduce the bill at one of the most peevish and disorderly times of a peevish and disorderly parliament, and at the very moment when political attention was distracted by the outbreak of the Crimean War. Derby determined that the result of the last vote in Convocation made it impossible to oppose the principle of the bill at the second reading, but he and his henchmen in the Commons were briefed by an Oxford delegation led by the Vice-Chancellor to play havoc with the details in committee.[85] These tactics were reinforced by a phalanx of radicals led by Blackett and

Heywood who shared Liddell's disillusionment with the conservative nature of the bill, and were supported by the London allies of the Oxford liberals.[86] Their first effort was to delay the bill irreparably by referring it to a select committee, and when this failed they attacked it clause by clause. They overthrew the Chancellor's nomination of one head and one professor to the Council, and it was never restored. They also substituted sectional election for congregational election of Council, the radicals in the name of independence for professors, the tories to rescue the choice of heads from a caucus of Tractarians.[87] Congregation, the invention of the royal commission, was now discovered to be a means of securing the permanent ascendancy of the Tractarian party. Furthermore, in committee as in Convocation, the privileges of schools were a very thorny topic. Sir William Heathcote who was sympathetic to the bill was still more sympathetic to the claims of Winchester upon New College, and carried an instruction to the committee that they be specially provided for.[88] This in itself threatened the bill's general arrangements with schools at the very time that the delaying tactics of the radicals and tories seemed likely to carry the day. By the beginning of June, 27 clauses relating to the university had been passed, but 31 relating to the colleges remained, and to these 75 amendments had been tabled. In this shape the bill had no hope at all of getting through the Lords before the end of the session. Gladstone was low in spirits,[89] but determined to fight. He abandoned the whole of the complicated arrangements for college statutes which the bill had contained, and made the reform of the colleges a simple matter of arrangement between the college and the commissioners, a college being given the right to reject any scheme of the commissioners by a two-thirds majority.[90] This arrangement, however, gave a cue to another loyal Wykhamist, Roundell Palmer, to carry an amendment enabling the governing body of any of the privileged schools to veto any ordinance for the abolition of their preference by a two-thirds majority.[91] Jeune was heart-broken at the prospect of his college being put at the mercy of the corporation of Abingdon. To Gladstone, with whom he had been in touch at every stage of the bill, he confessed

> I have the bitterness to know that two years of life and labour on the commission, odium incurred here, and lately increased, loss of private friendship, have been undergone in vain; and that any improvements which may be made under the bill as it now stands in the colleges, will only serve to place mine in a worse relative position. If I have contributed to the good of others it has been to my own great evil . . . it had been better for me at least and the college that I had not returned to it. The object

nearest to my heart frustrated, academic life now offers me little but mortification.[92]

Gladstone was equally mortified;[93] his Congregation had been so badly mauled that Heathcote recommended him to drop it altogether,[94] and the opening of foundations was threatened. Worse, however, was to befall; on June 22, after all Gladstone's promises to preserve the church character of the university, James Heywood moved the abolition of the tests, and in a good house obtained a majority of 91.[95]

This division caused universal surprise and consternation among Gladstone's friends, but it had been long prepared and sprang from one of the basic weaknesses of the coalition ministry. For some months the dissenting interests had been getting increasingly restive. When the blue book had been first published the dissenting journals had renewed their claim to a place in the national educational bodies (while admitting that few dissenters would make use of the opportunity),[96] but everything seemed to go against them. The Scottish university tests found few friends in the House other than Sir Robert Inglis,[97] but Heywood could make no progress against the English tests.[98] During the winter of 1853–4 the *Census of religious worship* was published which was not only damaging to the defenders of the establishment, but enabled the dissenters to claim that they now formed half of the church-going portion of the nation.[99] This fillip to the dissenting ego, however, was more than counterbalanced by the neglect they suffered in the formation of the coalition government and in the general trend of legislation. In the early months of 1854 half the divisions in the Commons were on ecclesiastical questions, and under government leadership they went consistently against the dissenting interest. The Irish Ministers' Money Bill, the Canadian Clergy Reserves Bill, the Church Building Acts Continuance Bill, Lord Blandford's Episcopal and Capitular Estates Bill, all pointed to parliamentary support for Anglican privilege, and in the very week that Heywood moved against the university test, the cabinet took the lead in defeating Clay's Church Rate Abolition Bill. One of the leading dissenting members was reported as saying that

> the coalition is formed upon the basis of giving the dissenters nothing; and I am glad it is so for that tells us what we have to do.

This temper was inflamed by the nonconformist press to a pitch not seen since the worst of the schools question in the later 'forties, and the ommission of any concessions to dissenters in the Oxford bill seemed not only a characteristic piece of ministerial machiavellianism, but an ideal question on which the dissenters could sink their differences.[100]

The Protestant Dissenting Deputies formed a committee of M.P.s who favoured religious liberty, and when the Oxford bill was expected they got up a petition in favour of the abolition of matriculation tests, had it signed by dissenting leaders like Heywood, Peto and Miall, radicals like Cobden and Hume, and Catholics like O'Connell, and presented to Russell on March 3, by a deputation which included Baden Powell of Oxford and J. J. Sylvester of Cambridge.[101] Russell was probably not quite candid with this deputation for he sent them away with the impression that

> although the Cabinet could not themselves propose such a measure as that asked by the Memorialists, they would not oppose it if proposed on the part of dissenters by independent members of the House.[102]

This was an invitation to agitation; the Liberation Society set its machine to work, petitions from congregations and corporations poured in, and the unitarian apostles James Martineau and J. H. Thom elicited public opinion in the usual form at a great public meeting in Liverpool. Another public meeting was planned in the City for the eve of the debate, and although the exigencies of the parliamentary time-table caused it to be cancelled, the maximum publicity was obtained for Heywood's motion by arranging that it should be made when the report was brought up.[103] On this occasion too the dissenters could reckon on more than the usual anti-ministerial voting by the conservatives. There were Cambridge members who saw no reason for the greater strictness of the Oxford matriculation test, and above all there was Lord Derby who had never forsworn the opinions he had expressed twenty years before in favour of the admission of dissenters. When Lord Stanley hinted broadly in the course of the debate that there was no foundation for the assertions of the government that Heywood's clause would never get through the House of Lords, it was plain that the cancellarial dignity sat lightly on his father's shoulders, and 50 tories trooped off into the nonconformist lobby.[104]

Though the result was a surprise, considerable forces had evidently conspired to produce it, and, particularly when Heywood determined to claim no more than a modest admission to the B.A. degree, Gladstone felt that the verdict of parliament could not be challenged; moreover the situation in which the basic education of the university was open to all, while the teaching and government remained firmly in the hands of the church, afforded ground for a stand upon principle. This at least was what Provost Hawkins had been campaigning for for twenty years, to the great wrath of the Tractarians.[105]

Their keynote now was anguish and dismay; Pusey, Marriott, Haddan, Keble (who had had a premonition that reform of any kind might mean the end of the university's connexion with the Church of England)[106] vied with each other in prophecies of woe, and began to talk of withdrawing from Oxford.[107] Pusey attempted to get the Hebdomadal Board to petition against the clause, but such was the confusion in that venerable body, that at one stage Jeune obtained a majority in favour of retaining only government and teaching in the hands of the church and that finally all motions fell to the ground and nothing was done.[108] Nor was Pusey more successful; his friends declared

> 1) there is little time. 2) Gladstone has set a bad example of pooh-poohing non-residents, as if all wisdom resided in the young M.As. So [he] gave it up.[109]

The great resistance of 1834 was not to be repeated, and soon the idea began to spread that all was not yet lost.[110] But attention was now focused on the House of Lords where the fate of the bill was no less remarkable than in the Commons.

The high-church press left the Lords in no doubt that they should keep the government to its pledges in regard to the test,[111] and Derby was embarrassed with advice from Symons, Hawkins and Gaisford; the main new point was that private halls took on a very different aspect if the test was to be repealed.[112] Proceedings in the upper house, however, travestied all expectations. It was quickly apparent that because of De La Warr's estimate of 'the temper of the House,'[113] or because (as he privately admitted to Hawkins) Derby's opinions as to the desirability of admitting dissenters remained unchanged,[114] or, as was widely alleged, because he wanted to get off to the races,[115] the university chancellor was not going to make a fight. No conservative whip was put on, and when the government peers found themselves unexpectedly in a majority, Goldwin Smith persuaded Gladstone to get them to reverse some of the changes which had been made in the bill in the Commons. Congregational election of the Hebdomadal Council was restored, and some of the sting was taken out of Roundell Palmer's clause protecting the privileged schools.[116] The admission of dissenters was 'combated only in the 'inaudible observations' by a noble lord unknown to the reporters' and by the silent votes of five bishops,[117] and the bill went back to the Commons much as the government wanted it. Their minority in the Lords had saved the day for the majority in the Commons.

As a result of an extraordinary chain of circumstances Oxford was now to be governed on principles somewhat different from any of those recommended during the previous four years. At the top, as the tutors had suggested, was an elected council consisting of the Vice-Chancellor and Proctors with six heads, six professors and six members of Convocation. The electing body, however, was to be Congregation, an institution which the tutors had not originally wanted at all, but not the Congregation which the Oxford liberals had wanted as late as the launching of the bill, for the official element in it was now to be swamped by the inclusion of all residents. The principles governing the opening of foundations were also the outcome of parliamentary controversy, and as in any case college regulations had to be approved by the commissioners their effect was obscure. Gladstone's friends among the tutors were the biggest gainers by the changes, but they were annoyed by the repeal of the tests as far as the bachelor's degree. This repeal made changes in the examination system almost inevitable, though the bill had originally avoided the question of studies, and put a different complexion upon the provision for private halls. Small wonder that Keble was chagrined about Gladstone,[118] or that diehard tories like Philip Bliss, Principal of St. Mary Hall, should see betrayal everywhere.[119]

The elections to the new council at the beginning of the next session bore out the balance of opinion in the university for the last few years. Tractarian meetings were held in Oriel with a view to promoting Pusey and others,[120] and Sewell

> took occasion for the text, 'Young men exhort to be sober-minded' to exhort the younger members of the university . . . to take especial care to avoid the company of dissenters should any intrude under the new bill; to warn them not to give Caesar, Jeremiah or Queen Victoria the things which belonged to the Church; and to join with him in as large amount of passive resistance to the decision of the legislature as was compatible with their position.[121]

The elections were quiet and there was a distinguished list of successful candidates. The elected heads were Williams (New College), Scott (Balliol), Hawkins (Oriel), Gaisford (Christ Church), Jeune (Pembroke), Symons (Wadham); the professors Hussey, Pusey, Daubeny, Cardwell, J. M. Wilson, Donkin; the members of Congregation were H. L. Mansel, J. B. Mozley, Dr. Lightfoot (Rector of Exeter), R. Michell, and Osborne Gordon. For the last place there was a tie between Charles Marriott and Mark Pattison. The two striking features about this council were its relatively conservative character,[122] and the wide range of interests represented. Scholarship was there in the persons of Gaisford, Daubeny, Wilson and Scott; the men of business of the old board in Cardwell, Hawkins, Williams and Jeune; the Tractarians in Pusey and Mozley. The great outcry against the new council came from the liberals who could hardly have expected much more than the two seats obtained by Wilson and Jeune,[123] and had only themselves to blame that when the tie between Marriott and Mark Pattison was resolved by a fresh poll, the liberal vote was divided by the nomination of Thomson of Queen's, and Marriott got in by five votes.[124] Despite liberal abuse the council proved itself a business-like body, and one of the unexpected results of its meetings was the growth of mutual respect between Jeune and Pusey as each observed the other's business capacity. Indeed, election to the Council and the Crimean War between them effected a notable broadening in Pusey's outlook. The one extended his range of acquaintance and gave scope to his administrative talents; the other led him to the newspapers, and away from his exclusive addiction to theology into current literature and affairs.[125]

The Council began by appointing committees to clear up its procedure and to make recommendations on the new statutes required under the Act, especially those concerning the admission of dissenters and the establishment of private halls.[126] The outlook for the dissenters was at first not bright. Robert Scott, Master of Balliol, proposed to enforce a test on members of his college (a dubious proposal finally vetoed by the college Visitor)[127] and the committee appointed by the Hebdomadal Board reported that no changes should be made in the examination statute to ease the scruples of dissenters.[128] Jeune found this proposition too painful to contemplate, and regarded it as 'treating Christianity like mythology;' in January 1855 he got another committee appointed which finally recommended that the present system be retained for Anglicans, while those who declared themselves to be dissenters be excused from examination in religious knowledge and required to bring up extra books in Greek and Latin instead.[129] In March a statute to this effect was promulgated in Congregation, which met for the first time on legislative business. To the dismay of Gladstone (who was being faced by a new campaign from Heywood)[130] old Dr. Macbride proposed an amendment which would have the effect of reintroducing an examination in religious knowledge for dissenters, but he was strongly opposed by Pusey and Jeune.[131] The amendments proposed created an interesting procedural complication, for when they had been considered and rejected by the Hebdomadal Council, and the draft statute came again before Congregation, the Vice-Chancellor ruled that the statute could only be accepted or rejected without discussion and that proceedings should be in Latin. Dr. Marsham, Warden of Merton, who was out to kill the new statute, protested but was put down, and the new statute accepted by a considerable margin.[132]

This statute proved to be satisfactory as long as the tests lasted, except in one embarrassing case. This was shortly raised by Sir

Culling Eardley, a baronet of advanced evangelical convictions. Eardley had been at Oriel a generation before, and though a member of the Church of England had had conscientious scruples about subscribing the XXXIX Articles, and had consequently gone away without his degree. He now applied to have his name restored to the books of the college with a view to proceeding B.A., but found that he must either subscribe or declare himself 'extra ecclesiam', a sentence of excommunication he was unwilling to accept. On August 15, 1855, his case was discussed in the House of Lords, and the Lord Chancellor pronounced that the university was acting contrary to the intention of the act. Eardley, however, took his personal grievance no further, as he was now involved in a scheme to establish an evangelical college in Oxford in which nonconformists and their anglican fellow-travellers should dwell together under the aegis of Lord Shaftesbury.[133]

This case revealed the difficulties under which the university now laboured in its legal obligation to draft a private halls statute. The question of halls and especially private halls occasioned heart-searching and controversy out of all proportion to the results finally achieved. Halls were sanctioned in the blue book, but it cost Marriott a sharp struggle to get the Tutors' Association to give them a blessing,[134] and there were further difficulties when Gladstone took up the scheme. When the crisis was upon them the Hebdomadal Board were prepared to offer a subsidy towards the building of a hall in return for strict measures against luxury; to provide against theological extravagance, however, the principals of new halls were to be nominated by the Chancellor. The Tractarian party as a whole came out against this, and the proposal was defeated in Convocation.[135] Meanwhile Marriott had been urging Gladstone to make provision for private halls in his bill, and was rewarded by clauses which empowered the university to make regulations under which the Vice-Chancellor might license M.As. to open private halls within a mile and a half of Carfax, to make regulations for their government and for the attendance of the students upon Divine Worship, and to make provision for their aggregation into one or more great halls of the university. At once the heads of the Tractarian party who had been seeking a hall for themselves for years, and especially Pusey and Keble, exploded in anguish at the thought of immense numbers of halls opening under the inspiration of theological parties, and a general relaxation of discipline, and Gladstone was hard put to, to get them to trust in the good sense of the university.[136]

After the act was passed, both Pusey and Marriott were put on the Council committee to draft the new statute, but it was not now legally possible for them to prevent a statute being made, and in any case Marriott succumbed to illness which by midsummer 1855 put an end to his active career. The committee finally produced a statute which provided

> that in order to obtain a licence to open a private hall the candidate must be a member of Convocation, 28 years old at least, known in the university by recent residence, recommended by sufficient testimonials, & the occupier of a house approved by the Vice-Chancellor. He shall also on receiving his licence sign a declaration binding him to the proper government of it.
>
> His deputy shall also be a member of Convocation, & any tutor appointed by him shall have subscribed the 39 Articles.

In May 1855 this statute passed Convocation without opposition,[137] but Keble was still not satisfied, for the requirement of recent residence put paid to the men most fitted in his view to stem the evils of the times.[138]

After all the Tractarian agitation and all the rumours that the Roman Catholics were returning,[139] it was the evangelicals who took immediate advantage of the statute, and set up a hall under E. A. Litton, an Irishman, a double first and former fellow of Oriel, whose theological work is still read. The ultimate intentions of this plan were suggested in notices in the dissenting press offering cheap residence and protection against infidelity and Tractarianism. Early in 1856 the pillars of the Evangelical Alliance announced their intention of transforming Litton's hall into a grand Protestant Hall governed by trustees, and of seeking exemption for their members from the university examinations in divinity in return for a certificate that they had passed an equivalent examination in the hall. These concessions were never forthcoming, the Alliance produced no great supply of undergraduates, and when Litton obtained preferment in Gloucestershire in 1860 the enterprise came to an end.[140] The other new hall was opened by George Butler, son of a former Dean of Peterborough who

> obtained a license as occupier of a large house in the best part of Oxford, & issued an advertisement addressed rather to anxious parents & men of taste and information than to Poor Scholars. Both he and Mrs. Butler [were] agreeable and accomplished persons,[141]

but they were even less successful than Litton in filling their hall. Goldwin Smith's expectation that private halls would become uneconomic through competition for sites proved ludicrously exaggerated,[142] and the development of private halls was frustrated by all those factors which had long led Jeune to insist on the superiority and cheapness of endowed colleges.

The party strife which underlay the apprehensions occasioned by the private halls ruffled the old public halls also, and great efforts to galvanise them into new usefulness were made by one of the Oriel high-churchmen, D. P. Chase. He had been elected into a fellowship along with A. H. Clough, and in recent years had diversified his labours as tutor and senior Proctor during the crisis of 1853–4 by curious experiments with home-made Turkish baths.[143] Chase endeavoured to prevent dissenters being exempted from the divinity examinations when the new statute was passed in 1855,[144] and he was full of the Tractarian party's enthusiasm for the education of poor clergy under discipline.

In January 1854 Chase submitted a paper to Lord Derby, who as Chancellor was Visitor of the halls, urging that they be made more useful. As things stood Magdalen Hall was doing useful work and was a considerable college in its own right; St. Mary Hall, of which Chase had been Vice-Principal for five years, was doing some educational work, but was never full; St. Alban and New Inn Halls were accomplishing nothing and were in any case too small to pay their way. Once the headship ceased to carry a seat on the Hebdomadal Board it might be difficult to find Principals. The unspecialised teaching of the halls had been deprived of whatever virtue it might have had by the extension of university studies, and their reputation was depressed by their receiving migrants from the colleges. It seemed to Chase to be foolish to talk of creating new halls until the old ones were full; what was needed was to concentrate the existing class of hall students at Magdalen Hall and St. Edmund Hall, to try to fill the others with the sons of poor clergy, and to provide for the teaching by appointing as Principals not the present leisured gentlemen, but working tutors who were supported by fellowships at other colleges. At present this was forbidden by the statutes. In the case of St. Mary Hall, the Principal should be a fellow of Oriel College which the hall buildings adjoined, and the college should be asked to furnish the rooms of the hall, fix the rents and admit the men to the college lectures. In return the hall would cease to admit migrants, and raise its matriculation standards to those of the college. However the Chancellor was none too anxious to have his patronage limited to the fellows of Oriel, and some of the latter thought it impossible

> to embody in the educational working of a college a number of scholars of a poorer class without danger to the social status of the College . . . noone thinks it our duty to transfer our labour from one class of society to another. To say nothing of the loss of respectability; it would also be a diminution . . . of usefulness . . .

The scheme for affiliating St. Mary Hall to Oriel therefore fell through. Chase, however, managed to get the statute which forbade the head of a hall to hold a fellowship repealed, and on the dying recommendation of Philip Bliss succeeded as Principal. His reforms were now limited to letting out some rooms to frugal scholars, refusing to accept migrants and arranging combined tuition with St. Alban Hall,[145] where there had been even more far-reaching changes.

In 1855 St. Alban Hall was empty, and St. Edmund Hall which until the retirement of Vice-Principal John Hill in 1851 had been full of young evangelicals, was almost empty; Edmund Hobhouse, fellow of Merton, a high-churchman in the confidence of Bishop Wilberforce, had a scheme for filling them both. He

> made a Concordat with the Principal of St. Edmund Hall, to receive, free of tuition and room-rent, 10 men, (sons if such offer, of poor clergymen), on condition of my vesting in Trustees' hands a sum of money sufficient to pay a V. Principal. I have vested £5000 and 10 men are now enjoying an university education all of whom would else have had the extremest difficulty to obtain [it] . . . and all of whom are desirous of entering the ministry.[146]

The evangelical hold upon St. Edmund Hall had been broken by the appointment of John Barrow as Principal in 1854,[147] but it was a bold high-church move to purchase the entry. Hobhouse's next design was upon St. Alban Hall. He first sounded the Principal, Dr. Cardwell, whether he would transfer the site and building to Merton for use as an affiliated hall in exchange for Merton property in North Oxford; Hobhouse, however, could not convert his own college to this scheme, and Cardwell refused the Warden's offer to buy the hall outright. Hobhouse then proposed to make the Principal

> an annual payment of £50 for the repairs of the Hall, £200 per annum to the V. Principal for the tuition and government of the hall, & a supplementary sum to the Mancipal to make amends for deficiencies and damage; on the condition of allowing the V.P. & ten poor scholars to occupy [the] only available rooms, without the payment of any rent or fees usually paid to the Principal.

Cardwell, a stout opponent of the Tractarians, had some qualms about the party with whom he was dealing, but felt that as long as he kept the admissions in his own hands all would be well. With new private halls advertising for men, and with New College and Magdalen taking in commoners, he had scant hopes of putting his hall to educational use in any other way, and he agreed to the plan. Hobhouse begged for money assiduously in high-church circles, but in 1858 he became Bishop of Nelson in New Zealand, and the subscriptions went on with greater difficulty under the management of William Jacobson, regius professor of divinity. In 1860 Cardwell died and the benefaction was withdrawn, though W. C. Slater whom Derby raised from Vice-Principal to Principal, made efforts to continue a scheme for frugal men. Like Litton's evangelical hall, however, Hobhouse's charity showed that it was difficult even for well-organised church parties to obtain a permanent result with an unendowed hall, and already Lord Derby was coming to think that there was little future for the halls except in close connexion with the colleges.[148]

It was the colleges which provided the chief work of the executive commission appointed under the act. The original names had been chosen with a view to minimising opposition in the university. At the head was the earl of Ellesmere, an able peer of liberal inclinations who long ago had been one of the promoters of the London University; in the more recent past he had incurred the wrath of the Tractarians by condoning the marriage of widowers with their deceased wives' sisters,[149] so he was balanced by one of the straitest set, Mr. Justice Coleridge, and another lawyer of high-church sympathies deeply respected by him, Sir John Awdry,[150] who had ventured into print on the question of university reform. The final two members were to be churchmen, and first the bishop of Ripon, C. T. Longley, sometime student of Christ Church and headmaster of Harrow, and a future primate. As a sop to the liberals the last place was to go to a member of the royal commission, and as the bishop of Norwich was ill, and in any case *persona non grata* in Oxford, it fell to the man regarded by Pusey as least noxious, G. H. S. Johnson, Dean of Wells.[151] The important choice of secretaries was governed by the same consideration of balance; Goldwin Smith represented the liberal, and S. W. Wayte, fellow and tutor of Trinity, and secretary to the Tutors' Association, the conservative wing of the Oxford reformers, and they proved a capable and co-operative pair.[152] Harmony was never a characteristic of the commission,[153] and the names were received in parliament with such a torrent of abuse from the liberals that Coleridge came close to resigning before the bill got to the House of Lords.[154] When it was decided to leave the college questions to be negotiated by the commission, two more commissioners were appointed, and again high church fears that the balance was to be upset where not fulfilled. The new members were

> Lord Harrowby and Mr. Cornewall Lewis—a respectable peer of negative views [i.e. evangelical leanings] and active habits, and a clever laborious Whig, capable of thinking for himself, and not destitute of candour, fairness and temper.[155]

The university and colleges had a year's grace in which to prepare their schemes, and the commission had barely got going in the Michaelmas term of 1855 when Cornewall Lewis resigned and was succeeded by Edward Twisleton. Twisleton was an aristocratic version of Goldwin Smith.

> He was of a quick, impulsive temperament, enthusiastic. . . . His politics were, like those of his ancestors, Liberal. At Oxford or soon after leaving it, he became a student of German philosophy and theology, and he imbibed the spirit of German Rationalism. His mind was disturbed by questions as to the possibility of divine revelation, and . . . he found no way of escaping from his difficulties. . . .[156]

Sir William Heathcote groaned that the applecart would now be upset,[157] and so it immediately proved.

Among the colleges which had proceeded furthest with the revision of their statutes was Exeter, which sought to safeguard its foundations, now that the matriculation test was abolished, by enacting that all scholars and fellows were to be members of the Church of England, or of some church in communion with her. At the beginning of the Michaelmas term, the liberal dean of Wells made a spirited protest against such college tests and also against the obligation of fellows to enter holy orders. College tests he considered to be contrary to the spirit of the act, the law requiring nothing more than the tests imposed by the Act of Uniformity. Obliging fellows to take orders was bad for individuals, for the university and for the church.[158] No sooner had Twisleton been appointed to the Board than the commissioners agreed to accept the Exeter statutes as a model for other colleges; at once, with the support of the dean, he again opposed college tests but they were in a minority of two. On January 10, 1856 they moved again on the Balliol statutes, and were again defeated, and a month later Twisleton produced an elaborate memorandum showing that[159]

> all general arguments which have been used founded in the supposed intention of Parliament that dissenters should not be admitted into college fellowships, appear to me inapplicable to the precise point now under consideration. For it seems to be a direct contravention of the policy of existing laws to regard anyone as a dissenter who will conform to the liturgy of the Church of England. The laws advisedly refrain from making inquisition of lay fellows as to whether their theological opinions are identical with those of the Church of England provided only that they themselves are conformists and to deal with such conformists as dissenters involves the attempt of prying into and

investigating delicate questions which it was the obvious intention of the legislature to leave undefined and untouched.

This conflict of opinion was the more serious as James Heywood
was setting the wheels turning for an attack in parliament against
the latest batch of college statutes approved by the commissioners.
He was lobbying for parliamentary support and arranging through
Mark Pattison for a petition to come up from Oxford, while Pattison
himself was extracting advice from a somewhat reluctant dean of
Wells.[160] Moreover, the coalition of tory and radical which had
abolished the matriculation test seemed likely to form again. Without
weighing the political consequences D. P. Chase had written to Sir
John Pakington to claim support for his defence of the 'indigentes.'
Chase's argument was that the act bound the colleges to make
ordinances for promoting the main designs of founders and donors.
Amongst these was that their bounty should be enjoyed by those
who needed it, an eleemosynary end which the commissioners were
determined to oppose.[161]

Twisleton and the dean of Wells had indeed attempted to abolish
all restrictions on the amount of private property compatible with
tenure of a fellowship at Balliol, but had ended as usual in a minority
of two,[162] and the proposal at Oriel attacked by Chase was that a
private income of £500 should disqualify, and that indigence should
be specifically provided for by the conversion of fellowships into
exhibitions.[163] Provost Hawkins and Chase, however, wanted the right
to pay attention to indigence in their elections without being bound
by definite limits, and answered the argument that they ought to elect
the most able man by the assertion that 'persons who do not need a
Tutor's salary will not undertake a Tutor's work.'[164] The commissioners, however, refused to accept a petition of conservative residents
in favour of the Oriel position,[165] and after petitioning the Privy
Council the college had finally to yield.[166] Nor, on this occasion,
did Heywood and Pakington find parliament willing to upset the
machinery it had so laboriously set in motion,[167] and Heywood
exposed himself to ridicule by objecting to the rule that

> the fellows of Lincoln should henceforth be deprived of their
> fellowships 'for notorious incontinence.' He says (we give his
> words) 'that the deprivation of a fellow for notorious inconti-
> nence *when celibacy is compulsory, and the custom of absolute
> monastic seclusion is generally known not to prevail in the Univer-
> sity of Oxford,* appears to be impracticable under existing
> circumstances.' He therefore objects to the retention of the old
> rule on this head.[168]

When an appeal went up to the Privy Council on the question

whether dissenters might qualify for fellowships as Twisleton urged, there was a real possibility that the commissioners might resign, and be replaced by a much more radical body; but again the corner was turned.[169]

In the end the work of the commission turned out as its composition had suggested from the beginning. With the aid of supplementary acts the commission completed its labours in 1858 to the applause of reformers of the high-church kind. The *Guardian* declared that

> it applied itself without noise or bustle, but with great judgement and unremitting energy, to its task, and by dint of much hard work no little skill and tact, and a general spirit of fairness, candour and courtesy, it accomplished in the space of four years, all that it had been appointed to do, with a single exception . . . there cannot be a doubt that they have performed a very considerable work, on the whole well; that, without compromising the main principles of the Act of Parliament, they have dealt tenderly with the Colleges; that their spirit has been conservative and conciliatory; that they have laboured to reform, not to root up; to invigourate, not to revolutionise, the Oxford system.[170]

To the diligence and conciliatory spirit of the commissioners their correspondence[171] and the number of professorial endowments they wheedled from unwilling colleges bear ample testimony. Nevertheless, the very conservative character of the reform was bound to disappoint the more visionary liberals. No-one doubted that even the partial opening of foundations did a great amount of good, but in Mark Pattison's words

> this sweeping away of local claims was nearly all the good that the Commission of 1854 effected. After all the contention about the professoriate what the Commission did in this direction was without method—crude, sporadic.[172]

Though Gladstone hoped to have staved off state intervention indefinitely, the liberals were by no means satisfied, and were shortly to find the remaining academic subscriptions a worse burden than they had suspected. The 'single exception' which had rebuffed the offers of the commission was St. John's College. The anglocatholic press had no use for Dr. Wynter in any case, and could find no words too hard for the stubborn determination of his college to keep for its own members both the advantages of its own close foundations and the opportunities of the new open foundations elsewhere. In 1861, however, a committee of the privy council compelled the college to accept a settlement even less palatable than that which the commissioners had offered.[173]

15

CHAPTER X

OXFORD REFORMED

Oxford *is* a queer place; it is getting into a strange state. Many of the older men liberal and reasonable; the young tutors, who have too much power, in a violent state of reactionary obstructiveness.

SIR THOMAS DYKE ACLAND to his wife, November 3, 1865.
A. H. D. ACLAND, *Memoir and Letters of Sir Thomas Dyke Acland*, p. 256.

THE violent controversies of the early 'fifties effected surprisingly little change in the balance of forces in Oxford. After the secessions to Rome which followed the Gorham Judgment, and as the Tractarian juniors ebbed away to country livings, Pusey felt himself to be fighting a solitary battle against the inroads of rationalism. On a broader stage, the deference of Lord Palmerston to Shaftesbury's advice on matters of church patronage, 'those unnatural alliances of the evangelicals with the liberals,' were evidence to him that evangelicalism had sold the pass. On the other hand Pusey admitted in 1858 that there were questions on which he could carry the Hebdomadal Council with him, that his influence there was growing no less, and (indifferent preacher as he was) his sermons retained their magnetism.[1]

Pusey's confused estimate of his own standing was due not simply to his bookish inability to comprehend those who differed sharply from him, but to the undoubtedly perplexing course of Oxford liberalism. Unlike Liddell and his allies the majority of the Oxford liberals had accepted Gladstone's reform, and the more enterprising were already looking for a reconstruction of Oxford studies. Mark Pattison had his plan,[2] and the blue book supplied another. Moreover, the opening of fellowships to competition gave new opportunities to progressive intellect, which no-one seized more eagerly than Jowett and the other successful tutors of Balliol. In the later 'fifties the colonisation of other colleges by Balliol men went on apace, and with it went the extension of liberal influence. Nowhere did this process have a greater impact than at All Souls. Here the executive commissioners found that the process of turning a club into a college was a good deal more difficult than that of opening a close foundation. They apparently played with the idea of vesting the election of fellows in a mixed board composed partly of members from outside the college. In the end, elections were left, as in other societies, to a college meeting, but it was laid down that none but first-class men or university prizemen should be eligible, and there should be no regard to birth or family circumstances. From the beginning, however, there were complaints in the liberal press that gross injustice was being done in elections to fellowships at All Souls,[3] and when the college received its ordinances from the Commissioners early in 1857, it passed a by-law which was considered by three young fellows of Balliol origin, A. G. Watson, W. H. Fremantle, and Godfrey Lushington, to be completely evasive. Under the by-law the examination was placed in the hands of a small committee and then

> the Fellows sat round the common room and the names were proposed one by one; but there was no assurance that the thirty or forty electors had examined the papers, and a report made by a small body of examiners gave little information; indeed it usually stated that all the candidates were worthy of becoming fellows. Some of the ablest young men were put aside . . .

The common room then elected the new fellows according to what they considered their merits, but with no special reference to their aptitudes for law and modern history. The three fellows obtained a sympathetic opinion from the executive commissioners, and appealed to the college Visitor, the Archbishop of Canterbury. The Archbishop's opinion was received in October 1859 and was not encouraging, and so the fellows went to the Queen's Bench. For the next two years the case was heard and heard again, the expenses being paid by outside liberals as various as Frederick Temple and Lord Lansdowne. And it accorded well with the eighteenth-century flavour of the whole conflict that the issue was not settled when the dissident fellows received a favourable verdict; the college then framed a new by-law which forbade an examiner to make any report except upon the papers he had marked and even this might not be done at the general meeting at which social claims were discussed. Finally in 1864 this evasive device was set aside by the Archbishop on the advice of Sir John Coleridge and Dr. Twiss.[4] By such means the liberals battered open the doors even of All Souls.

In a different way the open competition for fellowships led to radical changes at Christ Church. The executive commissioners had felt debarred from dealing with the constitutional anomalies which arose from the double status of the House as college and cathedral. Under the new ordinances the senior students received the emoluments of fellows, but the government remained firmly in the hands of the Chapter. From the beginning so loyal a son of the House as Osborne Gordon had prophesied that under the changed circumstances students would not be content with their inferior status.[5] When the poor recent performance of Christ Church in the schools became a target for criticism in the press,[6] when it became necessary to seek able staff in competition with other colleges, and when the

senior students began to complain that they had insufficient money
for educational purposes, a settlement was clearly urgent, and in 1866
the issues between the Chapter and the students were referred for
arbitration to the Archbishop of Canterbury, Sir John Coleridge,
Sir John Awdry, Edward Twisleton and Sir Roundell Palmer. The
referees rapidly and unanimously conceded the justice of the students'
case, and new statutes were drawn up by which certain revenues were
reserved to the Chapter to pay their salaries and maintain the
cathedral, while the senior students were to share with the Chapter
the government of the House and the management of the remaining
revenues.[7] This victory too was in some sense a liberal gain, for it
ended the unchecked rule of a Chapter which, even with Liddell in
the Deanery, was the most conservative governing body in Oxford.

The university liberals also profited from twenty years of almost
unbroken whig and liberal government patronage after the act of
1854. In 1855 Gaisford died, and Liddell not only succeeded him at
Christ Church but secured his chair of Greek for Jowett.[8] In the
following year A. P. Stanley returned to Oxford as regius professor
of ecclesiastical history, adding a much needed social grace to the
Oxford liberal armoury. His winsome ways, his preaching, his
breakfast parties, his poaching on Pusey's preserves by giving critical
courses on the Old Testament under the guise of ecclesiastical history,[9]
his Sunday night talks on the New Testament, did more than anything else to sustain and recruit the party during the next few years.
Even conservative patronage seemed to play into liberal hands in
1858, for Lord Derby acknowledged Goldwin Smith's services as
secretary to the executive commission by installing him regius professor of modern history.[10] Conservative preferment did nothing to
cool Goldwin Smith's propagandist zeal, for he at once plunged into
controversy against Mansel's conservative Bampton Lectures, and
dismayed even liberals by emulating a course of Bamptons in his
own inaugurals.

> We have in a pamphlet of ninety pages, nearly all the leading
> problems in theology, morals, and metaphysics. Amongst the
> preliminary questions disposed of are the attributes of the
> Creator and the character of Christ—the origin of evil and a
> future state—the immortality of the soul and the sanctions of
> morality—the doctrines of free will and necessity—the philos-
> ophy of the Absolute and the theory of the Inconceivable.
> Comte and Hegel, Mr. Mansel and Mr. Mill, Mr. Buckle and
> Mr. Darwin, are refuted in successive paragraphs, or tossed
> upon the horns of a lively dilemma. And all this in two lectures
> upon the Study of History! And à propos of a proposal to reduce
> that study to a method.[11]

Nevertheless, from a liberal point of view, Goldwin Smith was a good exchange for his predecessor, H. H. Vaughan, whose sterile tenure of the chair was the worst possible advertisement for the professorial system he advocated.

Seniority was bringing other liberals to the fore. Conington became the first Corpus professor of Latin in 1854. At the same time Max Müller, suspect as a German and a friend of the Chevalier Bunsen, became Taylorian professor, and in the following year Benjamin Brodie became professor of chemistry. By 1858 it was Francis Jeune's turn to succeed as Vice-Chancellor; his enthusiasm for reform, like that of William Thomson who attained dignity as Provost of Queen's in 1855, ebbed somewhat once the act and his own public recognition were safe, but his vigour and competence were unabated, and he did much to get the new government of the Hebdomadal Council working. 'Everything cannot go exactly as we wish,' declared Max Müller, 'but the avalanche rolls in the right direction.'[12]

Deriving in part from the great tide of preferment, and reinforcing the liberal tendency among the younger men, were important changes in the Greats school, which still held unchallenged primacy among Oxford studies. For twenty years or more the philosophical element in the Greats school had been steadily increasing in importance. The development of the Oxford examination system had gradually raised the level of linguistic achievement among the honours men, and transferred attention from the language to the substance of the books they brought up. In consequence ancient history and philosophy gained in weight, the latter especially, for the school had always been biased towards an abstract intellectual discipline by the importance attached to logic. In the generation before 1850 the university curriculum had gradually taken cognizance of the new branches of learning which had grown up outside, and Oxford philosophy had caught up with intellectual currents from which it had been formerly isolated. Sir William Hamilton had enjoyed a vogue in the schools, and then Oxford studies in Aristotle had been put on a scientific basis by contact with German philology. All these changes were given vivid prominence by the Examination Statute of 1850. Scholarship was now examined at Honour Moderations and the final school was left unencumbered for the examination of history and philosophy. So striking at that moment were the prospects of Oxford philosophy, that Mark Pattison saw in them the key to the future development of the university, and in a remarkable essay persuaded himself that his own years as a college tutor had witnessed the culmination of the whole history of higher education.[13]

Certainly the years which followed the new statute saw great changes in the reading offered for the school. Jowett introduced Plato's *Republic* and Bacon's *Novum Organon* as standard books,

and out of the Hegelian well drew a course on the history of philosophy as part of the apparatus of philosophy itself. All these became
essential equipment for the first-class man.[14] For a number of years
the study of Butler (first introduced by Dr. Hampden) and of the
Scottish philosophers, Dugald Stewart, Reid and Hamilton went on,[15]
but the influence of Butler is said to have been killed by Mark
Pattison (who certainly wrote against it), and Montagu Burrows
(the conservative seaman who matriculated as a married man at the
age of 33 and became Chichele Professor of Modern History in 1862)
claimed to have been the last to take up Butler's *Analogy* in the
schools in 1856.[16] By the early 'sixties the influence of all other
English writers was overshadowed by that of John Stuart Mill.
Mill's immense range, his logic, metaphysics, politics and economics,
and his consistency strengthened his impact upon the Oxford school,
and not only was he liberal in the political sense, but, as E. S. Talbot
recalled, he helped to unsettle the faith of Oxford churchmen by his
skill in accounting for what they imagined to be ultimate data, and
especially conscience. Much more important, Mill's inductive lines
of thought combined with the influence of Oxford Hegelianism to
produce startling changes in the outlook of the English catholics of
the next generation. Pusey and his friends had based a deductive
theology upon a clear and authoritative revelation, and commanded
men to obey it; but long before the truth came out in the publication
of *Lux Mundi* in 1889, the younger post-tractarians had been
attracted by a view of religion as explaining not only the church but
the world, and were not commanding but appealing for loyalty to
Christ on the basis of an inductive theology. They sought to show
how the best and truest things were fulfilled in Him.[17] The full dis-
comfort of the chasm which opened was felt by H. P. Liddon who
stood upon Pusey's side, and was unable to bridge the gulf; he is
now convicted by catholic writers of 'anti-critical conservatism,'[18]
and had probably done most of what he could for his party in Oxford,
before he became a canon of St. Paul's in 1870. In short the trans-
formations in the Oxford catholic party which had been begun by
the experience of opposition, by their support of Gladstone's tortuous
political evolution, by the harmonising of religion and culture in an
incarnational theology by men like Richard Church[19] who were
writing for an Anglican public in the *Guardian*, were confirmed by
the developments in the Greats school. Liberal catholicism and still
more, liberalism unqualified, seemed to be the intellectual outcome
of the dethronement of old authority in the schools.

Yet the history of the university would not have taken the course
it did in the twenty years between the two commissions, if the liberals
had carried the day in the way they expected, and some later writers
have supposed. There was a good deal of resistance to liberal advance

both on the intellectual level and in college politics. The Bampton Lectures, often a guide to current concern, had been delivered in the early 'fifties by a series of evangelical and liberal preachers, but in 1858 H. L. Mansel of Magdalen attempted to demolish liberal rationalism in his course on *The limits of religious thought examined*, while in the following year George Rawlinson of Exeter dealt with modern criticism in the *Historical evidences of the truth of the scripture records stated anew, with special reference to the doubts and discoveries of modern times.*[20] Mansel's lectures were delivered to packed congregations at St. Mary's, and created a considerable sensation when they were published, going into numerous editions at home, abroad, and in America. He attempted to dispose of the rationalist claim to determine what was and what was not revelation, by asserting the absolute nature of God to be inconceivable. By this argument Mansel exposed himself to violent controversy with Goldwin Smith and F. D. Maurice, and displeased some even of the Oxford orthodox,[21] but his friends hailed him as a new Bishop Butler, and it was no doubt the determined efforts they made to get his works established as standard texts for the schools that aroused the wrath of Goldwin Smith.[22]

The enemies of liberalism were strong in intrigue as well as vigorous in argument. In 1851 the fellows of Lincoln after manoeuvres of astonishing tortuousness elected James Thompson their Rector instead of Mark Pattison, and the deep gloom which overcame him heralded the onset of mental illness like that which had already overwhelmed his father and brought misery to the family at Hauxwell rectory.[23] An equally famous liberal disappointment came in 1854 when Robert Scott was elected Master of Balliol in preference to Jowett. By this date nearly half the fellows of Balliol were Jowett's pupils and he was given some reason to expect a reward for his labours as tutor. What Jowett seems never to have realised, however, and what is concealed by his biographers' slighting references to his opponents' adopting 'the expedient of bringing up a candidate from the country,' was that nine years before, on the prospect of a vacancy, the intention of the college had been to bring up Robert Scott, Rector of Duloe, and joint editor with Liddell of the famous Greek Lexicon.[24] The senior fellows now saw no reason to exchange the eminently respectable pretensions of Scott for the more recent merits and dubious orthodoxy of Jowett. Though dismayed, Jowett was not crushed by this defeat like Pattison, but he had to wait longer for his reward; in 1861 Pattison became a most unsatisfactory Rector of Lincoln, but it was 1865 before Jowett could get his way in Balliol College meetings, and 1870 before he succeeded to the headship.

There were more equivocal episodes elsewhere. In 1866, for example, after Dr. Jeune had departed for higher things, the authorities of

Pembroke were accused by the liberals of serious misdemeanours in their fellowship election. The Master was said to have deterred a number of candidates from presenting themselves by saying that several of the fellows had decided in advance whom they would elect, but still ten candidates, some of whom had distinguished records, entered for the examination. The successful candidate, however, was the man named in advance by the Master, who six years previously had obtained a second class, and had since failed several times in Pembroke elections. He had, however, acted as tutor to the passmen in the college, and it was alleged that a considerable portion of the examination questions were taken from the books on which he lectured. The *Times* made a feature of the case, one of the defeated candidates alleged that such episodes were not rare under the present system, and the odour was intensified by discrepancies in the replies of the Master and fellows.[25]

Much more serious from a liberal point of view than an occasional interruption in the free trade in fellowships, was the general failure of the colleges to endow the new chairs directed by the ordinances of the university commissioners. Magdalen which was reputed to spend £6000 p.a. in augmenting college livings,[26] created only two of the four chairs for which it was responsible (the first going to H. L. Mansel), and the colleges together established only half a dozen. As it also proved difficult to increase the emolument of the older chairs, even the limited hopes of strengthening the university which had been entertained by the executive commission, steadily faded.

As elections to the Hebdomadal Council succeeded each other, the fruits of university democracy suggested that, from a liberal viewpoint, Liddell had been wise in his generation. After the disappointments of the first election things went hopefully for the liberals for a while. In Michaelmas Term 1855 Bartholomew Price beat strong evangelical and high-church candidates for the seat vacated by Professor Donkin, though J. E. Sewell of New College defeated Mark Pattison for that resigned by Charles Marriott.[27] Eighteen months later in an election openly 'regarded as a struggle between the old stagers and the progressive men of the university,' Dr. Cradock, the highly-connected and whiggish Principal of Brasenose, routed Dr. Plumptre, Master of University, who had been Vice-Chancellor under the old system.[28] In the following autumn the only change which resulted from the retirement of half the Council brought in J. M. Wilson, the liberal of Corpus. In the by-elections which followed, however, the aged Dr. Cotton of Worcester beat the liberal Thomson of Queen's and Jowett, who had been beaten in the first round, was overwhelmed by Dr. Hawkins in a by-election by 89 votes to 11.[29] In 1858 when Dr. Jeune vacated his seat on becoming

Vice-Chancellor, Liddell succeeded him unopposed. This, however, was the high-watermark of liberal influence in the Council; their draft examination statutes received a fearful drubbing at the hands of Congregation, and they lost a great opportunity to consolidate their position at the election of 1860 when the aged evangelical heads of Worcester and Wadham retired. Both liberals and conservatives tried their hand with election lists, and the result was a drawn battle; three new members were elected, E. T. Turner (Brasenose, conservative), J. R. T. Eaton (Merton, liberal-conservative), and A. P. Stanley (liberal).[30]

After this check the liberal tide seemed to be running out. In 1863 Frederic Bulley, President of Magdalen, displaced Dr. Cradock,[31] and in 1864 Dr. Hawkins beat him again for the place vacated by Dr. Jeune.[32] Even high-churchmen with some propensities to university reform fell under the hammer; in 1865 a howl went up from the *Guardian* when George Rawlinson, the old pillar of the Tutors' Association, was beaten by Henry Wall of Balliol, the main-spring of the revived Derbyite political organisation in the university, and an opponent of the new studies. Rawlinson was the victim of the 'scandalous misrepresentation' that he was pledged to vote for the abolition of the university tests.[33] In 1866 conservatives were jubilant, for the only change went in favour of Pusey's right-hand man, H. P. Liddon; the liberals had given up trying to carry Jowett and Pattison, but their most popular man, Henry Smith of Balliol, Savilian professor of geometry, failed to secure a place.[34] Since 1860 there had been sufficient organisation for each side to accuse the other of caucus politics, and in 1869 each party produced a two-man list for each of the three-man constituencies; with the impulse of a liberal triumph in the general elections, with divisions amongst the conservatives and with the instinct to drop their most notorious candidates, the liberals carried the first two places in the constituencies for heads and professors, and were defeated only in the election of ordinary M.A.s.[35] But the liberal volcanoes on the Hebdomadal Council became extinct even quicker than those on the Treasury Bench, and in 1872 Liddon celebrated 'a great conservative victory' in both the professors' and the Masters' constituencies, Jowett's usual drubbing in the former being thoroughly administered on this occasion by Stubbs.[36]

If the liberals had shown prolonged weakness in the Council elections conducted by the residents in Congregation, they were of course still weaker in Convocation, where the railways strengthened the hold of the non-resident M.A.s. Even after the reforms of the executive commission, the chief business of the university was still the management of examinations and the election of its burgesses and Chancellor. The last word in legislation and the whole conduct of elections remained with Convocation, and each cast a curious light upon the balance of forces in the university.

The Examination Statute of 1850 which governed most of the academic activity of the university had been a compromise. On the one hand the advocates of the natural sciences and history had secured their recognition in the schools; on the other the advocates of Greats had secured their continued supremacy, for every candidate must pass in their school before proceeding to another. Passes in two schools were required for the B.A. degree. In the end the forces of opposition in the university, liberal and to a lesser degree anglo-catholic, had favoured the broadening of the schools, and the forces of conservatism had taken their stand upon the supremacy of the classics. Neither side remained altogether satisfied with the compromise, and two subsequent liberal manifestos, the blue book of 1852 and Pattison's essay on 'Oxford Studies' of 1855, set forth the general objects which the liberals entertained, before they had been harrowed into adjusting their ends to their means. The practical outcome was in each case the same; there should be an attempt to comprehend the universe of knowledge in Oxford studies, but no more than a single specialised final school should be required for the arts degree. The appointment of examiners should be vested in boards which should settle examination policy.[37] To secure this programme—the so-called 'liberation of studies'—was the chief object of the liberal, 'progress' or 'movement' party in the first decade of the reformed system.[38] It followed, *per contra*, that the orthodox saw in the defence of the heathen classics the bulwark of Christianity, and that the conservatives regarded themselves as defending a liberal education against the liberals.

By 1857 when liberal influence on the Council was nearing its peak, there existed sufficient dissatisfaction with the statute of 1850 to suggest that changes might be well received. It was widely felt that since scholarship had been removed from the final to an intermediate examination, and other schools had been created, no one knew what a first-class meant. Again despite the efforts of the commissioners to open the university, matriculations diminished steadily in the 'fifties and were less than they had often been in the seventeenth century. One reason for this was thought to be that, to work for two schools, men were residing longer, and that this, in conjunction with the fact that competition for open scholarships caused them to come up at a later age, was deterring some from coming up at all.[39] The second school, moreover, was widely regarded as a useless dispersion of energy, and many were disquieted by the number of candidates who did well in their first school, but were plucked in their second. The result was that when the draft statute was going through Council only Pusey and Mansel opposed it with any determination.[40] The proposal was to make Moderations equivalent to the old final examination of the days before 1830, including history, ethics and rhetoric so far as they could be learned in the classical writers; one final school must be chosen from a list of five, the Greats school being divided into two, according to the recommendations of Pattison and the blue book, a school of classical literature and philology, and a school of moral philosophy and metaphysics. The ill-fated boards of studies also reappeared.[41]

The Council seem to have been surprised by the storm which broke when the statute came before Congregation on March 3, 1857,[42] and at first they could find no defender other than Mansel, who admitted that he would have preferred another scheme altogether. Yet there was obvious room for reproach. It was argued that the new system had been working for too short a time to justify a major upheaval.[43] By dividing the Greats school the university must destroy whatever was left of public recognition of the Oxford first-class. Nor could Moderations candidates compass in the time available all the work required for the final school of 1830, which had in any case been jettisoned after six years as unsatisfactory.[44] A heavy examination at Moderations must interrupt steady reading for the final school.[45] Inevitably a neglected vested interest found its defenders; there seemed no reason why the study of ancient history in modern authors should be excluded from both the first and the second public examinations.[46] Jowett wanted a single final school but disliked most of the other proposals. The result was that for the first time under the new system, the Hebdomadal Council was routed, and compelled to think again.

Their second thoughts were ready for the Trinity term, and consisted in the abandonment of almost everything except the *idée fixe* of a single final school. Moderations were to remain as at present. The final classical school was not only not to be divided but was to have poetry and scholarship restored to it. The clause which the last draft had contained repealing compulsory attendance on professors' lectures was dropped in deference to professorial protests,[47] but the boards of studies remained.[48] When the statute came before congregation on May 12, however, the tutors were in no way appeased. E. A. Freeman made his usual complaints of the separation of ancient from modern history, and the junior Proctor, Meyrick of Trinity, unfurled the banner dear to the conservatives in the next few years, claiming that the statute must mean the extinction of classical education. Once the classical grind ceased to be compulsory the passmen would give it up after Mods., and before long the classmen would follow them. In a more moderate vein it could be argued that it was rash to leave undergraduates to seek the softest option among the final schools. The boards of studies also came in for criticism, and the final result was a humiliation of the Council as complete as that in March.[49]

> The university heard awful rumours that the Council was about to resign en masse—then, that it was to lose some of its most brilliant members—finally, that it was to follow the example of ministries which have blundered, and sacrifice its Jonah; but after expectation had been wrought to the highest pitch, it was baulked in the cruellest manner—*nothing happened* . . .[50]

Certainly the Council could hardly complain of J. P. Tweed's advice that they would do well another time to circulate their proposals and consult interested parties in advance.[51]

A year later the Council's hand was forced by changes in the regulations at Cambridge which reduced the necessary standing for a degree. With her own numbers still falling, Oxford was in no position to stand out for stiffer requirements than her ancient rival.[52] A committee of the Council sent a circular to the tutors, examiners and other influential residents, asking their opinion whether changes were desirable in the present regulations as to standing at graduation, and the residence and examinations required for the B.A. degree. A host of suggestions was considered, and taking into account the growing conviction that the present length of residence and the number of 'plucks' were both excessive, Vice-Chancellor Jeune (who had throughout been the engineer of the new schemes and had himself graduated under the system of 1830) introduced the new statute in Congregation on March 15, 1859. Jeune took good care to claim that the consensus of academic opinion underlay the Council's proposals that the standing for the B.A. degree should be diminished to twelve terms (i.e. three years, reckoning Easter and Act terms separately), that there should be one major examination instead of two, with a single mixed school for passmen and an option among the four schools for classmen.[53] A warning note, however, had been sounded by the conservative Montagu Burrows, who saw much merit in the compromise of 1850,[54] and members of Congregation showed scant disposition to own what had been represented as the consensus of their opinion. A number of liberals wished to use the statute as a basis for their own amendments, but the general reaction was wildly hostile, and George Rawlinson alleged that the standard in the non-classical honour schools would be less than the proposed mixed pass degree.

> There was a charming *naïveté* in the remarks with which the Vice-Chancellor wound up his two days' debate—a debate in which thirty-two persons had spoken, and all except some three or four had found fault with the proposition made to them—

'that, on the whole, he thought the Statute had met with a very fair amount of support, and that opinions were really less divided than he had anticipated.'

But all that could be salvaged of the statute was the reduction in the standing for the degree to three years—even compulsory attendance upon professors' lectures was abolished. The confusion of opinion brought about by the debate was illustrated by a memorial widely signed by a motley mixture of conservatives and liberals calling for an end to Moderation Honours, the great device of the statute of 1850 for extracting more work in the earlier years of the undergraduate course.[55]

After the defeat, J. P. Tweed of Exeter, again posing as a candid friend to the Council, recommended that the least change to meet the need would be to permit even less standing before graduation, to exempt classmen in Greats from the necessity of sitting a second school, and to give analagous relief to classmen in other schools.[56] The latter proposal in fact proved to be the Council's hope when the next move was made in 1863. Towards the end of the previous year a memorial had been submitted to the Council signed by 82 members of Congregation, mostly tutors and professors, pleading the hardship of men who obtained the highest honours in Greats, but failed to reach pass standard in the two or three weeks they then had to prepare for their second school. Similarly, those whose object was to obtain honours in the other schools were often of full standing for a degree before they had cleared off their classical pass requirements. The solution was to grant a degree to all those placed in the first three classes of any of the schools.[57] When Liddell introduced the statute in Congregation in March, however, he adopted Tweed's cautious policy, recommending that a degree be allowed for a third class in classics, and a second in the other schools, which represented about the same amount of work.[58] Even so the statute had got through the Council by only one vote,[59] and the conservatives were ready with all their guns loaded. The whole plan, they claimed, involved the abandonment of classics as an Oxford education. The Oxford principle had always been that specialisation should come after the first degree whereas the new proposals amounted to the beginning of professional education. If it was urged that the new statute only reduced the minimum classical requirement from six books to five, the reply came that the last year's work even in the pass school was the most valuable; and the claim that the way must be cleared for the final schools suggested that other changes must follow to the detriment of the elementary classical requirements. The next step would be the full programme of the blue book or the London University. E. A. Freeman, of course, would have nothing but his panacea of school of ancient and modern history.[60] However, the fact that the liberal caucus had whipped in signatures to the memorial gave them a good start in the voting in Congregation, the vested interests created in the new studies by the statute of 1850 grew stronger with every year that passed, and at this fourth attempt the new examination statute passed Congregation by 97 votes to 58.[61]

The conservatives, however, were not yet beaten. The statute must still go to Convocation, and the cry was industriously spread through the country that the classics were in danger; one Midland headmaster was heard to declare that 'if this statute passes, my living is gone.'[62] The appeal to Convocation created an issue in itself, for under the reformed constitution the primacy of the residents in matters of domestic regulation had never hitherto been questioned. While the *Guardian*, rallying to the support of the more liberal among the high-church tutors, claimed that the overwhelming bulk of the working residents had voted in the majority in Congregation, Montagu Burrows computed that the professors and tutors were evenly divided and, therefore, that it was proper for the non-residents to exercise a casting vote.[63] Stubbs and Freeman, at the conservative and liberal poles in politics, were brought together in favour of non-resident intervention by a common concern for high-grade history, and a common scorn for the pretensions of the residents. As Stubbs put it:

> I think that non-residents are far better judges of results than the Balliolized idiots who get classes under the new, and so should vote for going no further from the old system than is done already. If men wont work, why should they, and why are the good to be sacrificed for the bad, and a good man deprived of an honourable first class, that men who are only bribed to work may be honoured with a dirty little first in Nat. Phys. or whatever it is?[64]

While the Easter vacation was taken up with this conservative hue and cry, the liberals did little, and when the Council made the mistake of bringing on the statute immediately the university reassembled, its fate was sealed; the majority being 199 to 145.

This defeat caused immense bitterness among the liberals and there was a sharp division in their caucus whether to press the statute again at once (as Conington wished), or whether to press for the full equality of the schools as advocated in their memorial; the more resolute liberals led by Goldwin Smith and supported by the scientists carried the latter course. Council, however, were unprepared to make a move until after the next elections in the autumn, and so there was peace for six months before the attempt was made to wear down the patience of the non-residents.[65]

Meanwhile the liberal organisation was improved, but there was little difference in the subsequent pattern of events. The Council was moved by a memorial now bearing the signatures of 103 members of Congregation, and when Liddell introduced the statute requiring simply a third class in any school on December 1, he could claim that

> out of 36 professors, 23 had signed it [the memorial], while only 8 were known as its opponents; and out of 89 tutors and lecturers who were members of Congregation, 55 had signed it, while only 18 were among its known opponents.

Such men could not possibly wish to injure classical studies; indeed the statute was expected to attract men from the pass schools to Greats. In spite of this impressive support, the opponents of the statute gave it a closer run than before and were defeated by only 92 votes to 82. Burrows could still claim, therefore, that opinion in Oxford was evenly divided and all depended again on Convocation.[66] This time both sides whipped up their supporters and the statute passed the last hurdle by a majority of 38 in a poll of 524. The *Times* hailed this division as a great victory for the party of radical change in the university, and although the friends of the statute generally played down its importance, it is not surprising that conservatives were alarmed at changes which implied the surrender of any claim by the university to supply a single liberal education, a surrender which had been demanded by the royal commissioners and Mark Pattison in the name of progress and the triumph of philosophy.[67] C. L. Dodgson of Christ Church threw up his examinership in protest at the degradation of both classics and mathematics which was in prospect.[68] But a new principle had been irrevocably written into Oxford examination system and the next round of alterations was to see the Oxford conservatives trying to make the best of it.

At the time of the Oxford University Act the new constitution had been accepted by all the Oxford liberals except Liddell and his immediate friends, but the long struggle to force through the new Examination Statute and other battles like it soured them with Congregation altogether. Convocation was even worse from a liberal point of view, and it was the more galling that the liberals had no sooner begun to take Gladstone to their hearts, than it became impossible to carry his election any longer.

When Gladstone resigned from Palmerston's government in February 1855 he was in great ill-odour with his constituents, and his party organisers seriously considered whether they should withdraw him in the event of an election.[69] The Derbyite-evangelical coalition was still hostile; there were men who thought their own college ill-dealt with in the University Act; there were many who felt that Gladstone had betrayed them in admitting dissenters. Pre-eminent among these were Keble and Pusey; unless their mood of bitterness changed Gladstone must lose many of his warmest friends, and the best comfort Sir William Heathcote could report was that Keble thought he might vote for Gladstone rather 'as it were *in faith* than that he thought himself able to justify what had passed.' Arthur Haddan thought they might scrape home but devoutly hoped they would not have to try. There were liberal speculations that Gladstone might join the Radicals; if he did he must lose his connexion with Oxford.[70] By the time Palmerston had dissolved parliament in 1857 Gladstone's treatment of the Prime Minister as an idol before whom he could not bow (as he put it)[71] had done him good with his tory constituents, and Richard Greswell felt sure that all would go smoothly. In this election, however, the parties made a great set upon the splinter groups and both the Peelites and the dissenters suffered sharply. Gladstone's position was particularly vulnerable because his inveterate enemies among the evangelicals were now in happy partnership with Lord Palmerston, and hoping for a full share of the loaves and fishes. They had formerly acted with the Derbyites but were now plotting with a whig club in London which hoped to please Palmerston by annoying Gladstone. They had a candidate to hand in Lord Blandford, the church reformer, who had recently broken with Lord Derby and joined the premier. Gladstone himself was ready to fight one contest, though he assured his friends he would not fight another. In the end, however, no enthusiasm could be created for Blandford, and Gladstone was elected not only unopposed, but without prejudice to his future in the constituency.[72]

For the next two years Gladstone was in the wilderness, and the year 1859 in which he reached one of the crises of his career, proved appropriately stormy. Towards the end of 1858 he accepted an official mission in the Ionian Islands, and early in the new year, the lawyers discovered that by accepting this office he had not only vacated his seat in parliament but made himself incapable of re-election until he had ceased to hold it. A device was discovered for evading the difficulty, but in the middle of the negotiations the telegraph broke down; Gladstone arranged with Vice-Chancellor Jeune to delay the by-election till the last possible moment, but his legal adviser Phillimore was still on tenterhooks that 'some *Recordite* would be put up to poll two or three votes and claim to be returned before a committee.' The re-election, however, went unchallenged.[73]

In April Pusey was grieved by the threat of a Holy Week election; Sir William Heathcote was reported to be retiring from his seat owing to ill-health and a host of competitors were said to be aspiring to his place.[74] In fact Heathcote continued to sit, and it was Gladstone who vacated his seat under the most startling circumstances. On June 11 he voted with Disraeli on a motion of confidence, the loss of which brought down the tory government; a week later he was in office as Chancellor of the Exchequer under Palmerston. In 1857 his hostility to Palmerston had assisted his passage in Oxford; now he had taken office under him after what seemed to be an act of utter inconsistency. Inevitably there was an outcry at Oxford, and at such a juncture Gladstone chafed at the muzzling effects of Oxford etiquette. His committee, however, discountenanced his suggestion that he should come down to address Convocation; such an act would 'shock the nervous system' of the few Oxford neutrals, and would not reach country voters who came in late. Gladstone accepted that

> a contest for the university stretches me to be cut upon the operating table, instead of dying sword in hand. Nature pants and struggles to amend conditions so disadvantageous—

but his patience was clearly wearing thin.[75]

Some explanation, however, was clearly essential, and so in a letter to Provost Hawkins which was widely reprinted, Gladstone elucidated what he claimed to have been a perfectly clear decision. Palmerston had offered him a place despite his previous support of Derby's government, and he had felt constrained to accept because the Premier was sound on the Italian question, and the tories had shown themselves incapable of settling the other chief issue of the day, that of parliamentary reform. He would be reunited with men with whom he had served harmoniously under Aberdeen, and if the government contained radicals as well, the fact must be faced that no ministry could now stand which did not embrace a wide range of opinion.[76] This explanation satisfied very few in Oxford, and Gladstone was pestered with enquiries.[77] Richard Greswell, the chairman of his Oxford committee, (who had been invited to join a conservative committee in South Lancashire) spoke for many in finding Gladstone altogether too liberal.[78] The junior Proctor and others had to be reassured that Gladstone would not scrap the armed forces and seek peace at any price.[79] And there were the usual church questions. H. P. Liddon sought assurances that Gladstone would put a brake on the Divorce Bill and upon Palmerston's propensity to liberal and evangelical church appointments, but finally worked hard for the Oxford committee.[80] Others asked him to prevent the government's taking up the abolition of church rates or Dillwyn's schools bill.[81] George Rawlinson concluded that if Roundell Palmer were put up, Gladstone would lose his seat.[82]

In fact a more unequivocally tory candidate was found in Lord Chandos, the conspiracy being hatched at the Whitsuntide business meeting of the college then most obviously under the liberal hammer —All Souls—and led by the Hon. Frederick Lygon who, with the

16

fall of the Derby ministry, had just lost office as an admiralty lord.[83] The other erring college, St. John's, which had defied the executive commission, supplied the chairman of Chandos's committee in Mansel, a fanatical worker in Standing, and an indispensable tory figurehead in President Wynter.[84] Gladstone's London chairman went over to his opponent, and Stafford Northcote refused to serve him further. The Carlton Club came into the fray, and Richard Greswell embarrassed Gladstone's Oxford committee by writing a strong unauthorised protest to Lord Derby, part of the reply being printed to suggest that Derby disapproved of the contest.[85]

A hard fight followed, but Gladstone eventually came home by 1050 votes to 860, a much larger margin than in the last contest.[86] The Tractarian remnant were still faithful to their man, and the evangelicals, hitherto the most fanatical of Gladstone's opponents, and staunch allies of the Derbyites, with sublime indifference to politics now came out for him as the colleague of a Premier who put his church patronage in the hands of Lord Shaftesbury;[87] the only notable Oxford evangelicals who voted for Chandos were Dr. Cotton, Provost of Worcester, and Dr. Symons, Warden of Wadham. This invaluable reinforcement could obviously not be relied on in any future contest. The second great change was that the whole Oxford liberal phalanx accepted Gladstone for the first time.[88] In a constituency like Oxford their support was bound to be an embarrassment, how great an embarrassment the Oxford liberals were intellectually incapable of grasping. According to Goldwin Smith's doctrine of progress, liberal backing was a guarantee of security:

> As the poll goes on it becomes more apparent that you have with you all the men of distinction and all the young. The opposition is in fact the last kick of the most impracticable kind of Toryism, academical and political, Toryism which in the person of the Derby government has fallen by its own hand and for ever.[89]

As regards the men of distinction, it was true that for the first time Gladstone was widely supported by the heads of houses, only eight of whom voted for Chandos; on the other hand Hawkins reckoned that the wildest opposition to Gladstone was among the young M.A.s,[90] and George Rawlinson computed that 'of the 58 masters *lowest* [in seniority] on our list, exactly 28 voted for each candidate.'[91] Gladstone's 'juniors' who had trounced the heads a dozen years before were now men of consequence or non-resident, and neither he personally, nor the liberals, were holding the younger generation. The setbacks in Congregation which the liberals suffered in the 'sixties were foreshadowed in Convocation in 1859. There were two other unpleasant consequences of the election. The expense of advertisements and bringing up voters produced bills of over £1000, most of which Gladstone had to pay himself.[92] The carefree days of free election in Oxford were over, and, as well as uncertainty, an expense similar to that of a moderate sized borough was added to the member's liabilities. There was finally the question of his future in the seat. In 1857 he had declared himself ready to fight one contest and no more; now he reported to Robert Scott, Master of Balliol, that

> with respect to the future I was under the impression when I read the closing notice of the Chandos (London) committee that it was a distinct announcement of a contest on the next vacancy . . . Mr. Seymer assures me that this is *not* so, and disapproves of a renewal of the contest. As to the former point, he thinks he speaks the sense of the committee, but as to the latter I do not know why those who (the mass of them) have fought one & the same battle four times over, might not fight it forty if the span of human life were long enough. The regret therefore with which the past in this respect inspires me is not mitigated by turning my view upon the probable future.[93]

The events of the next two years strengthened the public impression that Gladstone would not contest Oxford again. His financial policies and his clash with the House of Lords over the Paper Duties seemed to mark him out as a liberal; the death or retirement of his old political intimates were compelling Gladstone to choose between isolation and a new political turn; the development of contentious church questions,[94] and Palmerston's unrepentant dependence upon Lord Shaftesbury in church patronage,[95] continued to vex his constituents. When, therefore, in the spring of 1861 a bill was going through parliament to create an extra seat in South Lancashire, there was no great surprise when the *Times* reported that a delegation from the county had offered Gladstone the seat and that he had accepted.[96] He at once wrote to the Vice-Chancellor denying the report, but it was obvious from the tone of proceedings in the Hebdomadal Council that opposition was again brewing, and H. G. Liddell formed the impression that Gladstone would not be their member much longer.[97] Nevertheless, Gladstone's old friends and supporters were anxious that he should stay and impressed him deeply with their personal loyalty. In midsummer the offer from South Lancashire actually arrived in the shape of a memorial signed by 8000 electors, a number which seemed to ensure his election. By this time it was unmistakably clear that Gladstone would never have any peace in Oxford,[98] but there was a new complication.

Gladstone's friends had given it out that if he should withdraw they would nominate Roundell Palmer who was then out of the house, and who in personal distinction and religious standpoint was another

Gladstone, with the advantage of being somewhat more conservative in his politics. The outright tories wished to promote Gladstone's old secretary, Sir Stafford Northcote, but he regarded Palmer as having the highest claim to the Oxford seat after Gladstone, and would not stand. On June 23, however, the Lord Chancellor died, and in the resulting cycle of legal promotions Roundell Palmer became Solicitor General and was brought into the house for Richmond. In conservative eyes this immediately branded him as a traitor to the cause, and Northcote consented to enter the lists.[99] Gladstone now had to weigh not only the advice he received that Oxford was safer than South Lancashire,[100] but whether, if he accepted, Roundell Palmer could carry Oxford for their friends.[101] While this elaborate calculus was proceeding, advanced canvassing on both sides was going on in the constituency,[102] but all was in vain, for finally Gladstone determined to stay.

Gladstone's decision not to create a vacancy in Oxford was doubtless also influenced by the terms of a new bill which was going through parliament while he was negotiating with South Lancashire, and which became law on August 1, 1861. The University Elections Act affords a curious illustration of the ambiguous attitudes of the parties towards parliamentary reform, and also of the special position of the universities. One of the reasons for the arrangement of the Hebdomadal Council elections in three constituencies under the act of 1854 had been to test out a scheme for the 'representation of minorities' with a view to its wider extension; there was now a feeling that something must be done about the question of parliamentary reform on which the last Derby ministry had foundered, and so the universities were marked out for another experiment, the postal vote, in a bill introduced by the rising liberal member for East Sussex, John Dodson.[103] The university constituencies were peculiarly apt for this experiment for there were probably no others with so large a proportion of non-resident voters, and certainly no others in which literacy might be presumed throughout the electorate. Much was made of the hardships suffered by poor curates in coming up to vote, though in fact M.A.s who could not afford to exercise their privileges did not generally keep their names on the books. Nevertheless, a scheme to enable voters to exercise the franchise which the law allowed was bound to win liberal support. On the conservative side, Derby felt committed to the principle because his reform bill of 1859 had given the option of this device to every constituency in the kingdom,[104] while others who did not share Pusey's view that the clergy were disillusioned with the tory party,[105] supported it to strengthen the clerical interest in the university seat.[106] As it was supposed at the time that about nine-tenths of the residents voted, about three-quarters of the London M.A.s, and only about half the country clergy, it was plain that the postal vote could easily cost Gladstone his seat, and would certainly do so if he had recently done violence to clerical prejudice. These considerations not only made Gladstone very uneasy about the bill, but turned many of his supporters against it, liberals like Dr. Jeune,[107] decaying whigs like Provost Hawkins,[108] moderate men like Professor Jacobson. A good deal of delicacy was felt about moving a petition against the bill in Convocation since the interests of non-residents were involved,[109] but a petition got up against it informally was signed by 93 residents, many of them influential.[110] The Rector of Exeter got Gladstone to present the petition, but warned him that to say a word in its favour might cost him his seat.[111] On the other hand a number of the liberals, especially Goldwin Smith, felt that nothing ought to override the principle of enabling voters to vote,[112] and amongst the 50 residents who signed a petition in favour of the bill were others who deplored the influence of parsons, but deplored paying their travelling expenses still more.[113] To complete the confusion, an important amendment was carried in committee, which turned the bill into a scheme for voting by proxy, for the voting papers were now to be delivered to the poll by the voters' nominees. This opened spectacular possibilities of abuse, and not only upset Sir William Heathcote who had favoured the original principle,[114] but turned Gladstone fiercely against the bill on the third reading.[115] It was, nevertheless, difficult to think of a case for depriving voters of their franchise, and the bill passed.

The next half-dozen years saw a period of intensive conservative organisation in Oxford, beginning with the launching of the anti-Gladstonian *Church and State Review* by Montagu Burrows and George Anthony Denison, and culminating in the purchase of the *Oxford Times* in the party interest by a group of dons[116] with the support of the aristocracy of the county,[117] and the promotion of men like Mansel and Stubbs during the third Derby ministry. In July 1864 this process provoked a brief spasm of liberal anger. In the previous year a Conservative Association had been founded to promote the cause among undergraduates, and a grand anniversary dinner was held partly to cheer them on, and partly to fly a kite for Gathorne Hardy, the candidate whom the party intended to run against Gladstone at the next vacancy.[118] At this dinner Lord Robert Cecil laid it down that 'every Churchman must be a good conservative, and every conservative a good Churchman,' (a view which George Rolleston, Linacre professor of anatomy, called upon Pusey to repudiate);[119] and Dr. Wynter, President of St. John's, and private secretary to the Chancellor, replied to the toast to Lord Derby as party leader. Professor Conington immediately made a vehement protest against this, as a grievous abuse of Wynter's official position, a position which the liberals on the Hebdomadal Council had already tried to bring to an end. Lord Derby would take no instruction in political etiquette, but the episode revealed the growing sense among the liberals that the constitution of the university was being twisted against them.[120]

The conservative dinner brought into the open an intrigue which had been proceeding covertly for some months. That old warhorse Archdeacon Denison had come to the conclusion that Gladstone would never resign the seat, but would have to be ejected; that Stafford Northcote would never undertake the task and another candidate would have to be found. In April 1864 he carried a meeting of conservative M.P.s with him, and secured the appointment of a committee which decided to promote Gathorne Hardy, and laid the foundation of his committees in Oxford and London; before the end of the Long Vacation they had collected more than a thousand promises of votes.[121] Keble made a spirited protest against this activity when the date of the election was not even known,[122] but canvassing spread far beyond Oxford, and local committees were established in the country, sometimes with professional agents, to work the constituency in a quite novel way;[123] when voting papers were eventually issued the agents would be able to make sure that the promises were kept. All the activity had one unexpected effect, for it encouraged prospective candidates to fish for votes in Gathorne Hardy's constituency, and drew from him embarrassed equivocations that he was not trying to dispossess Gladstone of his seat, but merely willing to accept it if elected.[124]

Hardy was probably the strongest candidate whom Gladstone had yet faced. Of evangelical stock, he had moved steadily towards high-church views, though he had no sympathy for the ritualism which was beginning to disquieten Pusey and to divide the high-church ranks. Since 1859 he had been regarded as one of the coming men in the party, and if he had none of Gladstone's intellectual eminence, he was a respectable embodiment of the newly furbished doctrine that every churchman should be a good conservative, and vice-versa. As denominational issues emerged again in the 'sixties, the alliance of conservatism and churchmanship began to be proclaimed with a vehemence not heard for many years. The new tory star, Lord Robert Cecil, fervently believed in it,[125] while conservative churchmen of the sort compared by Henry Hoare, the agent to the Oxford Churchmen's Union, 'to buttresses, because they never entered a church,'[126] took note that the church seemed immensely strengthened by the financial reorganisation which had taken place since 1850. Furthermore, it seems clear from Denison's account, that the decisive encouragement to the political tories to try another campaign against Gladstone, came from high-churchmen who had forsaken him. The defection of the majority of the fellows of Exeter at the last election aroused hopes of more defections to come. Pusey was uneasy,[127] Greswell was in despair,[128] and the increasing intimacy between Gladstone and eminent dissenters[129] lent itself to innuendoes of all kinds.

Over and over again, and supremely in an article in the *Quarterly* which appeared on the eve of the poll, Lord Robert Cecil pressed home the identification of church interests with those of the conservative party. In his view the basic issue in English politics since the Solemn League and Covenant was the issue between the church and dissent. The dissenters were powerless to injure the church except in alliance with the liberal rationalising party within—but it was these two factions that made up the liberal party; wherever liberalism triumphed dissent triumphed too. In throwing in his lot with the liberals Gladstone considered the church of less importance than the French Treaty. He had voted against the church on the Burials Bill and the Oxford Tests Bill, and he had not stopped the government from harrassing church schools, nor kept them to the support of church rates. As for the notion put about by the liberal anglo-catholics in the *Guardian* that the church was above allying herself with a particular political party, and that the church's representative at Oxford ought not to be challenged for affronting the party shib-boleths,[130] this was an ideology produced by the schism of the Peelites, who, in ceasing to be conservatives, obstinately refused to admit that they were becoming liberals.[131]

If this line was admirably calculated to encourage divisions among the high-churchmen, so also were Palmerston's church appointments. A deputation led, apparently, by Goldwin Smith and William Thomson, went up from the Oxford liberals to urge that Gladstone must be allowed to do something for his high-church friends or he would lose his seat, but this only resulted in the elevation of Thomson (who was reckoned an evangelical) to the see of Gloucester, and a year later to York—another scandal in high-church eyes.[132] And when at the eleventh hour Palmerston raised William Jacobson, regius professor of divinity, to the see of Chester, as a deliberate election gambit,[133] it was too late.

Two things added a final touch of plausibility to the conservative image. On the one hand the Liberation Society increased the vigour of their activities towards the end of 1864, and so divided the liberal vote by their doctrine that every good dissenter should be a liberal, and every good liberal a Liberationist, that they cost J. D. Coleridge a safe liberal seat at Exeter.[134] The Liberation Society seemed to be the living proof of the doctrine of the *Quarterly*. Finally, in March 1865, Gladstone who had long felt reservations about the establishment in Ireland, came out against it so roughly as to convince observers as politically different as Stafford Northcote and James Bryce that he had thrown away his seat.[135] Gladstone's Oxford friends were, however, still willing to promote him,[136] and although when the poll drew near and it became important for him to determine whether he should accept a fresh invitation from South Lancashire, they well knew that they had fewer promises than Hardy's committee, they would not accept Gladstone's suggestion that the whole conflict be settled on the basis of a scrutiny.[137] The Vice-Chancellor prepared for almost everything that might go wrong with the polling or the voting papers by soliciting legal opinions from Roundell Palmer,[138] and on July 13 polling began.

On the first day Hardy led Gladstone, and steadily increased his lead every succeeding day, the final figures being:

Sir William Heathcote	3,236
Gathorne Hardy	1,904
W. E. Gladstone	1,724

Apart from the result, which had seemed probable from the beginning,[139] the voting falsified almost every expectation. The voting papers gave very little trouble—about one per cent were spoiled—and virtually ended the system of pairing which, in a three-cornered election, was liable to abuse.[140] Much more important, although a huge proportion of the constituency voted and used the new voting papers, the new system seemed to have no influence on the result. Of the voters who had been on the register in 1859 who did not vote then but voted now (with the aid of the papers) 476 voted for Gladstone and 483 for Hardy.[141] The propaganda for the alliance of church and conservatism may have had some influence on the foundations of Hardy's victory, which lay in a net gain of 98 voters from Gladstone's ranks of 1859, but it did not prevent greater confusion than ever in the church vote. The one church party solidly to support Gladstone was the liberal group. The evangelicals, hitherto the most compact of all the parties, were hopelessly divided; many voted again for Gladstone and the patronage of Shaftesbury, but others marched against him at the dictates of the *Record*, which had

> for some time been endeavouring to unmask the secret policy of the Romanising party in the Church, and their willingness to throw overboard the Church of Ireland . . . that extreme party whose religious principles are sufficiently elastic to include in their embrace a Stanley, a Colenso and a Mill, provided they are allowed to chant choral services in their churches, to offer sacerdotal sacrifices at their altars amidst clouds of incense, diversified with the mummeries of processional pomp, the

haberdashery of curious vestments, and the graver scandals of the secret confessional.[142]

If Gladstone lost some evangelical votes which he had had in 1859, it was much more important that the division in the high church party was fully confirmed. Liddon wept.

> That our friends should have enabled the Carlton Club and the *Record* to carry out their wishes is one of the saddest episodes in the history of the Church Movement.[143]

Pusey concluded that 'the High Church are broken to bits.'[144] The unrelenting advocacy of Gladstone's cause by the *Guardian* created great bitterness amongst those high-churchmen who were not prepared to accept the soundness of Gladstone's church principles as a guarantee of his politics,[145] and this exacerbated the differences which the advanced ritualists were already causing in the Oxford Church Union. A year later a meeting of the Union under the chairmanship of the tory, Professor Burrows, and appropriately fumigated by incense paper, gathered to hear a paper advocating advances in ritual. To this paper Burrows made a somewhat hostile reply, and his 'sentiment was hissed, and his whole speech interrupted by cries of "No" &c.'[146] Burrows thereupon resigned from the Union, with Christopher Wordsworth and others bought the *English Churchman*, changed the title to *The Churchman*, and tried to run it against the *Guardian*.[147] This feud in its turn helps to explain the sudden liberal gains in the next Hebdomadal Council election in 1869.

If Gladstone's defeat was brought about by the defection of catholic Churchmen who had formerly supported him, the margin was immensely increased by a factor which had begun to operate even in 1859—his failure to hold the young. Of the voters who had been placed upon the register since 1859, 689 voted for Hardy but only 547 for Gladstone. Against this failure with the younger generation it was a hollow boast in Gladstone's friends to claim a great superiority in university distinctions, examinerships and so forth.[148] Though the rapid growth of high-church sentiments among the young was a feature of the period, Goldwin Smith refused to believe it, and stoutly maintained that

> a good many of the *recent* Masters were not *young* Masters, but old men who had not taken their M.A. and were brought up to do it for the purpose of this election.[149]

The remedy was to repeal the university tests which kept out only men who would have voted for Gladstone. In this state of mind Goldwin Smith saw an omen of the separation of church and state when, on the day of Gladstone's defeat, the Bible fell from the hand of the statue of James I in the quadrangle of the Bodleian.[150]

Gladstone and his friends acknowledged that the defeat had done much to weaken his power to assist the church,[151] dissenters calculated that 'movement may confidently be expected in the ecclesiastical policy of the country,'[152] but the one thing which no party could yet see was that the violent display of party animosity had taken the university a long way on the road out of politics. Gladstone's friends had been driven into pleading that the university elections should be essentially non-political, and their enemies had ensured that no politician of the first rank would again occupy the seat. Certainly Gladstone went to South Lancashire with relief, 'unmuzzled' because he could address his constituents and fight contests among them on equal terms with his opponents, cheering the liberals in the country with his new-found freedom, but leaving the liberals in the university with some unpleasant stock-taking.

CHAPTER XI

THE LIBERALS AND THE TESTS

We Liberals are therefore left . . . a head without a body. We must reconstruct our party . . . The two cardinal points of policy to be concurrently pursued are first, an alliance at Oxford between liberals & intelligent conservatives on the neutral ground of interest in education & secondly the pressing forward in Parliament, on the hustings & at meetings (as we see our way) of the abolition of the university tests. On this latter question our appeal must be to the country.

C. S. ROUNDELL to J. BRYCE, July 24, 1865.
Bodl. Bryce MSS. Box 30.

BY 1865 it was unmistakable that the liberals had lost ground in the Hebdomadal Council, were not strong in Congregation, and in Convocation had been parted from the only parliamentary candidate they had any hope of carrying. By 1869 even Goldwin Smith had given up the delusion that young Oxford must be liberal and concluded that

> the hope of the Oxford Liberals lay not in any contest in Oxford itself—a narrow avenue, where the enemy has long been and still is entrenched in overwhelming strength, but victory in an ampler field. Liberalize the national legislature & the national legislature will liberalize Oxford at a stroke without waste of time and all this chronic bitterness.[1]

This liberal frustration had been expected by neither party a dozen years before, and requires some explanation. Part of the explanation certainly lies in the very unpleasing personalities of the liberal leaders themselves. The Oxford liberals specialised in disciples rather than friends and were cordially detested not only by their enemies but by each other. Mark Pattison was notoriously misanthropic after his failure to gain the headship of his college. Jowett had nursed a number of ugly animosities from his youth up. After all Goldwin Smith's services to the executive commission he could dismiss him as a man with 'a crack in his skull.'[2] At the time of the *Essays and Reviews* Jowett thought him likely to 'libel us and go over to the Heads of Houses.' After pursuing a line of his own on examination reform throughout the 'fifties Jowett had the temerity to rebuke Frederic Harrison for not toeing the line on questions of subscription.[3] Colleagues received equally short shrift. The following on T. H.

Green came oddly from a Jowett who in his youth had been a great worshipper of German superiority.

> He intoxicates himself and others with Kant and does not see that these dead German philosophies cannot be revived and end in nothing . . . His character does great good here; his teaching almost harm.
>
> I am afraid that Green can never make a great and solid reputation unless he alters his method and thinks more for himself; and also until he recognizes the greatness of men like Locke and other masters of philosophy.[4]

In later years too when Jowett had brought Fremantle back to the college as theological tutor and chaplain, he discouraged his work.[5] It is small wonder that Jowett like Pattison was absent from his Common Room for years on end.

James Bryce, an optimistic and healthy man, offered this account of his fellow liberal, William Thomson:

> Thomson is no favourite here . . .; he was disliked as despotic in Queen's, sneered at by liberals for having gone over from Broad Ch. to the side of the quasi-persecutors & his elevation is generally ascribed to a prudent worship of the νάνας οὐκ ἀδίκως. By most people here his abilities—except for negotiation and intrigue, were thought little of: his books were poor, his sermons ambitious, with little real merit.[6]

To E. A. Freeman who was never long away from Oxford in the early years of the History School, it proved 'the hollowness of Oxford liberalism that they cannot see through such a humbug' as Liddell, who was a rogue as well as a 'blockhead and blunderer.'[7] Goldwin Smith's capacity for believing passionately in whatever issue was agitated at the moment, gave some strength to the party,[8] but he was also 'a great element of bitterness and strife;'[9] he did not scruple to make an assault upon Stanley's *Edinburgh Review* article on the *Essays and Reviews*, and his angry replies to Frederic Harrison's rough handling of his lectures on the 'Study of History' spilled over into the *Daily News*.[10] The one animosity which all the Oxford liberals shared was an inveterate aversion to Froude, who, they rightly suspected, would one day be forced into the regius chair of modern history by a liberal government. Goldwin Smith went for him in the press,[11] and Bryce and Freeman were prepared to pull every wire against him when Goldwin Smith retired.[12]

The only one of the Oxford liberal leaders who was generally popular as a person was A. P. Stanley. Whatever his limitations as a scholar, however deplorable his lack of enthusiasm for a fight, Stanley was an excellent man at the breakfast party, and in personal propaganda had a touch unrivalled by the others. After his departure for the Deanery of Westminster in 1864, the party lacked anyone of his obvious personal piety, and even their friends began to remark that the

> Liberals seem to want either the inclination or the courage to deliver themselves of a healthy religion for undergraduate benefit . . . apart from controversy and personality.[13]

Stanley's departure was a double blow to the liberals. Immense liberal pressure was brought to bear to replace him with G. G. Bradley, another liberal who had taught at Rugby and was now headmaster of Marlborough; in due course he succeeded Stanley at Westminster, and laid the foundations of his biography.[14] Lord Shaftesbury triumphed again, however, and the successful candidate, W. W. Shirley, brought joy to the heart of the *Record*.[15] Not only had the liberals lost a leader but the way was wide open for their great rival, H. P. Liddon, Pusey's right-hand man, who developed the art of personal propaganda and influence to a degree never attained on the other side.[16] How powerful this could be even upon a liberal is well illustrated in the correspondence of Edward Kaye Jupp who at one point makes the contrast with the liberals explicit. Jowett, he remarks,

> is an old man, rather small, with what many call a beautiful face, but extremely shy, and with hardly a word to say—a striking contrast to his opponent L[iddon], whose conversation is said, I believe with truth, to be more fascinating than that of any other man.[17]

Liddon was also a notable, if somewhat histrionic preacher, and already the high-church party had won the chief influence in the Oxford pulpit. Finally, although the Oxford churches and college chapels avoided the ritualistic extravagances of advanced churches elsewhere, there was a steady raising of the tone. Liddell agreed to important changes in the Cathedral, and Henry Nettleship chuckled at

> the Lincoln men wringing from Fowler and Mark [Pattison] a consent to chant the canticles & Psalms on Sundays in chapel, and actually doing it in a hoarse but not unforcible manner, while agony is written on the faces of those two eminent men. I tell Mark that instead of yielding to requests of this kind the clerical members of the college should deliver bi-terminal sermons: a jolly discipline the restoration of wh. is much to be wished but perhaps hardly to be expected (as someone I believe once said as his version of the Commination Service address).[18]

But Pattison like Liddell now rarely entered the pulpit.

The issue of religion was crucial for the liberals and far more important than their personal failings. Their own friends complained that 'their liberalism consists in expecting everybody to think as they do theologically.'[19] Conington and T. H. Green who refused to do so, found themselves not only ill-regarded, but cut off from the main body on the important question of the university tests.[20] Furthermore, their theological denials hardened their opponents against them and sharply limited their influence.

The most aggressive of the party was Jowett, and his intention of asserting a place in the church by right of open conquest rather than by infiltration, led to a series of famous cases which it is not necessary to recount in detail. Some of the shrewdest comments on Jowett's theology, as upon Newman earlier, came from outside the church. His *Epistles of St. Paul* of 1855 was quickly appreciated by unitarians.

> The whole of Mr. Jowett's book appears to us in the light of a theological manifesto, for the pronunciation of which his exposition of St. Paul's Epistles is regarded as a convenient opportunity . . . What next? Mr. Jowett does everything that the Church or the law requires him to do in order to prove himself a Churchman, and yet it is plain upon the surface of his writings that, in the sense in which the term is generally understood, he is no Churchman at all.

Perhaps the essay on casuistry which he included in the book, with its arguments against over-scrupulousness cast light on his own position.[21] For the moment, however, the only penalties were a conspiracy by Golightly which led to Jowett's being summoned to subscribe the articles again before the Vice-Chancellor,[22] and a course of lenten sermons by preachers, high-church and low, designed by the Vice-Chancellor to controvert his teaching on the atonement.[23] T. H. Green felt he had ample liberty as a Christian, but Jowett, was

> determined not to submit to this abominable system of terrorism which prevents the statement of the plainest facts, and makes true theology or theological education impossible.[24]

The 'system of terrorism' had in fact been quiescent since the degradation of W. G. Ward, and the Tractarian party which had then been claiming comprehension had since quietly established its right to continue; but Jowett's bid for freedom in the *Essays and Reviews* of 1860 provoked its revival in full force. This time the unitarian reviewer saw in Jowett's essay

> an undesigned but effectual justification of Unitarianism. Here are the principles of interpretation which are taught to our

divinity students while at college; here are the principles of interpretation which underlie the teachings given by our ministers from the pulpit; here are even the results of the same principles of interpretation as set forth in our Unitarian manuals and embodied in our Unitarian sermons.[25]

There was, nevertheless, little disposition in Oxford at first to make any reply except by the controversy which Jowett invited;[26] an evangelical association from the West of England put pressure on Vice-Chancellor Jeune, but he assured the Chancellor that

> where there is much intellectual activity it is certain that every possible hypothesis will be discussed and supported. Individual faiths may be wrecked, but the faith will as ever gain by the disputes,[27]

and the Hebdomadal Council refused to bring a heresy case before so unsuitable a tribunal as Convocation.[28] When, however, Frederic Harrison in the *Westminster Review* exposed the divisions among the Oxford liberals by insisting that the book overthrew Christianity altogether, scoffed at the authorities of church and university for taking no action, and concluded that

> noone that knows the religious state of the universities could doubt that such a book would be eagerly welcomed, but welcomed only as a partial instalment. Few perhaps are aware how far the decay of belief extends beneath these walls,

he issued a challenge which was speedily accepted.[29] Most of the Oxford contributors to the *Essays and Reviews* were not subject to episcopal jurisdiction, and after counsel's opinion had been obtained that Jowett had put forward views plainly at variance with the XXXIX Articles,[30] three of the divinity professors, Pusey, Heurtley and Ogilvie, attempted to catch him in the Chancellor's court, a tribunal hitherto employed for the recovery of petty debts. This case, however, collapsed when the Vice-Chancellor's assessor refused to exercise his discretion to let the case go forward. Meanwhile Stanley had been struggling vainly to get the endowments of Jowett's Greek chair increased, but every move was blocked by their political or religious opponents, and by those who could think of better things to do with the money. Not until 1865 when the Christ Church chapter were brought by the researches of E. A. Freeman and Charles Elton to acknowledge that in the 16th century they had received specific estates for the endowment of the chair was the increment secured. This attempt to keep Jowett on a salary of £40 p.a. when professorial stipends were generally being raised, was widely condemned as censuring bad theology by bad morality.

There were other deplorable examples of *odium theologicum* also. An attempt to whip up feeling against Jowett was made in December 1860 when there was an enormous assembly in Convocation for the election of the Boden Professor of Sanskrit. The contest was between Max Müller and Monier-Williams, an evangelical, on whose behalf the machinery of conservative political agitation had been working at full capacity for months. He had a London committee including Sir Brook Bridges, Sir Stafford Northcote and Yarde-Buller, and an Oxford Committee with Henry Wall as secretary. Besides being regarded as a safe man in religion, Monier-Williams derived some advantage from the terms of the bequest, which had missionary objects in view. Max Müller's one claim was that he was much the better candidate, but he was suspected of being infected by Bunsen, was known to be a liberal, and had friends who did not organise on his behalf till the last moment. Nevertheless, the coalition of liberal and catholic which supported Gladstone supported Müller; there were Pusey, Keble and Church, Bradley, Lake and Price, with even Macbride from the evangelical party. Numbers were too much for distinction, however, and Williams was a handsome victor.[31]

The theological agitation which began while the polling was on, soon caused the situation to deteriorate. Not much more than a year later, when the university was preparing to welcome the Prince of Wales, and the Hebdomadal Council was going through his nominations for honorary degrees, Pusey was able to get Kingsley removed from the list by threatening opposition to the last ditch.[32] Then in February 1864 when a large body of graduates assembled to vote the new Examination Statute a committee of high-churchmen and evangelicals launched a declaration that the Church of England

> maintains without reserve or qualification, the Inspiration and Divine Authority of the whole Canonical Scriptures, as not only containing but being the Word of God; and further teaches, in the Words of our Blessed Lord, that the 'punishment' of the 'cursed' equally with the 'life' of the 'righteous' is 'everlasting.'

Their 'proceedings were interrupted by a compact mass of liberals who took advantage of the wide terms of the invitation to make speeches and otherwise annoy' them,[33] but the declaration, designed to isolate the liberal churchmen, was rapidly signed by 11,000 clergy, and forwarded to the Archbishop of Canterbury. This privately organised attempt to cow a party in the church by power of public exposure showed how the 'abominable system of terrorism', which Jowett imagined in 1858, had finally come to pass, justifying itself by the legal judgments upon the *Essays and Reviews*.

Pressure of this kind, added to the fact that Jowett's teaching was acknowledged as unitarian by those who might best be expected to know, underlay the steady set-backs of the Oxford liberals in the early 'sixties, and their rapid addiction to a venomous anti-clericalism. At the same time the cases thrown up by the *Essays and Reviews* and the terrorism of the Oxford Declaration showed the need for a change in the present clerical subscriptions. On the side of the governors of the church this was recognised by the appointment of the royal commission upon clerical subscription in 1864, and the passing of the Clerical Subscription Act in the following year. On the side of the Oxford liberals it produced a rigid determination to be finished with subscriptions altogether, if not in the church at large, then at least in the university.

The ball was set rolling by Stanley in a *Letter to the Bishop of London*,[34] pleading the hardship of subscriptions both academic and clerical, and making it clear that he was pleading the cause of churchmen not dissenters. From a moderate high-church view point J. B. Mozley was

> sorry the Oxford Liberals have taken to *aggression*. For Stanley's attack on the Articles must be taken as such. It is very well to claim for their faith to be tolerated, but this is rather like an attempt to make you give up yours. It is evident that it has been forced upon Stanley by the go-aheads of Oxford, and that he does not like his task.[35]

In a temperate pamphlet Mozley pointed out that Articles IX to XVII which caused most of the difficulty, and raised the enigmas of grace and freewill, were couched in the language of scripture, and that the real problems were presented by the Bible and not by the discipline of the Church of England.[36] Other Oxford men, including Ogilvie from the divinity faculty, made their replies[37] and the temperature was still rising when in the following year the liberal attack was renewed with far more vigour. Liddell under the title 'Subscription no security,' asked

> why ecclesiastical bodies exact Declarations or Subscriptions from persons invested with authority in the Church, while other societies find it unnecessary to take such precautions,

and could find no satisfactory answer.[38] Goldwin Smith came out fiercely against the academic tests, which he characterised as immoral, useless and injurious to the university and to the country at large. Furthermore, the dead hand of orthodoxy prevented the university from fulfilling its ancient role.

> If we . . . inquire to which of the two antagonistic elements of the medieval intellect the Universities belonged, to that which was sacerdotal and reactionary or to that which was scientific

17

and progressive, we shall find . . . the universities were the very centres of science and progress: to the sacerdotal and reactionary party, they were the objects of deserved suspicion.[39]

History never failed to point a moral to Goldwin Smith, and in the same vein the *Westminster Review* warned the clergy against taking up the position of the *parti prêtre* in France, incapable of doing good, and only capable of plotting and intriguing with despots to hold back the tide. The English Church was losing its hold on the intelligent laity, but progress would not stop.[40] George Rolleston, in a more moderate vein, pressed upon Pusey that

> if I have to choose between a Court of Star Chamber and the imposition of subscription I will choose the former. It seems to me that as you can control a man's words and his actions, you should attempt that, and in a Christian country it is the duty of the state to prevent anything from being done or said . . . contrary to Christianity. But . . . you cannot control a man's thoughts . . .[41]

Unfortunately for the liberals their strongest argument, that the tests in no way inhibited the discussion of unorthodox opinions in Oxford,[42] was one to frighten waverers, and H. R. Bramley of Magdalen rubbed the point home by showing that the two sides in the dispute held totally different views of what religion was. On the one side it was regarded as kind of rational investigation not unlike other kinds; on the other side it was conceived as a dogmatic system which had to be received as it stood.[43] In this style Mark Pattison had aroused the wrath of H. P. Liddon by a sermon 'on education as a perfecting of the faculties, not a communication of truth.'[44] Provost Hawkins too, who as a young man had opposed the matriculation test, and had later advocated strict application of the graduation tests to the Tractarians, saw no ground for radical concessions to the liberals.[45] And the conservatives could take comfort from the folly of Goldwin Smith's assertions that if Christians were divided in doctrine, they were united in ethics.

While these debates were proceeding the first moves had been made from Cambridge.[46] In 1862 Edward Pleydell-Bouverie, who had been an undergraduate at Trinity College, Cambridge, and was son of the earl of Radnor who had tried to get rid of the university tests a generation before, presented a petition widely signed by Cambridge residents for the repeal of the provision in the Act of Uniformity which required all college fellows to sign a declaration of conformity with the liturgy, and on May 5, 1863 he introduced a bill to this effect.[47] Under the terms of the bill a college might, if it wished, elect dissenters (though not Roman Catholics) into fellowships. This bill at once brought out the difference between the objects of the liberals in the two universities. The mathematical education of Cambridge had always attracted dissenters, among whose higher social ranks there was some discontent at the reluctance of the Cambridge commissioners to extend their rights.[48] Moreover, dissenters became Senior Wrangler 19 times in the thirty years 1860 to 1889,[49] and there were colleges which felt sore at not being able to elect them into fellowships, though they employed them for teaching as praelectors.[50] In Oxford, on the other hand, dissenters were almost unknown, for their schools did not generally give the classical grounding required;[51] the great question here was the relief of the Anglican liberal conscience, and Christian orthodoxy was much more immediately threatened than at Cambridge. The Oxford liberals, therefore, got up a petition asking baldly for the removal of all tests required for academical degrees.[52] This petition, however, was pared and pruned away in order to collect 106 signatures, and after having been botched about for months arrived in parliament too late to obtain any notice.[53] The university corporately and a group of non-residents petitioned against Bouverie's bill (the liberals were beaten in Convocation by 182 votes to 51), and the bill was finally withdrawn at the second reading, there being insufficient time to take it any further.[54]

Plainly greater efficiency would be required for the next attempt, and the liberal defeat in Convocation gave no encouragement to expect official support in the university. The Oxford liberals, therefore, sought an outside impulse by working closely with non-residents in London, and although the grievances of dissenters were of far less practical consequence in Oxford than in Cambridge, they went further than the Cambridge men had ever done to secure the backing of the nonconformist wing of the liberal party. Benjamin Brodie had already been encouraging the nonconformists of Manchester,[55] and Goldwin Smith put the committee in touch with that powerful agitator, Edward Miall.[56] His *Nonconformist* accordingly began to scourge the dissenters for not taking more interest in the campaign, and to laud the Oxford liberals for going out of their way to extend the advantages they were seeking to nonconformists.[57] This association with the nonconformist politicians led inevitably to a great meeting at the Free Trade Hall in Manchester, on April 6, 1866. Addresses were given by Frederick Temple, by W. C. Sidgwick and G. C. Brodrick of Merton and others, resolutions were passed against the tests and the whole was designed to show that the voice of the people would brook no delay.[58] In retrospect Goldwin Smith declared that 'our alliance with Manchester . . . made our cause that of a party in the nation.'[59] but the flirtations which led up to the alliance had a comic aspect. One Manchester radical summed up Goldwin Smith's weakness better than his Oxford friends, 'and thought him a rabid, useless, fanatical declaimer.' On the other side, James Bryce whose Scottish experience ought to have prepared him for prospecting in Manchester, confessed that

> people sick of a southern squirearchy admire far off these Lancashire politicians; near at hand the roughness and the dirt are seen.[60]

The truth was that the nonconformist world at large cared very little for admission to universities, and especially to Oxford, which was known to be full of Puseyism and other bad influences. The advanced men of Manchester admitted that

> we want sadly a knot of scholarly minded speakers here! The League, that ought to have died when the Corn Laws finally gave way, trained economical speakers of some ability, & a certain number of political haranguers; but we have no other prominent leaders of thought. There is a most respectable and intelligent community who would rally about a well arranged demonstration; but of our own resources we could scarcely get a couple of first-class resolutions decently, much less ably, proposed and seconded.[61]

Hence the importation of the Oxford liberal circus to the Free Trade Hall. Nevertheless, the alliance with nonconformity ensured that the question of the tests got into the liberal election programmes after the Reform Act of 1867,[62] and the nonconformist ebullience of the years which immediately followed helped to put an additional screw upon a reluctant Gladstone.

Before this consummation there were many preliminary skirmishes to be fought. The campaign in 1864 was centred upon a bill promoted by John Dodson, who had brought in the University Elections Bill of 1861, to secure the abolition of all tests for Oxford degrees. The Oxford liberals did their best to whip up support, and Edward Miall and the Liberation Society lent their aid on the strict understanding that no amendment should be accepted which excluded nonconformists from the benefit of the bill. This was a matter of importance because the bill provided that no graduate should take any office in or out of the university until he had made a declaration of membership of the church. The risk was that the 'Cambridge compromise,' or declaration of *bona fide* membership of the church, might be extended from office-holding to the M.A. degree. In that case the Oxford liberals could subscribe without qualms, but dissenters would be no further forward. Gladstone's attitude was enigmatic, but he might well carry part of the liberal party with him in support of some such amendment.

By 1861 Gladstone had attained a position in regard to the tests which changed little until he became premier of a reforming ministry. Lay subscriptions which were required nowhere outside the university were an abuse, and he thought that degrees in general should be freed from them. The university should be opened as widely as was compatible with its government and teaching remaining in Anglican hands. In exceptional cases chairs should be opened to individuals outside the church by special statute, and it should be possible for nonconformists to open private halls. College emoluments should also be opened where there was no connexion with the governing body. The test for a governing or teaching office should be a subscription or declaration of *bona fide* church membership. With these views Gladstone deplored the Oxford Petition of 1863, regarded Dodson's bill as impossible in its original shape, and was quite accurately regarded by the Oxford liberals as a pillar of the tests.[63] On the other hand, he was the despair of the high-churchmen with his language that the church must be defended from her friends, that she must agree with her adversary while he was in the way, and that the theological conservatives were foolish in resisting a settlement while it could still be obtained on reasonable terms.[64] Keble was in deep grief that 'the true, old, loyal, Laudian, believing Oxford' had gone, and could not see how to stop the new Oxford contaminating other places.[65] Liddon was in a white fury believing that Gladstone conceded the principle while contesting the details.[66] And it proved that no party was prepared to accept the standing ground which Gladstone was now recommending.

Dodson's immediate problem, however, was the certainty that Gladstone and others might try to amend his bill in committee, and that whatever assurances he gave Miall and the Liberation Society, he might not be able to stop them. The second reading of the bill passed by 211 votes to 189 (Heathcote being a teller for the 'Noes', and Gladstone abstaining), the various hostile parties proposing to reshape the bill at the next stage.[67] When the bill went into committee in June, Dodson knew that neither the Oxford liberals nor the nonconformists would brook any concession; the London committee

> held a meeting at which twelve M.P.s, Dean Stanley, Jowett and some eight or ten Oxford Professors, Goldwin Smith, Bp. Colenso, Maurice, John Bright, Miall, J. Martineau, P. Taylor, Greg, Huxley etc. etc., met and spoke, using identical sentiments —Anglicans, Broad Churchmen, Neo-Christians, Non-Christians, Papists, Unitarians, Quakers, and Agnostics all together, . . . [Harrison] suggested (to a few friends) that a declaration should be drawn up in the following form—bother the 39 Articles—and then have it signed by all present.[68]

Petitions from the nonconformist colleges were organised; the view that subscription should be replaced by a declaration of *bona fide* church membership was controverted by a petition from Scotland pointing out that this would exclude presbyterians who were now comprehended; and on June 10, a great public meeting was held at Freemason's Tavern, Great Queen Street, at which resolutions were passed in favour of Dodson's bill and Bouverie's bill. Of the 120 persons who signed the petition at once more than half were Oxonians, and of these a third had been educated at Balliol. This great agitation and the refusal of Dodson to accept a clause,[69] had the effect of paralysing Gladstone's intentions to amend the bill, even though Heathcote tried to catch him between the horns of a dilemma.

> It was rather for you ... to give effect to your expressed opinions in favour of a considerable modification of the Bill, with a view to passing it, than for those who were content with the alternative of its rejection.[70]

The result was that, contrary to all expectation, the bill was reported without amendment,[71] and Heathcote declared war upon it on the third reading. His motion that the third reading be deferred three months was, nevertheless, lost by ten votes, and a desperate scramble followed to whip members in from the clubs and Opera House for the crucial division. Fifty more members were brought in for the division on the third reading which ended in a tie, 170 having voted on each side. The Speaker, seeing that the tide was turning against the bill, did not exercise his casting vote, but put the motion 'that the bill do pass,' which was lost by 173 to 171.[72] The *Nonconformist* growled furiously that

> the Prime Minister had not once voted for the bill, the Home Secretary [Sir George Grey] walked out of the House to avoid voting, and the Chancellor of the Exchequer [Gladstone] and the Attorney General [Roundell Palmer] gave the two votes which constituted the hostile majority. The cause of Liberalism has ... been sacrificed by the Liberal ministers. The opposition have triumphed because they have allies on the Treasury Bench.[73]

As an alternative measure Bouverie's bill was immediately brought forward and although it received a substantial defeat,[74] the liberal leaders were going to find it difficult to avoid accepting some measure of this kind.[75]

After the meeting at the Freemason's Tavern a committee of five was formed for promoting the whole cause of university reform, the members being John Dodson, Mountstuart Grant Duff, Liberal member for Elgin Boroughs, Frederic Harrison, C. S. Roundell, fellow of Merton, and C. S. Bowen, fellow of Balliol.[76] In November 1864 this committee attempted to link up with the Oxford liberals to revive Dodson's bill of last session as part of a larger programme. Early in February 1865, however, Dodson had to relinquish control of the bill on being appointed Chairman of Ways and Means,[77] and G. J. Goschen, who had raised the question of the tests in his address when he was elected liberal member for the City of London in 1863,[78] brought in what was virtually Dodson's bill again;[79] plans for combining it with Bouverie's were postponed.[80]

A number of circumstances raised liberal hopes. The University of Durham removed its tests except in the theology faculty.[81] C. S. Roundell button-holed Gladstone at a public luncheon and tried to give him an impulse towards repeal of the tests by deluding him with the idea that young Oxford was panting for a wide measure of university reform. Gladstone, who had his Oxford election to face, appeared much moved, but said that he found his Oxford friends obstructive.[82] In debate he was more hostile than in the previous year, and although the bill obtained its second reading by 16 votes, it had to be withdrawn owing to the lateness of the session.[83] A few days later Gladstone's connexion with the university seat was severed.

The Oxford liberals were in no doubt as to the consequences of Gladstone's defeat. 'Our present organisation is shattered. We have to begin all anew . . . Our party is dissolved, the bond which connected Liberals & High Churchmen having been snapped asunder.'[84] Their disillusionment with the reformed university constitution came to a head. After the liberal defeats in the Hebdomadal Council in 1866 Goldwin Smith passionately denounced the caucus system which had been turned against them, and attacked the clerical influence in Congregation given by the right of the clergy of the city to vote as resident members of the university. To him this was the sufficient cause of liberal weakness.[85] Whether the liberals proposed excluding the non-educational members of Congregation, or balancing them by introducing senior non-residents,[86] they were exposed to the damaging charge of wishing to rig the constitution of the university in the party interest. In these dire straits C. S. Roundell, who had taken Balliol liberalism into a fellowship at Merton, suggested to James Bryce a tortuous policy, in a letter which is worth quoting at length because it affords the key to the manoeuvres of the next few years.[87]

> We Liberals therefore are left . . . a head without a body. We must reconstruct our party; &, as it seems to me, from within & from without—from within, & as an immediate step, on the basis of a common interest in the work & development of education; & for the future from without, by the admission of dissenters to the governing body.

So only can we hope to make head against the inveterate professional bigotry of the rank and file of Convocation as it is. Therefore it seems to me, the two cardinal points of policy, to be concurrently pursued are first, an alliance at Oxford between liberals & intelligent conservatives on the neutral ground of interest in education & secondly the pressing forward in Parliament on the hustings & at meetings (as we see our way) of the abolition of the university tests.

On this latter question our appeal must be to the country. A third point, intermediate between the other two, & of the most immediate and pressing importance (but one which we must speak of only between ourselves & with muffled lips) is the abolition of the clerical restriction on the fellowships.

As you probably are aware this question will be brought on by me at Merton in October as well as by your party at Oriel. Let us fight this battle with a resolution to win, but with the very utmost circumspection. To carry either college would be in effect to give a prerogative vote in the university. For the like reason, failure would probably retard the movement for years.

The years following Gladstone's defeat saw a curious mixture of conflict and co-operation between the Oxford liberals and conservatives of both the political and theological kind.

The liberals were inevitably irked by the turning tide of preferment. Goldwin Smith gave up his chair in 1866, having spent more time in addressing the Liberation Society than in advancing his subject, and was succeeded by that quintessential high-church conservative, William Stubbs. J. R. Green did not miss the barbs in Stubbs's inaugural;

> The chair was not to be a chair of politics, but of simple sheer work. Perhaps the great political lesson to be learnt was not that 'the stupid party' were on one side, the intelligence on the other, but that both sides had their stupid, their intelligent part . . . Then came the religious close . . . the old simple lesson that the world's history led up to God, that modern history was but the broadening of His Light in Christ! . . . conceive the thoughts of young liberalism.[88]

In theology their lack of constructive power cost the liberals dear. In 1867 the Ecclesiastical History chair went to H. L. Mansel, and in the following year he was succeeded by a high-churchman, William Bright. If these were appointments of a conservative ministry, this could not be said of Liddon's election in 1870 to the Ireland chair of exegesis; to him Pusey ascribed the chief influence in turning the tide towards belief among the talented young men of the university.[89]

Twice in 1868 the liberals took a heavy fall from the conservatives, even though on the second occasion, the parliamentary election, they were able to rally some of their old support from the high-church party. The first conflict came upon the perennially vexed topic of the study of theology. From time to time the old complaints revived that Oxford's claim to be the right arm of the church was belied both by the inadequacy of the divinity required for the B.A. degree, and by the worthlessness as training for ordinands of the short courses put on by the divinity professors.[90] In the later 'forties and 'fifties, the liberals tried repeatedly to establish a theology school, if possible under the management of a board, so that the English clerical wilderness might be fertilised by the pure streams of modern knowledge, and Robert Hussey, regius professor of ecclesiastical history, had also had a scheme in agitation just before his death in 1856.[91] Pusey and his friends, however, opposed the establishment of a school for the very reasons which led the liberals to favour it, and blocked all progress with the arguments that all professional training should come after the arts degree, that the consolidation of the other new schools should not be jeopardised by the launching of a fifth, and, most of all, that sacred studies should not be demeaned by becoming 'an arena for the sort of emulation and display' produced by the competition for honours.[92]

Only with a great struggle did the liberals succeed in reforming the Voluntary Theological Examination. This examination had been established in 1842 amidst the blackest suspicions of the Tractarians,[93] but had been a total failure as the bishops did not attach any professional advantage to it; in the first few years half a dozen candidates passed, but no more presented themselves thereafter.[94] In 1860 an effort was made to revive the examination, and by a system of classification to give it some of the stimulus of the competition for honours. Pusey, however, pronounced judgment against it, and the whole substance of the statute was rejected in Congregation.[95] In 1863, however, there were signs of a changing atmosphere. Dr. Jeune moved that the Johnson Scholarships and Denyer prizes, which had accomplished little for the encouragement of theological studies, should be consolidated as theological scholarships, and awarded on the results of the Voluntary Theological Examination. This meant, as Pusey put it, that every candidate who prepared himself properly would receive what he sought, while the three best would receive something more. Though no-one thought that this arrangement would answer every need, it was generally agreed to be an improvement, passed Congregation easily, and attracted 52 successful candidates in the first twelve years of its operation.[96]

As the decade proceeded two things became clear. In the first place, as Conington admitted frankly, the Oxford liberals became a spent force in theology, and virtually all the work done in this field was done by the high-churchmen.[97] The liberals ascribed their failures to clerical mob rule based on the tests, the conservatives to the defeats of the liberal standpoint. Then secondly, the recent gains of the orthodox might be seriously jeopardised if the tests should be removed by parliamentary action. It was important to the conservative theological party to capitalise their present advantages. The nature of their tactics is indicated in Liddon's diary.

> Dec. 20, 1867.
> . . . went to Burgon's rooms where I met Woollcombe and Bright. We discussed the state of things in Oxford for 2 hours. Decided
> 1. to watch the examiners & try to bring about some change in the final philosophical school,
> 2. to try to set up a school of theology. Burgon will write a letter to the Vice-Chancellor.

> February 11, 1868.
> Meeting at Balliol to discuss resistance to the Liberal policy in Woollcombe's rooms. We agreed to draw up a petition to the Abp. of C.—to attempt the separation of the Philological & Philosophical Schools, and to establish a Theological School.[98]

To disinfect the Greats school by removing the philosophy (as for other reasons Pattison had formerly proposed) proved to be altogether beyond their power, but in a very short time they had secured their theology school, and Congregation had witnessed its most remarkable exchange of parts.

The first shot was fired in a pamphlet from J. W. Burgon, fellow of Oriel and Vicar of St. Mary's, a wild and unscrupulous controversialist, who was a constant embarrassment to his friends. In his exaggerated way he claimed that theology as a separate study was nearly extinct in Oxford, but there was no denying his assertion that

> . . . we . . . are knowingly training up a large body of young men to be clergymen, to whom we are careful to impart *no special knowledge* of that science which, *almost in the same hour* that they leave us, they are expected publicly to profess and teach.

Moreover, as the age of graduation was steadily increasing, it was hopeless to expect professional studies to be undertaken after the arts degree.[99] Pusey introduced the statute in Congregation in June 1868, and candidly owned that changed circumstances in the university had led him to change his opinion and support a proposal which he had long bitterly opposed. Jowett, without any such confession, introduced Pusey's argument of yesteryear, declaring himself 'old-fashioned enough to think the subject of theology too sacred for the arena of an honour school.' There was a further reversal of form, when Pusey recommended that the new school be placed under the management of a board, a system which he had bitterly opposed in earlier years, while the liberals opposed a board which was to be composed of the Vice-Chancellor, Proctors and divinity professors with three elected clerical members of Convocation. Finally the principle of the school was carried in Congregation, but the board was lost.[100]

In November Pusey introduced a new proposal by which the board should be composed of the Vice-Chancellor and Proctors, three of the six divinity professors elected by their fellows, and the three examiners of the preceding year. He twitted the liberals with their new fondness for the antiquated system of entrusting the appointment of examiners to the Vice-Chancellor and Proctors. The liberals nevertheless pressed their new case with great vigour, and Henry Smith, Savilian professor, now the most able and respected of them, made a good point of the anomaly of organising this one school so that Congregation should have no control over it. Again the decision was postponed by very narrow margins,[101] and before the matter came on again in May 1869 there was a lively exchange of pamphlets. Pusey now proposed to have a board of four divinity professors and the Vice-Chancellor and Proctors, and claimed that this clerical majority was an essential precaution against the day when the repeal of the university tests removed all guarantee of orthodoxy from the other members. The liberals made great play with the idea that Pusey was erecting a test of opinion under the guise of an examination of knowledge, but the real difficulty was that they did not share the high-church view that theology was a science based upon the fundamentals of Christianity as received by the church. Pusey's pamphlet nevertheless had its effect and in Congregation the alliance of churchmen of various shades who had concluded that theology must be salvaged somehow, was reinforced by a defection of moderate liberals. The result was that in the biggest division for some years the statute was carried in Congregation by 116 votes to 61.[102]

There was intense liberal anger at this defeat. Goldwin Smith declared that

> Pusey will find that he has won 'a white elephant' and that before long it will trample down his own ranks. If candidates are rejected for their opinions, this will soon get wind, and there will be controversies more damaging to Puseyism than the bestowal of a Theological First Class on Strauss. Any veto on the appointment of an examiner will have the same effect in a still greater degree.[103]

His fears were given colour by Pusey's desperate efforts to get Liddon to refuse the offer of a canonry at St. Paul's and to

> remain to work the Theological School, and prevent it getting into the hands of the rationalists. He became very pathetic and emphatic—almost femininely so.[104]

But to some of its founders, especially J. W. Burgon, the school proved a disappointment, and it was to show, as the foundation of the English school was to show on a larger scale later, that the establishment of a school would not provide a stimulus to a study unless adequate teaching were provided. For various reasons this was not forthcoming in theology.[105] More immediately, the conflict over the establishment of the school had shown up an alarming weakness in the university constitution. It had always been the practice of the Hebdomadal Council to submit draft statutes to Congregation in portions to be voted upon separately, in order to define the areas in which there was disagreement. In this way it had been possible to revise the proposals for a theology board after the principle that the school should be established had been accepted. The opponents of the statute, however, obtained counsel's opinion in January 1869 that the statute could not legally be submitted to Convocation until it had been once more promulgated in Congregation as a whole. The liberals' opportunity for last ditch opposition to the statute in May 1869 was thus purchased at the cost of the suggestion that almost all the legislation since 1854 had been irregularly passed. The Hebdomadal Council then sought an independent legal opinion which confirmed the worst, and a special act had to be obtained to validate the university statutes.[106]

Meanwhile, the long battle over the university tests was reaching its climax. Between 1866 and 1868 the parties seeking a relaxation of the tests joined forces, and the question was advanced to the point where it became apparent that great changes would follow as soon as there was a liberal majority in the Commons. In 1866 Bouverie introduced his bill again on the ground that he must try his fortune in a new parliament. On this occasion he piloted it to the third reading, but the debate was then adjourned, and as the end of the session pressed, Bouverie withdrew the bill.[107] At the same time the bill for the abolition of the Oxford tests previously managed by Dodson and Goschen, who was now in office, was introduced by a young barrister who had recently entered the House as liberal member for Exeter, J. D. Coleridge. He had been prevailed on to take charge of the bill as a means of disarming opposition, for as the son of Sir John Taylor Coleridge, the friend and biographer of Keble, and as one brought up in the straitest of high-church sets, he might satisfy the timid that no harm to the church was contemplated. Yet Coleridge was a man in whom the light of faith was virtually out, and had been replaced by a vigorous radicalism. Already in 1860 Coleridge had written to his father:

> You have a compensating influence which I never can or shall have, I mean a real belief in and affection for the religious system in which God has cast your lot. I get no help from Anglicanism for all my deepest and strongest needs. What can a Protestant body say to Jowett and Co. except persecute them? And it is because I see how strong rationalism is in reason, and how powerless I am without a church against it, that I am so intolerant to the Germans.

Even this scruple had now ebbed, and he was persuaded to take charge of the bill by such extreme liberals as Jowett, G. C. Brodrick and Grant Duff.[108] The ambiguities in his personal position nevertheless stood out clearly in the debate. In a maiden speech of wholly unusual eloquence and charm, Coleridge introduced a bill which by opening the university and leaving the colleges untouched sought to accomplish a very minor change. Inevitably the commentators asked what deep significance in the bill aroused such advocacy.[109] The pressure put upon candidates at the election had its effect, and the second reading was carried triumphantly by 217 votes to 103, Gladstone and Heathcote both being in the minority.[110] A fortnight later the great meeting in the Free Trade Hall was held, but like so many private members' measures, the bill got pushed to the end of the session and was withdrawn before it was out of committee.[111]

There were three other matters worthy of note in this campaign. The Oxford liberals made an effort to get up college petitions in favour of Bouverie's bill, but they failed to get a majority in Merton, and seemed likely only to succeed in Lincoln, so the enterprise was dropped.[112] When the university petitioned against Coleridge's bill the liberals failed to appear in Convocation at all.[113] Since 1864 they had concluded that they must suffer discreditable defeats and it was better ostentatiously to abstain.[114] Their main hopes turned now upon destroying the political standing of the university. Then Gladstone began to screw up his resolution to face a change. When Coleridge's bill came on he determined to keep out of the fray until there was evidence that a settlement could be reached, and he was convinced that there was 'no tenable ground of defence which absolutely draws the line between the university and the colleges.'[115] The following September he confessed privately to Liddon and the Bishop of Salisbury that

> the present state of things was unmaintainable: that if left as it was there might be a few years resistance followed by a measure sweeping away everything. The best compromise

possible was a measure dealing with the whole question—providing that ½ the fellows of each college should be in Holy Orders in the Ch. of England. The advanced liberals would dislike this, but Parliament would certainly close with it.[116]

This proposal was shortly to bear odd fruit.

Finally Provost Hawkins who as usual was not quite in sympathy with any party, and had voted for the university petition against the bill, even though regretting that it contained no hint of any willingness to accept concession,[117] began to move the Hebdomadal Council to substitute for the present subscriptions for the higher degrees the declaration of assent from the Clerical Subscription Act of 1865, omitting the clause which applied only to clergymen. Early in 1868 this amendment was adopted.[118]

The year 1867 saw the two schemes for university opening move a little nearer success, and a little nearer to making common cause. Coleridge introduced his bill knowing that the majorities he had won last year would restrict his opponents to proceeding by amendment rather than rejection. In fact the scope of his bill was extended to include Cambridge by an amendment moved by Henry Fawcett, the Cambridge radical. To this extent the cause of the two universities was now allied. Fawcett, however, also brought in Bouverie's old bill; this bill suffered more from amendment than the other, but both passed the Commons, and were only defeated in the Lords.[119] As the *Nonconformist* remarked, their Lordships had accepted the Reform Bill, and 'to be compelled to satisfy one such demand upon them at the expense of their traditional principles is no doubt accounted more than enough for a single session.'[120]

The old parliament ran for another session, but with elections under the new franchise in view the liberals stepped up their campaign, and conservative churchmen began to cast about desperately for a settlement while there was still time. The London reform committee prepared the bill in strictest secrecy, and in Oxford only Goldwin Smith, Jowett, Liddell, J. M. Wilson and Thomas Fowler were admitted to the discussion.[121] The outcome was that Bouverie's bill and Coleridge's bill were consolidated and brought in as one measure. The bill now proposed to repeal the tests for all degrees other than those in divinity, and for all lay university offices. It also proposed to repeal the acts bearing upon college offices, leaving the colleges free to open them or not as they wished. The Oxford conservatives were now in real alarm and Woollcombe and his friends, recognising that the university's automatic petitions to parliament had ceased to produce any response, got up an address to the Archbishop of Canterbury.[122] The conclusion of the address lacked nothing in emphasis:

We cannot too strongly represent to your Grace that this is no
common contest, no party question; it is not even a question
between the Church and Dissent. The battle is for Christian
faith and Christian morals. It is for our very life.[123]

This declaration aroused a good deal of mirth in the liberal press.
It ought to have meant that the high-churchmen were preparing to
secede as they had often threatened in the past, but everyone knew
they were not.[124] As the *Express* remarked:

That chorus of Trappists, who look so solemn under the stage
moonlight as they dig their graves to the accompaniment of the
violon-celli, make us all feel very penitential, but the honest
fellows who are harrowing a sentimental public are not a bit
distressed. They have sung this dirge a hundred times before, and
keep time and tune with admirable ease.[125]

There were also high-churchmen who thought the address which
was presented to the Archbishop in March with 1800 signatures,
somewhat foolish. D. P. Chase considered it contrary to both policy
and justice to exclude otherwise qualified persons from Convocation,[126] and the cleft in the anglo-catholic movement was openly
revealed when the *Guardian* concluded that the tests were now
finished, and could not be defended against attack from without
when they were crumbling from within.[127] The Oxford liberals, nevertheless, got up a petition asking for the opening of the university
'without any interference with the religious worship of the University
or Colleges, with religious instruction, or with the religious inter-
course between tutor and pupil.'[128] Sixty of the 105 tutors and
lecturers in the university signed, but no great advance in liberal
sentiment could be recorded.[129]

The debate on second reading of the bill in the Commons was
marked by an intelligent speech on the conservative side by Beresford
Hope who argued that the parties supporting the bill were irrecon-
cilable one with another, and that they were playing the game of
Grant Duff and his friends who cared as little for dissent or practical
education as they did for the church, and who stood

upon their own pedestals—self-sent apostles of a new philosophy
of which the foundation is the denial of all authority—icono-
clasts of traditionary beliefs, on the ruins of which they profess
to rear the temple of a system, of which the main condition is
the unfettered recognition of free thought on all questions.

The bill, nevertheless, passed its second reading by 198 votes to 140,
but then had to be withdrawn as the end of the session was near.[130]
Conservative churchmen expected no reprieve, and the summer

witnessed a startling development of the idea which Gladstone had
planted in the minds of Liddon and his friends. In March Liddon
made a desperate attempt to win Gladstone from the liberal side by
suggesting that

> we should rejoice if one half of the property of the colleges, or
> even one half of the colleges themselves could be alienated from
> the church and made over to the various dissenting bodies, if
> only the rest could be really secured to her.[131]

When Gladstone did not respond Liddon published his plan in the
Guardian and initiated a lively correspondence.[132] In August there
was a great sensation when Pusey formally proposed his plan to the
Wesleyans, and published a letter in the *Times* arguing that the
church must face up to disestablishment. Of this the repeal of the
tests was an instalment, and the nation must be made to face the
question of the means by which disestablishment was to be effected;
the method of secularisation embodied in Coleridge's bill was not
the only method—property could be shared out among the denomi-
nations, and the principle of unmixed education preserved. This
plan, so reminiscent of the way Pusey had in the past turned to the
evangelicals when in desperate straits, miscarried; the Wesleyans had
nothing to lose by holding their hand, they were entering upon their
liberal and free church period, and were in any case being wooed by
the *Record* and the *Times* at the same moment. Nevertheless Liddon
continued to pin his hopes to the plan.[133] Unfortunately for Liddon,
Coleridge's bill now formed a plank in the platforms of all the
liberal groups, and took second place in their election addresses only
to the Irish church question; C. S. Roundell reckoned that there
were a dozen young university liberals standing for election for the
first time, and they alone made a considerable stir.[134]

Nor did Oxford escape the breeze, for shortly before the election,
Sir William Heathcote announced his retirement from the seat on
grounds of health. At once the London conservatives who had been
interfering in Oxford for so long, put up J. R. Mowbray, Judge-
Advocate General, a respectable, but minor, conservative politician.
Immediately afterwards a meeting in Magdalen nominated the man
who had been second to Gladstone as Oxford's most distinguished
son, Roundell Palmer. Like Gladstone, Roundell Palmer was distinguished equally as a scholar and a churchman, he was a former
Peelite who had compromised his career through independence, but
was now a liberal; on the other hand he had been unwilling to follow
Gladstone on the Irish church question. A dozen years before
Palmer might have succeeded in a dream for which he was the last
politician to be willing to sacrifice a career, but the great cleavage
in the high-church movement between what was already recognisable

as liberal catholicism, and the party which still had the odour of Tractarianism upon it was altogether fatal. The *Guardian* and the *Times* trumpeted the superior personal claims of Palmer, but conservatives were not without reason in condemning the notion of an unpolitical election. Palmer's support was more exclusively liberal than Gladstone's had ever been, though there was the usual difficulty in securing extreme liberal votes for a churchman. This alone tended to drive conservative churchmen to the other side. Finally Pusey concluded that after his strenuous opposition to Coleridge's bill he could not vote for a candidate, however sympathetic, who would not pledge himself against it. Roundell Palmer, however, was unwilling to compromise his ability to get the best bargain he could for the church by pledges in advance and would give no promise. As the evangelicals had already computed that there would be one vote more for the Irish church if a conservative were returned for Oxford and Palmer for Richmond than if Palmer were returned for Oxford and Lord Zetland brought in another liberal for Richmond, the game was up. Palmer was left with the liberals, a few churchmen like Lord Salisbury who put merit first, and those high-churchmen who were still in the train of Gladstone and the *Guardian*; on November 11 a comparison of promises between the committees revealed that he could not win, and his nomination was withdrawn.[135] The liberal retreat and the Tory predilection for politicians of no consequence nevertheless conspired together to take the university a step further out of politics.

The great liberal triumph at the polls elsewhere did not immediately advance the repeal of the tests. Coleridge, now Solicitor-General, introduced virtually the same bill as the previous year, but although he had the support of members of the government as individuals, Gladstone was still in the last degree reluctant to take the matter up, and the bill was not a ministerial measure.[136] It was certain, however, that the liberal majority would not only pass the bill, but would keep sending it up to the Lords until they gave way. There was thus a difficult problem of tactics for churchmen. The Primate talked about creating a number of university fellowships which should be free from tests,[137] Liddon talked of abandoning Oxford altogether,[138] Roundell Palmer concluded that the time had come to accept the bill and amend it. He therefore introduced amendments to safeguard religious worship instruction and discipline in the colleges according to their statutes, and carried them with conservative support. In this course he had the support of Edward Talbot, who became the first Warden of Keble, and secured an advantage which was not lost in the later campaigns.[139] The bill went easily through the Commons, but was contemptuously thrown out by the Lords on a motion for the previous question.[140]

The least the conservatives could do, however, as the Chancellor's life ebbed away in the autumn, was to make sure that they had a candidate ready who would not fail his duty in the Lords like Derby in 1854. A. P. Forbes, the turbulent Bishop of Brechin, put forward Lord Salisbury before Derby died,[141] and the cause was enthusiastically taken up by All Souls;[142] according to his own account Salisbury declined on the ground that the Chancellor 'should be less of a partizan & more of a scholar' but was prevailed upon to stand by the assurance that his nomination would be the most likely to spare the university a contest.[143] Eighteen months before the liberals had been ready to run a candidate,[144] probably Gladstone,[145] but after their failure with Roundell Palmer they had no hope now, and Salisbury's election was carried through in a thin Convocation by 37 votes to one unexpectedly cast for Lord Carnarvon, the High Steward.[146] There was some liberal soreness at this smooth passage, and Pusey soon concluded that he had been misled into refraining from opposition,[147] but the conservative leader in the Lords seemed now to be firmly tied to the university's cause, and in 1870 did all that could be done to save the tests.

From the end of the previous session, there had been pressure from liberals and nonconformists for the government to take the matter in hand,[148] and towards the end of the year the pressure was increased. In October the Congregational Union declared its resolution to accept no settlement by which any section of the community should be excluded 'on account of its religious beliefs from either of the universities, or any of their colleges or from any of their emoluments, offices or advantages,'[149] and in November W. E. Forster, on a visit to the Liverpool Mechanics Institute, was confronted by a powerful deputation led by William Rathbone M.P., the eminent unitarian, demanding the opening of both universities and colleges.[150] The liberal parties in the universities came to the same resolution in December at important meetings at St. John's College, Cambridge, and at Corpus Christi in Oxford. The *Times* which had been cool when Coleridge had begun his campaign five years before, now tuned up in his favour, and on December 15 Gladstone received deputations from each of the universities and from the dissenters. Each of them asked the government to take up the cause, and each wanted college tests to be removed by statute, rather than left to be fought over college by college under permissive legislation. Each found that Gladstone still had misgivings, and that he feared the pressure upon government time would be so great in the coming session that he could not take up the subject at once. He also urged the universities to agree together before the next bill went into the house.[151]

The plea of pressure on the time-table, despite the demands of the Irish Land Bill and the Education Bill, occasioned a good deal of liberal uneasiness that the ministry was not in earnest,[152] though Lowe privately convinced Jowett that all was well.[153] The draft bill which included the compulsory opening of the colleges was sent down to Oxford and agreed by Liddell on behalf of the Oxford liberals, who also agreed to except the headships from the operation of the bill in deference to the wishes of the Cambridge party.[154] The usual meetings were held in the country in support of the bill,[155] and it was noteworthy that the conservatives could raise hardly any counter demonstration,[156] apart from petitions from the universities.[157] The active organisers of the Oxford petitions were Gladstone's old allies, E. C. Woollcombe of Balliol and Provost Hawkins.[157] There was little heart in conservative resistance in the Commons, and only 66 members could be brought to oppose the second reading.[158] The chief embarrassment, indeed, came from the Oxford liberals. On June 13 Lord Edmond Fitzmaurice moved that the heads be not excepted from the operation of the bill, and the Oxford liberals assembled at Balliol under the chairmanship of Jowett on June 4 to pass resolutions in his support and sign a petition to Gladstone. Liddell did his best to dissuade them from breaking their understanding to defer to the Cambridge view, but Jowett thought the fact that Fitzmaurice was moving the amendment was evidence that the government was really indifferent, and he would not give way.[159] Gladstone, however, was trying to present the bill as the fruit of common university opinion, and to convince conservatives like Provost Hawkins that he was saving them from a much worse fate,[160] and asked Fitzmaurice to postpone his amendment until he could be released from his engagements to the university deputations.[161] The amendment in due course was carried and the question then was whether at the tail end of a session the bill could be carried through the upper house.

The debate in the Lords was enlivened by involutions of ethics on the part of Dr. Ellicott, Bishop of Gloucester, and of tactics on the part of Lord Salisbury, on whom the last hopes of the Oxford conservatives centred. The Bishop of Gloucester had just scandalised high-churchmen by supporting Dean Stanley in his invitation to the Bible Revisionists (including the unitarian Vance Smith) to take communion in Westminster Abbey, but he was not prepared to admit dissenters to the university.[162] Salisbury's problem was that

> the difficulty of getting a sufficiently large attendance at the extreme end of the session prevented us from dealing with the measure by way of amendment; for our amendment would certainly have been rejected by the House of Commons, & then we should have come to a vote on the question of accepting the

bill in its original form at a time when the mass of peers would certainly have been away.[163]

He therefore played for time by referring the bill to a select committee.[164]

As in the previous year the dissenters and university liberals began to growl again in order to make the government take up the bill, and threatened to extend it to the abolition of clerical fellowships.[165] Augustus Wilkins, professor of Latin at Manchester, rubbed home the point that the liberals would be lost without dissenting support in the boroughs and must be prepared to pay for it,[166] though most of the nonconformist journalists did not disguise the fact that the lead on this issue had always been taken by liberal graduates 'who have already attained the object of their intellectual ambition although not always the accompanying emoluments.'[167] In January 1871 a deputation from the Liberation Society reinforced by the leaders of the Cambridge academic dissenters, Aldis and Goodman, waited upon Gladstone to inform him that they wanted nothing less than the whole bill and the abolition of clerical fellowships.[168] The comedy of the last campaign was that when Salisbury had lost all hope of success,[169] and had to press all the other tory leaders into the contest against their will,[170] Gladstone had less heart than ever to press home his advantage. He now absolutely refused to go beyond the terms of Coleridge's last bill, and before the session gave the party the choice between having him take over the bill as a ministerial measure unchanged, or leaving it in private hands on their own terms.[171]

Gladstone was asked to take over the bill. It was recommended in the Queen's speech and brought in on the first day of the session; but although the bill reached the House of Lords in a month, the politics of Gladstone's university legislation had changed very little. In committee Fawcett moved the abolition of the clerical restrictions, and the government defeated his amendment by only 22 votes with the aid of the conservatives against their own supporters.[172] Meanwhile Salisbury had secured the reappointment of his select committee, and there was a pause in the upper house until the committee had reported. The report showed what was on other grounds clear enough, that while men like C. S. Roundell and Jowett would not give an inch there were both liberals and nonconformists who hesitated before the complete abolition of the tests;[173] this gave Salisbury an opportunity to move a number of amendments. Tutors should be required to make a declaration to teach nothing contrary to the doctrine and Divine authority of the Old and New Testaments, the headships should be exempted from the bill and colleges should have no power to alter the statutes which imposed clerical restrictions.

These amendments were carried by derisory majorities,[174] and the proposed declaration was accurately described by Archdeacon Denison as 'an imposture upon the public.'[175] It was certain that the Commons would reject the amendments, and the Oxford conservatives had no spirit left. Woollcombe called a meeting at the lodgings of the Provost of Oriel to discuss whether, upon the rejection of his amendments in the Commons, Salisbury should be asked to defeat the bill; only eleven met, and they decided by the majority of a single vote (Hawkins and Liddon being in the majority) not to make the request.[176] The Commons rejected Salisbury's amendments, and when the bill came back to the Lords he failed to carry his tutors' declaration by forty votes.[177] The battle was now over, the bill passed, and the struggle went into liberal propaganda 'as illustrating both the moderation of Liberal Policy, and the perverse obstinacy of Conservative opposition.'[178]

The more thoughtful dissenters now began to ponder the pastoral consequences of their new advantage,[179] and G. H. Curteis delivered his Bampton Lectures with the hope of elucidating the church's connexions with the state and conciliating 'those who are conscientiously . . . endeavouring to subvert her influence and to destroy her vantage-ground for doing good.'[180] In the second successive year a great blow had been struck in favour of mixed as distinct from denominational education. The difficulties which had arisen in the case of the university tests, however, gave no great encouragement for the next contest which was already brewing in Ireland. For a number of years there had been rumours that Newman was to return to Oxford as the head of a Catholic Hall or mission, and he actually purchased a site, but Manning was opposed to every move, and the Catholic bishops concluded with the least feasible of all schemes, and attempted to deter Catholic parents from sending their sons to the English universities, while providing no Catholic alternative.[181] In Ireland where the question was also coming to a head, and English radicals like Fawcett were anxious to apply the English solution to Trinity College,[182] the difficulties created by Catholic intransigence and by Gladstone's personal scruples were infinitely worse, and in 1873 the Irish University Bill was to bring about his resignation.[183]

Even in Oxford the downfall of the tests coincided with some curious outbursts of intolerance. Salisbury submitted a list of candidates for honorary doctorates on the occasion of his installation as Chancellor in 1870, and immediately ran into trouble from two quarters. Pusey took exception to the names of Darwin, Huxley and Tyndall on theological grounds, and threatened to create a scene in Convocation if their degrees were proposed, while Jowett strongly objected to Keppel and Cockburn. Salisbury admitted that the latter had had natural children, but claimed that he had behaved respectably since entering public life, and that a university which had honoured Palmerston had no room for scruples. The scientists he was reluctantly prepared to surrender, whereupon Henry Smith and some other members of council threatened to wash their hands of the whole proceeding. However, though Acland failed to make any impression upon Pusey's construction of the theory of evolution, Liddon did, and peace was restored when Pusey withdrew his opposition to Darwin's name. Ironically, Darwin was too ill to attend the ceremony, and a motion of Liddell's in the Hebdomadal Council that the degree be conferred *in absentia* produced a tie, and so was lost.[184]

The following year the threatened division in Convocation actually took place. Liddon earnestly advocated the award of the degree of D.C.L. to Döllinger of Munich. The high-church press did not disguise their conviction that both in Germany and England Döllinger was now fulfilling the role which ought to have been filled by Newman. The liberals were as determined that the University should not give its sanction to the notion that infallibility resided somewhere in the church as ever the high-church party had been to prevent the reverse, and Thorold Rogers opposed the degree in Convocation. In this case he was reinforced by Roman Catholics, who held that Liddon was fomenting trouble in their church; prominent among them was R. F. Clarke, who for many years had been tutor at St. John's and who upon his recent conversion had been deprived of his membership of the college, and received at Trinity. He and ten other resident Catholics addressed a protest to the Pope, but the degree was carried in Convocation.[185]

A few months later J. W. Burgon was protesting, from the side of the high-churchmen, against the appointment of Temple as a Select Preacher.[186] The board which nominated the Select Preachers had only recently been an object of liberal suspicion,[187] but the boot was now on the other foot, and in 1872, with the support of Woollcombe and Golightly, Montagu Burrows and H. R. Bramley, Burgon launched a full campaign against the nomination of A. P. Stanley. In 1865 when there had been talk of putting Stanley forward, Liddon and Pusey had been prepared to lead the attack,[188] but they now considered that such nominations were to be expected when Liddell was Vice-Chancellor, and that no useful purpose was served by creating a dispute in Convocation which was no longer an exclusively Anglican body. Eventually Stanley obtained his appointment by 349 votes to 287, E. M. Goulburn, Burgon's friend and biographer, resigned from his preachership, and Jowett heaved a sigh of relief, knowing that he could not have won with any other candidate.[189] *Odium theologicum* was not yet dead in Oxford, but the repeal of the tests made it much more difficult to use the machinery of the university for persecution.

CHAPTER XII

OXFORD AND NATIONAL EDUCATION

The further reforms which are called for originate in the intellectual activity of the universities themselves, even more than in that spirit of the age which is supposed to be always seeking to criticize and remodel. A restless educational fervour has taken possession of the most able residents and a propagandist spirit has been developed which desires to carry university teaching and university influence to every corner of the land.

Times, Aug. 21, 1873, p. 9.

IN 1871 as in 1865 the liberals were hoping that the repeal of the tests would strengthen them not only in Congregation but in Convocation where 'the growth of a body of nonconformist graduates ... might form as trustworthy a phalanx on the side of progress and reform as the country clergy now supply to the ranks of a stubborn conservatism.'[1] The fulfilment of this hope must clearly be long delayed, however, and so they bent their energies to the other aspect of their policy, the effort to recruit allies on the basis of a common interest in educational reform, and to see if further changes in the university would make it more receptive to liberal ideals. To the older generation of high-churchmen the cause which had come second only to the defence of the tutorial system had been that of university extension, especially in the interests of poor ordinands, and when they began to move again in 1865, the opportunity was ripe for the liberals to steal their thunder.

In the early 'sixties the expectations entertained by the royal commissioners from the opening of the university seemed to have been dismally disappointed. Matriculations fell steadily during the Crimean War when commissions were easy to purchase, and with the opening of the Civil Service at home and in India to competition they recovered only slowly; nor was there a decisive step forward until 1865. After this matriculations increased steadily for the rest of our period, though the grand total of 784 last attained in 1621 was not equalled till 1883. It was in 1865, when the university seemed to be the only stationary institution in the country, and there was fresh talk of meeting the shortage of clergy from sources outside the universities,[2] that the question of extension was taken up again in the high-church press.[3] Early in November a number of churchmen called on the Vice-Chancellor to press for action to increase the

number of clergy. When the question had been agitated in the
'forties the Hebdomadal Board had been able to point to the large
number of unoccupied rooms, but now, with the recent increase in
matriculations and the generally extended residence, there were said
to be not more than eight sets unoccupied in the town, if New Inn
Hall were excepted. The problem was now much more difficult, and
when in response to a notice from the Provost a great gathering
not only of high-churchmen but of liberals assembled at Oriel on
November 16, a great variety of views as well as great concern were
expressed.[4] As the meeting was too large to take practical action, it
resolved that each college and hall should have power to name one
member to form a committee. This committee appointed six subcommittees, one to consider each of the main proposals, and before
the end of the year they were at work.[5]

The views of the high-churchmen who had originally agitated the
question were embodied in the first committee which considered 'the
suggestion for extending the university by founding a college or hall
on a large scale, with a view not exclusively, but especially to the
education of persons needing assistance and desirous of admission
into the Christian Ministry.' This was plainly a revival of Marriott's
poor scholars' hall, and the committee, the chairman of which was
W. W. Shirley, regius professor of ecclesiastical history, included
such well-known high-churchmen as Pusey, Richard Greswell,
J. W. Burgon, and William Ince, as well as Burrows, Bernard and
H. L. Mansel. The second committee was to examine the nostrum
of its chairman, the Provost of Worcester, and seek the best means
of enlarging the existing halls and colleges. The third was to consider
the liberal scheme championed by the blue book of permitting
undergraduates to reside in lodgings, and besides the chairman,
Dean Liddell, included such prominent liberals as Sir Benjamin
Brodie, Bartholomew Price and Goldwin Smith. The fourth, under
the Warden of Merton, which was politically mixed in composition,
was to consider whether the colleges should have power to permit
undergraduates to go into lodgings after two years' residence. The
fifth committee formed in response to a pamphlet put out by
Professor Daubeny,[6] had him in the chair, and was

> to consider the means of extending the benefits of an Oxford
> University education to young men of slender means intended
> for the profession of medicine.

The last committee considered another far-reaching liberal scheme,
the possibility of university extension by the affiliation of other places
of liberal education. Goldwin Smith was chairman of a liberal
committee which included Professors Acland, Rolleston, Henry
Smith and Thorold Rogers, as well as G. E. Thorley of Wadham,

W. C. Sidgwick of Merton, and J. R. Magrath of Queen's. Liberals noted with delight that

> the high-churchmen who started the thing are rather astonished [at] the properties & characteristics of their offspring.[7]

All the committees reported enthusiastically in favour of their own schemes, and their views were widely discussed in the press and in the country.[8] All had a bearing on the discussions in the university in the next few years, and two of them, one liberal and the other conservative, bore speedy fruit. The proposal to found a large new college with a view to providing economical education for ordinands became known from the time of its publication as the 'Keble scheme.'[9] The committee argued that while colleges were reorganising their finances under the provisions of the College Estates Acts they could not provide the money for building and endowing a new college, and the money must come from private subscription. An opportunity for this was provided unsought by the death of John Keble on March 29, 1866. Gladstone immediately wrote to Liddon proposing that a memorial be erected, and at the funeral Liddon persuaded a number of friends to give it the form of a Keble College. Throughout the next months Liddon watched over the plan and caused offence in liberal quarters by insisting that A. P. Stanley be excluded from the great meeting at Lambeth at which the appeal was launched.[10] Thus even before the first subcommittee had reported, a scheme to carry out its recommendations was in being, and had already a strongly marked party character which was bound to provoke opposition.[11] Nevertheless the project prospered, there were foundation ceremonies in 1868, and Liddon, who had been a storm-centre at Cuddesdon a few years before, had the wisdom not to accept repeated offers of the headship. With the university tests obviously doomed, it was inevitable that the high-church party should seek to keep Keble an Anglican oasis in the desert,[12] and the result was strenuous liberal opposition to the New Foundation Statute of 1871 under which the college became part of the university. Thorold Rogers who had been dispossessed of the chair of political economy by a tory conspiracy in 1868,

> called upon Convocation to remember that he now pledged himself to oppose the introduction of any sectarian institution whether Dissenting, Buddhist, or Mahomedan, equally with Keble College,[13]

and H. A. Pottinger sought desperately to prove that the whole plan was illegal.[14] The real danger to the Keble conception, however, was pointed out in an unlikely quarter, Edward Miall's *Nonconformist*.

If any religious body had the necessary funds at its disposal it could hardly spend them worse than in founding a college and endeavouring to secure it by tests for its own purposes. . . It is highly probable that in a generation or two the college might become a focus of the very opposite school of ideas from those in whose interest it was founded. There is no real guarantee that Keble may not in a few years be a nest of Evangelicals or Rationalists.[15]

This Liddon found to his cost before the college had been functioning for a decade. His diary records a

Keble College meeting about the Scholarships from 12.15 until 4.30. A very earnest debate. I proposed a resolution (1) 'That it is inconsistent with the principles on wh. K.C. was founded to offer an education to any undergraduate who is not a member of the Ch. of E. & of Churches in communion with it.' This was carried after more than three hours debate: & then 2 subordinate resolutions (2) confining the scholarships given by the college to matriculated members of it and (3) inviting the Gorum & other Trustees to bring the Gorum & Wilbraham Scholarships into harmony with Resolution 1. . . The Warden I fear was much vexed. But it could not be helped. We were drifting, and a decisive effort was needed in order to arrest the downward course.[16]

But the effort was not decisive. A year later we read:

Keble College Council. . . The scholarship question again put off. The Warden vexed. But he sees he will have to give way.[17]

When Liddon discovered that liberalism had seeped into Pusey House as well his cup of misery was complete.

Another benefactor was nevertheless willing to gamble on the effect of a test. Baring offered a foundation of £30,000 on the condition that the fellows should be members of the Church of England, a condition which led Brasenose College to decline the offer. However a scheme was launched to transform Magdalen Hall into Hertford College with the aid of the endowment, and as soon as the conservatives returned to power in 1874 an act was passed for the purpose, a Convocation filled with an unusually large contingent of non-resident clergy going through the farce of assenting to it. Liberal suspicion of the act was mollified by a final clause specially introduced to the effect that nothing in the act should be construed to repeal any of the provisions of the University Tests Act. By the end of 1875 it was clear that the college was accepting Baring's conditions, and that the creation of the college had become a means of withdrawing Magdalen Hall from the operation of the Tests Act. Reports spread that the Liberation Society was assembling candidates to test the legality of the case, and in December 1875 A. I. Tillyard, a Cambridge nonconformist, applied to the college for permission to compete for a fellowship. They said he could be examined if he wished, but the fellowship could only be awarded to an Anglican. He then applied to the Queen's Bench for a mandamus to direct the college to examine him properly, and the mandamus was granted. The Court of Appeal reversed the judgment, and opened a way for benefactors to restrict the operation of the Tests Act.[18] Before any had done so, however, a second body of executive commissioners had ended the independent existence of all the halls except St. Edmund Hall.

If the report of the first subcommittee became known from the beginning as the Keble scheme and led to prolonged skirmishing between the liberals and the high-church party, the report of the third subcommittee on allowing undergraduates to live in lodgings became known as Temple's scheme, and had equally far-reaching results. In giving evidence to the royal commission, Frederick Temple had advocated the foundation of affiliated halls, but he now pressed on the Master of Balliol that the college monopoly must be ended, and a lodging-house system introduced.[19] The subcommittee argued that this was the only means of providing for university extension without capital outlay and commercial risk. There were no insuperable problems of undergraduate discipline in lodgings in Cambridge or in Scotland, and an efficient system of licensing lodgings together with the admission of men who wished to live economically should achieve a reasonable result.[20]

No sooner had the committee reported than Balliol put forward a scheme for building and furnishing lodgings in the town to let cheaply to men who would receive free tuition in the college, and have an opportunity of winning small exhibitions.[21] To carry out this plan Balliol required a relaxation of the university rules regarding residence within college walls, and applied to the Hebdomadal Council on October 29, 1866.[22] To this proposal there were two kinds of opposition. On the one hand there was the high-church belief that the college system kept the men under some kind of pastoral oversight, and on the other it was recognised that the requirement of residence was a protection as much for bad colleges as for good undergraduates. Any regulation by which colleges were freed from the restrictions on their intake imposed by their physical accommodation might lead to the absorption of the whole university into Balliol—a consummation complacently viewed by Jowett.[23] The result was that the Council dallied for a session and as usual the liberal press perceived the dark manoeuvres of clerical conspiracy.

The Council has treated this scheme most unworthily. They
first appointed a committee to examine it, which, with some
insignificant restrictions, reported in its favour. When the
adoption of this report was moved, Dr. Pusey, we believe,
moved, as an amendment, that another committee should be
appointed to consider all the reports on which we have been
commenting. How entirely this was a mere measure of obstruc-
tion was shown by Dr. Pusey declining to nominate his committee after the amendment had been carried. Eventually, we
believe, a committee was nominated by someone else; but the
practical result of these manoeuvres has been to shelve the
Balliol scheme,[24]

and divert the college to establishing Balliol Hall under the charge
of T. H. Green. And meanwhile parliamentary intervention was
again threatened.

On March 12, 1867, William Ewart, member for Dumfries burghs
and an advanced liberal, obtained leave to bring in a bill to open
the universities of Oxford and Cambridge to students not residing
in a college or hall, and on the second reading there was a lively
debate. Gladstone supported the bill on the grounds that plans for
private halls had failed, and that there had never been a time when
Oxford was more full of zealous teachers or did less for the poorer
class of students. The liberal press applauded the bill, the Oxford
liberal caucus opposed a university petition against it in Convocation
(W. C. Sidgwick of Merton making 'an extempore Latin speech which
elicited both laughter and applause'), and the bill obtained a second
reading by 14 votes. However, like most private members' measures,
the bill failed to get through before the end of the session, and it
was referred to a select committee.[25]

The select committee of July 1867 gave the Oxford liberals an
opportunity to air the schemes they had been nurturing in recent
years, and perhaps to achieve a triumph like the blue book of 1852.
Benjamin Brodie saw in the admission of non-collegiate students an
opportunity to develop the professorial system, the educational
virtues of which were proved in the college triumphs of the Balliol
professors, Jowett, Wall and Henry Smith. C. S. Roundell took up
the question of the redistribution of college revenues, and waxed
bitter against the clerical influence in colleges. Liddell argued
strongly for the lodgings system and said that Christ Church had
had no trouble with a considerable number of freshmen who had
had to live out while one of the buildings had been pulled down.
He admitted that he had been heavily defeated in the Council when
proposing the plan the previous term but intended to bring the
matter on again after the Long Vacation. Both Liddell and Roundell

wanted to see a reduction in the membership of Congregation. Jowett expressed himself in favour of the lodgings system, but opposed the plan recommended by Goldwin Smith's subcommittee of affiliating new colleges in the country to the university, with a view to granting exemptions from part of the residence normally required.[26] Pusey thought that parliamentary proceedings ought to be stayed as the Keble scheme was certain to go through, the Balliol plan morally certain, and some scheme for permitting part of the residence requirements to be fulfilled outside Oxford would probably be passed. Nevertheless the evidence, particularly the Oxford evidence, was of a strongly liberal cast, and its dissemination in the press was bound to encourage the liberals in their hopes of making university reform an issue in the reformed elections to which they were now looking forward.[27]

The debates on Ewart's bill and the evidence of the select committee had two important consequences which must be discussed in turn. In the first place, as Pusey had suggested, they made it morally certain that the university would agree to some form of the Balliol plan, if only to avoid a parliamentary settlement; and in the second, they gave a fresh impulse to the liberal discussions on the wider issues of university reform.

Just before the Long Vacation in 1867 the Hebdomadal Council published two draft statutes, the one empowering colleges to allow those students whom they educated free on account of poverty, to live in lodgings, the houses to be licensed by a lodgings delegacy; the other permitting students to spend their first four terms away from the university, and to commence residence in their fifth term provided that they had already passed their Responsions.[28] These statutes were promulgated in Congregation in November, and aroused violent controversy. Liberal speakers were extremely hostile to the provisions about gratuitous instruction and poverty, though the former had been included in the original Balliol scheme to sugar the pill, and there was great dissatisfaction with the way in which the Council handled the amendments which were made.[29] However, a ferocious skirmish between Liddell and Pusey and Liddon in the Hebdomadal Council in February 1868 was the turning-point,[30] and when the revised statute came back to Congregation in March, the high-church party raised very little fight.[31] By June the whole scheme was accepted in Convocation; the provision about poverty and gratuitous education had disappeared, and residence in lodgings was permitted not only to members of colleges but to students unattached to any college. For them tuition should be provided by a new race of university tutors.[32] The principle of Ewart's bill had been adopted by the university, and a step ahead of Cambridge had been taken.

There were even now men who believed that it must cost £100 p.a.

to live in lodgings if the cost of indispensable private tuition were included, and others who insisted that no one outside the present classes in the university could afford to delay his career by coming up.[33] The critics were, nevertheless, confounded when 40 men passed the first matriculation examination which the university had sponsored, entering as unattached students, and 75 members of colleges also went into lodgings. Numbers grew steadily until the unattached students were the equal of a moderate-sized college, and one third of all undergraduates were living out. It soon became necessary to separate the care of the men from the licensing of lodgings, and in 1870 two of the original delegates and enthusiasts for the scheme, G. W. Kitchin of Christ Church and G. S. Ward of Magdalen Hall, were appointed as stipendiary Censors with the duty of seeing that teaching was provided for their charges. The men themselves provided some corporate organisation for cheap catering, in 1870 the university resolved to

> fit up that portion of St. Mary's Church which for some time past has been used as a receptacle for the university fire engine as a chapel[34]

for them, and in 1872 made them a chapel in the old Convocation House and granted funds for a library.[35] It proved that economically minded men could pay their expenses in Oxford for £50 p.a., and that considerable numbers of nonconformists were prepared to seek an Oxford education freed from the snares of college life.[36] The Censors had their difficulties and their critics,[37] but they enabled the university to make a more rapid contribution to the education of the nation than would have been otherwise possible, and only J. W. Burgon continued to entertain suspicion of the spectacular vices of life in lodgings conjured up in conservative imaginations for years past.[38]

If Ewart's bill sealed the fate of the college monopoly it also brought into the open one of the wider movements for university reform which had arisen from the Oxford liberals' dissatisfaction with the constitution and intellectual condition of the university. The London committee which had formed at the time of Dodson's bill in 1864,[39] seem to have kept in touch informally, and in the spring of 1866 they resolved to meet in the Lincoln's Inn Chambers of Osborne Morgan, who as M.P. for Denbighshire in the next parliament was to prove a valiant university reformer. The original object seems to have been to produce a report on university extension and the professoriate for consideration at a future conference;[40] the conference was held at the Ship Hotel, Charing Cross (where Gladstone had formerly had his London committee rooms) on July 1st, 1867, just as the select committee on Ewart's bill was opening its hearings, while the report grew steadily into one of the most famous of all treatises on university reform, Mark Pattison's *Suggestions on academical organisation, with especial reference to Oxford*, published in the following year.[41]

The aim of the Ship Hotel conference was to produce 'a measure, which if taken up by our friends in parliament, may lead to a complete and permanent settlement,' and Gladstone,[42] John Dodson and other interested members of parliament were kept informed of the proceedings.[43] Twenty-two were present at the conference, the great majority of them Oxford liberals, resident like Liddell, Brodie, Thomas Fowler, Mark Pattison and J. M. Wilson, or resident in London like Frederic Harrison, C. S. Roundell and A. O. Rutson. There were M.P.s who were expected to take the lead in the cause, especially Grant Duff, Henry Fawcett and William Ewart, and two interested outside parties, Edward Miall, the proprietor of the *Nonconformist*, and the Principal of Owens College, Manchester, who might be concerned in any proposals for the affiliation of provincial colleges, and who was familiar at first-hand with the attitudes of the commercial classes towards higher education. It was notable that with the exception of W. L. Newman the entire phalanx of Balliol liberals was absent.

The memorandum which had been circulated before the conference gives a good idea of the state of opinion in the circle of which Pattison came to be the acknowledged head. It assumed that the university tests were doomed, that college tests would not last much longer, and that some form of residence in lodgings would be secured through Ewart's bill or otherwise. In short the two causes for which Jowett had fought were taken as virtually secure, and the conference turned to its serious business.

(3) the constitution of the university; the mode of appointing the Vice-Chancellor; the composition of Congregation; the restrictions on its power of initiation and debate; the power of non-residents exercised in Convocation.

(4) The enlargement of the power possessed by Colleges of amending their Ordinances and Statutes; an opinion having been recently given by high legal authority that the colleges have no power of amendment without the consent of a Visitor who is usually an ecclesiastic, and who has recently in the case of two colleges, put his veto on even a modified removal of clerical restrictions upon Fellowships.

(5) The redistribution of college revenues so as to secure not only good instruction in the university, but also the general advancement of science and learning. Under this head may be considered:—the tenure of fellowships with the view of rendering them in part terminable, and in part free from the restriction of

celibacy; the appropriation of fellowships to special studies; the reduction of sinecure fellowships; and the provision of a better staff of teachers either for each college separately, or for the university at large, by the help of contributions from the college funds.

The last point was taken first, and with liberals talking of giving college funds to the university, and Pusey thinking of giving them to the Wesleyans, it was evident that, as Palgrave put it, 'a plastic period' had begun in Oxford.[44]

Sir Benjamin Brodie strongly urged that the facts relating to college revenues should be elicited, and that the present system of prize fellowships was an inordinate waste of money. The increase in lay fellowships had led to an increase in non-residence and college revenues were being drained to subsidise London professional men; moreover, since the great inducement to an Oxford education was the bounties available as scholarships or fellowships, the age of matriculation was steadily increasing as candidates prepared themselves more thoroughly. Brodie had no doubt that the college system was an abuse from an educational point of view, that the university should be strengthened at the colleges' expense, and that there should be much greater appropriation of funds to new studies.

Inevitably a good deal of wrath was expended upon the university constitution. The conference thought the succession to the Vice-Chancellorship absurd, a view in which Lord Derby concurred, for in 1855 he had made an attempt to associate the Hebdomadal Council with him in a more rational choice, but had been rebuffed by members of the Council of all shades of opinion.[45] It was also laid down that Congregation could not become efficient until the non-academical element was eliminated, but amongst the changes suggested was the inclusion of non-resident fellows—a proposal which made it hard for the liberals to rebut clerical charges that they wished simply to gerrymander the constitution in their own interest.[46] Better points were made on the procedure of Congregation; members should have the right to put questions and to vote immediately after a discussion. A reformed Congregation ought to displace Convocation as the final authority in educational questions.

Lastly the issue was raised of the relations of colleges with their Visitors. C. S. Roundell's conspiracy to reduce the clerical restrictions upon fellowships at Merton[47] had ended in great bitterness. The college had almost unanimously agreed to pass an ordinance reducing the number of clerical fellowships by two-thirds. There was, however, a doubt whether this ordinance would require the consent of the Visitor, the Archbishop of Canterbury. Without prejudice to this question the college applied to the Primate who declared that in the interests of the church he could not sanction the measure. The Merton liberals resented this construction of the Visitor's duties, and applied to the Privy Council for a decision whether under the Act of 1854, they had the power of altering the ordinance without reference to the Visitor. The Privy Council declined their prayer without even hearing them by counsel.[48] The only solution seemed to be to seek an act of parliament. The conference thought also that Visitors should be deprived of their judicial functions. It wound up by appointing Goldwin Smith, Thomas Fowler and C. S. Roundell as a working committee for keeping the campaign on foot.

By the autumn the wires were being pulled with the leading liberals. Gladstone discussed a memorandum on the university question with Roundell Palmer,[49] and in December 1867 Earl Russell moved four resolutions on education, one of which declared that the ancient universities could be made more useful to the nation by the removal of restrictions and the better distribution of their revenues for purposes of instruction. These resolutions were negatived,[50] but they showed the success of the conference continuation committee in getting their policies written into the liberal programme; Goldwin Smith, for example had got Russell to drop his original demand for a new university commission—the last thing he wanted from a conservative government.[51] The intention seems to have been to tack the conference's proposals of reform to Coleridge's tests bill in the new session, but on Gladstone's advice the two projects were separated.[52] A draft bill 'for the extension and improvement of the University of Oxford and the colleges therein' was drawn up for Coleridge to introduce, and a meeting of Oxford residents sympathetic to its objects was summoned for May 30, 1868 at the Clarendon Hotel.[53] This bill contained the full programme; the small Congregation, the transfer of all the powers of Convocation to Congregation except the election of the Chancellor and burgesses and the conferring of honorary degrees, an executive commission with full powers to remodel college statutes and inquire into their finances with a view to transferring part of their funds to the university—all were there.[54] It was already too late in the session for another bill to be introduced, the clauses on the lodgings system were forestalled by the university and elections on the new franchise were to be held in the autumn.[55] The main effort of the reformers went therefore into propaganda, and the press was filled with discussions of academic technicalities with especial reference to Oxford.

In September 1867 Thorold Rogers read a paper to the British Association at Dundee on educational endowments, which led to a good deal of controversy, ridiculing the situation in which enormous endowments were consumed in educating a handful of men who paid their own way.[56] Goldwin Smith produced a characteristic version of the conclusions of the Ship Hotel conference, declaiming against the university constitution and the iniquitous clerical electioneering which had produced the conservative gains on the Council. He had no use for learned sinecures, but as he still wished to develop the professoriate he recommended putting an end to college teaching of the usual sort, and leaving the tutor simply to exercise moral oversight. College lectures should be a university function.[57] Bonamy Price, whose views had not developed since 1850, still wanted a professorial system, and hoped optimistically that the unattached students would provide the raw material on which university teaching could establish itself.[58] The *Edinburgh Review* insisted that in Oxford '*knowledge has absolutely no value at all,*' and that intellectual effort was devoted exclusively to the acquisition of prizes.[59]

This comment was in the Pattisonian vein, and the heaviest guns were brought by Pattison himself, whose *Suggestions on Academical Organisation* were found by his admirers 'really masterly; thoroughly thought out and articulated from beginning to end,'[60] and were undoubtedly framed more coherently and pitched at a higher level than any of the other versions of the liberal programme. Pattison made short work of most of Goldwin Smith's constitutional recommendations, while keeping within the general frame of the Ship Hotel conference. There was a touch of Newman in his defence of Convocation, for he doubted whether a wealthy institution like the university would be safe for a moment if it were handed over to the government of intelligence and severed from the professional and propertied interests represented in Convocation. To Pattison as to everyone else the endowments were coming to be the crux of the question. The bulk of the revenues at present went in subsidising education in scholarships, exhibitions and fellowships, a smaller amount in the payment of teachers, and very little indeed in the encouragement of science and learning. Open scholarships represented a very low standard of attainment, and went mainly to the classes who could afford a good school education. They helped to swell the standard of extravagance among men to whom the basic costs of an Oxford education were no great burden. Many of the prize fellowships held by non-resident fellows also served no useful purpose. Here was a fund which could be diverted to what ought to be the university's main end, the encouragement of science and learning. The doctrine that even to be an efficient educational body the university must first of all be a seat of science and learning was explicitly formulated, and supported by proposals which gained the name of 'the endowment of research.'

This doctrine was already far removed from that of the Pattison of 1855; his old view that 'the subject which demands our first care, and to the interests of which all others must be postponed, is the

Philosophy School,'[61] was now replaced by denunciations of the tyranny of examinations. In 1855 the key to the development of the university had been the triumph of philosophy; Pattison was now half-way to his morose position of 1876 when he saw 'philosophical initiative . . . crushed between the upper mill-stone of ecclesiastical terror, and the lower mill-stone of the competitive machine,' and thought that no redistribution of endowments 'would do anything towards raising a school of philosophy in this place, or in elevating our general studies to the point of contact with philosophy.'[62] If Pattison was already far from his old position he was also far from that of Jowett who believed that learning should be kept in close contact with teaching, that there was nothing wrong with colleges like Balliol, and that new chairs should not be endowed if the professors stood no chance of attracting a class.[63]

The one immediate reply from the conservative side came in the *Quarterly Review*, and it was remarkable for conceding many of the points that Pattison had made. English universities were admitted to be quite different from those in Germany. Examinations in Oxford had become too much ends in themselves, and the Greats school encouraged a superficial cleverness. The standard of the pass degree was admittedly too low. On the other hand it was argued that differences between English and German universities arose from different historical circumstances which had to be accepted. The movement for reviving the faculties of law, medicine and perhaps even divinity was hopeless, but it was no real reproach that these studies were cultivated outside the university. The standard of the pass degree should be raised—Pattison's intentions of ending pass degree work were preposterous. Moreover, the real trouble with the Greats school was that the demands of ancient history had driven candidates to take their philosophy from handbooks which were written only by utilitarians.

> It must be admitted that a School which gathers in the ablest youths, and then exposes them, *through its shallowness and superficiality*, to a very probable overthrow of their faith and morals, is not a very satisfactory thing.

Yet this was the very end which Pattison wanted to achieve, and which could only be furthered by the severance of the connexion of the university with the church.[64]

No feature of the life of the ancient universities of England received more criticism in these years than that which was peculiar to them—the fellowship system. It seemed to be generally admitted that funds consumed in fellows' stipends were funds wasted, and the prophecy made by Gladstone in 1854 when he was forced to give up his plan for certificates of study, that the public would not long tolerate the

existence of sinecure offices, even if they were distributed for merit,
seemed to be fulfilled to the letter.[65] The essence of the general
complaint was given by Thomas Arnold, the son of the great headmaster of Rugby:

> We ask for scholarly eminence, and we are presented with a
> successful *début* at the Old Bailey or the Chancery bar. We
> desiderate deep erudition, and are told to admire those eloquent
> leaders in the *Daily Trumpeter*. We call for scientific analysis,
> for profound research into the causes and conditions of pheno-
> mena, and from his fool's paradise on the top of Mont Blanc or
> the Devil's Peak, the first class man and fellow of his college,
> radiant and self-satisfied, invites us to marvel at his athletic
> performances.[66]

Whether the object of reformers was to subsidise undergraduates[67]
or scholarly research, there was a general set upon prize fellowships
granted for life after successful performance in one examination and
subject only to the condition of celibacy.[68] Moreover, the triumph of
Prussia in the war of 1870 revived attention to the continuing superiority of the German universities in research and advanced study.[69]
    Little could be said in defence of the 'idle fellowships'. There were
those like G. C. Brodrick of Merton who combined a Balliol faith
in the college system, with an assurance of the civilising mission of
non-resident fellows in metropolitan professions such as journalism
—his own leaders in the *Times*[70] being the thinly veiled object of
Arnold's sarcasm against the *Daily Trumpeter*. Sir John Awdry
attempted to argue that non-resident fellows broadened the vision of
college business meetings.[71] The best case against a change was
wittily put in an article in *Macmillan's Magazine* which concentrated
its fire upon the reformers' constructive deficiencies. Lay fellowships
had been introduced without any adequate attempt to weigh the
consequences of the loss of a career in the church; now by limiting
prize fellowships it was proposed to find resources to enable the
tutors to do without the inconveniences of celibacy. But Oxford
would never become a German university.

> Oxford, as it is, is a singularly perfect and delicate machine for
> the formation and regulation of opinion, and for the mainten-
> ance and diffusion of historical, literary, and philosophical
> knowledge. For these purposes it is as well fitted as any human
> institution can be expected to be. For the extension of knowledge
> it does not answer as well; it is rather doubtful whether it will
> ever be possible to persuade hundreds of men to make the
> extension of knowledge the business of their lives, in a time and

in a place where there are so many pleasanter things for the natural man to do.

In his cool attitude towards the German research worker the writer resembled the modern advocates of the Balliol tradition; the Germans had

> no genius in particular: they are simply meritorious hewers of wood and drawers of water in the temple of the Muses; they advance knowledge because it is their *métier*.

The Oxford system enabled men to delay the beginning of their career, and developed a civilised scepticism and suspense of judgment, qualities in which English life was lacking.

> It is . . . vain to promise that if we once make the profession of an Oxford tutor half as good for a family man as that of a Rugby master, the tutor will proceed to choose a line of study and to make discoveries . . .

Married tutors would take all the remunerative work they reasonably could, and degenerate into 'a thriving group of busy, finishing schoolmasters.'[72] Certainly the writer in *Macmillan*, disillusioned as he was at the prospect of real improvement in the plans canvassed in the 'seventies, would have been delighted by the conclusion of Lord Curzon in 1909 that there was 'a substantial and continuing identity' in the problems of university reform from 1850 onwards.[73]

Then the advocates of every special interest thought that the university served them badly. Thomas Arnold insisted that the new schools had been useful from the standpoint of examinations, but had not established themselves as effective disciplines from any loftier viewpoint;[74] and if the appearance of Stubbs's *Constitutional History* in three volumes between 1873 and 1878 might seem to suggest the contrary, Stubbs himself held the same view. He complained publicly that he could not collect a satisfactory lecture class and that his published work had 'met with a more appreciative and intelligent reception in Germany than in England.'[75] Similarly the best friends of the Oxford law school could claim little for it until it was severed from the history school in 1872; after that it developed rapidly, and lectures given in the school by Maine, Bernard, Holland, Pollock, Dicey, Anson and others grew into published works of great distinction.[76] T. D. Acland complained that elementary mathematics was discouraged because a modest accomplishment did a man no good.[77] Sir Henry Acland deplored the failure to concentrate all the scientific institutions around the museum,[78] while on the other hand Matthew Arnold regarded Salisbury as a dangerous Chancellor because religion he knows, and physical science he knows, but the immense work between the two, which is for literature to accomplish, he knows nothing of.[79]

Moreover there was steady criticism of the damage done to scholarship by the present regulations in Honour Mods.[80]

In one important respect the new examination system brought further changes in its train. In 1859 so conservative a man as D. P. Chase of St. Mary Hall had complained of the inadequate teaching available for the new schools. Only three or four tutors gave efficient teaching in mathematics, and there was scarcely anything for the schools of physical science or law and modern history, other than the lectures of professors. Private tutors still catered for the men who aimed at the highest honours, but they were increasingly caught up in college tuition, and as soon as they were, their round of routine work sapped their initiative and they were voted bores. The university was being killed by 'a superstitious reverence for the isolation of colleges.' Some form of college combination was desirable, and it would be immensely invigorating if academical instruction were thrown open to all graduates.[81] The first step was taken by a number of distinguished teachers in the school of law and modern history who began a scheme of joint lectures open without fee to members of the colleges of all those lecturers whose names appeared on the list; their example was followed by lecturers in divinity and mathematics. The much larger number of teachers in the Greats school rendered organisation more difficult in the classical line, but in 1868 Balliol and New College established a system of intercollegiate teaching which set an example to other colleges[82] and frightened high-churchmen as a device for propagating infidelity.[83] Not long afterwards a group of teachers in the Greats school advertised a combined list of lectures in the *Gazette* (a new university organ which was first published in 1870), and at Exeter Bywater and Pelham opened their lectures to members of other colleges on payment of a fee. In a variety of ways college isolation was breaking down, and both the college tutor and the professor were being shouldered aside by the intercollegiate lecturer as they had formerly been shouldered aside by the private tutor. These haphazard changes represented a great step forward from the old plan whereby each college sought out 'three or four walking encyclopaedias' of its own, but were totally unsystematic and uncontrolled. It was not simply the professor's loss when Stubbs 'found the junior assistant tutor advertising a course on the same subject and at the very same hours as [his] own.'[84]

The prospect of some relief from this disorder was opened by the final triumph of the 'liberation of studies.' In 1870 the principle was carried that there should be one pass school of a mixed character; that the other schools should all be honours schools, and that the lowest class in each should confer a degree. History should be separated from law. It took another eighteen months to settle all the details, to reach agreement on the examination in divinity, and above all to reorganise the Greats school. For this purpose a high-powered committee was established, half elected by Congregation (with the conservatives leading the poll but the liberals taking most places.) They ultimately defined the Greats school in its modern shape as consisting of (i) the Greek and Latin languages, (ii) a period of Greek and Roman history (as distinct from Greek and Roman history at large), and (iii) logic with moral and political philosophy described in very vague outline. By a choice of special subjects the candidate might impart some bias of his own to the school. These changes were generally reckoned an improvement, but whether the school continued to encourage 'a smattering of modern philosophical writers and the power of fluent writing upon many things with no sound knowledge of any' would clearly depend greatly upon the examiners.[85]

There were immediate potentialities in the belated triumph of another liberal principle lately attacked by the liberals in the case of the theological school, the establishment of boards of studies to supervise the six schools now available. These boards were composed of the professors of the subjects concerned together with an equal number of other persons. Thus the Modern History Board consisted of the regius professors of modern history and ecclesiastical history, the Chichele professors of modern history and international law, the Rawlinsonian professor of Anglo-Saxon, and the professor of political economy together with the three examiners in the school for the time being, and not more than three other persons co-opted by the board. The powers of the boards were narrowly limited to prescribing books, periods and special subjects, but they rapidly assumed some general charge of the interests of their studies.[86]

In 1873 the Vice-Chancellor sent a circular to the boards of studies and to the professors soliciting their views on the needs of the studies they represented. The replies to this circular were evidence both of the new standing of the boards, and of the expenditure to which the reformers wished to commit the university.[87] By June 1875 this material had been considered by a committee of the Hebdomadal Council, which stated the chief needs of the university in the way of capital expenditure as being £23,000 for new buildings for the Bodleian (together with an extra £2000 p.a. for general purposes), £4000 for the Botanic Gardens, £32,300 for university museums and laboratories, and £50,000 for the new examination schools. A special board should also be appointed to develop an Oxford counterpart of the extraordinary professoriate in a German university. Occasional lecturers and readers for a term of years should be appointed. Finally, the inadequate stipends of many professors should be increased. Even so no great provision was recommended for literary and historical studies. By no exercise of prudence could all these demands be met from the resources of the university and the Council expressed the pious hope that in future the salaries of professors would be more fully met from college resources. Plainly there would have to be parliamentary intervention to exact tribute on this scale.[88]

This point was underlined when in the following term the Hebdomadal Council asked the colleges to inform the Vice-Chancellor what contribution they were prepared to make for university purposes, and received from most colleges the answer that at present they were unwilling and unable to do anything.[89] When therefore in 1877 Lord Salisbury was preparing legislation for university reform the Hebdomadal Council appointed a fresh committee to take stock of their requirements, and again consulted the professors and boards of studies. With legislation in view no-one was modest in his claims, and when the committee finally reported to the Council, the university's requirements proved to have swollen significantly beyond those of 1873 or 1875.[90] In February 1878 the Hebdomadal Council through the Vice-Chancellor again consulted the boards of studies on the burning question of the arrangement of examinations, and the view which was already being canvassed that the honours schools should be examined once only in the session, at or after the end of the summer term.[91] Thus although in 1872 Thomas Arnold complained that of all the universities in the world only Oxford and Cambridge possessed no faculty organisation,[92] the boards of studies soon came to perform many of the functions elsewhere performed by faculties. Indeed the limitations of the boards became anomalous. Plainly the spontaneous growth of intercollegiate teaching might be converted into an efficient system of university instruction, but the boards of studies had no jurisdiction over it, and could not even draw up a time-table. Here were a series of interlocked questions which could hardly be solved by the university without some outside impulse.

Oxford, moreover, was aware that the country was groping towards the formation of a national educational system crowned by the universities. Among the first acts of the reformed university had been to take one great section of the schools of the country under its wing by the establishment of the Middle Class Examinations in 1857. Early in that year Thomas Dyke Acland set on foot a scheme for holding a voluntary examination at Exeter for boys from middle class schools in Devon, Cornwall and Somerset. The idea was that the boys should have some common standard against which to measure themselves, and that the parents should have some means of comparing the schools. Two inspectors of schools, one of whom was

Frederick Temple, were seconded by the Education Committee of the Privy Council to assist in the work. Without waiting for the first examination to prove itself a success, Acland and Temple were anxious to spread the idea to the country as a whole, and Temple saw great advantages in persuading the universities to take the lead. On February 25, 1857, he wrote to Robert Scott, Master of Balliol:

> Similar ideas are afloat everywhere; and it would require but a slight impulse to make the system general.
>
> The Government will not take this in hand; the Society of Arts is well enough as a leader of Mechanics' Institutes, but has neither the prestige nor the organisation to be more.
>
> Will there be any chance of inducing the Universities to step in? My plan is this:—
>
> That the University should appoint a competent Board of Examiners; that these examiners should be prepared to examine all boys between certain ages presented to them under certain regulations; that the examination should be divided into schools to cover the subjects at present most needed by boys in the middle class schools; that every boy who passes should have a Testamur from the examiners and the title Alumnus or Scholaris in Artibus of the University, and should be considered as in some sense matriculated; and that the expenses of the examination should be covered by a small fee from every candidate.

A committee of the Hebdomadal Council examined documents submitted by Acland and Temple, interviewed them personally, and reported that the university must answer the call made upon it and 'endeavour to extend its beneficial influence to the education of classes now for the most part beyond its reach.' There were liberals like Goldwin Smith who regretted the proposal as a great dispersion of effort,[93] and the high-church party in due course made a clamour about the difficulties created by religious examination,[94] but before the session was out the university had established the system, and Temple had persuaded Cambridge to follow suit. Oxford men had no doubt of the benefit to the schools of the university's reputation for honest examining, and thought it best to lead the schools in paths of liberal studies, before any other authority diverted them to technology or commerce.[95]

The new syllabuses were well received by both churchmen and dissenters,[96] and many hundreds of candidates came to seek the title of Associate in Arts conferred by the university. In 1870 women were admitted to the examination, and the Delegates for Local Examinations soon afterwards began to establish examinations based on those which the university held for undergraduates, for women over 18 years of age. After a triumph by Thorold Rogers's daughter, this

scheme led inevitably to pressure for the admission of women to
the university examinations proper.[97] In 1872 a speaker at the Social
Science congress advocated the development of the system so that
the middle classes could be examined locally for something like a
degree.[98] Thus if Temple's hopes that the university would inspect
as well as examine middle class schools were not fulfilled, Oxford
had begun to influence the education of many schools in the country,
and soon felt the consequences of its success.

The ready public acceptance of the university's examinations
created a demand for new ventures. In 1871 the *Guardian* called
upon the universities to examine the notoriously uneven work of
the theological colleges.[99] Towards the end of the following year the
Headmasters' Conference proposed that the universities should test
the general work of those schools which prepared large numbers of
men for university entrance, and regard the schools as sharing in the
preliminary work of the universities. It was also proposed that
certificates 'possessing a definite university value' should be awarded
to pupils at the ages of 16 and 19.[100] Despite fears that the growing
reluctance of young fellows to reside would make it impossible to
find enough examiners,[101] the university again proved eager to extend
its influence, and before the end of the session had passed a statute
establishing a joint delegacy with Cambridge to organise the examinations. The intentions of this statute went much further than the
Middle Class Examinations. The latter had cast light on the standards
of middle class schools only obliquely, through the results of their
selected candidates. The Joint Board now proposed to inspect the
work of the public schools through three types of examination, quite
apart from examinations for school leaving certificates. There should
be

> (a) An examination of the general work of the school extending
> to the whole or to such parts of the school as will enable the
> examiners to report generally upon the school work.
> (b) An examination upon any main subject or subjects of
> instruction . . . extending so far as will enable the examiners to
> report on the standard reached in that subject . . .
> (c) An examination of the higher division of the school, such
> that the examiners may report on the general work of that
> division to place the boys in order of merit, and to award
> scholarships, exhibitions and prizes.

Hitherto only the last of these types of examination had been held
by university examiners, and then only by private invitation from
individual schools.[102] Some schools such as Harrow were reluctant
to undergo this public ordeal, and the board had to fight off an
attempt by the Headmasters' Conference to stop publicity being

given to the results, but many schools, including many of the greatest, accepted fully the advantages which were offered by the examinations of the board, and were congratulated in the press for prudently staving off a public demand for state inspection under a Minister of Education. Moreover, the school leaving certificates came at once to possess much more than 'a definite university value.' The two universities accepted them (with certain qualifications) in place of Responsions and the Preliminary Examination, and most colleges accepted them in place of their matriculation examinations; thus a considerable step was taken towards the achievement of the ideal of Whately and Arnold, the substitution of a university for a college examination as a condition of matriculation. In addition the certificates were accepted by the College of Surgeons for its preliminary examination; by the Royal Institute of Architects and the General Council of Medical Education as evidence of having passed certain portions of their examinations; and by the Civil Service Commissioners in lieu of the non-competitive portions of the examinations for first appointments in the army, and for the Military Academy at Woolwich. In short the universities had now undertaken the supervision of most of the education in the country above the level of the National Schools, and were indirectly governing the standards of entry to professions whose education they had either let slip, or had never undertaken.[103]

Some of the liberals were now urgently pressing the ancient universities to occupy the same kind of strategic position in the world of higher education. The 'sixties and 'seventies saw the demand for higher education on the flood tide. From 1862 Oxford matriculations increased almost every year and multiplied by half in a decade. Owens College, which had almost collapsed from lack of support in the 'fifties (when Oxford matriculations also fell sharply) began a tremendous expansion which in the 'seventies led its somewhat optimistic authorities to forecast the early enrolment of 2000 students.[104] In 1874 Yorkshire College, Leeds was founded; in 1876 University College, Bristol; in 1879 Firth College, Sheffield; in 1880 Mason College, Birmingham; in 1881 University College, Liverpool. In 1877 the University of Durham from its own slender resources established a college at Newcastle. In 1873 lecturers from Cambridge began official extra-mural courses in Nottingham, Sheffield and elsewhere,[105] in response to local demand, and by 1877 the foundations of University College, Nottingham were being laid.[106] In 1875 a scheme was launched from the Mansion House under the auspices of the London Society for the Extension of University Teaching, a body which hoped for the joint support of the universities of Oxford, Cambridge and London. In 1876 the conservatives, supported by the advocates of the 'endowment of research', defeated in Convocation a proposal that Oxford should co-operate with so godless a body as the University of London, but the work went ahead nonetheless.[107] In 1877 the authorities of Owens College petitioned the Privy Council for the grant of a full university charter, and provoked the tribes of Yorkshire to climb on their bandwaggon before it was too late.[108] What attitude was Oxford to take to all these developments?

From Oxford as from Cambridge lecturers went abroad to the West of England and elsewhere, but the itinerants were never the main Oxford interest. As far back as 1850 William Sewell had sought to justify the preservation of the old Oxford he loved by advocating that colleges in the country be affiliated to the university, that redundant Oxford fellows should teach in them, and that the university should award external degrees.[109] This counsel of desperation bore no immediate fruit, but in 1863, T. E. Espin proposed that theological colleges in the country be affiliated to the university,[110] and in 1866, the sixth of the Oxford subcommittees on university extension undertook 'to frame the details of a scheme for the extension of the university by the affiliation of other places of liberal education.' This committee, packed with high-powered liberals under the chairmanship of Goldwin Smith, argued that the ancient universities could not for physical reasons cope with the whole liberal education of the growing professional classes, and that affiliated colleges in the country could well give an education which might entitle men to exemption from Moderations and thus reduce the residence required of them in Oxford.[111] The matter was canvassed again before the select committee on Ewart's bill in 1867, but Jowett who was then prepossessed by his scheme for getting men into lodgings opposed affiliation:

> I should say that education in another place is not the same thing as education at Oxford. Also I should find a difficulty in determining what are the places of education to be affiliated, and upon what terms are they to be affiliated? If you include colleges such as those at Birmingham or Manchester, why should you not include Eton or Rugby?

Jowett was, however, prepared to consider allowing eighteen months residence to anyone who was able to take Honour Mods.[112]

The question of affiliating local colleges came rapidly to demand a decision. On the one hand Owens College had become extremely restive under the yoke of the London University examination system and was thought to be anxious for affiliation to Oxford in the hope of improvement; and on the other, Oxford colleges themselves became involved in the development of higher education in Bristol, while Charles Neate of Oriel argued that there was no reason in law why some of the colleges either of Oxford or of Cambridge should not be transferred to the North of England, there to form nuclei of a new university, or to enlarge the foundation of Durham.[113]

Professor Jowett now underwent a crucial change of heart. Having secured his system of lodgings, he cast about for fresh worlds to conquer, and early in 1872 he got his college meeting to appoint a committee to consider how the benefits of university education could be extended to the large towns. The first concrete proposal came from Bristol. For a number of years lectures had been given by university men in Clifton, and in 1873 when the Bristol Medical School was rehoused, there was local talk about founding a college of science. Percival, the Headmaster of Clifton College seized the opportunity to urge the ancient universities to plant professorships in the chief provincial towns which should form faculties and remain an integral part of the parent university.[114] Jowett at once lent his support and spoke at the meeting held for the promotion of the Bristol University College in 1874. Percival had appealed for college fellows to be seconded to do the work, but Jowett's gift was the sum of £300 p.a. for five years from college funds.[115] Old William Sewell who had recently failed to persuade the *Quarterly* to carry an article recommending his plan of 1850,[116] now received his reward, for New College, of which his brother, J. E. Sewell, was Warden, came into the Bristol scheme on the same terms as Balliol.

Jowett and his friends now incorporated this plan into their general programme for university reform, reckoning that besides the foundations at Manchester, Durham and Newcastle, ten colleges were needed at Liverpool, Birmingham, Leeds, Bradford, Nottingham, Norwich, Bristol, Exeter, Plymouth and Merthyr Tydfil.[117] Even among the friends of university reform this scheme was sharply attacked upon two grounds. In the first place it was folly to give away Oxford funds to provincial towns; they had abundant money of their own if only they could be persuaded to expend it upon academic objects; what they needed was some portion of the learning and education which under the present Oxford system was recklessly exported into the London professions through non-resident fellowships.[118] This objection was of course felt most strongly by the advocates of the endowment of research, who could think of innumerable ways in which the university could spend college funds in Oxford.[119] In his evidence before the executive commission of 1877, Jowett conceded the force of the general criticism, though he claimed that 'some pecuniary assistance gives us a right and opportunity of taking part in' the provincial colleges,[120] and was warmly supported in this view by Percival of Clifton.[121]

The second line of criticism of the Bristol scheme was occasioned by rumours that Balliol and New College intended to obtain special facilities for Bristol students to obtain Oxford degrees, presumably by reducing the length of residence.[122] This was a matter for the university to decide, and many felt, as apparently Jowett had felt in 1867, that as what the university taught to passmen hardly justified any residence at all, the sole educational value of their course must consist in the residence itself, and no step should be taken down the slippery slope of reducing it. This, however, was precisely the proposal put by the authorities of King's College, London, who in 1874 sought affiliation to the universities of Oxford and Cambridge. These bodies, they declared, had assumed

> legislative and executive powers in all matters which concern the higher education of the country at large, and [were] therefore bound to exercise those powers as may be best for the promotion and superintendence of such education.[123]

They sounded the ground by holding a meeting in Oxford in the Clarendon Lecture-room on March 12, 1874, with the Vice-Chancellor in the chair. Heads and tutors attended in full force. The delegation from King's had two proposals to put:

> 1. That associates of King's College, and such other students as shall have attended the regular course of lectures at King's College for not less than two years, and specially distinguished themselves in the examinations, shall on the recommendation of the Principal, be excused their first year at the university, and be allowed to enter as second year undergraduates, provided that they pass any examinations which the university authorities may require.
> 2. Undergraduates of Oxford or Cambridge who have completed at least two years at the university shall be allowed to spend their last year in attendance in any of the three special schools at King's College (receiving all the advantages belonging to matriculated students) and to take their degrees at the usual time, if they can pass the prescribed university examinations.

The meeting was eloquently addressed by the university liberals, and by Ince and Bernard from the other side, and appeared strongly in favour of the first proposition, though chary of the second. Jowett, seconded by Thorold Rogers, moved that the University should receive such proposals as King's College had to make, and carried the motion without opposition.[124] The atmosphere was more cordial than that of a similar meeting at Cambridge, but the acceptance of a formal proposal was very far from guaranteed.

Liddon described how the matter came before the Hebdomadal Council on February 8, 1875:

In Council today Dr. Pusey moved the previous question on the report of the committee for shortening residence being presented with a view to admitting King's College & Owens College. His motion after a sharp debate was carried by a majority of 2. I certainly did not expect this result. Salwey & Wayte voted with us. Rolleston was evidently greatly vexed.[125]

When the matter got before Congregation on May 2, 1876, the liberals were unable to make any headway against the general reluctance to shorten residence, especially as the expense had been reduced by the admission of unattached students. The proposal was therefore defeated by 60 votes to 45.[126] The initial check in the Hebdomadal Council had been sufficient to launch Owens College into the only other possible scheme for escaping the thraldom of the University of London, the acquisition of a charter of their own. Robert Lowe who had for some years been making attacks upon academic endowments, now, as M.P. for the University of London, came out against the establishment of any other kind of university than the examining board which he represented, but it soon became clear that Owens would not only get a charter (if not necessarily upon the terms they desired), but that in any case they would no longer accept subordination to some other university by means of affiliation.[127] This prospect frightened so otherwise sympathetic a liberal as Goldwin Smith. Having seen in America the disastrous results of the free multiplication of universities, he was concerned to protect the public repute of the degrees granted at Oxford and Cambridge. Moreover, he was a prisoner of the notion, developed as an argument against the tests, that the universities were national institutions.

> If the number of national universities is to be increased, and the work of national education divided, the fund must be divided also. It would be absurd to leave two universities of the group grossly over-endowed, while the rest remained without adequate endowment . . . On the other hand there is a great deal to be said in favour of preserving the great historic centres and a national system

by means of the affiliated colleges his subcommittee had recommended in 1866.[128] This plan was heartily commended by W. C. Lake, now Dean of Durham, who had done precisely this in establishing the college at Newcastle.[129] In short, the desire to influence the whole development of higher education in the country, conspired with the desire to keep up the standard of work in the new colleges, and to preserve the endowments of the ancient colleges, in moving Oxford opinion towards a system of affiliation.

In 1878 the delegates for local examinations received increased

powers to establish lectures, teaching and examinations in the large
towns of England and Wales,[130] and in the following year with
University College, Nottingham, and Firth College, Sheffield, seeking
affiliation, a new attempt was made to pass a statute for the purpose.
In June 1879 the draft statute was brought before Congregation by
J. R. Magrath, Provost of Queen's. He claimed that the present
statute was of a more systematic character than that which had
foundered a few years before, and gave the university greater powers
in the regulation of studies. The university was already prepared to
accept the results of other examinations in place of Responsions, it
had already dispensed with college life for certain students, and it
was now asked to concede a year of residence to candidates prepared
elsewhere who could pass Moderations. Previous examinations for
such candidates should be prescribed by the delegates for local
examinations. The meeting which had been adjourned from a
previous day owing to a protracted discussion on the university
cricket ground was a thin one, but liberal speakers managed to carry
the principle and preamble of the measure.[131] In October there was a
stiffer fight and some of the details of the measure were lost,[132] but
on February 10, 1880 the statute went through Congregation by a
moderate margin, the liberal George Rolleston revealing a touch of
imperialism in the confession that

> it was true Owens College and Leeds were lost to the university,
> but as with the Sybilline books, the remainder must be secured
> on their own terms.[133]

In fact the only college to take immediate advantage of the new
opening was St. David's, Lampeter, but in due course the foundations
at Nottingham, Sheffield and Reading followed suit.

The immediate consequence of the agitation for the affiliation
statute was to complicate the labyrinthine contest about compulsory
Greek. In 1870 Lord Lyttelton, the chairman of the Endowed Schools
Commission, addressed a letter to the Vice-Chancellors of the English
universities, recommending that a knowledge of Greek should no
longer be required from all candidates for the arts degree. A considerable number of schools had already concluded that the minimum
requirements in Greek were not worth the trouble of attaining, there
were already many schools in which no Greek was taught, and it
could be argued that the only passmen for whom Greek was essential
were the ordinands, and for them it was a matter of professional
rather than of liberal education.[134] In Oxford the cue was taken up
by the science professors, but to the satisfaction of Liddon and the
conservatives, their efforts to get rid of the Greek requirement
collapsed in the Hebdomadal Council in March 1873.[135] It quickly
transpired, however, that no great progress would be made with

schemes of affiliation as long as Greek was indispensable, or as the *Times* coarsely put it,

> the truth is Oxford and Cambridge are . . . running a race with the University of London, and, yet more particularly, with Owens College.[136]

There was every inducement for Oxford's liberal empire-builders to find some substitute for Greek.

Early in 1877 it was reported that the Hebdomadal Council had been considering creating a degree in science alone, for which only one ancient language would be required at Responsions and Mods., a plan which the *Guardian* welcomed as a means for promoting more extensive use of Oxford's scientific apparatus, without tampering with the arts degree.[137] When the proposal came before Congregation in May, important realignments of opinion became evident. Henry Smith thought that the classical languages formed the ideal training for science and Liddon thought them the best possible prelude to studies in philology or the New Testament, but both recommended the measure as 'a timely sop to the wolves of non-classical education,' and the opposition came from those like Montagu Burrows and J. R. Magrath who were satisfied with the deduction that the proposal was 'a recommendation to drop Greek, and therefore mischievous to education.' However, the principle of the science degree, supported by some liberals as a means of connecting more students with Oxford and by Liddon as a device for chaining most men to Greek, was accepted by 63 votes to 40.[138]

Further progress was delayed for two years by the need to push on with the affiliation statute, and to take counsel's opinion on points raised by the proposed new faculty of natural science. The question was whether the university was competent to add any new faculty to those which had long been recognised, and if so, whether it might assign to degrees granted in the new faculty the rights belonging to the degree of Master of Arts—membership of Convocation and so forth. Two counsel agreed that the university might create the new faculty, but might not confer on graduates in natural science the privileges of the arts degree without a special act of parliament.[139] These opinions only added force to a violent attack upon the proposed statute when it came before Congregation in May 1879, delivered from the scientific camp by William Odling, Waynflete professor of chemistry. Odling insisted that

> either Greek was a necessity of liberal education, or it was not. If it was not why require it in the other schools of which the subject matter was quite alien to Greek—viz. the Modern History and Jurisprudence schools? If it was then the schools which excluded it from their necessary curriculum were at once

20

declared illiberal, and the B[achelorship of] N[atural] S[cience] would indicate to all the world a man who had received an illiberal education.

With the proposed science degree opposed by scientists and championed by the most conservative advocates of Greek the comedy was complete, and Thomas Fowler's discovery that

> a liberal education was of two kinds—one literary, the other mathematical and scientific. To the former Greek was essential, not to the latter,

fell somewhat flat.[140] Nevertheless, the principle was accepted by 57 votes to 20. By the following autumn Odling had carried the leading scientists with him in the demand for complete parity in the B.A. degree (though of course without Greek) and although the Hebdomadal Council offered to seek an act of parliament in order to give full privileges to a degree of Master in Natural Science, an amendment was carried in Congregation omitting all the clauses of the statute except the preamble. Council was thus left committed to a principle with nothing done towards it, and with no prospect of doing anything until the university was prepared to drop Greek from the arts requirements.[141]

In May 1880 the statute came before Congregation again, with assurances from Henry Smith that there would be no difficulty in securing an act of parliament to put things right for the new degrees. But Odling was not disposed to surrender the first opportunity the scientists had ever had for bullying the rest of the university. He declared that the statute was proposed in the interests of Greek rather than those of science. Henry Nettleship, Corpus professor of Latin, thought that the statute was 'imperfect, faulty and inopportune' and ignored the unity of liberal studies. On a division the statute was decisively rejected.[142] Before the end of the session the Master of University College invited a number of the friends of change to a meeting to discuss the prospects of omitting Greek from the compulsory requirements of the arts degree. Mark Pattison, D. B. Monro of Oriel, J. R. Magrath and other prominent liberals were present, and a number of resolutions were passed for relaxing the demands of Greek. In the main, however, the meeting was indecisive, for there was no unanimity on any of the resolutions, no discussion of the all-important question of a substitute for Greek, and a fairly general feeling that some knowledge of Greek and Latin should be required at matriculation.[143] So it transpired that in spite of constant complaints, compulsory Greek was saved by the filibustering of Professor Odling until 1919, and a very considerable march was stolen by Owens College, which in 1881, immediately after receiving a charter, opened degrees to candidates with no Greek or Latin.[144]

CHAPTER XIII

THE STATE AND THE SETTLEMENT

The first and broadest of all Liberal Principles is the unreserved recognition of Progress as the appointed law of all human institutions, civil or religious. . . . It was this principle . . . which applied to endowments produced the Charity Commission, the University Reform Acts, and the Endowed Schools Act, with many like measures to protect the interests of the living against the posthumous control of the dead.

G. C. BRODRICK, *What are Liberal Principles?* (1877).

So far as endowment is concerned, the Church of England is, with very few exceptions, disestablished in the university.

W. INCE, *The education of the clergy at the universities* (1882).

THE liberal victory at the polls in November 1868 almost guaranteed that the state would take a hand in the two great debates of the period as to what sort of place a home of liberal studies should be, and what place it should occupy in the educational system of the country. The university liberals kept up their barrage of propaganda,[1] and the conviction spread rapidly that the university machinery could not continue to function even on its present scale without some change. In particular the financial relations between the university and the colleges were overdue for revision. The increasing numbers of examinees were putting a great strain upon the accommodation traditionally available in the schools, a strain which would be increased if the decision were taken to induce undergraduates to do some work in the Trinity term by concentrating the honours examinations at the end of the session.[2] At the same time the stock of books in the Bodleian was increasing rapidly, and the library, if it retained its present site and character, must itself encroach upon the schools. The library or the schools would have to be rebuilt, and neither project could well be accomplished within the present straitened means of the university. By 1872 discussion had crystallised into two schemes; the first to erect a fire-proof building in the University Park and to transfer the Bodleian to it, and the second to erect new examination schools on the Angel site and surrender the use of the ancient schools to the Bodleian. The inconvenience of rendering the Bodleian inaccessible to students for a period led to the adoption of the latter scheme, and in June 1872 a delegacy of nine, headed by Vice-Chancellor Liddell, was appointed to secure a design.[3]

The rest of the story formed a comic chapter in the history of university patronage. The delegacy invited five architects to compete for a design, and three of them did so. The winning entry by J. O. Scott was recommended by the delegacy to Convocation on May 23, 1873 and decisively rejected.[4] The following December Council began again, and got Convocation, by a majority of four votes, to sanction the appointment of a fresh delegacy, and by a majority of two votes to agree to the mode of its election; however, the proposal that the delegacy should have an absolute discretion in the choice of a scheme was lost by one vote.[5] Even in 1875 there were efforts to reopen the whole question, as a party among the curators of the Bodleian hankered after a new library, and the prospect was opened of securing a more central position for the schools on the site of Hertford College.[6] By 1876 when the results of a further competition for the development of the Angel site were known, the shortage of accommodation had become urgent, and although C. E. Appleton of St. John's and the *Academy*, and other advocates of the 'endowment of research,' opposed such obeisance to the idol of examinations, T. Graham Jackson's design was accepted by great majorities.[7] The estimated cost of this building was £50,000 (about half the final cost, exclusive of the site and architect's fees) the borrowing of which imposed an enormous burden on the university, and when finally the building was completed in 1882, the incongruous furniture from the ancient schools had to be transferred to the palatial new quarters.[8]

Of all the schemes canvassed in the 'seventies, those arising from the interlocked requirements of the Bodleian and the examination schools were the most urgent. Bodley's librarian, H. O. Coxe, looked forward to the day when he would not be required to provide a home for rubbish as well as reputable literature, and the disciples of Mark Pattison hoped to diminish the importance of examinations, but it was clear that short of some great change in the policy of the university, expenditure upon a ruinous scale could not be avoided. All this was distinct from the claims for extra staff and equipment which were being made in every faculty. When in 1871, therefore, as soon as the question of the tests had been despatched, Lord Edmond Fitzmaurice asked Gladstone in the Commons whether he intended to proceed with university reform, he replied that he intended to institute an inquiry into the revenue and property of the university and colleges; he would appoint a royal commission if they would co-operate fully, a statutory commission if not.[9] In October the Vice-Chancellor confirmed the result of Gladstone's previous inquiries, that the university and colleges would give every assistance to a royal commission,[10] and early in the New Year the names of the members were announced. The duke of Cleveland, the chairman, Lord Clinton and Professor Price were the Oxford members, there were three Cambridge members, and Kirkman Hodgson M.P. represented the great unacademical British public. The commission of 1850 had failed to elicit authentic information about the wealth of the colleges and the university, and the reforms which they had recommended were thought to have greatly increased the wealth of the colleges; but a good many liberals especially at Cambridge would not accept the necessity for a financial inquiry, and wished to take advantage of the liberal majority in parliament to put their already formulated plans into effect. Nothing less than an immediate executive commission would do.[11] Five years later a tory government appointed an executive commission, and then many liberals cried that there ought first to have been a general commission of inquiry, though by this time every issue had been thoroughly aired in public.

Pattison put his case in advance of the Cleveland commission's report when he took the chair at a public meeting at the Freemasons' Tavern in London on November 16, 1872, a meeting which was attended by hand-picked representatives of the 'endowment of research' school from both the universities. Among the prominent Oxford speakers were Rolleston, Burdon Sanderson, and Benjamin Brodie, and a series of resolutions were adopted without opposition in favour of the 'adequate maintenance of mature study and scientific research.' Many of the familiar clichés of the modern universities were brought forward; Pattison and Rolleston claimed that 'a man who has not some notion of what original research means is not fit to be a teacher at all,' and Brodie argued that Waynflete's college statutes showed that the advancement and not simply the diffusion of knowledge was amongst the objects of the Oxford foundations. Pattison made it clear that he opposed the expenditure of university funds upon the promotion of education in the manufacturing districts, but thought his party would have to come to terms with the affiliation scheme.[12] The support of the *Nonconformist* which the Oxford liberals had enjoyed for some years now began to fail, for the endowment of research and Pattison's animus against scholarships were altogether beyond the ken of Edward Miall.[13] No new agitation seems to have sprung from the meeting in the Freemasons' Tavern, but Pattison's general cause was given an impulse in 1873 by the third report of the royal commission on scientific instruction and the advancement of science, which sharply criticised the poor endowment of scholarships and fellowships in science at Oxford,[14] and he was supported by Charles Appleton's *Academy*.

In October 1874 the Cleveland commission finally published their report and settled the framework within which the rival claims of the faculty system, the endowment of research, and university extension in the provinces must be adjusted.[15] At the time of the appointment of the commission Robert Lowe had been expounding the view that a university was in essence an examining board, and had created the impression that his object was first to turn the Irish universities into a joint examining board like that of London, and then to extend the system to Scotland, and perhaps finally to enable London to swallow up the other English universities. Endowments appeared to him simply a drag upon academic progress.[16] Even amongst liberals there were those who were not sorry that the fall of the liberal ministry had put such schemes out of court before the Cleveland commission reported. Two at least of the dark suspicions on which Lowe had played were then set at rest; the universities and colleges were shewn to be of relatively moderate wealth, and to be extremely economical in the management of their property. In round figures the disposable income of the university in 1871 was put at £32,000 and of the colleges at £330,000, the Cambridge figures exceeding in each case two-thirds of these sums. In short, the universities each did their work at the cost of one well-heeled duke, and not much could be obtained by expropriating or partitioning their funds. At the same time the colleges were commended for the management of their property; they were liberal and judicious landlords, and economical also. The press compared their management charges of £2 17s. 7d. per cent favourably with those of the Ecclesiastical Commissioners, and argued that there was no ground for handing over their estates to central management.[17]

A number of conclusions followed inescapably from these figures. The university clearly could not meet its impending expenses from its present income, let alone undertake any new obligations. Moreover, as its largest item of income consisted of fees and dues paid by members of the university, it could not increase its income without increasing the cost of Oxford education. In present circumstances this was impossible. The university must call on the resources of the colleges and the analysis of college expenditure showed which item would have to be sacrificed. The figures for 1871 had been as follow:—

	£	s.	d.
Heads	30,543	12	4
Fellows	101,171	4	5
Scholars and Exhibitioners	26,225	12	0
Professors (excluding Canons of Christ Church)	6,694	10	10
Augmentation of benefices	8,772	2	4
Management of estates	8,801	18	0½

Clearly the fellowships would again be the victims of university reform. Equally clearly, there was no useful margin anywhere for endowing provincial colleges. Owens College had been originally endowed with a sum almost equal to an entire year's expenditure upon fellowships, and had nearly collapsed in the first decade; the commissioners' figures supported the contention of Jowett's critics that Oxford could help the new foundations only by man-power not by money.

So far the report gave precision to the contentions of common-sense critics for many years, but in two respects, one of which was immediately challenged, it gave currency to false impressions. The commission itself underlined 'one point brought prominently out in the result of this inquiry, the great disparity between the property and income of the several colleges and the number of their members,' a point on which their terms of reference forbade them to enlarge. Everyone knew that of the wealthy colleges in Oxford only Christ Church had ever been a large educational establishment, but the details published in the report, and especially a synopsis of college revenues, were bound to provoke odious comparisons, and also to put the Oxford bursars on their mettle. On October 15, Godfrey Faussett, the Treasurer of Christ Church published a letter in the *Times* pointing out that the item of 'internal income' had been differently treated in different colleges; that in some cases it signified the bursar's gross receipts, in others his net profits. Christ Church for example was shown as spending £5000 on college servants and £1150 on the maintenance of the establishment, while Balliol returned nothing at all under the first heading and only £62 under the second.[18] C. S. Roundell, the liberal secretary to the commission, replied that the oddities in the accounts were due to the variety of college accounting methods, and that sufficient qualifications were to be found in the abstracts.[19] To this Faussett and the Senior Bursar of New College replied that if the college accounts could not be reduced to a common basis the synopsis should not have been printed.[20] A good deal of acrimonious correspondence followed between Roundell and dissatisfied Oxford bursars,[21] which culminated in a letter from 16 bursars stating that important parts of the report were inaccurate and likely to mislead, and a letter from G. G. Bradley, the liberal Master of University College, regretfully pointing out a long list of errors in the report's account of his own college not attributable to the college return.[22] The protesting colleges, unlike Balliol, had all been made to appear wealthier than they really were.

However odious the comparisons provoked by inaccuracies of detail in the computation of college resources, they were not as serious as one basic feature of the report. In ways to be discussed later, almost all the colleges had been improving their property, running out beneficial leases, and letting their estates at the rack-rent. The chief dividends of this policy were still to accrue, and by computing what they would yield the commission clinched the case for the transfer of college revenues to the university. The commission forecast increases of about £40,000 by 1885 with still more to come.[23] These figures suggested that the colleges in the next few years might double the income of the university without sacrificing anything which they now possessed. The commissioners accompanied their forecast with the caveat that these figures took no account of the charges upon loans which colleges had raised to tide them over their losses of fines, nor of the considerable expenditure which would be needed on their property as the leases fell in. Inevitably, however as no estimate was made of these outgoings, the gross increased receipts were treated as net profits, and an impression was created of growing college affluence beyond anything warranted by the circumstances of 1874. Nor did the commission point out that grave inroads might be made into these receipts by colleges which extended their usefulness by further building, still less that the receipts themselves might not accrue if there was a change in the economic climate.

Whatever its defects, the report now figured largely in the calcula-tions of the Oxford politicians, and it presented an acute dilemma to the liberals. Goldwin Smith was urging them to take the initiative,[24] but if they did so with a conservative government in power they might get a very distasteful settlement. Some liberals, especially amongst Pattison's friends, continued to urge that no executive commission should be appointed until a programme of reform should be drawn up like the blue book of 1852.[25] In default of this they continued skirmishing in the press and in 1876 fired three major salvoes, the *Essays on the endowment of research* edited by Charles Appleton, Mark Pattison's address to the Social Science Congress in Liverpool, and his article on 'Philosophy at Oxford' in the new journal *Mind*. The *Essays* which were written by Pattison and a number of his Oxford disciples contained little that was new, though Pattison delivered a solemn warning against the middle class notion that universities existed solely for purposes of education, and Charles Appleton tried to show that the endowment of research was economic in a sense that the endowment of teaching was not.[26] At Liverpool, Pattison in sparkling style denounced the government's intentions of confiscating the property of colleges without any clear idea of what to do with it. A fellowship was the grave of learning, and an effort must be made to unite the great body of scientific inquiry which went on outside the universities with the endowments within which were at present wasted upon youthful sinecurists.[27] In *Mind* he fulminated against the superficial learning which brought distinction in the schools and success in Oxford fellowship examinations but had to make the damaging admission that philosophy did not decay for lack of endowment.[28] Pattison was in the uncomfortable position of demanding

> a change of the atmosphere of the University, in the diffusion of the disinterested love of knowledge—it may be that legislation can do little to promote it.[29]

His assurances that he did not want to end the college system, were belied by his bitterness towards the friends of the colleges whether liberal or conservative, and if as he claimed, the professorial system in the last generation had been a failure because it was isolated from the main life of the university, there was perhaps little inducement to provide further endowment for research in advance of the change of heart on which everything must turn. Imbued with the idea that the whole purpose of a university was the pursuit of knowledge, he made no attempt to answer the charge that the best use of university funds for this purpose was to provide special subsidies or extra-ordinary chairs for men with particular projects or for distinguished scholars like Max Müller, as they came along.[30] Moreover, everyone knew that the profound scholarship for which Pattison's friends stood did not extend to theology.

If Pattison came almost to despise the functions of universities in educating men for service in the wider sphere of society, Jowett conceived this to be their true function, and the feud between the two, faithfully kept up by their disciples,[31] provided the chief entertainment in the Oxford liberal camp in the 'seventies. Goldwin Smith returned from experience of the uncollegiate American Universities convinced of the value of colleges,[32] but the chief spokesman for Jowett's party was now G. C. Brodrick, fellow of Merton; as a non-resident journalist and as a man who could commend the present order because fellows provided 25 per cent of the articles in the *Contemporary* and *Fortnightly* and a large but unknown proportion in the unsigned reviews, he embodied all that Pattison most deplored in the prize-fellowship system. In 1876 Brodrick replied to Pattison's campaigns by a series of letters in the *Times*, in which he gloried in the Balliol ideal.

> I believe the College system to be the very life and soul of the English university system, enabling it to reach a higher ideal—not of self-culture, but of education—than is realized in any other country. I believe the College tutor, by virtue of the several functions which he combines, to be capable of rendering the university educational services of a kind which cannot be rendered by any mere professor . . . I believe that except in physical science—where there are special reasons for the con-

centration of teaching—Oxford tutors have consistently done
more, not for education only, but for learning, than Oxford
professors, and that, in respect of conscientious devotion to
duty, they would gain largely by a comparison. I believe that,
since 1854, the rival systems have been fairly tried side by side,
in several important subjects; that in many instances professorial
classes have been gradually thinned by the superior efficacy of
collegiate lecturing; . . . I believe that fellowships, awarded as
they now are by academical merit, are the main spring, or
primum mobile, of English university education, as well as of
the college system.[33]

In this credo there were some shrewd points, but as Pattison's friends
were quick to reply, there was no answer to the charge that in Oxford
everything (and especially professorial lectures) was judged by the
examination system and the interests of learning were subordinated
to whatever would yield a dividend in examinations.[34] Moreover,
Brodrick was out of touch with current university feeling in still
deferring to the liberal shibboleths of the 'sixties. He was furious
with Salisbury for not restricting the powers of Convocation and the
membership of Congregation,[35] but these controversies had died away
remarkably in Oxford with the repeal of the university tests. While
the tests lasted party lines had been hard and fast, and the bias given
to the party struggle by the university constitution had made the
arrangements of 1854 a matter of bitter dispute. The repeal of the
tests, however, had done even more than the defeat of Gladstone to
take the university out of politics, and, though political differences
remained, questions of academic reform were now less readily to be
translated into party terms and constitutional bickering had died
away.[36]

   Jowett's friends had now obtained almost everything for which
they had campaigned, and how conservative liberals could now
become was illustrated by two papers written in 1875 and 1876 by
J. R. Magrath, fellow of Queen's, for a select society of persons
interested in university and college administration. Magrath wanted
to secure better management of college property, and some share
of the proceeds for the university; he wanted to abolish restrictions
of celibacy; but he declared that even if an executive commission
could realise all his hopes, he would 'much prefer that a commission
should not issue for the next twenty years at least.' Magrath reckoned
that it was not yet time to pass judgment on the reforms of 1854.
In six colleges, including three of the wealthiest and most important,
New College, Magdalen and St. John's, only a minority of the
fellows had been elected under the new ordinances, and great changes
were still probable. Christ Church had not yet freed itself from

ecclesiastical influence. Since 1871 the Privy Council had refused to sanction any changes in college statutes,[37] and at that time still fewer colleges were emancipated. In particular it had taken the juniors a long time to get control of the financial management of the colleges, and the present spate of reorganisation was a very unpromising time for a general change. Moreover, the country was obviously moving towards the creation of a national education system, and it was foolish to reorganise the university until the demands of that system were known. Much good could be done by enabling the colleges to resume their own reform, but the attempt to secure a final settlement on a large scale must be as burdensome as the last comprehensive examination statute.[38] In all this one is reminded of Jowett trying hard to remain a good liberal.[39]

In this state of relative content the liberal old guard under Liddell and Jowett did not shrink from a settlement imposed by a conservative government, and they took the lead by summoning a select meeting of their friends to the Deanery at Christ Church on February 1, 1875. This meeting was attended by S. W. Wayte, J. M. Wilson, and Bartholomew Price of the older generation, by G. G. Bradley, Henry Acland, Henry Smith and others of the younger, with Thomas Fowler and George Rolleston from Pattison's party. The meeting agreed with a few present dissenting that the government be asked to appoint an executive commission to

> direct its attention ... to the tenure of headships, fellowships & professorships; and the appropriation of funds at the disposal of the university & colleges, and also to the encouragement of learning and research in connexion with the university & colleges.

These resolutions were transmitted to Lord Salisbury,[40] and gave the conservative government a perfect opening to act before the liberals should return to power. Salisbury replied at once that the government would probably legislate if there was a general desire for reform.[41] A week later Disraeli announced in the debate on the Queen's speech that

> no government can exist which for a moment maintains that the consideration of University reform, and consequently legislation of some kind, will not form part of its duty,[42]

and the Cambridge authorities were stirred into considering what line they should take.[43] It was, however, a year before Salisbury introduced the Oxford bill into the Lords, and there was still conflict upon it in the cabinet.[44]

When the bill was finally published in March 1876, the credit was assumed by the Oxford high-church party, who ever since Disraeli's announcement had been meeting at Keble to draft a scheme to press upon the government.[45] Ritualists and anti-ritualists, liberal and conservative catholics, together with some political conservatives, had sunk their differences; they called for the immediate appointment of an executive commission to transfer college funds to the university for the purposes of enlarging the professoriate, for remunerating resident teachers more adequately, and supporting others engaged in study and learning. Funds should be reserved for the assistance of poor students. The powers of colleges to change their constitutions should be restricted. Non-resident fellowships should be reduced in number and limited in tenure to a term of years. Finally clerical fellowships should be retained in their present proportion to the whole, and candidates for them should be required to take Holy Orders not later than a year after their election.[46] This provision would prevent the practice well-known in Oxford and general in Cambridge, of laymen taking clerical fellowships as a prize for a term of years and resigning when the date for taking orders fell due. In so far as any policy could be divined from Salisbury's bill, this seemed to be it, and when in due course the commission was found to include not only Lord Selborne, who as Roundell Palmer had so often pleaded the cause of the church in Oxford, but the obstructive Lord Redesdale, and the buffoon of Oxford catholicism in J. W. Burgon, the worst fears of Mark Pattison and the extreme liberals seemed to have been fulfilled.

Lyulph Stanley who for some years had been a prominent wild man among the secularising liberals, became hysterical. Lord Salisbury's speech was 'insolent and untruthful.' The bill was 'as bad as possible.'

> It enables the Commissioners to reimpose clerical tests on offices now free from them. It enables them to direct funds to found new clerical offices. It subjects the colleges to the veto of the university in all alterations of the statutes to be made for them. It does not touch the present constitution of Congregation, nor the right of interference of Convocation in educational matters. And it enables the Commissioners by the wholesale suppression of lay fellowships and the preservation of clerical fellowships to revolutionize the governing bodies of the colleges in the interest of the sacerdotal party . . . by keeping the heads out of the bill it preserves their clerical restrictions . . .

In the same vein Stanley wrote in the *Nonconformist*,[47] galvanised the Liberation Society, and tried to stir up Pattison's party in Oxford, deploring the fact that Jowett was content with the bill.[48] And he was justified to the extent that in private Burgon was busily trying to stiffen Salisbury in the church interest, and thinking up schemes to defeat liberal hopes at the commission. 'They hate *me*, as cordially as I hate *them*:' he wrote, '& they know what a hopeless foe they have in me.'[49]

Salisbury, however, claimed in debate that the bill had no 'propagandist or theological bearings,'[50] his commission included eminent names in Mountague Bernard, Chichele professor of international law, Sir Henry Maine, Corpus professor of jurisprudence, Mr. Justice Grove, a distinguished scientist as well as judge, and M. W. Ridley an intelligent conservative back-bencher. Moreover, when a flood of suggestions for changes began to pour in from the university and colleges Salisbury showed himself unexpectedly willing to accept amendments. The Hebdomadal Council moved first and presented a number of suggested alterations to Convocation in the form of decrees, and got them accepted with great unanimity. They proposed among other things that the duration of the commissioners' powers should be reduced; that any statute proposed by the commissioners affecting the university should be communicated to the Hebdomadal Council; that the Oxford authorities should have the right to petition the Queen in Council on matters of policy as well as of law connected with the statutes; that the consent of the university to changes made by the commissioners in the college statutes should be required only for statutes affecting the university.[51] These points were reiterated in a very large number of college petitions,[52] Salisbury agreed to incorporate them in the bill, and met the charge that he was prescribing no policy to the commissioners by adding a preamble.[53] Even Jowett who had been defeated in a motion at the Hebdomadal Council to petition for a preliminary educational inquiry[54] was pleased.[55] As the colleges were given time in which to prepare schemes for their own reform, and three representatives on the commission when their own statutes were being drawn up, their interests were now well safeguarded and the circumstances which were to disappoint the hopes of the high-churchmen and the fears of the extreme liberals were already taking shape.[56]

The repeal of the tests had settled the last great issue which interested the general public in the universities,[57] and even in nonconformity there was very little concern for Lyulph Stanley and his friends to work upon. Having met the immediate vested interests Salisbury had a very quiet parliamentary passage. In both houses there was a call for a fresh inquiry, and in the Commons, Lord Francis Hervey declared that

> an indefinite extension of the Professoriate meant a number of luxurious residences, children in perambulators wheeled about in the Parks, picnics in Bagley Wood, carriages, champagne, and the abandonment of celibacy and culture.[58]

The bill, however, had no difficulty in passing the Lords or in receiving a second reading in the Commons. Unfortunately, the government showed very little drive in its legislative programme, and was beginning to make much of the Eastern Question; along with other promised legislation, the Oxford bill got no further, a Cambridge bill made hardly any progress at all, and the colleges were subjected to the inconvenience of having to make elections for at least another session under statutes which they almost all wished to change.

It was, nevertheless, in the conservative interest to secure a settlement while public interest in the university question continued so languid,[59] and Salisbury once again prepared to move by drawing the sting from his critics. The two great criticisms which he had not accepted in 1876 were that it was absurd to settle the universities in separate bills, and that the Oxford residents were not adequately represented on the commission by J. W. Burgon.[60] Towards the end of 1876, therefore, Salisbury prepared a new bill dealing with both universities through separate commissions, and got Maine and Burgon (to the latter's intense bitterness) to resign.[61] Burgon was replaced by James Bellamy, President of St. John's, a thorough conservative with the reputation of being a shrewd and sensible man;[62] a liberal was required to replace Maine, and after failing to secure Liddell,[63] Salisbury made the ideal second choice in Henry Smith. The bill which Gathorne Hardy introduced into the Commons in February 1877 was otherwise very similar to the bill of the previous year as amended in the Lords. The commissioners' powers were to terminate in 1881 instead of 1883, and they were to pay heed to the interests of education as well as those of religion, learning and research. The commission might reduce but not increase the present clerical restrictions upon fellowships. Appeal was to lie to a Universities Committee of the Privy Council instead of to the Judicial Committee, this new body to consist of the President of the Council, the Archbishop of Canterbury, the Lord Chancellor, the Chancellors of the universities, and up to two other members of the Privy Council appointed by the queen, one of whom at least was to be a member of the Judicial Committee.[64]

Except in committee the debates on the bill were very unexciting, altogether unlike those which had taken place on the bill of 1854 or even on the repeal of the tests. The main principles had been settled in the previous year, and only the details remained to be hammered out. The government was strong enough to defeat motions embodying the old liberal shibboleths of constitutional alteration in Congregation and Convocation, and the abolition of episcopal visitation, though Goschen carried the day for the liberals of Oriel by an amendment empowering the commissioners to separate the office of Provost from the canonry at Rochester.[65] In the Lords only one important amendment was accepted—Lord Morley's proposal that the commissioners be empowered to appropriate the property of any college for the benefit of the Bodleian, or to effect the complete or partial union of any college with any university institution.[66] The background to this apparently radical proposal was an article by C. H. Robarts, the librarian of All Souls, and a disciple of Mark Pattison, proposing to remedy the chronic poverty of the Bodleian by uniting his own college with it. Bodley's librarian would become Warden of All Souls, obtaining a good income and an official residence close to the Bodleian, other fellowships could be used for the support of sub-librarians and professors of bibliographical subjects, while the college library should become a regular law faculty library and a unit of the Bodleian.[67] However, as Charles Neate unkindly pointed out, the bill might almost have been described as a bill for the preservation of All Souls.

> If we look to its original author [Salisbury], he was an old fellow of All Souls; to its present introducer, he as well as his colleague in the representation of the University, has a son an actual fellow. If we look to the Commission, out of seven Commissioners there are two fellows of All Souls, who, with the three Commissioners to be appointed by the College, will equal in number all the rest.[68]

Moreover, the majority in the college meeting consisted of young lawyers, mostly from Balliol, who were equally unsympathetic to Robarts's scheme for the development of the Bodleian, and to an alternative pressed by the Warden, Montagu Burrows, Max Müller and other senior fellows, to rival Balliol in the education of candidates for the Indian Civil Service. All Souls, therefore, was committed to the support of further chairs in law, but otherwise remained unchanged 'as a social club with an intellectual qualification for admission.'[69]

The Universities of Oxford and Cambridge Act allowed the universities and colleges eighteen months until the end of 1878 to frame statutes for the commissioners' approval before their compulsory powers came into force. Meanwhile, the commission despatched circulars to the colleges and arranged sessions in Oxford for the purpose of taking information about the needs of the university between October 23 and November 5, 1877. These sessions immediately revealed one of the desiderata, for they took place in the Clarendon Hotel, the university having no accommodation which it could make available. The evidence given here and at further sessions in London the following February consisted of an enormous number of schemes for extra facilities of different kinds, some of them, such as the plan for medical education pressed by Acland and Lankester, very expensive indeed. On the other hand, there was cheerful counsel from one of the most respected of Oxford bursars, Alfred Robinson of New College. He held that the whole of the funds necessary for university requirements, even upon a most liberal estimate of what those requirements were, could be obtained out of increases in the college revenues which would accrue within the next twenty or thirty years; it was, therefore, erroneous to suppose that the development of the university must destroy the college system. The surpluses which had been expected by the Cleveland commission by 1895 would be garnered by 1890, and a good deal more would come in before the end of the century.[70]

The circumstances upon which these expectations were based formed a most interesting chapter in the nineteenth century history of the university, and one which had a great influence not only upon the reforming schemes of the 'seventies but also upon the policies pursued by Salisbury's commissioners.[71] Until the middle of the century, college property like church property had been generally let on a system of beneficial leases, by which the college had taken a small annual reserved rent together with a periodical fine for the renewal of the lease. Thus, for example, a tenant on a twenty-year lease would pay the reserved rent for six years and then pay a fine for the extension of his lease from fourteen years to twenty. Under this system the colleges practically incorporated the aristocracy and gentry of the country in their system of estate management, and college leases came to be used for family settlements, for the endowment of chairs and innumerable other purposes. Tenants and subtenants enjoyed security, and in the course of the previous century, the senior fellows in some colleges had come to enjoy dividing the fine amongst themselves, though, as rent paid fourteen years in advance, it should have been invested at compound interest for that period.

One of the difficulties of college leases, however, was that they could not be offered for more than forty years, and even with the prospect of renewal this was a great deterrent to building. In North Oxford, for example, where most of the land was college property, the only building was done by the most prosperous of Oxford tradesmen who were not discouraged by short leases from erecting large houses with plenty of land. The first real suburban development came by accident. The Board of Guardians acquired a few acres under a compulsory purchase order in order to rebuild the workhouse on a new site, but changed their plans before beginning to build. The college did not repurchase the property, which accordingly passed to a group of Oxford speculators. They in turn incongruously developed the Park Town estate in the middle of a large tract of agricultural land. Until colleges could run out their beneficial leases and issue longer leases, they were unable to develop their own property in this way.

Church and college property, moreover, obtained a bad name amongst reformers. Under the system of beneficial leases the land-lords had virtually lost control of their property, there was very little motive for improvement, farming was often poor, and buildings dilapidated. Under the combined pressure of public reproach and the need to maximise the yield of church endowments, the Ecclesi-astical Commissioners began to run out their beneficial leases which were much more valuable than those of the colleges. At the end of each lease the property would be let again at the full rack-rent. This resolution caused enormous consternation among the holders of church leases, and they formed the duke of Richmond's committee, popularly known as the Forty Thieves, to protect their interests. They obtained some concessions in the Church Estates Act of 1851, but a blow had been delivered to the confidence of tenants in the system of beneficial leases from which it could not recover, and the colleges were compelled to follow in the wake of the church.

In order to do so colleges needed twofold parliamentary assistance. They must be empowered to offer leases for more than forty years, and to borrow to bear the expenses of running out beneficial leases. To run out the leases meant not only that the colleges would have to forgo the fines, but that they would have to make good the dilapida-tions caused by tenants who had no interest in the renewal of the lease, before properties were let out again. Few colleges had reserve funds adequate to these demands, but recourse to credit seemed to be justified by the great increase in revenue which would eventually arise from the rack-rents. The Cleveland commission computed its increases in college incomes on the basis of the difference between reserved rents and rack-rents as leases fell in, but this happy day had been remote when the crisis arose in the middle of the century. The first attempts at legislation were made in 1856, and the major advance came with the Universities and College Estates Acts of 1858 and 1860 which were drawn up under the direction of experienced members of both universities, and especially of C. W. Lawrence, fellow of New College, and steward both of New College and of Christ Church. These acts authorised the colleges, with the approval of the Copyhold Commissioners to borrow such moneys as they could show were necessary by mortgage of any lands belonging to them. The loans were to be extinguished within thirty years. They were also empowered to sell land, the proceeds to be held by the Copyhold Commissioners for the purchase of other land.

Under these acts a vast deal of borrowing went on, and the spirit of improvement which was manifest in the endless tinkering with the examination and teaching system was manifest also in a great deal of agricultural investment. With prosperous farming it seemed possible to borrow for agricultural improvement, to recover the interest and

21

capital from the tenants within the thirty years and then claim the whole of the improved rent for the college. Already in 1871 loans and repayments were costing Lincoln £1250 p.a., Oriel £1800 p.a., Christ Church £7200 p.a., and New College in the previous decade had borrowed £28,335 to recoup the beneficiaries of fines not received, and another £25,000 for the extension of buildings which were not yet complete and producing an income.[72] Pipe-dreams of all kinds could flourish, and it required unusual prudence for a college like Brasenose to hold back, or for a liberal like J. R. Magrath to declare that the Cleveland commission's estimates of probable improvements in college revenues were valueless.[73]

In 1879, however, while the Selborne commission was deliberating on the division of the spoils, this proved disastrously to be the case. All property and especially agricultural land fell rapidly in value, and at the very moment when the profits of the changes in leases were expected to accrue there were sharp falls in rents.[74] This made circumstances difficult for those (on the whole smaller and poorer) colleges which had already completed the leasing of their property at the rack-rent, but was even worse for colleges which had borrowed heavily in anticipation of high rents which were not now going to accrue. Oriel was said to be suffering the worst, and at the end of 1880 the emoluments of the fellows were reported to have been reduced by nearly one half.[75] The colleges cast round for relief, and at the instance of Alfred Robinson, Bursar of New College, whose recent prophecies of affluence had been so dismally unfulfilled, the Universities and College Estates Amendment Act was passed in 1880.[76] In the course of the previous twenty years a good deal of college property had been sold and considerable sums of college money were held by the Copyhold Commissioners awaiting the purchase of new estates. These monies were invested in Consols at little more than three per cent, while colleges were paying four or five per cent on their mortgages. The act, therefore, permitted the colleges to borrow from themselves instead of going to the market, and considerable savings were made as many of the debts due to private mortgagees were paid off out of monies in the hands of the Copyhold Commission. Welcome as this relief was, the loans from the Copyhold Commissioners had to be repaid within the same period as the original loans, and the chief benefit of all the investment of the previous twenty years lay in the attraction offered to scarce tenants in a buyer's market; it was not often that college farms were left untenanted altogether.

This sudden financial deterioration coloured all the operations of the Selborne commission, and Mountague Bernard who succeeded Selborne as chairman after the latter had become Lord Chancellor in 1880, confessed himself 'unable to form any estimate of the future total income of the colleges which [he] should not regard as speculative.' The present revenue was very badly distributed, and most of the colleges were poor. Most of the current revenues were in any case consumed by vested interests and other unavoidable charges. The conclusion followed

> that no heavy *immediate* charge could be imposed on the Colleges for university purposes. No funds exist from which such charges could be met. And in imposing *prospective* charges it must be born in mind that the amount they will realize, and the time within which it will be realized, are matters of much uncertainty.[77]

Clearly the commission could give no support to the elaborate ambitions of the boards of studies, even as pruned by the Hebdomadal Council in 1877,[78] or to Acland's hopes of a medical school, and it must leave some elasticity in the arrangements in case the financial condition of the colleges continued to deteriorate. The commission hoped nevertheless ultimately to double the expenditure upon the Oxford professoriate, and to meet this contingency it invented the Common University Fund.[79] Each college was to cast up its accounts according to a common form and was to pay two per cent on all its net revenue thus computed; on all net revenue exceeding £5000 there would be additional taxation graduated according to the wealth of the college. The effect would be that a college having £5000 net revenue would pay £100, a college with £15,000 would pay over £1000, and a college with £25,000 would pay over £4000. Only the two per cent was payable at once, however, the additional taxation being imposed in instalments from 1885, and falling fully due in 1900. Provision was also made that in the early years of the fund the yield should be made up to £3000 from the University Chest.

The main purpose of the Common University Fund was to provide for the 'endowment of research'; it was to meet the stipends of readers, extraordinary professors and lecturers (and their pensions), grants for research expenses and apparatus, the improvement of libraries, and some quite distinct matters connected with unattached students. Building was not within the terms of the fund. The provision of university appointments was perforce limited, but appointments to six chairs and seven readerships were authorised, and before the end of the century a number of scholars were appointed extraordinary professors.

The first great battle in which the commissioners were involved was joined over their statutes prescribing the professors' terms of service. The professorial statutes (which were issued in November 1880) were the first which the commission produced, and this alone was made a matter of reproach by the liberal press. It was undeniably obscure what the functions of the professoriate were to be, and the provisions of the statutes suggested that they were to continue to be inferior to college tutors. Their obligations to reside and lecture were somewhat increased, they were to give private instruction and to examine the men who came to their lectures. Moreover, their pay was to be either £900 or £450 according to the importance of their subject in university teaching. They were to be subject to the supervision of a Visitatorial Board. At once the body of Oxford professors came out in protest (Max Müller complaining that professors 'were not much more than tolerated in the old Universities' and were '*not even prayed for at University sermons*'), and they obtained the support of the Hebdomadal Council. The *Guardian*, however, pointed out that there was no question of establishing a professorial system, that the professors must accept the consequences of increased usefulness and pay, and the commission took the view that 'an exclusive devotion to scientific inquiry or literary research . . . is not the proper business of a university professor.' The protests from Oxford and the clamours of the liberal press induced the commission to reduce the professor's supplementary chores to giving 'advice, . . . informal instruction . . . occasional or periodical examination . . . as he may judge to be expedient,' and to remove some of the more obnoxious features of the Visitatorial Board, but they were unwilling to make any major concession.[80]

The chief concession made by the commissioners to the notion of the professors as a regular estate of the university came with their establishment of the boards of faculties. As we have seen, the boards of studies had established themselves as an informal faculty organisation, and the commissioners created four faculties of Theology, Law, Natural Science (including mathematics and medicine) and Arts (including the rest). These boards were to consist of the professors and readers lecturing in the faculty *ex officio*, of elected members up to an equal number, and of some smaller number of co-opted members. The first object of these boards was to prepare and revise a lecture list, but they were also to elect members to sit on boards with the Vice-Chancellor and Proctors for the appointment of examiners, and they were each to be represented by one member on the delegacy to manage the Common University Fund. There was, therefore at least the theoretical possibility that through these elaborate processes of indirect election the professors might exercise an influence out of proportion to their numbers.

This suspicion underlay the fierce contest aroused by the new statute on the appointment of examiners. The old system of appointment by Vice-Chancellor and Proctors which continued everywhere except in the Theology School was increasingly unsuited to the multiplication of schools and the increase of knowledge, and the Hebdomadal Council wanted the commission to leave appointment of examiners to the boards of faculties. Knowing, however, that to innumerable Oxford men the present system seemed to guarantee college rights, the commissioners made a compromise by creating boards for each school, to consist of the Vice-Chancellor, the Proctors and three members of the appropriate faculty boards. There was an immediate counterblast. It was said that the Hebdomadal Council had only made their request by a majority of one vote with four members absent, and during Easter Term 1881 memorials against it signed by 155 members of Convocation were submitted to the commissioners and Hebdomadal Council. In June 1881 Convocation petitioned the Queen in Council against the statute but their petition was rejected. The cry, nevertheless, went up that the statute was an invasion of college rights such as even the commission of 1854 had not contemplated,[81] and although the liberal party in the university produced a memorial in favour of this ancient party shibboleth,[82] the matter was still unsettled when the powers of the commission ran out in 1882.[83] Lord Salisbury took up the cry in the House of Lords, claiming that the proposed alteration would destroy the character of the Greats school altogether and hand the control of university studies to the body of professors. To all this Camperdown replied that the Hebdomadal Council would never have asked for the statute if they had had any hope of securing the reform through the ordinary machinery of the university, and that some limit must be set to the powers exercised by Lord Salisbury in Oxford, in the Universities Committee of the Privy Council and in the Lords. At last the government carried the day, and the new examination system was adopted.[84]

The commission's dealings with the colleges gave rise to some ripe stories, such as that of Mark Pattison fuming at the reduction of his salary and the defeat of his attempts to transfer the religious instruction in the college to laymen,[85] and to one sharp and ironical dispute between the more conservative and more liberal members of the commission itself over the headship of Worcester. The conservatives (including Osborne Gordon and Lord Redesdale) wished to preserve the nomination to the office of Provost to the Chancellor, while the liberals, the traditional apologists of outside intervention, insisted that election be left to the fellows.[86] On the whole, however, the negotiations went peacefully.

Great inconveniences had arisen from the practice of the commission of 1854 of leaving the ancient statutes unrepealed in so far as they did not conflict with the new ordinances. The 1877 commission, therefore, abrogated all earlier statutes and ordinances, and substituted a new code for each college. In these they were content to follow the trends of the previous generation which were towards reducing the number of fellowships and towards special privileges for those willing to reside and do college work. In 1852 there had been over 500 fellowships with about 45 vacancies per year (as compared with 13 first classes in the two schools); in 1878 this number had been reduced to about 350, of which about 30 were suspended (as compared with about 50 first classes a year). Whereas at the time of the previous commission the great majority of the fellows were in Holy Orders and were looking forward to a college living, now the majority of fellows were laymen and even good college livings could often not be filled by the fellows. At the same time the offices of college tutor and lecturer were quite generally held by men who were not fellows of the college and did not reside in it. The result was that those colleges which had been able to revise their statutes had sought various inducements including permission to marry and live out of college in order to ensure that a reasonable proportion of their fellowships would be held by men who would undertake college work. This process was made general by the commission. Prize fellowships which had provoked so much criticism were to be limited to seven years duration and £200 p.a. in value. Every college was to have a proportion of official or tutorial fellows, who need not be elected by examination, and who might enjoy considerable advantages of tenure, permission to marry, the prospect of a pension, etc. in consideration of their services to the college, or, in some cases, to original scholarship. The effect of these arrangements at Magdalen, for example, was that instead of two-thirds of the college revenues being consumed by fellows under no obligations to educational work, only one-third would be so applied in future, and Bernard expected that ultimately, in the university as a whole, less than 100 prize fellowships would survive.[87]

The contentious matter was the question of clerical restrictions. Liberals like Lyulph Stanley had been convinced that the commission would limit prizes out of the open fellowships and leave the clerical fellowships untouched. In fact they took the line that there should be no restriction upon the free choice of the colleges except to fulfil the obligations imposed by the act of maintaining regular religious instruction and Divine Service. There were to be no clerical fellowships at colleges like All Souls, Merton, New College and Wadham where there had been no clerical restrictions before, nor at those like Exeter where the obligation to take Orders had been very long delayed. In most colleges, though the commissioners thought it likely that a considerable number of the men engaged in academical work would continue to be clergymen, they took no steps to ensure that more than one fellow would be in orders. It was an inevitable consequence of these provisions that the headships should also be opened to preserve some competition in the elections, and apart from the Deanery of Christ Church, the only clerical headship left was that of Pembroke, a college which could not afford to dispense with the canonry of Gloucester annexed to the Master's office.[88]

The statutes did not attain this final form without a contest. Conservative churchmen like Liddon and Burgon were deeply mortified at the church's losses when the draft statutes began to appear in 1880,[89] and they could use the argument that the act required the commissioners to pay heed to the founders' objects, which in some cases had been to create communities for theological study.[90] The fact that the commissioners were for the most part content to follow the wishes of the college representatives only proved how great was the lapse from grace. What might be in store was suggested by the efforts of the representatives of Lincoln to dislodge the Bishop of Lincoln from the office of Visitor.[91] The extremer liberals, however, were equally dissatisfied with the willingness of the commissioners to go with the majority in a few colleges including Christ Church, Magdalen and St. John's, who wanted more generous treatment of clerical fellows, and when a liberal government returned to office C. S. Roundell planned a demonstration. Early in 1880 a petition was got up against the requirement of Holy Orders for any office other than those required for the maintenance of religious instruction and Divine Service, and signed by the whole liberal phalanx at Oxford.[92] Another memorial with 800 signatures was presented to Gladstone urging him to support Roundell's motion.[93] James Bryce rubbed salt into the wound by an intemperate address to the Liberation Society in which he spoke of 'the liberal members of those [more clerical] colleges who are going to be handed over, bound hand and foot, to the mercies of a clerical majority' (notwithstanding the notorious liberalism of the Dean and his disciples like H. L. Thompson at Christ Church). He proposed to move for the opening of the chairs of Hebrew and ecclesiastical history to laymen, and in the latter case

> it ought to be, if not a positive disqualification, at any rate a disadvantage, to a man who stands for a chair of that kind, to be a clergyman of any religious body.[94]

There was some trembling among the Oxford liberals at the thought of removing all clerical restrictions, for many of them, including Jowett, wanted an irreducible minimum of clerical fellowships to carry out the purposes of the act.[95] On July 9, 1880, Roundell raised the matter in the Commons, declaring that as there was not time to bring in a bill he would move a resolution with a view to legislation the next session. Gladstone replied that the house ought to be chary of upsetting the main principles of previous legislation, and that

Roundell was trying to influence the commission by a resolution which had no force in law. In the end Roundell's motion, and Bryce's amendment about the ecclesiastical history and Hebrew chairs, were withdrawn.[96]

The demonstration, however, had its effect. Selborne, who was now Lord Chancellor, had to give up the chairmanship of the commission, and was succeeded by Mountague Bernard, the vacant place going to G. G. Bradley, Master of University College, a liberal divine in the tradition of Arnold, who was altogether less sympathetic to clerical fellowships than Selborne. At the time of the latter's resignation, the draft statutes of Magdalen were already in print, and provided that half the fellows should be in Holy Orders. These statutes were recalled, and by a majority of one vote the number of clerical fellowships was reduced to two.[97] St. John's after a long contest had its clerical fellowships also reduced to two, and Christ Church, where the burdens of religious instruction and Divine Service were unusually heavy, obtained no more than three clerical studentships. Bryce went on with a scheme, never put into force, of quartering a lay chair of oriental or semitic languages upon the endowments of the regius professor of Hebrew,[98] but the last round in the contest went to the bishop of Lincoln, Christopher Wordsworth. Thoroughly aggrieved at the attempt to deprive him of his visitatorial functions at Lincoln College, he refused to surrender his right to nominate a fellow. Worsted at the Privy Council, he took his case to the House of Lords, and so successfully convinced his peers of the iniquity of such interference with private property that he got the whole body of Lincoln College statutes thrown out, and the college remained tied to its old ordinances until 1925.[99]

The only other feature of the college settlement which caused much stir was among the matters first determined by the commission,[100] the total abolition of all the independent public halls; all were absorbed into colleges except St. Edmund Hall, which was partially united with Queen's. The commissioners believed that the creation of a body of unattached students had deprived the halls of any reason for existence; all the halls were in financial difficulties, and the dismal history of the strenuous efforts of the last forty years to revive them, argued cogently for transferring their property to colleges which could make more use of it. The halls, however, had their friends who appealed to Lord Salisbury not to agree to the diminution of his patronage,[101] not to exterminate useful bodies whose demise must be the signal for the opening of new private halls,[102] and above all not to countenance the flagrant avarice of the interested colleges.[103] Balliol got an early agreement to absorb New Inn Hall in order to further the training of candidates for the Indian Civil Service,[104] Queen's appeared to be the principal beneficiary of the partial union with St. Edmund Hall,[105] while E. A. Knox, sub-warden of Merton, revealed the qualities which later made him a formidable bishop of Manchester, by announcing his discovery that Merton owned a considerable portion of the house of the Principal of St. Alban Hall and the garden on which the chapel was built and did not propose to let these to any future Principal. This would drive the Principal into the premises of the hall itself which were already too small for economic working.[106] The *Times* pleaded in vain that the university was entitled to some recompense for the valuable assets which it was having to hand over,[107] and when no subsidies could be obtained from this source, the Principal of St. Mary Hall, as he had long foreseen, had to seek union with Oriel.[108] There was too much realism in the commissioners' settlement for Salisbury to stand in its way;[109] though no-one wept for Jowett at the prospect of the Tavern (as New Inn Hall was popularly known) being re-christened the Balliol Tap.[110]

With the halls were buried a generation of high-church hopes for the cheap education of the clergy under discipline, but neither this victory nor the remarkable sight of the university beginning the new session of 1882 with new statutes and with Jowett unchallenged at the helm as Vice-Chancellor,[111] did much to reconcile the liberals to the new order. Even at the last, Roundell and Bryce had moved a bill to alter the constitution of the Universities Committee of the Privy Council,[112] and Bryce bemoaned the conservatism of the commission. They had done nothing to make the professoriate useful, they had not taken nearly enough money from the colleges, and by requiring them rigidly to provide teaching for the main schools had wasted manpower and done much to injure the usefulness of the smaller societies. Even worse they had contributed nothing towards making the university more serviceable to the nation. The university was no nearer attracting the whole nation by cheap, technical and professional education, or improving education throughout the country. The commissioners neither cured the ills of Oxford nor required the colleges to spend funds elsewhere.[113] This argument (especially the plea for technical education) was applauded by E. A. Freeman who had lost none of his contempt for 'Cribmonger Jowett and that lot,'[114] but it was clearly based on an overestimate of the present wealth of the colleges and an underestimate of the way the commissioners had been inhibited by the agricultural depression. G. C. Brodrick made precisely the opposite complaint. The settlement

> was essentially socialistic—the spoliation of the Colleges as rich corporations, for the supposed benefit of the university, as a comparatively poor corporation.

So far from the college settlement being too rigid it was not rigid

enough, for the commissioners made a separate bargain with each
society, and so far from extorting too little college funds, they took
too much.

> Legislating during a 'boom' of agricultural prosperity, and
> assuming that it would continue, they enormously over-estimated
> the average rentals of colleges, and imposed on them contribu-
> tions quite out of proportion to their present revenues.

They also set a sorry example for democratic spoliation, which might
lead to demands for subsidies to provincial colleges. From the
opposite side to Bryce, Brodrick complained that no harmony had
been established between college and university teaching.[115]
Goldwin Smith also thought that the college system had been
uprooted with the end of celibacy, and nothing but barracks of
students left. Moreover, with the general sanction of marriage, college
revenues were now threatened by the personal interest of the fellows,
which would only become more dangerous as their families grew up.
The only check to this would be to put the universities under the
permanent visitatorial oversight of the Privy Council.[116] Now even
more than in an earlier generation, when religious grievances had
provided a common platform, the liberals were acrimoniously pursuing sectional causes, and it was not surprising that J. R. Green was
bewailing their declining hold upon the upper classes and pining for
'a higher and a more intelligent liberalism than we have now.'[117]
Equally angry and perplexed, however, were the high-churchmen
who had been engaged in agonising reappraisal ever since the repeal
of the tests. Only the *Guardian* and its sympathisers consistently
maintained the worthlessness of temporal supports, and thought that
clerical fellowships and headships did the church more harm than
good.[118] Yet as William Ince, who became regius professor of divinity
in 1878, and never ceased to urge the obligations of public service
upon the university,[119] pointed out, the 'disestablishment of religion'
was only one aspect of the problem of the church in Oxford. Long
before the repeal of the tests attendance at chapel had become
voluntary in some colleges, although this was still not general, and
all colleges had seen fit to cut their services to a quarter of an hour.
Never more than a handful of examination candidates had ever asked
for exemption from examination in divinity, and the standard of the
examination had risen since 1872, when it was made the responsibility
of a separate board; this helped to end the ancient abuse by which
the divinity examination had been stiffer for passmen than classmen,
and the examiners had been tempted to be particularly lax with the
men of most distinction in secular subjects.[120] On the other hand,
college instruction in divinity, which had always been inadequate,
was getting worse, not because of parliamentary legislation but

because of the pressure of other university examinations; by 1875 lectures on some of the more solid older books such as Butler's *Analogy*, Paley's *Horae Paulinae* and Davison on prophecy had gone out altogether. Moreover, the growth of historical method in the teaching for the Greats school made impossible such fantasies as William Sewell's old exposition of Plato as the great upholder of church principles against sophistry, scepticism and dissent. Among senior members of the university, theology had never been an obsession except during the 'thirties and 'forties, and now suffered from the growing dispersion of intellectual effort.

Mackarness, the Bishop of Oxford, perceived an anti-Christian conspiracy in Oxford bearing a curious resemblance to the clerical conspiracy perceived by the extreme liberals,[121] and in 1881 the Vicar of St. Mary's appealed to Salisbury for money for the restoration of the university church, on the surprising ground that if the present opportunity were lost 'religion, property, everything we hold dear' might succumb in two years.[122] But Ince was clear that 'an aggressive and proselytizing spirit of infidelity' was a thing unknown among Oxford teachers,[123] and a great deal of pastoral work was being better done than ever—though more commonly by societies and chaplaincies than by the authorities of college and university.[124] Nonconformists were gnashing their teeth that these influences were proving fatal to the dissent of their sons.[125] All manner of pastoral schemes were now on foot. Moody and Sankey in the Cornmarket, Wycliffe Hall to assist potential ordinands,[126] even a proposal for a special undergraduate church which should preserve men from the evils of compulsion in college chapels, of the theological vagaries of university sermons, and of the undesirable attentions of the opposite sex experienced in the parish churches.[127] None of these ventures could disguise the fact that the university as a corporate body now had no theological opinions. No longer a political oracle, Oxford was no longer a theological oracle either—but this was only partly due to the 'disestablishment of religion.' The last great heresy hunt which had begun in Oxford was Pusey's crusade against the *Essays and Reviews* of 1861; as the last volume of the *Life of Pusey* bears eloquent witness, the university was now as remote from the professional contests of the clergy as it was from those of the politicians. The great national controversies took place elsewhere. The liberal triumph in restoring the universities to the nation[128] had, at least in this sense, isolated them more completely than ever from the great currents of the national life.

The commission, moreover, had settled none of the problems which led to its appointment. A generation later when Lord Curzon as Chancellor took up the question of university reform, the old issues of the relations of the university and colleges, and of university extension, the old liberal grievances against the university constitution and the inadequate endowment of research, were still being agitated. Some of the changes which the commission itself had introduced had also worked indifferently. The boards of faculties greatly disappointed expectations and in the most important fields of Honour Mods. and Greats did not even succeed in producing a coherent lecture list. Equally unsatisfactory were the financial statements published annually by the university and colleges. These accounts omitted important matters, and enabled colleges bent on evading their responsibility to the university to reduce their net income by charging large sums to repairs and improvements. Further anomalies arose from the practices by which the wealthy colleges subsidised their kitchen from their external revenue while the poorer colleges made the kitchen subsidise the external revenue. Nor could these defects be blamed (as might some others) on the fact that the commission had no accurate idea of the size of the revenue of which it was disposing. All that could be said was that to those as far apart as Jowett and the liberal catholics of the *Guardian* who thought the college system was the secret of Oxford's usefulness, the heart of the university remained untouched and able to adapt itself to the demands of married fellows, and to the increased weight and variety of teaching for the honours schools.

REFERENCES

CHAPTER I

1 W. Crowe, *On the late attempt on His Majesty's person* (Oxford, 1786). This sermon is the more significant, as Crowe was noted for 'Whig, not to say republican propensities,' and obtained no more preferment. Lord Holland, *Further memoirs of the Whig Party* (London, 1905) pp. 321–2.

2 *Diary and letters of Madame D'Arblay* ed. Charlotte Barrett (London, n.d.) ii. 140–2; Bodl. MS. Top. Oxon. c. 296 fos. 3–14; *Journal and correspondence of Lord Auckland* [cited below as *Auckland Corr.*] (London, 1861–2) i. 386.

3 *Jackson's Oxford Journal* July 19, 1788.

4 University archives. MS. Conv. Reg. BK. 37 fos. 369–71; *Jackson's Oxford Journal* March 14, 1789.

5 *Hist. MSS. Comm. Fortescue MSS.* vii. 37.

6 *Parliamentary History* xxvi. 818 *seq.*, 831–2.

7 *Ibid.* xxviii. 16 *seq.*, 41.

8 Magdalen College MSS. D.6.3. George Horne to M. Routh, May 16, 1789. Peter Routh, father of the future President of Magdalen, noted the contrast between the 'Cambridge Heads of Houses returning thanks to Mr. Pitt and the University of Oxford taking no notice of their Chancellor.' Magdalen College MSS. D.5.9, Feb. 5, 1790.

9 University archives. MS. Minutes of Hebdomadal Meeting 1788–1803 fos. 27, 29–31, 35.

10 For Dolben's encomium upon the constitutional tendencies of the High Church party, *Parliamentary History* xxviii. 446.

11 Randolph referred to a unitarian 'sermon preached in Essex Street Chapel which if you are not harden'd will make your hair stand on end. I have long been hardened.' Bodl. MS. Top. Oxon. d. 353/2. fos. 21–3.

12 E. Tatham, *Letters to the Rt. Hon. Edmund Burke on Politics* (Oxford, 1791) pp. 92–4.

13 J. Hinton, *A vindication of the dissenters in Oxford* (London, 1792).

14 Bodl. MS. Top. Oxon. d. 354/2 fo. 74.

15 *Works of Vicesimus Knox* (London, 1824) iv. 158.

16 B.M. Add. MSS. 37909 fo. 1.

17 Bodl. MS. Top. Oxon. d. 353/2 fo. 47.

18 *Hist. MSS. Comm. Fortescue MSS.* ii. 300.

19 *Auckland Corr.* ii. 427.

20 B.M. Eg. MS. 2186 fo. 66. Cf. *Works of Samuel Parr* (London, 1828) vii. 343; viii. 151.

21 Magdalen College MSS. D.6.15 P. Homer to M. J. Routh, Sept. 24, 1792.

22 Bodl. MS. Top. Oxon. d. 353/2 fo. 49; *Correspondence of Edmund Burke* ed. Earl Fitzwilliam and Sir Richard Bourke (London, 1844) iii. 501, 521.

23 Bodl. MS. Add. D. 77 fo. 45.

24 *Works of Samuel Parr* vii. 646.

25 University archives. MS. Convocation Register 1793–1802 fos. 10–11; Bodl. MS. Top. Oxon. c. 236 fos. 13–18.

26 *Works of Samuel Parr* vii. 238.

27 E. Tatham, *Letters to Edmund Burke on politics*.

28 E. Tatham, *An address to the Rt. Hon. Lord Grenville, Chancellor of the University, upon great and fundamental abuses in that university* (Oxford, 1811) pp. 6–7.

29 Balliol College. MS. Jenkyns VI. MS. Letterbook of John Wills, Warden of Wadham, fo. 34.

30 Bodl. MS. Top. Oxon. d. 354/1 fos. 7, 9.

31 Balliol College. MS. Jenkyns VI. MS. Letterbook of John Wills, Warden of Wadham, fo. 61; G. V. Cox, *Recollections of Oxford* (2nd ed. London, 1870) p. 17. Further sums were raised in 1798 and 1803. *Ibid* pp. 35, 52; Bodl. MS. Top. Oxon. d. 354/2. fo. 28.

32 Bodl. MS. Top. Oxon. d. 354/2 fos. 33–4, 36; *Heber Letters 1783–1832* ed. R. H. Cholmondeley (London, 1950) p. 105; Cox, *Recollections* pp. 35–6; Balliol College. MS. Jenkyns VI, printed papers and MS. Diary of Richard Jenkyns, July 5, 1798; June 18, 1799.

33 University archives. MS. Hebdomadal Register 1803–23 fo. 47. When war broke out again in 1803, the university and the city formed a single volunteer force which was disbanded in 1813 when the threat of invasion ended. Cox, *Recollections* pp. 52, 74–5.

34 *Works of Samuel Parr* vii. 660.

35 *Ibid* vii. 287.

36 Bodl. MS. Top. Oxon. d. 354/2 fo. 55.

37 *Parliamentary History* xxii. 105.

38 *Monthly Review* xx. 86.

39 W. Field, *Memoirs of the life, writings and opinions of Rev. Samuel Parr* (London, 1828) i. 366–7.

40 *Works of Vicesimus Knox* iv. 165–7, 271, 274.

41 *University Notices 1826* (Bodl. G. A. Oxon. c. 42) p. 99; G. R. M. Ward and James Heywood, *Oxford University Statutes* [cited below as Ward & Heywood, *Statutes*] (London, 1844–51) ii. 139–142.

42 [J. Napleton] *A letter to the Rev. . . . M.A. Fellow of . . . College Oxford, on the case of subscription at matriculation* (Oxford, 1772).

43 Ward, *Georgian Oxford* chs. xv and xvi.

44 [J. Napleton] *Considerations on the residence usually required for degrees in the University of Oxford* (Oxford, 1772).

45 *University Notices 1662–1821* (Bodl. G. A. Oxon. b. 19) Broadsheets of March 20–22, 1820; *Letters of the earl of Dudley to the Bishop of Llandaff* [cited below as *Dudley-Copleston Corr.*] (London, 1840) p. 249. The Board refused any grace on a royal visit in 1835. University archives. MS. Hebdomadal Register 1833–41 fo. 64.

46 [J. Napleton] *Considerations on the public exercises for the first and second degrees in the University of Oxford* (n. pl., 1773).

47 *Works of Vicesimus Knox* i. 13–18, 340–342; iv. 273.

48 *Ibid.* iii. 373; iv. 259 *seq.*, 273.

49 *Ibid.* iv. 162, 272, 274.

50 *Ibid.* iv. 272.

51 *Ibid.* iv. 271–2.

52 *Memoirs of the life of Edward Gibbon* ed. G. B. Hill (London, 1900) pp. 49 *seq.*

53 *Monthly Review* xx. 79–80.

54 J. Hurdis, *A word or two in vindication of the university of Oxford* (n. pl. or d.). Hurdis explained the personal embarrassments in writing the pamphlet in a letter to Martin Routh, July 31, 1796. Magdalen College MSS. D.6.15.

55 S. Parr, *A Spital sermon* (London, 1801) pp. 107–113, 115–138.

56 An attempt to rehabilitate Tatham's reputation, which could well be taken further, is made in V. H. H. Green, *Oxford Common Room* (London, 1957) ch. 2.

57 Such as the replanning of the town, E. Tatham, *Oxonia explicata et ornata* (2nd ed. London, 1777).

58 E. Tatham, *The chart and scale of truth* (Oxford, 1790) i. 337 *seq.*, 360 *seq.*; E. Tatham, *Letter to the Rev. the Dean of Christ Church* (Oxford, 1807) p. 5.

59 James Bradley had been drawing large classes in experimental philosophy even in the middle of the century. *Miscellaneous works and correspondence of James Bradley* (Oxford, 1833) p. xxxviii.

60 E. Tatham, *A new address to the free and independent members of Convocation* (Oxford, 1810) pp. 16–17; B.M. Add. MSS. 38473 fo. 138; R. T. Gunther, *Early science in Oxford* (Oxford, 1923–45) xi. 195; *Oxford University Papers, 1660–1850* (Bodl. G. A. Oxon. b. 111) fo. 91.

61 Tatham, *op. cit.* pp. 16–18; *Annual biog[raphy] & Obit[uary]* xix. 470.

62 Bodl. MS. Add. D. 77 fo. 48. The Botany professor was required to produce medical qualifications and Sibthorp 'was compelled . . . to divulge the mortifying fact that not one of his few patients had survived his prescriptions.' Holland, *Further memoirs of the whig party* p. 322.

63 J. E. Stock, *Memoirs of the life of Thomas Beddoes* (London, 1811); Colchester MSS. J. Kidd to C. Abbot, Oct. 28, 1812. P.R.O. 30/9/16; T. Beddoes, *Memorial concerning the state of the Bodleian Library* (n. pl. or d.); Holland, *op. cit.* p. 324. Cf. Gunther, *op. cit.* i. 61–9, 202–4; xi. 277–8. He also turned against the war. T. Beddoes, *Where would be the harm of a speedy peace?* (Bristol, 1795).

64 G. C. White, *A versatile professor* (London, 1903) p. 207; Hurdis, *Vindication* p. 36.

65 Holland, *Further memoirs* pp. 338–9; J. Randolph, *Heads of a course of lectures in divinity* (n. pl. or d.).

66 MS. Letterbook of John Wills, Warden of Wadham fos. 141–3, 145 in Balliol College. MS. Jenkyns VI.

67 *Annual biog. & obit.* xii. 462 *seq.*; Colchester MSS. Cyril Jackson to C. Abbot, Sunday, 1807. P.R.O. 30/9/15.

68 University archives, MS. Minutes of Hebdomadal Meeting, 1788–1803 fos. 45–52; Holland, *Further Memoirs* p. 340.

69 *Annual biog & obit.* ix. 464. Wall had earlier been reader in chemistry. Gunther, *op. cit.* i. 61–6.

70 G. Pellew, *Life and correspondence of Lord Sidmouth* (London, 1847) i. 429.

71 *Hist MSS. Comm. Fortescue MSS.* v. 86–7.

72 Holland, *Further memoirs* p. 340. Cf. however, Gunther, *Early science in Oxford* xi. 118–9.

73 Cf. the course arranged at Christ Church in 1802 for Cecil Jenkinson, later 3rd earl of Liverpool. This consisted of college teaching in classics and the logic of Locke and his commentators, and professorial lectures on Euclid and natural science. B.M. Add. MSS. 38311 fos. 140–141. Cf. 38473 fo. 11.

74 *The correspondence of King George III* ed. Sir John Fortescue (London, 1927–8) vi. 382.

75 For an example of his taste for gossip see *The Diary and correspondence of Charles Abbot, Lord Colchester* ed. Charles, Lord Colchester (London, 1861) [cited below as *Colchester Diary*] ii. 496: 'Dr. Jackson . . . related all the particulars of the Regent's journey to Dover and back; and also the details of Colonel Campbell's private account of his conversation with Bonaparte, previous to his setting out with him from Fontainebleau to Elba.'

76 *Auckland Corr.* iv. 127–30.

77 *Diaries and correspondence of James Harris, first earl of Malmesbury* ed. 3rd earl of Malmesbury [cited below as *Malmesbury Diaries*] (London, 1844) iv. 214, 255, 259; *Colchester Diary* i. 422, 424, 430. Cf. Pellew, *Sidmouth* ii. 302–4.

78 *Malmesbury Diaries* iv. 302–6; *Colchester Diary* i. 522.

79 *Ibid* ii. 36, 97.

80 *Ibid* ii. 213–4; *Hist. MSS. Comm. Fortescue MSS* ix. 332.

81 H. Bathurst, *Memoirs of the late Dr. Henry Bathurst, Lord Bishop of Norwich* (London, 1837) i. 121.

82 B.M. Add. MSS. 40277 fo. 93.

83 E.g. to Peel in 1810: 'Work very hard, & unremittingly—work, as I used to say sometimes like a Tigur, or like a Dragon, if Dragons work more & harder than Tygurs.' B.M. Add. MSS. 40605 fo. 16 (Printed in C. S. Parker, *Sir Robert Peel* i. 29). Cf. J. Bagot, *George Canning and his friends* (London, 1909) i. 319–20.

84 *Annual biog. & obit.* xv. 136.

85 K. G. Feiling, *The second tory party 1714–1832* (London, 1938) p. 222.

86 Pellew, *Sidmouth* ii. 302; Bagot, *Canning & his friends* i. 39.

87 Parker, *Peel* i. 27.

88 Holland, *Further memoirs* p. 323; Cox, *Recollections* p. 174.

89 *Dudley-Copleston Corr.* p. 192; *Colchester Diary* ii. 525.

90 H. D. Beste, *Personal and literary memorials* (London, 1829) pp. 215–6.

91 Bodl. MS. Top. Oxon. d. 354/1 fo. 23.

92 A. Heber, *The life of Reginald Heber* (London, 1830) i. 449.

93 E. Tatham, *A letter to the Rev. the Dean of Christ Church . . .* (Oxford, 1807) p. 7.

94 B.M. Add. MSS. 38243 fos. 242–3 cf. fo. 221.

95 In 1854 Osborne Gordon explained to Gladstone that Christ Church 'prestige is owing mainly to the credit connected with the names of some of the nominees of the Dean and Canons, many of whom were appointed under high influence, and at once took or were in the way of being promoted, by merit or otherwise, to high positions in the world, and whose elevation reacted on the character and estimation of the whole society.' B.M. Add. MSS. 44379 fo. 227.

96 E.g. *The correspondence of the Rt. Hon. William Wickham* ed. W. Wickham (London, 1870) i. 87. cf. *The literary remains of Henry Fynes Clinton*, ed. C. J. Fynes Clinton (London, 1854) p. 214.

97 *Hist. MSS. Comm. Fortescue MSS.* vii. 37, 39.

98 Colchester MSS. C. Jackson to C. Abbot, June 5, 1807. P.R.O. 30/9/15.

99 *Dudley-Copleston Corr.* p. 192n.

100 E. H. Barker, *Parriana, or notices of the Rev. Samuel Parr* (London, 1828) i. 421.

101 MS. Colchester Diary. P.R.O. 30/9/33 fo. 21.

102 Duke of Buckingham and Chandos, *Memoirs of the courts and cabinets of George III* (London, 1855) iv. 340.

103 H. L. Thompson, *Christ Church* (London, 1900) pp. 179–80. Cf. Jackson's spirited battle with Lord Leicester in 1799, the latter having installed his mistress as deputy postmaster of Oxford, and she now using her house for immoral purposes. B.M. Add. MSS. 34454 fos. 171–3; 34455 fos. 170–8.

104 *The Diary of the Rt. Hon. William Windham, 1784–1810* ed. Mrs. H. Baring (London, 1866) p. 244.

105 On the operation of this system; Colchester MSS. S. Smith to C. Abbot, Nov. 20, 1812. P.R.O. 30/9/16; *The letters of King George IV 1812–30* ed. A. Aspinall (Cambridge, 1938) iii. 62, 63–4; B.M. Add. MSS. 38576 fos. 41–5; 34587 fos. 417–8; *Colchester Diary* iii. 320; Parker, *Peel* i. 322; *Reminiscences of Oxford by Oxford men* ed. L. M. Quiller-Couch. Oxford Historical Society xxii. 320.

106 *Dudley-Copleston Corr.* p. 192n.

107 University archives. MS. Minutes of Hebdomadal Meeting 1788–1803; E. Tatham, *A new address to the free and independent members of Convocation* (Oxford, 1810) p. 2.

22

108 *Times* April 25, 1800.

109 W. J. Copleston, *Memoir of Edward Copleston* (London, 1851) p. 63.

110 Broadsheet of May 20, 1800 in *University Notices 1662-1821* (Bodl. G. A. Oxon. b. 19); University archives. MS. Convocation Register 1793–1802 fos. 376–396; MS. Richard Jenkyns's Diary, May 21, 1800. Balliol College. MS. Jenkyns VI. This entry gives the names of the committee of heads who prepared the statute.

111 On this theme: R. Churton, *The will of God the ground and principle of civil as well as religious obedience,* (Oxford, 1790) pp. 8, 11; R. Churton, *Sermon preached before the university of Oxford . . . on . . . April* 19, 1793 (Oxford, 1793) pp. 15–17; Magdalen College MSS. D.6.3. W. Jones to M. J. Routh, March 5, 1792.

112 University archives. MS. Minutes of Hebdomadal Meeting 1788–1803 fo. 75.

113 *Heber Letters* p. 163; Balliol College. MS. Jenkyns VI. MS. Letterbook of John Wills fo. 6.

114 Cox, *Recollections* pp. 11–12, 21.

115 *British Magazine* 1800 pp. 425–6.

116 Ward & Heywood, *Statutes* ii. 29 *seq.*

117 *Ibid.* ii. 63.

118 *Ibid.* ii. 64, *seq.*

119 J. Bateman, *Life of the Rev. Daniel Wilson* (London, 1860) i. 65. Cf. University archives. MS. Hebdomadal Register 1803–23 fos. 109–111; broadsheet of June 5, 1807, *University Notices 1662–1821* (Bodl. G. A. Oxon. b. 19); *Report of Oxford University Commission* 1852. Evidence, p. 25.

120 Ward & Heywood, *Statutes* ii. 79.

121 *Ibid.* ii. 101–2.

122 University archives. MS. Hebdomadal Register 1803–23 fos. 63, 109–111, 115.

123 E. Tatham, *A fifth address to the free and independent Members of Convocation* (Oxford, 1808); E. Tatham, *A new address to the free and independent members of Convocation* (Oxford, 1810).

124 University archives. MS. Hebdomadal Register 1803–23 fos. 2, 10.

125 Tatham's pamphlets were collected under the title *Oxonia purgata* (London, 1812). Cf. *Hist. MSS. Comm. Fortescue MSS.* ix. 430.

126 E. Tatham, *Letter to the Dean of Christ Church* p. 10.

127 E. Tatham, *An address to the members of Convocation at large on the proposed statute of examinations* (Oxford, 1807) p. 6.

128 *The literary remains of Henry Fynes Clinton* p. 230.

129 E. Tatham, *A new address to free and independent members of Convocation* pp. 15–17.

130 J. E. Stock, *Memoirs of Thomas Beddoes* p. 24.

131 Bodl. MS. Top. Oxon. c. 236 fo. 20.

132 T. J. Hogg, *Life of Shelley* ed. H. Wolfe. i. 49.

133 Quoted in E. Dowden, *Life of Percy Bysshe Shelley* (London, 1886) i. 55-6.

134 Tatham, *New address* p. 17.

135 In 1787 it was said by a friend that Wm. Jackson might easily have had the Hebrew chair 'if he had but made good his pretensions to Hebrew learning.' Bodl. MS. Top. Oxon. d. 353/1 fo. 65.

136 R. Southey, *Letters from England by Don Manuel Alvarez Espriella* (London, 1807) ii. 77; J. W. Ward, Earl of Dudley, *Letters to Ivy* (London, 1905) p. 181; A. Heber, *Life of R. Heber* i. 499.

137 George Smith, *Bishop Heber* (London, 1895) p. 18.

138 Keble College MSS. Letters from John Keble to his sisters. John Keble to Elizabeth Keble, Nov. 15, 1807.

139 *The remains of the late Edward Copleston, D.D., Bishop of Llandaff* ed. R. Whately (London, 1854) p. 2.

140 W. J. Fitzpatrick, *Memoirs of Richard Whately* (London, 1864) i. 11-13.

141 *Heber letters* pp. 220-222.

142 MS. Oriel College Letters no. 389.

143 W. J. Copleston, *Memoir of Edward Copleston* p. 186.

144 Henry Kett, *Logic made easy* (Oxford, 1809); E. Copleston, *The examiner examined: or logic vindicated* (Oxford, 1809).

145 [E. Copleston] *Advice to a reviewer, with a specimen of the art* (Oxford, 1807); *Copleston's remains* p. 6.n.

146 *Heber letters* pp. 226-8, 238, cf. 243.

147 *Edinburgh Review* vii. 113 *seq.*

148 *Ibid.* xi. 279-283.

149 *Ibid.* xv. 40-53.

150 *Ibid.* xiv. 429-432.

151 M. L. Clarke, *Greek studies in England, 1700-1830* (Cambridge, 1945) p. 100.

152 A first, lame, defence was made by a correspondent to the *Times* Sept. 29, 1809.

153 E. Copleston, *A reply to the calumnies of the Edinburgh Review against Oxford* (2nd ed. Oxford, 1810) pp. 15-19.

154 E. Copleston, *A second reply to the Edinburgh Review* (Oxford, 1810) p. 16. This view was not shared by another Oxford defender, H. H. Drummond, *Observations suggested by the strictures of the Edinburgh Review* (Edinburgh, 1810).

155 Copleston, *Reply to calumnies.* pp. 111-3.

156 *Ibid.* pp. 133-4.

157 *Edinburgh Review* xvi. 180.

158 J. Davison, *Remains and occasional publications* (Oxford, 1841) pp. 347 *seq.*, 408 *seq.*

159 E. Copleston, *A third reply to the Edinburgh Review* (Oxford, 1811).

160 Cf. Philalethes, *A letter to the Rector of Lincoln College* (Oxford, 1807).

161 Copleston, *Memoir of Edward Copleston* pp. 47, 64.

162 University archives. MS. Hebdomadal Register 1803–23 fo. 375.

163 J. H. Newman, *On the scope and nature of university education* Discourse VI. A contemporary who began as an admirer of Copleston, but finally delivered much more radical attacks on Oxford in the *Edinburgh Review* was Sir William Hamilton. J. Veitch, *Memoir of Sir William Hamilton* (London, 1869) pp. 35–6.

164 Copleston, *Memoir of Edward Copleston* p. 188.

165 During Copleston's years as Provost, 1814–28, Oriel won 27 firsts, Christ Church 82.

166 *Dudley-Copleston Corr.* pp. 83–4, 107–8, 191–4.

CHAPTER II

1 University archives. MS. Convocation Register 1793–1802 fos. 440–1.

2 Colchester MSS. W. Vincent to C. Abbot, Nov. 7, 1806. P.R.O. 30/9/15.

3 Colchester MSS. Sir W. Dolben to Dean of Christ Church, July 11, 1806. P.R.O. 30/9/15.

4 *Heber letters* p. 263.

5 *Times* January 22, 1802.

6 In 1798 he had received an honorary D.C.L. as colonel of the university Volunteers. B.M. Add. MSS. 37909 fo. 5.

7 *Ibid.* fo. 9.

8 Ward, *Georgian Oxford* pp. 276–8; *Works of Samuel Parr* vii. 210.

9 T. Maurice, *Memoirs of the author of 'Indian Antiquities'* (London, 1820) ii. 9–10. Cf. Gibbon, *Memoirs* p. 80; *Annual biog. & obit.* ix. 449.

10 Parker, *Peel* i. 19; Lord Brougham, *Historical sketches of statesmen who flourished in the time of George III* (London, 1839–43) ii. 73–4.

11 Sir William Holdsworth, *History of English law* xiii. 676–80.

12 Magdalen College MSS. D.6.13 G. Hirst to M. J. Routh, July 18, 1793.

13 *Colchester Diary* i. 197.

14 P.R.O. 30/9/33 MS. Colchester Diary fo. 47.

15 Balliol College. MS. Jenkyns VI. Richard Jenkyns's MS. diary, March 23, 1801.

16 B.M. Add. MSS. 40266 fos. 134–5; University archives. MS. Hebdomadal Register 1803–23 fo. 114.

17 *Parliamentary History* xxxvi. 483–5.

18 Pellew, *Sidmouth* ii. 189.

19 *Times* June 2, 1802; June 13, 1803.

20 University archives. MS. Hebdomadal Register 1803–23 fos. 13–15, 75, 77–83, 145–7, 232–9; *Colchester Diary* i. 545–6; ii. 98, 147–8, 375, 390; Colchester MSS. P.R.O. 30/9/15 corr. between J. Parsons and

C. Abbot, April 25–May 24, 1808; S. Walpole, *Life of Spencer Perceval* (London, 1874) i. 281–4. A bill became law in 1812 and was taken further with Scott's support in 1817; *Parliamentary debates* xxxvi. 683; E. Halévy, *History of the English people in the nineteenth century* (Eng. tr. London, 1924–51). i. 442–5.

21 Balliol College. MS. Jenkyns VI. Richard Jenkyns's MS. Diary, May 7, 1805.

22 Cf. B.M. Add. MSS. 37909 fo. 13.

23 B.M. Add. MSS. 37909 fo. 26; Cf. E. S. Roscoe, *Lord Stowell* (London, 1916) p. 2.

24 B.M. Add. MSS. 37909 fo. 7.

25 *Ibid.* fo. 22. Routh, who died in 1854 in his hundredth year, had been the 'venerable President' even in 1795. B.M. Add. MSS. 22549 fo. 16.

26 *Reliquiae sacrae* (Oxford, 1814–48).

27 Oxford, 1823.

28 B.M. Add. MSS. 22549 fo. 16.

29 Who found a refuge for himself and his library at Magdalen in 1791 when threatened by the rioters who destroyed Priestley's house at Birmingham. Magdalen College MSS. D.5.23, cutting from *Times* Dec. 25, 1854.

30 Magdalen College MSS. D.5.8. M. J. Routh to Samuel Parr, Jan. 14, 1789.

31 Magdalen College MSS. D.5.12. Letter of Jan. 17, 1800.

32 Magdalen College MSS. D.5.23. Register p. 35.

33 *Heber letters* p. 242.

34 B.M. Add. MSS. 37887 fo. 11.

35 Magdalen College MSS. D.5.8. M. J. Routh to Samuel Parr, March 10, 1790.

36 Magdalen College MSS. D.5.12. Memorial attacking R.C. use of the word 'catholic'.

37 B.M. Add. MSS. 37909 fo. 22. This is quite clear despite J. B. Mozley's statements to the contrary in the obituary of Routh which he wrote for the *Times* Dec. 25, 1854 (Magdalen College MSS. D.5.23.).

38 *Works of Samuel Parr* vii. 648; Magdalen College MSS. D.5.8. M. J. Routh to S. Parr, May 22, 1792; cf. *Diary of the Rt. Hon. William Windham 1784–1810* p. 376.

39 A. P. Stanley, *Life and correspondence of Dr. Arnold* (London, 1901) pp. 7–8.

40 Bodl. MS. Add. D.77 fos. 58–9. A similar doctrine was expounded to Dr. Hughes for dissemination in the University (B.M. Add. MSS. 37909 fos. 14–19) and again to Sir John Coxe Hippisley. *Ibid.* fos. 52–3.

41 In 1800 he had been fancied for the Irish primacy. Duke of Buckingham, *Courts and Cabinets of George III.* iii 29, 44. Being resident in Oxford, Cleaver had confirmed and performed other episcopal duties during Bishop Smalwell's last infirmities. Bateman, *Life of Daniel Wilson* i. 56.

42 *Hist. MSS. Comm. Fortescue MSS.* vi. 68-92 *passim.*

43 B.M. Add. MSS. 37909 fo. 9; *Hist. MSS. Comm. Fortescue MSS.* vii. 285.

44 *Annual biog. & obit.* xix. 424-5.

45 Who in 1822 became Bishop of Calcutta.

46 *Heber letters* pp. 244-5, 263-5.

47 *Ibid.* pp. 199–200.

48 J. W. Burgon, *Lives of twelve good men* (London, 1891) p. 3.

49 *Heber letters* p. 198.

50 B.M. Add. MSS. 37909 fos. 22, 30.

51 *Ibid.* fo. 161.

52 *Ibid.* fos. 76, 197.

53 *Ibid.* fo. 64.

54 *Ibid.* fos. 32, 38, 99, 101. Robert Lukin who was sent down specially to University College, was on the whole discouraging. *The Windham papers* (London, 1913) ii. 254–61.

55 B.M. Add. MSS. 37909 fo. 44. When Portland became premier he made Marlow a prebendary of Canterbury.

56 *Ibid.* fo. 49.

57 B.M. Add. MSS. 37845 fo. 104. Cf. 37909 fo. 3.

58 *Ibid.* fos. 74, 89, 108, 121–5, 138; *Windham papers* ii. 255.

59 B.M. Add. MSS. 37909 fos. 92, 112; *Windham papers* ii. 257.

60 B.M. Add. MSS. 37909 fo. 119.

61 *Ibid.* fo. 130. In 1806 Tatham 'plumped' for Abbot against Heber, so the presumption is that he favoured Windham on this occasion.

62 *Heber letters* p. 198.

63 Magdalen College MSS. D.5.8. M. J. Routh to S. Parr, Oct. 23, 1806; D.5.19. W. Windham to M. J. Routh, April 27, 1807.

64 Especially by Archdeacon Churton, *The reality of the Powder Plot vindicated from some recent misrepresentations* (Oxford, 1806). In 1802 he had affirmed it to be Reformation doctrine that the Roman Church is the present representation of Anti-Christ. *Anti-Christ or the Man of Sin* (Oxford, 1804).

65 MS. Colchester Diary. P.R.O. 30/9/33 fo. 47.

66 B.M. Add. MSS. 37909 fo. 1.

67 *Ibid.* fo. 180.

68 *Colchester Diary* i. 259; MS. Colchester Diary June 29, 1805. P.R.O. 30/9/33. The first thought of the Chapter had been Thomas Grenville, brother of the marquis of Buckingham and Lord Grenville, but he was well provided for by the marquis, and unwilling to contest either the Speakership or the Oxford seat with Abbot. *Colchester Diary* i. 197, 411; *The Creevey Papers* ed. Sir Herbert F. Maxwell (London, 1904) i. 4; *Hist. MSS. Comm. Fortescue MSS.* vii. 128, 285; viii. 391; Colchester MSS. T. Grenville to C. Abbot, Oct. 17, 1806. P.R.O.

30/9/15; Buckingham, *Courts & cabinets of George III* iv. 87–8; *Parliamentary debates* viii. 11.

69 *Colchester Diary* ii. 17; MS. Colchester Diary Oct. 13, 1806. P.R.O. 30/9/34.

70 For such an occasion Marlborough and Auckland could patch up an arrangement for him, and Jackson felt his Oxford prospects were most convincing. MS. Colchester Diary June 29, 1805; Oct. 13–15, 1806. P.R.O. 30/9/33–4.

71 *Ibid.* May 12, July 1, 4, 5, 13, Oct. 13, 1806; Colchester MSS. C. Jackson to C. Abbot, Friday. P.R.O. 30/9/15.

72 MS. Colchester Diary July 8, 1806. P.R.O. 30/9/34; Colchester MSS. C. Jackson to C. Abbot, Aug. 20, 1806. P.R.O. 30/9/15.

73 Colchester MSS. S. Smith to C. Abbot, Nov. 4, 9, 1806. P.R.O. 30/9/15. Upon the advice of Hodson, Richard Heber refused to allow his friends to petition against Abbot's return upon these grounds. A. Heber, *Life of Reginald Heber* i. 322; *Heber letters* p. 214; Colchester MSS. R. Heber to C. Abbot, Nov. 9, 1806. P.R.O. 30/9/15.

74 The mass of correspondence relating to this confusion is to be found in P.R.O. 30/9/15, and especially in a MS. booklet in which Abbot summarised his grievances. Perceval's verdict was that though Abbot had read more into Richards's assurances than was warranted, there was no occasion for a quarrel between gentlemen since neither had tried to deceive the other. See also, MS. Colchester Diary Oct. 15–29, 1806. P.R.O. 30/9/34.

75 *An authentic copy of the poll* (Oxford, 1806).

76 *Heber letters* p. 244; A. Heber, *Life of R. Heber* i. 322.

77 *Heber letters* p. 215. Abbot was characterised as a 'nasty little stinking imp,' and 'the nasty little lick-spittle of the Duke of M[arlborough].'

78 University archives. MS. Hebdomadal Register 1803–23 fos. 119, 120–2; Colchester MSS. H. Richards to C. Abbot, March 10, 1807; C. Jackson to same, March 11, 1807, and n.d. P.R.O. 30/9/15.

79 *Literary remains of Henry Fynes Clinton* p. 26.

80 B.M. Add. MSS. 38242 fo. 68.

81 Colchester MSS. C. Jackson to C. Abbot n.d. [March 16, 1807] P.R.O. 30/9/15.

82 Colchester MSS. C. Jackson to C. Abbot, Sunday [April 19, 1807] P.R.O. 30/9/15.

83 University archives. MS. Hebdomadal Register 1803–23 fos. 124–6.

84 *Ibid.* fos. 179–81 (Another copy B.M. Add. MSS. 38243 fos. 249–50).

85 B.M. Add. MSS. 38473 fo. 220.

86 M. Roberts, *The Whig party 1807–1812* (London, 1939) p. 356.

87 Pellew, *Sidmouth* iii. 12, 14, 17–18; Devon C.R.O. Sidmouth MSS. Box J., Lord Grenville to Lord Sidmouth, Oct. 23, Nov. 4, 1809; Box F., N. Vansittart to Lord Sidmouth, Nov. 4, 1809.

88 B.M. Add. MSS. 38473 fos. 212–4, 220.

89 *Ibid.* fos. 332–4, 336–8; 38321 fos. 149–50; C. D. Yonge, *The life and administration of Robert Bankes, second earl of Liverpool* (London, 1868) i. 298–9.

90 H. Twiss, *Life of Lord Chancellor Eldon* (2nd ed. London, 1844) i. 360–1.

91 B.M. Add. MSS. 38473 fo. 220.

92 Magdalen College MSS. D.6.16. Charles Wetherell to M. J. Routh, Nov. 3, 1805.

93 B.M. Add. MSS. 38243 fo. 377.

94 Twiss, *Eldon* ii. 107–9; B.M. Add. MSS. 38473 fo. 337.

95 Devon C.R.O. Sidmouth MSS. Box K, H. Beeke to Lord Sidmouth, Nov. 17, 1809; Magdalen College MSS. D.5.8. Nov. 18, 1809. (Cf. *Works of Samuel Parr* vii. 666). Like the other candidates Beaufort had been talked of for several years. *Hist. MSS.*|*Comm. Fortescue MSS.* viii. 167.

96 Bagot, *Canning and his friends* i. 341–2.

97 Colchester MSS. Lord Sidmouth to C. Abbot, Nov. 24, 1809. P.R.O. 30/9/15; B.M. Add. MSS. 38473 fo. 337; 34567 fo. 85; *Times* Nov. 8, 1809.

98 B.M. Add. MSS. 38321 fos. 155, 163; Colchester MSS. S. Smith to C. Abbot, Nov. 3, 1809. P.R.O. 30/9/15.

99 Twiss, *Eldon* ii, 112, 114. This account shows signs of retouching, for, at the time, Eldon ascribed his candidature to the pressure not of the king, but of leading members of the university.

100 *Hist. MSS. Comm. Fortescue MSS.* viii. 167; *Colchester Diary* ii. 45. In 1807 he was working upon lists of voters. *Hist. MSS. Comm. Fortescue MSS.* ix. 359.

101 *Auckland Corr.* iv. 330.

102 *Hist. MSS. Comm. Fortescue MSS.* ix. 341.

103 *Ibid.* ix. 387–8.

104 H. Bathurst, *Memoirs of the late Dr. Henry Bathurst* (London, 1837) i. 95–6; Bodl. MS. Top. Oxon. d. 356 fo. 128; Devon C.R.O. Sidmouth MSS. Box J, Lord Grenville to Lord Sidmouth, Nov. 4, 1809; Colchester MSS. S. Smith to C. Abbot, Nov. 10, 1809. P.R.O. 30/9/15; B.M. Add. MSS. 38473 fo. 336.

105 *Ibid.* ix. 349, 373, 383, 404–5; *The Farington Diary* ed. J. Greig (London, 1923–8) vii. 146.

106 Devon C.R.O. Sidmouth MSS. Box K, H. Beeke to Lord Sidmouth, Nov. 17, 1809.

107 Twiss, *Eldon* ii. 111; *Hist. MSS. Comm. Fortescue MSS.* ix. 420; *A series of letters of the first earl of Malmesbury . . . from 1745–1820* (London, 1870) ii. 196–7.

108 *Auckland Corr.* iv. 333.

109 The duke of Grafton.

110 Twiss, *Eldon* ii. 110.

111 *Hist. MSS. Comm. Fortescue MSS.* ix. 383.

112 B.M. Add. MSS. 38321 fo. 162.

113 *Hist. MSS. Comm. Fortescue MSS.* ix. 426.

114 W. J. Copleston, *Memoir of Edward Copleston* p. 25.

115 *Hist. MSS. Comm. Fortescue MSS.* ix. 365.

116 *Ibid.* ix. 381.

117 Colchester MSS. W. Church to C. Abbot, Nov. 4, 1809. P.R.O. 30/9/15.

118 *Hist. MSS. Comm. Fortescue MSS.* ix. 365.

119 *Ibid.* ix. 373.

120 *Times* Nov. 20, 1809.

121 *Hist. MSS. Comm. Fortescue MSS.* ix. 374–5, 378, 393.

122 Broadsheet signed 'A member of Convocation,' *University Notices 1662–1821* (Bodl. G. A. Oxon. b. 19).

123 *Hist. MSS. Comm. Fortescue MSS.* ix 382.

124 Cox, *Recollections* p. 66; Buckingham, *Courts & Cabinets of George III* iv. 402; *Hist. MSS. Comm. Fortescue MSS.* ix. 390, 392, 396, 402–3, 422.

125 *A letter to the electors of the University of Oxford upon the present contest for the Chancellorship of that University.* (Oxford, 1809); Broadsheet headed *Memento*, 1809 in *University Notices 1662–1821* (Bodl. G. A. Oxon. b. 19).

126 *Hist. MSS. Comm. Fortescue MSS.* ix. 350; B.M. Add. MSS. 37909 fo. 256.

127 *Hist. MSS. Comm. Fortescue MSS.* ix. 343.

128 *Times* Dec. 6, 15, 20, 1809.

129 *A case of singular distress* in *University Notices 1662–1821* (Bodl. G. A. Oxon. b. 19).

130 *To members of Convocation* Oxford Dec. 11, 1809, *Ibid.*

131 *Heber letters* p. 230.

132 *Times* Dec. 2, 1809; *To the members of Convocation* Oxford, Dec. 12, 1809 in *University Notices 1662–1821* (Bodl. G. A. Oxon. b. 19.)

133 *Hist. MSS. Comm. Fortescue MSS.* ix. 364.

134 *Ibid.* ix. 395.

135 *Ibid.* ix. 401.

136 *Ibid.* ix. 364. Replies from the *Courier* were reprinted as a pamphlet one copy of which is in *University Notices 1662–1821* (Bodl. G. A. Oxon; b. 19).

137 *Hist. MSS. Comm. Fortescue MSS.* ix. 401.

138 *Bath Chronicle* Nov. 30, 1809 (B.M. Add. MSS. 37909 fo. 278).

139 *Hist. MSS. Comm. Fortescue MSS.* ix. 359–62 (for an abstract, *Colchester Diary* ii. 224).

140 Lord Holland, *Further memoirs of the whig party* p. 42.

141 *Times* Dec. 2, 1809; *Courier* Dec. 2, 1809 in *University Notices 1662–1821* (Bodl. G. A. Oxon. b. 19).

142 *Courier* Dec. 7, 12, 1809, in *University Notices 1662–1821* (Bodl. G. A. Oxon. b. 19); *Times* Dec. 5, 1809.

143 Buckingham, *Courts and cabinets of George III* iv. 401. The stages through which the figures were arrived at can be traced in *Hist. MSS. Comm. Fortescue MSS.* ix. 366, 369, 370, 372, 386, 400. One of Grenville's canvass books is preserved as Bodl. MS. Top. Oxon. b. 252. Cf. Bodl. MS. Top. Oxon. d. 356 fo. 130.

144 The constituency numbered less than 1300.

145 *Hist. MSS. Comm. Fortescue MSS.* ix. 400.

146 *Ibid.* 429.

147 Cox, *Recollections* p. 66.

148 *Auckland Corr.* iv. 335.

149 Colchester MSS. W. J[ackson] to C. Abbot, Dec. 18, 1809. P.R.O. 30/9/15.

150 *Hist. MSS. Comm. Fortescue MSS.* ix. 409, 411–412.

151 *Ibid.* ix. 429.

152 J. Coker, *Some reflections on the late election of a Chancellor for the University of Oxford* (Maidstone, 1809).

153 [E. Copleston] *A letter to John Coker Esq. of New College* (Oxford, 1810) pp. 14, 15. On these grounds Copleston seems to have favoured the admission of Jews to civil rights. *Copleston's Remains* p. 37.

154 J. Coker, *An answer to a letter addressed by the Rev. Edw. Copleston to John Coker* (Maidstone, 1810); *An answer to a second letter from Rev. Edw. Copleston* (Oxford, 1810). See also, *Remarks on the power of Proctors in Convocation* (Oxford, 1810).

155 Pellew, *Sidmouth* iii. 19.

156 e.g. *Hist. MSS. Comm. Fortescue MSS.* x. 3.

157 Twiss, *Eldon* ii. 115.

158 *Hist. MSS. Comm. Fortescue MSS.* ix. 419, 422.

159 T. J. Hogg, *Life of Shelley* ed. H. Wolfe i. 155–6.

160 Duke of Buckingham and Chandos, *Memoirs of the court of George IV, 1820–30* (London, 1859) i. 474.

161 Holland, *Further memoirs of whig party* p. 41. In 1814 it was recommended to Copleston as an 'excellent *hoax*' to put it about that Grenville would return to office, nothing being then less likely. *Dudley-Copleston Corr.* p. 49.

162 *Auckland Corr.* iv. 336.

163 *Colchester Diary* ii. 223; Colchester MSS. Letters between J. Parsons and C. Abbot, May 23, June 4, 1810. P.R.O. 30/9/15.

164 *Times* July 4, 1810.

165 W. D. Macray, *Annals of the Bodleian Library, Oxford* (2nd ed. Oxford, 1890) p. 290.

166 *Hist. MSS. Comm. Fortescue MSS.* x. 36.

167 *London Chronicle* July 5–6, 1810 (one copy in Balliol Coll. MS. Jenkyns I.).

168 *Times* July 6, 1810; but cf. Colchester MSS. Encaenia verses, 1810. P.R.O. 30/9/15.

169 Devon C.R.O. Sidmouth MSS. Box J, Bp. of Gloucester to Lord Sidmouth, July 25, 1810.

170 *Times* July 9, 10, 1810.

171 *Hist. MSS. Comm. Fortescue MSS.* x. 191–2.

172 Colchester MSS. J. Parsons to C. Abbot, April 17, 1812. P.R.O. 30/9/16.

173 *Ibid.* S. Smith to C. Abbot, April 17, 1812.

174 *Times* April 20, 1812.

175 *Parliamentary debates* xxii. 790.

176 *Times* April 24, 1812.

177 *Parliamentary debates* xxii. 840–1. A good many other hard things were said about the university in the later stages of this debate.

178 University archives. MS. Hebdomadal Register 1803–23 fo. 295.

179 Twiss, *Eldon* ii. 245.

180 B.M. Add. MSS. 34583 fo. 447.

181 A. Blomfield, *A memoir of Charles James Blomfield D.D. Bishop of London* (London, 1863) i. 30. Cf. *Works of Samuel Parr* vii. 135–8.

182 University archives. MS. Hebdomadal Register 1803–23 fos. 246, 248–9. Grenville dissented very forcibly and added his 'strong disapprobation of the terms in which it is expressed.' *Parliamentary debates* xxiv. 112–3.

183 *To the members of Convocation*, Nov. 10, 1812; *Catholic emancipation* Nov. 11, 1812. Both in *University Notices 1662–1821* (Bodl. G. A. Oxon. b. 19.)

184 Colchester MSS. S. Smith to C. Abbot, Nov. 12, 1812. P.R.O. 30/9/16.

185 *Times* Nov. 16, 1812.

186 University archives. MS. Hebdomadal Register 1803–23 fos. 302–10; *Hist. MSS. Comm. Fortescue MSS.* x. 370–380; *Auckland Corr.* iv. 410.

187 National Library of Wales. Ottley & Pitchford Hall MSS. Letter books of 3rd earl of Liverpool. Charles Cecil Cope-Jenkinson to C. H. Hall, Feb. 5, 1810.

188 A. Heber, *Life of R. Heber* i. 499; cf. Parker, *Peel* i. 251–2.

189 Colchester MSS. J. Webber to Lord Colchester, Dec. 21, 1817. P.R.O. 30/9/16.

190 *Ibid.* C. H. Hall to C. Abbot, Jan. 26, 1817; C. Abbot to C. H. Hall, Jan. 27, 1817; B.M. Add. MSS. 40344 fo. 41.

191 B.M. Add. MSS. 38275 fos. 63–4, 171–3; 40344 fo. 73; 40356 fos. 321, 323.

192 *Letters of King George IV* iii. 57.

193 Yonge, *Liverpool* iii. 387. Liverpool's letter to Hall refusing him a bishopric (B.M. Add. MSS. 38574 fo. 176) is printed in Yonge, *op. cit.* iii. 10–11, without Hall's name.

194 B.M. Add. MSS. 38298 fo. 170; 38299 fo. 162.

195 eg. *Letters of King George IV* ii. 550–51.

196 A. Heber, *Life of R. Heber* i. 499. Cf. the impressive roll of Christ Church luminaries when Pusey went up in 1819. H. P. Liddon, *Life of Edward Bouverie Pusey* (London, 1893–7) i. 23–4.

197 B.M. Add. MSS. 40342 fos. 117–20; *Times* May 30, 1823, p. 3; June 2, 1823, p. 3.

CHAPTER III

1 University archives. MS. Hebdomadal Register 1803–23 fo. 345.

2 *A correct account of the visit of His Royal Highness the Prince Regent* (Oxford, 1814). Cf. *An authentic account of the visit* (Oxford, 1814); Devon C.R.O. Sidmouth MSS. Box J, Lord Grenville to Lord Sidmouth, May 28, 1814, *et seq.*

3 *Times* June 15, 1814, p. 3.

4 Cox, *Recollections* p. 81.

5 Bodl. MS. Top. Oxon. b. 23 fo. 3b.

6 University archives. MS. Hebdomadal Register 1803–23 fos. 359–60: Devon C.R.O. Sidmouth MSS. Box J, Lord Grenville to Lord Sidmouth, Nov. 4, 1814.

7 University archives. MS. Hebdomadal Register 1803–23 fo. 349; *Farington diary* viii. 21.

8 In commemoration of his visit, the king of Prussia in 1818 presented the President of Corpus with 'a beautiful porcelain vase' made at Berlin. *Times* Aug. 24, 1818, p. 2.

9 Cox, *Recollections* pp. 88–9.

10 *Times* Oct. 19, 1818, p. 3; Bodl. MS. Top. Oxon. c. 31 fos. 3–4, 11.

11 For a fuller account of this election see N. Gash, *Mr. Secretary Peel* (London, 1961) pp. 211–18.

12 *Hist. MSS. Comm. Fortescue MSS.* x. 129.

13 Colchester MSS. Sir W. Scott to C. Abbot, Sept. 18, 1812. P.R.O. 30/9/16.

14 *Times* April 22, 1814.

15 *Colchester Diary* ii. 328.

16 Bagot, *Canning and his friends* i. 341–2.

17 *Colchester Diary* ii. 374, 384. J. W. Ward took his M.A. in order to vote for Canning. J. W. Ward, Earl of Dudley, *Letters to Ivy* ed. S. H. Romilly (London, 1905) p. 177.

18 *Colchester Diary* ii. 478, 497. For Canning's hopes in 1816, Bagot, *Canning and his friends* ii. 27.

19 *Colchester Diary* ii. 618–19; Colchester MSS. Lord Colchester to G. Canning, June 23, 1817. P.R.O. 30/9/16.

20 Parker, *Peel* i. 21.

21 B.M. Add. MSS. 40265 fo. 111.

22 Parker, *Peel* i. 179–80.

23 *Ibid.* i. 226, 250; Bagot, *Canning and his friends* ii. 45.

24 *Ibid*. ii. 50. It is apparent from Vansittart's controversy with John Coker (*Letters that have lately appeared in the Oxford and Cambridge papers . . . on the crusade of the nineteenth century collected . . . by Peter the Hermit* (London, 1812); N. Vansittart *Letter to John Coker Esq*. reprinted in *The Pamphleteer* no. 1. (London, 1813)) that the teaching received as 'novel' by Newman from Dr. Hawkins, that the inquirer should seek doctrine from the church, and merely verify it from Scripture (*Apologia Pro Vita Sua* (London, 1887) p. 9) was familiar in Oxford as a high-church argument against the Bible Society's policy of cooperating with dissenters in disseminating editions of the Scriptures without notes approved by church authority.

25 *Colchester Diary* iii. 5–8; Colchester MSS. S. Smith to C. Abbot. n. pl. or d. P.R.O. 30/9/16; Devon C.R.O. Sidmouth MSS. Box F, E. Goodenough to Lord Sidmouth, June 1, 1817.

26 B.M. Add. MSS. 40265 fo. 248.

27 B.M. Add. MSS. 40266 fos. 136, 145–8, 168.

28 Parker, *Peel* i. 251.

29 Colchester MSS. G. Canning to C. Abbot, May 29, 1817. P.R.O. 30/9/16.

30 Bagot, *Canning and his friends* ii. 45–6, 50–2, 54.

31 Colchester MSS. Lord Colchester to G. Canning, June 23, 1817. P.R.O. 30/9/16.

32 Described by Holland as 'galled . . . to the quick,' *Creevey Papers* i. 263.

33 Parker, *Peel* i. 252–3; B.M. Add. MSS. 40266 fos. 148–52.

34 *Ibid*. fo. 207; Colchester MSS. S. Smith to Lord Colchester, June 16, 1817. P.R.O. 30/9/16.

35 B.M. Add. MSS. 40266 fos. 168, 166.

36 Parker, *Peel* i. 252.

37 B.M. Add. MSS. 40266 fos. 145–6.

38 University archives. MS. Hebdomadal Register 1803–23 fos. 410–14; *Times*, Feb. 13, 1817, p. 3.

39 Tatham was arguing in 1816 as in 1797 for more currency, and if need be for more paper currency. E. Tatham, *Observations on the scarcity of money* (3rd ed. Oxford, 1816, reprinted in *The Pamphleteer* vii); E. Tatham, *A second letter to William Pitt on a national bank* (London, 1797). Cf. Green, *Oxford Common Room* p. 59.

40 Edward Copleston's *Letter to Rt. Hon. Robert Peel . . . on the pernicious effects of a variable standard of value . . .* (Oxford, 1819) was a prolonged attack on Vansittart and encouraged Peel to advocate the resumption of payments from the Bank.

41 The Drummond chair of political economy was endowed in 1825.

42 University archives. MS. Hebdomadal Register 1803–23 fos. 539–44. The previous term the Hebdomadal Board had taken measures against a pamphlet, *Christianity Unveiled*, on sale in Oxford, said to be replete with blasphemy. *Ibid*. fos. 531–2.

43 St. Edmund Hall. MS. Diary of John Hill, Nov. 11, 13, 29, Dec. 1, 1820; Bodl. MS. Autogr. d. 9 fos. 4, 6. George IV is said to have been hissed on his next journey through Oxford in September 1821. *Journal of Mrs. Arbuthnot 1820–32* ed. Francis Bamford and the duke of Wellington (London, 1950) i. 119.

44 University archives. MS. Hebdomadal Register 1803–23 fos. 587, 594–6; St. Edmund Hall. MS. Diary of John Hill, July 19, 1821.

45 Buckingham, *Courts of George IV* i. 87–8, 90, 98–9.

46 *Ibid.* i. 109.

47 *Ibid.* i. 52.

48 *Ibid.* i. 51.

49 See the correspondence, Magdalen College. Routh MSS. D.6/2, 4, 16, 18 *passim.*

50 Even from that stiff churchman John Keble. Keble College MSS. Miscellaneous bundle. R. Heber to J. Keble, Oct. 6, 1821.

51 For Nicholl's unsavoury dealings in the borough of Shaftesbury, *Letters of George IV* i. 312.

52 B.M. Add. MSS. 38259 fos. 132–4, 174–5, 230–1, 329, 345–6; 38260 fos. 40–1, 91.

53 Buckingham, *Court of the Regency* i. 278.

54 *Courier* Aug. 17, 1821 in *University Notices 1662–1821* (Bodl. G. A. Oxon. b. 19).

55 Colchester MSS. S. Smith to Lord Colchester, July 4, 1821. P.R.O. 30/9/16.

56 *From an anti-catholic member* Oxford, Aug. 14, in *University Notices 1662–1821* (Bodl. G. A. Oxon. b. 19).

57 These can be found in *University Notices 1662–1821* (Bodl. G. A· Oxon. b. 19).

58 *Heber letters* pp. 290–1; A. Heber, *Life of R. Heber* ii. 48. Vaughan Thomas, former fellow of Corpus, became famous in the 'thirties for his answers to Sir William Hamilton's attacks on the university, and for providing a protestant front for the Tractarian attack upon Dr. Hampden. His sermon had been preached at St. Mary's in 1816, and he now became extremely angry at the support given to Heber by the evangelical, Dr. Tournay, Warden of Wadham. V. Thomas, *Letter to Dr. Tournay* Oxford, 1821).

59 Broadsheet, Oxford, July 14, 1821, in *University Notices 1662–1821* (Bodl. G. A. Oxon. b. 19).

60 Colchester MSS. S. Smith to Lord Colchester, July 4, 1821. P.R.O. 30/9/16; *Oxford University Poll Book, 22–24 August 1821* (Oxford, 1821).

61 Magdalen College MSS. D.6.16. W. Cobbold to M. J. Routh, July 6, 1821; *Times* July 14, 1821, p. 3.

62 Broadsheet by Verax, Oxford, Aug. 18, 1821, in *University Notices 1662–1821* (Bodl. G. A. Oxon. b. 19).

63 *Heber letters* pp. 290–92. There had, however, been a great increase in matriculations under Hodson. *Brasenose Quatercentenary Monographs* vol. ii. part ii. p. 68.

64 *Heber letters* p. 301.

65 Magdalen College MSS. D.5.16. R. Heber to M. J. Routh, Jan. 17, 1826.

66 B.M. Add. MSS. 40342 fo. 179; 34569 fo. 280.

67 Peel remarked, 'Heber was so listless last session, and appeared to have such a horror of anything which might by possibility call him up in the House of Commons, that I am hardly surprised at his resignation.' B.M. Add. MSS. 40342 fo. 303.

68 *Report of the select committee on the Copyright Acts* in *Parliamentary debates* xxxviii. 1257 *seq.*

69 University archives. MS. Hebdomadal Register 1803–23 fo. 279.

70 54 Geo. III. c. 156.

71 University archives. MS. Hebdomadal Register 1803–23 fos. 325–7, 344–5.

72 B.M. Add. MSS. 40268 fo. 8.

73 University archives. MS. Hebdomadal Register 1803–23 fos. 465–7.

74 *Ibid.* fos. 487–92; (Another copy, B.M. Add. MSS. 40276 fos. 190–3).

75 *Quarterly Review* xxi. 196.

76 B.M. Add. MSS. 40342 fo. 3.

77 W. D. Macray, *Annals of the Bodleian Library, Oxford* (2nd ed. Oxford, 1890) p. 302. Such prodigality when important artistic works were being published without letterpress because of the crippling cost of delivering eleven copies to the copyright libraries, did the universities little credit. *Quarterly Review* xxi. 196.

78 University archives. MS. Hebdomadal Register 1803–23 fos. 468–9, 486–7; B.M. Add. MSS. 40274 fo. 201.

79 B.M. Add. MSS. 40276 fos. 127, 129, 194.

80 *Ibid.* fos. 283, 315; 40342 fos. 5–10.

81 *Parliamentary debates* xxxviii. 1257 *seq.*

82 *Ibid.* xxxviii. 1262.

83 B.M. Add. MSS. 40277 fo. 112.

84 *Parliamentary debates* xxxviii. 605–6.

85 B.M. Add. MSS. 40276 fo. 129; University archives. MS. Hebdomadal Register 1803–23 fos. 486–7.

86 B.M. Add. MSS. 40277 fo. 88.

87 *Parliamentary debates* xxxviii. 760–2, 1219.

88 MS. Diary of Frodsham Hodson as Vice-Chancellor 1818–1819, Bodl. MS. Top. Oxon. c. 31 fos. 114–15.

89 Buckingham, *Court of Regency* ii. 282–3, 286, 289.

90 Sir William Scott appears to have refused an invitation to serve, on the grounds that the unpaid would have no control over the paid commissioners. Pellew, *Sidmouth* iii. 224.

91 *Parliamentary debates* xl. 1339–41.

92 The correspondence is reproduced in *Curia Oxoniensis; or observations on the statutes which relate to the Vice-Chancellor's court, and power of searching houses.* (2nd ed. London, 1822).

93 B.M. Add. MSS. 40342 fos. 228–9. There is an amusing description of the relations between the Proctors and the night police in 1844 by Dean Church, *Life and letters of Dean Church* ed. Mary C. Church (London, 1895) p. 47.

94 B.M. Add. MSS. 40373 fos. 358–62.

95 B.M. Add. MSS. 40378 fo. 378.

96 B.M. Add. MSS. 40374 fos. 223–4, 227; 40378 fos. 74–5, 378–9; 40379 fos. 95–101, 250.

97 6 Geo. IV. c. 97 s.3.

98 B.M. Add. MSS. 40379 fos. 55, 89–95. There were sharp protests in the house from the radical Burdett and others, *Ibid.* fo. 251.

99 B.M. Add. MSS. 40342 fo. 286.

100 They were forbidden by the hospital rules to enter the Radcliffe.

101 University archives. MS. Minutes of the Hebdomadal Meeting 1823–33 fos. 59–60, 62, 64; B.M. Add. MSS. 40390 fos. 74–7.

102 Pellew, *Sidmouth* i. 370, 373–6, 464; ii. 514–9.

103 B.M. Add. MSS. 31229–32 *passim*.

104 B.M. Add. MSS. 31229 fos. 69–70.

105 Devon C.R.O. Sidmouth MSS. Box I Lord Sidmouth to Lord Grenville, Sept. 30, 1814; *Edinburgh Review* xv. 51; Copleston, *Reply to the Edinburgh Review* pp. 154, 172.

106 One of the unsuccessful candidates, John Penrose, solicited the chair on the strength of his research interests. B.M. Add. MSS. 38572 fo. 140; 38255 fos. 65–6.

107 See the bundle of papers on this subject in Devon C.R.O. Sidmouth MSS. Box I. Also B.M. Add. MSS. 40459 fos. 151–2.

108 G. C. White, *A versatile professor* p. 208.

109 *Ibid.* 163–5; Cox, *Recollections* p. 9; Bodl. MS. Top. Oxon. d. 354/1 fo. 4.

110 G. C. White, *A versatile professor* pp. 238–43.

111 B.M. Add. MSS. 38286 fo. 106.

112 *Times* Feb. 1, 1827, p. 4.

113 In 1817 Nares offered courses of 20 lectures on English and European history from the Romans to the Peace of 1763, and twelve lectures on political economy. *University Notices 1662–1821* (Bodl. G. A. Oxon. b. 19). For some years before his death he ceased to lecture. *Report of Oxford University Commissioners* 1852, Evidence p. 275.

114 The comment is Charles Lloyd's. B.M. Add. MSS. 40342 fo. 187.

115 Colchester MSS. Letters of Smith, Kidd, Abbot, Scott and Jackson, Oct.-Dec. 1812. P.R.O. 30/9/16.

116 University archives. MS. Hebdomadal Register 1803–23 fo. 253.

117 *Ibid.* fos. 290–1.

118 *Ibid.* fos. 498, 504; Mrs. Gordon, *Life and correspondence of William Buckland* (London, 1894) pp. 23–4.

119 Keble reported to his brother: 'Buckland is come with a diploma from the Geological Socty, at Petersburg, a bottle of red snow in his pocket, and a fixed opinion yt. there is no N.W. Passage. He has been in *Glamorgansh*. Verb. Sat.' Keble College MSS. Letters of J. Keble to T. Keble, 1807–49, n.d.

120 Yonge, *Liverpool* iii. 284–7; B.M. Add. MSS. 40342 fos. 187–9; Gunther, *Early science in Oxford* xi. 197–9.

121 Cecil Woodham-Smith, *Florence Nightingale* (Penguin ed.) p. 55; Gordon, *Life of Buckland* p. viii.

122 University archives. MS. Hebdomadal Register 1803–23 fos. 96–100.

123 *Ibid.* fo. 215.

124 University archives. MS. Minutes of Hebdomadal Meeting fos. 55, 89, 100; Cox, *Recollections* p. 84. Daubeny had already received a grant of £200 for equipment. Gunther, *Early science in Oxford* i. 74–5.

125 *Times* Jan. 13, 1819, p. 2. For senior members attending these lectures: St. Edmund Hall. MS. Diary of John Hill, March 28, 1821.

126 *Quarterly Review* xliii. 325 *seq.*; *Edinburgh Review* xxxi. 377–8; xxxv. 303. Cf. C. Babbage, *Reflections on the decline of science in England* (London, 1830). For a more favourable estimate *Times*, Nov. 6 1830, p. 3.

127 W. Ince, *The past history and present duties of the Faculty of Theology in Oxford* (Oxford, 1878) p. 24.

128 Buckingham, *Court of George IV* i. 52.

129 Richard Newton, Principal of Hertford, was made Canon of Christ Church in 1753. He died even sooner after his preferment than Hodson.

130 B.M. Add. MSS. 38286 fo. 352; 38369 fos. 313–14; 40342 fo. 194; 40344 fo. 61.

131 *Corr. of Geo. IV* ii. 499.

132 Parker, *Peel* i. 288; B.M. Add. MSS. 40265 fos. 219, 237; 40277 fo. 93; 40343 fo. 2.

133 B.M. Add. MSS. 40342 fo. 329.

134 Parker, *Peel* i. 438 *seq.*; B.M. Add. MSS. 38566 fo. 105; Devon C.R.O. Sidmouth MSS. Box J, Lord Colchester to Lord Sidmouth Feb. 1, 1827. Some observers thought that Lloyd gave good service to Peel, as to the University. *Three early nineteenth century diaries* ed. A. Aspinall (London, 1952) p. 118.

135 Lloyd's 'lectures had most nearly the character of the German lectures on Encyclopaedia, each lecture taking up half or perhaps all of a subject, and referring to the books in which these subjects could be studied in fuller detail.' W. Ince, *op. cit.* p. 25.

136 *Letters and correspondence of J. H. Newman* ed. A. Mozley (London, 1891) ii. 221.

137 *The Crypt* ii. 170.

138 University archives. MS. Minutes of Hebdomadal Meeting 1823–33 fos. 81, 163; Bodl. MS. Top. Oxon. b. 23 fo. 353.

139 Bodl. MS. Autogr. d. 9 fo. 2.

140 B.M. Add. MSS. 40342 fo. 257.

141 Balliol College. MS. Jenkyns VI. Lord Grenville to R. Jenkyns, Feb. 18, 1825.

142 *Times* Nov. 2, 1811.

143 B.M. Add. MSS. 40342 fo. 199.

144 5 Geo. IV. c. 36 cl. iv.

145 *Public Bills* 1825 vol. i.

146 Parker, *Peel* i. 385 (misdated 1826).

147 B.M. Add. MSS. 40378 fo. 109, 195. Richard Jenkyns, the Vice-Chancellor, even hoped to be able to borrow on Exchequer Bills, interest free, and at very long terms for repayment. Balliol Coll. MS. Jenkyns VI. Lord Grenville to R. Jenkyns, June 3, 1825.

148 B.M. Add. MSS. 40378 fos. 69, 239–42, 256–7, 352.

149 Hertford College had ceased to exist; its buildings were handed over to Magdalen Hall, thereby destroying what some considered an irreplaceable opportunity to expand the Bodleian (Colchester MSS. F. Barnes to Lord Colchester, April 14, 1818. P.R.O. 30/9/16); the Hall buildings acquired by Magdalen College were burned down. Magdalen College MSS. C.II. 3. 9.

150 *A few observations on All Souls College, Oxford, relative to the abuse of charities* (London, 1819); *Some animadversions on a pamphlet entitled 'A few observations on All Souls College, Oxford'* (Oxford, 1819).

151 Though Samuel Parr reckoned the election of Warden Shuttleworth in 1822 'a triumph of learning over pedantry and of constitutional principles over sacerdotal intolerance.' *Works of Samuel Parr* viii. 223.

152 For this paragraph generally, B.M. Add. MSS. 40342 fos. 198–201.

153 E. J. Whately, *Life of R. Whately* i. 46; S. Baring-Gould, *The vicar of Morwenstow* (London, 1899) p. 11; D. P. Chase, *General suggestions for the improvement of halls* (Oxford, 1854) p. 4.

154 E. J. Whately, *op. cit.* i. 46. Lloyd advised Peel to refuse Whately's appeal for money for building. B.M. Add. MSS. 40343 fo. 94.

155 Twiss, *Eldon* i. 87.

156 B.M. Add. MSS. 34457 fos. 52, 56–7; 34458 fos. 47, 425, 593.

157 Balliol College. MS. Jenkyns VI. Richard Jenkyns's Diary, Oct. 15, 1801.

158 Bodl. MS. Top. Oxon. d. 354/2 fo. 34.

159 Balliol College. MS. Jenkyns VI. Letters of Lord Grenville, Richard Jenkyns and James Blackstone, May–June 1825.

160 *Guardian* 1848 p. 583; Cox, *Recollections* p. 193. Cramer was a protégé of Charles Lloyd. B.M. Add. MSS. 40309 fo. 19.

161 Flysheet of 1829 in *Papers on new examination statute* (Bodl. G. A. Oxon. b. 21).

162 Bodl. MS. Top. Oxon. d. 15 fo. 4.

163 Cf. *The new statute* June 1, 1830, in *Papers on new examination statute* (Bodl. G. A. Oxon. b. 21.).

164 Daubeny made this point in his inaugural lecture. C. Daubeny, *Inaugural lecture on the study of Chemistry* (Oxford, 1823).

165 Bodl. MS. Top. Oxon. d. 15 fo. 72.

166 B.M. Add. MSS. 40342 fos. 358–9; Bodl. MS. Top. Oxon. d. 15 fos. 37–8, 41–7.

167 B.M. Add. MSS. 40342 fo. 360.

168 Cf. *A brief appeal to the good sense of the University of Oxford on classification of merit* . . . (Oxford, 1829).

169 [R. Walker] *A few words in favour of Professor Powell and the sciences* (Oxford, 1832).

170 And recently in *Reflections occasioned by the flirtations of Alma Mater and the Stagyrite* (Oxford, 1820).

171 MS. Oriel College Letters no. 562; [J. T. Round] *A few remarks suggested by the reprinting of the preface to Dr. Whately's 'Elements of Logic'.* (Oxford, 1829) (Bodl. G. A. Oxon. b. 21).

172 *A brief appeal to the good sense of the university* . . .

173 University archives. MS. Minutes of Hebdomadal Meeting 1823–33 fos. 1–8 and back of vol.; St. Edmund Hall. MS. Diary of John Hill, March 11, 1824.

174 Draft of examination statute annotated by Philip Bliss, Registrar (Bodl. G. A. Oxon. c. 40).

175 *Reflections on the project of changing the present examination statutes* (n. pl. or d. [Oxford, 1824]). (Bodl. G. A. Oxon. c. 40).

176 *Address to members of Convocation on the expediency of the proposed statute*, March 8, 1824 (Bodl. G. A. Oxon. c. 40).

177 *Papers on the examination statute, 1824* (Bodl. G. A. Oxon. c. 40); University archives. MS. Minutes of Hebdomadal Meeting 1823–33 fos. 9, 11.

178 Notice from the Vice-Chancellor Jan. 31, 1825 (Bodl. G. A. Oxon. c. 41); Ward & Heywood *Statutes* ii. 116 *seq.*

179 *Ibid.* ii. 131 *seq.*

180 University archives. MS. Minutes of the Hebdomadal Meeting 1823–33 fo. 101.

181 Bodl. MS. Top. Oxon. d. 15.

182 There were still advocates for the division not only of the second class, but also of the third. *Ibid.* fos. 31–2.

183 MS. Oriel College Letters no. 567.

184 MS. Oriel College Letters nos. 562, 563. It was Hampden who secured the adoption of a full fourth class with the publication of the names.

185 The alternatives recommended were four books of Euclid, or Greek or Roman history, or any ancient philosophical treatise.

186 The report is preserved in *Papers on new examination statute* (Bodl. G. A. Oxon. b. 21) cf. MS. Oriel College Letters no. 562.

187 *Agitate! Agitate! Agitate!* (Bodl. G. A. Oxon. b. 21).

188 *An address to the members of the lower division of the house of Convocation on the proposed examination statute* (Oxford, 1830). (Bodl. G. A. Oxon. b. 21).

189 Newman feared that, without a conservative statute, examiners would 'exclude Aristotle, and bring in modern subjects.' *Letters and corr.* i. 220.

190 University archives. MS. Minutes of the Hebdomadal Meeting 1823–33 fo. 121.

191 *Times* Nov. 27, 1830 p. 4; Ward & Heywood, *Statutes* ii. 160 *seq.*

192 MS. Oriel College Letters no. 746.

193 Bodl. MS. Top. Oxon. b. 23 fo. 298.

194 *Ibid.* fo. 557.

195 *The examination system* Oxford, Nov. 1, 1833 (Bodl. G. A. Oxon. b. 140); Bodl. MS. Top. Oxon. c. 236 fo. 23.

196 University archives. MS. Minutes of Hebdomadal Meeting 1823–33 fo. 189.

CHAPTER IV

1 *A memoir of Charles Louis Sand: including a narrative of the circumstances attending the death of Augustus von Kotzebue: also a defence of the German universities* (London, 1819).

2 *Ibid.* pp. xix–xx, xxxiii.

3 *Ibid.* p. 78n.

4 T. Hodgskin, *Travels in the North of Germany* (Edinburgh, 1820) ii. 265–9. Even German critics who thought that the English universities were politically preferable to their own were reported as taking a low view of their intellectual standing. *London Magazine* 1822 pp.166–72.

5 *Parliamentary debates* n.s. vii. 1292.

6 *Quarterly Review* xxiii. 446–8.

7 S. Parr, *A Spital sermon* p. 112. At the same time the liberal Crabb Robinson was making a first-hand acquaintance with the universities of Germany. He found much to admire, but deplored Paulsen 'the more than Priestly of Germany' whose 'cold deism . . . is miscalled rational Christianity.' *Crabb Robinson in Germany* ed. E. J. Morley (London, 1929) pp. 74–5, 103–4, 114–21, 150, 152–3.

8 *The correspondence of William Wilberforce* ed. R. I. and S. Wilberforce (London, 1840) ii. 394–6.

9 George Smith, *Bishop Heber* (London, 1895) p. 17.

10 H. J. Rose, *The state of protestantism in Germany* (2nd ed. Cambridge, 1829) pp. x, 1–2.

11 A. P. Stanley, *Life of Arnold* (1901 ed.) p. 71.

12 H. P. Liddon, *Life of E. B. Pusey* (London, 1893–7) i. 146 *seq.*

13 *Ibid.* i. 147.

14 John Hill, Vice-Principal of St. Edmund Hall, for example, probably read no German theology, but in 1824 met a young Lutheran ordinand at an evangelical tea-party at Wadham, who was much distressed at the liturgical policy of the king of Prussia. Hill himself several times

entertained Professor Tholuck of Berlin, at whose lectures Pusey later attended. St. Edmund Hall. MS. Diary of John Hill, Sept. 23, 1824; June 7, 1825. Cf. *The diary of the Rev. Wm. Jones 1777–1821* ed. O. F. Christie (London, 1929) p. 184.

15 B.M. Add. MSS. 40342 fos. 269–71, printed in H. H. Bellot, *University College, London 1826–1926* (London, 1929) pp. 216–17.

16 B.M. Add. MSS. 40342 fos. 273–4.

17 Cf. however, *Quarterly Review* xxxix. 133.

18 *Quarterly Review* xxxiii. 257 *seq.* This article was a very characteristic production of Edward Copleston, Provost of Oriel. W. J. Copleston, *Memoir of Edward Copleston* p. 105.

19 B.M. Add. MSS. 40342 fos. 332–3, 335.

20 *Quarterly Review* xxxvi. 216 *seq.* For the views of another candid friend: *West of England Magazine* 1828 pp. 225–34.

21 *Quarterly Review* xxxix. 128.

22 *Edinburgh Review* xliii. 326. See also, *ibid.* xlii. 222–3, 347 *seq.*

23 *Wesleyan Methodist Magazine* 3s. viii. 108 *seq.*

24 The duke of Wellington guaranteed the soundness of King's to the protestant constitution; but defaulted in passing Catholic emancipation. A letter by the earl of Winchilsea in the *Standard* describing the foundation of King's as 'a blind to the protestant and high-church party,' led to a duel between the two in which neither was injured. *Despatches, correspondence and memoranda of the duke of Wellington.* ed. 2nd duke of Wellington. 2s. v. 526.

25 Bodl. MS. Top. Oxon. b. 23 fo. 333.

26 University archives. MS. Minutes of Hebdomadal Meeting 1823–33 fos. 132–4.

27 *Ibid.* fo. 135. The same advice was given to Melbourne by the law officers of the Crown. Bellot, *University College, London* p. 221.

28 University archives. MS. Minutes of Hebdomadal Meeting 1823–33 fo. 136.

29 *Ibid.* fo. 137.

30 *Ibid.* fos. 139–40.

31 E.g. in Manchester (H. B. Charlton, *Portrait of a university, 1851–1951* (Manchester, 1951) p. 17) and in Yorkshire, where both liberals and the aristocracy favoured a foundation. *Quarterly Review* xxxix. 127; A. N. Shimmin, *The university of Leeds; the first half-century* (Cambridge, 1954) p. 3.

32 B.M. Add. MSS. 38292 fos. 257, 278–9.

33 Magdalen College MSS. D.5.8. M. J. Routh to S. Parr, Jan. 5, 1808.

34 B.M. Add. MSS. 40342 fo. 297.

35 *Ibid.* fo. 304.

36 Recognition of which was made in his appointment as university counsel in 1829. *Times* Feb. 25, 1829, p. 3.

37 *Colchester Diary* iii. 409; B.M. Add. MSS. 40342 fo. 303.

38 Oriel College. Treasurer's Muniments. MS. Papers on election of 1826. F. N. Rogers to E. Copleston, Feb. 17, [1826].

39 *Ibid.* J. Phillimore to Edward Copleston, Feb. 3, 1826; B.M. Add. MSS. 40342 fo. 305.

40 Buckingham, *Court of George IV* ii. 214.

41 See e.g. the correspondence of the Dean, Samuel Smith (B.M. Add. MSS. 40385) and Charles Lloyd (Add. MSS. 40342 fos. 297 *seq.*) Lloyd, however, confessed that 'the misery is that we have two whig censors of Christ Church; and all the whigs are for Canning.' (*Ibid.* fo. 309).

42 Lord Liverpool was doubtless right in reporting that Canning would not stand unless certain of election. B.M. Add. MSS. 40385 fo. 153.

43 *Times* Feb. 17, 1826, p. 3.

44 B.M. Add. MSS. 40385 fo. 132.

45 *Ibid.* fo. 151.

46 Oriel College. Treasurer's Muniments. MS. Papers on election of 1826. T. G. B. Estcourt to E. Copleston. Feb. 2, 1826.

47 In 1845 Estcourt would not follow Inglis in his opposition to the Maynooth bill. Parker, *Peel* iii. 175–6.

48 Devon C.R.O. Sidmouth MSS. Box H, T. G. B. Estcourt to Lord Sidmouth, Jan. 14, 1828. Earlier correspondence between the two is preserved in Box O.

49 Balliol College. MS. Jenkyns V. Thomas Arnold to Henry Jenkyns, Feb. 5, 1826.

50 *Parliamentary debates* n.s. xvii. 118.

51 Parker, *Peel* ii. 518.

52 *Parliamentary debates* n.s. xiv. 1243; xvii. 1265; xix. 371.

53 Oriel College. Treasurer's Muniments. MS. Papers on election of 1826; B.M. Add. MSS. 40342 fos. 311–14; Liddon, *Pusey* i. 90–1.

54 Oriel College. Treasurer's Muniments. MS. Papers on election of 1826. MS. Canvas list.

55 B.M. Add. MSS. 40343 fo. 92.

56 *Parliamentary debates* n.s. xvii. 1148.

57 Sir Robert Peel, *Memoirs* ed. Lord Stanhope and Edw. Cardwell (London, 1856) i. 64–8.

58 B.M. Add. MSS. 40343 fo. 189. The Dean of Christ Church reported 'a strong disinclination' in the university to petition. *Colchester Diary* iii. 553.

59 Peel, *Memoirs* i. 81–8; B.M. Add. MSS. 40343 fo. 241.

60 Peel, *Memoirs* i. 197.

61 B. L. Manning, *The Protestant Dissenting Deputies* ed. O. Greenwood (Cambridge, 1952) p. 234.

62 *Parliamentary debates* n.s. xviii. 688.

63 *Ibid.* xix. 118.

64 In 1827 the Vice-Chancellor informed Peel that 'we have deemed it desirable to retain the same form of words in our petition which we used on the late occasion—our object being to maintain consistency.' B.M. Add. MSS. 40390 fo. 68.

65 Notice of March 9, 1825 annotated by P. Bliss (G. A. Oxon. c. 41 no. 32).

66 Paper i, in *University Notices 1826* (Bodl. G. A. Oxon. c. 42).

67 University archives. MS. Minutes of Hebdomadal Meeting 1823–33 fo. 53.

68 B.M. Add. MSS. 40342 fo. 213; Parker, *Peel* i. 372.

69 *Ibid.* i. 477–81.

70 Flysheet dated Oxford, March 12, 1828 in Bodl. G. A. Oxon. b. 21.

71 This account is taken from a note by the Registrar, Philip Bliss, to *University Notices 1828* fo. 27 (Bodl. G. A. Oxon. c. 44). Cf. that of Charles Lloyd, Peel, *Memoirs* i. 311.

72 *Works of Samuel Parr* viii. 223; Shuttleworth was a friend of Lord Holland. *Life of Joseph Blanco White* ed. J. H. Thom. (London, 1845) ii. 194.

73 Balliol College. MS. Jenkyns V. J. Dornford to H. Jenkyns, Dec. 7, 1827.

74 The voluminous correspondence on this election shows that Thomas Mozley's story (*Reminiscences chiefly of Oriel College and the Oxford movement* (London, 1882) i. 39) that Hawkins owed his election to Newman is quite untrue. See J. W. Burgon, *Lives of twelve good men* pp. 207–9; *Letters & corr. of J. H. Newman* i. 174–6; Balliol College. MS. Jenkyns V; Keble College MSS. Corr. between J. Keble and J. Davison 1814–37, Feb. 9, 1828.

75 [R. Whately] *Letters on the Church* by an episcopalian (London, 1825) p. 93.

76 Keble College MSS. Corr. between J. Keble and J. Davison, June 23, 1827.

77 Twiss, *Eldon* iii. 56.

78 A good account of the mechanics of this election is given by N. Gash, 'Peel and the Oxford election of 1829,' *Oxoniensia* iv. 162 *seq.*

79 Merton, Oriel, New College, All Souls, Pembroke, Magdalen Hall, St. Alban Hall.

80 'The meeting originated in letters written by Short to several whigs, & was therefore principally attended by men of that cast. But a few *tories & true Protestants* attended and the whigs were quite contented to give them the lead.' Balliol College. MS. Jenkyns VI. Henry Hobhouse to R. Jenkyns. Feb. 14, 1829.

81 B.M. Add. MSS. 34570 fo. 163.

82 *Ibid.* fos. 146–51.

83 Pellew, *Sidmouth* ii. 387; iii. 108; Devon C.R.O. Sidmouth MSS. Box I.

84 A. Heber, *Life of R. Heber* i. pp. vii, 443, 459–61; ii. 62; G. Smith, *Bishop Heber* pp. 85, 354.

85 B.M. Add. MSS. 34570 fo. 148.

86 *Ibid.* fo. 154.

87 E. M. Forster, *Marianne Thornton. A domestic biography* (London, 1956) p. 77.

88 B.M. Add. MSS. 40394 fo. 286. He was regarded as a possible President of the British Association in 1847. Magdalen College. MS. B.II.2.2. Edward Sabine to C. G. B. Daubeny, Dec. 19, 1845.

89 Even Lloyd deplored some of Peel's theological notions.

90 *Letters & corr. of J. H. Newman* i. 200.

91 In Forster's phrase, 'Sir Robert . . . opposed everything except science and art.' *Marianne Thornton* pp. 176–7.

92 Both sides employed the newspaper press, and scores of pamphlets were produced, most of which are preserved in Bodl. G. A. Oxon. b. 21, c. 107, 8°145, and Hope 8°285.

93 B.M. Add. MSS. 40343 fo. 368.

94 *Letters & corr. of J. H. Newman* i. 203.

95 *Times* March 11, 12, 1829, p. 3.

96 *Letters & corr. of J. H. Newman* i. 200–3.

97 *Reply to an expostulatory letter* (Oxford, 1829) p. 4.

98 κ ὶ) οῖς κἀγαθοῖς (one copy in Bodl. G. A. Oxon. b. 21).

99 *An address to the members of Convocation of the university of Oxford* (Newport, 1829). This idea was worked out by Keble in socratic form. J. Keble, *Six Queries*, Fairford, Feb. 16, 1829 (one copy in Bodl. G. A. Oxon. b. 21).

100 *A circular of advice and justification from Inglis's committee* (Oxford, 1829).

101 *An expostulatory letter addressed to the members of the University of Oxford* (London, 1829).

102 Both are preserved in Bodl. G. A. Oxon. b. 21. For the pressure put on Blanco White by Hawkins and Pusey, Thom, *Life of J. B. White* i. 453; Oriel College. Treasurer's Muniments. MS. papers on Election of 1829.

103 *Two speeches delivered in Convocation on February* 26, 1829 (Bodl. G. A. Oxon. 8°145).

104 C. Girdlestone, *Substance of a speech for the Convocation House, Oxford* (Oxford, 1829).

105 B.M. Add. MSS. 34570 fo. 178. Cf. Foster, *Marianne Thornton* p. 89.

106 B.M. Add. MSS. 40399 fo. 10.

107 *The Greville memoirs 1814–1860* ed. Lytton Strachey & Roger Fulford (London, 1938) i. 260.

108 Keble College MSS. Corr. between J. Keble and J. Davison, 1814–37, Feb. 18, 1829.

109 Even in 1830 Hawkins felt that Oriel freedom of thought must be defended against high-church criticism. Balliol College. MS. Jenkyns V. E. Hawkins to H. Jenkyns, May 20, 1830.

110 This tortuous dispute may be followed in *John Henry Newman: Autobiographical writings* ed. H. Tristram (London, 1956) pp. 86–107; *Letters & corr. of J. H. Newman* i. 148–60, 191–2; MS. Oriel College Letters nos. 2–7, 1301–30, and the fascinating correspondence of Henry Jenkyns, fellow of Oriel, preserved with the papers of his brother at Balliol. MS. Jenkyns V.

111 A. R. Ashwell & R. G. Wilberforce. *Life of Samuel Wilberforce* (London, 1880–2) i. 45.

112 *Ibid.* i. 45. Cf. his father's opinion. *Private papers of William Wilberforce* ed. A. M. Wilberforce (London, 1897) p. 157.

113 A. P. Stanley, *Life of Arnold* p. 222.

114 St. Edmund Hall. MS. Diary of John Hill. May 5–12, 1828.

115 H. B. Bulteel, *A sermon on 1 Cor. II. 12.* (Oxford, 1831) p. 46. Bulteel's charge about testimonials is borne out by W. Cockburn, *Strictures on clerical education in the University of Cambridge* (London, 1809) p. 15, and H. Bathurst, *Memoirs of Dr. Henry Bathurst* i. 197–8. It was repeated by another seceding evangelical, J. C. Philpot, *Letter to the Provost of Worcester College, Oxford, on resigning his fellowship and seceding from the Church of England* (3rd. ed. London, 1835).

116 E. Burton, *Remarks upon a sermon preached at St. Mary's* . . . (Oxford, 1831) p. 5.

117 [W. Irons] *Strictures on Mr. Bulteel's sermon and Dr. Burton's remarks* (Oxford, 1831). For doubts as to the ascription of this pamphlet, Reynolds, *Evangelicals at Oxford* p. 98 n.2.

118 H. B. Bulteel, *A reply to Dr. Burton's remarks* (Oxford, 1831).

119 St. Edmund Hall. MS. Diary of John Hill. Aug. 10, 1831.

120 *Ibid.* Oct. 18, 1831.

121 *Ibid.* March 10, 1831.

122 H. B. Bulteel, *The doctrine of the miraculous interference of Jesus on behalf of believers* . . . (Oxford, 1832); *Letters of Rev. J. B. Mozley* (London, 1885) p. 25.

123 St. Edmund Hall. MS. Diary of John Hill. May 18, 1833.

124 Reynolds, *Evangelicals at Oxford* p. 98.

125 St. Edmund Hall. MS. Diary of John Hill. Jan. 1, 1832.

126 Bodl. MS. Top. Oxon. b. 23 fo. 144.

127 S. P. Rigaud, Savilian professor of astronomy.

128 J. Dornford, fellow of Oriel.

129 J. D. Macbride, Principal of Magdalen Hall.

130 Magdalen College. MS. B.II.2.2. W. Mills to C. G. B. Daubeny, Aug. 2, 1830; *A political diary 1828–1830 by Lord Ellenborough* ed. Lord Colchester (London, 1881) ii. 316–17.

131 Peel showed himself amiable towards the university by refusing to intervene. *Courier* July 23, 1830 (one copy in Bodl. MS. Top. Oxon. d. 16 fo. 27); *Times* July 26, 1830, p. 3.

132 [J. Wade] *The extraordinary black book* (new ed. London, 1832) pp. 49, 117.

133 Bodl. MS. Top. Oxon. b. 23 fos. 302, 305, 317a; St Edmund Hall. MS. Diary of John Hill. Nov. 25–7, 1830.

134 *Ibid.* May 9–13, 1831; Bodl. MS. Top. Oxon. b. 23 fos. 411–12, 415, 421–2, 424, 425, 429. A pamphlet bantered undergraduates for galloping about wearing party colours and attempting to influence votes. *Gentlemen Undergraduates* Oxford, May 4, 1831. (Bodl. G. A. Oxon. b. 21).

135 B.M. Add. MSS. 34570 fos. 417–18.

136 Bodl. MS. Top. Oxon. b. 23 fos. 372–3.

137 MS. Oriel College Letters nos. 356, 382.

138 University archives. MS. Minutes of Hebdomadal Meeting 1823–33 fos. 142–3.

139 Keble College MSS. Letters from John Keble to Thomas Keble 1807–49, two undated letters.

140 Bodl. MS. Top. Oxon. b. 23 fos. 377–8. The petition was carried by 76 votes to 39 with many abstentions, fo. 379. Cf. MS. Oriel College Letters no. 1152.

141 MS. Oriel College Letters no. 365.

142 Bodl. MS. Top. Oxon. b. 23. fos. 467–9, 476, 478, 482.

143 University archives. MS. Minutes of Hebdomadal Board 1823–33 fos. 173–4. Gladstone and his friends mobilised support for an undergraduate petition; C. Wordsworth, *Annals of my early life* (London, 1891) p. 84.

144 *Times* April 2, 1832, p. 2.

145 *Westminster Review* xv. 69. Cf. *Times* Dec. 5, 1832, p. 3.

146 Keble insisted that Oxford's 'usefulness' would go if she ceased to encourage 'loyalty'. MS. Oriel College Letters no. 472.

CHAPTER V

1 To this tendency, however, Liddon ascribed the various lapses from grace of W. G. Ward, F. Oakeley and Mark Pattison, Liddon, *Life of Pusey* ii. 216.

2 *Christian Observer* 1832, p. 88; 1834, pp. 258, 323.

3 *Ibid.* 1831, pp. 614–15; 1832, p. 88; 1833, pp. iii, 323; 1835, p. 520.

4 *Ibid.* 1834, pp. 446–7.

5 For the currency of this term before 1830, G. Dyer, *Academic Unity* (London, 1827) pp. xiii, xiv.

6 Congregationalists claimed that if their baker's dozen of colleges were located in one place they would 'constitute a university of much better pretensions than many on which princely and royal patronage have been largely bestowed.' R. W. Dale, *History of English Congregationalism* (London, 1907) pp. 627–8: Robert Vaughan, *Congregationalism: or the polity of the independent churches viewed in relation to the state and tendencies of modern society* (2nd ed. London, 1842) pp. 64–8.

7 *Nonconformist* June 21, 1871, p. 617.

8 *Christian Reformer* 1831, pp. 31–5, 67–75, 158–61. Cf. 1832, p. 305.

9 John Medway, *Memoirs of the life and writings of John Pye Smith* (London, 1853) p. 361; John Pye Smith, *The protestant dissent vindicated in a letter to Rev. Samuel Lee* (2nd ed. London, 1835) pp. 49–50. Pusey seems to have persuaded Pye Smith that abolition 'wd. make no difference to any dissenters except those [Socinians and Baptists] whom one wd. least wish to bring in.' Pusey Ho. MSS. Radnor Letters. E. B. Pusey to Lord Radnor, Oct. 24, 1834.

10 *Times* Feb. 25, 1833, p. 2; Nov. 14, 1834, p. 2; Wade, *Extraordinary black book* p. 49. Wm. Howitt in his best-selling *Popular history of priestcraft* (1833) concluded a rabid assault on the tests by asserting that 'the devil never found himself more in his element, since he descended from his position in the Tree of Knowledge in the garden of Eden, to mount those in Oxford and Cambridge', p. 283.

11 *Times* May 9, 1833, p. 3; May 11, 1833, p. 2.

12 *Parliamentary debates* 3s. ii. 29 *seq.*

13 *Oxford: academical abuses disclosed* (London, 1832) p. 23; *Extraordinary black book* p. 117.

14 'A proctor . . . can at all seasons resort to those dens of iniquity [the brothels], with power to clear the coast of all youngsters, thereby clearing the coast for himself.' *Times* April 8, 1830, p. 3.

15 *Westminster Review* xv. 56 *seq.*

16 *Parliamentary debates* 3s. iv. 982 *seq.*

17 *Ibid.* 3s. xii. 475; xxii. 751; xxviii. 772.

18 B.M. Add. MSS. 34571 fos. 39–40; Apsley Ho. MSS. P. Bliss to duke of Wellington, April 19, 1834; G. Rowley to same, May 4, 1834. Parliamentary papers on this subject are preserved in University archives. MS. N.W. 8. 1.

19 *Edinburgh Review* liii. 384 *seq.*

20 Veitch, *Memoir of Sir William Hamilton* p. 30.

21 Hamilton had an acknowledged influence upon the royal commission which reported in 1852. *Ibid.* 167–8.

22 *Edinburgh Review* liii. 386.

23 *Ibid.* liii. 397–8.

24 Cf. the opinion of the German liberal oracle, Baron Bunsen: 'The point I should have in view in England as in Germany, would be to unite the two methods—the English of tuition and spontaneous activity, and the German of a regular course of professorial lectures.' Frances, Baroness Bunsen, *A memoir of Baron Bunsen* (London, 1868) i. 420.

25 [Vaughan Thomas] *The legality of the present academical system of the University of Oxford asserted against the new calumnies of the Edinburgh Review* (Oxford, 1831) p. 5.

26 *Edinburgh Review* liv. 478 *seq.*; [Vaughan Thomas] *The legality of the present academical system of the university of Oxford reasserted* (Oxford, 1831).

27 J. S. Mill, 'The right and wrong of state interference with corporation and church property,' reprinted from the *Jurist* Feb. 1833 in *Dissertations and discussions* (London, 1859–75) i. 1 *seq.*

28 This point was made by Alexis de Tocqueville (among others); he thought that if the state took over college property, it could establish a better system at one-hundredth of the cost. *Oeuvres complètes* (Paris, 1865) viii. 313.

29 B.M. Add. MSS. 34571 fos. 247–8.

30 Newman, *Letters & corr.* i. 493; ii. 21; J. B. Mozley, *Letters* pp. 37–8; Keble College MSS. Letters of J. Keble to T. Keble n.d. [Jan. 1834]. Keble absurdly attributed Wellington's success to the radicals.

31 On him see N. Gash, *Politics in the age of Peel* (London, 1953) pp. 413 *seq.*; *E.H.R.* lxiii. 502 *seq.*

32 Bonham was evidently uninformed of the bitter divisions here.

33 The supporters of Peel.

34 B.M. Add. MSS. 40403 fo. 284.

35 *Ibid.* fo. 290.

36 *Ibid.* fos. 286–7. Informal approaches had clearly been made in November 1833, if not earlier, for Lord Sidmouth had sounded both Eldon and Wellington. Twiss, *Eldon* iii. 217–18; Parker, *Peel* ii. 227–8.

37 B.M. Add. MSS. 40342 fo. 285.

38 *Ibid.* fos. 220–2, 230, 234, 256–65 *passim; Journal of Mrs. Arbuthnot* i. 387; *Times* April 5, 1825, p. 5; April 25, p. 6; *Personal reminiscences of the duke of Wellington by Francis, Earl of Ellesmere* ed. Alicia, Countess of Strafford (London, 1902) p. 138.

39 Pellew, *Sidmouth* iii. 436; Devon C.R.O. Sidmouth MSS. Box H, J. Keble to Lord Sidmouth, May 9, 1833; Keble College MSS. Letters of J. Keble to T. Keble, broadsheet June 21, 1832; Duke of Buckingham and Chandos, *Memoirs of the courts and cabinets of William IV and Victoria* (London, 1861) ii. 43–4.

40 Parker, *Peel* ii. 227–8.

41 Apsley Ho. MSS. Duke of Wellington to T. Wintle, Nov. 30, 1833; Lord Talbot to duke of Wellington, Dec. 22, 1833.

42 B.M. Add. MSS. 40403 fos. 282, 291–2.

43 B.M. Add. MSS. 40343 fos. 84, 90.

44 B.M. Add. MSS. 40403 fos. 284–5, 293–5.

45 B.M. Add. MSS. 40404 fo. 3. On Eldon, however, cf. Twiss, *Eldon* iii. 217–18.

46 B.M. Add. MSS. 40309 fo. 19.

47 B.M. Add. MSS. 40404 fos. 9–12; Parker, *Peel* ii. 228–9; Apsley Ho. MSS. Printed requisition, Jan. 15, 1834.

48 Including the heads of Worcester (Whittington Landon), Balliol (Jenkyns), St. John's (Wynter), Brasenose (A. T. Gilbert), Trinity (Ingram), Wadham (B. P. Symons), Magdalen (Routh), Queen's (Fox), and St. Edmund Hall (Grayson). Apsley Ho. MSS. Jan. 14, 1834.

49 Edward Burton, regius professor of divinity, who had begun the negotiation with Talbot (B.M. Add. MSS. 40403 fo. 291) signed Peel's requisition; as did Canon Buckland also.

50 Apsley Ho. MSS. Lord Talbot to duke of Wellington, Jan. 14, 1834; Duke of Wellington to Lord Talbot, Jan. 17, 1834; Duke of Wellington to T. Wintle, Jan. 16, 1834; T. Wintle to duke of Wellington, Jan. 17, 1834.

51 Parker, *Peel* ii. 229–31.

52 *Ibid.* ii. 231; BM. Add. MSS. 40404 fos. 34–5.

53 Apsley Ho. MSS. C. A. Ogilvie to duke of Wellington, Jan. 18, 19, 1834; T. Wintle to duke of Wellington, Jan. 22, 1834.

54 Parker, *Peel* ii. 236. There were sore feelings also in Oxford. Newman, *Letters & corr.* i. 27.

55 Twiss, *Eldon* iii. 218.

56 *Ibid.* iii. 219.

57 *Ibid.* iii. 231.

58 Apsley Ho. MSS. G. Rowley to duke of Wellington, May 20, 30, 1834; Duke of Wellington to Vice-Chancellor, May 31, 1834; *The Creevey papers* ii. 279. An embarrassingly circumstantial account of this transaction was published by the *Times* June 10, 1834, p. 5.

59 Bodl. Wynter Papers. MS. Dep. d. 6. fo. 153.

60 MS. Knowsley Papers 157/11. Copy of speech. In 1837 Bliss asked him for the headship of St. Mary Hall, but Wellington enjoyed no opportunity to exercise his patronage till 1848. B.M. Add. MSS. 34572 fos. 150–1.

61 *Greville Memoirs* iii. 46.

62 *Jackson's Oxford Journal* June 14, 1834.

63 J. B. Mozley, *Letters* p. 41; Twiss, *Eldon* iii. 231–2. Cf. Buckingham, *Courts of William IV and Victoria* ii. 103.

64 *Ibid.* ii. 86; *Greville memoirs* iii. 25.

65 *Edinburgh Review* lix. 505–9; *Times* June 18, 1834, p. 3; *Hilarity of the monks of Oxford* (G. A. Oxon. b. 111 (270)).

66 For an example of this, J. B. Mozley, *Letters* p. 41.

67 *Christian Reformer* 1834, p. 77.

68 *Ibid.* 1834, pp. 161 *seq.*

69 *Ibid.* 1834, pp. 257–8, 337–8.

70 *Parliamentary debates* 3s. xxi. 874 *seq.*, 994 *seq.*

71 *Ibid.* 3s. xxii. 497.

72 Peel was being pressed by Provost Hawkins to adopt a liberal view of the matriculation test (B.M. Add. MSS. 40404 fos. 104, 117) and in the Tamworth Manifesto conceded that the civil advantages obtained by Anglican graduates in the professions of law and medicine 'ought to undergo modification.' Peel, *Memoirs* ii. 64.

73 *Supra* p. 66.

74 *Parliamentary debates* 3s. xix. 120 *seq.*

75 University archives. MS. Minutes of Hebdomadal Meeting 1823–33 fos. 205, 206; Bellot, *University College, London* p. 226.

76 *Ibid.* pp. 230–1.

77 Apsley Ho. MSS. Corr. between duke of Wellington and G. Rowley Feb. 15, 16, 18, March 8 (2), 13, 15 (2), 16 (2), 18, 21, 1834; University archives. MS. Hebdomadal Register 1833–41 fos. 13, 14, 16, 19, 22; Newman. *Letters & corr.* ii. 29.

78 University archives. MS. Hebdomadal Register 1833–41 fo. 17.

79 W. Sewell, *A second letter to a dissenter* (Oxford, 1834).

80 University archives. MS. Hebdomadal Register 1833–41. fo. 52.

81 *Parliamentary debates* 3s. xxii. 899 *seq.*

82 Connop Thirlwall, *A letter to the Rev. Thomas Turton on the admission of dissenters to academical degrees* (Cambridge, 1834). On this as on other occasions Pusey had immediate cause to regret his public statements on political matters, and explained that he meant that although Oxford religious education was not adequate for the clergy it was excellent for the laity. Pusey Ho. MSS. Radnor Letters. E. B. Pusey to Lord Radnor, Aug. 28, 1834.

83 C. Wordsworth, *On the admission of dissenters to reside and graduate in the University of Cambridge* (Cambridge, 1834).

84 Bonamy Price was at this time a scholar of Worcester, and an assistant master at Rugby; he was elected Drummond professor of political economy in 1868.

85 B.M. Add. MSS. 44353 fo. 130. The Rugby men were also hoping to get up a petition.

86 Thomas Arnold, *Principles of church reform.*

87 Cf. Sir James Graham's judgment on his years at Christ Church (1810–12). 'I was never once called upon to attend any lectures either upon theology or divinity; I never received any religious instruction whatever, apart from that which I derived from enforced attendance at chapel, and I am ashamed to say that I never during the whole period of my residence heard a single sermon.' C. S. Parker, *Life and letters of Sir James Graham* (London, 1907) i. 12.

88 W. Sewell, *Thoughts on the admission of dissenters to the university of Oxford* (Oxford, 1834). Cf. *Oxford University Magazine* (Oxford, 1834) pp. 95 *seq.* 248 *seq.* On this magazine see Lord Selborne, *Memorials. Part 1, family and personal* (London, 1896) i. 139–40, 164.

89 W. Sewell, *The attack upon the university of Oxford* (Oxford, 1834). Sewell decried the Rugby hopes of promoting social solidarity through the mingling of classes at the universities. pp. 6, 59.

90 G. Moberly, *A few remarks on the proposed admission of dissenters into the university of Oxford* (Oxford, 1834). Whately replied to this that in some colleges there were no divinity lectures at all. E. J. Whately, *Life and corr. of R. Whately* i. 228.

91 G. Horne, *A letter to Lord North concerning subscription to the XXXIX articles* (ed. Oxford, 1834). This pamphlet, first published during the subscription crisis of 1772 was now re-edited by Vaughan Thomas. Bodl. Bliss B. 210 no. 23.

92 Liddon, *Pusey* i. 301.

93 *Parliamentary debates* 3s. xxv. 815 *seq.*

94 *Ibid.* 3s. xxv. 643.

95 University archives. MS. Hebdomadal Register. 1833–41 fo. 2; Apsley Ho. MSS. E. Cardwell to duke of Wellington, April 19, 1834.

96 St. Edmund Hall. MS. Diary of John Hill, April 21–3, 1834.

97 Apsley Ho. MSS. E. Burton to duke of Wellington, April 24, 1834.

98 Apsley Ho. MSS. V. Thomas to duke of Wellington, April 26, 1834.

99 B.M. Add. MSS. 44354 fo. 34.

100 B.M. Add. MSS. 44281 fo. 6.

101 Apsley Ho. MSS. Duke of Wellington to Vice-Chancellor, May 7, 1844. Instead of a subscription to the articles the Cambridge authorities required a declaration of membership of the church; it seems to have been accepted that dissenters who were prepared to conform during their residence might be received.

102 Apsley Ho. MSS. G. Rowley to duke of Wellington, May 4, 1834.

103 On June 2 the Board warmly thanked Vaughan Thomas for the services which had caused it so much embarrassment. University archives. MS. Hebdomadal Register 1833–41 fos. 33–4.

104 *Parliamentary debates* 3s. xxiv. 356, 632 *seq.* Opportunist unitarians were already confessing that the dissenters had done much to spike their own guns. *Christian Reformer* May 1834, p. 423.

105 *Parliamentary debates* 3s. xxv. 815 *seq.*

106 Buckingham, *Courts of William IV and Victoria* ii. 115.

107 E. J. Whately, *Life and corr. of R. Whately* i. 225. When the storm had been brewing in April Whately told Hawkins candidly that 'we have cried "the wolf" so often without occasion, that now the wolf does come, no-one will attend to us.' MS. Oriel College Letters no. 204.

108 *Select works and memoirs of Rev. Joseph Fletcher D.D.* ed. Rev. Joseph Fletcher jnr. (London, 1846) pp. 408–9; Pusey Ho. MSS. Radnor Letters. Vassall Holland to Lord Radnor, Sept. 2, 4, 11, 16, 1834.

109 Veitch, *Memoir of Sir William Hamilton* pp. 166–7; Pusey Ho. MSS. Radnor Letters. J. Allen to Lord Radnor, March 3, 1835.

110 *Edinburgh Review* lx. 202 *seq.* 422 *seq.*

111 *Some memorials of R. D. Hampden, bishop of Hereford* ed. Henrietta Hampden (London, 1871) p. 33.

112 *Ibid.* p. 6.

113 MS. Oriel College Letters no. 434. Four years later he was more cautious in his assessment. *Ibid.* no. 413.

114 Balliol College. MS. Jenkyns VI. Lord Grenville to R. Jenkyns, April 20, 1833.

115 R. D. Hampden, *Observations on religious dissent* (Oxford, 1834).

116 R. D. Hampden, *Postscript to observations on religious dissent* (London, 1835).

117 Hampden, *Observations* pp. 39–40. Hampden's friend Arnold also wrote, but did not publish, a pamphlet in favour of the admission of dissenters. A. P. Stanley, *Life & correspondence of Dr. Arnold* p. 293.

118 Apsley Ho. MSS. Duke of Wellington to Vice-Chancellor, August 27, 1834.

119 Apsley Ho. MSS. Duke of Wellington's corr. with E. Cardwell and the Vice-Chancellor, Nov. 3–10, 1834.

120 Apsley Ho. MSS. Duke of Wellington's corr. with E. Cardwell and the Vice-Chancellor, Nov. 17–18, 1834; University archives. MS. Hebdomadal Register 1833–41 fos. 39, 40.

121 W. Sewell, *Thoughts on subscription* (Oxford, 1834) p. 1. Cf. *Standard* Nov. 13, 1834 and *Morning Chronicle* Dec. 3, 1834 both quoted in *Christian Reformer* 1834, p. 875; 1835, p. 62; *Times* Nov. 14, 1834, p. 2; *Greville memoirs* iii. 100–1.

122 Apsley Ho. MSS. Duke of Wellington to Vice-Chancellor, Nov. 18, 1834.

123 Apsley Ho. MSS. E. Cardwell to duke of Wellington, March 5, 1835.

124 *Parliamentary debates* 3s. xxvi. 576 *seq.*

125 Apsley Ho. MSS. E. Cardwell to duke of Wellington, March 5, 1835. There is a copy of the return in Bodl. G. A. Oxon. c. 25 (9).

126 Apsley Ho. MSS. Duke of Wellington to E. Cardwell, March 3, 1835.

127 Apsley Ho. MSS. E. Cardwell to duke of Wellington, March 2, 1835.

128 Apsley Ho. MSS. E. Cardwell to duke of Wellington, March 23, 1825; University archives. MS. Hebdomadal Register 1833–41 fo. 50.

129 [G. Faussett] *A few plain reasons for retaining our subscription to the Articles* . . . (Oxford, 1835); B.M. Add. MSS. 34571 fo. 380.

130 W. Sewell, *Postscript to thoughts on subscription* (Oxford, 1835).

131 V. Thomas, *Letter to the duke of Wellington* (Oxford, 1835).

132 [F. D. Maurice] *Subscription no bondage* (Oxford, 1835); *Life of F. D. Maurice* ed. F. Maurice (3rd ed. London, 1884) i. 168 *seq.*, 181 *seq.*

133 St. Edmund Hall. MS. Diary of John Hill, May 20, 1835.

134 J. B. Mozley, *Letters* p. 46; Keble College MSS. Letters of Archdeacon Froude to J. Keble, Nov. 20, 1834; Letters of J. Keble to T. Keble n.d. [April 1835].

135 [H. W. Wilberforce] *The foundations of the faith assailed in Oxford* . . . (London, 1835).

136 [E. B. Pusey] *Questions respectfully addressed to members of Convocation on the subjoined declaration* (Oxford, 1835).

137 [E. Hawkins] *Oxford matriculation statutes: answers to the 'Questions' addressed to members of Convocation* (Oxford, 1835). Copleston described this pamphlet as 'a sensible temperate & useful admonition to a well-meaning but rather shatter-brained man' (MS. Oriel College Letters no. 401). Pusey rejoined with *Subscription to the Thirty-Nine Articles* (Oxford, 1835).

138 [C. P. Eden] *Self-protection the case of the articles* (Oxford, 1835).

139 All the sheets published by residents were collected and ascribed to their authors by Philip Bliss in Bodl. Bliss B. 210.

140 A quantity of Pusey's correspondence with non-residents is in the Pusey Papers at Pusey House.

141 R. E. Prothero, *Life and correspondence of A. P. Stanley* (2nd ed. London, 1894) i. 145. Arnold declared: 'It makes me half daft to think of Oxford and the London University, as bad as one another in their opposite ways, and perpetuating their badness by remaining distinct instead of mixing.' Stanley, *Arnold* p. 361.

142 Prothero, *Stanley* i. 146.

143 That Burton would take this line had been probable even then. E. Burton, *Thoughts on the separation of church and state* (London, 1834) p. 47.

144 [B. P. Symons] *A letter to a non-resident friend upon subscription . . .* (Oxford, 1835).

145 Pusey Ho. MSS. Radnor Letters. Lord Radnor to Sir W. Hamilton, March 21, 1835. Cf. MS. Oriel College Letters no. 403.

146 Pusey Ho. MSS. Radnor Letters. R. D. Hampden to Lord Radnor, May 21, 1835.

147 Pusey Ho. MSS. Radnor Letters. May to July 1835.

148 Cf. the suggestions of Edward Denison, fellow of Merton, *A review of the state of the question respecting the admission of the dissenters to the universities* (London, 1835).

149 Pusey Ho. MSS. Radnor Letters. R. D. Hampden to Lord Radnor, May 21, June 2, 16, 18, 21, 1835.

150 F. Oakeley, *Letter to the duke of Wellington* (Oxford, 1835).

151 Apsley Ho. MSS. Duke of Wellington to Vice-Chancellor, June 14, 18, 19, 1835.

152 Apsley Ho. MSS. E. Cardwell to duke of Wellington, June 18, 1835; Pusey Ho. MSS. Radnor Letters. R. D. Hampden to Lord Radnor, June 18, 1835; University archives. MS. Hebdomadal Register 1833–41 fos. 55–6.

153 Pusey Ho. MSS. Radnor Letters. Vassall Holland to Lord Radnor, Friday.

154 Apsley Ho. MSS. E. Cardwell to duke of Wellington, June 20, 1835; G. Rowley to duke of Wellington, June 21, 1835; Pusey Ho. MS. Radnor Letters. R. D. Hampden to Lord Radnor, June 21, 1835; University archives. MS. Hebdomadal Register 1833–41 fo. 56. The petition was voted in Convocation by 91 to 4. *Times* June 26, 1835, p. 7.

155 *Parliamentary debates* 3s. xxix. 496 *seq.*

156 *Ibid.* 3s. xxix. 534.

157 University archives. MS. Hebdomadal Register 1833–41 fo. 65.

158 *Ibid.* fos. 66, 68, 73; *Summary of proposed alterations in university oaths* (Oxford, 1836), (Bodl. G. A. Oxon. b. 23).

159 Apsley Ho. MSS. E. Cardwell to duke of Wellington, Feb. 5, 1836.

160 *The following hints on the alterations proposed in the statutes relating to the oaths are respectfully submitted to members of Convocation* (n. pl. or d. [Oxford, 1836]), (Bodl. G. A. Oxon. b. 22).

161 In October 1835, Melbourne regarded him as a safe candidate for a bishopric. *Lord Melbourne's papers* ed. Lloyd C. Sanders (2nd ed. London, 1890) p. 496.

162 Liddon, *Pusey* i. 365–6.

163 *Lord Melbourne's papers* pp. 496, 498; MS. Oriel College Letters no. 414.

164 Whately, however, told Hawkins he suspected that he sought the advice of whichever of his old friends he thought would concur with him. MS. Oriel College Letters no. 257.

165 Though Newman was now arrogantly prepared to doubt whether Burton was 'ever . . . fixed, ever saw the Truth.' Liddon, *Pusey* i. 368.

166 Liddon, *Pusey* i. 368–9; Newman, *Letters & corr.* ii. 162–3.

24

167 MS. Oriel College Letters no. 413.

168 In the Pusey Papers at Pusey House is a whole bundle of drafts in Pusey's hand of objections to the appointment of Hampden to the regius chair.

169 J. B. Mozley, *Letters* p. 50.

170 Liddon, *Pusey* i. 369.

171 The previous summer Lord Holland had bewailed 'that the Dons of the University are great favourites at Court, & have through the Chancellor of Dublin [Cumberland] the means of earwigging the K.' Pusey Ho. MSS. Radnor Letters. Vassall Holland to Radnor n.d. [July 1835]. 'Earwigging' the king to take ecclesiastical patronage into his own hand was now one of Pusey's wilder hopes. B.M. Add. MSS. 44281 fo. 23.

172 *Lord Melbourne's papers* pp. 498–500.

173 'The question about Hampden seems to me simple. If he had preached & published heresy, let him be tried by the proper judge . . . What they are now doing is merely lynch law.' Thomas Arnold to W. W. Hull. March 17, 1836. Stanley, *Arnold* p. 399.

174 St. Edmund Hall. MS. Diary of John Hill. Feb. 24–6, 1836.

175 J. B. Mozley, *Letters* p. 52.

176 See the applications for the headship, Apsley Ho. MSS. Feb. 1836; Newman, *Letters & corr.* ii. 175. In the following year the duke seems to have tried to dislodge Hampden from the Hall on charges of non-residence. *Memorials of Hampden* pp. 91–2.

177 Apsley Ho. MSS. E. Cardwell to duke of Wellington, Feb. 11, 1836; MS. Oriel College Letters. no. 413.

178 Apsley Ho. MSS. E. Cardwell to duke of Wellington, Feb. 29, March 4, 1836. Dr. Jenkyns, Master of Balliol, made a strenuous effort to get Martin Routh, President of Magdalen to turn out for the meeting. Feb. 29, [1836] Magdalen College MSS. D.5.17.

179 St. Edmund Hall. MS. Diary of John Hill. March 1, 1836.

180 *Ibid.* March 2, 1836. Arthur Haddan later calculated that at least 50 of the 82 signatories of the declaration of March 10 were not Tractarians, and only 3 went over to Rome. B.M. Add. MSS. 44183 fos. 4–10.

181 St. Edmund Hall. MS. Diary of John Hill. March 4, 1836; Apsley Ho. MSS. E. Cardwell to duke of Wellington. March 4, 1836.

182 St. Edmund Hall. MS. Diary of John Hill. March 10, 1836.

183 Apsley Ho. MSS. E. Cardwell to duke of Wellington. March 7, 11, 1836.

184 *The propositions attributed to Dr. Hampden by Professor Pusey compared with the text of the Bampton lectures* (London, 1836). The substance of this charge was admitted by Liddon, *Pusey* i. 376–7.

185 *Specimens of the theological teaching of certain members of the Corpus committee* (London, 1836).

186 Prothero, *Stanley* i. 161.

187 St. Edmund Hall. MS. Diary of John Hill. March 17, 1836.

188 *Ibid.* March 22, 1836. Bonamy Price expected that 'these high-church Newmanitish people will try and get their Proctors' power of veto done away with, and when the hole for reform is made, all the water will run out' (A. H. Clough, *Correspondence* i. 42). J. B. Mozley gives a characteristic description of the scene, *Letters* p. 54. Cf. *Letters of Frederic, Lord Blachford* ed. G. E. Marindin (London, 1896) p. 29.

189 *Edinburgh Review* lxiii. 225. Hampden was delighted by the article. B.M. Add. MSS. 34617 fo. 407.

190 University archives. MS. Hebdomadal Register 1833–41 fo. 77.

191 Vaughan Thomas, *Letters addressed by large bodies of clergy to those members of Convocation who met in the common room of Corpus Christi during the controversy of 1836.* (Oxford, 1842). Cf. University archives. N.W. 21.4. Memorial of Sheffield clergy.

192 This opinion was reprinted in the *Report of the Oxford University Commission* 1852, App. D. pp. 52–3.

193 Apsley Ho. MSS. E. Cardwell to duke of Wellington, May 5, 1836; G. Rowley to same, May 5, 1836: Opinion of Philip Bliss.

194 Reprinted in *The state of parties in Oxford* (London, 1836). Cf. *Memorials of Hampden* pp. 66–7.

195 *Times* March 18, 1836, p. 15; March 19, p. 4; March 23, p. 5; May 7, p. 7.

196 *Copleston's Remains* p. 56n.

197 *Wesleyan Methodist Magazine* 1836, pp. 311, 312.

198 *Christian Observer* April 1836 p. 256.

199 *State of parties in Oxford* p. 15.

200 *The Laudian code of statutes; 1636* ed. J. Griffiths (Oxford, 1888) p. xxiv.

CHAPTER VI

1 University archives. MS. Hebdomadal Register 1833–41 fos. 93–4; Apsley Ho. MSS. E. Cardwell to duke of Wellington, Feb. 27, 1837.

2 MS. Oriel College Letters no. 1335.

3 University archives. MS. Hebdomadal Register 1833–41 fos. 97–9; Apsley Ho. MSS. A. T. Gilbert to duke of Wellington, March 13, 1837; Lord Radnor to same, March 13, 1837; Duke of Wellington to Vice-Chancellor, March 16, 1837.

4 *Parliamentary debates* 3s. xxxvii. 1001–43.

5 *An historical vindication of the leading principles contained in earl Radnor's bill* (London, 1837).

6 Apsley Ho. MSS. Duke of Wellington to Vice-Chancellor, April 12 1837.

7 Apsley Ho. MSS. Duke of Wellington to Vice-Chancellor, April 18, 1837.

8 University archives. MS. Hebdomadal Register 1833–41 fo. 102; Apsley Ho. MSS. A. T. Gilbert to duke of Wellington, April 20, 27 (2) 1837; E. Cardwell to same, April 28, 1837.

9 .E.g. Merton, Ornsby, *Hope-Scott* i. 128–32, 167, cf. 273–4; and Oriel, Oriel College Treasurer's MSS. Provost Hawkins to Vice-Chancellor, May 26, 1837. It is instructive to compare Newman's judgment that there were 'only two things . . . not in substance . . . observed' in the Oriel statutes (Sir J. T. Coleridge, *Memoir of Rev. John Keble* (2nd ed. Oxford, 1869) i. 248–9) with that of Copleston, who thought the college would be defenceless at a public inquiry. MS. Oriel College Letters no. 1338.

10 E.g. Queen's; *Times* July 26, 1838, p. 3; W. Thomson, *An open college best for all* (Oxford, 1854) p. 40. Cf. Magdalen; Selborne, *Memorials Pt. I, family and personal* i. 227–32.

11 Exeter College MS. Register Oct. 31, 1843.

12 *Parliamentary debates* 3s. xxxviii. 509–30, 658–75. Pryme withdrew his motion upon the intimation of the government that the Crown ought to 'be left to act upon its own sense of public duty.'

13 Apsley Ho. MSS. Duke of Wellington to Vice-Chancellor, May 9, 1837.

14 In 1836 Newman undertook to supply a quarter of the contents; in 1838 he became sole editor and the *Critic* became the Tractarian party organ. T. Mozley, *Reminiscences chiefly of Oriel college and the Oxford movement* (2nd ed. London, 1882) i. 414–16.

15 *British Critic* Oct. 1837, p. 401.

16 *Quarterly Review* lix. 439 *seq*. esp. 474–5. Cf. Wm. Sewell's argument in the *Times* (April 18, 1837, p. 7) that in the case of 'absurd and impracticable' statutes, 'there is a dispensation in the very nature of the oath.'

17 Which consisted of R. Jenkyns, Master of Balliol, T. Gaisford, Dean of Christ Church, B. P. Symons, Warden of Wadham, E. Cardwell, Principal of St. Alban Hall, and P. Wynter, President of St. John's.

18 University archives. MS. Hebdomadal Register 1833–41 fos. 115, 117. There were 21 titles in the Caroline Code.

19 University archives. MS. Hebdomadal Register 1833–41 fo. 116.

20 Apsley Ho. MSS. E. Cardwell to duke of Wellington, Nov. 2, 1837.

21 Newman, *Letters & corr.* ii. 246.

22 Sewell also thought that the proposal to abolish the matriculation oath 'impugns all acknowledged principles of a sound moral education, and also the practice of the church herself in the rite of Baptism.'

23 The chief opposition writers were Vaughan Thomas, William Sewell, B. Harrison, and E. Greswell: for the Board, Symons, Cardwell, Hayward Cox (Hampden's Vice-Principal at St. Mary Hall), R. Jenkyns, and G. H. S. Johnson who later sat on the royal commission. Their papers are preserved in Bodl. G. A. Oxon. b. 23. See also E. Greswell, *Letter to the duke of Wellington* (Oxford, 1837); Vaughan Thomas, *Reasons for protesting against the principle upon which a general revision of the statutes of the University has been undertaken . . .* (Oxford, 1838).

24 Apsley Ho. MSS. Duke of Wellington to E. Cardwell, Nov. 5, 1837. In 1842 Sewell pledged himself to obtain an authoritative decision on the right of Convocation to be consulted in advance on the general

principles of measures. Bodl. Wynter Papers. MS. Dep. d. 5 fos. 1–15; *Christian Remembrancer* ix. 137.

25 University archives. MS. Hebdomadal Register 1833–41 fos. 119–20. A further protest against general revision was made through the Proctors in October 1838. *Ibid.* fos. 149–50.

26 Apsley Ho. MSS. A. T. Gilbert to duke of Wellington, Nov. 23, 1837. The matriculation oath to observe the statutes was abolished. *Times* Nov. 27, 1837, p. 6.

27 *Parliamentary debates* 3s. xxxix. 1384–402.

28 B.M. Add. MSS. 34567 fos. 43, 53; 34572 fo. 116.

29 Reprinted in the *Times*, July 16, 1838, p. 5. Whately asked the peers to give legislative assistance to colleges which could not otherwise mend their statutes. (MS. Oriel College Letters no. 225). Not all the speeches were reported in *Parliamentary debates* 3s. xliv. 1–9. At least half a dozen colleges claimed to be actively revising their statutes. Apsley Ho. MSS. R. L. Cotton to duke of Wellington, June 22, 1838.

30 Apsley Ho. MSS. G. Rowley to duke of Wellington, Jan. 14, 1835.

31 University archives. Hebdomadal Register 1833–41 fos. 117–18.

32 *Ibid.* fo. 120.

33 Apsley Ho. MSS. E. Cardwell to duke of Wellington, March 19, 1838; University archives. MS. Hebdomadal Register 1833–41 fos. 130–32.

34 Cox, *Recollections* p. 301.

35 In 1836, Bliss, the Registrar, had hinted broadly to the aged Edward Nares, that he ought to resume the duties of the modern history chair B.M. Add. MSS. 34572 fo. 5.

36 Pusey's influence, for example, was now at its peak, but recruits for his elementary class declined from 8 to 1 per term. Bodl. Wynter Papers MS. Dep. d. 3 fo. 13.

37 University archives. MS. Hebdomadal Register 1833–41 fos. 146–7.

38 Apsley Ho. MSS. A. T. Gilbert to the duke of Wellington, Feb. 22, 1839.

39 See Charles Daubeny's two flysheets of Feb. 24, and March 11, 1839.

40 On this see Robert Hussey, *An examination of the statutes Tit. IV and Tit. V with hints for establishing a system of professorial teaching* (Oxford, 1839) p. 34.

41 Prothero, *Stanley* i. 224, 230–2; *Hints on the formation of a plan for the safe and effectual revival of the professorial system in Oxford* (Oxford, 1839).

42 *Considerations of a plan for combining the professorial system with the system of public examinations in Oxford* (Oxford, 1839). Cf. Mark Pattison's comment. Bodl. MS. Pattison 6 fo. 76.

43 Who wrote the article 'Oxford—tutors and professors' in *Quarterly Review* lxvi. 162.

44 See also the broadsheets preserved in Bodl. G. A. Oxon. c. 55.

45 Apsley Ho. MSS. A. T. Gilbert to duke of Wellington, March 14, 1839; Cox, *Recollections* p. 306.

46 University archives. MS. Hebdomadal Register 1833–41 fo. 174.

47 Apsley Ho. MSS. A. T. Gilbert to duke of Wellington, June 4, 1839.

48 Apsley Ho. MSS. A. T. Gilbert to duke of Wellington, Dec. 23, 1839; University archives. Hebdomadal Register 1833–41 fos. 189–93, 197–9.

49 *Ibid.* fos. 204–5, 213.

50 Apsley Ho. MSS. A. T. Gilbert to duke of Wellington, May 23, June 19, 1840; E. Cardwell to same, June 1, 18, 1840.

51 University archives. MS. Hebdomadal Register 1833–41 fo. 226; Apsley Ho. MSS. E. Cardwell to duke of Wellington, Dec. 16, 1840.

52 University archives. MS. Hebdomadal Register 1833–41 fos. 231–2.

53 University archives. MS. Hebdomadal Meeting Register 1841–54 fo. 22.

54 MS. Oriel College Letters no. 1012.

55 *Second report of the Ecclesiastical Commissioners* (1836) p. 11; *Fourth report* (1836) pp. 10–11.

56 University archives. MS. Hebdomadal Register 1833–41 fos. 104–5, 107.

57 *Ibid.* fos. 216–17; Apsley Ho. MSS. Lord John Russell to duke of Wellington, June 3, 1840.

58 Biblical criticism was provided for in 1843 with the foundation of the Dean Ireland chair.

59 This lengthy correspondence is preserved in the University archives. MS. N.W. 21.5.

60 C. Perry, *Clerical education considered with especial reference to the universities* (London, 1841). This pamphlet carried the support of the Bishop of Lichfield.

61 The voluminous correspondence dealing with this question (including Gaisford's defeat of Sir James Graham's attempt to put the new professors under financial security for the performance of duty) is to be found in Apsley Ho. MSS. E. Cardwell to duke of Wellington, Feb. 15, May 17, 1841; May 12, 1842; P. Wynter to same, Feb. 27, 1841; Bodl. Wynter Papers MS. Dep. d. 4 *passim*; B.M. Add. MSS. 40459 fos. 113–15, 118–27, 145, 168, 216, 222, 224–32; 40499 fos. 176–9; 40506 fos. 241, 243, 301–2, 339, 341; 40507 fos. 7, 9.

62 Liddon, *Pusey* ii. 285, printed with some errors from Bodl. Wynter Papers MS. Dep. d. 3 fo. 16.

63 *Ibid.* fos. 10–14.

64 Newman, *Letters & corr.* ii. 317. The other interest of this comment is that Newman had obtained information which was still being treated as 'top secret' by the Board. Apsley Ho. MSS. E. Cardwell to duke of Wellington, Dec. 16, 1840.

65 *British Critic* July 1842.

66 *The new degree of candidate in theology* (Oxford, 1842).

67 See H. W. Wilberforce's article in *Christian Remembrancer* 1845 pp. 133 *seq.* Cf. J. B. Mozley, *Letters* p. 132.

68 *Christian Remembrancer* ix. 154.

69 *Memorials of Hampden* pp. 141–3; Pusey Ho. MSS. Corr. of Isaac Williams with T. Keble, n.d. [c. May 23, 1842].

70 Apsley Ho. MSS. E. Cardwell to duke of Wellington, Dec. 2, 1839.

71 After much perplexity John Hill supported him. St. Edmund Hall• MS. Diary of John Hill, June 7, 1842; *Chrs* 1 *1 Observer* 1839, pp. 349–60; 1844, p. 297; Newman, *Letters & corr.* i 296, 398. Cf. MS. Oriel College Letters no. 216.

72 Apsley Ho. MSS. E. Cardwell to duke of Wellington, May 23, 1842.

73 Pusey Ho. MSS. Corr. of C. P. Golightly with W. J. Bricknell, July 1, 1842. This became a constant theme of the high-church party (cf. the *Guardian's* fulminations against Bunsen's appearance on Exeter Hall platforms in the later 'forties) but there had been regular points of alliance as well as of conflict between the two parties for over twenty years.

74 Prothero, *Stanley* i. 310–11.

75 The leaders took a less active part than in 1836. Newman, *Letters & corr.* ii. 397. Liddon, *Pusey* ii. 288–9.

76 See flysheet of May 26, 1842, Bodl. G. A. Oxon. b. 24.

77 *The Hampden question revived by the Hebdomadal Board* (Oxford, 1842); *The censure of 1836 still necessary* (Oxford, 1842).

78 Apsley Ho. MSS. E. Cardwell to duke of Wellington, June 7, 1842. On July 20, the Board took no action upon the resolution in Hampden's favour of a numerous meeting at St. Mary Hall held under the chairmanship of Charles Daubeny. University archives. MS. Hebdomadal Meeting Register 1841–54 fo. 26.

79 The way Newman and Pattison comforted themselves with this image long after the reality had changed is shown in *British Critic* 1838 pp. 144–5; Bodl. MS. Pattison 6 fo. 6.

80 On this episode see Ward, *Georgian Oxford* pp. 89–90.

81 *Edinburgh Review* lxvi. 396 *seq.*

82 *Christian Observer* 1839, p. 64. The Chancellor's opposition to a church was blunter. 'I don't think that an addnl. church is necessary in Oxford, and I don't feel any disposition to subscribe to defray the expense thereof.' Apsley Ho. MSS. Duke of Wellington to J. D. Macbride, Feb. 25, 1839.

83 On his views see E. M. Goulburn, *Reminiscences of C. P. Golightly* (Oxford, 1886) p. 12.

84 *Times* March 23, 1841, p. 6; Newman, *Letters & corr.* ii. 333. Cf. *Life & letters of Dean Church* p. 26.

85 The most famous of these was Froude's *Remains* (1837), but a lesser known later jewel was Rev. G. D. Haughton's treatise *On sex in the world to come* (1841).

86 *Corr. of A. H. Clough* i. 81.

87 Keble College MSS. Letters of J. Keble to T. Keble, June 3, 1839. Cf. *Letters of Lord Blachford* p. 42.

88 Bodl. MS. Top. Oxon. e. 165 p. 4.

89 Magdalen College MSS. D.5.14. F. C. Balfour to Martin Routh May 26, 1836.

90 *Edinburgh Review* lxxvi. 464 *seq.*

91 Stanley, *Arnold* p. 559.

92 Apsley Ho. MSS. Duke of Wellington to Vice-Chancellor, Dec. 29, 1839.

93 E. J. Whately, *Life of Whately* i. 484.

94 *Correspondence of J. H. Newman with J. Keble and others 1839–45* (London, 1917) pp. 36–9.

95 Keble College MSS. Corr. of Sir J. T. Coleridge with J. Keble, n.d. and Feb. 8, 1842.

96 Keble College MSS. Letters of J. Keble to T. Keble, n.d. and July 18, 1841.

97 Newman, *Letters & corr.* ii. 296. Cf. MS. Oriel College Letters no. 1012.

98 The whigs kept Dr. Shuttleworth, Warden of New College, waiting till 1840 for the see of Chichester, and he died a year and four months later (Cox, *Recollections* p. 323); Arnold, whose regius chair of modern history was the last preferment in Melbourne's gift, survived less than a year. After Hampden no other Oxford whigs received anything.

99 B.M. Add. MSS. 40459 fo. 146.

100 He forbade B.N.C. men to attend Hampden's lectures. Apsley Ho. MSS. A. T. Gilbert to duke of Wellington, Nov. 16, 1836; Jan. 19, 1837; E. Cardwell to same, Dec. 5, 7, 1836.

101 *Autobiography of Isaac Williams* ed. Sir G. Prevost (London, 1892) pp. 145–6.

102 This appointment was by no means popular. MS. Oriel College Letters no. 248; Pusey Ho. MSS. Corr. of I. Williams with T. Keble, 'Monday evening ½ past 7.' Cf. E. Hodder, *Life & work of 7th earl of Shaftesbury* (London, 1886) i. 399.

103 B.M. Add. MSS. 40459 fos. 252, 257; 40512 fos. 55–61.

104 Apsley Ho. MSS. E. Cardwell to duke of Wellington, March 10, 1841.

105 B.M. Add. MSS. 40554 fos. 284–9, 393.

106 *Ibid.* fos. 382–8.

107 B.M. Add. MSS. 40459 fo. 230.

108 B.M. Add. MSS. 40561 fos. 311, 313–17.

109 J. D. Dalgairns gave a hilarious account of the contretemps at Balliol in 1843. The fellows persuaded the Master to let Pugin rebuild the ruinous portions of the college, but after the designs had won approval he opposed them as a popish influence. The fellows thereupon refused to rebuild the Master's lodgings which were already unfit for habitation. To complete the comedy, the leaders of the Pugin party were the liberals who got W. G. Ward turned out of his lectureship. Keble College MSS. Letters presented by Dr. Hermitage Day (2 letters of April 1843). Cf. W. Ward, *William George Ward and the Oxford Movement* (London, 1889) pp. 154–5.

110 B.M. Add. MSS. 40567 fos. 409–12; 40568 fos. 49, 53, 55–8; Balliol College. MS. Jenkyns VI. Sir R. Peel to R. Jenkyns, May 30, 1845; Bp. of Llandaff to same, June 9, 1845.

111 Which formed the basis of his *Kingdom of Christ* (1838).

112 MS. Oriel College Letters no. 419; B.M. Add. MSS. 34572 fo. 120; A. H. D. Acland, *Memoir and letters of Sir Thomas Dyke Acland* (printed London, 1902) pp. 75, 81.

113 Liddon, *Pusey* ii. 263. In 1846 Pusey admitted to Keble that he had gone wrong on this issue and on the Jerusalem bishopric. *Ibid.* iii. 57.

114 Keble College MSS. Corr. of Sir J. T. Coleridge with Keble, Nov. 30, 1841; Pusey Ho. MSS. Corr. of I. Williams with T. Keble, Nov. 21, 1841; Bodl. MS. Pattison 44 fos. 75–6; E. Hodder, *Shaftesbury* i. 388–98.

115 B.M. Add. MSS. 40469 fo. 122; 44236 fos. 1–3; 44343 fo. 29.

116 Liddon, *Pusey* ii. 266–7.

117 Newman obstinately refused to credit the strength of the opposition. *Ibid.* ii. 267.

118 *Oxford unmasked; or an attempt to describe some of the abuses of that university* . . . (London, 1842).

119 J. Garbett, *Is unauthorised teaching always schismatical?* (London, 1844).

120 Bodl. Wynter Papers MS. Dep. d. 5 fos. 141–8. Cf. Cox, *Recollections* p. 338.

121 Liddon, *Pusey* ii. 306 *seq.* Liddon's MS. sources are now in the Bodleian. Wynter Papers. MS. Dep. d. 3.

122 Bodl. Wynter Papers. MS. Dep. d. 3 fo. 157.

123 Bodl. Wynter Papers. MS. Dep. d. 4. fo. 348.

124 *Inquirer* June 10, 1843, p. 354.

125 *Edinburgh Review* lxxxi. 399 *seq.*

126 *Inquirer* Nov. 4, 1843, p. 689.

127 *Christian Reformer* 1839, p. 932; 1845, p. 439; *Inquirer* 1845, p. 433; *Edinburgh Review* lxxxi. 474; *Parliamentary debates* 3s. lvii. 65–72, 451–2, 972–4, 1245–8; lxxi. 317–21; lxxiv. 465; lxxx. 11–23; lxxxii. 277, 871; cvi. 1343.

128 Keble College MSS. Letters presented by Dr. Hermitage Day. J. D. Dalgairns to J. M. Gresley, Dec. 10, 1844.

129 Liddon, *Pusey* ii. 340.

130 Cox, *Recollections* p. 328; Bodl. Wynter Papers MS. Dep. d. 3 fo. 94; 4 fos. 316–40.

131 B.M. Add. MSS. 34575 fos. 85, 89.

132 Bodl. Wynter Papers MS. Dep. d. 4 fo. 343.

133 Liddon, *Pusey* iii. 113–28 *passim*.

134 Apsley Ho. MSS. E. Cardwell to duke of Wellington, Dec. 12, 1842.

135 *Copies of the correspondence in the case of the regius professor of divinity and Mr. Macmullen* (Oxford, 1844); Bodl. Wynter Papers. MS. Dep. d. 5. fos. 20–68; University archives. MS. N.W. 21.7; J. B. Mozley, *Letters* pp. 151–2; *The new examination for divinity degrees* (Oxford, 1844); [Charles Marriott] *A few words to the resident members of Convocation* . . . (Oxford, 1844;) *The Theological Statute* (Oxford, 1844); broadsheets of Feb. 21 & March 7, 1844. The new

Principal of St. Edmund Hall postponed his divinity disputations for six months 'in consequence of the prevailing cavillings and determination of the tractarian party to put any hindrance they can, by vexatious opposition to public business, especially in reference to Divy Degrees.' St. Edmund Hall. MS. Diary of John Hill, June 25, Dec. 11, 16, 1844. Cf. *Oxoniensia.* xxiv. 92, 93.

136 St. Edmund Hall. MS. Diary of John Hill, Oct. 6, 1843; Bodl. Wynter Papers MS. Dep. d. 4. fo. 427.

137 A useful account of this episode, based on most of the available material, is given by J. S. G. Simmons, 'The Duke of Wellington and the Vice-Chancellorship in 1844' *Bodleian Library Record* v. 37 *seq.*

138 Keble College MSS. Letters presented by Dr. Hermitage Day. J. D. Dalgairns to J. M. Gresley, Sept. 5, 1844.

139 Pusey Ho. MSS. Corr. of E. B. Pusey with Sir William Heathcote, Sept. 23, 1844. Pusey later ungraciously claimed that he had taken up the cause in the hope of keeping Newman in the church. Keble College MSS. Corr. of E. B. Pusey with J. Keble [Oct. 27] 1844.

140 Liddon, *Pusey* ii. 413.

141 Keble College MSS. Corr. of J. T. Coleridge with J. Keble, Sept. 28, October 2, 1844; J. B. Mozley, *Letters* p. 154; Cf. however, Pusey Ho. MSS. Corr. of E. B. Pusey with Sir Wm. Heathcote, J. W. Awdry to same, Oct. 1, 1844.

142 Pusey Ho. MSS. Corr. of E. B. Pusey with Sir Wm. Heathcote, Sept. 21, 23, 27, 1844.

143 B.M. Add. MSS. 44247 fo. 218. They were, however, right in supposing Symons had condemned Pusey.

144 Keble College MSS. Unbound corr. of E. B. Pusey with J. Keble, Sept. 1844; [John Griffiths] *Letters with a few remarks concerning rumours which have long been in circulation to prejudice the appointment of the Warden of Wadham to the Vice-Chancellorship* (printed but not published, Oxford, 1844).

145 MS. Oriel College Letters nos. 43–50; Pusey Ho. MSS. Corr. of C. P. Golightly with W. S. Bricknell, *passim.*

146 *Bodleian Library Record* v. 46–7.

147 Bodl. Wynter Papers. MS. Dep. d. 4 fos. 427–8.

148 MS. Oriel College Letters no. 45; B.M. Add. MSS. 34575 fos. 406–7.

149 The committees' sheets are preserved in Bodl. G. A. Oxon. b. 25.

150 St. Edmund Hall. MS. Diary of John Hill, Oct. 8, 1844.

151 Liddon, *Pusey* ii. 413.

152 University archives. MS. Hebdomadal Meeting Register 1841–54 fos. 88–9.

153 University archives. MSS. W.P.γ3 (7); W.P.γ4.2.

154 MS. Oriel College Letters no. 47. For Ward's case in general: W. Pugh & R. G. Chapman, 'Henry Wall's Notes, 1844,' *Oxoniensia* xxiv. 83 *seq.*

155 E. J. Whately, *Life of R. Whately* ii. 60–3.

156 MS. Oriel College Letters nos. 54–8. The official papers of the case are in University archives. MS. N.W. 21–8.

157 Pusey Ho. MSS. Letters to Dr. R. Scott, B. Jowett to R. Scott, [June 1841]; A. C. Tait to same, Oct. 12, 31, 1841; R. Scott to A. C. Tait n.d. [Nov. 1841]; Balliol College. MS. Jenkyns VI. W. C. Lake to R. Jenkyns, July 1, 1844.

158 Liddon, *Pusey* ii. 415.

159 Keble College MSS. Letters presented by Dr. J. Hermitage Day. J. D. Dalgairns to J. M. Gresley, Dec. 10, 1844.

160 Pusey Ho. MSS. Corr. of C. Marriott with E. B. Pusey [Dec. 29] 1844.

161 E. J. Whately, *Life of R. Whately* ii. 78.

162 A. C. Tait, *Letter to the Vice-Chancellor* (London, 1845); Balliol College. MS. Jenkyns VI. A. C. Tait to R. J. Renishaw, Dec. 30, 1844; Jowett MSS. Box. E, 2 letters, B. Jowett to A. P. Stanley, Jan. 1845. Cf. *Life of F. D. Maurice* i. 391 *seq.*; Abbot & Campbell, *Jowett* i. 111-16.

163 B.M. Add. MSS. 44247 fo. 239.

164 *Memorials of Hampden* pp. 117-18.

165 These papers are preserved in University archives. MS. N.W. 21.8.

166 Much of the correspondence relating to this is in Pusey Ho. MSS. Ollard Papers Box II.

167 J. B. Mozley, *Letters* pp. 161-2.

168 B.M. Add. MSS. 44206 fos. 1-22 (Other copies in MS. Oriel College Letters Gl. 1-5, 66-8).

169 B.M. Add. MSS. 44236. fos. 5-6.

170 R. Hussey, *Reasons for voting upon the third question to be proposed to Convocation on 13th inst.* (Oxford, 1845); Bodl. Wynter Papers MS. Dep. d. 3 fos. 146, 151.

171 Prothero, *Stanley* i. 337-8.

172 E.g. Abbot & Campbell, *Jowett* i. 93-4.

173 B.M. Add. MSS. 44281 fo. 28.

174 *Ibid.* fo. 28; University archives. MS. Hebdomadal Meeting Register 1841-54 fos. 92-3.

175 Bodl. G. A. Oxon. 4°25 (13).

176 B.M. Add. MSS. 44281 fo. 33.

177 Ward forfeited his fellowship by marriage, having, as W. D. Christie remarked, preached celibacy as he subscribed the articles, in a non-natural sense. *Parliamentary debates* 3s. lxxix. 405.

178 St. Edmund Hall. MS. Diary of John Hill, July 5, 1845.

179 Apsley Ho. MSS. B. P. Symons to duke of Wellington, Dec. 22, 1845.

180 Reynolds, *The evangelicals at Oxford* p. 125.

181 E.g. Keble College MSS. Letters of J. Keble to T. Keble [1842].

182 Crabb Robinson, *Diary* iii. 204-5.

183 B.M. Add. MSS. 40470 fos. 305-8. Printed in D. C. Lathbury, *Correspondence on church and religion of W. E. Gladstone* (London, 1910) i. 342-7.

184 W. Sewell, *The attack upon the University of Oxford in a letter to earl Grey.* (2nd ed. London, 1834) p. 6.

185 University archives. MS. Hebdomadal Register 1841–54 fos. 46, 60; Bodl. Wynter Papers. MS. Dep. d. 3. fo. 94.

186 Bodl. Wynter Papers MS. Dep. d. 4 fo. 366; *Tradesmen & undergraduates* (London, 1844); *Christian Observer* 1844, pp. 147 *seq.*; *Quarterly Review* lxxiii. 98–9.

187 J. W. Burgon, *Twelve good men* pp. 281–2.

188 B.M. Add. MSS. 40470 fos. 307–8; 44735 fos. 42–3.

189 University archives. MS. Hebdomadal Meeting Register 1841–54 fo. 87.

190 Abbot & Campbell, *Jowett* i. 120.

191 Cf. *New regulations on medical degrees* Aug. 1, 1840 (Bodl. G. A. Oxon. c. 59).

192 University archives. MS. Hebdomadal Register 1833–41 fo 101.

193 Cox, *Recollections* p. 321.

194 University archives. MS. Hebdomadal Meeting Register 1841–54 fos. 25, 34–7.

195 *Parliamentary debates* 3s. lxxxii. 715.

196 Francis Jeune found it 'painful . . . that many of the attached members of the church have been led to doubt whether the learning we impart be indeed useful learning; whether the religion which we teach be indeed true religion.' F. Jeune, *The studies of Oxford vindicated* (Oxford, 1845) p. 4.

197 *Edinburgh Review* lxxvi. 378.

198 *Corr. of J. H. Newman with J. Keble and others* p. 58.

199 Apsley Ho. MSS. P. Wynter to duke of Wellington, Nov. 8, 1840.

200 G. R. M. Ward. *An appeal to the bishop of Winchester, visitor of Trinity College, Oxford on the misappropriation of the endowments of that society.* (Oxford, 1839).

201 Apsley Ho. MSS. E. Cardwell to duke of Wellington, Oct. 8, 1839.

202 G. R. M. Ward, *The statutes of All Souls College, Oxford.* (London, 1841).

203 Apsley Ho. MSS. E. Cardwell to duke of Wellington, Oct. 15, 1839.

204 Apsley Ho. MSS. Duke of Wellington to E. Cardwell, Oct. 17, 1839; Same to Vice-Chancellor, Dec. 27, 1839; A. T. Gilbert to duke of Wellington, Jan. 8, 1840.

205 J. B. Mozley, *Letters* pp. 97–9, 101.

206 *British Critic* 1840, p. 358; R. Ornsby, *Memoirs of J. R. Hope-Scott* (London, 1884) i. 178–90; *Corr. of J. H. Newman with J. Keble and others* pp. 56–9.

207 G. R. M. Ward, *The foundation statutes of Bishop Fox for Corpus Christi College . . .* (London, 1843) p. xliii.

208 *Oxford university statutes* vol. i. ed. G. R. M. Ward (London, 1845); vol. ii. ed. G. R. M. Ward and J. Heywood (London, 1851).

209 For the above see *Manchester Guardian*, Oct. 19, 1897, p. 12; Oct. 20, 1897, p. 3.
210 J. O. Halliwell, *The foundation documents of Merton College, Oxford* (London, 1843) p. xi.
211 1st ed. London, 1845; 2nd ed. London, 1846.
212 London, 1843. See vol. i. p. vi; ii pt. ii. 597 *seq*. Cf. *Inquirer*, 1843, p. 517.
213 *English universities* ii. pt. i. p. 246.
214 *Parliamentary debates* 3s. lxix. 855–915. Cf. B.M. Add. MSS. 34575 fo. 66.
215 Manning, *Protestant Dissenting Deputies* p. 372.
216 *Parliamentary debates* 3s. lxxiv. 1459, 1465.
217 *Ibid.* 3s. lxxix. 393–452. Cf. *Inquirer* 1845, p. 241.

CHAPTER VII

1 *Guardian* 1848, p. 450.
2 Cox, *Recollections* p. 355.
3 Pusey Ho. Liddon's MS. transcripts of Pusey's corr. with J. Keble. i. fo. 423.
4 *Times*, Jan. 9, 1846, p. 3; Jan. 16, p. 4; Jan. 27, p. 5; March 25, p. 6.
5 Bodl. MS. Pattison 47 *passim*; M. Pattison, *Memoirs* pp. 222–3.
6 W. Sewell, *The danger and safeguard of the young in the present state of controversy* (Oxford, 1848) pp. 16–17. Cf. *Oxford Magazine* May 1847, pp. 141–8.
7 Sewell, *op. cit.* p. 18.
8 Lord Selborne, *Memorials Part I, family and personal, 1766–1865* ii. 64.
9 *Christian Observer* Jan. 1850, p. 6.
10 MS. Oriel College Letters no. 297.
11 Liddon, *Pusey*, iii. 116.
12 Bodl. MS. Pattison 47 fo. 134.
13 Even in 1844, however, Froude was reported to have 'become regularly Germanized, and talked unreservedly about Strauss, miracles, etc.' Abbot & Campbell, *Jowett* i. 111.
14 MS. Exeter College Register fos. 152–3. On March 15, 1858, Froude sought to win the Rector's support for his candidacy for the regius chair of modern history by an abject recantation of his folly, and the assurance that he had purchased the copyright of the offending book and was now seeking 'to clear the English Reformation and the fathers of the Anglican Church from the stains which have been allowed to gather on them.' *Ibid.* fo. 216. Cf. W. H. Dunn, *James Anthony Froude* (Oxford, 1961) i. 135 *seq.* 226–7.
15 *Corr. of A. H. Clough* i. 249.
16 F. Oakeley, *Remarks on the study of Aristotelian and Platonic ethics as a branch of the Oxford system of education* (Oxford, 1837) p. 11.

17 Balliol College. Jowett MSS. Box E, B. Jowett to A. P. Stanley [June 1846], [Aug. or Sept. 1847]. In 1841 Vaughan unsuccessfully contested the moral philosophy chair.

18 *Edinburgh Review* xc. 305; lxxxi. 394–5.

19 *Letters of William Stubbs* ed. W. H. Hutton (London, 1904) p. 20.

20 *Corr. of A. H. Clough* i. 38.

21 Goldwin Smith, *Reminiscences* ed. A. Haultain (New York, 1910) p. 73.

22 In 1848 he made a spirited attempt to curb the activities of J. W. Burgon, the high-churchman, as librarian of the Union. J. B. Mozley, *Letters* p. 193.

23 'A divine of the Arnold school, with all its excellences, but with its faults exaggerated . . . a clear and decisive writer; an earnest & bold preacher; not caring about learning or authority, but stating the truth fearlessly as he finds it.' E. Cardwell to Lord Derby, March 15, 1858. MS. Knowsley Papers Box 93/3.

24 F. A. Iremonger, *William Temple, Archbishop of Canterbury* (London, 1948) p. 12.

25 *Letters of Benjamin Jowett* ed. E. Abbot and L. Campbell (London, 1899) p. 167.

26 *Correspondence of A. H. Clough* i. 90.

27 *Ibid.* i. 38.

28 Abbot & Campbell, *Jowett* i. 68. It is characteristic of Jowett that in this, his version, of John vii. 17, 'His will' is rendered by 'the works.'

29 Goldwin Smith, *Reminiscences* p. 83.

30 *Letters of Benjamin Jowett* pp. 2, 4.

31 Balliol College. Jowett MSS. Box. F, B. Jowett to R. R. W. Lingen, Aug. 18, 1846.

32 Abbot & Campbell, *Jowett* i. 124. Cf. The dissenters 'are narrow-minded dogs as they have again and again shewn.' Balliol College. Jowett MSS. Box F, B. Jowett to R. R. W. Lingen, Sept. 22, 1846.

33 Though admitting that he only half-understood the *History of Philosophy*. Abbot & Campbell, *Jowett* i. 117.

34 *Ibid.* i. 142.

35 *Ibid.* i. 412.

36 Balliol College, Jowett MSS. Box E, Florence Nightingale to E. Abbot, Jan. 4, 1895.

37 H. L. Thompson, *Henry George Liddell. A memoir* (London, 1899) p. 52.

38 Abbot & Campbell, *Jowett* i. 165–6.

39 Goldwin Smith, *Reminiscences* p. 103.

40 The tory Edward Cardwell described him as 'an excellent scholar & highly accomplished.' MS. Knowsley Papers Box 93/3. March 15, 1858.

41 J. B. Mozley, *Letters* p. 320.

42 M. Pattison, *Memoirs* p. 89; J. R. Magrath, *The Queen's College* (Oxford, 1921) ii. 168–9; B.M. Add. MSS. 44218 fos. 79–82.

43 Balliol College. Jowett MSS. Box E, B. Jowett to A. P. Stanley, Sept. 9, [1850].

44 Keble College MSS. Corr. of J. Keble with T. Keble, [?1831], [?1833].

45 D. Macleane, *History of Pembroke College, Oxford* (Oxford, 1897) pp. 445–6.

46 MS. Oriel College Letters no. 425.

47 Bodl. Wynter Papers. MS. Dep. d. 5 fo. 100.

48 *Pages from the diary of an Oxford lady, 1843–62* ed. M. J. Gifford (Oxford, 1932) p. 5. For the rest of this case see Bodl. Wynter Papers MS. Dep. d. 5 fos. 97–110; Macleane, *Pembroke College* pp. 463–4.

49 B.M. Add. MSS. 44363 fos. 230–3.

50 Apsley Ho. MSS. Master of Pembroke to duke of Wellington, June 1838.

51 *Ibid.* See the correspondence between Jeune and the duke of Wellington, 1849.

52 F. Jeune, *The studies of Oxford vindicated* (Oxford, 1845).

53 Liddon, *Pusey* iii. 101.

54 *Times* Nov. 18, 1847, p. 3.

55 MS. Knowsley Papers. Box 93/3. March 15, 1858.

56 *Liberty! Equality! Fraternity!* [Oxford, 1848] (Bodl. G. A. Oxon. b. 26).

57 Bodl. MS. Pattison 50 fo. 404.

58 On Conington: *The recollections of the Very Rev. G. D. Boyle* (London, 1895) pp. 145 *seq.*; Mark Pattison, *Memoirs* p. 249; *Memorials of W. C. Lake* ed. K. Lake (London, 1901) p. 74. There is a memoir by H. J. S. Smith prefixed to *Miscellaneous writings of John Conington* ed. J. A. Symonds (London, 1872). Cf. *Macmillan's Magazine* xxi.146.

59 *Prospective Review* v. 2.

60 Abbot & Campbell, *Jowett* i. 173. The draft is in Balliol College Jowett MSS. Box E.

61 *Commons Journals* ci. 21; *Parliamentary Papers* 1846 vol. xxxii. no. 765.

62 *British Quarterly Review* iii. 358–76. This interesting article distinguished the functions of universities in different types of state.

63 B.M. Add. MSS. 34576 fo. 144.

64 Abbot & Campbell, *Jowett* i. 188.

65 *Ibid.* i. 187–8; Balliol College. Jowett MSS. Box F, B. Jowett to R. R. W. Lingen, Sept. 22, 1846.

66 *Morning Post* reprinted in *Guardian* Jan. 6, 1847, p. 582. Cf. Jan. 26, p. 62. Both the university burgesses suspected the same thing. B.M. Add. MSS. 34576 fo. 348; J. B. Mozley, *Letters* p. 182.

67 *Guardian* 1847, p. 73.

68 *Ibid.* 1847, p. 89.

69 The principal editor was the radical and dissenting postmaster, Mr. Warne. B.M. Add. MSS. 44181 fo. 10.

70 The *Magazine* ran till April 1848 when it was amalgamated with the rabidly liberal and even shorter-lived *Christian Enquirer* edited by Henry Stebbing, editor of the *Athenaeum*. See also *Christian Reformer* June 1847, p. 366; March 1848, p. 182; *British Quarterly Review* v. 559.

71 *Times* April 22, 1847, p. 4.

72 B.M. Add. MSS. 44208 fos. 13–14.

73 Balliol College. Jowett MSS. Box F, B. Jowett to R. R. W. Lingen [Oxford, July 14, 1847]; Abbot & Campbell, *Jowett* i. 188–92.

74 *Inquirer* 1847, p. 754; 1848, pp. 65, 81.

75 D. A. Winstanley, *Early Victorian Cambridge* (Cambridge, 1940) p. 221.

76 It was said that Horsman and Bonamy Price were the moving spirits behind this petition. B.M. Add. MSS. 44367 fo. 141.

77 *Guardian* 1848, pp. 333, 354, 550; *Royal commission of inquiry in the universities of Oxford and Cambridge* (n. pl. or d.). Bodl. G. A. Oxon. c. 64 (163).

78 The Vice-Chancellor was delighted (Apsley Ho. MSS. B. P. Symons to duke of Wellington, July 1, 1848). The duke replied on July 19, urging the university again to broaden the basis of its studies, reform its statutes and reduce undergraduate expenses.

79 *Guardian* 1848, pp. 543–5, 560–1. The *Times* also became much less friendly to the university system. 'What the Crown practically acknowledges by appointing a professor, the university practically denies by withholding his class.' *Times* Aug. 24, 1848, p. 4.

80 For the genesis of this movement; Liddon, *Pusey* iii. 79–81. A copy is printed in *Six letters addressed to the editor of the Oxford Herald* (Oxford, 1846) (Bodl. G. A. Oxon. 8°77 (18)) and another in *Report of the Oxford University Commission* 1852 Appendix p. 55.

81 'I do not know anything that would be a greater trial of faith than to throw oneself into such a crowd.' Pusey Ho. MSS. Corr. of C. Marriott with E. B. Pusey, Aug. 8, 1845.

82 J. W. Burgon, *Twelve good men* App. G. pp. 480–1; Boyle, *Recollections* pp. 109–10.

83 W. Sewell, *Journal of a residence at the college of St. Columba in Ireland* (Oxford, 1847) pp. xv–xvii.

84 This notion with its overtones of past disputes at Oriel again provoked the wrath of the *Edinburgh Review* (1848) lxxxviii. 183.

85 B.M. Add. MSS. 44251 pt. I. fo. 1. Cf. MS. Oriel College Letters no. 1072.

86 Liddon, *Pusey* iii. 83.

87 *Guardian* 1851, p. 449.

88 Pusey Ho. MSS. Corr. of C. Marriott with E. B. Pusey, *passim*; B.M. Add. MSS. 44281 fo. 38; 44251 pt. I. fos. 1–2.

89 Later, Beresford-Hope; the builder of All Saints, Margaret Street, London.

90 Keble College MSS. Letters of J. Keble to T. Keble, May 8, 1846; Liddon, *Pusey* iii. 87–9; A. H. D. Acland, *Memoir and letters of Sir T. D. Acland* (printed, London, 1902) p. 131 (this letter should be dated 1846); B.M. Add. MSS. 44251 pt. I. fos 4–7; Pusey Ho. MSS. Corr. of C. Marriott with E. B. Pusey, April 11, [1846].

91 B.M. Add. MSS. 44251 pt. I. fos. 3, 10; Pusey Ho. MSS. Corr. of C. Marriott with E. B. Pusey, Nov. 9, 1845.

92 Apsley Ho. MSS. E. Cardwell to duke of Wellington, March 16, 1846. The report was filed at the end of MS. Hebdomadal Meeting Register 1841–54 no. 43, and printed in *Report of the Oxford University Commission* 1852 App. pp. 55–7.

93 B.M. Add. MSS. 44362 fo. 109–110; 44363 fo. 5.

94 *Oxford Protestant Magazine* i. 121–22; *Parliamentary Papers* 1850 vol. xlii. Return of matriculations, 1845–9.

95 C. Marriott, *University extension and the poor scholar question* (Oxford, 1848) p. 10. With matriculations averaging about 400 annually, this was a considerable addition.

96 J. W. Mackail, *Life of William Morris* (London, 1907) i. 32.

97 *Guardian* 1848, p. 11; *Times* Jan. 1, 1848, p. 6; Jan. 5, p. 7; Jan. 6, p. 3; Jan. 8, p. 3; Jan. 12, p. 4; May 20, p. 5; Aug. 7, 1849, p. 4; Aug. 13, pp. 4, 5; Oct. 18, p. 4; Oct. 19, p. 4; Oct. 20, p. 7; *Oxford tradesmen versus the insolvent Jennings* (Oxford, 1848); *Resolutions of a meeting of Oxford tradesmen . . . Oct. 13, 1849* (G. A. Oxon. c. 65 (125)); University archives. MS. Hebdomadal Meeting Register 1841–54 fos. 105, 152, 166.

98 *Guardian* 1851, p. 533. Cf. University archives. MS. Hebdomadal Meeting Register 1841–54 fo. 118.

99 Woollcombe was conservative in politics and theology, and was a great bugbear to both Mark Pattison and Jowett. Pattison, *Memoirs* p. 178.

100 O. Gordon, *Considerations on the improvement of the present examination statute . . .* (2nd ed. Oxford, 1847) p. 76; E. C. Woollcombe, *University extension and the poor scholar question* (Oxford, 1848). Cf. *Six letters addressed to the editor of the Oxford Herald.*

101 According to the calculations of C. P. Eden, fellow of Oriel.

102 Abbot & Campbell, *Jowett* i. 120, 183, 212, 223, 280. At the crucial time Temple was serving as principal of Kneller Hall (1849–55). Cf. Prothero, *Stanley* i. 363.

103 Pusey Ho. MSS. Corr. of C. Marriott with E. B. Pusey, 1846 *passim*: B.M. Add. MSS. 44251 pt. I. fos. 8–10.

104 Sir J. T. Coleridge, *A memoir of the Rev. John Keble* (2nd ed. Oxford and London, 1869) i. 332.

105 *Guardian* 1849, pp. 745, 752, 781.

106 B.M. Add. MSS. 44251 pt. I. fos. 28–30.

107 W. Sewell, *Suggestions for the extension of the university* (Oxford, 1850).

108 MS. Oriel College Letters nos. 791–3.

109 B.M. Add. MSS. 44386 fos. 196–8.

110 University archives. MS. Hebdomadal Meeting Register 1841–54 fos. 120, 123, 148, 212, 217, 226, 227–8, 231.

111 £200 was a figure commonly spent at this time.

112 B.M. Add. MSS. 44363 fos. 230–1.

113 Cf. M. Wilkinson, *Expenses of undergraduates* (London, 1845).

114 For expectations of Cardwell's candidature before the vacancy was declared; Balliol College. Jowett MSS. Box F, B. Jowett to R. R. W. Lingen [April 12, 1847].

115 Goldwin Smith, *Reminiscences* p. 187; Selborne, *Memorials, family and personal* i. 450–1.

116 Jenkyns (Balliol), Ingram (Trinity), Cardwell (St. Alban Hall), Harington (B.N.C.), Jeune (Pembroke), Thompson (St. Edmund Hall), Hampden (St Mary Hall), Cramer (New Inn Hall), Plumptre (University), Hawkins (Oriel), Wynter (St. Johns).

117 Hampden professed not to mind who stood (even Lord Ashley) provided he was a strong anti-Tractarian; but like a good many other heads he finally abstained. *Memorials of R. D. Hampden* pp. 119–20.

118 J. B. Mozley, *Letters* p. 182. W. C. Lake, however, supported Gladstone without much optimism. E. H. Coleridge, *Life and correspondence of John Duke, Lord Coleridge* (London, 1904) i. 185–6.

119 *Guardian* 1847, p. 297. The charge was partially withdrawn, p. 312.

120 B.M. Add. MSS. 44276 fos. 79–80.

121 Gladstone had not sought re-election when he vacated his seat for Newark on becoming colonial secretary in 1845.

122 He regarded the Oxford members as 'representatives of the Church in the House of Commons.' Lathbury, *Corr. of W. E. Gladstone on church and religion* ii. 12.

123 A memoir of Greswell is given in Burgon, *Twelve good men* pp. 292–306.

124 He is said to have refused both the Presidency of Corpus and the divinity chair at Durham in order to devote himself to his studies. T. Fowler, *History of Corpus Christi College* (Oxford, 1893) p. 318.

125 R. Greswell, *Improvements in Port Meadow. A letter to the Mayor of Oxford* April 24, 1865.

126 Magdalen College MSS. D.5.16. R. Greswell to M. J. Routh, Jan. 17, 1844. On this controversy, Burgon, *Twelve good men* p. 414.

127 Apsley Ho. MSS. A. T. Gilbert to duke of Wellington, Jan. 17, 1839; Bp. of Oxford to same, Jan. 18, 1839.

128 He unsuccessfully applied for St. Mary Hall in 1847. Apsley Ho. MSS. R. Greswell to duke of Wellington, Dec. 7, 1847.

129 B.M. Add. MSS. 40537 fos. 59–67.

130 B.M. Add. MSS. 44181 fos. 60–1.

131 *Oxford Protestant Magazine* June 1847, pp. 187 *seq.*

132 B.M. Add MSS. 44276 fo. 109.

133 On these points see Lathbury, *op. cit.* ii. 7–16; B.M. Add. MSS. 44736 fo. 256.

134 *Times* May 17, 1847, p. 4. Gladstone was attacked alike by the *English Churchman* and the *Morning Post.* B.M. Add. MSS. 44276 fo. 100.

135 B.M. Add. MSS. 34576 fos. 373. Cf. *Guardian* 1847, p. 312.

136 'He denies that he said "millions rejoice in potatoes." He said nothing of the kind . . . What then did he say? "Millions rejoice in oatmeal and potatoes." There the Doctor takes his stand and glories in the dictum.' *Times* Feb. 18, 1846, p. 5.

137 St. Edmund Hall. MS. Diary of John Hill. May 17, 22, 1847.

138 B.M. Add. MSS. 44365 fos. 229–36. Characteristically Sewell was soon threatening to resign from Round's committee. *Ibid.* fos. 388–9.

139 Marsham (Merton), Fox (Queen's), Foulkes (Jesus), Cotton (Worcester), Macbride (Magdalen Hall).

140 Garbett, for example, publicly championed Gladstone. B.M. Add. MSS. 44247 fo. 337.

141 B.M. Add. MSS. 44181 fos. 3–4. Christ Church refrained from taking any organised part.

142 The propaganda is summarised in Morley, *Gladstone* (1908 ed.) i. 244–6. Collections of the election squibs are to be found in *A. W. Haddan's Election Book* (Bodl. G. A. Oxon. 4°56); Bodl. G. A. Oxon. b. 24; B.M. Add. MSS. 40617; 44565; Balliol College. MS. Jenkyns VI.

143 *Guardian* 1847, p. 329.

144 e.g. B.M. Add. MSS. 44276 fo. 117.

145 F. D. Maurice, *Thoughts on the duty of a protestant in the present Oxford election* (London, 1847).

146 *Times* July 24, 1847, p. 4.

147 J. B. Mozley, *Letters* p. 185. Haddan had been one of Newman's curates at St. Mary's and was a frequent correspondent of the *Guardian* of which his brother had been a founder. F. Meyrick, *Memories of life at Oxford and elsewhere* (London, 1905) pp. 14–15.

148 *Guardian* 1847, p. 488.

149 J. B. Mozley, *Letters* p. 184. Cf. Coleridge, *Life of Lord Coleridge* i. 186.

150 Keble College MSS. Letters of J. Keble to T. Keble, June 9, 1847.

151 Coleridge, *Memoir of Keble* ii. 341–3.

152 Balliol College. Jowett MSS. Box F, B. Jowett to R. R. W. Lingen, Dec. 3 [1847]; Box E, B. Jowett to A. P. Stanley [1847, 8].

153 Pusey Ho. MSS. Corr. of C. Marriott with E. B. Pusey, Nov. 23, 1847; Jan. 14, 1848.

154 *Guardian* 1847, p. 699.

155 *Guardian* 1848, p. 5; Apsley Ho. MSS. E. Cardwell to duke of Wellington. Dec. 30, 1847; B.M. Add. MSS. 34577 fo. 21.

156 B.M. Add. MSS. 34577 fos. 3–15, 29–30, *passim.*

157 The juniors on their part were sharply rebuked by the liberal press. *Inquirer* 1847, p. 785.

158 R. Whately, *Statements and reflections respecting the church and the universities* (2nd ed. Dublin, 1848). Cf. *Guardian* Jan. 19, 1848, p. 41.

159 *Times* Nov. 19, 1847, pp. 4, 5; Nov. 20, pp. 5, 6.

160 Instead Hinds became Bishop of Norwich in 1849.

161 *Times* Dec. 10, 1847, p. 6. Jacobson had had a nonconformist education. Burgon, *Twelve good men* pp. 367 *seq.*

162 B.M. Add. MSS. 44367 fo. 47.

163 Lathbury, *op. cit.* i. 80.

164 B.M. Add. MSS. 44221 fo. 1.

165 St. Edmund Hall. MS. Diary of John Hill, Dec. 4, 1847.

166 B.M. Add. MSS. 44281 fo. 53; Keble College MSS. Letters of J. Keble to T. Keble. St. Thos. 1847.

167 B.M. Add. MSS. 44181 fo. 21.

168 B.M. Add. MSS. 44206 fo. 23 (MS. Oriel College Letters G1. 69).

169 B.M. Add. MSS. 44181 fos. 24–8.

170 B.M. Add. MSS. 44181 fo. 21; 44367 fo. 43.

171 MS. Oriel College Letters no. 270.

172 On this see Magdalen College MS.B. II.2.2. J. Heywood to G. C. B. Daubeny, Nov. 25, 1846.

173 University archives. MS. Hebdomadal Meeting Register 1841–54 fos. 103, 106; *Oxford University statutes* ii. 364–8.

174 B.M. Add. MSS. 34582 fos. 121–4.

175 O. Gordon, *Considerations on the improvement of the present examination statute* . . . In March, the divinity professors had urged the Board to reform the divinity examinations. University archives. MS. Hebdomadal Meeting Register 1841–54 fo. 117.

176 Abbot & Campbell, *Jowett* i. 192–3.

177 *Guardian* 1848, p. 182.

178 *Ibid.* 1849, p. 77.

179 University archives. MS. Hebdomadal Meeting Register 1841–54 fo. 137.

180 [B. Jowett & A. P. Stanley] *Suggestions for an improvement of the examination statute* (Oxford, 1848); Abbot & Campbell, *Jowett* i. 193.

181 R. Hussey, *Remarks on some proposed changes in the public examinations* (Oxford, 1848) p. 19.

182 *Guardian* 1848, pp. 228, 241–2.

183 R. Walker, *Letter to the Vice-Chancellor on improvements in the examination statute* (Oxford, 1848).

184 C. G. B. Daubeny, *Brief remarks on the correlation of the natural sciences* (Oxford, 1848).

185 H. W. Acland, *Remarks on the extension of education at the University of Oxford* (Oxford, 1848).

186 T. H. Haddan, *Remarks on legal education with reference to the suggested introduction of legal studies in Oxford* (London, 1848); B.M. Add. MSS. 44276 fos. 148–50.

187 J. B. Mozley, *Letters* p. 198.

188 *Guardian* 1849, pp. 125, 142, 157–8.

189 MS. Oriel College Letters no. 292; *Corr. of A. H. Clough* i. 247.

190 *Ibid.* i. 248.

191 *The fourth school* (Bodl. G. A. Oxon. c. 65 (179)).

192 *Guardian* 1849, p. 157. See also the collection of flysheets in Bodl, G. A. Oxon. b. 26.

193 Balliol College. Jowett MSS. Box F, B. Jowett to R. R. W. Lingen [March 16, 1849]; *Guardian* 1849, pp. 173–4.

194 The voting is conveniently set out in the *Times*, March 21, 1849, p. 8.

195 *Guardian* 1849, pp. 189–90, 205–6; *Oxford Herald*, March 24, 1849.

196 B.M. Add. MSS. 44181 fo. 54; Balliol College. Jowett MSS. Box E. B. Jowett to A. P. Stanley [Dec. 1849, misdated 1851?].

197 E. M. Goulburn, *J. W. Burgon* (London, 1892) i. 211–12.

198 *Guardian* 1849, pp. 791, 793, 803–4.

199 Jowett, *Letters* p. 168. The syllabus was finally drawn up by Dr. Jeune, Master of Pembroke. University archives. MS. Hebdomadal Meeting Register 1841–54 fo. 180.

200 *Guardian* 1850, pp. 224, 253.

201 See *The professorial boards* by B. D. and *The objections of B. D. to 'Professorial boards' answered* in Bodl. G. A. Oxon. b. 26.

202 St. Edmund Hall. MS. Diary of John Hill, April 23, 1850.

203 *Guardian* 1850, p. 297; *Times* April 24, 1850, p. 5.

204 University archives. MS. Hebdomadal Meeting Register 1841–54 fos. 187–8.

205 *Times* May 15, 1850, p. 5.

206 Efforts were made to persuade Gladstone to use his influence with Guizot. B.M. Add. MSS. 44367 fos. 107–8, 123–4.

207 *Times* July 3, 1848, p. 4.

208 *Guardian* June 29, 1848, p. 419.

209 Jowett, *Letters* p. 166. Punch amusingly lampooned them all. *Times* July 13, 1848, p. 8.

210 *Times* July 5, 1848, p. 6.

211 He was made M.A. and full professor in 1854.

212 Greswell raised £3500 of which he subscribed £500 himself. MS. Knowsley Papers Box 8, R. Greswell to duke of Wellington, May 3, 1853.

213 Cox, *Recollections* pp. 366, 380; B.M. Add. MSS. 44181 fos. 47, 55, 60–7; Bodl. MS. Acland d. 95 fos. 15, 34; Magdalen College MSS. D.5.16. R. Greswell to M. J. Routh, July 30, 1849; *Guardian* 1851, pp. 449, 453, 467; H. M. & K. D. Vernon, *A history of the Oxford Museum* (Oxford, 1909) pp. 48–50.

214 *Edinburgh Review* lxxxix. 499–517; *Prospective Review* v. 1–16; *Inquirer* 1849, pp. 258, 338; *Guardian* 1849, p. 321.

215 Balliol College. Jowett MSS. Box E, B. Jowett to A. P. Stanley [1848, 9] [1849]; Box F, same to R. R. W. Lingen [March 13, 1849]; Jowett, *Letters* p. 166.

216 *Parliamentary debates* 3s. cx. 691 *seq.*

217 B.M. Add. MSS. 44181 fo. 52; *Guardian* 1850, p. 308. In January 1850, however, Wellington had been certain that a commission would be issued. Bodl. MS. Top. Oxon. e. 80 fo. 6.

218 *Inquirer* 1850, pp. 178, 184, 256. The *Christian Reformer* still supported him, April 1850, p. 242.

219 Prothero, *Stanley* i. 419–20.

220 *Pages from the diary of an Oxford lady* p. 16.

221 *Parliamentary debates* 3s. cx. 747–55.

222 Winstanley, *Early Victorian Cambridge* p.226.

223 Cf. *Fraser's Magazine* July 1850, p. 86.

224 Abbot & Campbell, *Jowett* i. 178; *Memorials of W. C. Lake* p. 78.

225 E. H. Thomson, *Life and letters of William Thomson, Archbishop of York* (London, 1919) pp. 26–9.

226 *Times* May 20, 1850, p. 4; June 3, p. 5; June 12, p. 5; June 22, p. 8.

227 B.M. Add. MSS. 44230 fos. 229–34. Cf. E. A. Litton, *University reform* (London, 1850).

228 *Fraser's Magazine* July 1850, p. 87; Apsley Ho. MSS. Hebdomadal Board to duke of Wellington, May 16, 1850. Cf. B.M. Add. MSS. 44566 fo. 156.

229 B.M. Add. MSS. 34578 fo. 75.

230 B.M. Add. MSS. 44251 pt. I. fo. 17.

231 B.M. Add. MSS. 34578 fo. 99; 44251 pt. I. fos. 18–22; 44369 *passim.*

232 *Parliamentary debates* 3s. cxii. 1455–525.

233 Apsley Ho. MSS. F. C. Plumptre to duke of Wellington. Aug. 16, 1850; B.M. Add. MSS. 34578 fos. 123–5; Bodl. MS. Top. Oxon. e. 80 fos. 15–19.

234 Apsley Ho. MSS. Lord John Russell to duke of Wellington, Aug. 7, 1850; Bodl. MS. Top. Oxon. e. 80 fo. 15.

235 For a humorous forecast of this combination of evangelicalism and liberalism. [W. Sewell] *The university commission, or Lord John Russell's postbag* (Oxford, 1850) pp. 20–1.

236 Goldwin Smith, *Reminiscences* pp. 104–5; Selborne, *Memorials, family and personal* i. 142.

237 Goldwin Smith, *Reminiscences* p. 102.

238 Balliol College. Jowett MSS. Box E, B. Jowett to A. P. Stanley, Sept. 9 [1850].

239 B.M. Add. MSS. 34578 fos. 150–1.

240 Apsley Ho. MSS. E. Cardwell to duke of Wellington, Oct. 22, 26, 29, 1850; University archives. MS. Hebdomadal Meeting Register 1841–54 fos. 195–6; J. B. Mozley, *Letters* pp. 205–6.

241 *Parliamentary debates* 3s. cx. 1159–60; cxi. 1146–58; *Guardian* 1850, p. 813; 1852, p. 45.

242 G. E. Corrie, *Brief historical notices of the interference of the Crown with the affairs of the English universities* (Cambridge, 1839) pp. 99–100.

243 J. W. Pycroft, *The Oxford University Commission* (Oxford and London, 1851). Cf. B.M. Add. MSS. 34578 fos. 310–552 *passim.*

244 University archives. N.W.4.1. (*Guardian* 1851, p. 249); This opinion and others obtained at the time were reprinted in the *Report of the Oxford University Commission* 1852, Appendix pp. 21 *seq.*

245 Bodl. MS. Top. Oxon. c. 286 fos. 3–12.

246 B.M. Add. MSS. 44370 fos. 88–9, 226–7; J. B. Mozley, *Letters*, p. 206. After an appeal to the Visitor, Corpus resolved to co-operate. Fowler, *Corpus Christi College* pp. 320–1. So did All Souls and Merton.

247 Similar advice had been received by both Wellington and Gladstone. C. P. Cooper, *Letter to the duke of Wellington* . . . (London, 1851); Apsley Ho. MSS. W. E. Gladstone to duke of Wellington, April 25, 1850.

248 C. N[eate], *In the matter of the petition of the university against the commission of enquiry*, May 19, 1851 (Bodl. G. A. Oxon. c. 67 no. 155).

249 *Guardian* 1851, p. 385.

250 J. B. Mozley, *Letters* p. 207.

251 R. T. Davidson & W. Benham, *Life of Archbald Campbell Tait* (London, 1891) i. 163.

CHAPTER VIII

1 Cf. *Guardian* 1852, p. 45; *Quarterly Review* xciii. 155.

2 H. L. Thompson, *Liddell* p. 127.

3 Davidson & Benham, *Tait* i. 165; Prothero, *Stanley* i. 431–2. As it was, Jeune entered an anonymous disclaimer (*Report* p. 167) to the majority's opposition to terminable fellowships. B.M. Add. MSS. 44221 fo. 9.

4 *Report*. Evidence pp. 19–21.

5 *Ibid.* Evidence pp. 112–13. Scott said he gave evidence because he dreaded the consequences of leaving the whole testimony to men who wanted 'the entire demolition of the old Oxford system.' B.M. Add. MSS. 44295 fo. 307.

6 *Report*. Evidence pp. 138–9.

7 B.M. Add. MSS. 44218 fo. 96.

8 H. L. Thompson, *Liddell* p. 127.

9 *Report*. Evidence pp. 82–92.

10 *Ibid.* Evidence pp. 30–40.

11 *Quarterly Review*. lxi. 215.

12 M. Pattison, *Memoirs* p. 258.

13 *Report*. Evidence pp. 41–50.

14 Now detached from Oxford tutorial politics, Newman was recommending this blend for his new university in Ireland. F. McGrath, *Newman's University. Idea and Reality* (London, 1951) pp. 120–21.

15 *Report* pp. 6–7.

16 *Ibid.* pp. 14–16.

17 *Ibid.* pp. 35–54.

18 H. L. Thompson, *Liddell* p. 127; Davidson & Benham, *Tait* i. 168.

19 *Report* pp. 54–6.

20 *Ibid.* pp. 60–83.

21 *Ibid.* pp. 87–103.

22 *Ibid.* pp. 104–7.

23 *Ibid.* pp. 108–9.

24 Veitch, *Memoir of Sir William Hamilton* p. 167.

25 *Report* p. 136.

26 *Report* pp. 143–6.

27 B.M. Add. MSS. 44566 fos. 297–8.

28 The college had little control over the succession of scholars and fellows who came up to Balliol from Tiverton on the Blundell's foundation, and made very odious comparisons between them and the distinguished scholars who were elected in the other foundations, which were all open. Abingdon School, being in a state of decay, sent Pembroke few poor natives of the town who were worth electing; such good scholars as the college received through this channel were boys from elsewhere who qualified by lodging temporarily with the masters of the school. *Report* p. 177.

29 *Report* pp. 149–69.

30 *Ibid.* pp. 172–80.

31 *Times* May 22, 1852, p. 6; *Guardian* 1852, p. 345.

32 *Guardian* 1852, p. 45.

33 *Times* Aug. 28, 1852, p. 8.

34 *Guardian* 1852, p. 681.

35 *Edinburgh Review* xcvi. 232 *seq.*

36 *Prospective Review* viii. 347–92.

37 *British Quarterly Review* xvi. 289–357.

38 *Guardian* 1852, pp. 384, 401.

39 *Ibid.* 1852, pp. 424–5, 441.

40 *Ibid.* 1852, pp. 489, 521, 569.

41 *Ibid.* 1852, p. 696.

42 *Christian Remembrancer* xxv. 192–212.

43 *Quarterly Review* xciii. 152 *seq.*

44 *Guardian* 1853, pp. 645, 660–1, 693.

45 C. Daubeny, *Can physical science obtain a home in an English university?* (Oxford, 1853).

46 *Times* June 26, 1852, p. 8; B.M. Add. MSS. 44372 fo. 149; 44251 fos. 46–7.

47 B.M. Add. MSS. 44318 fos. 7–12.

48 *Guardian* 1852, p. 377; *Times* June 11, 1852, p. 8.

49 Magdalen College MSS. D.6.20. E. H. Hansell to M. J. Routh, Dec. 31, 1850.

50 J. B. Mozley, *Letters* pp. 207–8; H. A. Wilson, *Magdalen College* (London, 1899) pp. 244–7.

51 MS. Knowsley Papers Box 8, H. Harris to Lord Derby, Feb. 3, 1854 printed in *Correspondence respecting the proposed measures of improvement in the universities and colleges of Oxford and Cambridge*, presented to Parliament 1854, p. 72 (cited below as *Corr. on improvement of Oxford*). At one stage there seems to have been a majority of one in favour of an application for an enabling act. J. B. Mozley, *Letters* p. 224; Selborne, *Memorials, family and personal* ii. 195.

52 Wilson, *op. cit.* p. 234n. The vested interest of existing demies was however preserved. The last demy of the old system resigned in 1877, at the age of sixty, having held his demyship nearly 42 years. The fellowship to which he would have succeeded became vacant soon afterwards.

53 Magdalen College MSS. C.I.2.13.

54 MS. Knowsley Papers Box 8, M. J. Routh to Lord Derby, Feb. 24, 1854.

55 B.M. Add. MSS. 44221 fo. 219.

56 MS. Knowsley Papers Box 8, James Norris to Vice-Chancellor, Dec. 28, 1853, printed in *Corr. on improvement of Oxford* p. 15; B.M. Add. MSS. 44318 fos. 15–18; 44378 fos. 46–7, 94–5, 100; T. Fowler, *Corpus Christi College* p. 324.

57 *Report*, pp. 203–5.

58 B.M. Add. MSS. 44376 fo. 227–8.

59 J. Barrow, *The case of Queen's College, Oxford* (Oxford, 1854).

60 Compare with the conservative views of the present Provost, John Fox. MS. Knowsley Papers Box 8, J. Fox to Vice-Chancellor, Jan. 6, 1854. Printed in *Corr. on improvement of Oxford* pp. 12–13.

61 W. Thomson, *An open college best for all* (Oxford, 1854). The college was sharply rebuked by A. C. Tait in the *Edinburgh Review* xcix. 182–3.

62 B.M. Add. MSS. 44376 fos. 227–8.

63 MS. Knowsley Papers 157/10. E. Cardwell to Lord Derby, May 4, 1853; MS. Letter Book 182/1 fos. 87–96.

64 MS. Knowsley Papers Box 8, F. Jeune to Lord Derby, June 15, 1853. In this box there are a number of letters from Jeune about disciplinary cases and reforms at Pembroke.

65 Macleane, *Pembroke College* pp. 448–50; B.M. Add. MSS. 44221 fo. 11. Cf. *Corr. on improvement of Oxford* pp. 18, 34.

66 *Correspondence between Lord Viscount Palmerston, the Chancellor of the University, and the Board of Heads of Houses and Proctors* (Oxford, 1854) p. 4.

67 Most of these are in MS. Knowsley Papers Box 8. They are printed in *Corr. on improvement of Oxford*.

68 For the St. John's proposals, W. C. Costin, *The history of St. John's College Oxford, 1598–1860* (Oxford, 1958) pp. 258–60.

69 Cradock who was 'nearly connected with Lord John Russell having married Miss Lister, formerly Maid of Honour to the Queen' (B.M. Add. MSS. 44376 fo. 238) was elected President in December 1853. He was regarded by his friends as 'a scholar and a gentleman, thoroughly well-disposed towards University progress and improvement, and thoroughly able—as he has shown as Treasurer at Worcester [Cathedral]—to carry his theories into practical effect.' (B.M. Add. MSS. 44376 fo. 240); and assessed for conservative patronage by Dr. Cardwell as 'a professed reformer; with average talent and acquirement; a sensible and impressive preacher; a good specimen of a producible man.' (MS. Knowsley Papers 93/3. E. Cardwell to Lord Derby, March 15, 1858). He obtained no further preferment.

70 B.M. Add. MSS. 44740 fos. 15–23.

71 Keble College MSS. Corr. of W. E. Gladstone with J. Keble, June 30, 1852.

72 W. E. Gladstone, *A letter to Rt. Rev. William Skinner, D.D. Bishop of Aberdeen and Primus, on the functions of laymen in the church* (London, 1852).

73 And they could point to the fact that he was being hailed by the dissenters as a voluntaryist. *Morning Herald* June 4, 1852 (cutting in Bodl. G. A. Oxon. 8° 208).

74 B.M. Add. MSS. 44372 fo. 174. Cf. fos. 47–53.

75 B.M. Add. MSS. 44208 fo. 23.

76 B.M. Add. MSS. 34578 fo. 672.

77 B.M. Add. MSS. 44181 fos. 75–9; MS. Oriel College Letters Gl. 11.

78 *Guardian* 1853, p. 10.

79 B.M. Add. MSS. 44181 fo. 80–1; 44183 fos. 20–3; 44118 fo. 31. Keble College MSS. Corr. of E. B. Pusey to J. Keble, n. pl. or d. (Answer to Keble's letter of May 10, 1852).

80 B.M. Add. MSS. 44181 fo. 83; 44372 fos. 39–40.

81 B.M. Add. MSS. 44181 fos. 86–100.

82 *Ibid.* fos. 109–11. There is a copy of the counter-declaration in Balliol College. MS. Jenkyns I. The papers of this election as a whole are conveniently collected in *A. W. Haddan's Election Papers, 1852* (Bodl. G. A. Oxon. Fol. A. 129).

83 B.M. Add. MSS. 44181 fos. 124–6; 44206 fo. 51.

84 H. A. Woodgate, *Is Mr. Gladstone inconsistent with his former position?* (Oxford, 1852); J. Keble, *A letter to Sir Brook W. Bridges* (Oxford, 1852). Keble's open championship of Gladstone is interesting in view of the fact that his advisers had thought it prudent to remove Pusey's name from his committee, even though he was willing once again to serve. B.M. Add. MSS. 44251 Pt. I. fos. 41–5.

85 Bodl. Wynter Papers MS. Dep. d. 5 fos. 150–2. Cf. *Guardian* 1852, pp. 456–7.

86 MS. Knowsley Papers 156/3. P. Wynter to Lord Derby, June 26, 1852; MS. Private Letter Book no. 180/1 fo. 188; MS. Letter Book no. 179/2 fo. 131.

87 Liddell was half-converted by Gladstone's assurances to Stanley (B.M. Add. MSS. 44236 fos. 258–61); Jeune had been expected to join the opposition B.M. Add. MSS. 44118 fo. 31.

88 For Haddan's analysis, B.M. Add. MSS. 44183 fos. 36–41.

89 Bodl. Wynter Papers. MS. Dep. d. 5 fos. 216–17; B.M. Add. MSS. 44372 fos. 298–332; 44373 fos. 7–11. Cf. Edward Hawkins, Provost of Oriel, who 'except in stirring times of peculiar interest, . . . only read a weekly newspaper.' (B.M. Add. MSS. 44206 fo. 57. (MS. Oriel College Letters Gl. 72.)).

90 Cox, *Recollections* p. 386. For a variation on this story see *Times*, Sept, 24, 1852, p. 4.

91 B.M. Add. MSS. 34579 fo. 43.

92 Pusey Ho. MSS. Letters from Dr. Pusey to Dr. Bull, *passim*. (All these letters are undated and unfoliated.)

93 B.M. Add. MSS. 44372 fos. 339–40, 345–7; *Morning Herald* Oct. 14, 1852 (cutting in Add. MSS. 34579 fo. 117). Cf. Add. MSS. 44181 fos. 142–3.

94 B.M. Add. MSS. 44183 fos. 49–52; *Guardian* 1852, p. 632.

95 *Letters of Queen Victoria*. First series ed. A. C. Benson and Viscount Esher (London, 1907) ii. 456.

96 B.M. Add. MSS. 34579 fos. 45, 48.

97 MS. Knowsley Papers MS. Letter Book 181/2 fos. 7–9.

98 B.M. Add. MSS. 34579 fo. 45.

99 *Ibid.* fos. 51–2. Wilberforce's letters confirm the accuracy of the story Michell relates.

100 Ashwell and Wilberforce, *Life of Samuel Wilberforce* ii. 150.

101 MS. Knowsley Papers 156/3. Bishop of Oxford to Lord Derby, Sept. 17, 1852.

102 [William Sewell] *Misgivings on the requisition to Lord Derby* (Printed, 1852).

103 *Times* Sept. 24, 1852, p. 4; *Guardian* Sept. 22, 1852, p. 632.

104 Morley, *Gladstone* i. 327–8.

105 G. A. Denison, *The coalition of 1852* (London, 1853).

106 Ashwell and Wilberforce, *Life of Samuel Wilberforce* ii. 159.

107 B.M. Add. MSS. 44281 fo. 74.

108 H. Stowell, *Address to electors of University of Oxford.* (London, 1853); *Nonconformist* Jan. 5, 1853, p. 2.

109 Cox, *Recollections* p. 389.

110 Bodl. Wynter Papers. MS. Dep. d. 5. fos. 152–88; B.M. Add. MSS. 34579 fos. 168–96, *passim*; 34582 fo. 406.

111 B.M. Add. MSS. 44181 fos. 146–7.

112 The printed papers of this election are conveniently collected in *A. W. Haddan's Election Papers, 1853* (Bodl. G. A. Oxon. 4°57).

113 On Lempriere: Costin, *St. John's College* p. 252. In 1861 Lempriere published a tract advocating the cause of the Southern States (*The American crisis considered*) which was roughly handled by Gladstone's friends in the *Guardian* (Oct. 9, 1861, p. 928).

114 For these tortuous manoeuvres: B.M. Add. MSS. 44181 fo. 151; 44276 fos. 253–57; *Guardian* 1853, pp. 5–10; *Times* Jan. 5, 1853, p. 4; Sir Stafford H. Northcote, *A statement of facts connected with the election of the Rt. Hon. W. E. Gladstone as member for the University of Oxford* (Oxford, 1853). Wynter claimed to have accepted Lempriere's assurances that Chandos would stand, and to have been engaged in trying to get him to retract his refusal when Lempriere advertised Perceval's candidacy (Bodl. Wynter Papers MS. Dep. d. 6. fos. 71–98). Major Beresford was also involved in this conspiracy, and was so disgusted at the way the Oxford committee disowned him when the scandal came out, that he refused to sign a petition against the Oxford University Bill six months later. B.M. Add. MSS. 34579 fos. 629–32.

115 B.M. Add. MSS. 44208 fos. 31–2, 39.

116 B.M. Add. MSS. 44206 fo. 55 (MS. Oriel College Letters Gl. 14); 44276 fo. 289; 44343 fo. 185; 44570 fo. 83.

117 B.M. Add. MSS. 44206 fo. 60 (MS. Oriel College Letters Gl. 73); 44181 fo. 160.

118 B.M. Add. MSS. 44570 fo. 83.

119 *Times* Jan. 16, 1853, p. 4.

120 B.M. Add. MSS. 44183 fo. 31; 44208 fos. 21–4.

121 B.M. Add. MSS. 44206 fo. 64; 44528 fos. 79–80. Some of Gladstone's friends said openly that he would not stand again. Bodl. MS. Acland d. 69 fo. 28.

122 *Times* Jan. 7, 1853, p. 4. A correspondent of the *Guardian* proposed a postal ballot. *Guardian* Feb. 2, 1853, p. 72.

123 University archives. MS. Hebdomadal Meeting Register 1841–54 fos. 262–3.

124 16 and 17 Vict. c. 68.

125 MS. Oriel College Letters no. 164; B.M. Add. MSS. 44372 fos. 178–9.

126 Abbot & Campbell, *Jowett* i. 225; *Corr. of A. H. Clough* ii. 363.

127 *Guardian* 1853, p. 56; J. B. Mozley, *Letters* p. 217; *Letters of Sir George Cornewall Lewis* ed. Rev. Sir Gilbert Frankland Lewis (London, 1870) p. 267.

128 'I look upon the National Club as a mischievous body, whose extreme pretensions and views must not be encouraged, but which must be kept . . . in good humour by civility, and by the negative means of avoiding in debate, or in meetings of the party, language which may unnecessarily "froisser" their pet views.' MS. Knowsley Papers MS. Letter Book 182/1. Lord Derby to Disraeli, Nov. 14, 1853.

129 *Guardian* 1853, p. 75.

CHAPTER IX

1 Edward Cardwell subsequently moved that six members of Convocation be invited to join the committee, but was defeated. University archives. MS. Minutes of committee appointed by Hebdomadal Board to consider the commissioners' recommendations, N.W.8.10 fo. 5.

2 *Guardian* 1852, pp. 717, 761. Wellington communicated this information to the Board with the characteristic injunction that they should adopt measures to meet the points made in the report. University archives. MS. Hebdomadal Meeting Register 1841–54 fos. 247–8; *Guardian* 1852, p. 727.

3 *Ibid.* 1852, p. 728; B.M. Add. MSS. 44183 fo. 55; *Reports of the Oxford Tutors' Association* No. 1 (Oxford, 1853) p. 4.

4 *Memorials of W. C. Lake* pp. ix, 76–7; B.M. Add. MSS. 44230 fo. 239.

5 *Reports of the Oxford Tutors' Association* No. 1.

6 B.M. Add. MSS. 44282 fos. 209–12; *Guardian* 1852, p. 836; 1853, p. 58.

7 *Reports of the Oxford Tutors' Association* No. II.

8 B.M. Add. MSS. 44282 fos. 217–22; 44230 fos. 250–3; 44528 fos. 107, 121.

9 *Guardian* 1853, p. 341.

10 J. B. Mozley, *Letters* pp. 217–19.

11 *Guardian* 1853, pp. 323, 325.

12 B.M. Add. MSS. 44282 fos. 223–4.

13 *Reports of the Oxford Tutors' Association* No. III (Oxford, 1853).

14 B.M. Add. MSS. 44282 fos. 223–4; 44529 fo. 15; 44230 fos. 262–4 (printed in *Memorials of W. C. Lake* pp. 180–90).

15 *Reports of the Oxford Tutors' Association* No. IV. (Oxford, 1854).

16 For Gladstone's correspondence with the tutors while the report was being compiled B.M. Add. MSS. 44282 fo. 225; 44230 fos. 268–77.

17 The liberal H. B. Barry, fellow of Queen's, insisted that by the early months of 1854 the Association was being maintained by an unrepresentative score of the 120 tutors. H. B. Barry, *Remarks on the three proposals for reforming the constitution of the University of Oxford*. (Oxford, 1854).

18 MS. Knowsley Papers 157/12. R. L. Cotton to Lord Derby, Nov. 16, Dec. 6, 1852; J. W. Henley to Lord Derby, Dec. 10, 1852; 157/10. Edward Cardwell to Lord Derby, Nov. 2, 1852; University archives. MS. Hebdomadal Meeting Register 1841–54 fos. 251–3, 255, 257, 259–62.

19 B.M. Add. MSS. 44206 fos. 83–8; 44528 fos. 93, 95–7, 121 (MS. Oriel College Letters Gl. 21, 23).

20 B.M. Add. MSS. 44528 fos. 123–5.

21 *Edinburgh Review* xcix. 174; *Correspondence between Lord Palmerston, the Chancellor of the University and the Board of Heads of Houses and Proctors*. Delegates Room. Feb. 25, 1854.

22 *Diary of an Oxford Lady* p. 26.

23 MS. Knowsley Papers MS. Letter Book 182/1 fos. 79–84.

24 *Guardian* 1853, p. 397.

25 Keble College MSS. Letters of E. B. Pusey to J. Keble Vol. I. Two undated letters of May and June 1853, and another (in the same volume) of the same period to Charles Marriott.

26 B.M. Add. MSS. 44251 pt. I fos. 74–6.

27 MS. Oriel College Letters no. 426.

28 *Report and evidence upon the recommendations of Her Majesty's commissioners for inquiry into the state of the University of Oxford.* (Oxford, 1853).

29 *Guardian* 1854, p. 9.

30 *Report and evidence.* Evidence pp. 2–3.

31 *Ibid.* Evidence pp. 1–173. This evidence is summarised in Liddon, *Pusey* iii. 381–6.

32 *Correspondence between Lord Palmerston, the Chancellor of the University, and the Board of Heads of Houses and Proctors.* Delegates Room. Feb. 25, 1854.

33 University archives. MS. Hebdomadal Meeting Register 1841–54 fos. 291, 298.

34 These proposals were worked out by Hawkins in consultation with Pusey (B.M. Add. MSS. 44206 fo. 114). Marriott was taken by surprise. Add. MSS. 44251 pt. I fo. 82.

35 H. H. Vaughan, *Oxford reform and Oxford professors* (London, 1854).

36 E. B. Pusey, *Collegiate and professorial teaching and discipline* (Oxford, 1854); *A reply to Professor Vaughan's strictures on the third report of the Tutors' Association*, by one of the Committee (Oxford, 1854).

37 B.M. Add. MSS. 44376 fo. 246; 44377 fos. 193, 199; 44230 fos. 278, 283–4, 288; *Guardian* 1854, p. 136. There is a copy of the petition in *University Reform Papers, 1854* (Bodl. G. A. Oxon. c. 70).

38 B.M. Add. MSS. 44183 fos. 77–80.

39 B.M. Add. MSS. 44236 fos. 262–3, 266–71; 44377 fos. 253–5. Gladstone gave a broad hint to Liddell himself that the Government favoured the tutors' line. Add. MSS. 44529 fo. 49.

40 B.M. Add. MSS. 44343 fo. 240.

41 *Memorials of W. C. Lake* p. 190; Selborne, *Memorials, family and personal* ii. 191–2; J. B. Mozley, *Letters* pp. 223–4; MS. Oriel College Letters no. 1089.

42 For an elaborate conspectus of press comment: *Guardian* 1854, p. 77.

43 B.M. Add. MSS. 44271 fos. 49–53; 44281 fos. 103–42; 44377 fos. 201–2, 205, 218; Pusey Ho. MSS. Corr. of E. B. Pusey with Sir W. Heathcote, Feb. 13 [1854]; Keble College MSS. Corr. of E. B. Pusey with J. Keble Vol. II n.d. [Feb. 16, 1854]; MS. Knowsley Papers 157/12. R. L. Cotton to Lord Derby, letters from Feb. 10 to Feb. 25, 1854; Box 8, Lord Palmerston to Lord Derby, Feb. 16, 1854; (This letter was drafted by Gladstone who would give no ground. B.M. Add. MSS. 44743 fos. 143–9). MS. Letter Book 182/2. fos. 220–2; Box 8, E. B. Pusey to Lord Derby, Feb. 23, 27, 1854.

44 C[harles] M[arriott], *How are we to vote on the proposed constitution for the University?* Feb. 20, 1854.

45 *Guardian* 1854, pp. 151–2, 165, 173, 182–3; B.M. Add. MSS. 44282 fo. 246.

46 MS. Oriel College Letters Gl. 10.

47 B.M. Add. MSS. 44236 fo. 261. Cf. 44318 fo. 10.

48 B.M. Add. MSS. 44183 fo. 52.

49 *Ibid.* fo. 57.

50 *Diary of an Oxford lady* p. 20.

51 *Corr. of A. H. Clough* ii. 373.

52 B.M. Add. MSS. 44206 fos. 103–4.

53 B.M. Add. MSS. 44376 fos. 210–15.

54 *Ibid.* fos. 218–19; 44529 fo. 16.

55 B.M. Add. MSS. 44376 fos. 246–51; 44743 fos. 2–12.

56 *Ibid.* fos. 119–20; 44377 fo. 215. The comments of Lord Chancellor Cranworth are in Add. MSS. 44580 fos. 45–7. Drafts of clauses on fellowships were also circulated. Add. MSS. 44183 fos. 72–5.

57 B.M. Add. MSS. 44743 fos. 119–20.

58 B.M. Add. MSS. 44377 fo. 19.

59 B.M. Add. MSS. 44743 fos. 130–1.

60 B.M. Add. MSS. 44377 fos. 113–15.

61 *Ibid.* fos. 10–14.

62 B.M. Add. MSS. 44183 fos. 77–8; 44236 fo. 264.

63 B.M. Add. MSS. 44377 fo. 206; 44230 fos. 318–20.

64 B.M. Add. MSS. 44377 fos. 273–4.

65 B.M. Add. MSS. 44183 fos. 108–9; 44251 pt. I fo. 130; 44374 fos. 9–10, 33–4.

66 B.M. Add. MSS. 44230 fo. 275; 44236 fos. 272–3.

67 B.M. Add. MSS. 44251 pt. I fo. 103, 144, 149, 170–1.

68 B.M. Add. MSS. 44183 fos. 66–70; 44230 fos. 313–16; 44377 fos. 207–8, 237.

69 B.M. Add. MSS. 44183 fos. 85, 93–4, 99–100. But cf. 44282 fos. 256–9.

70 B.M. Add. MSS. 44236 fo. 272; 44378 fo. 46. After the bill was published the Oxford liberals, together with some liberal M.P.s petitioned Russell against this provision. Add. MSS. 44236 fos. 274–8.

71 B.M. Add. MSS. 44378 fos. 26, 33–4, 78–82.

72 B.M. Add. MSS. 44282 fos. 251–4.

73 B.M. Add. MSS. 44378 fo. 34.

74 A copy of the bill in its original shape was printed in the *Guardian* 1854, pp. 248–9.

75 B.M. Add. MSS. 44378 fo. 44.

76 *Ibid.* fo. 70; 44281 fos. 143–4. Keble also was much grieved by most of the intended reforms. Coleridge, *Memoir of Keble* ii. 380–90.

77 B.M. Add. MSS. 44281 fo. 149.

78 B.M. Add. MSS. 44221 fos. 23–4, 29–30, 37, 43–4, 49–54; 44282 fos. 268–71.

79 *Guardian* 1854, pp. 257, 262, 264–5; MS. Oriel College Letters nos. 72–4.

80 *Guardian* 1854, p. 285; B.M. Add. MSS. 44183 fos. 106–9; 44282 fos. 272–4.

81 B.M. Add. MSS. 44379 fos. 143–8.

82 B.M. Add. MSS. 44208 fo. 97. Liddell's biographer asserts (H. L. Thompson, *Liddell* p. 146) that he refused to serve on the commission, though pressed to do so, but I have found no trace of the transaction in Gladstone's correspondence.

83 B.M. Add. MSS. 44378 fos. 269–72, 285; 44236 fos. 272–80; 44206 fo. 140; 44221 fo. 57; 44230 fo. 324. The extreme liberal line was that the artificial ascendancy of the clergy in Oxford was bad for the university, the church and the clergy, and in any case formed no barrier to the influence of sceptical literature. *A selection from Goldwin Smith's correspondence* ed. A. Haultain (London n.d.) p. 6.

84 Bodl. MS. Acland d. 68 fos. 8–11. Liddell who ascribed all the feuds of the university to Gladstone's 'culpable weakness' (MS. Acland d. 69 fos. 30–3) received no further offers of preferment, until the death of Stanley in 1881, when he felt too old to succeed to the Deanery of Westminster.

85 MS. Knowsley Papers MS. Letter Book no. 182/1. Lord Derby to Vice-Chancellor, April 1, 1854.

86 B.M. Add. MSS. 44381 fo. 69.

87 *Guardian* 1854, pp. 348, 357.

88 B.M. Add. MSS. 44208 fo. 76, 82–91.

89 B.M. Add. MSS. 44221 fos. 109, 114.

90 *Guardian* 1854, p. 451.

91 Selborne, *Memorials, family and personal* ii. 200–1.

92 B.M. Add. MSS. 44221 fos. 146–7; MS. Knowsley Papers Box 8, F. Jeune to Lord Derby, July 6, 1854; *Diary of an Oxford lady* p. 49. There was also much distress in Jesus, where the college had determined to open its foundations to natives of the principality subject to a *ceteris paribus* preference. B.M. Add. MSS. 44381 fos. 169–70.

93 B.M. Add. MSS. 44221 fo. 150.

94 B.M. Add. MSS. 44208 fo. 92.

95 *Parliamentary debates* 3s. cxxxiv. 511–95.

96 *Prospective Review* viii. 382 *seq.*; *British Quarterly Review* xvi. 324 *seq.*

97 *Guardian* 1853, p. 469.

98 *Ibid.* p. 476; *C. J.* cviii. 758.

99 eg. *Christian Reformer* June 1854, p. 384; *Letters of Sir G. C. Lewis* p. 282; B.M. Add. MSS. 44183 fo. 135.

100 *Eclectic Review* May 1854, 5s. vii. 611–21; *Inquirer* March 25, 1854, p. 178; June 24, 1854, pp. 385–6; *Nonconformist* May 3, 1854, p. 365.

101 Manning, *Protestant Dissenting Deputies* p. 373; there is a copy of the petition in Bodl. G. A. Oxon. b. 137 (23).

102 *Christian Reformer* April 1854, p. 247; *Inquirer* March 25, 1854, p. 178.

103 *Christian Reformer* July 1854, pp. 414–21, 442–3; *Nonconformist* March 29, 1854, pp. 257–8; May 3, p. 365; June 21, 1854, p. 505; *Inquirer* March 25, 1854, p. 187; April 1, pp. 196–7; April 15, pp. 226–7; April 22, p. 245; April 29, p. 266; July 1, p. 405.

104 *Parliamentary debates* 3s. cxxxiv. 556; *Nonconformist* June 28, 1854, p. 525.

105 B.M. Add. MSS. 44206 fos. 143–60; 44251 pt. I fo. 232; Lathbury, *Letters on church and religion of W. E. Gladstone* i. 217–18.

106 Coleridge, *Memoir of Keble* ii. 404.

107 Liddon, *Pusey* iii. 399; J. Keble, *A few very plain thoughts on the admission of dissenters to the University of Oxford* (Oxford, 1854); B.M. Add. MSS. 44183 fos. 133–4; 44251 pt. I fos. 230, 233–6. Cf. 44282 fos. 300–16.

108 B.M. Add. MSS. 44221 fos. 164–9; University archives. MS. Hebdomadal Meeting Register 1841–54 fos. 337–9; Keble College MSS. Corr. of E. B. Pusey with J. Keble Vol. II. n. pl. or d. (in fact June 27, 1854).

109 Keble College MSS. Corr. of E. B. Pusey with J. Keble Vol. II. n. pl. or d. (two letters, one ansd. July 6, 1854). There is a copy of the first of these at Pusey Ho. Liddon's MS. transcripts of Pusey's corr. with J. Keble IV n.p. Marriott's proposal to prepare a petition of non-residents sprang from a scheme he had already concocted with Lord Robert Cecil and Frederick Meyrick for a petition of residents (F. Meyrick, *Memories of my life at Oxford and elsewhere* (London, 1905) pp. 87–8; MS. Knowsley Papers 157/12. R. L. Cotton to Lord Derby, July 1, 1854). There is a copy of the flysheet they prepared, pressing the parallel with the crisis of 1834, in Magdalen College MSS. D.7.4.

110 Abbot & Campbell, *Jowett* i. 278–9.

111 *Guardian* 1854, pp. 523, 530–1.

112 MS. Knowsley Papers Box 8. T. Gaisford to Lord Derby, June 21, June 30, 1854; E. Hawkins to Lord Derby, July 5, 1854; B. P. Symons to Lord Derby, July 6, 1854.

113 MS. Knowsley Papers Box 8. Lord De la Warr to Lord Derby, 12, 13, 17 July, 1854.

114 MS. Knowsley Papers MS. Letter Book 182/2. Lord Derby to Provost of Oriel, July 6, 1854.

115 *Guardian* 1854, p. 546; Selborne, *Memorials, family and personal* ii. 201–2.

116 Goldwin Smith, *Reminiscences* pp. 106–7.

117 *Guardian* 1854, p. 539.

118 *Letters of Frederic, Lord Blachford* ed. G. E. Marindin (London, 1896) p. 158.

119 P. Bliss, *Reliquiae Hearnianae* (2nd ed. London, 1869) iii. 189–91.

120 *Nonconformist* Oct. 25, 1854, p. 883.

121 *Inquirer* Oct. 28, 1854, p. 683.

122 MS. Knowsley Papers 157/10. Edward Cardwell to Lord Derby, Oct. 25, 1854; B.M. Add. MSS. 44251 pt. I fo. 245.

123 Abbot & Campbell, *Jowett* i. 279; Bodl. MS. Autogr. d. 6 fo. 29; *Memoirs of Archbishop Temple* ed. E. G. Sandford ii. 536–7; *Diary of an Oxford lady* p. 52; B.M. Add. MSS. 44183 fos. 137–9; 44221 fos. 199–200.

124 *Guardian* 1854, pp. 839, 843; Bodl. MS. Pattison 50 fos. 397–401. Flysheets for this election are in Bodl. G. A. Oxon. b. 28.

125 Liddon, *Pusey* iii. 405; Pusey Ho. W. Tuckwell's MS. Reminiscences of E. B. Pusey; B.M. Add. MSS. 44221 fo. 208.

126 The Provost of Oriel raised a hare immediately as to whether the creation of a new Congregation in the act involved the abolition of the old. B.M. Add. MSS. 44221 fos. 201–2.

127 MS. Knowsley Papers 157/10. E. Cardwell to Lord Derby, Nov. 7, 28, 1854, Jan. 29, 1855; Balliol College. Jowett MSS. Box E, B. Jowett, to A. P. Stanley, n.d. [1854].

128 The committee was in any case a conservative one; B.M. Add. MSS. 44221 fos. 203–5, 210–11.

129 B.M. Add. MSS. 44221 fos. 212–15, 224–5; University archives. MS. Minutes of Hebdomadal Council 1854–66 fos. 20, 27; MS. Reports to Hebdomadal Council 1855–64, p. 4.

130 *Guardian* 1855, p. 193.

131 *Ibid.* p. 197; B.M. Add. MSS. 44218 fos. 101–3; 44221 fos. 219–21. The flysheets on this question are in Bodl. G. A. Oxon. b. 28.

132 Cox, *Recollections* pp. 406–7; R. Bullock-Marsham [Open letter to the Vice-Chancellor, March 13, 1855]; *Guardian* 1855, p. 211; B.M. Add. MSS. 44221 fo. 229.

133 B.M. Add. MSS. 44529 fo. 190; 44206 fos. 177–8; *Parliamentary debates* 3s. cxxxix. 2139–41; Sir Culling Eardley, *The rights of the laity in the universities* (London, 1856); *Guardian* 1854, p. 791. The tone of anger in Gladstone's correspondence with Hawkins on this case contrasts oddly with the sympathy he expressed to Eardley. MS. Oriel College Letters Gl. 33.

134 B.M. Add. MSS. 44282 fo. 211.

135 University archives. MS. Hebdomadal Meeting Register 1841–54 fos. 307, 310; C. Marriott, *A few words on the statute for new halls . . .* (Oxford, May 17, 1854); B.M. Add. MSS. 44251 pt. I fo. 224.

136 B.M. Add. MSS. 44251 pt. I fos. 96–102, 105–6; 44281 fos. 95–102, 153–4; 44218 fos. 56–7, 70–3; Pusey Ho. MSS. Corr. of E. B. Pusey with Sir William Heathcote, May 9, [1854]; Coleridge, *Memoir of Keble* ii. 382–5.

137 Pusey Ho. MSS. Liddon's Transcripts of Pusey's corr. with J. Keble IV [misdated? Aug. 1854]; Keble College MSS. Corr. of E. B. Pusey with J. Keble I [Nov. 1854], [ansd. June, 1855]; B.M. Add. MSS. 44221 fos. 203–8; 44582 fos. 49–50; MS. Knowsley Papers 157/10. E. Cardwell to Lord Derby, March 15, May 19, 1855.

138 Coleridge, *Memoir of Keble* ii. 388.

139 McGrath, *Newman's University* pp. 379–81.

140 *Guardian* 1855, p. 771; 1856, p. 24; *Nonconformist* Aug. 15, 1855, p. 615; Jan. 23, 1856, p. 49. Cf. Dec. 3, 1856, pp. 913–14; MS. Knowsley Papers 157/10. E. Cardwell to Lord Derby, Dec. 26, 1855; 161/5. D. Williams to Lord Derby, March 21, April 2, 1857.

141 *Guardian* 1855, p. 771; MS. Knowsley Papers 157/10. E. Cardwell to Lord Derby, Dec. 26, 1855.

142 B.M. Add. MSS. 44303 fo. 8.

143 *Corr. of A. H. Clough* i. 117; B.M. Add. MSS. 34582 fo. 274.

144 *Guardian* 1855, p. 197.

145 Some of the material correspondence is printed in D. P. Chase, *General suggestions for the improvement of the halls under the visitation of the Chancellor of the University of Oxford.* The full original correspondence is in MS. Knowsley Papers 159/1. Correspondence of D. P. Chase with Lord Derby; also 161/5. D. Williams to Lord Derby, Oct. 20, 1856; Box 8. D. P. Chase to Lord Derby, April 30, 1855 to October 1856 with enclosures; 157/12. R. L. Cotton to Lord Derby, Nov. 26, 1857; 156/3 Bp. of Oxford to Lord Derby, Nov. 20, 22, 1857; 157/11 Php. Bliss to Lord Derby, Jan. 1, 11, 1856; MS. Letter Book 182/2 fo. 179; MS. Letter Book 183/1 fos. 154–61; MS. Oriel College Letters no. 614; D. P. Chase, *Education for frugal men at the University of Oxford* (Oxford, 1864). In 1867 Chase made an unsuccessful effort to persuade Lord Derby to sever the headship of Oriel from the canonry of Rochester to which it was annexed and transfer the canonry to the Principalship of St. Mary Hall. MS. Knowsley Papers. Letter Book no. 194/1 fos. 165–9.

146 Bodl. MS. Top. Oxon. d. 35 fo. 25.

147 *Guardian* Oct. 4, 1854, p. 759.

148 MS. Knowsley Papers 157/10. E. Cardwell to Lord Derby, Dec. 21, 26, 1855; Nov. 4, 1856; 157/11. P. Bliss to Lord Derby, Jan. 11, 1856; MS. Letter Book no. 183/1 fos. 327–30, 334–40; MS. Letter Book no. 188/2 fos. 240–1, 332–4; Box 101. W. C. Salter to Lord Derby, Aug. 7, 1863; Bodl. MS. Top. Oxon. d. 35 *passim*; Bodl. Wynter Papers MS. Dep. d. 4. fos. 460–4, 476; B.M. Add. MSS. 44218 fos. 119–20; D. P. Chase, *Education for frugal men* pp. 15–19.

149 B.M. Add. MSS. 44208 fo. 60.

150 MS. Oriel College Letters nos. 1085–6.

151 B.M. Add. MSS. 44281 fo. 161.

152 On the choice of secretaries: B.M. Add. MSS. 44208 fo. 73; 44118 fos. 69–70; 44303 fos. 22, 25; 44744 fo. 72; 44208 fos. 94–5.

153 B.M. Add. MSS. 44303 fo. 131.

154 E. H. Coleridge, *Life and correspondence of John Duke, Lord Coleridge* (London, 1904) i. 232–3; B.M. Add. MSS. 44208 fos. 96–7; 44221 fo. 131; 44183 fo. 115; 44206 fo. 137.

155 *Guardian* 1854, pp. 451, 475.

156 Selborne, *Memorials, family and personal* i. 226–7.

157 B.M. Add. MSS. 44208 fo. 128.

158 MS. Papers of the Oxford University Commission. P.R.O. H.O. 73/40 pp. 54–6.

159 P.R.O. H.O. 73/40 pp. 65–6, 72–3, 80–6. A year later Twisleton made a vain assault upon clerical fellowships. pp. 166, 172–7.

160 *Guardian* 1856, p. 145; Bodl. MS. Pattison 51 fos. 196–7, 202–8, 214–15, 221.

161 D. P. Chase, *The rights of 'indigentes' in respect to college foundations* (Oxford, 1856); *Guardian* 1856, p. 243.

162 P.R.O. H.O. 73/40, p. 74.

163 B.M. Add. MSS. 44303 fos. 98–101.

164 B.M. Add. MSS. 44206 fos. 183–7.

165 P.R.O. H.O. 73/38 p. 180.

166 MS. Knowsley Papers 159/1. D. P. Chase to Lord Derby, May 19, 1857.

167 *Parliamentary debates* 3s. cxl. 2015–33; cxli. 467.

168 *Guardian* 1856, p. 445.

169 *Ibid.* 1856, p. 277.

170 *Ibid.* 1858, p. 565.

171 P.R.O. H.O. 73/37–40. There is much information also in Goldwin Smith's correspondence with Gladstone. B.M. Add. MSS. 44303 fos. 64–135.

172 M. Pattison, *Memoirs* p. 304.

173 Costin, *St. John's College* pp. 260–78; *Guardian* 1858, pp. 561, 566.

CHAPTER X

1 Keble College MSS. Corr. of Rev. E. B. Pusey with Rev. J. Keble (both series) [Early Feb. 1856], [May 1858], [11 June, 1858], [May 5, 1860].

2 Mark Pattison, 'Oxford Studies' in *Oxford Essays, 1855*.

3 *Times* Nov. 9, 1855, p. 5; Nov. 10, 1855, p. 6.

4 *Times* Nov. 28, 1859, p. 6; Jan. 9–14, 1861, *passim*; Sept. 27, 1864, p. 8; Bodl. MS. Top. Oxon. a 6 fo. 153; *Recollections of Dean Fremantle* (London, 1921) pp. 62–4; cf. James Heywood, *Academic reform and university representation* (London, 1860) p.v. A recent attempt by Sir Geoffrey Faber to state a case for the college in opposition to the views of both the executive commissioners and the courts (*Jowett* (London, 1957) pp. 202–4), breaks down on the ground that the examination system which the liberals championed and he disliked was imposed by the act and, *mutatis mutandis*, was operated by other colleges. The commissioners imposed on All Souls the special obligation towards law and modern history with the deliberate object of encouraging the school by appropriating endowments to it.

5 B.M. Add. MSS. 44389 fo. 166.

6 *Times* Dec. 17, 1859, p. 6; Dec. 20, 1859, p. 3.

7 *Times* July 13, 1867, p. 8; *Guardian* 1867, p. 156; Thompson, *Liddell* p. 144; Bodl. MS. Top. Oxon. c. 309 fos. 2–31. The new ordinances were enacted by 30 & 31 Vict. c. 76.

8 *Letters of Queen Victoria* 1st series iii. 188.

9 *The Ecclesiastic* 1866 p. 545.

10 MS. Knowsley Papers MS. Letter Book No. 185/1 fo. 12.

11 *Westminster Review* n.s. xx. 295.

12 *Life and letters of the Rt. Hon. Friedrich Max Müller* ed. his wife (London, 1902) i. 173–4.

13 Mark Pattison, 'Oxford Studies' in *Oxford Essays, 1855.*

14 *Edinburgh Review* cxxxiv. 306.

15 *Times* April 3, 1858, p. 9. This letter is an interesting example of the pace of change for it is plainly somewhat behind the times.

16 *Autobiography of Montagu Burrows* ed. S. M. Burrows (London, 1908) pp. 200–1. For Goldwin Smith's hostility to Butler; *Recollections of Dean Boyle* p. 282. Provost Hawkins told a story of a tutor who 'said to his class when Butler's name was mentioned, "Bp. Butler! Bp. Butler was a fool." ' B.M. Add. MSS. 44206 fo. 314.

17 E. S. Talbot, *Memories of my early life* (London, 1924) pp. 41–3, 78.

18 A. M. Ramsey, *From Gore to Temple* (London, 1960) pp. 7–8.

19 On him see B. A. Smith, *Dean Church. The Anglican response to Newman* (London, 1958).

20 For comments upon these, *Guardian* 1858, p. 237; 1859, p. 262.

21 J. B. Mozley, *Letters* p. 240.

22 Burgon, *Twelve Good Men* pp. 339–46; M. Burrows, *Pass and class* (Oxford, 1860) p. 143.

23 Compare the accounts of the election in Pattison's *Memoirs* pp. 272 seq. and V. H. H. Green, *Oxford Common Room* ch. vii.

24 B.M. Add. MSS. 40568 fo. 55. Cf. Abbot & Campbell, *Jowett* i. 228–30.

25 *Times* March 27, 1866, p. 10; March 29, p. 7; March 30, p. 4; March 31, p. 10; April 4, p. 9; April 5, p. 10; *Guardian* 1866, pp. 333, 346, 370.

26 *Times* March 28, 1876, p. 5.

27 *Times* Oct. 24, 1855, p. 9; Nov. 22, 1855, p. 10.

28 *Guardian* 1857 p. 95.

29 *Times* Oct. 22, 1857 p. 6; Oct. 23, 1857 p. 6.

30 *Times* Oct. 23, 1860 p. 7; *Guardian* 1860, pp. 904, 927; Bodl. MS. Pattison 53 fos. 350, 402.

31 *Guardian* 1863, p. 1003. Bulley sought election 'chiefly with a view to prevent in these unhappy times as much *mischief* as I could.' Christ Church. Salisbury MSS. Frederic Bulley to Lord Salisbury, July 25, 1870.

32 *Times* March 4, 1864, p. 12.

33 *Guardian* 1865, p. 1099.

34 *Times* Oct. 23, 1866, p. 7; *Guardian* 1866, p. 1096; *The Ecclesiastic* Dec. 1866, pp. 543–4.

35 *Times* Oct. 15, 1869, p. 4; Oct. 18, p. 8; Oct. 22, p. 7; *Guardian* 1869, pp. 1160, 1187; Liddon House. MS. Diary of H. P. Liddon, Oct. 21, 1869.

36 *Ibid.* Oct. 22, 1872; *Times* Oct. 23, 1872, p. 7.

37 *Report of the royal commission on the University of Oxford* 1852 pp. 60 *seq.; Oxford Essays, 1855* pp. 293–4.

38 *Times* Dec. 2, 1863, p. 12 (Stanley's speech).

39 A later analysis of these questions was given in W. W. Shirley, *Ought our honours to be given without limit of age?* (Oxford, 1865).

40 Keble College MSS. Corr. of E. B. Pusey to J. Keble [11 June, 1858].

41 Vice-Chancellor's notice, December 1856. Bodl. G. A. Oxon. b. 29.

42 *Times* March 5, 1857, p. 9; Cox, *Recollections* p. 425; *Guardian* 1857, pp. 190–1.

43 *The educational changes proposed in the new Examination Statute*, (n. pl. or d. [Oxford, 1857]).

44 *Guardian* 1856, pp. 977–8; 1857, p. 277.

45 Robert Walker, *Remarks on . . . the proposed form of Statute respecting the examinations for the degree of B.A.* (Oxford, 1857).

46 *Ancient History and the new Statute* (n. pl. or d. [Oxford, 1857]) (Bodl. G. A. Oxon. c. 73 (341)); *Guardian* 1857, p. 169; *Reasons for dissenting from the proposed examination statute . . .* (n. pl. or d. [Oxford, 1857]), (Bodl. G. A. Oxon. b. 29).

47 Robert Walker, *Remarks . . .*; C. Daubeny, *Reasons for voting in favour of clauses 2 and 3 . . . relative to the attendance on the lectures of professors.* (Oxford, 1857).

48 *Times* April 2, 1857, p. 11.

49 *Times* May 13, 1857, p. 12.

50 *Guardian* 1859, p. 171.

51 J. P. Tweed, *The vote on the Examination Statute* (Oxford, 1857).

52 *Guardian* 1859, p. 235; MS. Knowsley Papers MS. Letter Book 185/2 fos. 167–9.

53 *Guardian* 1859 p. 235; *Times* March 16, 1859 p. 12; March 17, 1859 p. 5.

54 [Montagu Burrows] *Is educational reform required in Oxford and what?* (Oxford, 1859). (For the authorship, M. Burrows, *Autobiography* p. 208); *Guardian* 1859, p. 171.

55 *Guardian* 1859, pp. 261, 279; Flysheet by an ex-tutor, Oxford May 5, 1859 (Bodl. G. A. Oxon. b. 29); *Times* June 8, 1859, p. 10; July 4, 1859, p. 10; Cox, *Recollections* p. 442.

56 J. P. Tweed, *The least change which suffices, best* (Oxford, 1859).

57 Broadsheet 'for the Hebdomadal Council only' (n. pl. or d. [Oxford, 1862]) Bodl. G. A. Oxon. c. 78 (341).

58 *Guardian* 1863, p. 232.

59 *Ibid.* p. 463.

60 For these discussions; *Ibid.* pp. 253, 285, 333, 441, 463–4; E. A. F[reeman]. *The new Examination Statute* [n. pl. or d. (1863)]. See also the flysheets in *University Notices 1859–64.* (Bodl. G. A. Oxon. b. 30).

61 *Times* March 13, 1863 p. 5.

62 *Guardian* 1863, p. 464.

63 *Guardian* 1863, p. 392; M. Burrows, *On which side is the majority of the professors, and tutors?* April 20, 1863 (cf. the anonymous reply in Bodl. G. A. Oxon. b. 30); Liddon Ho. MS. Liddon Diary March 23, 1863.

64 *Letters of William Stubbs, Bishop of Oxford 1825–1901* ed. W. H. Hutton (London, 1904) p. 96. Cf. *Guardian* 1863, p. 333, 438. See the reply by J. E. Thorold Rogers, *The new Examination Statute* (n. pl. or d. [Oxford, 1863]) Bodl. G. A. Oxon. b. 23.

65 *Guardian* 1863, pp. 438, 441; *The new Examination Statute* April 29, 1863 (Bodl. G.A. Oxon. b. 30); Bodl. Bryce MSS. Box E 30. J. Conington to James Bryce. October 2, 1863; MS. Knowsley Papers Box 101. J. P. Lightfoot to Lord Derby, Aug. 29, 1863.

66 *Guardian* 1863 pp. 1144–5, 1168, 1193, 1201, 1215; 1864, p. 107; *Times* Dec. 2, 1863, p. 12.

67 *Guardian* 1864, pp. 157, 202; *Times* Feb. 26, 1864, pp. 8, 9; *A true view of the new statute* Feb. 19, 1864; *The new examination statute* Oxford, 1864 (Both the above are in Bodl. G. A. Oxon. b. 30); W. E. Buckley, *A new view of the new statute* Feb. 16, 1864.

68 C. L. Dodgson, *The new examination statute*. Christ Church, March 2, 1864.

69 A. Lang, *The life letters and diaries of Sir Stafford Northcote, first earl of Iddesleigh* (2nd ed. London, 1890) i. 114.

70 B.M. Add. MSS. 44343 fo. 283; 44183 fos. 141–55; 44208 fos. 119–20; Bodl. MS. Pattison 51 fo. 33. Liberal support was forthcoming from Goldwin Smith and Dr. Jeune. B.M. Add. MSS. 44303 fos. 75–6.

71 Bodl. MS. Acland d. 68 fo. 20. Cf. B.M. Add. MSS. 44183 fo. 165; 'I think his mode of conducting public affairs is alike dangerous and dishonourable.'

72 B.M. Add. MSS. 44181 fos. 193–205; 44183 fos. 151–56; 44208 fos. 187–90; 44387 fo. 168–9; *Guardian* 1857, pp. 185, 210, 257.

73 Morley, *Gladstone* i. 455; B.M. Add. MSS. 44181 fo. 212; 44221 fo. 250; 44277 fo. 110; MS. Oriel College Letters Gl. 43.

74 *Times* April 7, 1859, p. 12; April 8, p. 5; April 9, p. 5; *Guardian* 1859, p. 326; B.M. Add. MSS. 44281 fo. 206; MS. Oriel College Letters no. 1025.

75 Morley, *Gladstone* i. 469; B.M. Add. MSS. 44206 fo. 232; 44236 fo. 293; 44391 fo. 376; 44530 fo. 39. Cf. T. Gladstone, *Letter to the Vice-Chancellor*, Fasque, Laurencekirk, Jan. 24, 1860.

76 B.M. Add. MSS. 44206 fo. 217 (MS. Oriel College Letters Gl. 47); 44295 fo. 361; 44530 fo. 39; 44209 fos. 38–40 (partly printed, Morley, *Gladstone* i. 468).

77 B.M. Add. MSS. 44206 fos. 227–33 (MS. Oriel College Letters Gl. 81).

78 B.M. Add. MSS. 44181 fos. 216–17, 222–3.

79 B.M. Add. MSS. 44391 fo. 374; 44530 fos. 37–8. See the collection of election flysheets in *University Notices, 1856–9.* (Bodl. G. A. Oxon. b. 29). Also in Bodl. G. A. Oxon. c. 75; *Shall we reject Mr. Gladstone?*

(Oxford, 1859); *Mr. Gladstone's premiership* (London, 1860); *Guardian* 1859, pp. 535–76 *passim*.

80 B.M. Add. MSS. 44237 fo. 1; Liddon Ho. MS. Liddon Diary June 28, 1859.

81 B.M. Add. MSS. 44282 fo. 344; 44391 fos. 372, 391.

82 B.M. Add. MSS. 44282 fo. 339.

83 B.M. Add. MSS. 44181 fo. 230. The Warden followed the fellows somewhat reluctantly, *Ibid* fo. 225; 44391 fo. 366.

84 B.M. Add. MSS. 44181 fo. 230.

85 B.M. Add. MSS. 44181 fos. 230–33; 44236 fos. 295–6; 44530 fos. 38, 39; 44209 fo. 44; MS. Oriel College Letters Gl. 48; MS. Knowsley Papers MS. Letter Book 186/2 fos. 145–7.

86 *An authentic copy of the poll for a burgess to serve in parliament for the University of Oxford* (Oxford, 1859).

87 Cf. B.M. Add. MSS. 44221 fo. 264; 44303 fo. 141.

88 B.M. Add. MSS. 44221 fo. 264.

89 B.M. Add. MSS. 44303 fo. 144. Cf. Morley, *Gladstone* i. 469.

90 B.M. Add. MSS. 44206 fo. 228.

91 B.M. Add. MSS. 44282 fo. 343.

92 B.M. Add. MSS. 44181 fos. 236–9; 44392 fos. 329–30.

93 Pusey Ho. MSS. Letters to Dr. Robert Scott; W. E. Gladstone to R. Scott, July 6, 1859 (There is a copy in B.M. Add. MSS. 44295 fos. 365–6.). Cf. *Guardian* 1859, p. 587.

94 B.M. Add. MSS. 44395 fos. 176–8, 182–3, 184–7.

95 Keble College MSS. Corr. of J. T. Coleridge with John Keble, July 15, 1860; B.M. Add. MSS. 44281 fos. 280–1.

96 B.M. Add. MSS. 44181 fo. 241.

97 B.M. Add. MSS. 44395 fos. 212–13; 44281 fos. 266–7; 44221 fo. 293; 44236 fo. 303.

98 B.M. Add. MSS. 44209 fo. 107.

99 Selborne, *Memorials, and family personal* ii. 364–5, 367; Coleridge, *Life of John Duke, Lord Coleridge* i. 268–9. The odd position of the Tractarians (with whom Palmer had always been associated) at this time is illustrated by the fact that Pusey, convinced that Derbyite conservatism had no principles, wished to put his name on Palmer's committee, only to find that Keble, seeing no good in a whig government, was likely to join Northcote's Committee. Keble College MSS. Corr. of E. B. Pusey with J. Keble [July 8, 1861].

100 B.M. Add. MSS. 44206 fos. 247–51 (MS. Oriel College Letters Gl. 83–5); 44181 fos. 249–50.

101 B.M. Add. MSS. 44396 fo. 186 (printed in Ashwell & Wilberforce, *Life of Samuel Wilberforce* iii. 20), 230–1, 240–3.

102 B.M. Add. MSS. 44396 fos. 162–7, 178–9; Bodl. MS. Pattison 54 fo. 387; *Oxford University Election* (Oxford, 1861); *Times* July 8, 1861, p. 6; July 9, p. 10; July 12, p. 10; *Guardian* 1861, pp. 644, 668, 685.

103 *Guardian* 1861, p. 645. Heathcote appears to have expected the extension of this system: MS. Knowsley Papers Box 99. F. Jeune to Lord Derby, Feb. 15, 1861.

104 MS. Knowsley Papers MS. Letter Book no. 188/2 fos. 159–63.

105 Liddon, *Pusey* iv. 195–7.

106 Cf. A. E. Gathorne Hardy, *Gathorne Hardy, first earl of Cranbrook, a memoir* (London, 1910) i. 149–50.

107 B.M. Add. MSS. 44221 fo. 294. Jeune was examined before the Select Committee on the bill. *Parliamentary Papers, England* 1861 vol. xiv. p. 4.

108 B.M. Add. MSS. 44206 fos. 238–47; MS. Oriel College Letters Gl. 52, (82–3).

109 B.M. Add. MSS. 44396 fo. 221.

110 Bodl. MS. Top. Oxon. a. 6 fo. 151.

111 B.M. Add. MSS. 44396 fo. 28; Ashwell & Wilberforce, *Life of Samuel Wilberforce* iii. 20.

112 B.M. Add. MSS. 44209 fos. 82–3. Cf. Pusey: Add. MSS. 44281 fo. 265.

113 Bodl. MS. Top. Oxon. a.6 fo. 151; B.M. Add. MSS. 44396 fo. 29.

114 B.M. Add. MSS. 44209 fos. 111–13; MS. Knowsley Papers Box 99. W. E. Gladstone to Lord Derby, July 21, 1861.

115 *Parliamentary debates* 3s. clxv. 832–43. Other debates on the bill; *Ibid.* 3s. clxii. 1014–21; clxv. 253–71, 580–1, 1343, 1469–77.

116 Including Frederic Bulley, President of Magdalen, H. H. Cornish, Principal of New Inn Hall, Montagu Burrows, H. L. Mansel and Henry Wall.

117 See the prospectus and advertisement, February 1867, in Bodl. G. A. Oxon. c. 83 (349–50).

118 Gathorne Hardy, *Memoir* i. 163. Cf. Keble College. Miscellaneous MSS. Gathorne Hardy to J. Keble, July 27, 1863.

119 Pusey Ho. MSS. Corr. of George Rolleston with E. B. Pusey [n.d.].

120 Bodl. Wynter MSS. Dep. d. 4 fos. 478, 481–3; MS. Knowsley Papers MS. Letter Book 190/1 fos. 17–20; *Times* June 13, 1864, p. 8. Wynter was, however, deterred from becoming Chairman of Gathorne Hardy's election committee in 1865; MS. Knowsley Papers Box 103. P. Wynter to Lord Derby, May 2, 1865.

121 G. A. Denison, *Notes of my life, 1805–1878* (Oxford and London, 1878) pp. 334–7. See the requisition to Gathorne Hardy in Bodl. G. A. Oxon. c. 80 (367); *Guardian* 1864, p. 684; Keble College MSS. Corr. of E. B. Pusey with J. Keble [1864 soon after July 27].

122 B.M. Add. MSS. 44404 fo. 108; *Guardian* 1864, pp. 1176, 1199–200, 1223.

123 B.M. Add. MSS. 44282 fos. 349–50; *Guardian* 1865, p. 737.

124 Gathorne Hardy, *Memoir* i. 167–72.

125 Meyrick, *Memories of Oxford* pp. 88–9.

126 Gathorne Hardy, *Memoir* i. 169.

127 Keble College MSS. Corr. of E. B. Pusey with J. Keble [August 1894]

128 B.M. Add. MSS. 44277 fos. 242–3.

129 Morley, *Gladstone* i. 575–6.

130 e.g. *Guardian* 1865, pp. 460, 716–17.

131 *Quarterly Review* cxviii. 193 *seq.* Cf. the election circular in Bodl. G. A. Oxon. c. 81 (358); *Is Mr. Gladstone the right man for Oxford?* [1865].

132 F. Max Müller, *Autobiography* p. 270; Goldwin Smith, *Reminiscences* pp. 284–5; Ashwell & Wilberforce, *Life of Samuel Wilberforce* iii. 161–2.

133 Hodder, *Life of Shaftesbury* iii. 199–200.

134 *Guardian* 1864, pp. 804, 815; Coleridge, *Life of Lord Coleridge* ii. 134.

135 Lang, *Life of Stafford Northcote* i. 223; Bodl. MS. Bryce 9 fo. 71; Morley, *Gladstone* i. 580.

136 B.M. Add. MSS. 44277 fos. 242–4.

137 B.M. Add. MSS. 44218 fos. 127–36; 44209 fos. 170–1; 44277 fos. 245, 249.

138 The opinions are in University archives, N.W.4.2.

139 The forecasts of Hardy's canvassers proved remarkably accurate, Gathorne Hardy, *Memoir* i. 176, 178.

140 *Guardian* 1865, p. 908.

141 On this and other points, E. W. Urquhart, *The late Oxford University election* (London, 1865).

142 Quoted in *Guardian* 1865, p. 738.

143 J. O. Johnston, *Life and letters of Henry Parry Liddon* (2nd ed. London, 1904) p. 99; Liddon Ho. MS. Liddon Diary July 18, 1865; B.M. Add. MSS. 44282 fo. 350.

144 Liddon, *Pusey* iv. 199–200.

145 *Guardian* 1865, p. 498; Urquhart, *The late Oxford University election*.

146 *Guardian* 1866, p. 1203.

147 Burrows, *Autobiography* pp. 209–27.

148 J. W. Caldicott, *An analysis of the poll book in the recent election of two burgesses to serve in Parliament for the University of Oxford* (London, 1866).

149 B.M. Add. MSS. 44303 fos. 156, 167.

150 Goldwin Smith, *Reminiscences* p. 285.

151 Ashwell & Wilberforce, *Life of Samuel Wilberforce* iii. 162; *Guardian* 1865, p. 836.

152 *Nonconformist* 1865, p. 573.

CHAPTER XI

1 Bodl. MS. Bryce 16 fo. 14.

2 Balliol Coll. Jowett MSS. Box E, B. Jowett to A. P. Stanley, Feb. 27 [1856]. Cf. an undated letter of 1854 and another of 1862.

3 *Letters of Benjamin Jowett* pp. 14–16.

4 Balliol Coll. Jowett MSS. Box F, B. Jowett to J. A. Symonds, Dec. 28, 1880.

5 *Recollections of Dean Fremantle* pp. 106–8.

6 Bodl. MS. Bryce 9 fos. 3–6.

7 Bodl. MS. Bryce 5 fos. 70–3, 132; 6 fo. 22.

8 Bodl. Bryce MSS. Box E 30. H. Nettleship to J. Bryce, Feb. 21, 1866.

9 *Letters of Matthew Arnold 1848–88*. ed. G. W. E. Russell (Oxford, 1895) i. 135.

10 *Westminster Review* n.s. xx. 293–334; *Guardian* 1861, pp. 970, 983.

11 *Corr. of A. H. Clough* ii. 557; Bodl. MS. Pattison 52 fo. 153. Cf. Balliol Coll. Jowett MSS. Box E, B. Jowett to A. P. Stanley [1862].

12 Bodl. MS. Bryce 9 fos. 82–4. Cf. Ch. Ch. Salisbury MSS. W. C. Lake to Lord Cranborne, July 28, Nov. 26, 1866.

13 Bodl. Bryce MSS. Box E 30. H. Nettleship to J. Bryce, Feb. 21, 1866.

14 B.M. Add. MSS. 44281 fos. 296–303; 44236 fo. 313; 44318 fo. 48. Cf. Ch. Ch. Salisbury MSS. W. C. Lake to Lord Cranborne, Nov. 26, 1866.

15 *Guardian* 1863, p. 1142.

16 *The Ecclesiastic* Dec. 1866, p. 545; June 1868, p. 274–5.

17 *Correspondence of a junior student of Christ Church, Oxford, 1868–70* (n. pl. or d.) pp. 66 *et passim*.

18 Bodl. Bryce MSS. Box E 30. H. Nettleship to J. Bryce, Feb. 21, 1866.

19 Bodl. MS. Bryce 5 fo. 73.

20 Conington, *Miscellaneous Writings* p. xl.; R. L. Nettleship, *Memoir of Thomas Hill Green* (London, 1906) p. 44.

21 *Christian Reformer* 1856, pp. 413–31.

22 For correspondence upon this, Pusey Ho. MSS. Letters to Dr. Robert Scott, Master of Balliol.

23 Meyrick, *Memories of Oxford* pp. 101–3.

24 Abbot & Campbell, *Jowett* i. 275.

25 *Christian Reformer* 1860, p. 598.

26 *Guardian* 1861, pp. 321–2.

27 MS. Knowsley Papers Box 100. F. Jeune to Lord Derby, Oct. 5, 1862.

28 University archives. N.W.21.10. Memorial of the Clerical and Lay Association for the maintenance of Evangelical Principles for the Western District; *Guardian* 1861, p. 341.

29 *Westminster Review* n.s. xviii pp. 293–332.

30 *Case whether Professor Jowett in his Essay and Commentary has so distinctly contravened the doctrines of the Church of England that a court of law would pronounce him guilty; with the opinion of the Queen's Advocate thereon* (London, 1862).

31 *Guardian* 1860, pp. 951–2, 1032, 1033; *Times* June 11, 1860, p. 9; June 27, p. 12; Aug. 8, p. 9, Oct. 22, p. 7; Oct. 29, p. 67; Dec. 8, p. 9. Pusey reckoned that Müller suffered by association with Jowett even before the great agitation began. B.M. Add. MSS. 44281 fo. 261.

32 MS. Knowsley Papers. MS. Letter Book 189/2 fos. 126–9; Box 101. J. P. Lightfoot to Lord Derby, May 27, June 1, 1863. For the new method of balloting for honorary degrees; *Ibid.* Box 100. P. Wynter to Lord Derby, May 19, 1862.

33 Liddon Ho. MS. Liddon Diary Feb. 25, 1864; *Nonconformist* 1864, pp. 161, 164.

34 A. P. Stanley, *Letter to the Bishop of London on the state of subscription in the Church of England and in the University of Oxford* (Oxford and London, 1863).

35 J. B. Mozley, *Letters* 254–5.

36 J. B. Mozley, *Subscription to the Articles. A letter to the Rev. Professor Stanley* (Oxford, 1863).

37 C. A. Ogilvie, *On subscription to the Thirty-Nine Articles as by law required of candidates for Holy Orders and of the Clergy* (Oxford, 1863). Cf. W. J. Irons, *The proposed surrender of the Prayer Book and Articles of the Church of England* (London, 1863).

38 *Macmillan's Magazine* ix. 465–73; x. 174–5.

39 Goldwin Smith, *A plea for the abolition of tests in the University of Oxford* (Oxford, 1864) p. 32.

40 *Westminster Review* n.s. xxv. 384 *seq.*

41 Pusey Ho. MSS. Corr. of George Rolleston with E. B. Pusey, April 23, 1864. Osborne Gordon and others thought Rolleston was making a very odd choice indeed. B.M. Add. MSS. 44400 fos. 290–1.

42 Liddell might have done well to say in public, what he admitted in private, that orthodoxy had social supports far more powerful than the tests. Bodl. MS. Acland 69 fo. 48.

43 H. R. Bramley, *An answer to Professor Goldwin Smith's plea for the abolition of tests in the University of Oxford* (London, 1864).

44 Liddon Ho. MS. Liddon Diary, Nov. 3, 1861.

45 E. Hawkins, *Notes upon subscription, academic and clerical* (Oxford, 1864); E. Hawkins, *Additional notes upon subscription* (Oxford, 1866); E. Hawkins, *Religious education, academical and collegiate* (Oxford, 1870).

46 For an account of the Cambridge movement for the repeal of the tests; D. A. Winstanley, *Later Victorian Cambridge* (Cambridge, 1947) ch. III.

47 *Parliamentary debates* 3s. clxx. 1228–43.

48 *Christian Reformer* 1860, pp. 122–3; *Nonconformist* 1860, p. 661.

49 H. S. Skeats and C. S. Miall, *History of the Free Churches of England, 1688–1892* (London, 1891) p. 625n.

50 H. Fawcett, 'On the exclusion of those who are not members of the established church from fellowships and other privileges of the English universities,' *Macmillan's Mag.* iii. 411–16.

51 Bodl. MS. Pattison 54 fo. 244. One dissenter, left stranded in 1861 when Litton's Hall closed down 'made a round of Oxford Colleges in the hope of being allowed to enter one, in which he should not be compelled to attend the reading of the Litany in the College chapel . . . [Liddell took him in at Christ Church] but no other Oxford Head offered to make any concession to the young man's conscientious

scruples' (MS. Pattison 54 fos. 97, 239–40). The situation seemed a little easier when C. P. Scott was seeking entrance at the end of 1864 (Balliol Coll. MS. 421 no. 29). Cf. however the case of James Bryce. H. A. L. Fisher, *James Bryce* (London, 1927) i. 39.

52 B.M. Add. MSS. 44318 fos. 41, 43.

53 Bodl. MSS. Bryce 9 fos. 23, 27; Box E 30. J. M. Marshall to J. Bryce, May 15, 1863; Frederick Lygon, *University Tests* (Oxford and London, 1864); *Times* July 6, 1863, p. 9; July 9, p. 12; July 10, p. 12; July 13, 1863, p. 5; MS. Knowsley Papers Box 101. J. P. Lightfoot to Lord Derby, June 30, July 4, 5, 8, 1863; F. Jeune to Lord Derby, July 27, 1863. After all the alterations the liberal Henry Acland would not sign. B.M. Add. MSS 44091 fos. 49–53. Cf. Add. MSS. 44401 fo. 24 (misdated 1865).

54 *Parliamentary debates* 3s. clxxi. 1386 *seq.*

55 *Nonconformist* 1863, p. 304.

56 Bodl. Monk Bretton MSS. Goldwin Smith to J. G., Dodson, March 29, 1864; 'Notes of Miall's letter to G. Smith.'

57 *Nonconformist* 1864, pp. 261, 457–8, 537.

58 *Abolition of tests at the Universities of Oxford and Cambridge* ed. G. C. Brodrick (London, 1866); *Nonconformist* 1866, p. 283.

59 Bodl. MS. Bryce 16 fo. 14.

60 Bodl. MS. Bryce 9 fos. 58–9.

61 Bodl. Bryce MSS. Box E 30. R. D. Darbishire to J. Bryce, July 3, 1865; C. S. Roundell to J. Bryce, July 27, 1865.

62 *Nonconformist* 1868, pp. 824, 1111.

63 For Gladstone's views; B.M. Add. MSS. 44277 fo. 165; 44752 fo. 311; 44401 fos. 39–41; 44091 fo. 55 (another copy Bodl. MS. Acland d. 68 fos. 30–3); Monk Bretton MSS. W. E. Gladstone to Sir George Grey, June 22, 1864; G. C. Brodrick, *Memories and Impressions, 1831–1900* (London, 1900) pp. 238–9. Cf. his rebuff to Baldwin Brown in 1865; Lathbury, *Corr. on church and religion of W. E. Gladstone* i. 219–20.

64 Ashwell & Wilberforce, *Life of Samuel Wilberforce* iii. 81; MS. Oriel College Letters Gl. 55–6.

65 B.M. Add. MSS. 44402 fos. 254–7; Keble College MSS. Corr. of W. E. Gladstone with J. Keble, March 31, April 20, 1864.

66 Liddon Ho. MS. Liddon Diary, March 15, 16, 1864; B.M. Add. MSS. 44237 fos. 3–6.

67 *Parliamentary debates* 3s. clxxiv. 102–61.

68 Letter of Frederic Harrison in his *Autobiographic Memoirs* (London, 1911) i. 355.

69 *Parliamentary debates* 3s. clxxx. 222–3.

70 B.M. Add. MSS. 44209 fos. 154, 158. For other correspondence on Gladstone's immobility; Add. MSS. 44318 fo. 51; 44206 fos. 257–65 (MS. Oriel College Letters Gl. 86, 88).

71 *Parliamentary debates* 3s. clxxvi. 466–7.

72 *Ibid.* pp. 666–80.

73 *Nonconformist* 1864, p. 537.

74 *Parliamentary debates* 3s. clxxvi. 1391–1408.

75 The organisation of this whole campaign is revealed in Dodson's own papers, now preserved in a box of miscellaneous political papers in Bodl. Monk Bretton MSS. See also L. Campbell, *On the nationalisation of the old English Universities.*

76 Bodl. Monk Bretton MSS. C. S. Roundell to J. G. Dodson, Nov. 23, 1864. This letter shows that the formation of the Committee was antedated in Lewis Campbell, *op. cit.*

77 Bodl. Monk Bretton MSS. C. S. Roundell to J. G. Dodson, Dec. 19, 1864, Feb. 6, 8, 1865; J. G. Dodson to C. S. Roundell, Nov. 25, 1864, n.d. [Feb. 5 or 6, 1865].

78 A. D. Elliott, *Life of Lord Goschen* (London, 1911) i. 60–1.

79 *Times* March 28, 1865, p. 11.

80 Bodl. Monk Bretton MSS. E. S. Foulkes to J. G. Dodson, Nov. 21, 1864.

81 *Nonconformist* 1865, p. 163.

82 Bodl. Bryce MSS. Box E 30. C. S. Roundell to J. Bryce, June 24, 1865.

83 *Parliamentary debates* 3s. clxxx. 185–250.

84 Bodl. Bryce MSS. Box E 30. C. S. Roundell to J. Bryce, July 24, 1865.

85 Goldwin Smith, *The elections to the Hebdomadal Council. A letter to Rev. C. W. Sandford.* (Oxford, 1866). The elections were still being fought on party lines in the early years of this century. Lord Curzon, *Principles & methods of university reform* (Oxford, 1909) pp. 22–3.

86 Bodl. MS. Bryce 9 fo. 19.

87 Bodl. Bryce MSS. Box E 30. C. S. Roundell to J. Bryce, July 24, 1865.

88 *Letters of John Richard Green* ed. L. Stephen (London, 1891) pp. 175–6.

89 B.M. Add. MSS. 44281 fo. 327. Cf. Goldwin Smith's attack on Liddon in the *Daily News* for using his lectures to organise a party. Liddon Ho. MS. Liddon Diary. Nov. 11, 1866.

90 E.g. *Guardian* 1859, p. 348; 1862, p. 685.

91 *Times* Nov. 29, 1856, p. 8.

92 E. B. Pusey, *Summary of objections against the proposed Theological Statute* (Oxford, 1854); [M. Burrows] *Is educational reform required in Oxford, and what?* p. 25n.

93 *Supra* p. 110.

94 W. Ince, *The past history and present duties of the Faculty of Theology in Oxford* (Oxford and London, 1878) p. 39; *Guardian* 1860, pp. 216–18.

95 *Times* Feb. 24, 1860, p. 10; March 2, p. 5; May 11, p. 12; May 25, p. 5; *The new Theological Statute* May 19, 1860 (Bodl. G. A. Oxon. b. 30); Keble College. MSS. Corr. of E. B. Pusey with J. Keble, [c. March 7, 1860].

96 *Guardian* 1863, pp. 260, 277, 414; *Times* March 13, 1863, p. 12.

97 J. Conington, *The Theological Statute* (n. pl. or d. [1869]).

98 Liddon Ho. MS. Liddon Diary.

99 J. W. Burgon, *Plea for a fifth school* (Oxford, 1868); Bodl. MS. Eng.
    th. d. 15 fo. 1. On Burgon see E. M. Goulburn, *John William Burgon*
    (London, 1892) e.g. ii. 163, 194.

100 *Times* June 4, 1868, p. 6; *Guardian* 1868, p. 673; Liddon Ho. MS.
    Liddon Diary, June 8, 1868; Pusey Ho. MSS. Corr. of G. Rolleston
    with E. B. Pusey, June 13, 18, 1868; *The new Theological Statute*
    (Bodl. G. A. Oxon. c. 84 (470)).

101 *Times* Nov. 11, 1868, p. 11; Nov. 21, p. 11; E. B. Pusey, *The Divinity
    School* Nov. 19, 1868; G. Rolleston, *The proposed school of theology*
    (Oxford, Nov. 30, 1868); R. P. Smith, *Letter to Rolleston* (Oxford,
    Dec. 4, 1863); Pusey Ho. MSS. Corr. of G. Rolleston with E. B. Pusey,
    Nov. 24–5, 1868.

102 *Guardian* 1869, p. 593; *Times* May 20, 1869, p. 5 (where the division is
    reported as 121–61); Liddon Ho. MS. Liddon Diary May 19, 1869
    (for Henry Smith's analysis of the voting); E. B. Pusey, *The proposed
    statute for a Theological School*, May 12 [1869]; H. J. S. S[mith].
    The proposed School of Theology Whit. Monday 1869; J. W. Burgon,
    To Professor H. J. S. Smith May 18, 1869.

103 Bodl. MS. Bryce 16 fo. 13; E. L. Stanley, *Oxford University reform*
    (London, 1869) pp. 9–10.

104 Liddon Ho. MS. Liddon Diary Feb. 6, 1870 (Partly printed in J. O.
    Johnston, *Life and letters of H. P. Liddon* p. 120).

105 J. W. Burgon, *Plea for the study of divinity in Oxford* (Oxford and
    London, 1875) Goulburn, *Burgon* ii. 32, 90; Cf. D. P. Chase; *Guardian*
    1879, pp. 7, 46, 81; W. Ince, *The past history and present duties of the
    Faculty of Theology in Oxford*.

106 *Times* Feb. 2, 1869, p. 7; March 24, p. 11; April 21, p. 12. For the
    legal opinions Bodl. G. A. Oxon. c. 85 (110, 423); 32 & 33 Vict. c. 20.

107 *Parliamentary debates* 3s. clxxxi. 1257–64; clxxxii. 2013–61; clxxxiii.
    2008–19.

108 E. H. Coleridge, *Life of Lord Coleridge* i. 264, 259–60, ii. 40–1, 56–7.

109 *Times* March 22, 1866, p. 8; *Guardian* 1866, p. 325.

110 *Nonconformist* 1866, p. 241.

111 For the debates: *Parliamentary debates* 3s. clxxxii. 659–715; clxxxiv.
    307–44.

112 Bodl. MS. Pattison 56 fo. 179.

113 *Times* March 19, 1866, p. 10.

114 Bodl. Monk Bretton MSS. Goldwin Smith to J. G. Dodson, March 9,
    1864. Cf. *Times* May 7, 1868, p. 5.

115 MS. Oriel College Letters Gl. 57.

116 Liddon Ho. MS. Liddon Diary, Sept. 4, 1866.

117 MS. Oriel College Letters no. 1294. For the concessions he was
    prepared to make: B.M. Add. MSS. 44206 fos. 271–6. (Another copy
    of one of these letters is in MS. Oriel College Letters Gl. 91).

118 University archives. MS. Minutes of Hebdomadal Council 1866–1879
    fos. 27, 32, 63; *Times* Jan. 23, 1868 p. 6; *Guardian* 1868, p. 131.

119 For the debates on Coleridge's bill: *Parliamentary debates* 3s. clxxxv. 296–7, 1419–26; clxxxviii. 83, 1655–8, clxxxix. 43–75. On Fawcett's bill, *Ibid.* 3s. clxxxvii. 1248–82; clxxxviii. 962–3; clxxxix. 1048–50.

120 *Nonconformist* 1867, p. 617.

121 Bodl. Bryce MSS. Box E 30. MS. Memorandum on the bill in an envelope addressed by C. S. Roundell to James Bryce, post-marked Dec. 21, 1867; B.M. Add. MSS. 44303. fos. 180–1.

122 B.M. Add. MSS. 44414 fos. 99–102.

123 The memorial was reprinted in the *Guardian* 1868 p. 277; *Times* March 3, 1868, p. 4.

124 *Saturday Review* 1868 i. 304–5.

125 Quoted in *Nonconformist* 1868, p. 220.

126 D. P. Chase, *A few words on the Oxford address to the Archbishop of Canterbury* (Oxford, 1868).

127 *Guardian* 1867, p. 420; 1868, pp. 281, 316, 344, 373. One of the most uncomfortable liberal high-churchmen was Richard Church, who did not mind being abused by Pusey as a trimmer, but was reluctant to accept Gladstone's offers of preferment in case he was attacked as a time-server (B.M. Add. MSS. 44127 fos. 131–2). Only after the repeal of the tests did he accept the Deanery of St. Paul's.

128 Bodl. MS. Bryce 9 fos. 117–18; B.M. Add. MSS. 44303 fos. 185–7.

129 *Parliamentary debates* 3s. cxcii. 1012 *seq.*

130 *Parliamentary debates* 3s. cxc. 926–7; cxcii. 209–32, 1012–25; cxciii. 426–71.

131 B.M. Add. MSS. 44237 fos. 27–34.

132 *Guardian* 1868, pp. 357–8, 389, 402, 443, 515.

133 *Guardian* 1868, pp. 949, 952–3; *Nonconformist* 1868, pp. 833, 858; Johnston, *Liddon* pp. 131–3. Cf. D. P. Chase, *The de-Christianising of the colleges of Oxford* (London, 1869). The Wesleyans, nevertheless, had mixed feelings about opening the door to 'the audacity of rationalism, and the scheming of Popery—the two great enemies of truth.' *Wesleyan Methodist Magazine* July 1870, p. 654.

134 *Nonconformist* 1868, pp. 824, 1111.

135 Earl of Selborne, *Memorials, personal and political* (London, 1898) i. 100–11; *Times* Oct. 9, 1868, p. 7; Oct. 13, p. 5; Oct. 14, p. 3; Oct. 16, p. 6; Oct. 22, p. 7; Oct. 26, p. 6; Nov. 12, p. 7; *Guardian* 1868, pp. 1137, 1174, 1176, 1185, 1199, 1228, 1251, 1273, 1281; B.M. Add. MSS. 44303 fos. 188–9; *Saturday Review* 1868 ii. 644–5. For the election papers, Bodl. G. A. Oxon. c. 221, G. A. Oxon. c. 84 (509–17 *passim*).

136 Morley, *Gladstone* i. 710.

137 Liddon Ho. MS. Liddon Diary March 8, 1869.

138 Johnston, *Liddon* pp. 116–17

139 Selborne, *Memorials, personal and political* i. 125–6.

140 *Parliamentary debates* 3s. cxciv, 272–3, 1041–54, 1415–59; cxcvii. 767–98; cxcviii. 125–45; *Times* July 20, 1869, p. 9.

141 *Guardian* 1869, p. 1165.

142 Ch. Ch. Salisbury MSS. MS. College Resolution Oct. 25, 1869.
143 Bodl. MS. Acland d. 74 fos. 34–7.
144 Bodl. Wynter MSS. Dep. d. 4 fos. 518–19 (There is a copy in Knowsley MSS. MS. Letter Book 197/1 fos. 1–2); *Guardian* 1868, p. 277.
145 Cf. *Times* Oct. 25, 1869, p. 10.
146 *Times* Nov. 13, 1869 p. 9; *Guardian* 1869 pp. 1276, 1347.
147 Ch. Ch. Salisbury MSS. Lord Salisbury to Dr. Pusey, May 24, 1870.
148 *Parliamentary debates* 3s. cxcviii pp. 451–3; *Times* July 22, 1869, p. 5.
149 *Congregational Year Book, 1870* (London, 1870) pp. 91–2, 95–105. In 1868 the first political resolutions of the Cheshire Congregational Union had been in favour of Coleridge's Bill. F. J. Powicke, *A history of the Cheshire County Union of Congregational Churches* (Manchester 1907) p. 49.
150 *Nonconformist* 1869, pp. 1092–3; *Inquirer* 1869, pp. 738–40; *Times* Nov. 11, 1869, p. 6. Cf. Nov. 12, 1869, p. 6. This leader, like others in the same vein, was probably written by G. C. Brodrick, fellow of Merton.
151 *Times* Dec. 3, 1869, p. 7; Dec. 6, p. 5; Dec. 7, p. 4; Dec. 9, p. 9; Dec. 11, p. 12; Dec. 17, p. 9; *Guardian* 1869, pp. 1353, 1374–5, 1417; *Inquirer* 1869, p. 782; *Nonconformist* 1869, p. 1162.
152 *Times* Jan. 18, 1870; *Parliamentary debates* 3s. cxcix. 591, 1146.
153 Bodl. Bryce MSS. Box E 30. H. G. Liddell to J. Bryce, March 10, 1870.
154 B.M. Add. MSS. 44236 fos. 315–16.
155 *Times* Feb. 5, 1870, p. 5; May 23, p. 7.
156 *Guardian* 1870, pp. 201, 415, 635, 662; B.M. Add. MSS. 44206 fos. 279–87.
157 Ch. Ch. Salisbury MSS. E. C. Woollcombe to Lord Salisbury, July 12, 1870.
158 *Parliamentary debates* 3s. cci. 1192–255; *Times* May 24, 1870, p. 9.
159 *Guardian* 1870, p. 709; B.M. Add. MSS. 44236 fos. 323–30; 44427 fos. 40–1, 64–5.
160 MS. Oriel College Letters Gl. 60. Hawkins poured out his chagrin to Salisbury; Ch. Ch. Salisbury MSS. E. Hawkins to Lord Salisbury, July 9, 1870. Old Dr. Symons thought that if headships became generally open to laymen all virtue would go out of the university. *Ibid.* B. P. Symons to Lord Salisbury, July 30, 1870.
161 *Parliamentary debates* 3s. cci. 1947–80.
162 *Guardian* 1870, pp. 847, 879–80, 1039.
163 MS. Oriel College Letters no. 1173.
164 *Parliamentary debates* 3s. cciii. 196–232.
165 *Times* Sept. 24, 1870 p. 4; Dec. 6, p. 7; *Congregational Year Book 1871* (London, 1871) p. 78.
166 A. S. Wilkins, *Our national universities* (London, 1871) pp. 320–1.
167 *Inquirer* 1871, p. 99.

168 *Nonconformist* 1871, p. 76.

169 MS. Oriel College Letters no. 1174.

170 Kimberley Journal June 13, 1871, *Camden Miscellany* xxi. 22.

171 Coleridge, *Life of Lord Coleridge*, ii. 176-7. (partly printed in Morley, *Gladstone* i. 710); *Nonconformist* 1871, p. 169.

172 *Parliamentary debates* 3s. cciv. 499-528; *Times* Feb. 21, 1871, p. 7; *Nonconformist* 1871, p. 169.

173 *Report from the Select Committee of the House of Lords on University Tests, Parliamentary Papers*, 1871, Vol. IX. Cf. *Wesleyan Methodist Magazine* 1870, p. 654; Ch. Ch. Salisbury MSS. G. Rolleston to Sir Roundell Palmer, June 21, 1870; G. Rolleston to Vice-Chancellor (Leighton) July 9, 1870.

174 *Parliamentary debates* 3s. ccvi. 338-98.

175 *Guardian* 1871, p. 582.

176 Ch. Ch. Salisbury MSS. E. C. Woollcombe to Lord Salisbury, June 5, 1871.

177 *Parliamentary debates* 3s. ccvi. 1962-73.

178 G. C. Brodrick, *Political Studies* (London, 1879) p. 185.

179 E.g. B. A. Gregory, 'Methodism and the University of Oxford,' *City Road Magazine* 1871, pp. 492-9. (There is a copy of this article in the Hobill Collection, *Methodist History* xiv at Hartley-Victoria College, Manchester.)

180 G. H. Curteis, *Dissent in its relation to the Church of England* (London, new ed. 1892) p. x.

181 E. S. Purcell, *Life of Cardinal Manning* (London, 1896) ii. 288-303. In 1863 E. S. Foulkes, a former fellow and tutor of Jesus, now a Roman Catholic, had attempted to open a Catholic hall in Oxford, and had subsequently supported John Dodson's campaign against the tests. University archives. N.W.4.2. E. S. Foulkes to the Vice-Chancellor, Sept. 30, 1863; Bodl. Monk Bretton MSS. E. S. Foulkes to J. G. Dodson, Nov. 14, 21, 1864; Feb. 16, 1865.

182 *Parliamentary debates* 3s. ccvii. 1163-5; ccviii. 694-753.

183 T. W. Moody and J. C. Beckett, *Queen's, Belfast 1845-1949* (London, 1959) i. 277-89.

184 Ch. Ch. Salisbury MSS. T. K. Leighton to Lord Salisbury, May 20, 1870; Lord Salisbury to T. K. Leighton, May 23, 1870; H. J. S. Smith to Lord Salisbury, May 26, June 1, June 6, 1870; Lord Salisbury to unknown correspondent May 28, 1870. J. B. Atlay, *Sir Henry Wentworth Acland Bt. A memoir* (London, 1903) pp. 347-9; University archives. MS. Minutes of Hebdomadal Council, 1866-79 fos. 204-5; F. Darwin, *Life and letters of Charles Darwin* (London, 1888) ii. 126; L. Huxley, *Life and letters of T. H. Huxley* (London, 1903) ii. 13-14 (Huxley obtained his degree in 1885). A few years earlier Pusey had conducted a correspondence with George Rolleston on the implications of his beliefs for biological studies. Pusey Ho. MSS. Corr. of G. Rolleston with E. B. Pusey. Cf. C. A. Heurtley's flysheet against Tyndall, June 18, 1873.

185 *Times* June 7, 1871, p. 9; June 9, p. 9; *Guardian* 1871, pp. 668, 700. See the flysheets in Bodl. G. A. Oxon. b. 140. On Clarke; *Guardian* 1869, p. 1319; *Inquirer* 1870, p. 3.

186 *Times* Nov. 27, 1871, p. 9; *Guardian* 1871, p. 1421, 1505.

187 *Guardian* 1868, p. 1363.

188 Liddon Ho. MS. Liddon Diary, Nov. 18, 1865.

189 Prothero, *Stanley* ii. 226–9; *Times* Dec. 7, 1872, p. 9; Dec. 9, p. 9; Dec. 10, p. 9; Dec. 11, p. 4; Dec. 12, p. 9; Dec. 16, p. 8; *Guardian* 1872, pp. 1534, 1539, 1577; W. R. W. Stephens, *Life and letters of E. A. Freeman* ii. 65; Goulburn, *Burgon* ii. 78–80; Bodl. MS. Eng. th. d. 10; Johnston, *Liddon* pp. 240–1.

CHAPTER XII

1 Wilkins, *Our national universities* p. 320.

2 MS. Knowsley Papers. MS. Letter Book 189/1 fos. 252–6.

3 *Guardian* 1865, pp. 331, 363, 421–2.

4 *Guardian* 1865, pp. 1169, 1177–8; Liddon Ho. MS. Liddon Diary Nov. 16, 1865.

5 *Guardian* 1865, p. 1291.

6 C. Daubeny, *A letter to the Provost of Oriel on university extension* (Oxford and London, 1865).

7 Bodl. Bryce MSS. Box E 30. Edward Donner to J. Bryce, Dec. 13, 1865.

8 *North British Review* March 1867, pp. 224–39; *Macmillan's Magazine* xv. 224–7; *Saturday Review* 1867, i. 49, 108–9, 133–4; *Times* Aug. 6, 1866, p. 12; Aug. 9, p. 8; J. Rumsey, *Oxford Extension* (Oxford, 1868). The reports were printed as *University Extension, Reports of the subcommittees* (Oxford, n. d. [1867]).

9 *Guardian* 1866, p. 845; *Macmillan's Magazine* xv. 225. Cf. *Autobiography of Montagu Burrows* p. 246.

10 Johnston, *Liddon* pp. 110–14; Liddon Ho. MS. Liddon Diary, April–May 1866 *passim* e.g. April 23, 1866; Coleridge, *Life of Lord Coleridge* ii. 140–1; *Guardian* 1866, p. 685.

11 *Guardian* 1866, p. 1204.

12 J. Wordsworth, *Keble College and the present university crisis* (Oxford, 1869).

13 *Guardian* 1871, p. 276.

14 H. A. Pottinger, *The University of Oxford and Keble College. I The Decree, II The Statute* (both Oxford, 1871).

15 *Nonconformist* 1870, p. 631.

16 Liddon Ho. MS. Liddon Diary, March 6, 1880. The Warden was E. S. Talbot.

17 *Ibid.* Feb. 1, 1881. The strictness of the Keble conception had occasioned another contest in the *Guardian* in 1878 (pp. 616, 682–3). Montagu Burrows and Burgon contended that the college had its origin in Marriott's scheme for a poor scholars' hall, while Liddon and Pusey insisted that its object was to keep alive the memory of Keble and the *Christian Year*.

18 Liddon Ho. MS. Liddon Diary, Feb. 20, 1874; B.M. Add. MSS. 44303 fos. 192–3; *Times* May 5, 1874, p. 13; June 4, p. 7; Nov. 27, 1875, p. 7; Nov. 30, p. 10; Dec. 6, p. 10; Dec. 7, p. 10; July 2, 1877, p. 9; *Nonconformist* 1878, pp. 446, 634.

19 *Memoirs of Archbishop Temple* i. 118–19.

20 *University Extension. Reports of the subcommittees* pp. 41–52.

21 Abbot & Campbell, *Jowett* i. 377–8.

22 University archives. MS. Minutes of Hebdomadal Council 1866–79 fos. 12, 13.

23 Abbot & Campbell, *Jowett* i. 433. Cf. *Guardian* 1867, p. 633.

24 *North British Review* March 1867, pp. 236–7.

25 *Parliamentary debates* 3s. clxxxv. 1704–8; clxxxvii. 1613–45; clxxxviii. 585; *Times* June 5, 1867, p. 8; June 7, p. 9. Cf. *Saturday Review* 1867, i. 786–7; ii. 46–7.

26 Jowett was much encouraged by the reception of his evidence. Abbot & Campbell, *Jowett* i. 424. This letter (now in Balliol Coll. Jowett MSS. F.) was written to Florence Nightingale.

27 *Parliamentary Papers* 1867 xxiii. *Special report from the select committee on the Oxford and Cambridge Universities Bill.* This evidence was summarised in the *Guardian* 1867, pp. 1229–30; 1868, pp. 42–3, 72–3, 97–8, and commented upon in *Edinburgh Review* cxxvii. 157–9; *Nonconformist* 1867, pp. 784–5, 810–11.

28 *Times* June 20, 1867, p. 14.

29 *Guardian* 1867, pp. 1220, 1248; *The Hebdomadal Council and the Lodging Statute* Oxford, Dec. 6, 1867. This pamphlet may have been written by Henry Smith; see *Times* Dec. 10, 1867, p. 4; Dec. 13, p. 8.

30 Liddon Ho. MS. Liddon Diary, Feb. 17, 1868. Cf. April 29, 1868.

31 *Guardian* 1868, pp. 337, 361; *Times* March 13, 1868, p. 12; March 28, p. 9.

32 *Guardian* 1868, pp. 687, 829, 853; *Times* May 21, 1868, p. 11; June 4, p. 6; June 18, p. 8.

33 *Times* Sept. 8, 1868, p. 7; Sept. 17, p. 4; Sept. 18, p. 6; Sept. 19, p. 8;

34 *Times* Oct. 15, 1870, p. 12.

35 *Guardian* 1872, pp. 163, 1511.

36 *Guardian* 1870, p. 1272; *Times* Oct. 16, 1872, p. 9. A third of the first entry were nonconformists (*Leisure Hour* Oct. 1, 1869, p. 668). See also *Paper issued by the Delegates for Licencing Lodging Houses* Aug. 5, 1868 (Bodl. G. A. Oxon. c. 84 (268)); *Report of the Delegati ad Aedes Licentiandas* Oxford, June 1869 (Bodl. G. A. Oxon. 250 (9)); R. L. Abbot, *The non-collegiate students; a brief sketch of their history* (Oxford, 1894).

37 *Guardian* 1872, p. 1480; J. Rumsey, *The unattached students of Oxford* (Oxford, 1876). The gradual tendency to impose collegiate organisation on the unattached students also received strong liberal criticism. E. Hatch, *The proposed 'University Hall.'* (Oxford, April 23, 1881).

38 J. W. Burgon, *Our present lodging-house system immoral* (Chichester, 1876); J. W. Burgon, *The late Vicar of St. Mary's in explanation*

(Oxford, 1876); *Saint and soubrette, or chops and tomato sauce.* (Oxford, 1876); University archives. MS. Reports to Hebdomadal Council 1865–9 no. 57.

39 *Vide supra* p. 246.

40 Bodl. MS. Pattison 56 fos. 160–3, 166–7, 212–3.

41 (Edinburgh, 1868) p. 1.

42 B.M. Add. MSS. 44303 fos. 171–3.

43 For the 'private and confidential' proceedings of the conference. Bodl. Monk Bretton MSS.

44 B.M. Add. MSS. 44270 fo. 88.

45 MS. Knowsley Papers. Box 157/10. E. Cardwell to Lord Derby, Nov. 16, 19, 21, 26, 1855; MS. Letter Book 183/1 fos. 300–7, 311–3; 95/2, Corr. of Lord Derby and R. Michell, Sept. 24, 30, 1858.

46 *The Ecclesiastic* Dec. 1866 p. 550.

47 *Vide supra* p. 248.

48 *Parliamentary Papers* 1867 xiii. *Special report from the Select Committee on the Oxford and Cambridge Universities Bill* p. 17.

49 B.M. Add. MSS. 44755 fos. 206–7.

50 *Parliamentary debates* 3s. cxc. 478–506.

51 B.M. Add. MSS. 44303 fos. 177–9.

52 *Ibid.* fos. 180–2. Cf. Bodl. Bryce MSS. Box E 30. MS. Memorandum (c. Dec. 21, 1867).

53 *University extension and improvement* May 20, 1868. (Bodl. G. A. Oxon. c. 84 (456)).

54 *Draft of a proposed bill for the extension and improvement of the university of Oxford and the colleges therein.* May 18, 1868 (Bodl. G. A. Oxon. c. 84 (462)).

55 *Nonconformist* 1868, p. 1111.

56 Correspondence between J. E. T. Rogers and Professor Masson. Oxford, Nov. 6, 1867 (Bodl. G. A. Oxon. c. 83 (419)); *The paper read at Dundee, and the University of Oxford* Nov. 25, 1867 (Bodl. G. A. Oxon. c. 83 (422)); *Fraser's Magazine* lxxix. 1–15. Cf. Charles Neate, 'Endowments,' *Macmillan's Magazine* xxii. 387–93.

57 Goldwin Smith, *The reorganization of the University of Oxford* (Oxford, 1868).

58 B. Price, 'Oxford,' *Fraser's Magazine* Nov. 1868.

59 *Edinburgh Review* cxxvii. 157–9.

60 Bodl. Bryce MSS. Box E 30. H. Nettleship to J. Bryce. Jan. 6, 1868.

61 *Oxford Essays, 1855,* p. 294.

62 M. Pattison, 'Philosophy at Oxford,' *Mind* i. 82–97.

63 Abbot & Campbell, *Jowett* i. 379.

64 *Quarterly Review* cxxiv. 386 *seq.*

65 *Times* May 5, 1873, p. 8.

66 T. Arnold, *The revival of the faculties at Oxford* (Oxford and London, 1872) p. 4.

67 T. C. Snow, *The endowment of education* (Printed, 1877).

68 H. A. Morgan, *Tenure of fellowships*; Abbot & Campbell, *Jowett* ii. 123.

69 'We have been lately witnessing in the elasticity with which every branch of Prussian organisation bore the tremendous strain laid upon it by the war, *the fruits of the effectiveness of the German university system*. Our breakdown at the Crimea is distinctly traceable to the ineffectiveness of our superior education.' Arnold, *Revival of the faculties* pp. 7–8. Cf. *Macmillan's Magazine* xxxvii. pp. 148 *seq.*

70 For an example of the rather feeble efforts of the *Times* to discountenance the 'scramble for plunder' among fellowships, *Times* Dec. 17, 1872, p. 9.

71 *Guardian* 1876, p. 678 (cf. p. 39); MS. Oriel College Letters no. 1234.

72 *Macmillan's Magazine* xxv. 300–6. Jowett who was now possessed by a contempt of tutors like that of the unreformed heads of his own young days used much stronger language. Abbot & Campbell, *Jowett* ii. 154–5.

73 Curzon, *Principles and methods of university reform* p. 17.

74 Arnold, *Revival of faculties* p. 4–5.

75 W. Stubbs, *Two lectures on the present state and prospects of historical study delivered on the 17th and 20th May, 1876.* (printed but not published).

76 J. Bryce, *Legal studies in the University of Oxford* (London, 1893); B.M. Add. MSS. 44447 fos. 363–4. Improvement in Oxford was stimulated by talk in 1871 of the establishment of a legal university. *Guardian* 1871, p. 121.

77 T. D. Acland, *The discouragement of elementary mathematics in general education at Oxford* (Oxford, 1867).

78 Sir Henry W. Acland, *Oxford and modern medicine* (Oxford, 1890).

79 Matthew Arnold, *Letters* ii. 35.

80 T. D. Acland, *General education and special studies* (Oxford, 1871); T. L. Papillon, *Oxford scholarship and honour moderations* (Oxford, 1880).

81 D. P. Chase, '*The voluntary system*' applied to academical instruction (Oxford, 1859).

82 Jackson, *Bywater* pp. 65–6; Balliol College. Jowett MSS. F, B. Jowett to J. Nichol, March 21, 1868.

83 Liddon Ho. MS. Liddon Diary, Dec. 23, 1867.

84 Stubbs, *Present state of historical study* p. 7.

85 *Times* March 24, 1870, p. 12; *Guardian* 1870, p. 575; 1872, pp. 481, 1013–14.

86 C. H. Firth, *The faculties and their powers* (Oxford, 1909) p. 6.

87 University archives. W.P. 7.1. Reports and papers on university requirements and reform. No. 1; *Times* June 18, 1874, p. 10.

88 *Times* June 18, 1875, pp. 6, 11; J. Wilkinson, *Oxford University reform* (Oxford, 1875).

89 *Questions submitted to colleges, and the answers communicated by the several societies, printed only for the private use of those societies and of the Hebdomadal Council* (Oxford, 1875), (Bodl. G. A. Oxon. 8° 1001 (14)).

90 *Statement of the requirements of the university adopted by the Hebdomadal Council on the 19th of March 1877, with the papers upon which it was founded* (Oxford, 1877), (Bodl. G. A. Oxon. 8° 296 (13)).

91 *Guardian* 1878, pp. 253, 341.

92 T. Arnold, *Revival of the faculties*.

93 *Oxford Essays, 1858*, pp. 284–5.

94 *Guardian* 1864, pp. 427, 429, 479, 499; *The newest struggle for principle at Oxford* (reprinted from the *English Churchman* April 28, 1864); Pusey Ho. MSS. Monograph on the middle class examinations by E. B. Pusey; Corr. of George Rolleston with E. B. Pusey, n.d; Liddon's MS. Transcripts of Pusey's corr. with J. Keble [May 3, 1861]; Liddon Ho. MS. Liddon Diary, March 21, 1865.

95 For this episode: *Memoirs of Archbishop Temple* ed. E. G. Sandford i. 129–32; ii 540–55; A. H. D. Acland, *Memoir and letters of Sir Thomas Dyke Acland*, (printed London, 1902) pp. 179 *seq.*; University archives. *Reports to Hebdomadal Council 1855–64* no. 37 (printed copies of this and other related documents are in *University Notices 1856–9* (Bodl. G. A. Oxon. b. 29) at June 1857).

96 *Times* Nov. 25, 1857, p. 8; Jan. 26, 1858, p. 4; *Nonconformist* 1857 pp. 428, 455, 474, 494, 854; 1858, pp. 208, 522, 693, 793, 836.

97 *Guardian* 1870, p. 415; Ch. Ch. Salisbury MSS. J. E. Thorold Rogers to Lord Salisbury, April 6, 1877, Cf. Balliol Coll. Jowett MSS. Box E, B. Jowett to L. Campbell, Oct. 28, 1875.

98 *Times* Sept. 16, 1872, p. 8.

99 *Guardian* 1871, pp. 36, 129.

100 *Times* Jan. 4, 1873, p. 7; Jan. 13, p. 9.

101 *Times* April 23, 1873, p. 9.

102 *Times* Dec. 22, 1873, p. 9; *Guardian* 1873, p. 1621.

103 *Times* Sept. 7, 1874, p. 8; *Guardian* 1872, p. 1486; 1874, p. 1156; 1875, p. 519; 1877, p. 1280.

104 *Times* Oct. 9, 1873, p. 9.

105 *Times* Jan. 29, 1873, p. 6; June 4, 1874, p. 7.

106 *Guardian* 1877, p. 1337.

107 *Times* July 30, 1875, p. 9; Feb. 19, 1879, p. 9; *Guardian* 1876, pp. 780, 873.

108 *Times* April 5, 1878, p. 4; May 17, p. 4.

109 W. Sewell, *Suggestions for the extension of the university submitted to the Vice-Chancellor* (Oxford, 1850).

110 *Guardian* 1863, p. 277. A similar plea was urged in 1872, *Guardian* 1872, p. 1477.

111 *Report of the subcommittee on extension by affiliation* pp. 6–7.

112 *Parliamentary Papers* 1867 xiii. *Special report from the Select Committee on the Oxford and Cambridge Universities Bill* p. 134.

113 Charles Neate, 'Endowments,' in *Macmillan's Magazine* xxii. 391.

114 J. Percival, *The connection of the universities and the great towns* (London, 1873).

115 Abbot & Campbell, *Jowett* ii. 57–61.

116 Ch. Ch. Salisbury MSS. W. Sewell to Lord Salisbury, May 13, 1870.

117 See Jowett's pamphlet on university reform, 1874, pp. 8, 26, in Balliol Coll. Jowett MSS. E, printed in Campbell, *Nationalization of old English universities* pp. 183–208; C. S. Parker, *Academical endowments* (London, 1875). Bryce had long reached the same conclusion. Fisher, *Bryce* i. 111.

118 *Times* Sept. 23, 1875, p. 7; *Guardian* 1875, p. 519.

119 Bodl. MS. Pattison 57 fo. 30.

120 Abbot & Campbell, *Jowett* ii. 128.

121 *Times* Nov. 27, 1877, p. 4.

122 *Guardian* 1875, p. 519.

123 J. B. Mayor, *Affiliation of local colleges to Oxford and Cambridge* (London, 1874).

124 *Times* March 14, 1874, p. 5; *Guardian* 1874, pp. 324, 385.

125 Liddon Ho. MS. Liddon Diary, Feb. 8, 1875. On the proposal of Owens College, cf. Bodl. MS. Pattison 57 fo. 30.

126 *Guardian* 1876, p. 608; *The proposed statute on affiliated colleges* April 24, 1876 (Bodl. G. A. Oxon. b. 140).

127 Bodl. MS. Acland d. 68 fos. 44–9; L. Playfair, *On teaching universities and examining boards* (Edinburgh, 1872); *Macmillan's Magazine* xxxv. 407–16; xxxix. 12–16; *Times* June 14, 1879, p. 7; *Guardian* 1877, p. 213.

128 *Times* Nov. 7, 1877, p. 8. The view that the university revenues should be distributed among the chief provincial towns was expressed at the Social Science Congress in 1874. *Guardian* 1874, p. 301.

129 *Times* Nov. 17, 1877, pp. 6, 9.

130 *Times* Feb. 21, 1878, p. 6; March 6, p. 10.

131 *Times* June 14, 1879, p. 7; *Guardian* 1879, p. 741.

132 *Times* Oct. 30, 1879, p. 8.

133 *Times* Feb. 11, 1880, p. 10.

134 S. Taylor, *On French and German as substitutes for Greek in university pass examinations* (London, 1870).

135 Liddon Ho. MS. Liddon Diary, March 19, 1873.

136 *Times* May 23, 1879, p. 9.

137 *Guardian* 1877, p. 156.

138 *Guardian* 1877, p. 748.

139 *Guardian* 1879, p. 1441.

140 *Times* May 23, 1879, pp. 9, 10. A vigorous correspondence between Odling and Liddon followed; *Times* May 27, 1879 p. 9; May 31, p. 7 and in later numbers. Cf. *Times* June 3, 1879, p. 9.

141 *Guardian* 1879, p. 1677.

142 *Times* April 28, 1880, p. 7.

143 *Guardian* 1880, p. 713.

144 *Times* April 16, 1881, p. 9.

CHAPTER XIII

1 E.g. E. L. Stanley, *Oxford University Reform* (London, 1869); *Macmillan's Magazine* xx. 124–29; A. S. Wilkins, *Our national universities.* There was a good deal written from Cambridge at the same time, e.g. H. A. Morgan, *The tenure of fellowships considered* (London, 1871). Liberal animus was sharpened by the failure of Oriel College to get an act severing the headship from its ecclesiastical preferments. The bill was thrown out by a select committee of the Lords, so that colleges must await a general settlement to obtain any extension of lay influence. Ch. Ch. Salisbury MSS. E. Hawkins to Lord Salisbury, March 10, 1869; B.M. Add. MSS. 44206 fo. 286 (MS. Oriel College Letters Gl. 94); *Guardian* 1869, p. 513.

2 One of the themes of the pamphleteers of the 'seventies was the great growth of extravagant expenditure in college balls in the Commemoration season, and the enormously increased popularity of boating, cricket, and other summer sports (G. W. Kitchen, *Letter to the Vice-Chancellor . . . on the summer term and Commemoration week* (Oxford, 1869)), and the possibility of moving examinations to the end of the session was much canvassed.

3 Jackson, *Bywater* p. 71. For a fuller account of these episodes, Sir Edmund Craster, *History of the Bodleian Library 1845–1945* (Oxford, 1952) pp. 130–4.

4 *Guardian* 1873, p. 704.

5 *Ibid.* p. 1564.

6 *Guardian* 1875, pp. 264, 303, 535; *Times* April 22, 1875, p. 12.

7 *Guardian* 1876, p. 812.

8 *Times* May 9, 1882, p. 10.

9 *Times* July 18, 1871, p. 6.

10 University archives. N.W.8.6. W. E. Gladstone to Vice-Chancellor, Oct. 24, 1871 (printed in *Guardian* 1871, p. 1292 and the Report of the Cleveland Commission 1874); B.M. Add. MSS. 44236 fos. 333–5.

11 *Times* Nov. 3, 1871, p. 7; Dec. 26, p. 7; Dec. 28, p. 7; *Nonconformist* 1871, p. 1217; *Guardian* 1871, p. 1481.

12 *Guardian* 1872, pp. 1477, 1485–6; *Times* Nov. 23, 1872, pp. 4, 9; Dec. 17, p. 9.

13 *Nonconformist* 1872, p. 1209.

14 *Times* Aug. 21, 1873, p. 9; Aug. 26, p. 7.

15 *Report of the commissioners appointed to inquire into the property and income of the Universities of Oxford and Cambridge, Parliamentary Papers* 1873 xxxvii.

16 Bodl. MS. Acland d. 68 fos. 44–9; Playfair, *On teaching universities and examining boards.*

17 *Times* Oct. 10, 1874, p. 9.

18 *Times* Oct. 15, 1874, p. 9.

19 *Times* Oct. 22, 1874, p. 5.

20 *Times* Oct. 26, 1874, p. 6.

21 *Times* Nov. 11, 1874, p. 5; Nov. 13, p. 5; Dec. 1, p. 10.

22 *Times* Dec. 16, 1874, p. 9; Dec. 21, p. 6. One of the protesting bursars was West of Lincoln who had conflicted with Roundell while the report was being compiled. Green, *Oxford Common Room* p. 252. Faussett sent a copy of the protest to the Chancellor, Lord Salisbury. Ch. Ch. Salisbury MSS. R. G. Faussett to Lord Salisbury, Dec. 12, 1874.

23 *Report* i. 32.

24 Goldwin Smith, *Oxford University and the forthcoming report of the Commission.* Cf. B.M. Add. MSS. 44303 fo. 194.

25 Ch. Ch. Salisbury MSS. J. Bryce to Lord Salisbury, May 3, 1876. Pattison insisted that Salisbury's bill embodied no policy. (*Guardian* 1876, pp. 1374–5.) The duke of Cleveland himself urged a further enquiry (*Parliamentary debates* 3s. ccxxvii. 1686), and a motion of Jowett to the same effect was defeated at the Hebdomadal Council by 14 votes to 8. University archives. MS. Minutes of Hebdomadal Council 1866–79 fo. 428.

26 *Essays on the endowment of research* (London, 1876).

27 *Guardian* 1876, pp. 1357, 1359, 1361, 1375.

28 *Mind* i. 82–97.

29 *Guardian* 1876, p. 1375.

30 *Guardian* 1876, pp. 201, 873.

31 Liddon Ho. MS. Liddon Diary, Oct. 23, 1875 (the explanation of this is given in the *Guardian* 1875, p. 1368); C. S. Parker, *Academical endowments* (London, 1875).

32 Goldwin Smith, *Oxford University and the forthcoming report of the commission* reprinted from *Oxford Chronicle* May 30, 1874; *Minutes of evidence taken by Oxford University commissioners* pp. 104–5; *Parliamentary Papers* 1881 lvi.

33 C. G. Brodrick, *Political studies* (London, 1879) pp. 551–2 (Cf. Brodrick *Memories and impressions* p. 182; D. Roll-Hansen, *The Academy 1869–79* (Copenhagen, 1957) p. 78). Brodrick conveyed to Pattison privately some interesting information about these letters. Bodl. MS. Pattison 57 fos. 262–5.

34 Sidney Colvin, 'Fellowships and national culture,' *Macmillan's Magazine* xxxiv. 136–42.

35 Brodrick, *Political studies* p. 548. Cf. Brodrick 'The universities and the nation', *Contemporary Review* June 1875, p. 71.

36 *Times* March 27, 1876, p. 7. J. R. Thursfield, the writer of this letter, had been a prominent liberal politician in the previous decade. Significantly one of the last pamphlets of the old style was by H. A.

Pottinger who maintained that the tests were still in force in Oxford (H. A. Pottinger, *University tests. A short account of the contrivances by which the acts of parliament abolishing tests and declarations have been evaded at Oxford* (London, 1873)). The decline in the political temperature of the university also fostered the liberal cause in the elections to the Hebdomadal Council. There was little change in October 1875 when Burrows replaced Liddon, and Jowett replaced Fowler, though Pusey's circle was plunged into gloom at the defeat of their candidate by an enemy of ritualism (Liddon Ho. MS. Liddon Diary, Oct. 18, 21, 23, 24, 1875; *Times* Oct. 22, 1875, p. 10; *Guardian* 1875, p. 1368; Johnston, *Liddon* pp. 242-3). In October 1878, the liberals swept the board, securing the majority seats in all three divisions, and showing so decisive a lead that Liddon refused to contest a by-election with Professor Rolleston. (*Times* Oct. 23, 1878, p. 6; Liddon Ho. MS. Liddon Diary, Oct. 22, 23, 1878). And in 1881 when the reforms of the new university commission had to be put into force the parties arranged that there should be no contest, even though the choice of candidates gave an additional seat to the liberals (*Times* Oct. 24, 1881, p. 11). These gains more than offset another liberal fiasco in the parliamentary by-election of 1878 when Henry Smith was routed by J. G. Talbot, a minor conservative politician, and brother of the Warden of Keble. On this election (which is chiefly interesting for the antagonisms among the high-church and conservative groups) see: Bodl. MS. Bryce 6 fos. 26, 164; Brodrick, *Memories and impressions* pp. 238-9, 241; *Times* April 20, 1878, p. 9; *Guardian* 1878, pp. 545, 603-4, 641, 649, 701, 713, 756; *Nonconformist* 1878, p. 354; Johnston, *Liddon* pp. 246-7.

37 In 1871 the Privy Council had determined that the consent of the Visitor was not necessary to changes in the college ordinances made by the executive commission of 1854, but on the representation of Salisbury they agreed to allow no changes in the statutes affecting the fellowships and revenues of any college until the Cleveland commission reported (*Parliamentary debates* 3s. ccxvi. 10-13). Two Oxford colleges with schemes suspended by this decision were Brasenose and Oriel, where a strenuous agitation was being led by Jowett's friend, D. B. Monro, to open the office of Provost to laymen by severing it from the canonry at Rochester. Hawkins's ultimate failure to maintain the ecclesiastical character of the office enabled Monro to succeed him as Provost. On this episode, MS. Oriel College Letters Nos. 616-29; Ch. Ch. Salisbury MSS. J. W. Burgon to Lord Salisbury, May 13, 1876; E. Hawkins to same, April 1, 1871; April 8, 1872; June 29, 1877; July 20, 1881; Lord Salisbury to E. Hawkins, July 22, 1881; D. P. Chase to W. E. Gladstone, Nov. 2, 1871; B.M. Add. MSS. 44206 fo. 286 (MS. Oriel College Letters Gl. 94); E. Hawkins, *Notices concerning the design, history, and present state of Oriel College, with respect to the ecclesiastical character of the institution and of the Provostship* (Rochester, 1875); Balliol College. Jowett MSS. E, B. Jowett to L. Campbell, April 2, 1875.

38 J. R. Magrath, *University reform* (Oxford, 1876).

39 Balliol College. Jowett MSS. F, B. Jowett to R. B. D. Morier, Oct. 23, 1879.

40 Ch. Ch. Salisbury MSS. H. G. Liddell to Lord Salisbury, Feb. 1, 1875; *Times* Feb. 6, 1875, p. 9.

41 Bodl. MS. Acland d. 74 fos. 46–7.

42 *Times* Feb. 20, 1875, p. 9.

43 *Guardian* 1876, pp. 220, 233.

44 Liddon Ho. MS. Liddon Diary, March 23, 1876; *Guardian* 1876, p. 204.

45 *Church Quarterly Review* xii. 221 (cf. *Guardian* 1880, p. 817); Liddon Ho. MS. Liddon Diary, March 12, Nov. 3, 1875.

46 Ch. Ch. Salisbury MSS. Petition of Resident Members of Congregation to Lord Salisbury, March 17, 1875. Among the high-churchmen who signed were E. S. Talbot, D. P. Chase, J. B. Mozley, E. B. Pusey, W. Bright, J. W. Burgon, H. P. Liddon, W. Stubbs, Montagu Burrows, E. C. Woollcombe and John Wordsworth; among the conservative politicians were F. Bulley, T. K. Leighton, W. Jackson and J. Bellamy, the heads of Magdalen, All Souls, Queen's, and St. John's respectively.

47 *Nonconformist* 1876, p. 234. For Stanley's authorship, Bodl. MS. Pattison 57 fo. 223.

48 Bodl. MS. Pattison 57 fos. 220–3, 228–9, 232–3 (cf. MS. Pattison 60 fo. 119); *Times* March 28, 1876, p. 5.

49 Ch. Ch. Salisbury MSS. J. W. Burgon to Lord Salisbury, March 18, 25, April 3, 20; May 13, 1876; Goulburn, *Burgon* ii. 145–6.

50 *Parliamentary debates* 3s. ccxxix. 102.

51 *Times* March 18, 1876, p. 12; March 22, p. 7.

52 Many of these petitions are to be found in the Salisbury MSS. and they are there summarised in a MS. schedule entitled 'Suggestions by various colleges of the University of Oxford on the University of Oxford Bill.' Cf. Bodl. MS. Pattison 57 fos. 228, 234.

53 *Parliamentary debates* 3s. ccxxviii. 347, 598–9.

54 University archives. MS. Minutes of Hebdomadal Council 1866–79 fo. 428. At the same meeting 'a motion by the Rector of Exeter in favour of a fund being made available for disposal on grounds of poverty was rejected by 14 to 6.' It was thus the middle party which had triumphed on the Hebdomadal Council and with the government.

55 Balliol Coll. Jowett MSS. E, B. Jowett to L. Campbell [1876]. At a meeting at Balliol in May attended by Goschen, there was a general desire that the bill should pass, and a good deal of opposition to the motion that a preliminary inquiry was necessary. *Guardian* 1876, p. 608.

56 For example, among the amendments accepted by Salisbury were others bringing the headships within the action of the commissioners (and thus opening the possibility of lay headships) and requiring the commissioners to make provision for religious instruction (thus ensuring the retention of some clerical fellowships). *Parliamentary debates* 3s. ccxxviii. 1950.

57 *Times* April 8, 1876, p. 11.

58 *Parliamentary debates* 3s. ccxxix. 1735–6.

59 *Times* June 16, 1877, p. 11; *Guardian* 1877, p. 404.

60 There had been much criticism of Burgon's appointment in both houses (*Parliamentary debates* 3s. ccxxviii. 932; ccxxix. 1721) and even his high-church friends could find little to say for him (Ch. Ch. Salisbury MSS. C. H. Daniel to Lord Salisbury, March 31, 1876;

Guardian 1876, p. 905). He also chose this inconsiderate moment to attack the Oxford lodging-house keepers in the interests of under-graduate morals—so threatening conservative votes for the town. See ch. XII n. 38.

61 *Parliamentary debates* 3s. ccxxxii. 585; Goulburn, *Burgon* ii. 149–50.

62 *Guardian* 1877, p. 244.

63 Ch. Ch. Salisbury MSS. H. G. Liddell to Lord Salisbury, Jan. 25, 1877.

64 For the terms of the bill; *Guardian* 1877, p. 253; *Times* Feb. 17, 1877, p. 9.

65 *Parliamentary debates* 3s. ccxxxiv. 1802.

66 *Times* July 17, 1877, p. 9.

67 C. H. Robarts, 'University libraries and professional colleges,' *Macmillan's Magazine* xxxiii. 326–39; *Guardian* 1877, p. 1580. Cf. Craster, *History of the Bodleian* p. 50.

68 C. Neate, *The universities reform bill* (n. pl. or d. [1877]) p. 11.

69 Ch. Ch. Salisbury MSS. Montagu Burrows to Lord Salisbury, Nov. 8, 1878; [Printed] A paper presented to H.M. University Commissioners by the Warden and seven fellows of All Souls College, July 23, 1878; [Printed] Report on selected Indian Civil Service candidates, pre-sented by a committee of the Warden, Bernard, Buller, *et. al.*; *Guardian* 1880, pp. 1705–6.

70 The evidence was published in *Parliamentary Papers* 1881, lvi.

71 For the following see *Fraser's Magazine* n.s. cxxxvii. 590 *seq.*; C. L. Shadwell, *The universities and college estates acts, 1858 to 1880, their history and results* (Oxford, 1898); *Journal of the Royal Statistical Society* lv. 2; lviii. 36; lxvii. 585, lxxvi. 737.

72 *Report of the Cleveland Commission* pp. 66, 76–7, 80, 102.

73 J. R. Magrath, *University Reform* p. 9.

74 For the impact of this in an individual college: Green, *Oxford Common Room* pp. 289 *seq.*

75 *Guardian* 1880, p. 1829.

76 In the debates on this bill there was remarkable liberal animosity against college borrowing. *Parliamentary debates* 3s. ccliv. 1177 *seq.*

77 Bernard, *Letter to Gladstone* p. 13.

78 *Vide supra*, p. 280.

79 This and the other statutes created by the commission are contained in *Statutes made for the University of Oxford and the Colleges and Halls therein* . . . (Oxford, 1882).

80 Bernard, *Letter to Gladstone* pp. 15–23; *Times* Nov. 9, 1880, pp. 4, 9; Dec. 8, pp. 5, 6, 9; Dec. 21, p. 10; Dec. 25, p. 11; March 11, 1881, p. 9; *Guardian* 1880, pp. 1581, 1617–18, 1668–9; 1881, pp. 281, 385. [H. F. Pelham and W. W. Jackson] *A few words on the proposals of the Oxford University Commission* (Oxford, 1880); *Memorial to the Oxford University Commission* (Oxford, Dec. 6, 1880).

81 Ch. Ch. Salisbury MSS. E. Evans to Lord Salisbury, June 7, July 10, 1881; [Printed] *Vote in Convocation* June 13 [1882]; Bernard, *Letter to Gladstone* pp. 27–8; *Guardian* 1880, p. 1789; 1881, pp. 385, 693, 846.

82 *Times* Aug. 4, 1881, p. 5; *Guardian* 1881, pp. 878, 1116.

83 Ch. Ch. Salisbury MSS. G. C. Brodrick to Lord Salisbury, May 28, 1882; J. R. Magrath to same, June 30, July 5, 1882; E. Moore to same, June 15, 1882; *Times* May 8, 1882, p. 8; *Guardian* 1882, pp. 458–9.

84 *Parliamentary debates* 3s. cclxxi. 765, 1381; cclxxii. 1055–9.

85 Liddon Ho. MS. Liddon Diary, Nov. 11, 1880.

86 Ch. Ch. Salisbury MSS. O. Gordon to Lord Salisbury, Jan. 14, May 12, Aug. 29, 1881; Lord Salisbury to Mountague Bernard, Dec. 11, 1880; Mountague Bernard to Lord Salisbury, Dec. 6, 1880, April 29, 1881; T. W. Jackson to Lord Salisbury, Jan. 10, 1881.

87 Bernard, *Letter to Gladstone* pp. 29–35; *Guardian* 1880, p. 1705.

88 *Guardian* 1881, p. 781.

89 Liddon was the writer of the unsigned article 'The recent fortunes of the Church in Oxford,' *Church Quarterly Review* xii. 201–42 (see Johnston, *Liddon* p. 253); J. W. Burgon poured out his wrath from the pulpit of St. Mary's in a sermon published as *The disestablishment of religion in Oxford, the betrayal of a sacred trust: words of warning to the University* (Oxford, n.d.). Cf. Ch. Ch. Salisbury MSS. J. W. Burgon to Lord Salisbury, May 17, Dec. 13, Holy Innocents, 1880.

90 C. Wordsworth, *A letter to the University of Oxford Commissioners* (n.d. or pl. [1879]).

91 Christopher Wordsworth, *A letter to members of Lincoln College, Oxford, on certain proposed changes in their college* (Lincoln, 1880).

92 Bodl. MS. Top. Oxon. c. 236 fos. 25–61.

93 *Times* July 8, 1880, p. 10.

94 Reprinted from the *Nonconformist* in the *Guardian* 1880, p. 707 and Burgon, *Disestablishment of religion* App. C.

95 B.M. Add. MSS. 44464 fos. 200–3; 44465 fos. 32–4; Jowett, *Letters* 39–40; *Times* July 9, 1880, p. 5. Widespread fears that religious instruction might be divorced from church connexion were revealed in a petition to Gladstone signed by men of all religious parties in January 1880. Bodl. G. A. Oxon. b. 140.

96 *Parliamentary debates* 3s. ccliv. 102–33.

97 Clerical anger at this change of front is illustrated in Burgon, *Disestablishment of religion* App. A; J. Wordsworth, *The church and the universities* (Oxford, 1880) p. 10.

98 Bodl. MS. Bryce 10 fo. 36; 11 fos. 64–6.

99 Green, *Oxford Common Room* pp. 254–60.

100 *Times* Nov. 22, 1879, p. 10.

101 Ch. Ch. Salisbury MSS. E. R. Dukes to Lord Salisbury, June 21, 1881.

102 Ch. Ch. Salisbury MSS. E. Evans to Lord Salisbury, Feb. 14, 1880.

103 Ch. Ch. Salisbury MSS. W. J. Priest to Lord Salisbury, March 1, 1882.

104 Ch. Ch. Salisbury MSS. B. Jowett to Lord Salisbury, Feb. 11, 26, 1878; June 3, 1879; Balliol Coll. Jowett MS. F, B. Jowett to R. B. D. Morier, March 7, 1878.

105 Ch. Ch. Salisbury MSS. G. Hill to Lord Salisbury, Dec. 6, 1881, March 30, 1882.

106 Ch. Ch. Salisbury MSS. E. A. Knox to Lord Salisbury, June 6, 1879.

107 *Times* May 14, 1881, p. 12.

108 D. P. Chase, *Oxford University Bill* (Oxford, 1876); Ch. Ch. Salisbury MSS. [Printed] Sketch of a statute for the 'complete union' of Oriel College and St. Mary Hall. Proposed by the Principal of St. Mary Hall; E. Hatch to Lord Salisbury, March 12, 1882.

109 *Guardian* 1881, p. 781; Bernard, *Letter to Gladstone* p. 44.

110 Ch. Ch. Salisbury MSS. E. Evans to Lord Salisbury, June 3, 1879. The Tavern was 'a name given to New Inn Hall, not only from its title "New Inn," but also because the buttery is open all day, and the members of the Hall can call for what they please at any hour, the same as in a tavern.' Cuthbert Bede [i.e. E. Bradley]. *The adventures of Mr. Verdant Green* (London, n.d.) p. 185n.

111 Burgon, however, made a strenuous private effort to get Salisbury to appoint Pattison (who had once declined) instead of Jowett. In his view 'the difference between the two men is this:—P[attison] was a devoted disciple of Newman's—and though he has drifted clean away into Heaven-knows-what, he is at least not *actively* mischievous . . . the other man (J[owett]) is bent on doing mischief—and has an extraordinary, as well as (to me) unaccountable amount of influence.' Ch. Ch. Salisbury MSS. July 7, 10, 1882.

112 B.M. Add. MSS. 44236 fos. 369–70; *Commons Journals* cxxxvii. 16, 18, 92.

113 J. Bryce, 'The future of the English universities', *Fortnightly* March 1883, pp. 381–403.

114 Bodl. MS. Bryce 6 fos. 90–2.

115 Brodrick, *Memories and impressions* pp. 169–71. Brodrick's complaint that colleges were over-taxed was borne out by the next royal commission which found that the stipends of fellows had often been inadequate and that some colleges had had to change their statutes and reduce the number of fellows. *Report of royal commission on Oxford and Cambridge Universities*, 1922, p. 23.

116 *Guardian* 1881, p. 1871; B.M. Add. MSS. 44303 fos. 221–2.

117 *Letters of J. R. Green* pp. 480–1.

118 Cf. Liddon Ho. MS. Liddon Diary, Jan. 1, 1880.

119 W. Ince, *The internal duties of the university in prospect of external changes* (Oxford and London, 1878); Ince also urged the folly of withdrawing clerical education from Oxford, as the perils to faith which were found there were no different from those of society at large; W. Ince, *The education of the clergy at the universities* (Oxford, 1882).

120 Pusey Ho. MS. Corr. of George Rolleston with E. B. Pusey n.d. [c. 1872].

121 J. F. Mackarness, *A charge delivered to the clergy of the diocese of Oxford* (Oxford, 1875) pp. 13–14; Jackson, *Bywater* pp. 77–80; Liddon Ho. MS. Liddon Diary, June 14, 1881.

122 Ch. Ch. Salisbury MSS. E. Ffoulkes to Lord Salisbury, Sept. 23, 1881.

123 On the above; W. Ince, *Religion in the University of Oxford* (Oxford and London, 1875). There is a good deal of other evidence in favour

of this view. The power of competitive examinations in Oxford told immensely against proselytisation or the rigging of elections in the interests of either religion or scepticism.

124 *Guardian* 1875, p. 1305.

125 *Guardian* 1881, p. 557; *Nonconformist* 1881, p. 471.

126 Wycliffe and Ridley Hall at Cambridge were twin foundations. *Guardian* 1877, pp. 880, 894, 920, 922, 974.

127 *Spiritual destitution at Oxford* (Oxford, 1876) [in Bodl. G. A. Oxon. 4° 405].

128 This point is developed in J. P. C. Roach, 'Victorian universities and the national intelligentsia,' in *Victorian Studies* iii. 131–50.

INDEX

Abbot, Charles, Lord Colchester, 9, 10, 11, 27–8, 38, 41–2, 43, 326 nn 61, 68, 327 nn 73–4, 77.

Aberdeen, Lord, 176, 178, 225.

Academy, 292–3.

Acland, Sir Henry Wentworth, Regius professor of medicine, 148, 262, 264, 277, 299, 303, 307, 397 n 53.

Acland, Sir Thomas Dyke, 277, 280–1.

Addington, Henry, Lord Sidmouth, 9, 10, 23, 27, 28, 29, 30–6, 50, 68, 72, 348 n 36.

Albert, Prince Consort, 132, 137, 152.

Aldis, William Steadman, 260.

Aldrich, Henry, 18.

All Souls College, 26, 54, 55, 56, 161, 169, 210–11, 225, 258, 303, 310, 343 n 79, 375 n 246, 388 n 4, 412 n 46.

Althorpe, Lord, 88.

Anson, Sir William Reynell, Warden of All Souls College, 277.

Appleton, Charles Edward Cutts Birchall, 292–3, 296.

Arnold, Matthew, 137, 277.

Arnold, Thomas, Headmaster of Rugby School, 58, 64, 68, 75, 89, 101, 113, 130, 146, 157, 351 n 117, 352 n 141, 360 n 88.

Arnold, Thomas, son of the above, 276–7, 280.

Ashmolean Museum, 51.

Ashurst, William Henry, 68.

Auckland, Lord, 9, 32, 33, 327 n 70.

Awdry, Sir John, 118, 206, 212, 276.

Aylesbury, Lord, 67.

Baines, Edward, 92.

Balliol College, 5, 26, 31, 33, 38, 54, 56, 78, 82, 90, 108, 111, 114, 120, 130, 140, 141, 143, 144, 153, 156, 158, 161, 169, 185, 200–1, 207, 210, 211, 215, 217, 222, 227, 246–7, 250, 259, 267–9, 271, 275–8, 281, 285–286, 295, 297, 303, 312, 348 n 48, 354 n 178, 356 n 17, 360 n 109, 370 n 116, 376 n 28, 412 n 55.

Balliol Hall, 140, 268.

Bampton Lectures, 7, 50, 93, 100, 122, 133, 212, 215, 261.

Bandinel, Bulkeley, Bodley's Librarian, 45.

Baring, Thomas, 266.

Barnes, Frederick, Sub-dean of Christ Church, 41.

Barrow, John, Fellow of Queen's College, Principal of St. Edmund Hall, 168, 205.

Barry, Henry Boothby, Fellow of Queen's College, 168, 187, 381 n 17.

Bathurst, Bragge, 42.

Baur, Ferdinand, 131.

Beaufort, Duke of, 3, 31–6, 41, 328 n 95.

Beaufoy, Henry, 2.

Beddoes, Thomas, Reader in chemistry, 8, 51.

Bedford, Duke of, 4.

Beeke, Henry, Regius professor of modern history, 32, 50.

Bellamy, James, President of St. John's College, 302, 412 n 46.

Berdmore, Scrope, Warden of Merton College, 26.

Beresford, Major, 176, 380 n 114.

Bernard, Mountague, Chichele professor of International Law, 181, 264, 277, 286, 301, 306, 310, 312.

Bible Society, 2, 41, 333 n 24.

Blackett, John Fenwick Burgoyne, 195.

Blackstone, James, Principal of New Inn Hall, 55–6.

Blackstone, William, Principal of New Inn Hall, 55.

Blandford, Marquis of, 171, 177, 197, 224.

Bliss, Philip, Principal of St. Mary Hall, 72, 86, 102, 107, 127, 177, 200, 205, 339 n 174, 343 n 71, 349 n 60, 357 n 35.

Blomfield, Charles James, 37.

Blücher, Gerhard Lebrecht von, 40.

Bodleian Library, 8, 36, 45–6, 53, 234, 279, 291–2, 303, 335 n 77, 338 n 149.

Bonham, F. R., 84, 348 n 32.

Bouverie, Edward Pleydell-, 242–3, 246–7, 252–4.

Bowen, Sir Charles Synge Christopher, Fellow of Balliol College. 246

Bradley, George Granville, Fellow of University College, 137, 237, 240, 290, 295, 299, 312.

Bradley, James, Savilian professor of astronomy, 319 n 59.

Bramley, Henry Ramsden, Fellow of Magdalen College, 242, 262.

Brasenose College, 25–8, 29, 32, 33, 35, 37, 42, 43–4, 52, 54, 101, 105, 114, 154, 161, 169, 195, 216–17, 266, 306, 348 n 48, 360 n 100, 370 n 116, 411 n 37.

Bridges, Sir Brook, 171, 240.

Bridges, Thomas Edward, President of Corpus Christi College, 68.

Bright, John, 245.

Bright, William, Regius professor of ecclesiastical history, 248, 250, 412 n 46.

British Critic, 17, 50, 53, 105, 110, 125, 356 n 14.

British Quarterly Review, 135, 163.

Brodie, Sir Benjamin Collins, Waynflete professor of chemistry, 195, 213, 243, 264, 268, 271–2, 293.

Brodrick, George Charles, Fellow of Merton College, 243, 253, 276, 297–298, 313–14, 401 n 150, 410 n 33, 415 n 115.

Brougham, Henry, Lord, 46–7, 63, 64–5, 154.

Bryce, James, Lord Bryce, Fellow of Oriel College, 232, 236, 244, 247, 311–14, 397 n 51, 408 n 117.

Buckingham, Marquis and Duke of, 25, 32, 43, 326 n 68.

Buckland, William, Canon of Christ Church, 51, 337 n 119, 348 n 49.

Buckle, Henry Thomas, 212.

Bull, John, Christ Church, 85, 151.

Bulley, Frederic, President of Magdalen College, 167, 217, 389 n 31, 393 n 116, 412 n 46.

Bulteel, Henry Bellenden, Fellow of Exeter College, 17, 75–7, 345 n 115.

Burdett, Sir Francis, 24, 336 n 98.

Burgon, John William, Fellow of Oriel College, 132, 250, 252, 262, 264, 270, 300, 302, 311, 366 n 22, 403 n 17, 412 nn 46, 60, 414 n 89, 415 n 111.

Burke, Edmund, 4, 7, 15, 22, 26.

Burney, Fanny, 1.

Burrows, Montague, Chichele professor of modern history, 214, 220, 222–3, 229, 233, 262, 264, 289, 303, 393 n 116, 403 n 17, 411 n 36, 412 n 46.

Burton, Edward, Regius professor of divinity, 53, 76, 81, 91, 97, 99, 117, 348 n 49, 352 n 143, 353 n 165.

Butler, George, Fellow of Exeter College, 189, 203.

Butler, Samuel, 37.

Bywater, Ingram, Fellow of Exeter College, 278.

Cambridge, Duke of, 63.

Cambridge, University of, 9, 14, 32, 45–7, 49, 51, 54, 57, 60, 64, 65, 87, 88, 91, 97, 104, 109, 126–7, 135, 146, 168, 198, 220, 242–44, 254, 258–60, 267, 269, 280–87, 289, 294, 299–300, 302–3, 317 n 8, 347 n 10, 351 n 101, 396 n 46.

Campbell, Thomas, 64.

Camperdown, Lord, 309.

Canning, George, 9, 10, 29, 31, 41–4, 67–70, 72, 84, 332 n 17, 342 nn 41–2.

Canterbury, Archbishops of, 2, 52, 84, 98, 104, 110, 142, 211, 212, 240, 250, 254–5, 257, 272, 303.

Cardwell, Edward, Principal of St. Alban Hall, 95, 98, 100, 105, 107, 109, 114, 117, 134, 141, 142, 145, 151, 205–6, 356 nn 17, 23, 366 n 40, 370 n 116, 378 n 69, 381 n 1.

Cardwell, Edward, statesman, 141–4, 200, 370 n 114.

Carey, William, Censor of Christ Church, 12.

Carlisle, Lord, 84, 175.

Carnarvon, Lord, 258.

Caroline, Queen, 42.

Carpenter, Lant, 126.

Castlereagh, Lord, (1), 29.

Castlereagh, Lord, (11), 39.

Cathcart, Lord, 40.

Catholic Emancipation, 20, ch. II *passim*, 43–4, 70–5, 85, 341 n 24.

Catholic Vindicator, 172.

Cecil, Lord Robert, *see* Salisbury, Marquess of,

Census Act (1800), 27.

Chambers, Robert, Principal of New Inn Hall, 55.

Chancellor of the University, *see* North, Lord; Portland, Duke of, Grenville, Lord; Wellington, Duke of; Derby, Earl of; Salisbury,

Marquess of. *also* 4, 6, 23, 32, 37, 51, 66, 94, 118, 119, 133, 174, 177, 193, 196, 202, 229, 239, 258, 261, 273, 277, 309, 315, 317 n 8, 359 n 82, 410 n 22. Elections of, xiv, xv, 3, 9, 30–7, 67, 84–6, 174–6, 189, 217, 258.

Chandos, Marquis of, 72, 177, 225–7, 380 n 114.

Chase, Drummond Percy, Principal of St. Mary Hall, 186, 204–5, 208, 255, 278, 387 n 145, 412 n 46.

Cholmondeley, Hugh, Dean of Chester, 27–8.

Christ Church, 3, 4, 9–12, 16, 20, 22–3, 26–32, 38–9, 41–2, 44, 51–5, 67, 71–3, 84–6, 91, 108–10, 132, 140, 142, 144, 147, 161–2, 169, 175, 185, 191, 193, 200, 206, 211–12, 223, 237, 239, 268, 270, 295, 298–9, 305–6, 311–12, 320 n 73, 321 n 95, 326 n 68, 332 n 196, 337 n 129, 342 nn 41, 58, 350 n 87, 356 n 17, 371 n 141, 396 n 51.

Christian Observer, 81, 102, 111–12, 129.

Christian Remembrancer, 134, 164.

Christie, William Dougal, 127, 135–6, 363 n 177.

Church, Richard William, Fellow of Oriel College, 119, 122, 214, 240, 336 n 93, 400 n 127.

Church and State Review, 229.

Churchman, 233.

Churton, Ralph, 34, 44.

Clarence, Duke of, *see* William IV.

Clarendon Press, 2, 13, 151.

Clarke, Richard Frederick, 262.

Classical Studies in Oxford, 10, 13–16, 18–19, 60, 159–60, 164, 213, 218–19, 221–3, 278–9, 288–90, 309, 316.

Clay, Sir William, 197.

Cleaver, William, Principal of Brasenose College, 25, 29, 32, 325 n 41.

Clergy Non-Residence Bills, 23.

Cleveland, Duke of, 293–4, 305–6, 410 n 25, 411 n 37.

Clinton, Lord, 293.

Clough, Arthur Hugh, Fellow of Oriel College, 129, 130, 135, 137, 148, 158, 195, 204.

Cobbett, William, 47.

Cobden, Richard, 173, 198.

Cockburn, Sir Alexander James Edmund, 261.

Coker, John, 22, 35–6, 333 n 24.

Cole, John, Rector of Exeter College, 32, 37.

Colenso, John William, 232, 245.

Coleridge, John Duke, Lord Coleridge, 231, 252–4, 256–8, 260, 273, 400 n 119, 401 n 149.

Coleridge, Sir John Taylor, 114, 118, 138, 140, 206, 211–12, 252–3.

College Estates Acts, 265, 305–6.

Collinson, Septimus, Provost of Queen's College, 25, 26, 168.

Colquhoun, John Campbell, 171, 177.

Congregation, 149, 158–9, 160, 163–4, 181, 187, 192–3, 196–7, 199–201, 217–23, 226, 235, 247, 249–52, 255, 263, 265, 267, 271–3, 279, 287–90, 298, 300, 302, 386 n 126.

Congreve, Richard, Fellow of Wadham College, 130, 137, 157, 195, 366 n 22.

Conington, John, Corpus professor of Latin, 134, 157, 162, 187, 213, 222, 229, 238, 250.

Contemporary Review, 297.

Convocation of the University, xv, 6, 8, 14, 15, 21, 24, 29, 30, 33, 35–8, 57–9, 70–2, 74, 78, 88, 95–8, 100–2, 106–9, 114, 117–19, 121–3, 135, 138, 140, 143–4, 146, 149, 150–151, 154, 157, 159–60, 166, 180, 185–9, 194–6, 200, 203, 217, 222–3, 225–6, 229, 235, 239–40, 243, 248, 251–3, 258, 262–3, 266, 268–9, 271–4, 283, 289, 292, 298, 300–2, 356 n 23, 381 n 1.

Conybeare, John Josias, 64.

Cooke, John, President of Corpus Christi College, 25.

Copleston, Edward, Provost of Oriel College, 12–13, 16–20, 30, 32, 34–8, 42, 56, 60, 67–9, 71, 75, 78, 86, 99, 104, 114, 120, 125, 324 n 163, 330 n 161, 341 n 18, 352 n 137, 356 n 9.

Copyright, 45–6.

Corne, William, Censor of Christ Church, 41.

Cornish, Henry Hubert, Principal of New Inn Hall, 393 n 116.

Corpus Christi College, 25, 54, 67, 99–101, 111, 117, 125, 162, 167, 216, 258, 332 n 8, 334 n 58, 375 n 246.

Cotton, Richard Lynch, Provost of Worcester College, 75, 122–3, 138, 140, 194, 216–17, 226, 264, 371 n 139.

Courier, 34–5, 38, 44.
Cox, George Valentine, Esquire bedell, 128.
Cox, William Hayward, 86, 141, 157–158, 356 n 23.
Coxe, Henry Octavius, Bodley's Librarian, 292.
Cradock, Edward Hartopp, President of Brasenose College, 169, 187, 216–217, 378 n 16.
Cramer, John Anthony, Principal of New Inn Hall, 56, 86, 111–12, 114, 338 n 160, 370 n 116.
Crowe, William, Public Orator, 1, 317 n 1.
Cumberland, Duke of, 86, 354 n 171.
Curteis, George Herbert, Fellow of Exeter College, 261.
Curzon, Lord, 277, 315.

Daily News, 236, 398 n 89.
Dalgairns, John Dobree, 120, 124, 360 n 109.
Dampier, John Lucius, 153.
Darwin, Charles Robert, 212, 261–2.
Daubeny, Charles, professor of chemistry, 51–2, 82, 148, 153, 166, 200, 264, 337 n 124, 339 n 164, 357 n 39, 359 n 78.
Davison, John, Fellow of Oriel College, 19, 38, 42, 52, 315.
Dean(e), John, Fellow of Brasenose College, 30.
De La Warr, Lord, 199.
Denison, George Anthony, Fellow of Oriel College, 78, 150, 170, 176–7, 229–30, 261.
Derby, Earl of, Chancellor of the University, 155, 168–9, 171–6, 178, 180, 183–4, 186, 189, 194–5, 198–9, 204, 206, 212, 217, 223–6, 228–30, 258, 272, 387 n 145.
Dicey, Albert Venn, Fellow of All Souls College, 277.
Dickenson, William, 26.
Dickinson, Charles, 112.
Dillwyn, Lewis Llewelyn, 225.
Disraeli, Benjamin, 176, 178, 224, 299.
Divinity in Oxford, 8, 13, 52–3, 58, 65, 109–10, 117, 147–8, 160, 201, 203–4, 212, 249–52, 275, 278–9, 289, 308, 311–12, 314–15, 350 nn 87, 90, 358 nn 58, 61, 362 n 135, 372 n 175, 412 n 56.

Dodgson, Charles Lutwidge, Student of Christ Church, 223.
Dodson, John George, 228, 244–7, 252, 270–1, 398 n 75, 402 n 181.
Dolben, Sir William, 2, 21–3, 27–8, 317 n 10.
Döllinger, Johann Joseph Ignatius, 262.
Donkin, William Fishburn, Savilian professor of astronomy, 200, 216.
Dornford, Joseph, Fellow of Oriel College, 77, 345 n 128.
Dublin Review, 102.
Duff, Mountstuart Grant, 246, 253, 255, 271.
Durham, University of, 66, 110, 140, 247, 283, 285, 287, 370 n 124.

Eardley, Sir Culling, 202, 386 n 133.
Eaton, John Richard Turner, Fellow of Merton College, 217.
Eden, Charles Page, Fellow of Oriel College, 96, 120, 369 n 101.
Eden, Henley, 67.
Edinburgh Annual Register, 16.
Edinburgh Review, 17–19, 52, 56–7, 65–6, 82, 92, 112–13, 123–4, 130, 152, 163, 236, 274, 324 n 163, 368 n 84.
Eldon, Lord, High Steward of the University, 11, 24, 26, 29, 31–6, 43, 55, 70–2, 86, 328 n 99, 348 n 36.
Ellerton, Edward, Fellow of Magdalen College, 121, 125.
Ellesmere, Lord, 175, 206.
Ellicott, Charles James, 259.
Elmsley, Peter, Principal of St. Alban Hall, 37–8.
Elton, Charles Isaac, Fellow of Queen's College, 239.
Encombe, Lord, 72.
English Churchman, 118, 172, 233, 371 n 134.
Espin, Thomas Espinelle, Fellow of Exeter College, 284.
Estcourt, Thomas Grimston Bucknall-, 68, 75, 78, 141, 342 n 47.
Evangelicals at Oxford, 70–7, 80–1, 86, 96, 108, 111–12, 115, 122–3, 128, 133–4, 138, 143, 148, 151, 171–173, 175, 177, 202–3, 215, 223–4, 226, 232, 240, 257, 266, 340 n 14.
Evans, Evan, Master of Pembroke College, 216.
Eveleigh, John, Provost of Oriel College, 13, 31, 75.

Everett, Edward, 117, 119.
Ewart, William, 268–71, 284.
Examinations, 7, 9, 13, 16, 20, 56–60, 108, 146–7, 185, 187, 200, 275, 280–283, 288, 291, 409 n 2, 416 n 123.
Examination Statutes, general, 11, 129, 146–50, 159–60, 217–23, 249–51, 279
of 1800, 12–15, 17–18.
of 1803, 14.
of 1807, 14, 15, 18, 56.
of 1808, 14.
of 1809, 14, 15, 56.
of 1825, 58.
of 1826, 58.
of 1830, 60, 219–20.
of 1833, 124.
of 1850, 149–50, 157, 213, 218, 220, 222.
of 1855, 201, 204.
of 1864, 223, 240.
of 1869, 250–2.
Exeter College, 17, 37, 75, 86, 88–9, 129, 139, 146, 153, 169, 171, 181, 207, 215, 221, 229, 231, 278, 310, 412 n 54.
Express, 255.

Faber, Frederick William, 111.
Faussett, Godfrey, Margaret professor of divinity, 95, 110, 115, 121, 143, 177.
Faussett, Robert Godfrey, Treasurer of Christ Church, 295, 410 n 22.
Fawcett, Henry, 254, 260–1, 271, 400 n 119.
Firth College, Sheffield, 283, 288.
Fitzmaurice, Lord Edmond, 259, 292.
Fletcher, Joseph, 92.
Forbes, Alexander Penrose, 258.
Forster, William Edward, 258.
Fortnightly Review, 297.
Foulkes, Edmund Salisbury, Fellow of Jesus College, 402 n 181.
Foulkes, Henry, Principal of Jesus College, 371 n 139.
Fowler, Thomas, Fellow of Corpus Christi College, 255, 271, 273, 290, 299, 411 n 36.
Fowler, William Warde, Fellow of Lincoln College, 237.
Fox, Charles James, 3, 5, 24.
Fox, John, Provost of Queen's College, 348 n 48, 371 n 139, 377 n 60.
Frederick, Prince, 9.

Freeman, Edward Augustus, 150, 156, 219, 221–2, 236, 239, 313.
Fremantle, Sir William Henry, 43.
Fremantle, William Henry, Fellow of All Souls College, 211.
Fremantle, William Robert, 236.
Froude, James Anthony, Fellow of Exeter College, 129–30, 135, 236, 365 nn 13, 14.

Gaisford, Thomas, Dean of Christ Church, Regius professor of Greek, 18, 51, 71, 84–6, 109–10, 132, 150–1, 169, 194, 199–200, 212, 356 n 17, 358 n 61.
Garbett, James, 75, 115, 371 n 140.
Gathorne-Hardy, Gathorne, 229–33, 302, 393 n 120, 394 n 139.
Gauntlett, Samuel, Warden of New College, 42.
George III, King, 1, 8, 10, 29, 31–2.
George IV, King, as Prince of Wales, 9, 29, 32, 36.
as Regent, 10, 38–40, 42, 53.
as King, 43, 334 n 43.
German Universities, xvi, 61–7, 84, 136, 147, 152, 164, 166, 182, 187, 275–7, 279, 340 nn 4, 7, 347 n 24.
Gibbon, Edward, 6–7.
Gifford, S. L., 72–3.
Gilbert, Ashhurst Turner, Principal of Brasenose College, 105, 114–15, 118, 125, 142, 348 n 48, 360 n 98.
Gladstone, William Ewart, xv, 78, 89, 91, 115–16, 118, 121–2, 131, 137–8, 140–6, 153–4, 166, 168–79, 181–4, 187–93, 195–202, 209–10, 214, 223–234, 244–7, 253, 256–60, 265, 268, 270–1, 273, 275, 292, 298, 311, 321 n 95, 346 n 143, 370 nn 118, 121, 122, 371 nn 134, 140, 373 n 206, 375 n 247, 378 n 84, 379 n 87, 380 nn 113, 121, 381 n 16, 382 n 39, 384 nn 82, 84, 386 n 133, 388 n 171, 400 n 127, 414 n 95.
Globe, 102, 150.
Goderich, Lord, 69.
Golightly, Charles Pourtales, 111–12, 118, 121, 143, 238, 262.
Goodenough, Robert William, Censor of Christ Church, 41.
Goodman, Neville, 260.
Gordon, Osborne, Censor of Christ Church, 140, 147, 200, 211, 309, 321 n 95, 396 n 41.

Gore, Charles, 145.
Gorham Judgment, 112, 122, 170, 210.
Goschen, George Joachim, 247, 252, 302, 412 n 55.
Göttingen, University of, 62–3, 126.
Goulburn, Edward Meyrick, Fellow of Merton College, 262.
Graham, Sir James, 124, 142, 350 n 87, 358 n 61.
Graham, John, 146.
Grant, Charles, 72.
Grayson, Anthony, Principal of St. Edmund Hall, 348 n 48.
Green, John Richard, 249, 314.
Green, Thomas Hill, Fellow of Balliol College, 236, 238, 268.
Greg, William Rathbone, 245.
Grenville connexion, the, 10, 25, 28–30, 35, 42–4, 67.
Grenville, Lord, Chancellor of the University, xv, 3, 18–19, 28–38, 42–3, 45–6, 51–6, 66–7, 71, 74, 84–6, 93–4, 326 n 68, 330 n 161, 331 n 182.
Grenville, Thomas, 1, 10, 32, 326 n 68.
Greswell, Edward, Fellow of Corpus Christi College, 111, 142, 356 n 23, 370 n 124.
Greswell, Richard, Fellow of Worcester College, 111, 142, 151, 162, 171, 177–8, 224–6, 231, 264, 370 nn 123, 128.
Grey, Lord, 30, 77, 84, 87–8, 92.
Grey, Sir George, 246.
Griffiths, John, Fellow of Wadham College, 119.
Grove, Sir William Robert, 301.
Guardian, 134, 136, 142, 145, 147, 149–151, 154, 163–5, 172, 176, 181, 185, 194, 209, 214, 217, 222, 231, 233, 255–257, 282, 289, 307, 314, 316, 359 n 73, 371 n 147, 380 nn 113, 122, 403 n 17.
Guillemard, Henry Peter, Fellow of Trinity College, 119, 122.
Guizot, François Pierre Guillaume, 151, 373 n 206.

Haddan, Arthur West, Fellow of Trinity College, 144, 146, 171–3, 181, 192, 199, 224, 354 n 180, 371 n 147, 379 n 88.
Hall, Charles Henry, Dean of Christ Church, 12, 30, 38–9, 41, 52, 67, 193.
Hall, George William, Master of Pembroke 37, 133–4.
Hallam, Henry, 141.

Hamilton, Sir William, 82–3, 89, 92–3, 97–8, 103, 136, 160, 213, 324 n 163, 334 n 58, 347 n 21.
Hampden, Renn Dickson, Principal of St. Mary Hall, 58, 75, 86, 93, 96–7, 99–102, 110–12, 114, 116–17, 119, 121, 125, 132, 141, 144–5, 162, 214, 334 n 58, 339 n 184, 351 n 117, 353 n 161, 354 nn 173, 176, 356 n 23, 359 n 78, 360 nn 98, 100, 370 nn 116, 117.
Harding, Sir J. D., 177.
Harington, Richard, Principal of Brasenose College, 140, 154, 370 n 116.
Harrison, Benjamin, Student of Christ Church, 356 n 23.
Harrison, Frederic, Fellow of Wadham College, 130, 235–6, 239, 245–6, 271.
Hawkins, Edward, Provost of Oriel College, 58, 66, 70–1, 74–5, 78, 86, 93, 95–7, 99–100, 103, 114, 118, 120–1, 129, 140, 142, 146, 148, 172, 178, 184–5, 190, 198–200, 208, 216–217, 225–6, 229, 242, 254, 259, 261, 264, 333 n 24, 343 n 74, 344 nn 102, 109, 349 n 72, 351 nn 107, 113, 353 n 164, 370 n 116, 379 n 89, 382 n 34, 386 nn 126, 133, 389 n 16, 411 n 37.
Heathcote, Sir William, 118–19, 142, 170, 172, 178, 187–8, 194, 196–7, 206, 224, 229, 232, 245–6, 253, 256, 393 n 103.
Hebdomadal Board, 2, 4–5, 12–15, 23, 29, 37–8, 40, 42, 45–6, 49, 51, 54, 57–60, 66, 69, 76, 78, 80, 88, 90–2, 94–5, 97–102, 104–11, 114, 116, 118–21, 123–5, 138–42, 144, 146–7, 149–51, 153–4, 157–9, 166, 173, 175, 178–81, 183, 185–90, 194–5, 199, 202, 204, 264, 319 n 45, 333 n 42, 351 n 103, 358 n 61, 359 n 78, 381 n 2.
Hebdomadal Council, 132, 187, 191–3, 196, 199–201, 210, 213, 216–23, 227–8, 230, 233, 235, 239–40, 247, 252, 254, 262, 267–9, 272, 274, 279–81, 286–90, 292, 301, 307–9, 410 n 25, 411 n 36, 412 n 54.
Heber, Reginald, 11, 16, 25, 44, 63, 72.
Heber, Richard, 25–8, 33, 42–4, 67, 73, 75, 326 n 61, 327 n 73, 334 n 58, 335 n 67.

Magdalen Hall, 55, 70, 75, 77, 84–6, 112, 171, 177, 201, 240, 345 n 129, 371 n 139.

Mackarness, John Fielder, 315.

Mackintosh, Sir James, 6–7.

Macmillan's Magazine, 276–7.

Macmullen, Richard Gell, Fellow of Corpus Christi College, 117–18.

Macray, William Dunn, 45.

Magdalen College, 2–3, 7, 24, 28, 31, 43, 53–4, 67, 75, 97, 121, 125, 137, 161–2, 167, 205, 215–17, 242, 256, 298, 310–12, 325, 338 n 149, 348 n 48, 354 n 178, 356 n 10, 377 n 52, 393 n 116, 412 n 46.

Magdalen Hall, 19, 55, 70, 85, 112, 145, 171, 204, 266–7, 270, 338 n 149, 343 n 79, 371 n 139.

Magrath, John Richard, Provost of Queen's College, 265, 288–90, 298, 306.

Maine, Sir Henry James Sumner, 277, 301–2.

Manchester, xvi, 243–4, 313; 341 n 41.

Manning, Henry Edward, 140, 170, 261.

Mansel, Henry Longueville, Regius professor of ecclesiastical history, 63, 131, 156, 181, 200, 212, 215–16, 219, 226, 229, 248, 264, 393 n 116.

Mansfield, Lord, 85.

Markham, William, Dean of Christ Church, 9.

Marlborough, Duke of, 27, 32, 55, 327 nn 70, 77.

Marlow, Michael, President of St. John's College, 26, 31, 326 n 55.

Marriott, Charles, Fellow of Oriel College, 115, 120, 138, 140, 145, 151, 174, 184–5, 189, 195, 199–202, 216, 264, 382 n 34, 385 n 109, 403 n 17.

Marshall, Canon, 174.

Marsham, Robert Bullock-, Warden of Merton College, 71–2, 74, 85–6, 101, 111, 142–3, 172–3, 177, 189, 201, 264, 371 nn 136, 139.

Martineau, James, 198, 245.

Mason College, Birmingham, 283–4.

Maurice, Frederick Denison, 96, 115, 144, 215, 245.

Maurice, Peter, 112.

Maximilian, Archduke, of Austria, 40.

Medical Studies in Oxford, 124, 275.

Melbourne, Lord, 88, 95, 99–100, 111, 341 n 27, 353 n 161, 360 n 98.

Members of Parliament, election of, for the University, xiv, 21–8, 41–4, 59, 67–8, 71–5, 78–9, 141–5, 170–4, 176–9, 187–8, 190, 217, 223–34, 249, 273, 411 n 36.

Merton College, 26, 54, 71–2, 85, 101, 111, 126, 142–3, 158, 172, 201, 205, 217, 243, 246–8, 253, 264–5, 268, 272–3, 276, 297, 310, 313, 343 n 79, 356 n 9, 375 n 246, 401 n 150.

Metternich, Prince, 61.

Meyrick, Frederick, Fellow of Trinity College, 219, 385 n 109.

Miall, Edward, 198, 243–5, 265, 271, 293.

Michael, Grand Duke, of Russia, 40.

Michelet, Jules, 116.

Michell, Richard, Principal of Hertford College, 175, 200, 379 n 99.

Mill, John Stuart, 83–4, 131, 212, 214, 232.

Moberly, George, Fellow of Balliol College, 90.

Modern Languages in Oxford, 16, 151.

Molesworth, Sir William, 176.

Monro, David Binning, Fellow of Oriel College, 290, 411 n 37.

Moody, Dwight L., 315.

Morgan, Osborne, 270.

Morley, Lord, 302.

Morning Chronicle, 34, 42, 47, 134.

Morning Herald, 177.

Morning Post, 37, 371 n 134.

Morpeth, Lord, 113.

Morris, John Brande, Fellow of Exeter College, 113, 118.

Monier-Williams, Sir Monier, Boden professor of Sanskrit, 240.

Mowbray, John Robert, 256.

Mozley, James Bowling, Regius professor of divinity, 144, 167, 170, 181–2, 200, 241, 325 n 37, 412 n 46.

Müller, Max, Corpus professor of comparative philology, 151, 213, 240, 297, 303, 308, 373 n 211, 395 n 31.

Napleton, John, Fellow of Brasenose College, 6.

Nares, Edward, Regius professor of modern history, 50–1, 336 n 113, 357 n 35.

National Club, 171–2, 174, 177, 179, 380 n 128.

Neate, Charles, Fellow of Oriel College, 154, 284, 303.

Nettleship, Henry Corpus professor of Latin, 237, 290.

Neve, Timothy, Margaret professor of divinity, 8.

Newcastle, Duke of, 174–6.

New College, 22, 30, 35, 42, 54, 66, 70, 90, 95, 112, 141, 151, 161, 166, 169, 171, 191, 193, 195–6, 200, 205, 216, 278, 285–6, 295, 298, 304–6, 310, 343 n 79, 360 n 88.

Newdigate, Sir Roger, 51.

New Inn Hall, 55–6, 85, 111, 114, 204, 264, 312–13, 370 n 116, 415 n 110.

Newman, Francis William, Fellow of Balliol College, 126, 137.

Newman, John Henry, Fellow of Oriel College, xv, 19, 53, 63, 73–5, 81, 84, 90, 96, 99–101, 105–6, 109–10, 113–15, 118–20, 122, 124–6, 129, 131, 135, 145, 238, 261–2, 274, 333 n 24, 340 n 189, 343 n 74, 353 n 165, 356 nn 9, 14, 358 n 61, 359 n 79, 361 n 117, 362 n 139, 371 n 147, 376 n 14, 415 n 111.

Newman, William Lambert, Fellow of Balliol College, 271.

Newton, Richard, Principal of Hertford College, 337 n 129.

Nicholas, Grand Duke, of Russia, 40.

Nicholl, Sir John, 43–4, 67, 75, 334 n 51.

Nonconformist, 243, 246, 254, 265, 271, 293, 300.

Norris, Henry Handley, 93.

Norris, James, President of Corpus Christi College, 167.

North, Lord, Chancellor of the University, 2, 3, 8.

Northcote, Sir Stafford Henry, 226, 228, 230, 232, 240, 392 n 99.

Nowell, Thomas, Regius professor of modern history, 8.

Oakeley, Frederick, Fellow of Balliol College, 122, 346 n 1.

O'Connell, Daniel, 59, 71, 198.

Odling, William, Waynflete professor of chemistry, 289–90, 408 n 140.

Ogilvie, Charles Atmore, Regius professor of pastoral theology, 143, 151, 172, 239, 241.

Oriel College, 12–13, 16–17, 19–20, 28, 30–2, 37–8, 42–4, 46, 52, 54, 57–9, 67–8, 70–1, 74–5, 78, 84, 93, 99, 114, 129–30, 132, 138, 154, 161–2,

169, 172, 174–5, 180, 185, 188, 200, 202, 204, 208, 248, 250, 261, 264, 284, 290, 302, 306, 313, 341 n 18, 343 n 79, 344 n 109, 356 n 9, 368 n 84, 370 n 116, 379 n 89, 386 n 126, 387 n 145, 409 n 1, 411 n 37.

Owens College, Manchester, 126, 152, 159, 260, 271, 283–4, 286, 288–90, 295.

Oxford Herald, 47, 107, 147.

Oxford Protestant Magazine, 136, 143, 368 n 70.

Oxford Times, 229.

Oxford University Act (1854), 66, 193–202, 223.

Oxford University Gazette, 278.

Oxford Volunteers, 5, 9, 55, 318 n 33, 324 n 6.

Page, Francis, 21–3.

Pakington, Sir John, 188, 208.

Palgrave, Francis Turner, 272.

Palmer, Roundell, Earl of Selborne, 136–7, 153, 167, 188, 196, 199, 212, 225, 227–8, 232, 246, 256–8, 273, 300, 306, 312, 392 n 99.

Palmer, William, Worcester College, 109, 120.

Palmerston, Lord, 54, 169, 176, 186, 210, 223–5, 227, 231, 262, 391 n 71.

Parker, Charles Frederick, Fellow of Pembroke College, 133.

Parr, Samuel, 1, 4–5, 7, 11, 24–6, 37, 63, 325 n 29, 338 n 151.

Parsons, John, Master of Balliol, 13, 26, 31, 33, 35, 37–8, 56.

Pattison, Mark, Rector of Lincoln College, 129–30, 135, 157–8, 160, 182, 200–1, 208–10, 213–18, 223, 235–7, 242, 250, 271, 274–5, 290, 292–3, 296–300, 303, 309, 346 n 1, 359 n 79, 369 n 99, 410 nn 25, 33, 415 n 111.

Peel, Sir Robert, 9–10, 33, 38, 40–2, 45–50, 52, 54, 59, 64–5, 67–75, 85–6, 95–6, 111, 114, 119, 123, 138–9, 141–2, 144, 320 n 83, 335 n 67, 337 n 134, 338 n 154, 342 n 64, 344 n 89, 345 n 131, 348 n 30, 349 n 72.

Pegge, Sir Christopher, Regius professor of medicine, 9.

Pelham, Henry Francis, Fellow of Exeter College, 279.

Pembroke College, 37, 133–4, 141, 161–2, 168–9, 180, 187, 190, 192–3,

195, 200, 216, 311, 343 n 79, 370 n 116, 373 n 199, 376 n 28, 377 n 64.
Perceval, Dudley, 177–9, 188–9, 327 n 74, 380 n 114.
Perceval, Spencer, 28, 30, 177.
Percival, Ann, 126.
Percival, John, 285.
Perry, Charles, 110.
Perry, Walter C., 126.
Peto, Sir Samuel Morton, 198.
Phillimore, Joseph, Regius professor of civil law, 42, 67.
Phillimore, Sir Robert Joseph, 142, 225.
Philosophy in Oxford, *see* Logic and Philosophy in Oxford.
Philpotts, Henry, 74, 81, 119, 129.
Pitt, William, the Younger, 3, 9–10, 22, 24, 26, 28–9, 42, 317 n 8.
Plumptre, Frederick Charles, Master of University College, 216, 370 n 116.
Political Register, 47.
Pollock, Frederick, Fellow of Corpus Christi College, 277.
Poor Scholars' Hall, 123, 137–9, 264, 403 n 17.
Portland, Duke of, Chancellor of the University, 3–5, 9–11, 26, 28–31, 55, 326 n 55.
Port Meadow, 5, 142.
Potter, John, Regius professor of divinity, 52.
Pottinger, Henry Allison, 265, 411 n 36.
Powell, Baden, Savilian professor of geometry, 57, 60, 86, 132, 137, 153, 195, 198.
Price, Bartholomew, Sedleian professor of natural philosophy, 216, 264, 299.
Price, Bonamy, Drummond professor of political economy, 88, 130, 157, 195, 238, 274, 350 n 84, 355 n 188, 368 n 76.
Proctors, 5, 14, 30, 35, 37, 42, 47–8, 101, 119, 122, 149–50, 181, 183, 186–7, 200, 204, 219, 225, 251, 308–9, 336 n 93, 347 n 14, 355 n 188, 357 n 25.
Prospective Review, 135, 152, 163.
Prostitutes, 47–50, 321 n 103, 347 n 14.
Protestant Dissenting Deputies, 69, 87, 127, 198.
Pryme, George, 104–5, 356 n 12.
Public Works Loan Commissioners, 54.

Pusey, Edward Bouverie, Regius professor of Hebrew, 63–4, 78, 88, 91, 96, 99–101, 107, 110, 112, 115–16, 118, 120, 122, 128–9, 131, 135, 138, 145–6, 151, 174, 176, 184–9, 194–5, 199–202, 206, 210, 212, 214, 217–18, 224, 228–31, 233, 237, 239–40, 244, 248–53, 257, 261–2, 264, 268–9, 271, 286, 315, 332 n 196, 341 n 14, 344 n 102, 346 n 9, 350 n 82, 352 nn 137, 140, 354 nn 168, 171, 357 n 36, 361 n 113, 362 nn 139, 143, 378 n 84, 382 n 34, 392 nn 99, 102, 395 n 31, 400 n 127, 402 n 184, 403 n 17, 411 n 36, 412 n 46.
Pycroft, James Wallis, 154.

Quarterly Review, 17, 19, 46, 52, 63, 65, 105, 164, 231, 275, 285.
Queen's College, 25–6, 67, 125, 132, 137, 141, 153, 167–8, 201, 213, 216, 236, 288, 298, 312, 348 n 48, 356 n 10, 371 n 139, 381 n 17, 412 n 46.
Quinet, Edgar, 116.

Radnor, Lord, 35, 90, 92, 95, 97–9, 104–5, 107, 242.
Raine, Matthew, 37.
Randolph, John, Regius professor of divinity, 2, 5, 8, 317 n 11.
Rathbone, William, 258.
Rawlinson, George, Camden professor of ancient history, 181–2, 193, 215, 217, 220, 225–6.
Record, 111, 224, 232–3, 237, 256.
Redesdale, Lord, 175, 300, 309.
Revenues, of colleges, 42, 66, 82, 271–7, ch. XIII *passim;* of the university, 82, ch. XIII *passim*, 408 n 128.
Richards, Joseph Loscombe, Rector of Exeter College, 129, 146, 169.
Richards, Richard, 26, 28, 327 n 74.
Richmond, Duke of, 305.
Richmond, George, 73.
Ridley, Sir Matthew White, 301.
Rigaud, Stephen Peter, Savilian professor of astronomy, 51, 56, 77, 345 n 127.
Robarts, Charles Henry, Fellow of All Souls College, 303.
Robertson, Abraham, Savilian professor of geometry, 8.
Robinson, Alfred, Fellow of New College, 304, 306.

Rogers, Thorold, Drummond professor of political economy, 189, 262, 264–5, 273, 281, 286.
Rolleston, George, Linacre professor of anatomy, 229, 242, 264, 287–8, 293, 299, 396 n 41, 402 n 184, 411 n 36.
Rose, Hugh James, 64, 99.
Round, Charles Gray, 143–5, 170–1, 371 n 138.
Roundell, Charles Savile, Fellow of Merton College, 246–7, 256, 260, 268, 271–3, 295, 311–13, 410 n 22.
Routh, Martin Joseph, President of Magdalen College, 3, 24–6, 28, 31, 34, 43, 53, 73, 97, 125, 143, 167, 317 n 8, 319 n 54, 325 n 25, 348 n 48, 354 n 178.
Rowden, Edward, Fellow of New College, 171.
Rowley, George, Master of University College, 91.
Russell, Lord John, 70, 104–5, 109, 122, 133, 135, 137, 145–6, 152–5, 164, 169, 173, 176, 181, 184–7, 190, 192–3, 198, 378 n 69, 383 n 70, as Earl Russell, 273.
Rutson, Albert Osliff, Fellow of Magdalen College, 271.

St. Alban Hall, 38, 55, 58, 71, 86, 107, 141, 145, 158, 204–6, 313, 343 n 79, 356 n 17, 370 n 116.
St. Edmund Hall, 55, 75–6, 96, 174, 204–5, 267, 312–13, 340 n 14, 348 n 48, 362 n 135.
St. John's College, 5, 26, 31, 43–4, 84–6, 133, 156, 169, 172, 177, 191, 193, 195, 209, 226, 229, 262, 292, 298, 311–12, 348 n 48, 370 n 116, 412 n 46.
St. Mary Hall, 86, 93, 99, 177, 200, 204, 278, 313, 349 n 60, 354 n 176, 356 n 23, 359 n 78, 370 nn 116, 128, 387 n 145.
St. Mary's Church, 1, 27, 81, 96, 215, 250, 270, 315, 334 n 58, 371 n 147.
Salisbury, Marquess of, 257–61, 277, 280, 298–304, 309, 312–13, 315, 410 nn 22, 25, 411 n 37, 412 n 56, 415 n 111, as Lord Robert Cecil, 188, 229–31, 385 n 109.
Salwey, Herbert, Student of Christ Church, 287.

Sand, Charles Louis, 61.
Sanderson, John Scott Burdon, 293.
Sandon, Lord, 138–9, as Lord Harrowby, 175, 206.
Sankey, Ira D., 315.
Saunders, Augustus Page, 141.
Science in Oxford, 8–9, 13–19, 51–2, 56–60, 65, 108–9, 124, 146–8, 151, 160, 162, 166, 186, 217, 222, 277–8, 289–90, 308.
Scott, J. O., 292.
Scott, Robert, Master of Balliol College, 115, 132, 156, 200–1, 215, 227, 267, 281, 375 n 5.
Scott, Sir William, 22–4, 26, 28, 35, 40, 43, 45, 325 n 20, 335 n 90.
Scottish Universities, xvi, 65, 147, 165, 294.
Sedgwick, Adam, 126.
Select Preachers, 15, 102, 262.
Senior, Nassau, Drummond professor of political economy, 102.
Sewell, James Edward, 216, 285.
Sewell, William, Fellow of Exeter College, 88–9, 95, 101, 105–8, 111–113, 123–4, 128–9, 140, 143, 157, 171, 174, 176, 200, 284–5, 315, 350 n 89, 356 nn 16, 22–4, 371 n 138.
Shaftesbury, Lord, 226–7, 232, 237, as Lord Ashley, 138, 174–5, 202, 210, 320 n 117.
Shelley, Percy Bysshe, 16.
Sheridan, Richard Brinsley, 36.
Shirley, Walter Waddington, Regius professor of ecclesiastical history, 237, 264.
Short, Thomas Vowler, Censor of Christ Church, 71, 343 n 80.
Shuttleworth, Philip Nicholas, Warden of New College, 66, 70, 76, 90, 112, 338 n 151, 343 n 72, 360 n 88.
Sibthorp, John, Sherardian professor of botany, 8, 319 n 62.
Sibthorp, Richard Waldo, 75.
Sidgwick, William Carr, Fellow of Merton College, 243, 265, 268.
Sidmouth, Lord, see Addington, Henry.
Simeon, Henry, 5.
Slater, William Charles, Principal of St. Alban Hall, 206.
Smith, Goldwin, Regius professor of modern history, 128, 131–2, 135, 152–3, 161, 168, 179, 187, 199, 203, 206–7, 212–13, 215, 222, 226, 229,

231, 233, 235–6, 241–3, 245, 247–8, 251, 254, 264, 269, 273–4, 281, 284, 287, 296–7, 314, 388 n 171, 389 n 16, 391 n 70, 398 n 89.

Smith, Henry John Stephen, Savilian professor of geometry, 217, 251, 262, 264, 268, 289–90, 299, 302, 404 n 29, 411 n 36.

Smith, John, Savilian professor of geometry, 8.

Smith, John Pye, 64, 81, 346 n 9.

Smith, Samuel, Dean of Christ Church, 12, 54, 71, 342 nn 41, 58.

Smith, Vance, 259.

Smith, William, 69.

Smyth, John Henry, 47.

Somerset, Granville, 72.

Spencer, Lady Charlotte, 50.

Spry, John Hume, 141.

Standard, 177.

Stanhope, Lady Hester, 26.

Stanley, Arthur Penrhyn, Fellow of University College, 101, 108, 111, 121, 130, 131, 135, 140, 147–8, 152–3, 156, 161, 166, 195, 212, 217, 232, 236–7, 239, 241, 245, 259, 262, 265, 379 n 87, 384 n 84.

Stanley, Edward Lyulph, Fellow of Balliol College, 300–1, 310.

Statutes of the University (other than examination statutes, which see) 27, 94–5, 98–9, 102–3, ch. VI *passim*, 158, 161, 173, 183, 186, 189, 191, 202–3, 356 nn 16, 18, 357 nn 25–6, 29, 368 n 78.

Stowell, Hugh, 177.

Strauss, David Friedrich, 129, 131, 251, 365 n 13.

Stubbs, William, Regius professor of modern history, 130, 217, 222, 229, 248, 277–8, 412 n 46.

Surtees, Bessie, 55.

Sylvester, James Joseph, 198.

Symons, Benjamin Parsons, Warden of Wadham College, 75, 97, 107, 118–22, 133, 144, 199–200, 217, 226, 348 n 48, 356 nn 17, 23, 362 n 143, 401 n 160.

Tait, Archibald Campbell, Fellow of Balliol College, 108, 111, 120–1, 130, 133, 153, 156, 159, 377 n 61.

Talbot, Edward Stuart, Warden of Keble College, 214, 257, 266, 403 n 16, 411 n 36, 412 n 46.

Talbot, Lord, 85–6, 348 n 49.

Tatham, Edward, Rector of Lincoln College, 2, 4–5, 7, 9, 11–12, 15–16, 26, 42, 319 n 56, 322 n 125, 326 n 61, 333 n 39.

Taylor, Peter Alfred, 245.

Taylorian Institute, 151.

Temple, Frederick, Fellow of Balliol College, 130, 142, 152, 157, 211, 243, 262, 267, 281–2, 366 n 23, 369 n 102.

Temple, William, 130.

Test and Corporation Acts, 1–2, 26, 69–70, 73.

Tests, University, xiv, xv, 6, 64, 66, 69, 80–1, 87–98, 112–16, 120, 122–3, 130, 152, 159, 175, 197–9, 201–3, 207, 217, 231, 233, 235, ch. XI *passim*, 265–7, 273, 298, 349 n 72, 351 n 101, 363 n 177, 402 n 181, 411 n 36.

Thirlwall, Connop, 88, 132.

Thom, John Hamilton, 198.

Thomas, Vaughan, Fellow of Corpus Christi College, xv, 44, 83, 90–1, 95, 101, 107, 111, 143, 334 n 58, 350 n 91, 351 n 103, 356 n 23.

Thompson, Henry Lewis, Student of Christ Church, 311.

Thompson, James, Rector of Lincoln College, 215.

Thompson, William, Principal of St. Edmund Hall, 362 n 135, 370 n 116.

Thomson, William, Provost of Queen's College, 153, 168, 201, 213, 216, 231, 236.

Thomson, William, Reader in anatomy, 8.

Thorley, George Earlam, Fellow of Wadham College, 264.

Thornton, Marianne, 72.

Tillyard, Alfred Isaac, 267.

Times, 34, 37–8, 48, 67, 73, 79, 102, 128, 135, 139, 143–4, 151, 153, 163, 176, 178, 188, 216, 223, 227, 256–8, 276, 289, 295, 313, 356 n 16, 368 n 79, 406 n 70.

Tooke, William, 66, 88.

Tournay, William, Warden of Wadham College, 70, 334 n 58.

Tractarianism, 2, 17, 24, 33, 59, 66, 74–5, 81, 84, 86, 90–103, ch. VI *passim*, 128–9, 134–8, 141–3, 145, 151, 153, 164, 174–5, 177, 179, 181, 187, 189, 196, 198, 200, 202–6, 210,

218, 226, 238, 242, 249, 257, 334 n 58, 354 n 180, 355 n 188, 356 n 14, 362 n 135, 370 n 117, 392 n 99.

Trinity College, 13, 32, 125, 144, 169, 206, 219, 262, 348 n 48, 370 n 116.

Turner, Edward Tindal, Fellow of Brasenose College, 217.

Tutors' Association, 147–8, 180–4, 187, 191, 194, 202, 206, 217, 381 n 17.

Tweed, James Peers, Fellow of Exeter College, 220–1.

Twisleton, Edward, 207, 209, 212.

Twiss, Travers, Drummond professor of political economy, 177, 188, 211.

Tyler, James Endell, Fellow of Oriel College, 57, 114, 141.

Tyndall, John, 261.

Universities of Oxford and Cambridge Act (1877), 303.

University College, Bristol, 283–5.

University College, Liverpool, 283.

University College, Nottingham, 283, 288.

University College, Oxford, 22, 26, 31–2, 67, 91, 130, 132, 134, 137, 169, 216, 290, 295, 312, 325 n 54, 370 n 116.

University College, Reading, 288.

University Commissions, 104–5, 127, 136–7, 147, 152–3, 191–2, 298–300, 374 n 217.
    of 1850, 152–66, 169, 172, 174, 181–2, 185–6, 196, 218, 223, 293, 347 n 21.
    of 1854, 193, 196, 200, 206–9, 211, 216–18.
    of 1872, 293–6, 305–6, 411 n 37.
    of 1877, 267, 300–16, 411 n 36, 412 n 56.

University Elections Act (1861), 228, 244.

University Museum, 151–2.

Van Mildert, Regius professor of divinity, 41, 52.

Vansittart, Nicholas, 41, 50, 333 n 24.

Vaughan, Henry Halford, Regius professor of modern history, 113, 129–30, 135, 150, 153, 157, 159, 187, 195, 213, 366 n 17.

Vice-Chancellor of the University, 3–5, 13, 15, 28, 31–3, 35, 37, 41–2, 45–9, 54, 56–7, 60, 66, 69, 71, 74, 76–7, 88, 91, 94–5, 97–8, 100, 102–3, 105, 107–8, 115–16, 118–20, 125, 133, 142, 144, 149–51, 159, 169, 180–1, 183, 186, 193–5, 200–3, 213, 217, 220, 224, 227, 232, 238–9, 250–1, 262–3, 271–2, 279–80, 286, 288, 291–2, 308–9, 313, 338 n 147, 342 n 64, 368 n 76.

Victoria, Queen, 200.

Wadham College, 26, 54, 57, 70, 75, 97, 107, 118–19, 130, 133, 174, 200, 217, 226, 264, 310, 334 n 58, 340 n 14, 348 n 48, 356 n 17.

Walker, Robert, Fellow of Wadham College, 57, 108, 148, 157.

Wall, Henry, Wykeham professor of logic, 158, 217, 240, 268, 393 n 116.

Wall, Martin, Clinical professor, 8.

Walter, John, I., 34.

Ward, George Robert Michael, Fellow of Trinity College, 125–6.

Ward, George Sturton, 270.

Ward, John William, Earl of Dudley, 11, 20, 42, 332 n 17.

Ward, William George, Fellow of Balliol College, 100, 113, 115, 120–2, 130–1, 143–4, 238, 346 n 1, 360 n 109, 363 n 177.

Watson, Arthur George, Fellow of All Souls College, 211.

Watson, Joshua, 93.

Wayte, Samuel William, President of Trinity College, 206, 287, 299.

Wellesley, Lord Charles, 85, 174.

Wellington, Duke of, Chancellor of the University, 43, 68–9, 71–2, 77, 85–6, 88, 90–1, 94–8, 100, 102, 104–107, 113–14, 116–18, 124–5, 133, 138, 142, 153, 168, 174, 341 n 24, 348 nn 30, 36, 349 n 60, 354 n 176, 359 n 82, 368 n 78, 374 n 217, 375 n 247, 381 n 2.

Wenman, Thomas, Regius professor of civil law, 8.

Wesleyans, attitudes of, towards university education, 65–6, 102, 256, 271, 400 n 133.

Westminster Review, 81, 239, 242.

Westminster School, 12, 27, 132.

Wetherall, Sir Charles, 66–8, 72, 75 86, 88, 119.

Wetherell, Nathan, 26, 67.

Whately, Richard, Principal of St. Alban Hall, 16–17, 55, 57–9, 70–2,

74, 76, 86, 92, 99, 102, 112–13, 120–1, 129, 145–6, 153, 157, 338, n 154, 350 n 90, 351 n 107, 353 n 164, 357 n 29.

Whewell, William, 126.

White, Blanco, 70, 74–5, 344 n 102.

Wickham, William, 32.

Wilberforce, Henry William, 96.

Wilberforce, Samuel, 75, 175–6, 205, 379 n 99.

Wilberforce, William, 47, 63, 73.

Wilkes, John, 1.

Wilkins, Augustus, 260.

Wilkinson, John, 158.

William IV, King, as Duke of Clarence, 32, 40, as King, 77–8, 354 n 171.

Williams, David, Warden of New College, 141, 200.

Williams, George, professor of botany, 8.

Williams, Isaac, Fellow of Trinity College, 111, 114–15.

Wilson, Daniel, 75–6.

Wilson, Henry Bristow, Fellow of St. John's College, 132–3.

Wilson, Horace Hayman, Boden professor of Sanskrit, 157.

Wilson, John, President of Trinity College, 169.

Wilson, John Mathias, President of Corpus Christi College, 167, 187, 195, 200–1, 216, 254, 271, 299.

Windham, William, 4, 22, 24–6, 38, 326 n 61.

Wingfield, John, headmaster of Westminster School, 12.

Wintle, Thomas, Vice–president of St. John's College, 84.

Wiseman, Nicholas, Cardinal, 102.

Wood, George, 88, 93, 97.

Woodgate, Henry Arthur, Fellow of St. John's College, 57, 172.

Woollcombe, Edward Cooper, Fellow of Balliol College, 111, 140, 171, 181, 192, 250, 254, 259, 261–2, 369 n 99, 412 n 46.

Worcester College, 26, 75, 111, 123, 138–9, 142, 162, 169, 174, 194, 216–217, 226, 264, 309, 348 n 48, 350 n 84, 371 n 139.

Wordsworth, Christopher, 88, 172–3, 233, 312.

Wrightson, Henry, 137.

Wycliffe Hall, 315.

Wynn, Charles Watkin Williams, 67.

Wynter, Philip, President of St. John's College, 84, 115–20, 133, 169, 172–5, 177, 208, 226, 229, 348 n 48, 356 n 17, 370 n 116, 380 n 114, 393 n 120.

Wyse, Thomas, 135.

Yarde-Buller, Sir John Buller, 240.

Yarmouth, Lord, 40.

York, Duke of, 5, 10.

York, proposed university at, 55.

Yorkshire College, Leeds, 283–4, 288.

Zetland, Lord, 257.